Autism Spectrum Disorders: Diagnosis and Therapies

Autism Spectrum Disorders: Diagnosis and Therapies

Editor: Irene Wright

MURPHY & MOORE
www.murphy-moorepublishing.com

www.murphy-moorepublishing.com

MURPHY & MOORE

Cataloging-in-Publication Data

Autism spectrum disorders : diagnosis and therapies / edited by Irene Wright.
p. cm.
Includes bibliographical references and index.
ISBN 978-1-63987-065-3
1. Autism spectrum disorders. 2. Autism spectrum disorders--Diagnosis.
3. Autism spectrum disorders--Treatment. 4. Developmental disabilities. I. Wright, Irene.
RC553.A88 A98 2022
616.858 82--dc23

Murphy & Moore Publishing,
1 Rockefeller Plaza,
New York City, NY 10020, USA

ISBN 978-1-63987-065-3 (Hardback)

Contents

Preface

I am honored to present to you this unique book which encompasses the most up-to-date data in the field. I was extremely pleased to get this opportunity of editing the work of experts from across the globe. I have also written papers in this field and researched the various aspects revolving around the progress of the discipline. I have tried to unify my knowledge along with that of stalwarts from every corner of the world, to produce a text which not only benefits the readers but also facilitates the growth of the field.

Autism spectrum disorder consists of a group of developmental disabilities which present social and behavioral challenges. The different disorders which are a part of this group of disorders are Asperger's syndrome, pervasive developmental disorder not otherwise specified (PDD-NOS), and autistic disorder. The diagnosis of these disorders cannot be done through medical tests. Instead, it relies on observation of the behavior and development of a child. The therapies to manage autism spectrum disorders focus on providing intervention as early as possible to maximize their effectiveness. They generally help the children learn basic skills such as walking, talking and interacting with other people. This book includes some of the vital pieces of work being conducted across the world, on the diagnosis and therapies for autism spectrum disorders. It will also provide interesting topics for research which interested readers can take up. Students, researchers, experts and all associated with the research on these disorders will benefit alike from this book.

Finally, I would like to thank all the contributing authors for their valuable time and contributions. This book would not have been possible without their efforts. I would also like to thank my friends and family for their constant support.

Editor

1

Prenatal and Newborn Immunoglobulin Levels from Mother-Child Pairs and Risk of Autism Spectrum Disorders

*Judith K. Grether[1,2], Paul Ashwood[3], Judy Van de Water[4], Robert H. Yolken[5], Meredith C. Anderson[1], Anthony R. Torres[6], Jonna B. Westover[6], Thayne Sweeten[7], Robin L. Hansen[8], Martin Kharrazi[9] and Lisa A. Croen[2]**

[1] California Department of Public Health, Richmond, CA, USA, [2] Division of Research, Kaiser Permanente of Northern California, Oakland, CA, USA, [3] Department of Medical Microbiology and Immunology, University of California, Davis, CA, USA, [4] Department of Internal Medicine, University of California, Davis, CA, USA, [5] Johns Hopkins School of Medicine, Johns Hopkins University, Baltimore, MD, USA, [6] Center for Persons with Disabilities, Utah State University, Logan, UT, USA, [7] Department of Biology, Utah State University, Brigham City, UT, USA, [8] MIND Institute, University of California, Davis, CA, USA, [9] Genetic Disease Screening Program, California Department of Public Health, Richmond, CA, USA

Edited by:
John Vijay Sagar Kommu, National Institute of Mental Health and Neurosciences, India

Reviewed by:
Munis Dundar, Erciyes University, Turkey
Alka Anand Subramanyam, Topiwala National Medical College and BYL Nair Charitable Hospital, India

***Correspondence:**
Lisa A. Croen
lisa.a.croen@kp.org

Background: An etiological role for immune factors operating during early brain development in children with autism spectrum disorders (ASD) has not yet been established. A major obstacle has been the lack of early biologic specimens that can be linked to later diagnosis. In a prior study, we found lower risk of ASD associated with higher levels of maternally-derived total IgG and *Toxoplasmosis gondii* (Toxo) IgG in newborn blood spot specimens from children later diagnosed with ASD compared to population controls.

Methods: We obtained maternal mid-gestational serum specimens and newborn screening blood spots from the California Genetics Disease Screening Program (GDSP) for linked mother-baby pairs for 84 children with ASD and 49 children with developmental delay but not ASD (DD) identified from California Department of Developmental Services records and for 159 population controls sampled from birth certificates.Immunoglobulin levels in maternal and newborn specimens were measured by solid phase immunoassays and analyzed in logistic regression models for total IgG, total IgM, and Toxo IgG, and, for maternal specimens only, Toxo IgM. Correlations between maternal and newborn ranked values were evaluated.

Results: In both maternal and newborn specimens, we found significantly lower risk of ASD associated with higher levels of Toxo IgG. In addition, point estimates for all comparisons were <1.0 suggesting an overall pattern of lower immunoglobulin levels associated with higher ASD risk but most did not reach statistical significance. We did not find differences in maternal or newborn specimens comparing children with DD to controls.

Discussion: These results are consistent with evidence from our prior study and other published reports indicating that immune factors during early neurodevelopment may be etiologically relevant to ASD. Lowered immunoglobulin levels may represent suboptimal function of the maternal immune system or reduced maternal exposure to common infectious agents.

Conclusion: Patterns seen in these selected immunoglobulins may provide clues to mechanisms of early abnormalities in neurodevelopment contributing to ASD. We recommend further study of immunoglobulin profiles in larger samples of linked mother-baby pairs to evaluate possible etiologic relevance.

Keywords: autism, maternal infection, biomarkers, immune function

INTRODUCTION

Whether and how immune factors operating during fetal brain development are etiologically relevant to autism spectrum disorders (ASD) has not yet been determined. Numerous studies have documented atypical immune findings in some individuals already diagnosed with ASD. These include post-mortem brain tissue studies demonstrating evidence of chronic CNS inflammation in individuals aged 4–40 years old with ASD (Goines and Van de Water, 2010; Onore et al., 2012). More directly implicating a prenatal etiologic pathway, animal model studies have shown that autism-relevant behaviors can be induced in offspring following in utero exposure to antibodies derived from mothers with a child already diagnosed with ASD (Martin et al., 2008; Singer et al., 2009; Braunschweig et al., 2012), but not prenatal exposure to antibodies derived from serum of children with ASD (Morris et al., 2009). Other animal studies provide evidence that activation of the maternal immune system during pregnancy, either through infectious or non-infectious agents, can lead to atypical behaviors similar to those in ASD-affected children (Patterson, 2011). These findings are consistent with observational human studies that report maternal viral exposure (Chess, 1971; Deykin and MacMahon, 1979; Markowitz, 1983; Stubbs et al., 1984; Yamashita et al., 2003; Atladottir et al., 2012a; Zerbo et al., 2013) or inflammation (Brown et al., 2014) during pregnancy to be associated with increased risk of ASD in some children. Evidence for an association between prenatal infection and risk of other psychiatric disorders, such as schizophrenia and bipolar disorder, has also been reported (Buka et al., 2001a, 2008; Brown, 2011; Mortensen et al., 2011; Kneeland and Fatemi, 2013).

Despite this growing and complex body of research, questions regarding an etiologic role for immune factors in ASD remain to be resolved, impeded, in part, by a paucity of biologic specimens obtained during the presumed vulnerable period of fetal brain development and linked to later behaviorally-based diagnostic information. Routinely collected and archived specimens in California provide a resource for addressing some of these questions.

Using archived maternal specimens from California originally obtained during routine prenatal screening (Early Markers for Autism Study/EMA), Croen et al. (2008a) found differences in maternal mid-gestation antibody reactivity to human fetal brain protein in specimens from mothers of children with ASD compared to population-based controls. Although, the differences did not reach statistical significance, they are generally consistent with those based on maternal specimens obtained after an ASD diagnosis of an affected child (Dalton et al., 2003; Zimmerman et al., 2007; Braunschweig et al., 2008). Using the same prenatal specimens from the EMA project, Goines et al. (2011) reported a pro-inflammatory cytokine profile in mothers of children with ASD that was different from that of mothers of children without ASD.

In another California study, we measured neonatal levels of selected IgG, IgM, and IgA antibodies in archived newborn screening blood specimens to evaluate the hypothesis that higher antibody levels would be associated with a risk of ASD (Grether et al., 2010). In newborns, IgG antibodies are largely derived from the mother and transferred across the placenta to the fetus (Simister, 2003). Neonatal IgM and IgA antibodies are generally made by the fetus or neonate and serve as one set of putative markers of perinatal infection. In this earlier California study (Grether et al., 2010) in which we evaluated total IgG, IgM, and IgA as well as common viral antigen-specific immunoglobulins, we found no evidence of elevated immunoglobulin levels that would indicate increased prenatal infectious exposure in children with ASD, but we could not confidently rule out a role for all possible antigens or early transient exposures. Contrary to our hypothesis and of uncertain clinical significance, we found significantly lower ASD risk associated with higher levels of total IgG and *Toxoplasmosis gondii* (Toxo) IgG in the newborn specimens from the children with ASD. If supported by further research, these results may plausibly represent suboptimal humoral function in the maternal immune system and/or impaired transplacental transfer; the findings may also represent a protective effect in the controls in the postnatal period from earlier maternal exposure. As maternal specimens were not available for the children in that study, we were unable to further explore possible pathways.

We here report a case-control study using maternal mid-gestational as well as neonatal specimens from linked

Abbreviations: ASD, autism spectrum disorders; CNS, central nervous system; DDS, California Department of Developmental Services; CAT, category; CPD, The Center for Persons with Disabilities (CPD); DD, developmental delay; DSM IV, Diagnostic and Statistical Manual of Mental Disorders, 4th Edition; ELISA, enzyme-linked immunosorbent assay; EMA, Early Markers for Autism Study; GA, gestational age; GDSP, California Genetics Disease Screening Program; HIGH, the three higher quartiles (or categories); IgA, Immunoglobulin A; IgG, Immunoglobulin G; IgM, Immunoglobulin M; IRB, institutional review board; LOW, lowest quartile (or category); MDL, minimum detection level; OR, odds ratio; PBB, Project Baby's Breath; Q, quartile; RCOC, Regional Center of Orange County; SI, standardized international units; Toxo, Toxoplasmosis gondii; XAFP, expanded alpha fetoprotein.

mother-child pairs to re-evaluate total IgG, total IgM, and *Toxoplasma gondii* immunoglobulins in children with ASD compared to population-based controls. To assist with interpretation of results, we also included a group of children with other developmental disabilities, comparing their assay results to control values. The study sample comes from the Early Markers for Autism (EMA) Study, a population-based, nested case-control study designed to evaluate biologic markers of susceptibility and exposure in archived maternal mid-gestational and neonatal blood specimens from linked mother-baby pairs.

METHODS

Subjects

Study subjects were selected from the population of offspring born to women living in Orange County, California who were pregnant in 2000–2001 and enrolled in the State's Prenatal Expanded Alphafetoprotein Screening Program (Croen et al., 2008a) and for which specimens were available in the Project Baby's Breath (PBB) special research archive (see below). Three groups of children were identified: children with ASD, children with other developmental delay but not ASD (DD), and general population controls. Children with ASD or DD represent all children identified with these conditions who met the above criteria and who were enrolled with the Regional Center of Orange County (RCOC), one of 21 Regional Centers operated by the California Department of Developmental Services (DDS) to coordinate services for persons with ASD, developmental delay, and other developmental disabilities. Possible ASD cases were initially ascertained as clients receiving DDS services for autistic disorder or clients receiving services for other DDS-eligible conditions but who also had a code indicating ASD in the electronic record. Possible DD cases were initially ascertained as DDS clients without any evidence of ASD in the electronic records and with evidence of intellectual disability.

To confirm ASD or DD case status, we followed a protocol initially developed by the Metropolitan Atlanta Developmental Disabilities Surveillance Program (Autism and Developmental Disabilities Monitoring Network Surveillance Year 2006 Principal Investigators; Centers for Disease Control and Prevention (CDC), 2009), employing trained medical record abstractors to compile detailed diagnostic and clinical data from RCOC records for all children ascertained as possible ASD or possible DD. A pediatrician with certification in developmental and behavioral pediatrics (RH) then conducted expert clinical review of abstracted data to confirm ASD or DD case status using DSM IV criteria. Because of etiologic questions regarding co-morbid intellectual disability in children with ASD, children with ASD were further categorized by presence or absence of intellectual disability using DSM-IV criteria and based on standardized cognitive and adaptive assessments. Children with all scores <70 were coded as having ID; children with all scores ≥ 70 or some scores <70 and others ≥ 70 were coded as not having ID; children with no standardized scores in their chart were coded as "unknown."

Controls were randomly sampled from the birth certificate files, frequency matched to ASD cases by sex, birth month, and birth year in a 2:1 ratio; all past or current DDS clients were identified through statewide electronic files and excluded from the control population. Demographic variables for all subjects were obtained from live birth certificates.

Specimen Collection

Maternal mid-gestational specimens were retrieved from the Project Baby's Breath (PBB) prenatal screening specimen archive maintained by the California Genetic Disease Screening Program (GDSP), California Department of Public Health. Following the completion of routine prenatal screening conducted by GDSP, PBB had retained any remaining portions of specimens in three selected southern California counties and selected birth years for analysis in approved research studies. During the study period, prenatal screening was conducted for approximately 70% of pregnancies in the state (state law mandates that all women in the first half of pregnancy be offered the voluntary screening). Venous blood was collected at 15–20 weeks gestation in serum separator tubes by obstetrical care service providers and laboratories, and underwent expanded alpha fetoprotein (XAFP) screening at a single regional laboratory, typically within 7 days of collection (median time = 3 days). During transit via US Postal Service to the regional screening laboratory, no effort was made to control the temperature of the specimens. After testing, remaining portions of specimens were kept under refrigeration for 1–2 days and then stored at −20°C by the regional laboratory and PBB. Aliquots of the samples used for this study were shipped to the laboratory of Dr. Judy van de Water, UC Davis, and stored at −80°C until use with a single thaw prior to immunoglobulin testing. All samples were exposed to the same collection and storage protocols.

Newborn screening filter paper blood specimens were obtained from the newborn archive maintained by GDSP that conducts routine metabolic screening for all newborns in the state. Specimens from cases and controls were located, one spot bar-coded with a study identifier, and shipped on dry ice, without regard to case-control status, to The Center for Persons with Disabilities (CPD) at Utah State University. Working under aseptic conditions, researchers in the CPD lab prepared 96-well plates, each well containing two 3 mm diameter punches from one archived specimen. Since original blood draw and newborn screening, specimens have been stored at −20°C.

All prenatal and newborn specimens were then shipped on dry ice to the Neurovirology Laboratory, Johns Hopkins School of Medicine, for analysis, blinded to case-control status, using enzyme immunoassays as described below.

Laboratory Assays

We measured antibodies in both maternal and newborn specimens by solid phase immunoassays (ELISA). Maternal and newborn total IgG and total IgM levels were expressed as μg/ml. In maternal specimens, we also measured *Toxoplasma gondii* (Toxo) IgG with resulting levels expressed as standardized international units (SI) and Toxo IgM with resulting levels expressed as blank-adjusted optical density units. In newborn specimens, we measured Toxo IgG with resulting levels expressed as blank-adjusted optical density units. Assay results were not corrected for hematocrit or total protein and specimens lacking detectable signals for a specific assay were considered at the minimum detection level (MDL) for that assay.

Exclusions

Subjects (1 child with ASD, 3 children with DD, 1 control child) were excluded due to estimated gestational age <26.0 completed weeks (182 days; recorded on the birth certificate and based on LMP) or because age at blood draw was >7.0 days after birth according to the newborn screening record.

Statistical Methods

To take into consideration assay detection limits, unknown distributions of the immunoglobulins, and inadequate knowledge of the biologic significance of immunoglobulin levels measured in archived specimens, we conducted primary analyses treating the measured immunoglobulin values as categorical variables. Categories were constructed separately for each of the analytes based on percent of signals at the MDL for these assays: if ≤25% of controls were at the MDL, observations were divided into quartiles based on control values, with MDL values included in lowest quartile (Q1); if >25% of controls had values at the MDL, then MDL values were designated as the lowest category (CAT1) and remaining values were divided into three equal-sized categories based on control values. The exception to this was newborn total IgM, which had only a low and a high category due to limited distribution.

For comparisons between ASD and controls, and separately between DD and controls, we then conducted crude and adjusted analyses using logistic regression to estimate the risk of ASD (or DD) associated with each analyte separately, comparing the lowest category to each higher category using odds ratios (ORs) considered statistically significant if 95% confidence intervals did not include 1.0. Adjusted models included assay plate (5 maternal and 5 newborn) as additional independent variables and covariates associated with ASD (or DD) in these data ($p < 0.5$; **Table 1**). Due to small numbers of children with DD, we collapsed the three higher quartiles (or categories) into one group (HIGH) and used the lowest quartile (or category) as the reference group (LOW). We explored differences in immunoglobulin levels between children with ASD with ID and those with ASD without ID, comparing each of these subgroups to the control group. Small numbers of subjects in subgroups precluded the use of adjusted models.

To evaluate the association between maternal mid-gestational analyte signals and those detected in their children's newborn specimens, we computed Spearman rank-order correlation coefficients separately for cases and controls for the three analytes measured in both mothers and newborns (total IgG, total IgM, and Toxo IgG). Values at the MDL were treated as the lowest category, with measured signals above the MDL for each individual treated as categorical variables in the computations.

Institutional Review Board

This study was approved by the California Health and Human Services Agency Committee for the Protection of Human Subjects (IRB) and the Kaiser Permanente of Northern California Institutional Review Board, who granted a waiver of informed consent. The analytic laboratories operated under an IRB exemption as the samples were preexisting and did not have personal identifiers.

RESULTS

The final study group included 84 children with ASD, 49 children with DD, and 159 controls. No significant differences were found between ASD and controls on the matching variables (gender, birth month, birth year), nor for single or multiple birth, gestational age (GA), birth weight, days between birth and blood draw, and protein concentration in the newborn specimen (**Table 1**). Mothers of children with ASD were similar to controls with regard to parity, inter-pregnancy interval (number of months between birth of index child and prior live birth), GA at mid-gestational blood draw, and maternal weight at blood draw (**Table 1**). ASD cases were more likely than controls to have mothers who self-identified as white non-Hispanic, were older, and more educated.

Compared to the control children, children with DD were less likely to be male and born in the first study year (2000) or during the same birth months due to matching of the controls with the ASD group on these variables. Children with DD were also of lower birth weight and had a longer time between birth and blood draw than controls (**Table 1**). No differences in maternal characteristics were observed.

For the ASD study group, both newborn and maternal specimens were available for 80 mother-baby pairs and only maternal specimens were available for the remaining 4 mother-baby pairs; for the DD study group, both specimens were available for 45 pairs, only maternal specimen for 1 pair, and only newborn specimens for 3 pairs; for the controls, both specimens were available for 141 pairs, only maternal specimens for 6 pairs, and only newborn specimens for 12 pairs. Signals above the MDL were detected for total IgG and total IgM in all maternal and newborn specimens and for Toxo IgM in all maternal specimens. For the Toxo IgG assay, 93 maternal specimens were at the MDL (45% of ASD, 33% of DD, 27% of controls), as was one newborn specimen for a child with DD.

ASD vs. Controls

The distributions of each analyte for ASD cases and controls are shown in **Table 2**. In unadjusted analyses, measured levels of total IgG, total IgM, and Toxo IgM in mid-gestational specimens of mothers of children diagnosed with ASD were not significantly different from population control values but virtually all point estimates were substantially below 1.0 (**Table 2**). For Toxo IgG, significantly fewer mothers of children with ASD were represented in CAT3 and CAT4 than were mothers of controls (**Table 2**), indicating lower risk of ASD with higher measured antibody.

In unadjusted analyses, newborn specimens from children with ASD did not show significantly different levels from controls for total IgG or total IgM. For Toxo IgG, risk was reduced for signals above Q1, but only significantly so for Q2 and Q4 (**Table 2**). All ORs were below 1.0 in the newborn comparisons.

TABLE 1 | Demographic characteristics of children with Autism Spectrum Disorders (ASD), developmental delay without ASD (DD), and Control Subjects. Early Markers for Autism (EMA) Study, births 2000, 2001.

	Controls (*N* = 159)		Children with ASD (*N* = 84)			Children with DD (*N* = 49)		
Baby characteristics	***N***	**%**	***N***	**%**	***P*-value[a]**	***N***	**%**	***P*-value[a]**
GENDER								
Male	139	87.42	73	86.90	0.91	29	59.18	<0.0001
Female	20	12.58	11	13.10		20	40.82	
BIRTH YEAR								
2000	31	19.5	23	27.38	0.16	26	53.06	<0.0001
2001	128	80.5	61	72.62		23	46.94	
Birth Month					0.96			0.01
PLURALITY								
Singleton	156	98.11	81	96.43	0.42	47	95.92	0.34
Multiple	3.00	1.81	3	3.57		2	4.08	
	Mean	**(SD)**	**Mean**	**(SD)**	***P*-value[b]**	**Mean**	**(SD)**	***P*-value[b]**
Gestational age at birth (days)	271.01	(14.27)	272.12	(18.47)	0.63	266.33	(28.12)	0.27
Birth weight	3348.1	(616.09)	3416.1	(699.1)	0.44	2897.7	(827.22)	0.0008
Days between birth and blood draw	1.46	(0.94)	1.48	(0.71)	0.80	1.92	(1.43)	0.036
Protein concentration in newborn specimen (ug/ml)	6520.3	(1377.2)	6495.5	(1222.1)	0.89	6404.4	(1551.5)	0.62
Maternal characteristics	***N***	**%**	***N***	**%**	***P*-value[a]**	***N***	**%**	***P*-value[a]**
MATERNAL RACE/ETHNICITY								
White non-Hispanic	53	33.33	37	44.05	0.0005	9	18.37	*0.43*
White Hispanic: US Born	13	8.18	10	11.9		5	10.20	
White Hispanic: Not US Born	60	37.74	10	11.9		23	46.94	
Black	1	0.63	0	0.00		1	2.04	
Asian	28	17.61	19	22.62		9	18.37	
Other	4	2.52	8	9.52		2	4.08	
MATERNAL AGE								
<20	9	5.66	2	2.38	0.004	3	6.12	0.90
20–24	33	20.75	7	8.33		8	16.33	
25–29	48	30.19	18	21.43		18	36.73	
30–34	51	32.08	38	45.24		14	28.57	
35+	18	11.32	19	22.62		6	12.24	
MATERNAL EDUCATION								
< High school	49	30.82	7	8.43	<0.0001	22	44.90	0.23
High school graduate	39	24.53	15	18.07		9	18.37	
College	46	28.93	40	48.19		14	28.57	
Post graduate	25	15.72	21	25.3		4	8.16	
PARITY								
Primiparous	67	42.14	42	50.00	0.24	16	37.65	0.24
Multiparous	92	59.86	42	50.00		33	67.35	
INTER-LIVEBIRTH INTERVAL (MONTHS)								
0–12	16	17.58	8	20.00	0.68	4	12.50	0.52
13–24	19	20.88	10	25.00		10	31.25	
25–60	31	34.07	15	37.50		12	37.50	
>60	25	27.47	7	17.50		6	18.75	
	Mean	**(SD)**	**Mean**	**(SD)**	***P*-value[b]**	**Mean**	**(SD)**	***P*-value[b]**
Gestational age at blood draw (days)	118.78		119.76		0.35	118.37		0.75
Mother's weight at XAFP blood draw (lbs)	146.89	(33.78)	145.07	(26.72)	0.65	150.3	(39.3)	0.56

[a] *Chi-square test of association, comparing to controls.*

[b] *t-test for equality of means, comparing to controls.*

TABLE 2 | Association of antibodies and risk of ASD, distribution and crude odds ratios, EMA study, births 2000–2001.

	N at MDL	Category	Analyte	ASD	Controls	OR_{unadj}	95% CI
MATERNAL							
Total IgG (μg/ml)		Q4	>53.63	18	36	0.77	(0.36, 1.66)
		Q3	>46.59–53.63	28	37	1.17	(0.57, 2.37)
		Q2	>43.11–46.59	14	37	0.58	(0.26, 1.30)
	0	(Ref*) Q1	0–43.11	24	37		
Total IgM (μg/ml)		Q4	>65.96	15	35	0.55	(0.25, 1.19)
		Q3	>56.80–65.96	18	38	0.60	(0.29, 1.27)
		Q2	>29.56–56.80	22	37	0.76	(0.37, 1.56)
	0	(Ref*) Q1	0–29.56	29	37		
Toxo IgG (SI)		Cat 4	>18.6	8	37	**0.23**	**(0.09, 0.55)**
		Cat 3	>6.3–18.6	15	35	**0.45**	**(0.21, 0.96)**
		Cat 2	>0–6.3	23	35	0.69	(0.35, 1.38)
	78	(Ref**) Cat 1	0	38	40		
Toxo IgM (odu***)		Q4	>0.202	15	35	0.57	(0.26, 1.23)
		Q3	>0.172–0.202	22	38	0.77	(0.38, 1.56)
		Q2	>0.158–0.172	17	34	0.67	(0.32, 1.41)
	0	(Ref*) Q1	0–0.158	30	40		
NEWBORN							
Total IgG (μg/ml)		Q4	>61.18	18	38	0.66	(0.31, 1.38)
		Q3	>55.03–61.18	16	38	0.59	(0.27, 1.25)
		Q2	>51.63–55.03	18	38	0.66	(0.31, 1.38)
	0	(Ref*) Q1	0–51.63	28	39		
Total IgM (μg/ml)		Cat2	>1.20	29	66	0.75	(0.43, 1.31)
	0	(Ref**) Cat 1	0–1.20	51	87		
Toxo IgG (odu***)		Q4	>0.097	5	38	**0.14**	**(0.05, 0.39)**
		Q3	>0.066–0.097	23	38	0.64	(0.32, 1.27)
		Q2	>0.057–0.066	15	38	**0.42**	**(0.20, 0.88)**
	0	(Ref*) Q1	0–0.057	37	39		

Reference quartile (Q1) includes signals at and above the MDL based on control values.
**Reference category (Cat 1) only includes signals at the MDL. Values above the MDL divided into equal-sized categories based on control values.*
***Optical density units (blank adjusted).*
Bold means statistically significant.

After adjustment for laboratory plate, maternal age, and maternal education (**Table 3**$_{\text{Adj Column 1}}$), maternal specimens did not show significant difference between cases and controls for total IgG, total IgM, or Toxo IgM, although, as in the unadjusted analyses, virtually all point estimates were below 1.0. Higher levels of Toxo IgG were significantly associated with lower risk of ASD (Category 4 vs. Category 1) and the dose-response trend across the Toxo IgG categories reached statistical significance ($p = 0.038$). With further adjustment for maternal race-ethnicity (**Table 3**$_{\text{Adj Column 2}}$), the Toxo IgG results continued to indicate lower risk with higher levels with a dose-response pattern ($p = 0.039$). Further adjustment that included place of birth for white Hispanic mothers (US-born or not US-born) showed similar patterns that did not reach statistical significance (**Table 3**$_{\text{Adj Column 3}}$).

In adjusted models with newborn specimens, all ORs were below 1.0, with the comparison of Toxo IgG Q4 vs. Q1 reaching statistical significance (**Table 3**$_{\text{Adj Columns 1 and 2}}$). No dose-response pattern for newborn Toxo IgG was observed.

ASD with and without Intellectual Disability

Data on presence/absence of intellectual disability was available on 76% of the children with ASD, permitting identification of two subgroups: ASD with ID ($n = 34$) and ASD without ID ($n = 30$). Each of these subgroups was then compared separately to the control group and the resulting ORs for each analyte compared across the two subgroups. No statistically significant differences between the two subgroups were observed (data not shown). Small numbers of children precluded adjustment for covariates.

DD vs. Controls

In models adjusted for laboratory plate, gender, birth year, and days to blood draw, we found no association between risk of DD and any of the analytes when comparing the LOW and HIGH exposure categories. Odds ratios for the different analytes ranged from 0.71 to 1.28 with no apparent pattern and all confidence intervals included the null value (data not shown).

Correlations within Mother-Baby Pairs

Within mother-baby pairs, levels of total IgG measured in mothers during mid-gestation and in their newborns were not

TABLE 3 | Association of antibodies and risk of ASD, EMA study, births 2000–2001.

	OR^{a}_{adj}	95% CI	OR^{b}_{adj}	95% CI	OR^{c}_{adj}	95% CI
MATERNAL						
Total IgG						
Q4 vs. Q1	0.92	(0.39, 2.17)	0.87	(0.37, 2.08)	0.89	(0.37, 2.13)
Q3 vs. Q1	1.41	(0.63, 3.14)	1.39	(0.62, 3.12)	1.34	(0.59, 3.01)
Q2 vs. Q1	0.53	(0.22, 1.30)	0.51	(0.21, 1.25)	0.51	(0.21, 1.27)
Total IgM						
Q4 vs. Q1	0.46	(0.17, 1.27)	0.44	(0.16, 1.23)	0.42	(0.15, 1.21)
Q3 vs. Q1	0.63	(0.25, 1.61)	0.63	(0.25, 1.60)	0.71	(0.27, 1.85)
Q2 vs. Q1	0.68	(0.29, 1.62)	0.69	(0.29, 1.66)	0.75	(0.31, 1.82)
Toxo IgG						
CAT4 vs. CAT1*	**0.35**	**(0.13, 0.91)**	**0.33**	**(0.12, 0.86)**	0.40	(0.15, 1.11)
CAT3 vs. CAT1*	0.58	(0.25, 1.32)	0.53	(0.22, 1.24)	0.55	(0.23, 1.30)
CAT2 vs. CAT1*	0.86	(0.40, 1.86)	0.83	(0.38, 1.81)	0.86	(0.39, 1.87)
Toxo IgM						
Q4 vs. Q1	0.80	(0.32, 1.99)	0.78	(0.31, 1.94)	0.71	(0.28, 1.77)
Q3 vs. Q1	0.82	(0.36, 1.84)	0.78	(0.34, 1.78)	0.70	(0.30, 1.64)
Q2 vs. Q1	0.78	(0.33, 1.84)	0.74	(0.31, 1.78)	0.69	(0.28, 1.69)
NEWBORN						
Total IgG						
Q4 vs. Q1	0.77	(0.31, 1.89)	0.76	(0.31, 1.86)	0.70	(0.28, 1.76)
Q3 vs. Q1	0.65	(0.28, 1.48)	0.61	(0.27, 1.42)	0.64	(0.27, 1.48)
Q2 vs. Q1	0.75	(0.33, 1.69)	0.72	(0.32, 1.65)	0.72	(0.31, 1.66)
Total IgM						
HIGH vs. LOW**	0.67	(0.30, 1.49)	0.67	(0.30, 1.48)	0.77	(0.34, 1.75)
Toxo IgG						
Q4 vs. Q1	**0.25**	**(0.08, 0.79)**	**0.25**	**(0.08, 0.78)**	0.31	(0.10, 1.01)
Q3 vs. Q1	0.89	(0.41, 1.94)	0.90	(0.41, 1.96)	0.87	(0.39, 1.92)
Q2 vs. Q1	0.52	(0.23, 1.17)	0.52	(0.23, 1.18)	0.50	(0.22, 1.14)

[a] *Adjusted for laboratory plate, maternal age, maternal education.*
[b] *Adjusted for laboratory plate, maternal age, maternal education, maternal race/ethnicity (White non-Hisp., White Hisp., Other).*
[c] *Adjusted for laboratory plate, maternal age, maternal education, maternal race/ethnicity (White non-Hisp., White Hisp.-US Born, White Hisp.-Not US Born, Other).*
**Reference category (CAT1) only includes signals at the MDL. Values above the MDL divided into 3 equal-sized categories based on control values.*
***Reference category (LOW) includes all signals above but close to the minimum observed value for the assay, with remaining values lumped into one higher category.*
Bold means statistically significant.

correlated in the group of ASD cases ($r_\varphi = -0.03$), in controls ($r_\varphi = 0.04$), or in the DD group ($r_\varphi = 0.08$). Similarly, IgM showed no correlation between levels in maternal and newborn specimens in the ASD group ($r_\varphi = 0.04$), the control group ($r_\varphi = -0.03$) or the DD group ($r_\varphi = -0.0.26$, $p = 0.08$). In contrast, Toxo IgG levels in maternal and newborn specimens were correlated within ASD cases ($r_\varphi = 0.34$, $p < 0.002$) and within population controls ($r_\varphi = 0.53$, $p < 0001$) but not in the DD group ($r_\varphi = 0.11$, $p = 0.47$).

To further explore an association between low Toxo IgG and ASD, we evaluated mother-baby ASD and control pairs in which both mother and newborn Toxo IgG levels were in the reference range (see **Table 2**) compared to pairs in which either or both the maternal or the newborn values were above the reference range. The logistic model (adjusted for laboratory plate only) yielded an OR of 0.24 (95% CI 0.10, 0.56), consistent with a lower risk of ASD associated with higher levels of Toxo IgG.

DISCUSSION

This ASD case-control study is the first to report immunoglobulin levels measured in both maternal mid-gestational and newborn specimens from linked mother-baby pairs. The immunoglobulins were selected based on our prior California study using newborn specimens in which lower risk of ASD was associated with higher assay levels for total IgG and Toxo IgG (Grether et al., 2010).

The results reported here are consistent in many, but not all, respects to those we reported earlier. In the current study, the results for both total IgG and Toxo IgG suggest, but do not statistically confirm, a lower risk of ASD associated with higher levels of the analytes in newborn specimens, similar to the earlier findings but not reaching statistical significance, perhaps because of the smaller number of subjects available for this current study. In the maternal specimens, lower risk of ASD appeared to be associated with higher measured levels of Toxo IgG, reaching statistical significance for several comparisons with a dose-response pattern indicating a protective association. However, this association no longer reached statistical significance in models controlling for maternal place of birth, suggesting that the ASD case and controls differences we see with Toxo IgG may be a function of place of birth, as country of origin is a significant factor influencing exposure to Toxo (Jones et al., 2001).

The ORs for most comparisons, both maternal and newborn, were substantially below the null value, suggesting an overall pattern of lower measured levels of these immunoglobulins in ASD mother-baby pairs, even though some risk estimates did not reach statistical significance. Whether these patterns would become more statistically robust with a larger number of subjects cannot be determined from this one study. No differences were detected in immunoglobulin levels between subgroups of ASD defined by presence/ absence of intellectual disability, but sample sizes were small. Analyses of the analytes in specimens from a heterogeneous group of children with DD and their mothers failed to show any associations or possible patterns when compared to the controls, and small numbers of children with DD prevented detailed analysis.

Within mother-baby pairs, the levels of total IgG for mothers and their offspring were not statistically correlated for any of the three groups of subjects; nor were mother-baby values correlated for total IgM. Absence of correlation is, perhaps, not surprising given the elapsed time between maternal mid-gestational and newborn blood draws, the limitation of one time-point during pregnancy, and the multitude of antigens and immune response represented in these total measurements (Buka et al., 2001b). In contrast, signals for antigen-specific Toxo IgG show moderate and statistically significant correlation between maternal mid-gestational and newborn values for both ASD and population control pairs, despite the limitations related to time of specimen collection. Within the context of this study, we are unable to determine if the presence of Toxo IgG represents recent or distant exposure (Toxo IgG can persist for several years), but to our knowledge, none of the children in either the ASD or population control groups showed clinical manifestations of congenital Toxoplasmosis. For the DD group, no correlations were observed within mother-baby pairs for any analytes, perhaps because of the greater number of children of low gestational age in this subgroup (transfer of IgG antibodies from mother to baby occurs late in gestation).

Because this study employs different specimens and assays than those used in clinical settings, the clinical significance of the differences observed here is unclear. However, the overall consistency of our results with those found in our prior study (Grether et al., 2010), of higher ASD risk associated with lower immunoglobulin signals, is potentially informative. Taken together, these results are consistent with the evidence from other studies indicating that atypical maternal immune function during fetal life may contribute in some way to the development of ASD in a subset of children (Croen et al., 2008a; Goines et al., 2011; Brown et al., 2014).

In the prior study, we raised the question of whether the higher risk of ASD associated with lower newborn immunoglobulin signals might represent impaired placental transport. Based on the current study, this does not seem likely since the ASD maternal specimens showed the same overall pattern of lower immunoglobulin levels compared to controls as seen in the newborn specimens.

A plausible explanation for lower immunoglobulin levels associated with ASD is suboptimal function of the maternal immune system; exposure to common antigens may not elicit a full or typical maternal immune response, contributing to development of ASD in offspring. Whether and how suboptimal maternal immune function may impact fetal neurodevelopment remains to be explicated. Another possible explanation is that the lower immunoglobulin levels associated with ASD may simply represent reduced maternal exposure to common infectious agents. That some version of the "hygiene hypothesis" during early neurodevelopment may be relevant to ASD risk was previously offered by Becker (2007) based on parallel epidemiological, morphometric, molecular, and genetic patterns between ASD and other inflammatory disorders such as asthma.

Infants and young children who lack the robust immune protection provided by maternally-derived immunoglobulins, whether from suboptimal maternal immune function or reduced maternal exposure, might be expected to be more vulnerable to infectious exposures after birth, perhaps contributing to higher risk for ASD. However, studies have failed to consistently show an association between increased frequency of postnatal infectious illnesses and risk for ASD (Rosen et al., 2007; Atladottir et al., 2010, 2012b). Whether postnatal exposure to *Toxoplasmosis* as a specific antigen may be related to higher risk for ASD has not, to our knowledge, been investigated.

Animal studies have documented a link between maternal infectious exposure (and non-infectious activation of the maternal immune system) during pregnancy and autistic-like behaviors in offspring (Patterson, 2011). A number of early human studies also indicated that maternal infectious illnesses during pregnancy, although uncommon, may be more frequent in the history of children with ASD than in controls (Chess, 1971; Deykin and MacMahon, 1979; Markowitz, 1983; Yamashita et al., 2003). More recent studies are inconsistent (Atladottir et al., 2012a; Zerbo et al., 2013; Brown et al., 2014). Further studies based on medical record documentation may be informative, at least for more severe infections/fevers, as would prospective studies that document maternal illness during pregnancy.

In interpreting the results of our study, several strengths and limitations need to be considered. Strengths include population-based identification of subjects and the prospective specimen collection, permitting analysis of biological markers of infections during early fetal and neonatal neurodevelopment. However, our modest sample size limited our statistical power, especially for DD group for which our null results may not be generalizable. The diagnostic information we used to select the ASD and DD groups relied on DDS service agency reports with expert review by experienced clinicians. Other studies, in which the ASD diagnosis has been validated through comprehensive clinical assessment, have indicated a very high level of diagnostic validity for children enrolled in DDS with an ASD (Hertz-Picciotto et al., 2006; Croen et al., 2008b; Hallmayer et al., 2011). Our laboratory assays were fully blinded to case-control status and conducted in research laboratories with extensive experience in these research assays. However, the assays are not comparable to clinical ones, limiting our ability to interpret the biologic relevance of the results in a clinical framework. Since we did not measure all antigen-specific immunoglobulins, our results should not be interpreted as ruling out the possibility that exposure to some specific antigens not evaluated here might increase risk of ASD. Bias related to laboratory procedures can reasonably be ruled out as an explanation for our overall patterns of lower antibody levels in the ASD group, but undetected bias in initial selection of subjects must be considered as a possible explanation.

CONCLUSION

Taken as a whole, and if supported by further research, our results suggest that early immunoglobulin patterns in ASD mother-baby pairs may be etiologically informative; we recommend further studies that include prenatal and newborn specimens from linked mother-baby pairs to evaluate these immunoglobulins and other immune markers and possible effect modification associated with gene-pool factors or geographic differences in maternal exposure.

AUTHOR CONTRIBUTIONS

JG provided direction to the conception and design of the study, acquisition of data, conducted analysis and interpretation of data, and prepared the manuscript. PA contributed to conception and design of the study, analysis and interpretation of data, and revision of the manuscript for important intellectual content. JV contributed to conception and design of the study, preparation of specimens, analysis and interpretation of data, and revision of the manuscript for important intellectual content. RY contributed PA contributed actively to conception and design of the study, analysis and interpretation of data, and revision of the manuscript for important intellectual content. MA contributed to conception and design of the study, analysis and interpretation of data, and revision of the manuscript for important intellectual content. AT contributed to conception and design of the study, preparation of specimens, analysis and interpretation of data, and revision of the manuscript for important intellectual content. JW contributed to preparation of specimens, analysis and interpretation of data, and revision of the manuscript for important intellectual content. TS contributed to preparation of specimens, analysis and interpretation of data, and revision of the manuscript for important intellectual content. RH contributed to conception and design of the study, acquisition of data, and revision of the manuscript for important intellectual content. MK contributed to conception and design of the study, acquisition of data, analysis and interpretation of data, and revision of the manuscript for important intellectual content. LC contributed to the conception and design of the study, acquisition of data, analysis and interpretation of data, and review and revision of the manuscript. All authors read and approved the final manuscript.

FUNDING

Study funded by the National Institute of Environment Health Sciences, 5R01ES016669.

ACKNOWLEDGMENTS

We thank Daniel Smith, DrPH, California Department of Public Health, for statistical consultation.

REFERENCES

Atladottir, H. O., Henriksen, T. B., Schendel, D. E., and Parner, E. T. (2012a). Autism after infection, febrile episodes, and antibiotic use during pregnancy: an exploratory study. *Pediatrics.* 130, e1447–e1454. doi: 10.1542/peds.2012-1107

Atladottir, H. O., Henriksen, T. B., Schendel, D. E., and Parner, E. T. (2012b). Using maternally reported data to investigate the association between early childhood infection and autism spectrum disorder: the importance of data source. *Paediatr. Perinat. Epidemiol.* 26, 373–385. doi: 10.1111/j.1365-3016.2012.01296.x

Atladottir, H. O., Thorsen, P., Schendel, D. E., Ostergaard, L., Lemcke, S., and Parner, E. T. (2010). Association of hospitalization for infection in childhood with diagnosis of autism spectrum disorders: a Danish cohort study. *Arcyh. Pediat. Adoles. Med.* 164, 470–477. doi: 10.1001/archpediatrics.2010.9

Autism and Developmental Disabilities Monitoring Network Surveillance Year 2006 Principal Investigators; Centers for Disease Control and Prevention (CDC) (2009). Prevalence of autism spectrum disorders - Autism and Developmental Disabilities Monitoring Network, United States, 2006. *MMWR. Surveill. Summ.* 18, 58, 1–20.

Becker, K. G. (2007). Autism, asthma, inflammation, and the hygiene hypothesis. *Med. Hypotheses.* 69, 731–740. doi: 10.1016/j.mehy.2007.02.019

Braunschweig, D., Ashwood, P., Krakowiak, P., Hertz-Picciotto, I., Hansen, R., Croen, L. A., et al. (2008). Autism: maternally derived antibodies specific forfetal brain proteins. *Neurotoxicology* 29, 226–231. doi: 10.1016/j.neuro.2007.10.010

Braunschweig, D., Golub, M. S., Koenig, C. M., Qi, L., Pessah, I. N., Van de Water, J., et al. (2012). Maternal autism-associated IgG antibodies delay development and produce anxiety in a mouse gestational transfer model. *J. Neuroimmunol.* 252, 56–65. doi: 10.1016/j.jneuroim.2012.08.002

Brown, A. S. (2011). Exposure to prenatal infection and risk of schizophrenia. *Front. Psychiatry.* 2:63. doi: 10.3389/fpsyt.2011.00063

Brown, A. S., Sourander, A., Hinkka-Yli-Salomäki, S., McKeague, I. W., Sundvall, J., and Surcel, H. M. (2014). Elevated maternal C-reactive protein and autism in a national birth cohort. *Mol. Psychiatry* 19, 259–264. doi: 10.1038/mp.2012.197

Buka, S. L., Cannon, T. D., Torrey, E. F., and Yolken, R. H. (2008). Collaborative study group on the perinatal origins of severe Psychiatric Disorders. Maternal exposure to herpes simplex virus and risk of psychosis among adult offspring. *Biol. Psychiatry* 63, 809–815. doi: 10.1016/j.biopsych.2007.09.022

Buka, S. L., Tsuang, M. T., Torrey, E. F., Klebanoff, M. A., Bernstein, D., and Yolken, R. H. (2001a). Maternal infections and subsequent psychosis among offspring. *Arch. Gen. Psychiatry* 58, 1032–1037. doi: 10.1001/archpsyc.58.11.1032

Buka, S. L., Tsuang, M. T., Torrey, E. F., Klebanoff, M. A., Wagner, R. L., and Yolken, R. H. (2001b). Maternal cytokine levels during pregnancy and adult psychosis. *Brain Behav. Immun.* 15, 411–420. doi: 10.1006/brbi.2001.0644

Chess, S. (1971). Autism in children with congenital rubella. *J. Autism Child. Schizophr.* 1, 33–47.

Croen, L. A., Braunschweig, D., Haapanen, L., Yoshida, C. K., Fireman, B., Grether, J. K., et al. (2008a). Maternal mid-pregnancy autoantibodies to fetal brain protein: the early markers for autism study. *Biol. Psychiatry* 64, 583–588. doi: 10.1016/j.biopsych.2008.05.006

Croen, L. A., Matevia, J., Yoshida, C. K., and Grether, J. K. (2008b). Maternal Rh D status, anti-D immune globulin exposure during pregnancy, and risk of autism spectrum disorders. *Am. J. Obstet. Gynecol.* 199, 234.e1–e6. doi: 10.1016/j.ajog.2008.04.044

Dalton, P., Deacon, R., Blamire, A., Pike, M., McKinlay, I., Stein, J., et al. (2003). Maternal neuronal antibodies associated with autism and a language disorder. *Ann. Neurol.* 53, 533–537. doi: 10.1002/ana.10557

Deykin, E. Y., and MacMahon, B. (1979). Viral exposure and autism. *Am. J. Epidemiol.* 109, 628–638.

Goines, P. E., Croen, L. A., Braunschweig, D., Yoshida, C. K., Grether, J., Hansen, R., et al. (2011). Increased midgestational IFN-γ, IL-4 and IL-5 in women bearing a child with autism: a case-control study. *Mol. Autism.* 2:13. doi: 10.1186/2040-2392-2-13

Goines, P., and Van de Water, J. (2010). The immune system's role in the biology of autism. *Curr. Opin. Neurol.* 23, 111–117. doi: 10.1097/WCO.0b013e3283373514

Grether, J. K., Croen, L. A., Anderson, M. C., Nelson, K. B., and Yolken, R. H. (2010). Neonatally measured immunoglobulins and risk of autism. *Autism Res.* 3, 323–332. doi: 10.1002/aur.160

Hallmayer, J., Cleveland, S., Torres, A., Phillips, J., Cohen, B., Torigoe, T., et al. (2011). Genetic heritability and shared environmental factors among twin pairs with autism. *Arch. Gen. Psychiatry* 68, 1095–1102. doi: 10.1001/archgenpsychiatry.2011.76

Hertz-Picciotto, I., Croen, L. A., Hansen, R., Jones, C. R., Van de Water, J., et al. (2006). The CHARGE study: an epidemiologic investigation of genetic and environmental factors contributing to autism. *Environ. Health Perspect.* 114, 1119–1125. doi: 10.1289/ehp.8483

Jones, J. L., Kruszon-moral, D., Wilson, M., McQuillan, G., Navin, T., and McAuley, J. B. (2001). Toxoplasma gondii infection in the United States seroprevalence and risk factors. *Am. J. Epidemiol.* 154, 357–365. doi: 10.1093/aje/154.4.357

Kneeland, R. E., and Fatemi, S. H. (2013). Viral infection, inflammation and schizophrenia. *Prog. Neuropsychopharmacol. Biol. Psychiatry* 42, 35–48. doi: 10.1016/j.pnpbp.2012.02.001

Markowitz, P. I. (1983). Autism in a child with congenital cytomegalovirus infection. *J. Autism Dev. Disord.* 13, 249–253.

Martin, L. A., Ashwood, P., Braunschweig, D., Cabanlit, M., Van de Water, J., and Amaral, D. G. (2008). Stereotypies and hyperactivity in rhesus monkeys exposed to IgG from mothers of children with autism. *Brain Behav. Immun.* 22, 806–816. doi: 10.1016/j.bbi.2007.12.007

Morris, C. M., Zimmerman, A. W., and Singer, H. S. (2009). Childhood serum anti-fetal brain antibodies do not predict autism. *Pediatr. Neurol.* 41, 288–290. doi: 10.1016/j.pediatrneurol.2009.04.014

Mortensen, P. B., Pedersen, C. A., McGrath, J. J., Hougaard, D. M., Norgaard-Petersen, B., et al. (2011). Neonatal antibodies to infectious agents and risk of bipolar disorder: a population-based case-control study. *Bipolar Disord.* 13, 624–629. doi: 10.1111/j.1399-5618.2011.00962.x

Onore, C., Careaga, M., and Ashwood, P. (2012). The role of immune dysfunction in the pathophysiology of autism. *Brain Behav. Immun.* 26, 383–392. doi: 10.1016/j.bbi.2011.08.007

Patterson, P. H. (2011). Maternal infection and immune involvement in autism. *Trends Mol. Med.* 17, 389–394. doi: 10.1016/j.molmed.2011.03.001

Rosen, N. J., Yoshida, C. K., and Croen, L. A. (2007). Infection in the first 2 years of life and autism spectrum disorders. *Pediatrics* 119, e61–e69. doi: 10.1542/peds.2006-1788

Simister, N. E. (2003). Placental transport of immunoglobulin G. *Vaccine* 21, 3365–3369. doi: 10.1016/S0264-410X(03)00334-7

Singer, H. S., Morris, C., Gause, C., Pollard, M., Zimmerman, A. W., and Pletnikov, M. (2009). Prenatal exposure to antibodies from mothers of children with autism produces neurobehavioral alterations: a pregnant dam mouse model. *J. Neuroimmunol.* 211, 39–48. doi: 10.1016/j.jneuroim.2009.03.011

Stubbs, E. G., Ash, E., and Williams, C. P. (1984). Autism and congenital cytomegalovirus. *J. Autism Dev. Disord.* 14, 183–189.

Yamashita, Y., Fujimoto, C., Nakajima, E., Isagai, T., and Matsuishi, T. (2003). Possible association between congenital cytomegalovirus infection and autistic disorder. *J. Autism Dev. Disord.* 33, 455–459. doi: 10.1023/A:1025023131029

Zerbo, O., Iosif, A. M., Walker, C., Ozonoff, S., Hansen, R. L., and Hertz-Picciotto, I. (2013). Is maternal influenza or fever during pregnancy associated with autism or developmental delays? Results from the CHARGE (CHildhood Autism Risks from Genetics and Environment) study. *J. Autism Dev. Disord.* 43, 25–33. doi: 10.1007/s10803-012-1540-x

Zimmerman, A. W., Connors, S. L., Matteson, K. J., Lee, L. C., Singer, H. S., Castaneda, J. A., et al. (2007). Maternal antibrain antibodies in autism. *Brain Behav. Immun.* 21, 351–357. doi: 10.1016/j.bbi.2006.08.005

2

Resting State Functional Connectivity MRI among Spectral MEG Current Sources in Children on the Autism Spectrum

Michael Datko [1,2]*, *Robert Gougelet* [1], *Ming-Xiong Huang* [3] *and Jaime A. Pineda* [1,2]

[1] Cognitive Science, University of California San Diego, La Jolla, CA, USA, [2] Neurosciences, University of California San Diego, La Jolla, CA, USA, [3] Department of Radiology, University of California San Diego, La Jolla, CA, USA

Edited by:
Roma Siugzdaite,
Ghent University, Belgium

Reviewed by:
Lutz Jäncke,
University of Zurich, Switzerland
Jesus M. Cortes,
Biocruces Health Research Institute, Spain

***Correspondence:**
Michael Datko
mdatko@ucsd.edu

Social and communicative impairments are among the core symptoms of autism spectrum disorders (ASD), and a great deal of evidence supports the notion that these impairments are associated with aberrant functioning and connectivity of various cortical networks. The present study explored the links between sources of MEG amplitude in various frequency bands and functional connectivity MRI in the resting state. The goal of combining these modalities was to use sources of neural oscillatory activity, measured with MEG, as functionally relevant seed regions for a more traditional pairwise fMRI connectivity analysis. We performed a seed-based connectivity analysis on resting state fMRI data, using seed regions derived from frequency-specific amplitude sources in resting state MEG data in the same nine subjects with ASD (10–17 years of age). We then compared fMRI connectivity among these MEG-source-derived regions between participants with autism and typically developing, age-matched controls. We used a source modeling technique designed for MEG data to detect significant amplitude sources in six frequency bands: delta (2–4 Hz), theta (4–8 Hz), alpha (8–12 Hz), beta (12–30 Hz), low gamma (30–60 Hz), and high gamma (60–120 Hz). MEG-derived source maps for each participant were co-registered in standard MNI space, and group-level source maps were obtained for each frequency. For each frequency band, the 10 largest clusters resulting from these *t*-tests were used as regions of interest (ROIs) for the fMRI functional connectivity analysis. Pairwise BOLD signal correlations were obtained between each pair of these ROIs for each frequency band. Each pairwise correlation was compared between the ASD and TD groups using *t*-tests. We also constrained these pairwise correlations to known network structures, resulting in a follow-up set of correlation matrices specific to each network we considered. Frequency-specific MEG sources had distinct patterns of fMRI resting state functional connectivity in the ASD group, but perhaps the most significant was a finding of hypoconnectivity between many sources of low and high gamma activity. These novel findings suggest that in ASD there are differences in functionally defined networks as shown in previous fMRI studies, as well as between sets of regions defined by magnetoencephalographic neural oscillatory activity.

Keywords: autism, magnetoencephalography, fMRI, functional connectivity, multimodal

INTRODUCTION

Autism spectrum disorders (ASD) are characterized by social and communicative impairments, as well as repetitive and stereotyped behaviors (DSM-V, American Psychiatric Association (APA), 2013). It is well established that these impairments may result from aberrant anatomy and functional connectivity, defined as inter-regional correlations in the time-course of the fMRI BOLD signal (Biswal et al., 1995), within and between various cortical networks (Vissers et al., 2012). These atypical patterns of functional connectivity may underlie the disordered information integration characteristic of the ASD brain (Brock et al., 2002), therefore accounting for the myriad symptoms along the autism spectrum (Belmonte et al., 2004).

Unsurprisingly, functional connectivity in the ASD population is largely idiosyncratic across tasks (Vissers et al., 2012), methodologies (Müller et al., 2011), and behavioral symptoms (Hahamy et al., 2015). Findings include hypoconnectivity in some systems (Just et al., 2004, 2007; Kana et al., 2006, 2007), and hyperconnectivity in others (Welchew et al., 2005; Mizuno et al., 2006; Turner et al., 2006; Noonan et al., 2009; Shih et al., 2010). More recent studies have refined the characterization of functional connectivity in ASD, highlighting the contrast between within-network and out-of-network connectivity patterns, and argue for reduced within-network integration along with increased out-of-network connectivity, which ultimately results in reduced network segregation in ASD (Fair et al., 2009; Rudie et al., 2011, 2013; Shih et al., 2011; Fishman et al., 2014; Nebel et al., 2014). This characterization is supported by observations from Keown et al. (2013) and Supekar et al. (2013), who found functional hyperconnectivity in children with ASD across multiple networks, and from Pérez Velázquez and Galán (2013), who found an increase in information gain in the absence of external stimuli in ASD subjects, possibly as a consequence of hyperconnectivity and network cross-talk.

Current understanding about the neurophysiological etiology of ASD may shed light on the functional connectivity abnormalities observed during rest and task performance. It has been hypothesized that in ASD, cortical GABAergic interneurons may fail to preserve proper excitation/inhibition dynamics during development, causing irregularities in synaptic pruning and network maturation (Hensch, 2005; Coghlan et al., 2012; Rosenberg et al., 2015). In a recent study on adults with ASD, low GABA concentrations in visual cortex were shown to correlate with decreased performance on a binocular rivalry task (Robertson et al., 2016). In addition to these GABAergic interneuron dysfunctions, abnormalities in cortical minicolumns in the frontal cortex (Casanova et al., 2002), as well as enlarged frontal gray and white matter (Carper and Courchesne, 2005; Courchesne and Pierce, 2005), may also contribute to the functional connectivity issues in ASD. Whatever the sources of the abnormalities seen in ASD are, functional connectivity remains an important metric in elucidating the neurophysiological substrates of the disorder.

Non-invasive electrophysiological measures like EEG and MEG have been crucial in providing converging evidence for functional connectivity abnormalities in ASD (Vissers et al., 2012). These biophysical signals are often examined in spectral bands prescribed in the literature: delta (0–4 Hz), theta (4–8 Hz), alpha (8–12 Hz), beta (12–30 Hz), low gamma (30–60 Hz), and high gamma (60+ Hz), many of which exhibit abnormal patterns in ASD compared to typically developing controls. Subjects on the spectrum show reduced interhemispheric coherence in the gamma band (Peiker et al., 2015), a finding that provides support for the weak central coherence hypothesis of autism. Barttfeld et al. (2011), on the other hand, found distinct EEG connectivity patterns within the delta range during rest in an ASD population. These subjects lacked long-range connections, with most prominent deficits in fronto-occipital networks, and increased short-range connections in lateral-frontal networks. But while electrophysiological approaches provide important results like these on their own, the complementary use of MEG and fMRI can provide both millisecond and millimeter precision capable of spanning the multiple orders of temporal and spatial magnitudes involved in neocortical processing (Dale et al., 2000; Dale and Halgren, 2001; Liu et al., 2006; Salmelin and Baillet, 2009).

Research on these modalities suggests that the cortical neuronal activity that generates measurable electromagnetic fields imposes metabolic demands that are discernable by fMRI BOLD (Dale et al., 2000; Dale and Halgren, 2001; Logothetis et al., 2001; Arthurs and Boniface, 2002; Logothetis, 2002, 2003, 2008; Logothetis and Wandell, 2004). In particular, power in the mid-gamma band (60–120 Hz) has been shown to positively correlate with BOLD signals, whereas beta (13–30 Hz) power shows a negative correlation with BOLD (Conner et al., 2011). The higher co-localization of gamma band synchronous activity with fMRI BOLD becomes relevant in the discussion of ASD when considering that GABAergic interneurons are responsible for generating the gamma cortical oscillation (Cardin et al., 2009), and there may be dysfunction among GABAergic interneurons in ASD (Coghlan et al., 2012). Indeed, the combined use of MEG and fMRI to investigate functional connectivity could provide important new insights into the functional properties of gamma activity in ASD. Yet despite the complementarity of these two methods, there is a lack of cross-modal investigations that link measures of MEG and fMRI connectivity in autism.

The present study explored the links between MEG current source amplitudes in various frequency bands and functional connectivity MRI (fcMRI) in a resting state. More specifically, we performed a seed-based connectivity analysis on fMRI data, with seed regions based on amplitude sources from MEG data within a subgroup of subjects. We then compared connectivity among these regions between participants diagnosed with ASD and typically developing controls. First, we predicted that MEG amplitude sources for each frequency band would be located in areas previously associated with those frequencies for both ASD and typically developing controls. For instance, we predicted that alpha sources would be concentrated in visual areas, while areas associated with the mu rhythm centered more on somatosensory and premotor cortex (Pfurtscheller et al., 2006; Bernier et al., 2007). Furthermore, beta sources were expected near the central gyrus but also to extend to more frontal areas (Jensen et al., 2005). We predicted theta sources would be located in midline frontal and prefrontal areas (Iramina et al., 1996), while gamma sources were expected to show a sparse and widely distributed pattern (Cardin et al., 2009). We further predicted that ASD would show abnormal resting state fMRI connectivity patterns among regions corresponding to MEG current sources in the various frequency bands. Based on previous observations of reduced within-network integration (Rudie et al., 2011, 2013), we predicted that MEG current sources falling within the same networks would show hypoconnectivity in ASD.

METHODS

Participants

Nine participants with high-functioning autism (mean age = 13.1 ± 2.59, range = 10–17; 1 female; mean WASI IQ = 96.1 ± 15.6, range = 72–121; mean ADOS Communication and Social Interaction score = 13.7 ± 3.14, range = 12–20) were scanned with both MEG and fMRI. A clinical psychologist collaborator verified autism diagnoses through the administration of the ADOS test (Rutter et al., 2012). Nine age-matched, typically developing (TD) participants (Mean age = 10.6 ± 2.75, range = 8–16; 3 female; mean WASI IQ = 118.33 ± 13.1, range = 103–138) completed both resting state fMRI and anatomical MRI scans, but not MEG scans. TD participants had no major diagnoses and did not have ASD siblings or parents. Groups did not differ significantly for age ($p = 0.14$), but were not matched for WASI IQ ($p = 0.005$). All participants gave informed consent or assent, and read forms describing the nature of the experiment and their rights as participants. There were two different age-appropriate forms, one for children ages 7–12 and the other for ages 13–17.

MEG Data Collection and Preprocessing

Participants in the ASD group completed two back-to-back, 4-min resting state MEG scans, during which they were instructed to keep their eyes open with their gaze directed at a fixation point, and let their mind wander. MEG data were collected for ASD participants using the Elekta/Neuromag Vectorview whole-head MEG system. Data were sampled at 1000 Hz and were bandpass filtered between 0.1 and 330 Hz. Eye blinks and eye movements as measured via electrooculography (EOG), and heart activity as measured by electrocardiogram (ECG) were collected MEG sensor data were filtered for movement-related artifacts using the program MaxFilter (Taulu et al., 2005). Feeding continuous magnetic sinusoidal signals to five head position indicator coils allowed for subjects' head positions to be continuously collected. These signals are used to continuously adjust the coordinate transformation from the device to the head frame of reference, necessary for applying MaxFilter. These signals were removed from the data *post-hoc*, in addition to interference from other magnetic sources (e.g., 60 Hz line frequency and its harmonics). The spatiotemporal signal space separation (tSSS) method was used in this case to remove noise and artifacts originating from outside the brain (Taulu et al., 2004b, 2005). By continuously tracking the subjects' head positions, we minimized the influence of movement artifacts on our analyses, a common consideration when working with the pediatric ASD population.

Precautions were taken to ensure head stability: foam wedges were inserted between the subject's head and the inside of the unit. During collection, the head positions were measured to ensure that head movement across different sessions was <5 mm (usually 2–3 mm). The ECG artifacts in the MEG data were also removed when the MEG data were passed through MaxFilter. This feature of MaxFilter has been described previously (Taulu et al., 2004a,b; Song et al., 2008).

Sensor data were co-registered with subjects' anatomical MRI scans for accurate source localization. To co-register the MEG with MRI coordinate systems, three anatomical landmarks (i.e., left and right preauricular points, and nasion) were measured for each subject using the Probe Position Identification system (Polhemus, USA). By identifying the same three points on the subject's MR images using MRILAB software developed by Elekta/Neuromag, a transformation matrix involving both rotation and translation between the MEG and MRI coordinate systems was generated. To increase the reliability of the MEG-MRI co-registration, ~300 points on the scalp were digitized with the Polhemus system, in addition to the three landmarks, and those points were co-registered onto the scalp surface of the MR images.

MEG Analysis

We used a source modeling technique (Fast-VESTAL) designed for MEG data, which consists of two steps (Huang et al., 2014). First, L1-minimum-norm MEG source images were obtained for the dominant spatial (i.e., eigen-) modes of the sensor-waveform covariance matrix. Next, accurate source time-courses were obtained using an inverse operator constructed from the spatial source images of Step 1. This approach has been successfully used to obtain comprehensive MEG source-magnitude images covering the entire brain for different frequency bands of resting-state brain rhythms (Huang et al., 2014). The six different frequency bands of interest in the present study were: delta (2–4 Hz), theta (4–8 Hz), alpha (8–12 Hz), beta (12–30 Hz), low gamma (30–60 Hz), and high gamma (60–120 Hz).

In the present study, each of the artifact-free, 8-min long, resting-state MEG sensor-space scans were bandpass filtered for each frequency band of interest. The sensor-waveform covariance matrix was calculated and used to obtain MEG frequency band source magnitude images that cover the whole brain for each subject following the fast-VESTAL procedure (Huang et al., 2014). An Objective Prewhitening Method was applied to remove correlated environmental noise and to select the dominant eigen-modes of the sensor-waveform covariance matrix (Huang et al., 2014).

For each frequency band, a three-dimensional image volume showing the locations and intensities of each amplitude source was obtained for each participant. These individual subject volumes were then aligned to standard Montreal Neurological Institute (MNI) space. Using the neuroimaging software suite Analysis of Functional Neuroimages (AFNI; Cox, 1996), we then performed a one-sample t-test with a whole-brain field-of-view to determine the most significant amplitude sources at the group level. The resulting images met an uncorrected voxel wise statistical threshold of $p < 0.02$, and were cluster corrected for

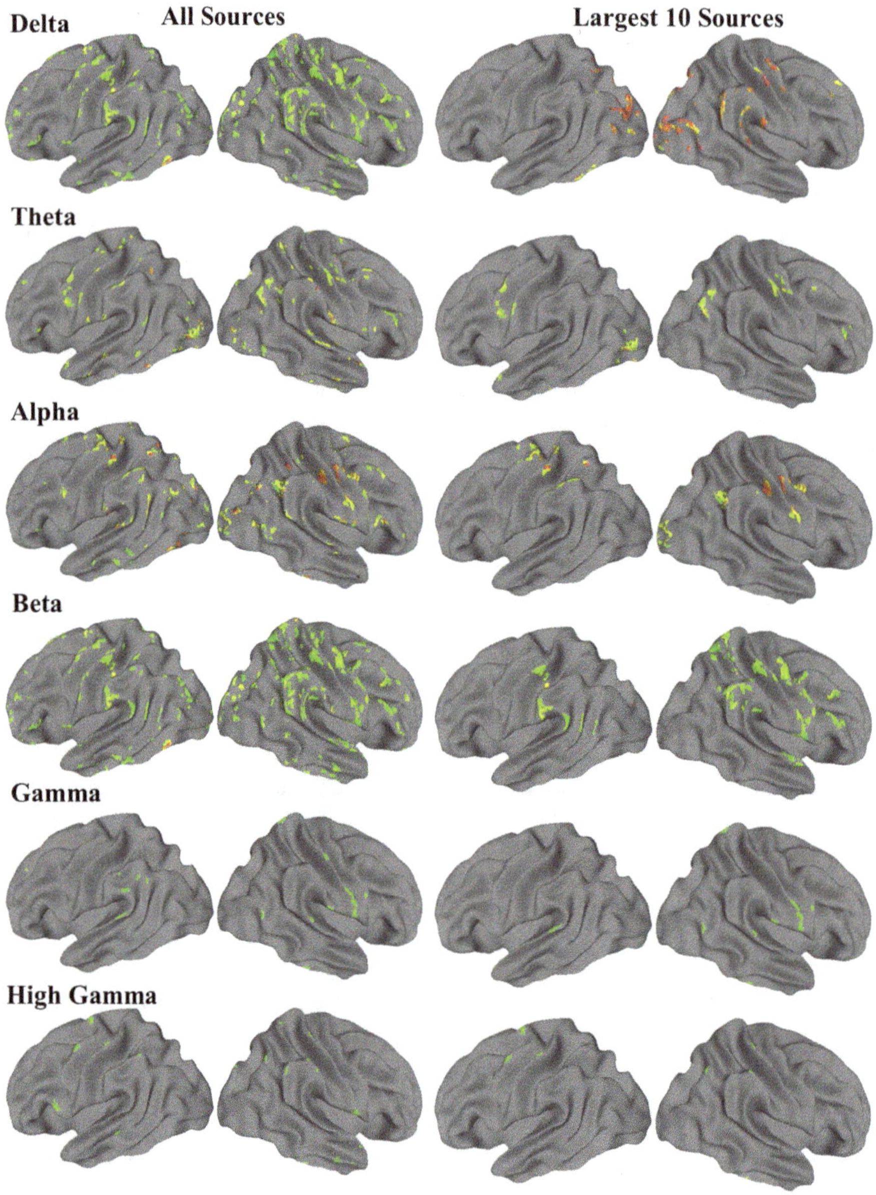

FIGURE 1 | Group-level MEG-derived source maps for each frequency band. The first column shows all sources that were significant at corrected $p < 0.01$, while the second column shows the 10 sources with the most voxels.

multiple comparisons at $p < 0.01$. For each frequency band, the 10 clusters with the largest volumes resulting from these t-tests were saved as regions of interest (ROIs) for the fMRI functional connectivity analysis (**Figure 1**).

fMRI Data Collection and Preprocessing

For ASD subjects, resting state and anatomical imaging data were acquired on a GE 1.5T Excite MRI scanner. The anatomical scan was acquired as a standard high-resolution anatomical volume with a resolution of $0.94 \times 0.94 \times 1.2\ mm^3$ using a T1-weighted 3D-IR-FSPGR pulse sequence. Functional T2*-weighted images were acquired with a single-shot gradient-recalled, echo-planar pulse sequence, as a single 7:48-min scan with 156 whole-brain volumes (TR = 3000 ms, TE = 40 ms, flip angle = 90°, FOV = 240 mm, 40 axial slices, $4 \times 4 \times 4\ mm^3$ resolution).

For TD subjects, resting state and anatomical imaging data were acquired on a GE 3T MR750 scanner with an eight-channel head coil. High-resolution anatomical images were obtained using a standard T1-weighted inversion recovery spoiled gradient echo sequence (TR = 8.108 ms, TE = 3.172 ms, flip angle 8°, 172 slices, $1\ mm^3$ resolution). Functional T2*-weighted images were acquired using a single-shot gradient-recalled, echo-planar pulse sequence, in one 6:10-min resting state scan consisting of 185 whole brain volumes (TR = 2000 ms, TE = 30 ms, flip angle 90°, FOV = 220 mm, 64×64 matrix, $3.4 \times 3.4 \times 3.4\ mm^3$ resolution, 42 axial slices).

The instructions to participants during resting state fMRI scans were identical to those received by ASD participants in the resting state MEG scans: they were told to keep their gaze on a fixation point, and remain awake. While ASD and TD groups were scanned on different magnets, all other scanning procedures and instructions to participants were identical, and subjects were scanned by the same researcher (MD).

Anatomical MRI scans for each subject were reconstructed using AFNI (Cox, 1996), and were warped to standard MNI space using FSL's nonlinear registration program *fnirt* (Andersson et al., 2007; Jenkinson et al., 2012). Standard preprocessing procedures were performed for the anatomical and resting state fMRI data, including image reconstruction, registration to MNI standard space, motion correction, spatial blurring to 6 mm full width at half maximum, spectral bandpass filtering from 0.008 to 0.08 Hz, and regression of nuisance signals derived from motion parameters, white matter, and ventricles. Time points with motion exceeding 1.5 mm from the previous time point were censored from the final analysis to reduce erroneously high correlations resulting from head motion (Power et al., 2012).

fMRI Analysis

Using the ROIs derived from the MEG source amplitude images, pairwise correlations were obtained between the BOLD time series of each possible pair of regions. These pairwise correlations were performed separately for each of the six sets of ROIs, corresponding to each of the six frequency bands for which we modeled amplitude sources. Each pairwise correlation was also compared between the ASD and TD groups using t-tests, to determine which nodes of each frequency-source-based network showed abnormal connectivity in ASD. Prior to these between-group tests, Pearson product moment correlation values were converted into Z-scores using the Fisher transformation.

We also sought to determine the extent to which the VESTAL-derived MEG amplitude sources overlapped with various functionally defined cortical networks. To define cortical network structure, we used a set of ROIs derived from a cortical parcellation created by Gordon et al. (2014). In that parcellation, which is shared publicly by the authors (http://www.nil.wustl.edu/labs/petersen/Resources.html), the cortex is divided into 333 separate ROIs. The authors of that paper then organized the parcels into 13 communities, which corresponded to various resting state and task-related networks and were derived from the Infomap community detection method developed by Rosvall and Bergstrom (2008). We focused on seven of the parcel communities they describe: default mode network (DMN), somatomotor (combining their separate somatomotor hand and mouth communities into one), visual, cingulo-operculum, frontoparietal, dorsal attention, and ventral attention. To adapt those regions for the present study, the parcels from each of the seven communities were combined into seven different community masks. Since the original parcels were created from a very thin layer of cortex, we then dilated our community masks by 1 voxel in all directions, using the AFNI command 3dmask_tool. The resulting community masks used for the present study are shown in **Figure 2**.

We conducted two follow-up correlation analyses with network-based constraints. Notably, unlike the first analysis, all between-group tests were bonferroni-corrected for multiple comparisons to a corrected $p < 0.05$. First, we looked at the pairwise correlations specifically within MEG amplitude sources that overlapped strongly with one of the seven previously discussed networks. We defined "strong" overlap as an ROI with >50% of its voxels falling within the bounds of one of our dilated network masks. For this analysis, MEG-source-based ROIs were included regardless of the frequency band from which they were derived, as it is argued that multiple frequency oscillations could emanate from the same region (Mantini et al., 2007). For instance, 1 beta source ROI, 1 gamma source ROI, and 2 high gamma source ROIs overlapped with the cingulo-opercular network, and these were examined together within one correlation matrix. ROIs included in these network-constrained correlation matrices are listed in **Table 7**.

Second, we focused on ROIs that were derived from the *same* MEG frequency band and *also* overlapped (>50% of voxels in each ROI) with the same network. Therefore, this analysis was limited to networks for which we found at least two MEG sources in the same band. Pairwise correlations were obtained for a total of nine of these sets of correlations (listed in **Table 8**). Between-group t-tests were performed for each pairwise correlation, and these were bonferroni-corrected for the number of multiple comparisons in each set, to a corrected $p < 0.05$.

RESULTS

MEG Fast-VESTAL Spectral Current Sources

We performed one-sample t-tests across all ASD subjects for the fast-VESTAL output for each frequency band. We applied a threshold to these group-level source maps in a voxel wise fashion at $p < 0.02$, and were then corrected for multiple comparisons at the cluster level to $p < 0.01$. Here we only report detailed results from the largest 10 clusters for each frequency band, although this level of correction resulted in the following number of clusters for each band: delta: 129, theta: 91, alpha: 84, beta: 128, low gamma: 19, and high gamma: 22. Anatomical labels, volumes, and MNI coordinates for the largest 10 clusters for each frequency band are listed in **Tables 1–6**.

FMRI Functional Connectivity among Regions Derived from MEG Amplitude Sources

Our first analysis compared the pairwise correlations of the BOLD signal among MEG-based ROIs in each frequency band of interest. For each of the six frequency bands, there were 10 ROIs, resulting in a 10 × 10 pairwise correlation matrix and a total of 45 between-group comparisons for each band. In this analysis, there were no significant between-group differences after strict bonferroni correction for multiple comparisons in each matrix (45), so we report results that passed an uncorrected $p < 0.05$. See **Tables 1–6** for reference of the anatomical locations of the numbered ROIs to which we refer in each frequency

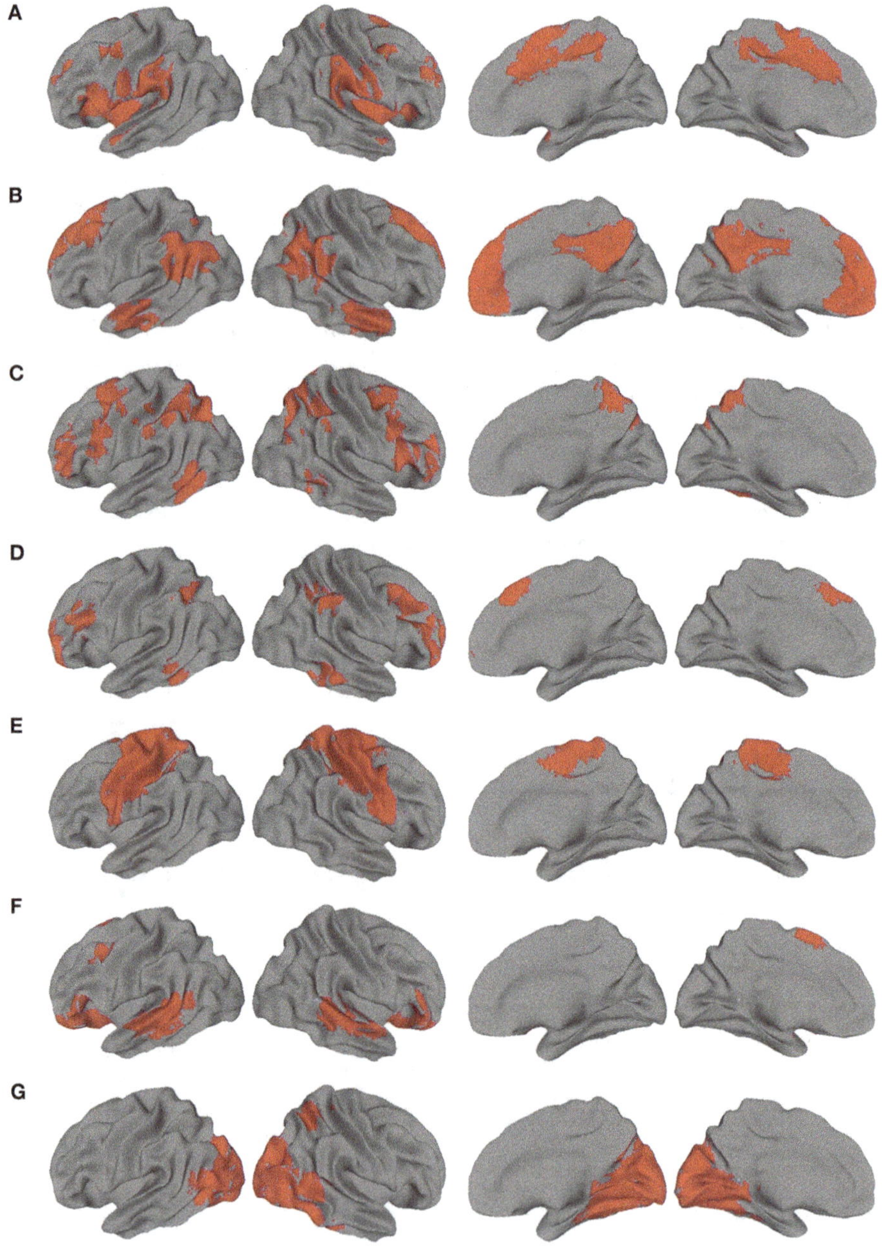

FIGURE 2 | Dilated network masks derived from the cortical parcellation from Gordon et al. (A) Cingulo-opercular, (B) Default mode network (DMN), (C) Dorsal Attention, (D) Frontoparietal, (E) Somatomotor, (F) Ventral attention, (G) Visual.

band. In the delta band, ASD showed hyperconnectivity between ROIs 1–4, 1–10, 6–10, and 7–10. Also in delta, ASD showed hypoconnectivity between ROIs 2–8, 2–9, 3–10, and 8–10. In theta, ASD showed hyperconnectivity between ROIs 1–7, 1–9, and 2–9, and hypoconnectivity between ROIs 4–6. In alpha, ASD showed hyperconnectivity between ROIs 1–2, 1–8, 1–10, 2–10, 3–10, and 8–10, and hypoconnectivity between ROIs 5–6, 5–9, and 5–10. In beta, ASD showed hyperconnectivity between ROIs 2–6, 4–10, and 6–8. In gamma, ASD showed hyperconnectivity between ROIs 2–3, 2–5, 4–7, 6–10, 7–10, and 9–10, and hypoconnectivity between ROIs 4–5. In high gamma, ASD showed hyperconnectivity between ROIs 1–4, and hypoconnectivity between ROIs 2–4, 2–9, 4–7, 7–8, and 8–10. See **Tables 1–6** and **Figure 3** for detailed summaries of these results.

The VESTAL-derived MEG amplitude sources overlapped with several of our dilated adaptations of the Gordon parcel communities. Details about the extent of these overlaps can be found in **Tables 1–6**. The 10 largest delta source clusters, totaling 842 voxels, overlapped with the following networks (each listed with number of overlapping voxels): DMN: 106, somatomotor: 80, visual: 280, frontoparietal: 18,

TABLE 1 | Delta band ROIs: Labels, Brodmann areas (BA), peak coordinates, size (voxels), and overlaps with networks.

ROI label	No. of voxels	Region	BA	x	y	z	DMN	SM	Vis	FP	Vent. attn.	Dor. attn.	C-O
1	134	L occipital	19	34	90	19	7 (5.2%)	0	120 (90%)	0	0	0	0
2	117	R precuneus	7	−18	78	52	0	0	51 (44%)	0	0	11 (9.4%)	0
3	106	R IPL	40	−66	39	28	44 (42%)	0	0	3 (2.8%)	0	2 (1.9%)	42 (40%)
4	83	L fusiform	37	49	69	−21	0	0	13 (16%)	5 (6%)	0	0	0
5	75	L SPL	7	28	69	61	21 (28%)	0	11 (15%)	0	0	5 (6.7%)	0
6	74	R IPl	40	−57	39	55	0	56 (76%)	0	0	0	10 (14%)	7 (9.5%)
7	73	R occipital	18	−24	99	1	0	0	61 (84%)	0	0	0	0
8	63	L cerebellum	7a	49	51	−48	0	0	0	0	0	0	0
9	60	R occipital	19	−42	84	22	13 (22%)	0	24 (40%)	0	0	0	0
10	57	L middle Frontal	9	−36	−37	46	21 (37%)	0	0	10 (18%)	0	2 (3.5%)	0

TABLE 2 | Theta band ROIs: Labels, Brodmann areas (BA), peak coordinates, size (voxels), and overlaps with networks.

ROI label	No. of voxels	Region	BA	x	y	z	DMN	SM	Vis	FP	Vent. attn.	Dor. attn.	C-O
1	58	L occ (V4)	18	43	84	−3	0	0	51 (88%)	0	0	0	0
2	46	L orbitofrontal	11	4	−37	−27	5 (11%)	0	0	0	0	0	0
3	44	L precentral	6	58	3	37	0	44 (100%)	0	0	0	6 (14%)	12 (27%)
4	43	R angular gyrus	39	−51	69	34	30 (70%)	0	0	0	0	0	0
5	36	R postcentral	2	−57	27	52	0	33 (92%)	0	0	0	1 (2.8%)	0
6	27	L V1	17	13	96	−18	0	0	7 (26%)	0	0	0	0
7	27	R IFG	46	−57	−31	19	0	0	0	7 (26%)	12 (44%)	2 (7.4%)	0
8	26	L ITG	20	58	36	−24	0	0	12 (46%)	8 (31%)	0	0	0
9	26	R middle frontal	6	−36	−1	43	11 (42%)	0	0	0	14 (54%)	12 (46%)	8 (31%)
10	24	L temporal pole	38	55	−10	−15	13 (54%)	0	0	0	0	0	7 (29%)

TABLE 3 | Alpha band ROIs: Labels, Brodmann areas (BA), peak coordinates, size (voxels), and overlaps with networks.

ROI Label	No. of voxels	Region	BA	x	y	z	DMN	SM	Vis	FP	Vent. attn.	Dor. attn.	C-O
1	88	L precentral	4	31	30	73	0	88 (100%)	0	0	0	8 (9.1%)	0
2	74	R Precentral	4	−42	15	52	0	72 (97%)	0	0	0	29 (39%)	6 (8.1%)
3	50	R occipital	18	−27	99	7	0	0	49 (98%)	0	0	0	0
4	42	L postcentral	2	49	33	58	0	13 (31%)	0	22 (52%)	0	0	22 (52%)
5	39	R cerebellum	8a	−12	69	−54	0	0	0	0	0	0	0
6	35	R angular gyrus	39	−54	60	34	32 (91%)	0	0	1 (2.9%)	0	1 (2.9%)	0
7	35	R precentral	6	−63	12	40	0	31 (89%)	0	0	0	0	6 (17%)
8	33	R precuneus	7	−21	78	49	0	0	19 (58%)	0	0	7 (21%)	0
9	31	L IPL	40	40	57	58	1 (3.2%)	0	4 (13%)	1 (3.2%)	0	4 (13%)	0
10	29	R precuneus	7	−3	54	67	0	5 (17%)	0	0	0	19 (66%)	0

ventral attention: 0, dorsal attention: 30, cingulo-operculum: 49. The 10 largest theta source clusters, totaling 357 voxels, overlapped with the following networks (each listed with number of overlapping voxels): DMN: 59, somatomotor: 93, visual: 70, frontoparietal: 15, ventral attention: 26, dorsal attention: 21, cingulo-operculum: 27. The largest alpha source clusters, totaling 456 voxels, overlapped with the following networks (each listed with number of overlapping voxels): DMN (33), somatomotor (224), visual (72), frontoparietal (24), dorsal attention (68), and cingulo-operculum (34). The 10 largest beta source clusters, totaling 734 voxels, overlapped with the following networks (each listed with number of overlapping voxels): DMN: 85, somatomotor: 331, visual: 46, frontoparietal: 35, ventral attention: 21, dorsal attention: 132, cingulo-operculum: 133. The 10 largest gamma source clusters, totaling 130 voxels, overlapped with the following networks (each listed with number of overlapping voxels): DMN: 9, somatomotor: 38, visual: 2, frontoparietal: 2, ventral attention: 0, dorsal attention: 20, cingulo-operculum: 16. The 10 largest high gamma source clusters, totaling 98 voxels, overlapped with the following networks (each listed with number of overlapping voxels): DMN: 10, somatomotor: 32, visual: 0, frontoparietal: 2, ventral attention: 0, dorsal attention: 7, cingulo-operculum: 15.

TABLE 4 | Beta band ROIs: Labels, Brodmann areas (BA), peak coordinates, size (voxels), and overlaps with networks.

ROI label	No. of voxels	Region	BA	x	y	z	DMN	SM	Vis	FP	Vent. attn.	Dor. attn.	C-O
1	121	R IPL	40	−45	45	46	1 (0.83%)	82 (68%)	0	0	0	68 (56%)	4 (3.3%)
2	98	R precentral	3	−45	18	55	1 (1%)	82 (84%)	0	0	1 (1%)	1 (1%)	13 (13%)
3	91	R STG	22	−60	−1	−6	13 (14%)	43 (47%)	0	0	3 (3.3%)	9 (9.9%)	29 (32%)
4	80	R IPL	40	−51	45	31	51 (64%)	1 (1.2%)	0	0	0	4 (5%)	30 (38%)
5	79	R mid frontal	9	−39	−22	34	1 (1.3%)	0	0	27 (34%)	15 (19%)	7 (8.9%)	4 (5.1%)
6	68	R SPL	7	−21	51	70	0	48 (71%)	0	0	0	39 (57%)	0
7	58	R/L cuneus	19	−6	90	28	0	0	43 (74%)	0	0	0	0
8	48	L IPL	2	43	30	43	0	46 (96%)	0	8 (17%)	0	4 (8.3%)	4 (8.3%)
9	46	L IPL	40	64	30	25	0	2 (4.3%)	0	0	0	0	46 (100%)
10	45	L pSTS	40	58	54	22	18 (40%)	0	3 (6.7%)	0	2 (4.4%)	0	3 (6.7%)

TABLE 5 | Gamma band ROIs: Labels, Brodmann areas (BA), peak coordinates, size (voxels), and overlaps with networks.

ROI label	No. of voxels	Region	BA	x	y	z	DMN	SM	Vis	FP	Vent. attn.	Dor. attn.	C-O
1	21	R precentral	6	−63	−1	31	0	20 (95%)	0	0	0	1 (4.8%)	1 (4.8%)
2	19	L postcentral	7	4	57	67	0	0	0	0	0	8 (42%)	0
3	15	R sup temporal	42	−66	30	16	0	0	0	0	0	0	4 (27%)
4	12	R cerebellum	7a	−48	45	−33	0	0	0	0	0	0	0
5	12	L mPFC	11	13	−61	−18	9 (75%)	0	0	2 (17%)	0	0	0
6	11	R ITG	20	−63	42	−24	0	0	0	0	0	0	0
7	11	R postcentral	7	−12	54	73	0	10 (91%)	0	0	0	9 (82%)	0
8	10	L pMTG	39	−57	69	13	0	0	2 (20%)	0	0	2 (20%)	0
9	10	L STG	22	64	36	16	0	0	0	0	0	0	6 (60%)
10	9	R postcentral	43	−66	9	19	0	8 (89%)	0	0	0	0	5 (56%)

TABLE 6 | High Gamma band ROIs: Labels, Brodmann areas (BA), peak coordinates, size (voxels), and overlaps with networks.

ROI label	No. of voxels	Region	BA	x	y	z	DMN	SM	Vis	FP	Vent. attn.	Dor. attn.	C-O
1	12	R med orbitofrontal	11	−12	−52	−24	2 (17%)	0	0	0	0	0	0
2	11	R cerebellum	8a	−33	45	−54	0	0	0	0	0	0	0
3	11	L precentral	6	25	12	73	0	9 (82%)	0	0	0	0	1 (9.1%)
4	10	L precuneus	7	4	69	64	0	0	0	0	0	1 (10%)	0
5	9	R inferior temporal	20	−63	39	−24	0	0	0	0	0	0	0
6	9	R SPL	7	−42	69	52	8 (89%)	0	0	0	0	0	0
7	9	R IPL	40	−54	39	58	0	0	0	0	0	3 (33%)	5 (56%)
8	9	L precentral	6	43	−1	58	0	5 (56%)	0	2 (22%)	0	3 (33%)	9 (100%)
9	9	L postcentral	1	49	27	61	0	9 (100%)	0	0	0	0	0
10	9	R postcentral	2	−42	36	67	0	9 (100%)	0	0	0	0	0

The first follow-up analysis included correlation matrices containing all ROIs overlapping with a specific network regardless of the MEG frequency band on which they were based. Overall, four networks overlapped with at least two ROIs each. Among the six ROIs that overlapped with the DMN (2 theta, 1 alpha, 1 beta, 1 gamma, 1 high gamma), there were no significant differences in connectivity between ASD and TD groups. Among the 16 ROIs that overlapped with the Somatomotor network (1 delta, 2 theta, 3 alpha, 4 beta, 3 gamma, 3 high gamma), there were three ROI pairs in which ASD showed *hypoconnectivity*: a delta to a high gamma ROI, theta to high gamma, and alpha to high gamma. Among the six ROIs that overlapped with the Visual network (2 delta, 1 theta, 2 alpha, 1 beta), there were no significant differences in connectivity between ASD and TD groups. Among the four ROIs that overlapped with the cingulo-operculum network (1 beta, 1 gamma, 2 high gamma), the ASD group showed *hypoconnectivity* between the gamma and a high gamma ROI. These results are further summarized in **Table 7** and **Figure 4**.

The second follow-up analysis looked only at correlations between sources that (a) were derived from the same MEG frequency band and (b) overlapped with the same network.

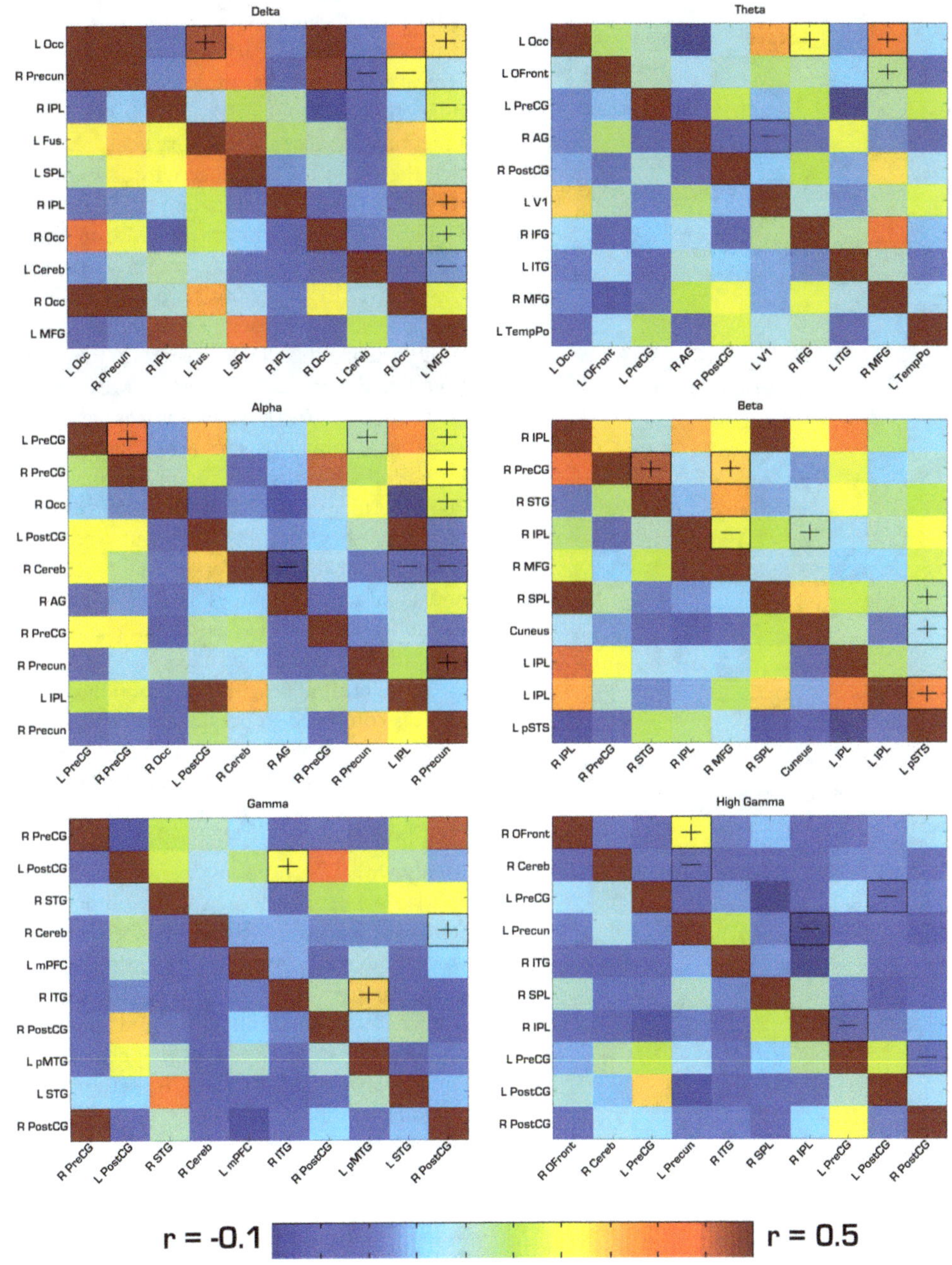

FIGURE 3 | Correlation matrices for ROIs derived from each frequency band. ASD correlations are in the top right triangle of each matrix, while TD correlations are in the bottom left. "–" and "+" indicates ROI pairs for which ASD trended toward hypo- or hyperconnectivity, respectively. In this first analysis, none of the group differences were significant after strict Bonferroni correction. Therefore, the group differences shown here had an uncorrected $p < 0.05$. Occ, Occipital; IPL, Inferior Parietal Lobule; SPL, Superior Parietal Lobule; PreCG, Precentral Gyrus; PostCG, Postcentral Gyrus; MFG, Middle Frontal Gyrus; Cereb, Cerebellum; Precun, Precuneus; STG, Superior Temporal Gyrus; MTG, Middle Temporal Gyrus; ITG, Inferior Temporal Gyrus; AG, Angular Gyrus; Ofront, Orbito Frontal Cortex; TempPo, Temporal Pole.

Overall, nine separate sets of correlations were performed based on this criteria. Three significant effects emerged from this analysis, all surviving bonferroni-correction for multiple comparisons at $p < 0.05$. In the ASD group, two alpha ROIs were *hyperconnected* to each other within the somatomotor network, two high gamma ROIs were *hypoconnected* to each other within the somatomotor network, and two high gamma ROIs were *hypoconnected* to each other within the cingulo-operculum network. See **Table 8** for a more detailed summary of results from this analysis.

TABLE 7 | ROIs used in network-constrained correlation matrices.

Network	Derived from MEG band	ROI label	Location	Percent overlap of ROI with network (%)
DMN	Theta	4	R angular gyrus	70
	Theta	10	L temporal pole	54
	Alpha	6	R angular gyrus	91
	Beta	4	R IPL	64
	Gamma	5	L mPFC	75
	High gamma	6	R SPL	89
Somatomotor	Delta	6	R IPL	76
	Theta	3	L precentral	100
	Theta	5	R postcentral	92
	Alpha	1	L precentral	100
	Alpha	2	R Precentral	97
	Alpha	7	R precentral	89
	Beta	1	R IPL	68
	Beta	2	R precentral	84
	Beta	6	R SPL	71
	Beta	8	L IPL	96
	Gamma	1	R precentral	95
	Gamma	7	R postcentral	91
	Gamma	10	R postcentral	89
	High gamma	3	L precentral	82
	High gamma	9	L postcentral	100
	High gamma	10	R postcentral	100
Visual	Delta	1	L occipital	90
	Delta	7	R occipital	84
	Theta	1	L occ (V4)	88
	Alpha	3	R occipital	98
	Alpha	8	R precuneus	58
	Beta	7	R/L cuneus	74
Cingulo-opercular	Beta	9	L IPL	100
	Gamma	9	L STG	60
	High gamma	7	R IPL	56
	High gamma	8	L precentral	100

DISCUSSION

The present study used a multimodal approach to investigate brain network dynamics in children with ASD, and provides new evidence for abnormal functional connectivity in cortical networks. The integration of both MEG and fMRI data collected during a resting state enabled groupwise comparisons of functional connectivity between MEG current sources for delta, theta, alpha, beta, and gamma bands. Our primary connectivity analysis was performed on fMRI data, while the ROIs derived from MEG amplitude-sources provided a novel framework within which to test that fMRI data. One advantage of this method is that MEG allowed us to localize important hubs of fast neuronal oscillations not normally detected with fMRI. Most studies define ROIs for connectivity analyses using data from task activation studies, anatomical atlases, meta-analyses, and data driven approaches such as independent component analyses. However, no study has explored the possibility of detecting novel differences between ASD and TD samples among regions that function as neuronal oscillatory generators. Another advantage is that the use of fMRI connectivity as an outcome measure allows us to compare our results to a large body of previous evidence. Unlike MEG, the literature on fcMRI in ASD is quite extensive.

Using a spectral MEG current source-modeling algorithm (fast-VESTAL) in resting state MEG scans, we found that the spatial distribution of spectral current sources in a group of ASD participants followed general patterns reported in a previous investigation of VESTAL-derived MEG sources in healthy adults (Huang et al., 2014). Alpha sources were highly concentrated in visual and somatosensory areas, in line with previous findings on both the mu rhythm and occipital alpha (Pfurtscheller et al., 2006; Bernier et al., 2007). Beta sources overlapped with some somatosensory alpha sources, but were concentrated in more anterior and fewer posterior regions compared to alpha. Low and high gamma sources showed a wider spatial distribution, including regions such as medial prefrontal cortex, precuneus, and inferior temporal gyrus.

To determine how the distribution of spectral MEG current sources compared to previously described resting state network structure, we looked at the number of voxels from each ROI that overlapped with an existing map of cortical parcel communities from Gordon et al. (2014). Delta ROIs overlapped largely with DMN and visual areas; theta ROIs overlapped somewhat evenly with DMN, visual, and somatomotor areas; alpha ROIs overlapped largely with somatomotor and visual areas; beta ROIs overlapped mostly with somatomotor areas, but also had considerable overlap with DMN, dorsal attention, and cingulo-opercular networks; gamma ROIs overlapped mostly with somatomotor, dorsal attention, and cingulo-opercular networks; and high gamma ROIs overlapped with somatomotor and cingulo-opercular networks. The pattern of activity that emerged was one where current sources of lower frequency bands (delta, theta) were found in areas associated with resting state activity, in line with electrophysiological findings on the DMN (Mantini et al., 2007). As expected, lower frequency sources were also found in primary sensory (visual and somatomotor) cortices (Pfurtscheller et al., 2006; Bernier et al., 2007). In contrast, higher frequency bands (beta, gamma, and high gamma) were associated with areas involved in higher-order sensory integration and attention regulation such as dorsal attention and cingulo-opercular networks. Notably, these sources were derived exclusively from an ASD group, yet they displayed a general distribution consistent with previous findings in healthy adults (Huang et al., 2014). This leaves open the possibility that, while MEG current sources have a typical distribution in ASD, there exist abnormalities in their functional, coordinated activity.

The results of our first analysis of functional connectivity in resting state fMRI data using seed ROIs based on MEG amplitude sources found pairs of regions showing trends toward differences between ASD and TD groups, although none proved statistically significant after correction for multiple comparisons. There was

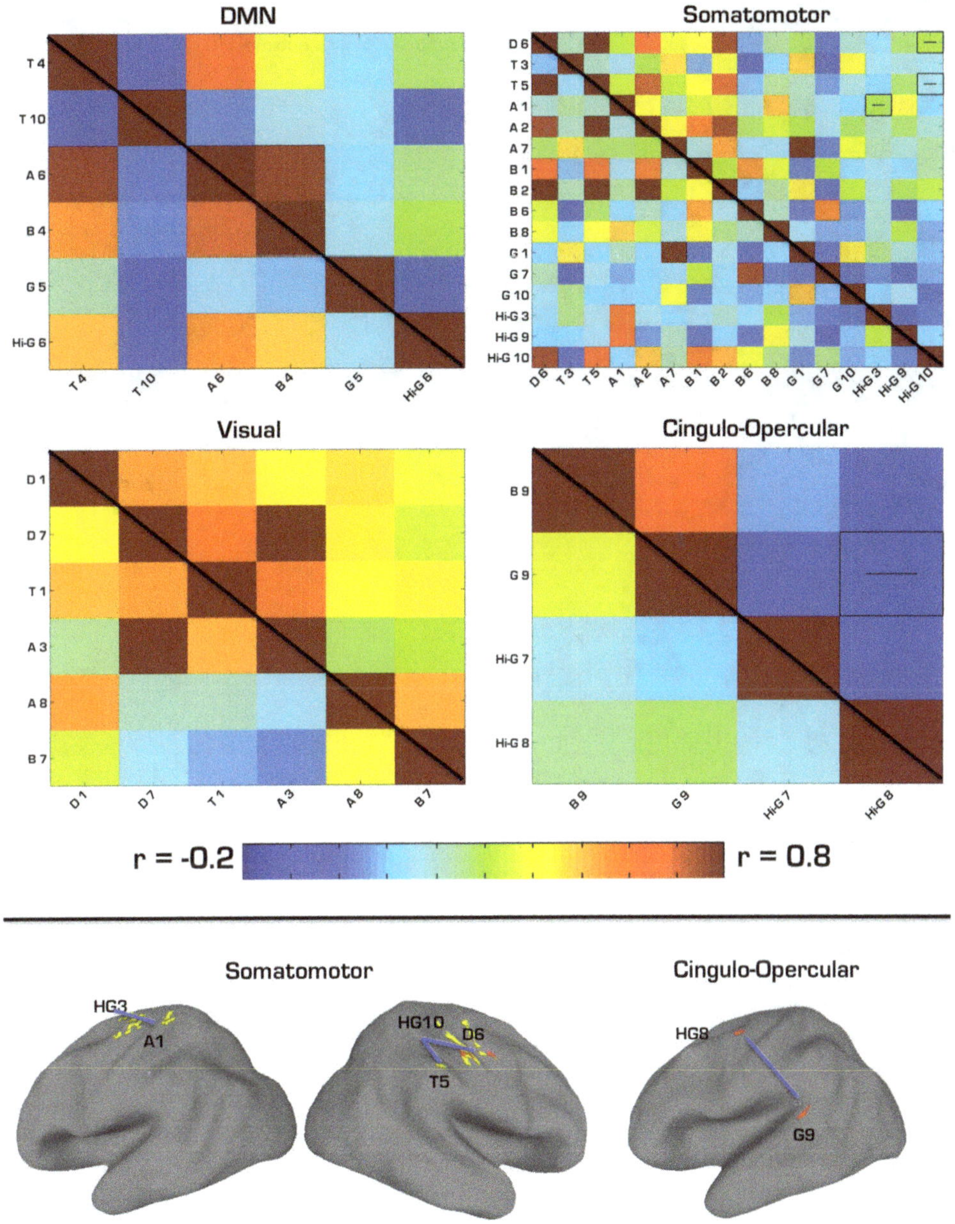

FIGURE 4 | (Top) Correlation matrices for network-constrained MEG source ROIs. ASD correlations are in the top right triangle of each matrix, while TD correlations are in the bottom left. Pairwise correlations with significant group differences ($p < 0.05$, Bonferroni corrected) are depicted by a "−" or "+" to indicate ASD hypo- or hyperconnectivity. Labels for each ROI correspond to the first letter of each ROI's frequency band, and the number it is associated with in **Tables 1–6**. **(Bottom)** Regions showing significant hypoconnectivity in ASD. Regions connected by blue lines correspond to those shown in the above correlation matrices as being hyperconnected.

a trend toward hyperconnectivity among alpha sources located in sensorimotor cortex, while an alpha source in the cerebellum showed a trend of hypoconnectivity to multiple regions in the parietal and temporal lobes. While not statistically significant in the present study, this trend is consistent with recent findings of cerebellum hypoconnectivity to supramodal cortical regions, including parietal and temporal regions (Khan et al., 2015).

We then performed two sets of follow-up correlation analyses based on the overlaps of our VESTAL-derived ROIs with previously described network structure. First, we looked at pairwise correlations between MEG-derived sources that overlapped with one of seven networks, based on the parcel communities described by Gordon et al. (2014). Unlike the first analysis, we used ROIs across any of the six frequency bands, as long as they overlapped with a network. This was done to highlight possible group differences in neural information encoding across multiple frequencies, in light of previous findings of abnormal coupling between different frequency

TABLE 8 | ROIs used in correlation matrices constrained by both network membership and frequency band of origin.

Network	Band	ROI label	Location	Percent overlap of ROI with network (%)	ASD vs. TD *P*-values for pairwise *r*
Visual	Delta	1	L occipital	90	0.14
		7	R occipital	84	
	Alpha	3	R occipital	98	0.4
		8	R precuneus	58	
DMN	Theta	4	R angular gyrus	70	0.82
		10	L temporal pole	54	
Somatomotor	Theta	3	L precentral	100	0.52
		5	R postcentral	92	
	Alpha	1	L precentral	100	0.01 (ROIs 1 and 2)
		2	R precentral	97	0.55 (ROIs 1 and 7)
		7	R precentral	89	0.10 (ROIs 2 and 7)
	Beta	1	R IPL	68	0.02 (1 and 2), 0.83 (1 and 6), 0.47 (1 and 8)
		2	R precentral	84	0.53 (2 and 6), 0.99 (2 and 8)
		6	R SPL	71	0.97 (6 and 8)
		8	L IPL	96	
	Gamma	1	R precentral	95	0.91 (1 and 7), 0.61 (1 and 10)
		7	R postcentral	91	0.25 (7 and 10)
		10	R postcentral	89	
	High gamma	3	L precentral	82	0.001 (3 and 9)
		9	L postcentral	100	0.43 (3 and 10)
		10	R postcentral	100	0.52 (9 and 10)
Cingulo-opercular	High gamma	7	R IPL	56	0.013
		8	L precentral	100	

bands in various disease states Voytek and Knight (2015). Hyperconnectivity of the BOLD signal between the MEG sources we identified could indicate problematic overcoupling between neuronal oscillations of different frequencies. Also unlike the first analysis, we found several between-group results that survived bonferroni correction for the number of pairwise correlations in each network's matrix. Within the somatomotor network, the ASD group showed *hypoconnectivity* in three ROIs based on high gamma MEG sources, including between a high gamma source in left postcentral gyrus to a delta source in right postcentral gyrus and to a theta source in right postcentral gyrus. Additionally, ASD was *hypoconnected* from a high gamma source in left precentral gyrus to an alpha source located more ventrally in left precentral gyrus. Within the cingulo-opercular network, the ASD group showed *hypoconnectivity* between a gamma ROI in right lateral visual cortex (V5) and a high gamma ROI in left precentral gyrus (Brodmann Area 6). In another follow-up fMRI correlation analysis, we further narrowed our focus to include only ROIs that overlapped with the same network and which were derived from the same MEG frequency band. ASD showed significant hypoconnectivity between two ROIs based on high-gamma sources within the somatomotor network. That group also showed hypoconnectivity between two other gamma ROIs (one low gamma and the other high gamma), which were instead located in the cingulo-operculum network. Thus, across both secondary analyses, there was a clear pattern of hypoconnectivity among many sources of gamma activity that overlapped with several networks. This pattern could represent the increased neural noise that is a consequence of dysfunctional inhibitory processing of GABAergic interneurons (Brock et al., 2002; Casanova et al., 2002; Brown et al., 2005; Wilson et al., 2007; Sun et al., 2012; Peiker et al., 2015). These stronger findings of within-network connectivity abnormalities support the notion of reduced within-network integration (Fair et al., 2009; Rudie et al., 2011, 2013; Fishman et al., 2014; Nebel et al., 2014), and recapitulate MEG and EEG findings on abnormal gamma connectivity, in ASD.

There were no significant differences between groups in any pairwise correlations among ROIs overlapping with the DMN, suggesting that electrophysiological activity may be relatively normal in ASD in this network. This is in contrast to some previous studies that have shown abnormal functional connectivity in DMN (Cherkassky et al., 2006; Monk et al., 2009; Lynch et al., 2013), but it could be the case that our VESTAL-derived MEG sources were located in unaffected sub regions of this network.

There are several limitations that call for caution in the interpretation of our results. First, we only collected MEG data from ASD subjects. It is possible that we would see a qualitatively different distribution of MEG amplitude sources if the VESTAL algorithms were performed on TD participants alone, or on a combination of ASD and TD participants. However, many other studies, including the initial report of the VESTAL source localization technique (Huang et al., 2014), have found source distribution patterns in neurotypical individuals were similar to those displayed by our ASD sample. Thus, while the exact locations of some current sources may differ between groups, their overall similarity to previously observed typical patterns justifies the use of these sources as the basis for the rest of our analyses. Another caveat to these results is that the TD and ASD groups were scanned on magnets of differing strength: 3T and 1.5T, respectively. Although the acquisition parameters differed between these scanners, the larger voxel size, longer TR, longer total scan length for the 1.5T scans ensured that the signal-to-noise ratio was comparable between both groups. Finally, groups were not matched for IQ, with ASD showing a lower full score on the WASI. In a follow-up analysis, we used participant IQ as a covariate in the between-group *t*-tests of pairwise functional connectivity between sources. Of the eight source pairs showing significant group differences before accounting for IQ, two pairs still showed significant differences after doing so. These included an alpha to a high gamma source within the somatomotor network ($p = 0.019$, hypoconnected in ASD), and a theta to a beta source within the visual network ($p = 0.005$, hyperconnected in ASD). The persistence of these effects after controlling for IQ is evidence that, despite a low sample size and suboptimal group matching, this novel approach to integrating resting state MEG and fMRI data was still able to detect group differences in brain connectivity between ASD and TD individuals. Thus, this approach could inform future studies with larger, well-matched samples.

The present study demonstrates a novel approach to a multimodal investigation of brain connectivity in ASD. By using an MEG-amplitude source modeling technique as the basis for fcMRI analyses, we found further evidence supporting the notion of aberrant functional connectivity in ASD. This is also is the first study to report ASD hypoconnectivity of the BOLD signal specifically between sources of MEG gamma oscillations, providing supporting evidence that dysfunctional inhibitory processing mediated by gamma oscillations may play an important role in the neuroetiology of ASD.

AUTHOR CONTRIBUTIONS

MD collected fMRI and MEG data, preprocessed and analyzed data, and wrote much of the manuscript. RG collected MEG data, preprocessed MEG data, and contributed to the manuscript. MH contributed the VESTAL algorithm that was used to analyze MEG data, and trained other authors in the use of VESTAL. JP collected MEG data, advised during data preprocessing and analysis steps, and contributed to the manuscript.

ACKNOWLEDGMENTS

The authors would like to thank the following individuals for their assistance with participant recruitment, data collection and analysis for this study: Anne Marie Angeles, Nicolette Castro, Thomas Donoghue, Matthew Goodman, Mike Metke, Megan Kirchgessner, Nicole Mlynaryk, Ashley Swan, and Michael Widdowson. The authors would like to thank the UC San Diego Academic Senate for funding this work (RN038B-Pineda).

REFERENCES

American Psychiatric Association (APA) (2013). *Diagnostic and Statistical Manual of Mental Disorders, 5th Edn.* Arlington, VA: American Psychiatric Association.

Andersson, J. L. R., Jenkinson, M., and Smith, S. (2007). *Non-Linear Registration, Aka Spatial Normalisation FMRIB Technical Report TR07JA2.* FMRIB Analysis Group of the University of Oxford.

Arthurs, O., and Boniface, S. (2002). How well do we understand the neural origins of the fMRI BOLD signal? *Trends Neurosci.* 25, 27–31. doi: 10.1016/S0166-2236(00)01995-0

Barttfeld, P., Wicker, B., Cukier, S., Navarta, S., Lew, S., and Sigman, M. (2011). A big-world network in ASD: dynamical connectivity analysis reflects a deficit in long-range connections and an excess of short-range connections. *Neuropsychologia* 49, 254–263. doi: 10.1016/j.neuropsychologia.2010.11.024

Belmonte, M. K., Allen, G., Beckel-Mitchener, A., Boulanger, L. M., Carper, R. A., and Webb, S. J. (2004). Autism and abnormal development of brain connectivity. *J. Neurosci.* 24, 9228–9231. doi: 10.1523/JNEUROSCI.3340-04.2004

Bernier, R., Dawson, G., Webb, S., and Murias, M. (2007). EEG mu rhythm and imitation impairments in individuals with autism spectrum disorder. *Brain Cogn.* 64, 228–237. doi: 10.1016/j.bandc.2007.03.004

Biswal, B., Yetkin, F. Z., Haughton, V. M., and Hyde, J. S. (1995). Functional connectivity in the motor cortex of resting human brain using echo-planar MRI. *Magn. Reson. Med.* 34, 537–541.

Brock, J., Brown, C. C., Boucher, J., and Rippon, G. (2002). The temporal binding deficit hypothesis of autism. *Dev. Psychopathol.* 14, 209–224. doi: 10.1017/S0954579402002018

Brown, C., Gruber, T., Boucher, J., Rippon, G., and Brock, J. (2005). Gamma abnormalities during perception of illusory figures in autism. *Cortex* 41, 364–376. doi: 10.1016/S0010-9452(08)70273-9

Cardin, J. A., Carlén, M., Meletis, K., Knoblich, U., Zhang, F., Deisseroth, K., et al. (2009). Driving fast-spiking cells induces gamma rhythm and controls sensory responses. *Nature* 459, 663–667. doi: 10.1038/nature08002

Carper, R. A., and Courchesne, E. (2005). Localized enlargement of the frontal cortex in early autism. *Biol. Psychiatry* 57, 126–133. doi: 10.1016/j.biopsych.2004.11.005

Casanova, M. F., Buxhoeveden, D. P., Switala, A. E., and Roy, E. (2002). Minicolumnar pathology in autism. *Neurology* 58, 428–432. doi: 10.1212/WNL.58.3.428

Cherkassky, V. L., Kana, R. K., Keller, T. A., and Just, M. A. (2006). Functional connectivity in a baseline resting-state network in autism. *Neuroreport* 17, 1687–1690. doi: 10.1097/01.wnr.0000239956.45448.4c

Coghlan, S., Horder, J., Inkster, B., Mendez, M. A., Murphy, D. G., and Nutt, D. J. (2012). GABA system dysfunction in autism and related disorders: from synapse to symptoms. *Neurosci. Biobehav. Rev.* 36, 2044–2055. doi: 10.1016/j.neubiorev.2012.07.005

Conner, C. R., Ellmore, T. M., Pieters, T. A., Disano, M. A., and Tandon, N. (2011). Variability of the relationship between electrophysiology and BOLD-fMRI across cortical regions in humans. *J. Neurosci.* 31, 12855–12865. doi: 10.1523/JNEUROSCI.1457-11.2011

Courchesne, E., and Pierce, K. (2005). Why the frontal cortex in autism might be talking only to itself: local over-connectivity but long-distance disconnection. *Curr. Opin. Neurobiol.* 15, 225–230. doi: 10.1016/j.conb.2005.03.001

Cox, R. W. (1996). AFNI: software for analysis and visualization of functional magnetic resonance neuroimages. *Comput. Biomed. Res.* 29, 162–173.

Dale, A. M., and Halgren, E. (2001). Spatiotemporal mapping of brain activity by integration of multiple imaging modalities. *Curr. Opin. Neurobiol.* 11, 202–208. doi: 10.1016/S0959-4388(00)00197-5

Dale, A. M., Liu, A. K., Fischl, B. R., Buckner, R. L., Belliveau, J. W., Lewine, J. D., et al. (2000). Dynamic statistical parametric mapping: combining fMRI and MEG for high-resolution imaging of cortical activity. *Neuron* 26, 55–67. doi: 10.1016/S0896-6273(00)81138-1

Fair, D. A., Cohen, A. L., Power, J. D., Dosenbach, N. U., Church, J. A., Miezin, F. M., et al. (2009). Functional brain networks develop from a "local to distributed" organization. *PLoS Comput. Biol.* 5:e1000381. doi: 10.1371/journal.pcbi.1000381

Fishman, I., Keown, C. L., Lincoln, A. J., Pineda, J. A., and Müller, R. A. (2014). Atypical cross talk between mentalizing and mirror neuron networks in autism spectrum disorder. *JAMA Psychiatry* 71, 751–760. doi: 10.1001/jamapsychiatry.2014.83

Gordon, E. M., Laumann, T. O., Adeyemo, B., Huckins, J. F., Kelley, W. M., and Petersen, S. E. (2014). Generation and evaluation of a cortical area parcellation from resting-state correlations. *Cereb. Cortex* 26, 288–303. doi: 10.1093/cercor/bhu239

Hahamy, A., Behrmann, M., and Malach, R. (2015). The idiosyncratic brain: distortion of spontaneous connectivity patterns in autism spectrum disorder. *Nat. Neurosci.* 18, 302–309. doi: 10.1038/nn.3919

Hensch, T. K. (2005). Critical period plasticity in local cortical circuits. *Nat. Rev. Neurosci.* 6, 877–888. doi: 10.1038/nrn1787

Huang, M. X., Huang, C. W., Robb, A., Angeles, A., Nichols, S. L., Baker, D. G., et al. (2014). MEG source imaging method using fast L1 minimum-norm and its applications to signals with brain noise and human resting-state source amplitude images. *Neuroimage* 84, 585–604. doi: 10.1016/j.neuroimage.2013.09.022

Iramina, K., Ueno, S., and Matsuoka, S. (1996). MEG and EEG topography of frontal midline theta rhythm and source localization. *Brain Topogr.* 8, 329–331. doi: 10.1007/BF01184793

Jenkinson, M., Beckmann, C. F., Behrens, T. E., Woolrich, M. W., and Smith, S. M. (2012). FSL. *Neuroimage* 62, 782–790. doi: 10.1016/j.neuroimage.2011.09.015

Jensen, O., Goel, P., Kopell, N., Pohja, M., Hari, R., and Ermentrout, B. (2005). On the human sensorimotor-cortex beta rhythm: sources and modeling. *Neuroimage* 26, 347–355. doi: 10.1016/j.neuroimage.2005.02.008

Just, M. A., Cherkassky, V. L., Keller, T. A., Kana, R. K., and Minshew, N. J. (2007). Functional and anatomical cortical underconnectivity in autism: evidence from an FMRI study of an executive function task and corpus callosum morphometry. *Cereb. Cortex* 17, 951–961. doi: 10.1093/cercor/bhl006

Just, M. A., Cherkassky, V. L., Keller, T. A., and Minshew, N. J. (2004). Cortical activation and synchronization during sentence comprehension in high-functioning autism: evidence of underconnectivity. *Brain* 127, 1811–1821. doi: 10.1093/brain/awh199

Kana, R. K., Keller, T. A., Cherkassky, V. L., Minshew, N. J., and Just, M. A. (2006). Sentence comprehension in autism: thinking in pictures with decreased functional connectivity. *Brain* 129, 2484–2493. doi: 10.1093/brain/awl164

Kana, R. K., Keller, T. A., Minshew, N. J., and Just, M. A. (2007). Inhibitory control in high-functioning autism: decreased activation and underconnectivity in inhibition networks. *Biol. Psychiatry* 62, 198–206. doi: 10.1016/j.biopsych.2006.08.004

Keown, C. L., Shih, P., Nair, A., Peterson, N., Mulvey, M. E., and Müller, R. A. (2013). Local functional overconnectivity in posterior brain regions is associated with symptom severity in autism spectrum disorders. *Cell Rep.* 5, 567–572. doi: 10.1016/j.celrep.2013.10.003

Khan, A. J., Nair, A., Keown, C. L., Datko, M. C., Lincoln, A. J., and Müller, R. A. (2015). Cerebro-cerebellar resting-state functional connectivity in children and adolescents with autism spectrum disorder. *Biol. Psychiatry* 78, 625–634. doi: 10.1016/j.biopsych.2015.03.024

Liu, Z., Ding, L., and He, B. (2006). Integration of EEG/MEG with MRI and fMRI. *IEEE Eng. Med. Biol. Mag.* 25, 46–53. doi: 10.1109/MEMB.2006.1657787

Logothetis, N. K. (2002). The neural basis of the blood-oxygen-level-dependent functional magnetic resonance imaging signal. *Philos. Trans. R. Soc. Lond. B Biol. Sci.* 357, 1003–1037. doi: 10.1098/rstb.2002.1114

Logothetis, N. K. (2003). MR imaging in the non-human primate: studies of function and of dynamic connectivity. *Curr. Opin. Neurobiol.* 13, 630–642. doi: 10.1016/j.conb.2003.09.017

Logothetis, N. K. (2008). What we can do and what we cannot do with fMRI. *Nature* 453, 869–878. doi: 10.1038/nature06976

Logothetis, N. K., Pauls, J., Augath, M., Trinath, T., and Oeltermann, A. (2001). Neurophysiological investigation of the basis of the fMRI signal. *Nature* 412, 150–157. doi: 10.1038/35084005

Logothetis, N. K., and Wandell, B. A. (2004). Interpreting the BOLD signal. *Annu. Rev. Physiol.* 66, 735–769. doi: 10.1146/annurev.physiol.66.082602.092845

Lynch, C. J., Uddin, L. Q., Supekar, K., Khouzam, A., Phillips, J., and Menon, V. (2013). Default mode network in childhood autism: posteromedial cortex heterogeneity and relationship with social deficits. *Biol. Psychiatry* 74, 212–219. doi: 10.1016/j.biopsych.2012.12.013

Mantini, D., Perrucci, M. G., Del Gratta, C., Romani, G. L., and Corbetta, M. (2007). Electrophysiological signatures of resting state networks in the human brain. *Proc. Natl. Acad. Sci. U.S.A.* 104, 13170–13175. doi: 10.1073/pnas.0700668104

Mizuno, A., Villalobos, M. E., Davies, M. M., Dahl, B. C., and Müller, R. A. (2006). Partially enhanced thalamocortical functional connectivity in autism. *Brain Res.* 1104, 160–174. doi: 10.1016/j.brainres.2006.05.064

Monk, C. S., Peltier, S. J., Wiggins, J. L., Weng, S. J., Carrasco, M., Risi, S., et al. (2009). Abnormalities of intrinsic functional connectivity in autism spectrum disorders. *Neuroimage* 47, 764–772. doi: 10.1016/j.neuroimage.2009.04.069

Müller, R. A., Shih, P., Keehn, B., Deyoe, J. R., Leyden, K. M., and Shukla, D. K. (2011). Underconnected, but how? A survey of functional connectivity MRI studies in autism spectrum disorders. *Cereb. Cortex* 21, 2233–2243. doi: 10.1093/cercor/bhq296

Nebel, M. B., Joel, S. E., Muschelli, J., Barber, A. D., Caffo, B. S., Pekar, J. J., et al. (2014). Disruption of functional organization within the primary motor cortex in children with autism. *Hum. Brain Mapp.* 35, 567–580. doi: 10.1002/hbm.22188

Noonan, S. K., Haist, F., and Müller, R. A. (2009). Aberrant functional connectivity in autism: evidence from low-frequency BOLD signal fluctuations. *Brain Res.* 1262, 48–63. doi: 10.1016/j.brainres.2008.12.076

Peiker, I., David, N., Schneider, T. R., Nolte, G., Schöttle, D., and Engel, A. K. (2015). Perceptual integration deficits in autism spectrum disorders are associated with reduced interhemispheric gamma-band coherence. *J. Neurosci.* 35, 16352–16361. doi: 10.1523/JNEUROSCI.1442-15.2015

Pérez Velázquez, J. L., and Galán, R. F. (2013). Information gain in the brain's resting state: a new perspective on autism. *Front. Neuroinform.* 7:37. doi: 10.3389/fninf.2013.00037

Pfurtscheller, G., Brunner, C., Schlögl, A., and Da Silva, F. L. (2006). Mu rhythm (de) synchronization and EEG single-trial classification of different motor imagery tasks. *Neuroimage* 31, 153–159. doi: 10.1016/j.neuroimage.2005.12.003

Power, J. D., Barnes, K. A., Snyder, A. Z., Schlaggar, B. L., and Petersen, S. E. (2012). Spurious but systematic correlations in functional connectivity MRI networks arise from subject motion. *Neuroimage* 59, 2142–2154. doi: 10.1016/j.neuroimage.2011.10.018

Robertson, C. E., Ratai, E. M., and Kanwisher, N. (2016). Reduced GABAergic action in the autistic brain. *Curr. Biol.* 26, 80–85. doi: 10.1016/j.cub.2015.11.019

Rosenberg, A., Patterson, J. S., and Angelaki, D. E. (2015). A computational perspective on autism. *Proc. Natl. Acad. Sci. U.S.A.* 112, 9158–9165. doi: 10.1073/pnas.1510583112

Rosvall, M., and Bergstrom, C. T. (2008). Maps of random walks on complex networks reveal community structure. *Proc. Natl. Acad. Sci. U.S.A* 105, 1118–1123. doi: 10.1073/pnas.0706851105

Rudie, J. D., Brown, J. A., Beck-Pancer, D., Hernandez, L. M., Dennis, E. L., Thompson, P. M., et al. (2013). Altered functional and structural brain network organization in autism. *Neuroimage Clin.* 2, 79–94. doi: 10.1016/j.nicl.2012.11.006

Rudie, J. D., Shehzad, Z., Hernandez, L. M., Colich, N. L., Bookheimer, S. Y., Iacoboni, M., et al. (2011). Reduced functional integration and segregation of distributed neural systems underlying social and emotional information processing in autism spectrum disorders. *Cereb. Cortex* 22, 1025–1037. doi: 10.1093/cercor/bhr171

Rutter, M., DiLavore, P. C., Risi, S., Gotham, K., and Bishop, S. (2012). *Autism Diagnostic Observation Schedule: ADOS-2*. Los Angeles, CA: Western Psychological Services.

Salmelin, R., and Baillet, S. (2009). Electromagnetic brain imaging. *Hum. Brain Mapp.* 30, 1753–1757. doi: 10.1002/hbm.20795

Shih, P., Keehn, B., Oram, J. K., Leyden, K. M., Keown, C. L., and Müller, R. A. (2011). Functional differentiation of posterior superior temporal sulcus in autism: a functional connectivity magnetic resonance imaging study. *Biol. Psychiatry* 70, 270–277. doi: 10.1016/j.biopsych.2011.03.040

Shih, P., Shen, M., Öttl, B., Keehn, B., Gaffrey, M. S., and Müller, R. A. (2010). Atypical network connectivity for imitation in autism spectrum disorder. *Neuropsychologia* 48, 2931–2939. doi: 10.1016/j.neuropsychologia.2010.05.035

Song, T., Gaa, K., Cui, L., Feffer, L., Lee, R. R., and Huang, M. (2008). Evaluation of signal space separation via simulation. *Med. Biol. Eng. Comput.* 46, 923–932. doi: 10.1007/s11517-007-0290-y

Sun, L., Grützner, C., Bölte, S., Wibral, M., Tozman, T., Schlitt, S., et al. (2012). Impaired gamma-band activity during perceptual organization in adults with autism spectrum disorders: evidence for dysfunctional network activity in frontal-posterior cortices. *J. Neurosci.* 32, 9563–9573. doi: 10.1523/JNEUROSCI.1073-12.2012

Supekar, K., Uddin, L. Q., Khouzam, A., Phillips, J., Gaillard, W. D., Kenworthy, L. E., et al. (2013). Brain hyperconnectivity in children with autism and its links to social deficits. *Cell Rep.* 5, 738–747. doi: 10.1016/j.celrep.2013.10.001

Taulu, S., Kajola, M., and Simola, J. (2004b). Suppression of interference and artifacts by the signal space separation method. *Brain Topogr.* 16, 269–275. doi: 10.1023/B:BRAT.0000032864.93890.f9

Taulu, S., Simola, J., and Kajola, M. (2004a). MEG recordings of DC fields using the signal space separation method (SSS). *Neurol. Clin. Neurophysiol.* 2004:35.

Taulu, S., Simola, J., and Kajola, M. (2005). Applications of the signal space separation method. *IEEE Trans. Signal Process.* 53, 3359–3372. doi: 10.1109/TSP.2005.853302

Turner, K. C., Frost, L., Linsenbardt, D., McIlroy, J. R., and Müller, R. A. (2006). Atypically diffuse functional connectivity between caudate nuclei and cerebral cortex in autism. *Behav. Brain Funct.* 2, 1. doi: 10.1186/1744-9081-2-34

Vissers, M. E., Cohen, M. X., and Geurts, H. M. (2012). Brain connectivity and high functioning autism: a promising path of research that needs refined models, methodological convergence, and stronger behavioral links. *Neurosci. Biobehav. Rev.* 36, 604–625. doi: 10.1016/j.neubiorev.2011.09.003

Voytek, B., and Knight, R. T. (2015). Dynamic network communication as a unifying neural basis for cognition, development, aging, and disease. *Biol. Psychiatry* 77, 1089–1097. doi: 10.1016/j.biopsych.2015.04.016

Welchew, D. E., Ashwin, C., Berkouk, K., Salvador, R., Suckling, J., Baron-Cohen, S., et al. (2005). Functional disconnectivity of the medial temporal lobe in Asperger's syndrome. *Biol. Psychiatry* 57, 991–998. doi: 10.1016/j.biopsych.2005.01.028

Wilson, T. W., Rojas, D. C., Reite, M. L., Teale, P. D., and Rogers, S. J. (2007). Children and adolescents with autism exhibit reduced MEG steady-state gamma responses. *Biol. Psychiatry* 62, 192–197. doi: 10.1016/j.biopsych.2006.07.002

3

Altered Onset Response Dynamics in Somatosensory Processing in Autism Spectrum Disorder

Sheraz Khan[1,2,3,4], *Javeria A. Hashmi*[1,2,3†], *Fahimeh Mamashli*[1,2,3], *Hari M. Bharadwaj*[1,2,3], *Santosh Ganesan*[1,2], *Konstantinos P. Michmizos*[5], *Manfred G. Kitzbichler*[1,2,3†], *Manuel Zetino*[1,2], *Keri-Lee A. Garel*[1,2], *Matti S. Hämäläinen*[2,3,6,7] and *Tal Kenet*[1,2,3*]

[1] Department of Neurology, Massachusetts General Hospital, Boston, MA, USA, [2] Athinoula A. Martinos Center for Biomedical Imaging, MGH/MIT/Harvard, Boston, MA, USA, [3] Harvard Medical School, Boston, MA, USA, [4] McGovern Institute for Brain Research, Massachusetts Institute of Technology, Cambridge, MA, USA, [5] Department of Computer Science, Rutgers University, Piscataway, NJ, USA, [6] Department of Radiology, Massachusetts General Hospital, Boston, MA, USA, [7] Department of Neuroscience and Biomedical Engineering, Aalto University School of Science, Espoo, Finland

Edited by:
Roma Siugzdaite,
Ghent University, Belgium

Reviewed by:
Tatiana Alexandrovna Stroganova,
Moscow State University of Psychology and Education, Russia
Bharat B. Biswal,
University of Medicine and Dentistry of New Jersey (UMDNJ), USA

***Correspondence:**
Tal Kenet
tal@nmr.mgh.harvard.edu

†Present Address:
Javeria A. Hashmi,
Department of Anesthesia, Dalhousie University, Halifax, NS, Canada;
Manfred G. Kitzbichler,
Behavioural and Clinical Neuroscience Institute, University of Cambridge, Cambridge, UK

Abnormalities in cortical connectivity and evoked responses have been extensively documented in autism spectrum disorder (ASD). However, specific signatures of these cortical abnormalities remain elusive, with data pointing toward abnormal patterns of both increased and reduced response amplitudes and functional connectivity. We have previously proposed, using magnetoencephalography (MEG) data, that apparent inconsistencies in prior studies could be reconciled if functional connectivity in ASD was reduced in the feedback (top-down) direction, but increased in the feedforward (bottom-up) direction. Here, we continue this line of investigation by assessing abnormalities restricted to the onset, feedforward inputs driven, component of the response to vibrotactile stimuli in somatosensory cortex in ASD. Using a novel method that measures the spatio-temporal divergence of cortical activation, we found that relative to typically developing participants, the ASD group was characterized by an increase in the initial onset component of the cortical response, and a faster spread of local activity. Given the early time window, the results could be interpreted as increased thalamocortical feedforward connectivity in ASD, and offer a plausible mechanism for the previously observed increased response variability in ASD, as well as for the commonly observed behaviorally measured tactile processing abnormalities associated with the disorder.

Keywords: autism spectrum disorders (ASD), magnetoencephalography (MEG), somatosensory cortex, feedforward, feedback, tactile sensing, cortical connectivity, biomarker

INTRODUCTION

Autism spectrum disorder (ASD) is diagnosed by hallmark abnormalities in social behavior, and has a complex genetic basis (Berg and Geschwind, 2012; Skafidas et al., 2014; Pramparo et al., 2015) with no clear disease etiology. The neural correlates of ASD have been extensively explored, using a wide range of paradigms and non-invasive neuroimaging methods. One of the more consistent findings in ASD is that the connectivity between different brain areas is abnormal in ASD (Khan et al., 2013). This has been explored using both anatomical connectivity measures

(Wolff et al., 2012; Mueller et al., 2013; Peeva et al., 2013) and functional connectivity measures (Kana et al., 2011; Müller et al., 2011; Wass, 2011; Vissers et al., 2012).

The prevailing hypothesis in the field (Rubenstein and Merzenich, 2003; Just et al., 2004), has been that long-range functional connectivity is reduced and local functional connectivity is increased in ASD (Belmonte et al., 2004; Minshew and Williams, 2007). However, evidence for this dual hypothesis is inconclusive. In particular, the hypothesis that long-range functional connectivity, i.e., connectivity between two spatially distinct brain regions, is universally reduced in ASD has been challenged by recent studies showing instances of both increased (Cerliani et al., 2015) and normal (Tyszka et al., 2014) long-range functional connectivity in ASD.

Previously, we proposed that the inconsistencies in long-range functional connectivity studies in ASD might be reconciled if the directionally of the connectivity, i.e., the direction in which two areas are connected, would be considered. Specifically, we proposed that long-range feedforward (bottom-up along the cortical hierarchy) connectivity would be abnormally increased in ASD, while feedback (top-down along the cortical hierarchy) long-range connectivity would be abnormally reduced (Khan et al., 2015; Kitzbichler et al., 2015). In particular, in our recent study of cortical responses to vibrotactile stimuli in ASD, we showed that long-range functional connectivity was indeed significantly increased in the ASD group in the feedforward direction, from the primary somatosensory cortex (S1), upwards toward the secondary somatosensory cortex (S2) (Khan et al., 2015).

In that same study, we also found a significantly increased onset response in S1 in the ASD group. While the response in S1 was significantly increased at onset in the ASD group, it was not possible to determine, based on our prior analysis, whether this increase was generated locally, or via abnormal long-range connectivity, such as reduced feedforward functional connectivity from the thalamus for instance. This question is important, because increased local connectivity and increased long-range functional connectivity might have a similar final signature in the cortex, but would be generated and mediated by substantially different neural mechanisms, and thus different neural abnormalities. Thus, delineating the neural mechanisms that underlie the observed abnormal response in ASD is absolutely essential for understanding the abnormal neurophysiology of ASD.

To address this question, we focused here on the transient component of the response, and specifically on the rising edge of the evoked response. This transient response window, 30–70 ms immediately following the onset of the cortical response, has not been previously studied in relation to abnormal tactile processing in ASD. Given its timing, this part of the response is most likely generated at least in part by feedforward inputs from the thalamus. However, the mere observation of an increased response amplitude during that period is not sufficient to indicate whether the processes leading to that increase are local, or generated by long-range connections. Here, to test our hypothesis, that the increase in the transient evoked response observed in ASD is due to feedforward inputs from subcortical regions, we applied a novel measure that indicates how activation of a small neural population spreads in adjoining areas to become locally synchronized (Khan et al., 2009). This method, which is referred to as Spatio-Temporal Divergence (S-T Div), uses techniques based on the concept of optical flow, and was recently adapted to map the time-course of spatiotemporal propagation of brain activity across different cortical region (Khan et al., 2011).

RESULTS

Spatial Localization of Evoked Response to Tactile Vibrations

As expected and as described previously (Khan et al., 2015), the cortical evoked responses to the 25 Hz vibrotactile stimulus (**Figure 1A**) localized to the contralateral (left) S1 and S2 (**Figure 1B**).

Sharper Evoked Response in ASD

There was no group difference in the latency of the response. The amplitude of the evoked transient response was slightly increased in the ASD group relative to the TD group, but this difference was not statistically significant (**Figure 2A**). In contrast, when the cortical response was examined over the onset time window in the time-frequency domain, i.e., with spectral specificity rather than averaging over the frequency domain as for the standard evoked response shown in **Figure 2A**, significant group differences emerged (**Figure 2B**, $p = 0.0470$, corrected). The difference arose primarily from the higher frequencies, at the 25–60 Hz range.

Increased Onset Response Divergence in ASD

We computed the spatio-temporal divergence (S-T Div) at the onset component of the response, and specifically at the rising edge of the first peak (30–70 ms). This was done by selecting the latency for each subject individually, computing S-T Div for that particular subject at their latency, and then averaging the results at the group level. At this time window, the ASD groups demonstrated significantly increased S-T Div in S1 (**Figure 3**, $p = 0.034$, corrected). As a control, we also examined S-T Div during the steady state component of the response ($t = 250$–550 ms). As expected, there were no significant group differences in this later time window.

Correlations with Behavioral Measures and Prior Neurophysiological Measures

The neurophysiologically derived S-T Div was negatively correlated with the behaviorally derived ADOS (ASD group, $P < 0.002$, $r = 0.74$, **Figure 4A**) and touch perception score (TD group, $P < 0.008$, $r = -0.58$; ASD group, $P < 0.02$, $r = -0.63$, **Figure 4B**). Because the participants are identical to those in our prior study (Khan et al., 2015), we also assessed whether the onset derived S-T Div correlated with the steady-state derived neurophysiological measures from our prior study. Our steady state measures consisted of the LFCi ("Local Functional Connectivity index"), which estimated local functional connectivity in S1 during the steady state component

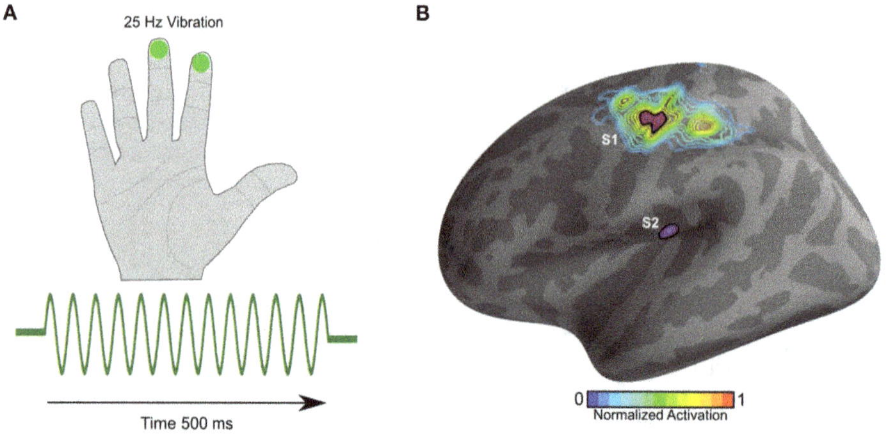

FIGURE 1 | Stimulus and source localization. (A) 500 ms train of pulses at 25 Hz (green trace) was delivered via a pneumatic stimulator and experienced as gentle vibrations on the index and middle right fingers. **(B)** The estimated cortical sources showing activation in S1 and S2. The contour plot represents average activation on the cortical manifold. The distance between adjacent contours is 10%.

of the response, and the GCS (Granger Causality score), which estimated the strength of feedforward connectivity from S1 to S2 during the steady state component of the response. Both were abnormal in the ASD group, with LFCi abnormally decreased, and the GCS abnormally increased. Our correlation analysis showed that LFCi was correlated with S-T Div for both the TD (**Figure 4C**, $P < 0.002$, $r = -0.66$) and ASD ($P < 0.007$, $r = -0.67$) groups. In contrast, S-T Div was not correlated with the GCS (**Figure 4D**).

Statistical Classification

Lastly, we tested whether S-T Div could be used to blindly classify participants with ASD (neuroimaging Biomarker) from TD participants, using a Linear Discriminant Analysis classifier (LDA). This approach evaluates the sensitivity and specificity, and thus the relevance, of the assessed neurophysiological measure to the behavioral phenotype. Using S-T Div alone, the classifier had 83.3% accuracy (80% sensitivity, 90% specificity). We then repeated the classifier computations using S-T Div alongside our two previously derived neurophysiological measures, LFCi, and GCS. The combination of these three neurophysiological features yielded a mean classification accuracy of 91.6%, with 95% specificity and 90% sensitivity (**Figure 5**, **Figure S1** and **Movie M1**). In our prior work the accuracy of the classifier was 89.7%. To assess whether adding the S-T Div measure significantly improved the classifier, the prior model (using LFCi, GCA) and the current model (using LFCi, GCA, S-T Div) were compared using the Akaike Information Criterion (AIC). The AIC score was −79.98 for the first model, and −92.17 for the second model. These scores, with a greater than 12-point difference, indicate that adding S-T Div significantly improved the model.

DISCUSSION

In the vast majority of studies, abnormal functional connectivity in ASD and abnormal evoked responses in ASD have been addressed separately. It is clear that functional connectivity and evoked responses are not independent from one another, but instead are tightly coupled. In our prior study using the same paradigm (Khan et al., 2015), we showed that the observed increases in steady state responses in the ASD group at 25 Hz in S2, were due to increased feedforward connectivity from S1. We also hypothesized that the observed increased onset response in S1 was due to increased feedforward connectivity from the thalamus, but were not able to test this hypothesis at the time.

The current method (S-T Div) allowed us to test this hypothesis indirectly, since it measures the flow (magnitude and velocity of spread) of neural activation in a given region and time window. The velocity at the onset of the response in S1, at the rising edge of the response, before local connections are strongly activated through recurrent loops, is likely to arise entirely or nearly entirely from feedforward connections into S1, primarily from the thalamus. While an increase in magnitude might arise from local recurrent connections, an increase in the velocity of spread can be attributed with relatively high certainty to an increase in feedforward inputs (Papadelis et al., 2012). Indeed, we found that at rising edge of the transient response in S1, this flow was greatly and significantly increased in ASD relative to TD.

Interestingly, as is evident from the time-frequency plots presented in **Figure 2B**, the evoked response in S1 in ASD is abnormally increased not only at the 25 Hz component of the response, but also at higher frequencies, including the 50 Hz component of the response. This seemingly contradicts our prior results. In our prior study (Khan et al., 2015), using a computational model and prior literature, we argued that only the 25 Hz component of the response, which was increased in ASD, is generated via feedforward connectivity, while the steady state of the 50 Hz component of the response, which was reduced in ASD, is generated via local connectivity within S1 and its immediate vicinity, i.e., horizontal connections across layers II/III. Simply put, why would the response in higher frequencies, and specifically around 50 Hz, be increased in ASD in the transient component immediately following the

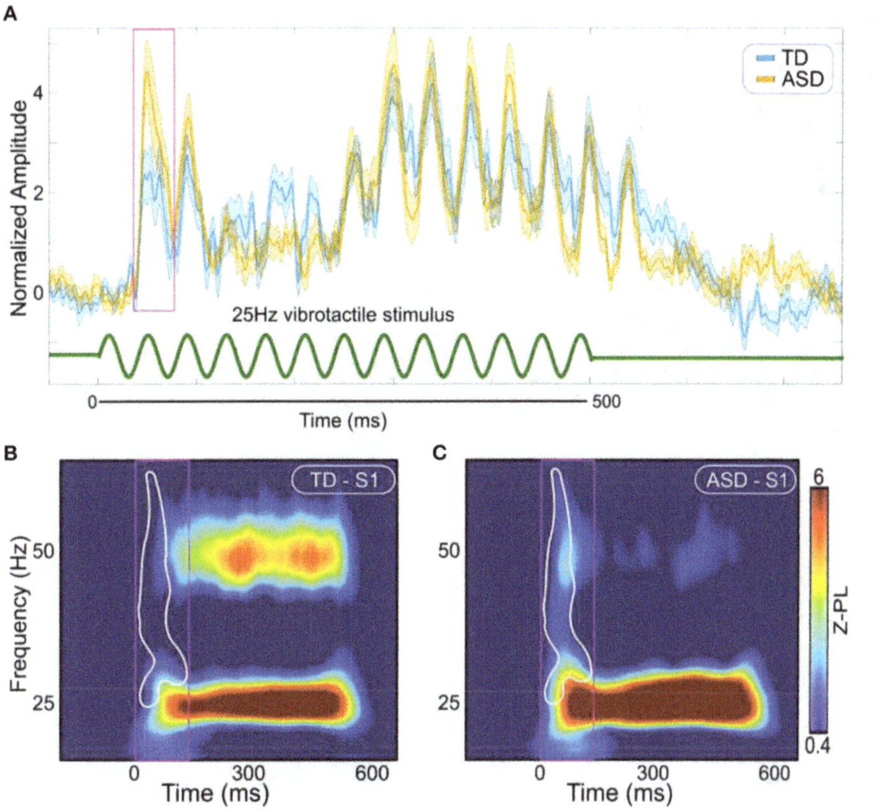

FIGURE 2 | Evoked responses. (A) Evoked responses in S1 (Orange ASD; Cyan TD). Stimulus is represented with green curve at the bottom. Magenta box shows the window for the first transient peak [30–70 ms]. **(B)** Time-frequency representations of Z-scored phase locking (Z-PL) at S1 in the TD group. **(C)** Time-frequency representations of Z-scored phase locking (Z-PL) at S1 in the ASD group. White contour outlines the region where the response was significantly increased in the ASD group ($p = 0.0470$, cluster corrected). Magenta boxes show time window for the transient response in the time-frequency domain [0–140 ms].

onset, but decreased during the steady state component of the response? If both the transient onset component and the steady state component of the cortical response were generated by the same neural mechanisms (local recurrent connections), the interpretation of the 50 Hz component of the response we proposed earlier would be inconsistent with the current proposed interpretation.

The logical resolution of this apparent conflict emerges from a line of studies affirming the fundamentally different nature of the onset component of the response relative to the steady state component (Nangini et al., 2006). For instance, somatosensory inputs from the thalamus to area 3b have been shown to evoke fast and slow adapting response patterns in non-human primates where one set of cortical cells respond only to stimulus onset and offset, while the other module respond throughout stimulus presentation (Sur et al., 1984). In contrast, the steady state response serves to more linearly convey detailed information about attended stimulus features (Ramcharan et al., 2005; Sherman, 2012). Furthermore, the corticothalamic pathways that would be most active during the onset component of the response, are largely distinct from the interareal corticocortical pathways that would be most active during the steady state component of the response (Petrof et al., 2012). Thus, the opposite patterns we observed in ASD for the onset component and the steady state components of the response around 50 Hz are not contradictory, as they are probably generated by at least partially independent neuronal assemblies.

That said, it is worthwhile to note that the strong correlation we observed between S-T Div and LFCi suggests that while these two temporally differentiated components of the response are distinct, they are not independent. However, from the current data, it is not possible to determine to what extent the abnormal response in ASD during the steady state component of the response is influenced by the initial abnormality in the onset component of the response. Since the two measures, S-T Div and LFCi, are correlated but not perfectly so, it is plausible that the reduced steady state response in ASD is a result both of the state of the neuronal assemblies following the increased onset response, alongside the previously discussed (Khan et al., 2015) inherent abnormalities in the local networks that mediate the steady state component of the response. Furthermore, the results from our classifier analysis indicate that the S-T Div analysis of the onset period adds independent information to the prior analyses of the steady state component of the response.

The differentiation proposed here between the feedforward dependent onset component of the response and the local

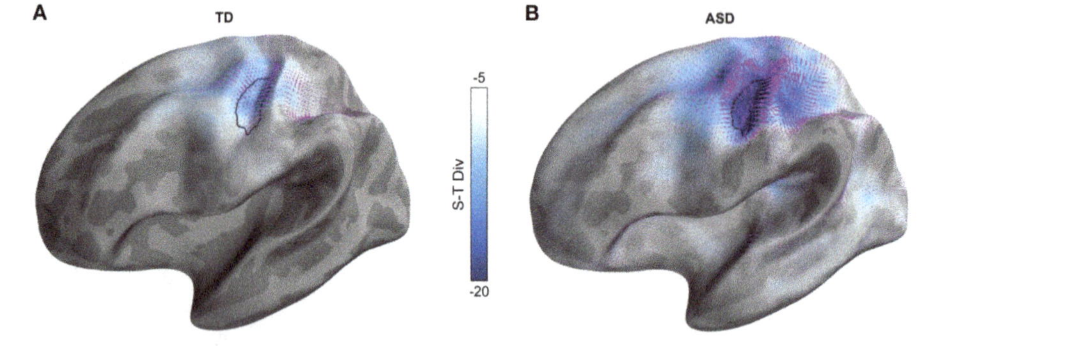

FIGURE 3 | S-T Div during the onset of the transient tactile response. S-T DIV in **(A)** The TD group, **(B)** The ASD group. The colormap represents the magnitude of divergence, and the purple vectors represent the velocity of the divergence. Black outline represents the area that is statistically significantly different ($p = 0.034$, cluster corrected) between the TD and ASD groups.

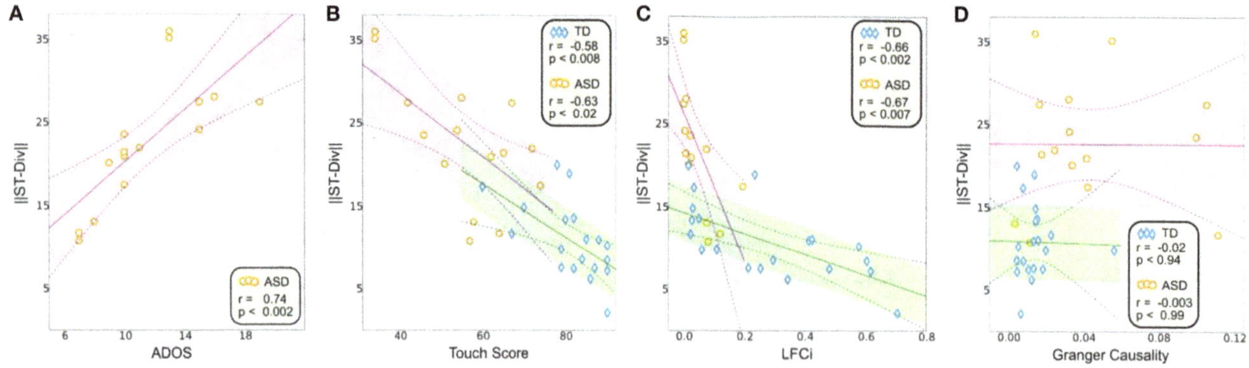

FIGURE 4 | Correlations between S-T Div and other measures. Correlation between S-T Div and: **(A)** ADOS score, **(B)** Touch score, **(C)** LFCi, and **(D)** GCS. The shaded areas (TD in green, ASD in purple) delineate the standard error, and the dashed lines encompass 95% of the confidence interval for the correlation.

feedback dependent steady state component of the response, is in line with studies of ASD that indirectly infer increased bottom-up perceptual processing tendencies in ASD (Neumann et al., 2006; Jarvinen-Pasley et al., 2008; Cook et al., 2012; Amso et al., 2014; Robertson et al., 2014). They are also in line with prior fMRI-based studies finding increased thalamocortical connectivity in ASD, in paradigms that were more likely to activate feedforward networks (Mizuno et al., 2006; Cerliani et al., 2015). These results are also intriguing in the context of a recent finding of increased inter-trial variability in ASD (Dinstein et al., 2012). Unmodulated, i.e., inconsistently gain controlled, feedforward inputs, as observed previously in ASD (Peiker et al., 2015), would likely result in more variable trial to trial onset responses. Lastly, these results are also relevant in the context of the high prevalence of behavioral sensory hypo- and hyper- sensitivities in ASD (Tommerdahl et al., 2007; Marco et al., 2011, 2012). Increased feedforward inputs and flow of sensory information would naturally result in hyper-sensitive behavior. It is possible that the observed hypo-sensitivities are due to generalized down regulation, as a compensatory strategy to the increased input intensities. Such a compensatory strategy would likely result in hypo-sensitivities.

An important limitation of the study is that this method does not directly measure thalamocortical feedforward connectivity from the specific thalamic nuclei, since no thalamic activation has been observed directly. Thus, the proposed interpretation, while relying strongly on known properties of response onset in early sensory cortex, and while fitting well with other studies, remains an indirect interpretation. Alternatively, other processes may also impact the observed abnormal dynamics of the onset response. For instance, it has been suggested that excitatory feedforward drive and feedback input from higher-order cortex or non-specific thalamic nuclei might also contribute to the onset component of the response (Cauller and Kulics, 1991; Jones et al., 2009). In addition, local interactions between excitatory and inhibitory circuits that occur before the M70 peak (Peterson et al., 1995) may also impact the abnormal dynamics observed here.

In summary, in our previous studies (Khan et al., 2015; Kitzbichler et al., 2015), we found increased forward cortical functional connectivity in ASD during the steady state component of the cortical response, from S1 to S2. We also found an increased onset response in S1 in the ASD group. In the present investigation we used the novel S-T Div measure to assess the dynamics of the onset response in S1. The observed

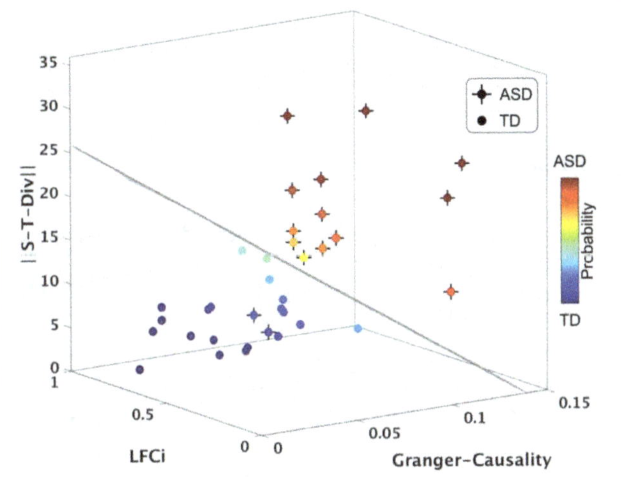

FIGURE 5 | Classifier results, using S-T Div, LFCi and Granger Causality. Visualization of LDA analysis using the full dataset. Each axis corresponds to each neurophysiological imaging feature. The probability of a participant having a diagnosis of ASD is shown as color of the sphere. Plain sphere represents the TD participants, while sphere with a cross represent ASD participants. The black line represents classification boundary (see also, **Figure S1** and **Movie M1**).

dynamics are consistent with an interpretation of increased feedforward thalamocortical connectivity. The interpretation proposed here of the result of the S-T Div measure, is consistent with the conjecture that stronger feedforward connectivity is likely characteristic of ASD, andmay underlie the behaviorally observed aberrant somatosensory and vibrotactile processing in ASD.

MATERIALS AND METHODS

Participants

Participants were 15 males diagnosed with ASD and 20 age-matched TD males, ages 8–18 (11.6 mean age). ASD participants had a prior clinically verified ASD diagnosis, met a cutoff of > 15 on the SCQ, Lifetime Version, and were assessed with either Module 3 ($n = 3$) or 4 ($n = 12$) of the ADOS (ADOS, Lord et al., 1999), administered by trained research personnel who had established inter-rater reliability. Individuals with autism-related medical conditions, e.g., Fragile-X syndrome, tuberous sclerosis, and other known risk factors, e.g., premature birth, were excluded from the study. All TD participants were below threshold on the SCQ and were confirmed to be free of any comorbid neurological or psychiatric conditions, and of substance use for the past 6 months, via parent and self-reports. The ASD and TD groups did not differ in verbal or nonverbal IQ, as measured with the Kaufman Brief Intelligence Test—II (Kaufman and Kaufman, 2004). Handedness information was collected using the Dean Questionnaire (Piro, 1998). Only right-handed participants were included in the study. Additional details on the participants are provided in **Table T1**. Participants overlapped in full with those studied in our prior publication on this paradigm (Khan et al., 2015). All the experimental protocols were approved by The Massachusetts General Hospital (MEG) Institutional Review Board and all procedures were carried out in accordance with the approved guidelines. Written informed consent was obtained from all subjects.

Experimental Paradigms and MEG Data Acquisition

Vibrotactile stimulation in the MEG consisted of pulses applied to the index and middle right fingers at 25 Hz using a custom made pneumatic tactile stimulator with latex tactor tips, based on a published design (Briggs et al., 2004). The duration of each stimulus train was 500 ms with an inter-stimulus interval of 3 s with a 500 ms jitter. The stimuli were presented while participants were watching a movie. Participants were instructed to not pay attention to the stimulation and not move their hands. Hands were kept still using an armrest, and a blanket positioned over the arm. The sequence of stimuli was presented using the psychophysics toolbox (www.psychtoolbox.org). A total of 100 trials were collected. The total recording time was 6 min per subject.

MEG data were acquired inside a magnetically shielded room (IMEDCO, Hagendorf, Switzerland) (Khan and Cohen, 2013) using a whole-head VectorView MEG system (Elekta-Neuromag, Helsinki, Finland), comprised of 306 sensors arranged in 102 triplets of two orthogonal planar gradiometers and one magnetometer. The MEG signals were acquired at 600 Hz, with a hardware bandpass filter set between 0.1 and 200 Hz. The position and orientation of the head with respect to the MEG sensor array was recorded continuously with help of four Head Position Indicator coils (Uutela et al., 2001; Zaidel et al., 2009). To allow co-registration of the MEG and MRI data, the locations of three fiduciary points (nasion and auricular points) that define a head-based coordinate system, a set of points from the head surface, and the sites of the four HPI coils were digitized using a Fastrak digitizer (Polhemus, Colchester, VT, USA) integrated with the Vectorview system. The ECG and EOG signals were recorded simultaneously to identify epochs containing heartbeats as well as vertical and horizontal eye-movement and blink artifacts. During data acquisition, on-line averages were computed from artifact-free trials to monitor data quality in real time. All off-line analysis was based on the saved raw data. In addition, 5 min of data were recorded from the room void of a subject before each experimental session for noise estimation purposes.

Structural MRI Data Acquisition and Processing

T1-weighted high-resolution magnetization-prepared rapid gradient echo (MPRAGE) structural images were acquired using a 3.0 T Siemens Trio whole body MR scanner (Siemens Medical Systems, Erlangen, Germany) and a 32 channel head coil. The in-plane resolution was $1 \times 1\ mm^2$, slice thickness 1.3 mm with no gaps, and a TR/TI/TE/Flip Angle 2530 ms/1100 ms/3.39 ms/7°. Cortical reconstructions and parcellations for each subject were generated using FreeSurfer (Dale et al., 1999; Fischl et al., 1999a). After correcting for topological defects, cortical surfaces were triangulated with dense meshes with ~130,000 vertices in each hemisphere. For visualization, the surfaces were inflated, thereby exposing the sulci (Dale et al., 1999).

MEG Data Pre-Processing

Cleaning and Motion Correction

The data were spatially filtered using the SSS method (Elekta-Neuromag Maxfilter software) to suppress noise generated by sources outside the brain (Taulu et al., 2004; Taulu and Simola, 2006). SSS also corrects for head motion between and within runs (Taulu et al., 2004). Cardiac and ocular artifacts were removed by signal space projection (Gramfort et al., 2013). The MEG data were then further low-pass filtered at 145 Hz to remove the HPI coil signals. The filtered data were then used for all further analyses.

Epoching

The data were epoched into single trials lasting 2.5 s, from 1000 ms prior to stimulus onset to 1500 ms following it. Epochs were rejected if the peak-to-peak amplitude during the epoch exceeded 1000 fT and 3000 fT/cm in any of the magnetometer and gradiometer channels, respectively. This resulted in the loss of 2–20 trials per participant. To maintain a constant signal to noise ratio across conditions and participants, the number of trials per condition per participant was fixed at 80, the minimum number of accepted trials that we had for each condition and participant. For participants that had more than 80 good trials, we selected 80 trials randomly from the available trials.

Transient Response Time Window Selection

For the standard evoked response (**Figure 2A**), we selected the first transient peak in the time window between 30 and 70 ms from stimulus onset, to evaluate latency and amplitude. For the response in the time-frequency domain, we needed to account for smoothing due to the convolution of the seven cycles complex Morlet wavelet with the data. Therefore, the time window of interest was 0–140 ms from stimulus onset.

Data Quality

There were no group differences in overall quality of the data, and the number of good (un-rejected) trials per condition was similar between groups and across conditions. For each participant, the same set of trials was used for all analyses.

Mapping MEG Data Onto Cortical Space

Source Estimation

The cortical source space consisted of 10,242 dipoles per hemisphere, corresponding to a spacing of approximately 3 mm between adjacent source locations. The forward solution was computed using a single-compartment boundary-element model (Hämäläinen and Sarvas, 1989). The individual inner skull surface triangulations for this model were generated with the watershed algorithm in FreeSurfer. The current distribution was estimated using the minimum-norm estimate by fixing the source orientation to be perpendicular to the cortex (Gramfort et al., 2014). The noise covariance matrix was estimated from data acquired in the absence of a subject prior to each session. We employed depth weighting to reduce the bias of the minimum norm estimates toward superficial currents (Lin et al., 2006).

Inter-Subject Cortical Surface Registration for Group Analysis

A morphing map to optimally align the cortical surface of each participant to an average cortical representation (FsAverage in FreeSurfer) was computed in FreeSurfer (Fischl et al., 1999b).

Data Analysis

Phase Locking

Inter Trial Phase Locking (PL) is a method to quantify phase synchrony across multiple trials. To compute PL, we convolved the epoched time series with a dictionary of complex Morlet wavelets (each spanning seven cycles). We then normalized the resulting complex coefficients by dividing by their absolute magnitude and averaging the unit-norm phasors across trials for each time-frequency bin. We then took their absolute value so that each number ranged between 0 and 1, with 0 representing a uniform distribution of phase angles and 1 representing perfectly synchronized phase angles, across trials (Tallon-Baudry et al., 1996; Makeig et al., 2002). Mathematically PL is defined as:

$$PL(f, t) = \frac{1}{N}\left|\sum_{n=1}^{N} e^{\phi^{k(f,t)}}\right|$$

Where $\emptyset^K$ represent instantaneous phase resulting from convolution of the trial with the complex Morlet wavelet, and N is the numbers of trials.

Z-PL (Normalized Phase Locking)

To compute Z-PL (**Figure 2**), we compared each PL value to a set of surrogate null distributions, to correct for statistical biases proportional to the number of epochs. This approach is non-parametric, and makes no a-priori assumptions besides the independence across the trials in the experimental data. The independence across trials was motivated by the fact that there was an average 3 s time interval between trials, and anticipation effects were eliminated because our experimental paradigm had a 500 ms jitter in Stimulus-Onset Asynchrony. Z-PL was computed as follows: each trial was first circularly shifted by a random lag ($\tau\epsilon(0, T]$, where T = period (1/f) in samples) and PL was computed on the shifted epoched data. This process was repeated 500 times. Z-PL was then computed by subtracting the mean and dividing by the standard deviation of the null distributions from the actual PL values.

S-T Div Decomposition

S-T Div is composed of two components. The first is the scalar component of the extent of divergence of the source estimates, i.e. the magnitude of the divergence, illustrated in **Figure 3** as a colormap. The second is the velocity of this divergence, illustrated in **Figure 3** with purple vectors, to represent both direction and magnitude. The S-T Div decomposition involves two steps: (i) The optical flow of distributed MEG/EEG MNE normalized estimates, where the relative maximum is set to be one unit for each individual subject, is computed on the cortical manifold. This step ensures that amplitude does not impact the result, so that different data sets where signal to noise may not be constant, can nonetheless be directly compared. (ii) Helmholtz-Hodge decomposition is then applied to the optical flow computed previously. The details and mathematics of the approach were published previously (Khan et al., 2011). Briefly, optical flow V is a vector field which defines the motion of scalar quantity *I*, defined on a surface *M* and at time *t*, such that:

$$\partial_t + \mathbf{g}(\mathbf{V}, \nabla_M I) = 0$$

Where $g(.,.)$ is the scalar product, modified by the local curvature of *M*. Given optical flow vector field **V** defined on a surface *M*, there exists: a scalar field U, a rotational vector field A, and a harmonic vector field **H** such that:

$\mathrm{V} = \nabla_M \mathrm{U} + \nabla \times \mathrm{A} + \mathrm{H}$ The scalar field U is the divergnce of the scalar field *I*, and $\mathbf{V}_{div} = \nabla_M \mathrm{U}$ is the divergence vector field component of vector field **V** defined on a surface *M* and at time *t*. Optical flow and S-T Div are availaible as part of open-source MEG/EEG toolboxes; Brainstorm (Tadel et al., 2011) and MNE-Python (Gramfort et al., 2013).

Lastly, it is important to note that S-T Div is not affected by the point spread of MNE solution. This is because S-T div is computed by taking the gradient in space and time. The point spread of MNE results from the regularization of the ill-posed inverse solution. Therefore, for a particular location in space, the spread is "constant" across different time points. Thus, because it is constant, taking the gradient cancels the impact of the point spread. This is discussed at length in prior publications on the topic (Khan et al., 2011).

Correlations Analyses

All correlation coefficients and the corresponding *P*-values were computed using Pearson correlation (**Figure 4**). Correlations resulting in significant *P*-values were then tested using Robust Correlation (Pernet et al., 2012), which strictly checks for false positive correlations using bootstrap resampling and 6 correlation tests (bootstrap Pearson correlation, bootstrap Spearman correlation, bootstrap Bend correlation, bootstrap Pearson skipped correlation and bootstrap Spearman skipped correlation). Significant correlations were further tested for survival of multiple comparison correction by controlling for family-wise error rate using maximum statistics through permutation testing (Groppe et al., 2011).

Linear Discriminant Analysis (LDA)

The performance of LDA was evaluated using 10-fold cross validation (a model validation technique for assessing how the results of a model will generalize to an independent data set). To perform this cross validation, both TD and ASD Subjects (35 total) were randomly partitioned into 10 equal size subsamples. Of the 10 subsamples, 9 subsamples were used as training data for model learning and then applied on the remaining subsample to test the validity of the model. The cross-validation process was then repeated 10 times, with each of the subsamples used once as the validation data. Scikit-learn Machine Learning in Python (Pedregosa et al., 2011) was used for the above analysis.

Akaike Information Criterion (AIC)

Given a set of models for the data, the Akaike Information Criterion (AIC) is a measure that assesses the quality of each model, relative to the remaining models in the set. The chosen model minimizes the Kullback-Leibler distance between the model and the ground truth. AIC takes into account both descriptive accuracy and parsimony, since it carries a penalty for increasing the number of free parameters. The model with the lowest AIC is considered the best model among all models specified for the data at hand. The absolute AIC values are not particularly meaningful since they are specific to the data set being modeled. The relative AIC value ($\Delta AIC_i = AIC_i - \min\{AIC_p\}$) is used to rank models: $\Delta AIC_i < 2$ suggest that models are basically equivalent, whereas a $\Delta AIC_i > 10$ indicates that the model with the minimum AIC ($\min\{AIC_p\}$) is significantly better than the alternative model (Akaike, 1992).

Statistical Analyses on Cortical Surface

Our statistical analyses (**Figure 3**) were based on cluster-based statistics which is a non-parametric method (Maris and Oostenveld, 2007; Maris et al., 2007) that also corrects for multiple comparisons. We used 1000 permutations and the test statistics used were Wilcoxon Rank Sum test.

AUTHOR CONTRIBUTIONS

SK and TK designed research; SK, FM, HB, SG, KG collected the data; SK, JH, FM, KM, MK, and MH analyzed the data; and SK, JH, MH, and TK wrote the paper. All authors reviewed the manuscript.

FUNDING

This work was supported by grants from the Nancy Lurie Marks Family Foundation (TK, SK, MK), Autism Speaks (TK), The Simons Foundation (SFARI 239395, TK), The National Institute of Child Health and Development (R01HD073254, TK), The National Center for Research Resources (P41EB015896, MH), National Institute for Biomedical Imaging and Bioengineering (5R01EB009048, MH), and the Cognitive Rhythms Collaborative: A Discovery Network (NFS 1042134, MH).

SUPPLEMENTARY MATERIAL

Figure S1 | ROCs showing performance of statistical classifier. We evaluated the performance of the classifier using the standard approach of measuring the area under the curve (AUC), where an AUC of 0.5 represents chance (dashed blacked line). Orange line, represent average ROC curve for 10-fold validation, standard error of the folds is represented as shaded area around the line. (AUC = 0.95).

Movie M1 | Rotating visualization of the 4D depiction of the LDA shown in Figure 5.

Table T1 | Participants in experimental paradigm. As expected, only ADOS scores and Touch scores were significantly different between the groups.

REFERENCES

Akaike, H. (1992). Data analysis by statistical models. *No To Hattatsu* 24, 127–133.

Amso, D., Haas, S., Tenenbaum, E., Markant, J., and Sheinkopf, S. J. (2014). Bottom-up attention orienting in young children with autism. *J. Autism Dev. Disord.* 44, 664–673. doi: 10.1007/s10803-013-1925-5

Belmonte, M. K., Allen, G., Beckel-Mitchener, A., Boulanger, L. M., Carper, R. A., and Webb, S. J. (2004). Autism and abnormal development of brain connectivity. *J. Neurosci.* 24, 9228–9231. doi: 10.1523/JNEUROSCI.3340-04.2004

Berg, J. M., and Geschwind, D. H. (2012). Autism genetics: searching for specificity and convergence. *Genome Biol.* 13, 247. doi: 10.1186/gb-2012-13-7-247

Briggs, R. W., Dy-Liacco, I., Malcolm, M. P., Lee, H., Peck, K. K., Gopinath, K. S., et al. (2004). A pneumatic vibrotactile stimulation device for fMRI. *Magn. Res. Med.* 51, 640–643. doi: 10.1002/mrm.10732

Cauller, L. J., and Kulics, A. (1991). The neural basis of the behaviorally relevant N1 component of the somatosensory-evoked potential in SI cortex of awake monkeys: evidence that backward cortical projections signal conscious touch sensation. *Exp. Brain Res.* 84, 607–619. doi: 10.1007/BF0 0230973

Cerliani, L., Mennes, M., Thomas, R. M., Di Martino, A., Thioux, M., and Keysers, C. (2015). Increased functional connectivity between subcortical and cortical resting-state networks in autism spectrum disorder. *JAMA Psychiatry* 72, 767–777. doi: 10.1001/jamapsychiatry.2015.0101

Cook, J., Barbalat, G., and Blakemore, S. J. (2012). Top-down modulation of the perception of other people in schizophrenia and autism. *Front. Hum. Neurosci.* 6:175. doi: 10.3389/fnhum.2012.00175

Dale, A. M., Fischl, B., and Sereno, M. I. (1999). Cortical surface-based analysis. I. Segmentation and surface reconstruction. *Neuroimage* 9, 179–194. doi: 10.1006/nimg.1998.0395

Dinstein, I., Heeger, D. J., Lorenzi, L., Minshew, N. J., Malach, R., and Behrmann, M. (2012). Unreliable evoked responses in autism. *Neuron* 75, 981–991. doi: 10.1016/j.neuron.2012.07.026

Fischl, B., Sereno, M. I., and Dale, A. M. (1999a). Cortical surface-based analysis. II: Inflation, flattening, and a surface-based coordinate system. *Neuroimage* 9, 195–207.

Fischl, B., Sereno, M. I., Tootell, R. B., and Dale, A. M. (1999b). High-resolution intersubject averaging and a coordinate system for the cortical surface. *Hum. Brain Mapp.* 8, 272–284.

Gramfort, A., Luessi, M., Larson, E., Engemann, D. A., Strohmeier, D., Brodbeck, C., et al. (2013). MEG and EEG data analysis with MNE-Python. *Front. Neurosci.* 7:267. doi: 10.3389/fnins.2013.00267

Gramfort, A., Luessi, M., Larson, E., Engemann, D. A., Strohmeier, D., Brodbeck, C., et al. (2014). MNE software for processing MEG and EEG data. *Neuroimage* 86, 446–460. doi: 10.1016/j.neuroimage.2013.10.027

Groppe, D. M., Urbach, T. P., and Kutas, M. (2011). Mass univariate analysis of event-related brain potentials/fields I: a critical tutorial review. *Psychophysiology* 48, 1711–1725. doi: 10.1111/j.1469-8986.2011.01273.x

Hämäläinen, M. S., and Sarvas, J. (1989). Realistic conductivity geometry model of the human head for interpretation of neuromagnetic data. *IEEE Trans. Biomed. Eng.* BME-36, 165–171. doi: 10.1109/10.16463

Jarvinen-Pasley, A., Wallace, G. L., Ramus, F., Happe, F., and Heaton, P. (2008). Enhanced perceptual processing of speech in autism. *Dev. Sci.* 11, 109–121. doi: 10.1111/j.1467-7687.2007.00644.x

Jones, S. R., Pritchett, D. L., Sikora, M. A., Stufflebeam, S. M., Hamalainen, M., and Moore, C. I. (2009). Quantitative analysis and biophysically realistic neural modeling of the MEG mu rhythm: rhythmogenesis and modulation of sensory-evoked responses. *J. Neurophysiol.* 102, 3554–3572. doi: 10.1152/jn.0053 5.2009

Just, M. A., Cherkassky, V. L., Keller, T. A., and Minshew, N. J. (2004). Cortical activation and synchronization during sentence comprehension in high-functioning autism: evidence of underconnectivity. *Brain* 127, 1811–1821. doi: 10.1093/brain/awh199

Kana, R. K., Libero, L. E., and Moore, M. S. (2011). Disrupted cortical connectivity theory as an explanatory model for autism spectrum disorders. *Phys. Life Rev.* 8, 410–437. doi: 10.1016/j.plrev.2011.10.001

Kaufman, A. S., and Kaufman, N. L. (2004). *Kaufman Brief Intelligence Test, 2nd Edn.* Circle Pines, MN: AGS Publishing.

Khan, S., and Cohen, D. (2013). Note: Magnetic noise from the inner wall of a magnetically shielded room. *Rev. Sci. Instrum.* 84, 056101. doi: 10.1063/1.4802845

Khan, S., Gramfort, A., Shetty, N. R., Kitzbichler, M. G., Ganesan, S., Moran, J. M., et al. (2013). Local and long-range functional connectivity is reduced in concert in autism spectrum disorders. *Proc. Natl. Acad. Sci. U.S.A.* 110, 3107–3112. doi: 10.1073/pnas.1214533110

Khan, S., Lefevre, J., Ammari, H., and Baillet, S. (2011). Feature detection and tracking in optical flow on non-flat manifolds. *Pattern Recognit. Lett.* 32, 2047–2052. doi: 10.1016/j.patrec.2011.09.017

Khan, S., Lefevre, J., and Baillet, S. (2009). Feature extraction from time-resolved cortical current maps using the Helmholtz-Hodge decomposition. *Neuroimage* 47(Suppl. 1), S79. doi: 10.1016/S1053-8119(09)70547-6

Khan, S., Michmizos, K., Tommerdahl, M., Ganesan, S., Kitzbichler, M. G., Zetino, M., et al. (2015). Somatosensory cortex functional connectivity abnormalities in autism show opposite trends, depending on direction and spatial scale. *Brain* 138, 1394–1409. doi: 10.1093/brain/awv043

Kitzbichler, M. G., Khan, S., Ganesan, S., Vangel, M. G., Herbert, M. R., Hämäläinen, M. S., et al. (2015). Altered development and multifaceted band-specific abnormalities of resting state networks in autism. *Biol. Psychiatry* 77, 794–804. doi: 10.1016/j.biopsych.2014.05.012

Lin, F. H., Witzel, T., Ahlfors, S. P., Stufflebeam, S. M., Belliveau, J. W., and Hämäläinen, M. S. (2006). Assessing and improving the spatial accuracy in MEG source localization by depth-weighted minimum-norm estimates. *Neuroimage* 31, 160–171. doi: 10.1016/j.neuroimage.2005. 11.054

Lord, C., Rutter, M., Dilavore, P. C., and Risi, S. (1999). *Autism Diagnostic Observation Schedule—WPS (ADOS-WPS).* Los Angeles, CA: Western Psychological Services.

Makeig, S., Westerfield, M., Jung, T. P., Enghoff, S., Townsend, J., Courchesne, E., et al. (2002). Dynamic brain sources of visual evoked responses. *Science* 295, 690–694. doi: 10.1126/science.1066168

Marco, E. J., Hinkley, L. B., Hill, S. S., and Nagarajan, S. S. (2011). Sensory processing in autism: a review of neurophysiologic findings. *Pediatric Res.* 69, 48R–54R. doi: 10.1203/PDR.0b013e3182130c54

Marco, E. J., Khatibi, K., Hill, S. S., Siegel, B., Arroyo, M. S., Dowling, A. F., et al. (2012). Children with autism show reduced somatosensory response: an MEG study. *Autism Res.* 5, 340–351. doi: 10.1002/aur.1247

Maris, E., and Oostenveld, R. (2007). Nonparametric statistical testing of EEG- and MEG-data. *J. Neurosci. Methods* 164, 177–190. doi: 10.1016/j.jneumeth.2007.03.024

Maris, E., Schoffelen, J. M., and Fries, P. (2007). Nonparametric statistical testing of coherence differences. *J. Neurosci. Methods* 163, 161–175. doi: 10.1016/j.jneumeth.2007.02.011

Minshew, N. J., and Williams, D. L. (2007). The new neurobiology of autism: cortex, connectivity, and neuronal organization. *Arch. Neurol.* 64, 945–950. doi: 10.1001/archneur.64.7.945

Mizuno, A., Villalobos, M. E., Davies, M. M., Dahl, B. C., and Müller, R. A. (2006). Partially enhanced thalamocortical functional connectivity in autism. *Brain Res.* 1104, 160–174. doi: 10.1016/j.brainres.2006.05.064

Mueller, S., Keeser, D., Samson, A. C., Kirsch, V., Blautzik, J., Grothe, M., et al. (2013). Convergent findings of altered functional and structural brain connectivity in individuals with high functioning autism: a multimodal MRI study. *PLoS ONE* 8:e67329. doi: 10.1371/journal.pone.0067329

Müller, R. A., Shih, P., Keehn, B., Deyoe, J. R., Leyden, K. M., and Shukla, D. K. (2011). Underconnected, but how? A survey of functional connectivity MRI studies in autism spectrum disorders. *Cereb. Cortex* 21, 2233–2243. doi: 10.1093/cercor/bhq296

Nangini, C., Ross, B., Tam, F., and Graham, S. J. (2006). Magnetoencephalographic study of vibrotactile evoked transient and steady-state responses in human somatosensory cortex. *Neuroimage* 33, 252–262. doi: 10.1016/j.neuroimage.2006.05.045

Neumann, D., Spezio, M. L., Piven, J., and Adolphs, R. (2006). Looking you in the mouth: abnormal gaze in autism resulting from impaired top-down modulation of visual attention. *Soc. Cogn. Affect. Neurosci.* 1, 194–202. doi: 10.1093/scan/nsl030

Papadelis, C., Leonardelli, E., Staudt, M., and Braun, C. (2012). Can magnetoencephalography track the afferent information flow along white matter thalamo-cortical fibers? *Neuroimage* 60, 1092–1105. doi: 10.1016/j.neuroimage.2012.01.054

Pedregosa, F., Varoquaux, G., Gramfort, A., Michel, V., Thirion, B., Grisel O., et al. (2011). Scikit-learn: machine learning in python. *J. Mach. Learn. Res.* 12, 2825–2830.

Peeva, M. G., Tourville, J. A., Agam, Y., Holland, B., Manoach, D. S., and Guenther, F. H. (2013). White matter impairment in the speech network of individuals with autism spectrum disorder. *Neuroimage Clin* 3, 234–241. doi: 10.1016/j.nicl.2013.08.011

Peiker, I., Schneider, T. R., Milne, E., Schottle, D., Vogeley, K., Munchau, A., et al. (2015). Stronger neural modulation by visual motion intensity in autism spectrum disorders. *PLoS ONE* 10:e0132531. doi: 10.1371/journal.pone.0132531

Pernet, C. R., Wilcox, R., and Rousselet, G. A. (2012). Robust correlation analyses: false positive and power validation using a new open source matlab toolbox. *Front. Psychol.* 3:606. doi: 10.3389/fpsyg.2012.00606

Peterson, N. N., Schroeder, C. E., and Arezzo, J. C. (1995). Neural generators of early cortical somatosensory evoked potentials in the awake monkey. *Electroencephalogr. Clin. Neurophysiol.* 96, 248–260.

Petrof, I., Viaene, A. N., and Sherman, S. M. (2012). Two populations of corticothalamic and interareal corticocortical cells in the subgranular layers of the mouse primary sensory cortices. *J. Comp. Neurol.* 520, 1678–1686. doi: 10.1002/cne.23006

Piro, J. M. (1998). Handedness and intelligence: patterns of hand preference in gifted and nongifted children. *Dev. Neuropsychol.* 14, 619–630. doi: 10.1080/87565649809540732

Pramparo, T., Pierce, K., Lombardo, M. V., Carter Barnes, C., Marinero, S., Ahrens-Barbeau, C., et al. (2015). Prediction of autism by translation and immune/inflammation coexpressed genes in toddlers from pediatric community practices. *JAMA Psychiatry* 72, 386–394. doi: 10.1001/jamapsychiatry.2014.3008

Ramcharan, E. J., Gnadt, J. W., and Sherman, S. M. (2005). Higher-order thalamic relays burst more than first-order relays. *Proc. Natl. Acad. Sci. U.S.A.* 102, 12236–12241. doi: 10.1073/pnas.0502843102

Robertson, C. E., Thomas, C., Kravitz, D. J., Wallace, G. L., Baron-Cohen, S., Martin, A., et al. (2014). Global motion perception deficits in autism are reflected as early as primary visual cortex. *Brain* 137, 2588–2599. doi: 10.1093/brain/awu189

Rubenstein, J. L., and Merzenich, M. M. (2003). Model of autism: increased ratio of excitation/inhibition in key neural systems. *Genes Brain Behav.* 2, 255–267. doi: 10.1034/j.1601-183X.2003.00037.x

Sherman, S. M. (2012). Thalamocortical interactions. *Curr. Opin. Neurobiol.* 22, 575–579. doi: 10.1016/j.conb.2012.03.005

Skafidas, E., Testa, R., Zantomio, D., Chana, G., Everall, I. P., and Pantelis, C. (2014). Predicting the diagnosis of autism spectrum disorder using gene pathway analysis. *Mol. Psychiatry* 19, 504–510. doi: 10.1038/mp.2012.126

Sur, M., Wall, J. T., and Kaas, J. H. (1984). Modular distribution of neurons with slowly adapting and rapidly adapting responses in area 3b of somatosensory cortex in monkeys. *J. Neurophysiol.* 51, 724–744.

Tadel, F., Baillet, S., Mosher, J. C., Pantazis, D., and Leahy, R. M. (2011). Brainstorm: a user-friendly application for MEG/EEG analysis. *Comput. Intell. Neurosci.* 2011, 879716. doi: 10.1155/2011/879716

Tallon-Baudry, C., Bertrand, O., Delpuech, C., and Pernier, J. (1996). Stimulus specificity of phase-locked and non-phase-locked 40 Hz visual responses in human. *J. Neurosci.* 16, 4240–4249.

Taulu, S., Kajola, M., and Simola, J. (2004). Suppression of interference and artifacts by the Signal Space Separation Method. *Brain Topogr.* 16, 269–275. doi: 10.1023/B:BRAT.0000032864.93890.f9

Taulu, S., and Simola, J. (2006). Spatiotemporal signal space separation method for rejecting nearby interference in MEG measurements. *Phys. Med. Biol.* 51, 1759–1768. doi: 10.1088/0031-9155/51/7/008

Tommerdahl, M., Tannan, V., Cascio, C. J., Baranek, G. T., and Whitsel, B. L. (2007). Vibrotactile adaptation fails to enhance spatial localization in adults with autism. *Brain Res.* 1154, 116–123. doi: 10.1016/j.brainres.2007.04.032

Tyszka, J. M., Kennedy, D. P., Paul, L. K., and Adolphs, R. (2014). Largely typical patterns of resting-state functional connectivity in high-functioning adults with autism. *Cereb. Cortex* 24, 1894–1905. doi: 10.1093/cercor/bht040

Uutela, K., Taulu, S., and Hämäläinen, M. (2001). Detecting and correcting for head movements in neuromagnetic measurements. *Neuroimage* 14, 1424–1431. doi: 10.1006/nimg.2001.0915

Vissers, M. E., Cohen, M. X., and Geurts, H. M. (2012). Brain connectivity and high functioning autism: a promising path of research that needs refined models, methodological convergence, and stronger behavioral links. *Neurosci. Biobehav. Rev.* 36, 604–625. doi: 10.1016/j.neubiorev.2011.09.003

Wass, S. (2011). Distortions and disconnections: disrupted brain connectivity in autism. *Brain Cogn.* 75, 18–28. doi: 10.1016/j.bandc.2010.10.005

Wolff, J. J., Gu, H., Gerig, G., Elison, J. T., Styner, M., Gouttard, S., et al. (2012). Differences in white matter fiber tract development present From 6 to 24 months in infants with Autism. *Am. J. Psychiatry* 169, 589–600. doi: 10.1176/appi.ajp.2011.11091447

Zaidel, A., Spivak, A., Shpigelman, L., Bergman, H., and Israel, Z. (2009). Delimiting subterritories of the human subthalamic nucleus by means of microelectrode recordings and a Hidden Markov Model. *Movem. Disorders* 24, 1785–1793. doi: 10.1002/mds.22674

4

Semi-Metric Topology of the Human Connectome: Sensitivity and Specificity to Autism and Major Depressive Disorder

Tiago Simas [1*] *and John Suckling* [1, 2]

[1] *Department of Psychiatry, University of Cambridge, Cambridge, UK,* [2] *Cambridge and Peterborough NHS Foundation Trust, Cambridge, UK*

Keywords: neuroimaging, functional connectivity, transitivity, semi-metricity, connectome

Edited by:
Roma Siugzdaite,
Ghent University, Belgium

Reviewed by:
Sebastiano Stramaglia,
University of Bari Aldo Moro, Italy
Maxime Taquet,
Harvard Medical School, USA

***Correspondence:**
Tiago Simas
ts526@cam.ac.uk

Functional Magnetic Resonance Imaging (fMRI) records the blood oxygenation level dependent (BOLD) endogenous contrast, a physiological surrogate for brain activity. Experimental and analytic procedures for fMRI remained largely unchanged in the decade following discovery of BOLD contrast, detecting localized magnitude changes in response to external stimuli. Observations of persistent patterns of activation present under a wide variety of cognitive conditions, now known as the default mode network (Raichle et al., 2001), led to significant changes in data acquisition and analysis; that is, fMRI data began to be acquired in task-absent states (so-called "rest") and the analysis proceeded by generation of the functional connectome (Bullmore and Sporns, 2009) that putatively supported the distributed exchange of information, and supplanted localized activity as the basic unit of interpretation.

The functional connectome is constructed from nodes (brain regions) connected by edges with associated strengths (edge weights) that represent functional proximity, often inter-regional synchronicity measured by Pearson's correlation of BOLD time-series. Other strengths can be estimated; for example, coherence, cross-correlation (Salvador et al., 2005) or spectral mutual information (Granger and Hatanaka, 1964; Granger and Lin, 1994; Simas et al., 2015) which may capture alternative properties of the connectome. With this approach, a large-scale functional organization of the brain has been proposed (Bota et al., 2015) and many common mental health disorders linked to the vulnerability of particular topological elements of the connectome (Crossley et al., 2014).

Through whatever means these graphical networks are generated, complex network analysis can be applied to characterize the topography and thus the presumed flow or exchange of information that the network represents (Watts and Strogatz, 1998; Barabási and Albert, 1999; Barrat et al., 2008). Examples are replete in natural and man-made systems: computer networks, transport infrastructure, social and ecological relationships, and microstructures of the central nervous system. Up to now, complex analysis of the functional connectome has been dominated by characterization with parameters derived from a graphical network that is sparse and frequently binary (Cao et al., 2014). These networks are mostly simply created by a threshold on the edge weights, focusing then on the clique of edges with high values. Properties like small-worldness (Watts and Strogatz, 1998; Achard et al., 2006; Bassett and Bullmore, 2006; Simas, 2012; Suckling et al., 2015) can be estimated, implicitly assuming that information flows preferentially and most efficiently along paths with the fewest edges.

The role of "weak" edges has arguably been underrepresented in the complex analysis of the functional connectome (Suckling et al., 2015), although sociological theory has long recognized their central role in the distribution of information through friendship networks (Granovetter, 1973, 1983). Moreover, the complete transfer of information via shortest paths, i.e., the fewest edges between two nodes, is only possible if there is available a map of the connectome available to plan the most efficient routes, in the same way as a traveler has a map of the metro to efficiently navigate a city. It seems unlikely that the brain has to hand a representation of its own connectome, even more so given the connectome is time varying (Hutchison et al., 2013) (what is often measured by the functional connectome is a time average). More likely is that information is transferred across the entire, fully-connected network taking advantage of the proletariat of weak edges, with broadcast dynamics a potential strategy for dissemination. Nevertheless, the shortest path is a good starting point for a more expansive conceptualization.

Networks that are not transitive with edge weights representing proximities have homologs in the isomorphic distance space that are semi-metric (Klir and Bo, 1995; Simas and Rocha, 2015) (**Figure 1**). In other words, there are edges in the distance space that violate the triangle inequality when enforced by distance closure . Thus, it is possible to distinguish a metric edge from a semi-metric edge by determining whether the shortest path is the direct path between nodes, or if it is via

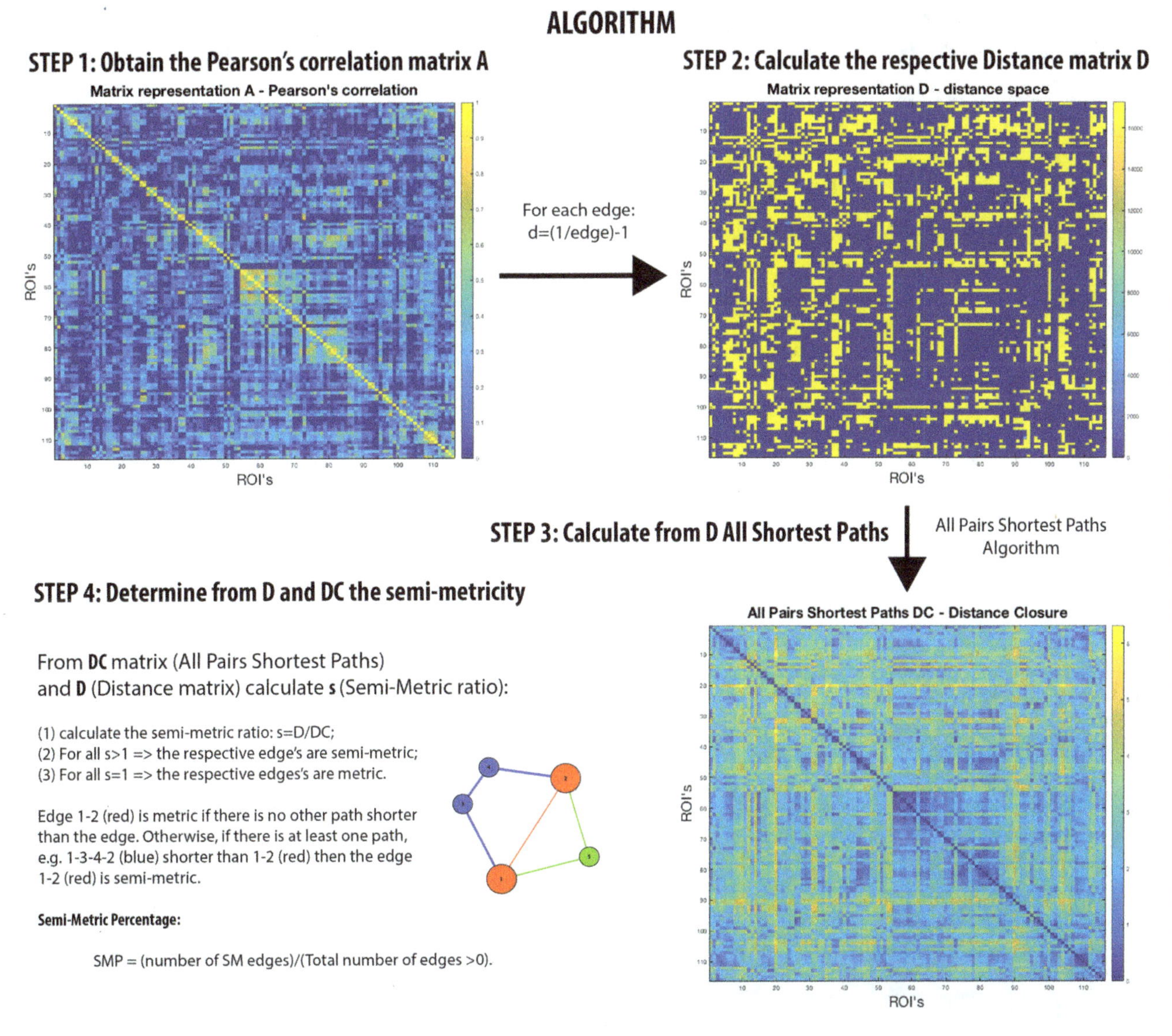

FIGURE 1 | Semi-metric analysis Algorithm on rs-fMRI with Pearson's correlation.

a circuitous route (and there may be more than one) involving additional nodes. This is a common phenomenon; for example, although it might be difficult to communicate directly with someone with whom you have no direct relationship, it is possible to transfer messages through intermediaries with whom you are mutually acquainted.

A semi-metric path in the functional connectome with edge weights estimated by Pearson's correlation between regional BOLD time-series, may be interpreted as the two regions synchronously co-activating along with all other regions involved the circuitous paths (Simas et al., 2015) (**Figure 1**). That is, there is a dispersion of communicability across the regions. Complementarily, metric connections do not have the significant involvement of other regions, and information exchange is constrained to the two regions. All non-trivially organized networks have some degree of semi-metricity, and in the healthy human functional connectome derived with Pearson's correlation they form around 80% of all the edges (Simas et al., 2015). There is also evidence that the degree of semi-metricity (i.e., transitivity) in anatomical networks predicts functional connectivity (Goñi et al., 2014).

Semi-metric analysis of the functional connectome (**Figure 1**) is sensitive and specific to psychopathologies (Peeters et al., 2015; Simas and Rocha, 2015; Simas et al., 2015; Suckling et al., 2015). Both positive and negative deviations in the global proportion of semi-metric edges, relative to neurotypical individuals, have been observed in Autism and Major Depressive Disorder respectively (Simas et al., 2015), occuring consistently across individuals in similar functional connections. Psychosis was also exclusively associated with only positive changes to semi-metricity, the severity of symptoms related to the magnitude of change (Peeters et al., 2015). However in Alzheimer's disease, both directions of effect were observed, with highly idiosyncratic patterns of change (Suckling et al., 2015). Together, these studies suggest that there exists an optimum value of semi-metricity both globally and locally that is associated with healthy brain function, and that disorders have their own particular pattern of change relative to control samples.

The human brain is the most complex system known. The evidence and analytic models to measure and predict its form and function have evolved toward an understanding of brain as a network of unceasing communication. Current tomographic technologies, like fMRI, limit the detectable time resolution and we are therefore only beginning to understand the topology of the connectome and how it might form the substrate for cognition and psychopathologies. Semi-metricity, and more generally the inclusion of all the brain's connections, is a next step toward a richer description of the functional topology and, subsequently, simulation and measurement of its complex dynamics and inter-regional information transmission.

AUTHOR CONTRIBUTIONS

Both authors made significant contributions to the drafting of the article.

FUNDING

This study was funded by the UK Medial Research Council (grant: G0802226), the National Institute for Health Research (NIHR) (grant: 06/05/01) and the Behavioural and Clinical Neuroscience Institute (BCNI), University of Cambridge. The BCNI is jointly funded by the Medical Research Council and the Wellcome Trust. Additional support was received from the NIHR Cambridge Biomedical Research Centre.

REFERENCES

Achard, S., Salvador, R., Whitcher, B., Suckling, J., and Bullmore, E. (2006). A resilient, low-frequency, small-world human brain functional network with highly connected association cortical hubs. *J. Neurosci.* 26, 63–72. doi: 10.1523/JNEUROSCI.3874-05.2006

Barabási, A.-L., and Albert, R. (1999). Emergence of scaling in random networks. *Science* 286, 509–512. doi: 10.1126/science.286.5439.509

Barrat, A., Barthelemy, M., and Vespignani, A. (2008). *Dynamical Processes on Complex Networks*. Cambridge: Cambridge University Press. doi: 10.1017/cbo9780511791383

Bassett, D. S., and Bullmore, E. (2006). Small-world brain networks. *Neuroscientist* 12, 512–523. doi: 10.1177/1073858406293182

Bota, M., Sporns, O., and Swanson, L. W. (2015). Architecture of the cerebral cortical association connectome underlying cognition. *Proc. Natl. Acad. Sci. U.S.A.* 112, E2093–E2101. doi: 10.1073/pnas.1504394112

Bullmore, E., and Sporns, O. (2009). Complex brain networks: graph theoretical analysis of structural and functional systems. *Nat. Rev. Neurosci.* 10, 312–312. doi: 10.1038/nrn2618

Cao, M., Wang, J.-H., Dai, Z.-J., Cao, X.-Y., Jiang, L.-L., Fan, F.-M., et al. (2014). Topological organization of the human brain functional connectome across the lifespan. *Dev. Cogn. Neurosci.* 7, 76–93. doi: 10.1038/nrn2618

Crossley, N. A., Mechelli, A., Scott, J., Carletti, F., Fox, P. T., McGuire, P., et al. (2014). The hubs of the human connectome are generally implicated in the anatomy of brain disorders. *Brain* 137, 2382–2395. doi: 10.1093/brain/awu132

Goñi, J., van den Heuvel, M. P., Avena-Koenigsberger, A., Velez de Mendizabal, N., Betzel, R. F., Griffa, A., et al. (2014). Resting-brain functional connectivity predicted by analytic measures of network communication. *Proc. Natl. Acad. Sci. U.S.A.* 111, 833–838. doi: 10.1073/pnas.1315529111

Granger, C., and Hatanaka, M. (1964). *Spectral Analysis of Economical Time Series*. Princeton, NJ: Princeton University Press.

Granger, C., and Lin, J.-L. (1994). Using the mutual information coefficient to identify lags in nonlinear models. *J. Time Ser. Anal.* 15, 371–384. doi: 10.1111/j.1467-9892.1994.tb00200.x

Granovetter, M. (1983). The strength of weak ties: a network theory revisited. *Sociol. Theory* 1, 201–233. doi: 10.2307/202051

Granovetter, M. S. (1973). The strength of weak ties. *Am. J. Sociol.* 78, 1360–1380. doi: 10.1086/225469

Hutchison, R. M., Womelsdorf, T., Allen, E. A., Bandettini, P. A., Calhoun, V. D., Corbetta, M., et al. (2013). Dynamic functional connectivity: promise, issues, and interpretations. *NeuroImage* 80, 360–378. doi: 10.1016/j.neuroimage.2013.05.079

Klir, G., and Bo, Y. (1995). *Fuzzy Sets and Fuzzy Logic: Theory and Applications*. New Jersey: Prentice Hall PTR.

Peeters, S., Simas, T., Suckling, J., Gronenschild, E., Patel, A., Habets, P., et al. (2015). Semi-metric analysis of the functional brain network: relationship with familial risk for psychotic disorder. *NeuroImage* 9, 607–616. doi: 10.1016/j.nicl.2015.10.003

Raichle, M. E., MacLeod, A. M., Snyder, A. Z., Powers, W. J., Gusnard, D. A., and Shulman, G. L. (2001). A default mode of brain function.

Proc. Natl. Acad. Sci. U.S.A. 98, 676–682. doi: 10.1073/pnas.98.2.676

Salvador, R., Suckling, J., Schwarzbauer, C., and Bullmore, E. (2005). Undirected graphs of frequency-dependent functional connectivity in whole brain networks. *Philos. Trans. R. Soc. B Biol. Sci.* 360, 937–946. doi: 10.1098/rstb.2005.1645

Simas, T. (2012). *Stochastic Models and Transitivity in Complex Networks*. PhD thesis, Indiana University.

Simas, T., Chattopadhyay, S., Hagan, C., Kundu, P., Patel, A., Holt, R., et al. (2015). Semi-metric topology of the human connectome: sensitivity and specificity to autism and major depressive disorder. *PLoS ONE* 10:e0136388. doi: 10.1371/journal.pone.0136388

Simas, T., and Rocha, L. M. (2015). Distance closures on complex networks. *Netw. Sci.* 3, 227–268. doi: 10.1017/nws.2015.11

Suckling, J., Simas, T., Chattopadhyay, S., Tait, R., Su, L., Williams, G., et al. (2015). A winding road: Alzheimer's disease increases circuitous functional connectivity pathways. *Front. Comput. Neurosci.* 9:140. doi: 10.3389/fncom.2015.00140

Watts, D. J., and Strogatz, S. H. (1998). Collective dynamics of 'small-world' networks. *Nature* 393, 440–442. doi: 10.1038/30918

5

One-Class Support Vector Machines Identify the Language and Default Mode Regions as Common Patterns of Structural Alterations in Young Children with Autism Spectrum Disorders

Alessandra Retico [1], Ilaria Gori [1,2], Alessia Giuliano [1,3], Filippo Muratori [4,5] and Sara Calderoni [4]*

[1] Pisa Division, National Institute for Nuclear Physics, Pisa, Italy, [2] Department of Chemistry and Pharmacy, University of Sassari, Sassari, Italy, [3] Department of Physics, University of Pisa, Pisa, Italy, [4] Department of Developmental Neuroscience, IRCCS Stella Maris Foundation, Pisa, Italy, [5] Department of Clinical and Experimental Medicine, University of Pisa, Pisa, Italy

Edited by:
Roma Siugzdaite,
Ghent University, Belgium

Reviewed by:
Luca Faes,
University of Trento, Italy
Suhash Chakraborty,
Hindustan Aeronautics Limited Hospital, India
Corrado Corradi-Dell'Acqua,
University of Geneva, Switzerland

***Correspondence:**
Alessandra Retico
alessandra.retico@pi.infn.it

The identification of reliable brain endophenotypes of autism spectrum disorders (ASD) has been hampered to date by the heterogeneity in the neuroanatomical abnormalities detected in this condition. To handle the complexity of neuroimaging data and to convert brain images in informative biomarkers of pathology, multivariate analysis techniques based on Support Vector Machines (SVM) have been widely used in several disease conditions. They are usually trained to distinguish patients from healthy control subjects by making a binary classification. Here, we propose the use of the One-Class Classification (OCC) or Data Description method that, in contrast to two-class classification, is based on a description of one class of objects only. This approach, by defining a multivariate normative rule on one class of subjects, allows recognizing examples from a different category as outliers. We applied the OCC to 314 regional features extracted from brain structural Magnetic Resonance Imaging (MRI) scans of young children with ASD (21 males and 20 females) and control subjects (20 males and 20 females), matched on age [range: 22–72 months of age; mean = 49 months] and non-verbal intelligence quotient (NVIQ) [range: 31–123; mean = 73]. We demonstrated that a common pattern of features characterize the ASD population. The OCC SVM trained on the group of ASD subjects showed the following performances in the ASD vs. controls separation: the area under the receiver operating characteristic curve (AUC) was 0.74 for the male and 0.68 for the female population, respectively. Notably, the ASD vs. controls discrimination results were maximized when evaluated on the subsamples of subjects with NVIQ $\geq$ 70, leading to AUC = 0.81 for the male and AUC = 0.72 for the female populations, respectively. Language regions and regions from the default mode network—posterior cingulate cortex, pars opercularis and pars triangularis of the inferior frontal gyrus, and transverse temporal gyrus—contributed most to distinguishing individuals with ASD from controls, arguing for the crucial role of these areas in the ASD pathophysiology. The observed brain patterns associate preschoolers with ASD independently of their age, gender and NVIQ and therefore they are expected to constitute part of the ASD brain endophenotype.

Keywords: features classification, One-class support vector machine, Brain Magnetic Resonance Imaging (MRI), autism spectrum disorders, preschool children

INTRODUCTION

Different approaches have been proposed to date to explore the clinical (Grzadzinski et al., 2013), genetic (De Rubeis and Buxbaum, 2015), and neurobiological (Hernandez et al., 2015) heterogeneity of Autism Spectrum Disorders (ASD), which are complex neurodevelopmental conditions affecting 1 in 68 children in USA (Centers for Disease Control Prevention, 2014), and are characterized by impairment in socio-communicative abilities, as well as restricted and stereotyped behaviors (American Psychiatric Association, 2013). The non-invasive and non-harmful Magnetic Resonance Imaging (MRI) is a promising tool to study and characterize ASD, as it allows the *in vivo* observation of the brain involvement in the disorder. Several post-processing methods to analyze brain MRI data were developed and a wide range of studies aimed to explore the predictive power of MRI by comparing the brain characteristics of patients with ASD and controls with the final aim of identifying reliable markers of ASD diagnosis (Ecker et al., 2010a,b; Jiao et al., 2010; Ingalhalikar et al., 2011; Calderoni et al., 2012; Wee et al., 2014; Zhou et al., 2014; Gori et al., 2015; Retico et al., 2016).

Machine-learning techniques, e.g., those based on support vector machines (SVMs; Vapnik, 1995), have been shown to be valuable tools to make predictive diagnoses in single subjects in a large variety of psychiatric and neurodevelopmental disorders (Wolfers et al., 2015), including ASD (Retico et al., 2014). They can be implemented for diagnosis prediction, for assessment of the disease progression and to evaluate the treatment effectiveness (Orrù et al., 2012). Machine learning refers to all procedures where the learning by example paradigm is implemented. In most cases conventional binary (also called two-class) classification algorithms are applied to image features to classify an unknown object into one of two pre-defined categories. The classification is particularly challenging when dealing with psychiatric disorders, as the reported neuroanatomical alterations are often very small and quite un-replicated among different studies. Subtle signs of pathology are difficult to catch especially in extremely heterogeneous conditions such as ASD.

In the present study, we propose the use of the One-Class Classification (OCC) or Data Description method (Moya et al., 1993), which, in contrast to two-class classification, makes a description of a single class of objects only (referred to as the positive class or target class) and detects which (new) objects resemble this target class, thus distinguishing them from examples considered outliers. Using OCC instead of two-class classification methods in standard binary classification problems, where objects from both the classes are at disposal, could result in worse recognition accuracy, as the complete knowledge encoded in the available training set is not fully exploited. However, OCC could provide more robustness in case of difficulties embedded in the nature of data, since they seek to describe properties of the target class instead of minimizing the classification error. Therefore, in case of difficult datasets (e.g., when the positive class is well-characterized, whereas the negative class is not sufficiently representative of the negative population) it could be useful to transform the binary classification problem into an OCC task.

The usefulness of OCC in the biomedical domain was already proved in a number of applications, e.g., the automatic recognition of the hypertension type (Krawczyk and Woźniak, 2015) or breast cancer biopsy and 3D optical coherence tomography (OCT) retinal image classification (Zhang et al., 2014) and on brain MRI data. In the latter domain OCC were implemented to learn multivariate normative rules on a group of healthy individuals, thus allowing the interpretation of the distance to the OCC boundary as an abnormality score (Mourão-Miranda et al., 2011; Sato et al., 2012a,b). Working on both voxel- and region-based features, Mourão-Miranda et al. (2011) investigated whether patterns of fMRI response to sad facial expressions in depressed patients would be classified as outliers in relation to patterns of healthy control subjects. They interestingly found out that most patients classified as non-outliers responded to treatments and most patients classified as outliers did not respond to treatments. Sato et al. (2012b) obtained an OCC-based abnormality index analyzing functional connectivity patterns of adults and children with Attention Deficit and Hyperactivity Disorder (ADHD), and found out that the ADHD patients differ significantly from the age-matched control group, showing instead stronger similarity to the group of younger control subjects.

We analyzed with OCC the features extracted from brain structural MRI data in order to measure the OCC performance in the discrimination of patients with ASD with respect to controls in the preschool age. Moreover, we used the OCC to define multivariate normative rules, i.e., we investigated the distribution of patterns of brain structures in control subjects to test the homogeneity of the latter sample and its potential to enable the definition of a robust boundary in relation to which the patients with ASD would be classified as outliers. To carry out a symmetry test, we investigated also whether a consistent neuroanatomical pattern among the ASD patients allows the definition of a robust boundary in relation to which the controls are classified as outliers.

Finally, the relative contribution of the anatomical brain features to the decision function was studied to localize the regions more involved in the one-class classifier boundary definition. To this purpose we extended to the case of OCC the previous literature referring to the generation of a *preimage* when non-linear kernel SVM are used to localize the relevant brain features (Schölkopf et al., 1999). Moreover, the permutation testing usually implemented in two-class classification problems (Mourão-Miranda et al., 2005; Wanh et al., 2007; Gaonkar and Davatzikos, 2013; Gori et al., 2015) was extended to the OCC formulation to allow assigning a statistical significance both to the classification performances and to the brain features contributing most to the OCC boundary definition.

MATERIALS AND METHODS

Participants and MRI Data Acquisition

A group of 21 male and 20 female preschoolers with ASD [mean age ± standard deviation (*SD*) = 49 ± 12 months; age range = 28–70 months] and a group of 40 control subjects matched by gender, age, non-verbal IQ (NVIQ), and socioeconomic status were selected for this case-control study (see **Table 1**).

Participants in the ASD group were recruited at the ASD Unit of IRCCS Stella Maris Foundation (Pisa), a tertiary hospital and research university in Italy. They were rigorously diagnosed with ASD according to the DSM-IV-TR criteria (American Psychiatric Association, 2000) by a multidisciplinary team including a senior child psychiatrist, an experienced clinical child psychologist and a speech–language pathologist during 3–5 days of extensive evaluation, and confirmed by the ADOS-G (Lord et al., 2000) administrated by clinical psychologists who met standard requirements for research reliability. ASD patients were included if their age was between 2 and 6 years and their NVIQ ≥ 30. Exclusion criteria were: (a) anomalies detected by MRI (b) neurological syndromes or focal neurological signs; (c) significant sensory impairment (e.g., blindness, deafness); (d) anamnesis of birth asphyxia, premature birth, or epilepsy; (e) use of any psychotropic medication; (f) absence of major dysmorphic features including microcephaly or macrocephaly; and (g) potential secondary causes of ASD determined by high-resolution karyotyping, DNA analysis of Fragile-X, or screening tests for inborn errors of metabolism (plasma and urine aminoacid analysis, urine organic acid measurement, urine mucopolysaccarides quantitation, plasma and urine creatine, and guanidinoacetate analysis). The control group was composed of 20 preschoolers with idiopathic developmental delay (DD), i.e., with NVIQ score < 70, and 20 preschoolers without developmental delay (noDD), i.e., with NVIQ score ≥ 70, recruited at the same hospital. Subjects with DD were included within the control group in order to obtain a match for NVIQ between patients and controls, as well as to increase the size of the data sample under investigation. The diagnosis of idiopathic DD was made after a negative thorough assessment for underlying causes, including audiometry, thyroid hormone disorders, high-resolution karyotyping, DNA analysis of Fragile-X and screening tests for inborn errors of metabolism. The control group was selected so as to meet the same exclusionary criteria as the ASD patients—except the criterion (g) specified above—with the further requirements of exclusion of ASD diagnosis (performed

TABLE 1 | Dataset composition and sample characteristics.

Variable	Subject group, mean ± std [range]							
	ASD (*n* = 41)				Controls (*n* = 40)			
Age (months)	49 ± 12 [28–70]				49± 14 [22–72]			
NVIQ	73 ± 22 [34–113]				73 ± 23 [31–123]			
	Males (*n* = 21)		Females (*n* = 20)		Males (*n* = 20)		Females (*n* = 20)	
Age (months)	50 ± 10 [34–70]		48 ± 13 [28 – 69]		48 ± 13 [24–70]		50 ± 16 [22–72]	
NVIQ	75 ± 22 [40–113]		70 ± 23 [34–113]		73 ± 23 [32–123]		72 ± 24 [31–106]	
	DD (*n* = 9)	no-DD (*n* = 12)	DD (*n* = 10)	no-DD (*n* = 10)	DD (*n* = 10)	no-DD (*n* = 10)	DD (*n* = 10)	no-DD (*n* = 10)
Age (months)	52 ± 11 [37–70]	48 ± 9 [34–66]	43 ± 14 [28–69]	54 ± 10 [36–69]	52 ± 13 [24–70]	45 ± 13 [30–65]	51 ± 14 [30–66]	50 ± 18 [22–72]
NVIQ	54 ± 8 [40–66]	91 ± 14 [70–113]	51 ± 10 [34–65]	89 ± 14 [73–113]	54 ± 11 [32–68]	92 ± 15 [74–123]	52 ± 13 [31–68]	93 ± 10 [73–106]

ASD, autism spectrum disorders; NVIQ, non-verbal intelligence quotient; std, standard deviation; DD, developmental delay (NVIQ < 70); no-DD, without developmental delay (NVIQ ≥ 70).

by a senior child psychiatrist and based on the DSM-IV-TR criteria), and no family history of ASD. ASD and DD patients underwent the brain MRI examination as a completion of the assessment pathway with the aim of excluding brain alteration, whereas noDD subjects performed brain MRI because of various reasons (including headache, seizures with fever, strabismus, cataract, paroxysmal vertigo, diplopia).

MRI data were acquired using a GE 1.5 T Signa Neuro-optimized System (General Electric Medical Systems) at IRCCS Stella Maris Foundation, fitted with 40 mT/m high-speed gradients. Within the MRI protocol for children a whole-brain fast spoiled gradient recalled acquisition in the steady-state T1-weighted series (FSPGR) was collected in the axial plane with repetition time 12.4 ms, echo time 2.4 ms, inversion time 700 ms, flip angle of 10°, yielding to contiguous axial slices with voxel size of $1.1 \times 1.1 \times 1.1$ mm^3. All children were sedated with a general anesthesia with a halogenated agent while spontaneously breathing. For all MRIs performed between September 2006 and February 2013 the same sequence of acquisition was used and the written informed consent from a parent or guardian of children was obtained. The research protocol was approved by the Institutional Review Board of the Clinical Research Institute for Child and Adolescent Neurology and Psychiatry.

Data Preprocessing and Feature Extraction

The preprocessing of the entire data set of structural MRI included the volumetric segmentation and cortical reconstruction by the Freesurfer image analysis suite version 5.1.0, documented and freely available online (http://freesurfer.net/; Fischl et al., 1999, 2004; Klein and Tourville, 2012). In the cortical parcellation step, Freesurfer assigns a neuroanatomical label to each location on the cortical surface according to a previously prepared atlas file. We used the Desikan-Killiany-Tourville (DKT) cortical atlas which divides the cerebral cortex into 62 structures (31 structures per hemisphere) (Klein and Tourville, 2012): 14 in the temporal lobe, 20 in the frontal lobe, 10 in the parietal lobe, 8 in the occipital lobe, and 10 in the cingulate cortex.

The following five surface-based features for each of the 62 DTK structures are computed: *Area* (white surface area in mm^2); *Volume* (gray matter volume in mm^3); *Thickness* (average cortical thickness in mm); *ThicknessStd* (standard deviation of cortical thickness in mm); *Mean-Curv* (integrated rectified mean curvature in mm^{-1}). The *Volume* is computed according to a surface-based method, as the average of the white and pial surface areas, multiplied by the cortical thickness. In addition we considered the white surface total area (in mm^2) and the mean thickness (in mm) of the cerebral cortex in the two hemispheres, thus obtaining a vector of 314 characteristics for each subject.

Feature Classification

We analyzed the brain image features with both standard two-class classifiers and OCC based on SVMs. The SVM (Vapnik, 1995) are quite extensively applied as conventional binary classification algorithms. They are supervised binary classifiers that require a training set of labeled input examples to learn the differences between the two sample classes, and a labeled test set to quantify the classification performance.

In the context of classification of brain images, each input example is a vector $\boldsymbol{x}$ of features extracted from each input image. The label **y** associated to each input example indicates its membership, e.g., "1" for vectors belonging to the patients class, "−1" for controls. Detailed information about two-class SVM can be found in (Pontil and Verri, 1997; Ben-Hur and Weston, 2010). Basically, during the training phase an optimization problem is solved to identify the largest-margin hyperplane ($\mathbf{w}\cdot\boldsymbol{x} + \mathrm{b} = 0$ for linear kernel SVM) allowing for an optimal separation of the training examples of the two classes. The goal is to find a vector **w** and a scalar b, which maximize the margin, i.e., the distance between the two classes in the direction of **w**.

The SVM can then predict the classification of an unlabeled input vector by checking on which side of the separating hyperplane the example lies.

The SVM belong to the class of kernel methods (Schölkopf and Smola, 2002; Shawe-Taylor and Cristianini, 2004), i.e., they depend on data only through dot products. To achieve good separation results even in case of non-linearly separable classes, the dot product can be replaced by a kernel function, which computes a dot product in some (possibly) higher dimensional feature space. This allows carrying out a linear classification in the feature space, without explicitly mapping in it the original observations. The separating hyperplane found in the feature space corresponds to a non-linear boundary in the input space. This property is commonly known as kernel trick. Formally, a kernel function is defined as a function that, given two observations $\boldsymbol{x}, \boldsymbol{x}' \in X$, satisfies $k(\boldsymbol{x},\boldsymbol{x}') = \phi(\boldsymbol{x})\,\phi'(\boldsymbol{x}')$, where X is the input space or domain and ϕ is a function mapping from X to a feature space. In this case, the prediction of the class membership of an unlabeled input vector is performed by mapping it into the feature space, and checking on which side of the separating hyperplane the example lies.

Among the non-linear kernel functions the Radial Basis Function (RBF) kernel is the most popular. It depends on the Euclidean distance between the examples and it is defined as $k(\mathbf{x},\mathbf{x}') = \exp(-\gamma \, ||\mathbf{x}-\mathbf{x}'||^2)$. The parameter γ determines the smoothness of the boundary (in the input space). Like the regularization parameter C in linear-kernel SVM, also the parameter γ is usually set using heuristics or tuned using cross-validation procedures.

Taking inspiration from the two-class SVM, Tax and Duin (2004) addressed the OCC problem by proposing a method to obtain a spherically shaped boundary around the target set. The method is called Support Vector Data Description (SVDD). During the training phase, an optimization problem is solved to minimize the volume of the sphere by minimizing the square of its radius, while demanding that the sphere contains most of the training objects. Similarly to what happens in two-class SVM, a regularization parameter C has to be set to control the trade-off between the sphere volume and the errors allowed in the target set.

Schölkopf et al. (2000) in presented a new formulation of two-class SVM, where the C parameter was removed and replaced with a new parameter ν with a more natural interpretation: it is an upper bound to the fraction of misclassifications and margin errors and a lower bound on the fraction of support vectors (SV). The authors showed that for certain parameter settings, the results of this new algorithm coincide with the conventional one. Moreover, desirable properties of previous SV algorithms are retained.

In 2001, Schölkopf and colleagues modified the previous approach (Schölkopf et al., 2000) to address the OCC problem and called the new algorithm single-class SVM. During the training phase of a single-class SVM, a hyperplane is placed such that it separates the target set from the origin with maximal margin. Similarly to the standard two-class SVM, when a more flexible data description is required, an implicit mapping of the data into another (possibly high dimensional) feature space is defined, such that the dot product in this feature space can be computed by evaluating a simple kernel function. An ideal kernel function would map the target examples onto a bounded, spherically shaped area in the feature space and outlier objects outside this area.

The constrained optimization problem to be solved is formulated as follows:

$$\text{Minimize}_{(\mathbf{w},\xi,\rho)} \ldots\ldots\ldots \tfrac{1}{2}||\mathbf{w}||^2 + \frac{1}{\nu N}\sum_{i=1}^{N} \xi_i - \rho \quad (1)$$

subject to

$$\mathbf{w}\,\boldsymbol{\phi}(\mathbf{x}_i) \geq \rho - \xi_i;\ i = 1, \ldots, N;\ \xi_i \geq 0. \quad (2)$$

where x_i are the target examples. The single-class SVM attributes a new point **x** to the target or the outlier class by evaluating which side of the hyperplane it falls on in the feature space.

As in two-class algorithm, the regularization parameter $\nu \in (0, 1]$ has to be set. Similarly to what happens in the two-class case, it can be interpreted as an upper bound on the fraction of training points outside the estimated region, and a lower bound on the fraction of support vectors. It is usually set based on its meaning or tuned using cross-validation procedures.

Although the method by Schölkopf et al. (2001) does not find a closed boundary around the data, it gives comparable solutions to Tax and Duin approach when the data is preprocessed to have unit norm (Tax and Duin, 2004). In particular, this happens when a RBF kernel is used. More in details, the solutions of the two approaches are identical when the same RBF kernel with γ and $C = 1/(\nu N)$, where N is the number of objects in the target set, are used, as reported by Sato et al. (2012a). In their practical implementation the two approaches operate comparably. Both perform best when the RBF kernel is used. Like in the two-class situation, the parameter γ can be set using heuristics or tuned using cross-validation procedures.

In this work, we first applied two-class SVM to the vector of 314 characteristics extracted for each subject of our datasets to obtain reference classification performances, and then we analyzed the same data with single-class SVM with RBF kernel. We performed the classification on the male subset and on the female subset separately, and then on the entire dataset. As pictorially shown in **Figure 1**, in contrast to the standard two-class classification approach to distinguish two well-characterized groups of subjects (**Figure 1A**), the OCC based on SVM can be implemented to make a multivariate description of the normative data, and thus to define a homogeneous baseline in comparison to which subjects with different diseases cluster out of the boundary enclosing the control group (**Figure 1B**). However, the latter approach relies on the hypothesis that the control group consists of typical individuals sharing a core of common distinctive features at neuroanatomical of functional levels, whereas non-typical individuals present alterations in many different ways, especially when highly heterogeneous condition are investigated, such as the ASD. Thus, in case the control class is not extremely homogeneous and it is matched to the patient class for many known aspects (e.g., age, gender, NVIQ) except for the presence of the disease condition, it may happen that OCC based on SVM capture common features according to which the patients can be described (**Figure 1C**). In the latter case, a boundary enclosing most patients can be identified, according to which most controls lie outside.

Pre-Image for RBF Kernel

In the linear kernel classifiers, the entries of the vector **w** can be directly considered as the relative weights of each characteristic for the decision function (Gori et al., 2015). Conversely, in the non-linear case (e.g., the RBF kernel), the interpretation of the vector **w** is non-intuitive and complex, since the separating hyperplane is found in the feature space. Since the map Φ is non-linear, we cannot generally assert that each vector **w** in the feature space will have a *preimage* under Φ, i.e., a point z in the input space such that $\Phi(z) = \mathbf{w}$. In the present work we used for the single-class SVM with RBF kernel the approach proposed in by Schölkopf et al. (1999) to generate *preimages* by approximating the inverse mapping from the feature space to the input space.

Additionally, to understand which features and which neuroanatomical regions drive the SVM boundary definition, we tailored the permutation testing method (Mourão-Miranda et al., 2005; Wanh et al., 2007; Gaonkar and Davatzikos, 2013; Gori et al., 2015) to the case of single-class classifiers.

RESULTS

Classification Performance

The Freesurfer pipeline was applied to preprocess the MRI of each subject according to the Freesurfer guidelines.

Patients with ASD and controls were matched on age and NVIQ, thus resulting in 20 matched case-control pairs in the female subset and in 19 matched case-control pairs and one group constituted by two patients and one control in the male subset, because of its dimensionality. We used these M (M = 20 for male and female subsets considered separately, M = 40 for the entire dataset) matched groups as subsets in a cross-validation procedure to evaluate the performance of the SVM classifiers: for each subset S_j, j = 1,...,M, we trained the SVM using the remaining subsets S_i, $i \neq j$, while retaining S_j as testing subset. Then we repeated the training and testing process for each subset, thus obtaining an estimate of the classifier performance on the entire dataset. Given the nature of the subsets, we refer

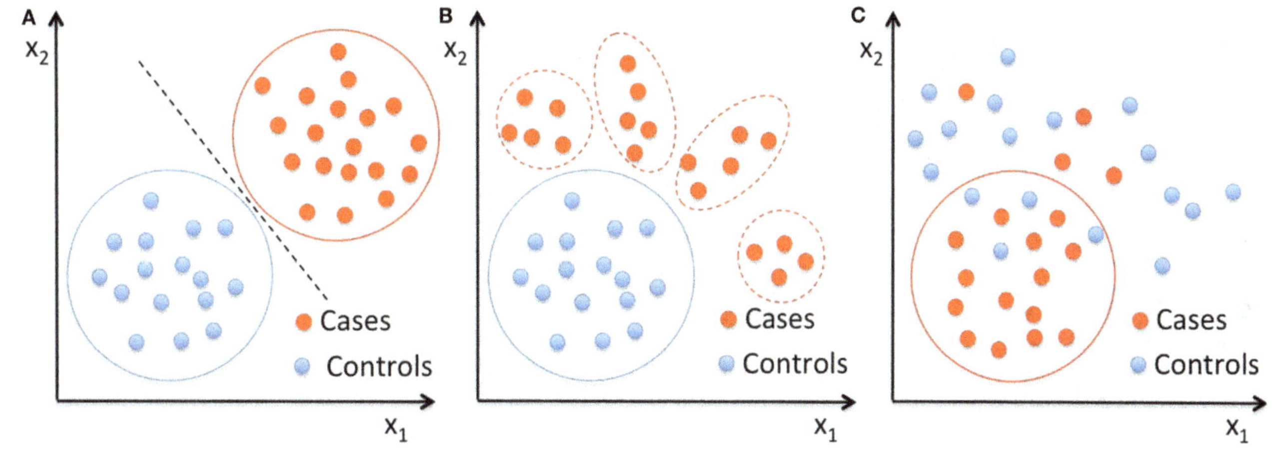

FIGURE 1 | Pictorial data representation in a two-dimensional space. (A) Classical application of a binary classifier to distinguish two well-characterized groups of subjects; **(B)** OCC approach based on the hypothesis that the control group is the homogeneous baseline in comparison to which, subjects with different diseases cluster out of the boundary enclosing the controls; **(C)** schematization of the OCC result in the case where common features associate the patients, thus the OCC boundary encloses most patients leaving outside most control cases. Solid lines are drawn around the groups entering the training of the classifiers, i.e., both case and control subjects are needed in training a binary classifier **(A)**, whereas only on control cases in **(B)** and only the patients' group in **(C)** are necessary to train a OCC, respectively.

to the cross-validation procedure we applied as leave-pair-out cross-validation (LPO-CV).

The performance of the SVM classifiers is evaluated in terms of the sensitivity (percentage of subjects with disease correctly identified, i.e., true positive rate) and the specificity (percentage of control subjects correctly identified, i.e., true negative rate). By varying the classifier decisional threshold, the trade-off between the sensitivity and the rate of false-positive detection can be represented in a curve known as Receiver Operating Characteristic (ROC) curve (Metz, 2006). The area under the ROC curve (AUC) is a global index to compare the ROC curves of different classifiers (Hanley and McNeil, 1982).

The LPO-CV scheme was implemented in the performance evaluation of both the two-class and the OCC SVM. A difference in the case of OCC SVM occurs only in the training step: to apply LPO-CV in the context of single-class classification we simply trained the single-class classifiers only on one class (target class) inside the cross validation, but tested it on both classes for the subset that was left out for testing.

To train and test two-class and single-class classifiers we used RapidMiner (http://rapidminer.com/) advanced analytics platform version 5.3, which includes both two-class and single-class SVM as a part of the LibSVM operator.

Two-Class Classification Performance

A standard two-class SVM classification with linear and RBF kernels was carried out to discriminate subjects with ASD from controls, including the optimization of the SVM free parameters during the training. We reported the results in **Table 2**. The best performances we obtained were: AUC = 0.74 by using the linear kernel for the male subset and AUC = 0.65 by using the RBF kernel for the female subset. The reported two-class SVM performance already take into account the regularization and kernel parameter optimization, carried out through the nested LPO-CV procedure. We obtained the best results with linear kernel for males and with RBF kernel for females. These results represent a reference classification performance to compare with the new OCC SVM approach we propose.

One-Class Classification Performance

We first performed single-class classification by setting $\nu = 0.1$ and γ using heuristics (i.e., as the inverse of the number of features). Then, following the procedure adopted in Mourão-Miranda et al. (2011), we carried out the optimization of the parameters ν and γ, within nested LPO-CV loops, as follows: at each iteration j of the outer LPO-CV scheme we had at disposal a subset $A_j = \{S_i\}_{i=1,...,N, i \neq j}$ for training. Before training, we performed an optimization procedure based on an internal LPO-CV twice. In the first run, we kept the parameter ν fixed at an initial value (0.1) and we performed a LPO-CV for several values of γ in order to find its optimal estimate (i.e., the one that maximizes the AUC). To cover a wide range of possible γ-values, we let this parameter vary first on a coarse grid (19 steps from 2^{-15} to 2^3 by power of 2); then, we refined the search in the interesting regions we identified. In the second run, we kept γ fixed at the optimal value and we performed a second optimization procedure to choose the optimal ν, using a coarse optimization with 10 linearly spaced values in the [0.01–0.5] range, then a fine search in [0.01–0.3] range using 20 linearly spaced values. A single-class SVM was finally trained on A_j using the optimal values of γ and ν and tested on the subset S_j left out in the outer LPO-CV scheme. This procedure was repeated for each j, each time leaving a different subset outside as test subset.

The intuitive approach for transforming a binary discrimination problem into a single-class task in the context of highly heterogeneous conditions like ASD is to use the control

TABLE 2 | The performances obtained in the ASD vs. CTRL classification with the two-class SVM, the OCC-SVM trained on the CTRL class, and the OCC-SVM trained on the ASD class are reported.

Two-class SVM				**Male sample**	**Female sample**
Training set	**Test set**	**Training specification**		**AUC**	**AUC**
ASD and CTRL	ASD and CTRL	linear-kernel SVM for males/RBF for females	optimized C/optimized ν, γ	0.74	0.65
	ASD and CTRL with NVIQ < 70			0.73	0.63
	ASD and CTRL with NVIQ ≥ 70			0.8	0.63

One-class SVM				**Male sample**	**Female sample**
Training set	**Test set**	**Training specification**		**AUC**	**AUC**
CTRL	ASD and CTRL	RBF	optimized ν, γ	0.50	0.50

One-class SVM				**Male sample**		**Female sample**	
Training set	**Test set**	**Training specification**		**AUC**	***p*-value**	**AUC**	***p*-value**
ASD	ASD and CTRL	RBF	optimized ν, γ	0.74	0.012	0.68	0.016
	ASD and CTRL with NVIQ < 70			0.64	0.19	0.65	0.05
	ASD and CTRL with NVIQ ≥ 70			0.81	0.016	0.72	0.05

One-class SVM				**Male and female sample**
Training set	**Test set**	**Training specification**		**AUC**
ASD male and females	ASD and CTRL males and females	RBF	optimized ν, γ	0.64
	ASD and CTRL males and females with NVIQ < 70			0.63
	ASD and CTRL males and females with NVIQ ≥ 70			0.65

All classification performances are obtained in a leave-pair-out cross validation scheme, where the classifier training parameters are optimized within nested loops. The performances of the classifiers were separately evaluated in most cases on the subsets of ASD and CTRL subjects with low and high NVIQ values. The permutation test was also performed to assign a statistical significance p-value to the AUC in the case of OCC classification of male and female samples. ASD, Subjects with Autism Spectrum Disorders; CL, chance level; CTRL, control sample; NVIQ, non-verbal intelligence quotient; RBF, Radial Basis Function; SVM, Support Vector Machine.

class as target class, figuring that it could enable the definition of a robust boundary, in relation to which the ASD patients would be classified as outliers. Consequently, we first trained a single-class SVM by considering only control examples to form the decision boundary, thus discarding information about the ASD class during the training phase.

This would be the optimal approach if the control class had characteristics of homogeneity, since the single-class SVM could capture the control class structure, by adjusting itself to its properties. This would allow recognizing ASD examples as outliers, even if the available ASD samples were not representative of the real ASD population, due to the extreme ASD heterogeneity.

However, the results obtained in this case in terms of AUC were not above the chance level, despite the optimization on of the parameters ν and γ.

Therefore, we repeated the same procedure using the ASD patient group as the target class to investigate whether there was a consistent neuroanatomical pattern among the ASD patients in relation to which the controls can be classified as outliers.

The results obtained in terms of AUC were: AUC = 0.73 for the male subset and AUC = 0.66 for the female subset by setting $\nu = 0.1$ and γ using heuristics; by optimizing the parameters ν and γ, AUC = 0.74 for the male subset and AUC = 0.68 for the female subset. We summarized in **Table 2** the classification results we obtained in the different classification experiments we conducted.

These results show that the control class does not have characteristics of homogeneity allowing recognizing ASD examples as outliers. Conversely, there is a common structure among the ASD patients that the OCC–SVM could capture. The OCC–SVM assigns to a test case a continuous output providing the confidence for it to belong to the target class or to be an outlier. To investigate whether the AUC performance obtained in the case-control discrimination were significantly above the chance level we implemented the permutation test. To obtain the null distribution of the AUC, we carried out a permutation test procedure in the training phase, tailoring it to the single-class classifiers. In a standard two-class classification the permutation test is performed by randomly exchanging several times the class labels (i.e., by randomly assigning positive and negative labels either to the ASD and the control cases) and repeating the classification procedure. In the OCC case, the training is performed on the target class only, e.g., the ASD class in our analysis. To find the null distribution for AUC, we permuted the group labels 10000 times, creating "artificial" training datasets where randomly chosen ASD cases were exchanged with their matched controls. Each "artificial" ASD dataset was then used to train one single-class SVM, i.e., to generate a decision function. We counted the number of times the AUC exceeded the value obtained with the real class labels. Dividing this value by the number of permutations provided a statistical significance for the AUC. The permutation testing procedure was applied separately for the male and the female subsets. We used the Matlab (The MathWorks, Inc.) interface to the LIBSVM package (http://www.csie.ntu.edu.tw/~cjlin/libsvm/) to train the single-class classifiers in the permutation test procedure, implementing the RBF parameter optimization as nested LPO-CV loops. The AUC values and the significance values of the permutation test are reported in **Table 2**.

Finally, to investigate the impact of some known heterogeneity factors present in the ASD sample, we estimated the OCC performance on the entire dataset, by using the group of both male and female subjects with ASD as the target class. We achieved AUC = 0.64 in the case-control discrimination. This slight performance decrease is not surprising and we ascribed it to the introduction of the gender as additional heterogeneity factor.

Another relevant heterogeneity factor in our data is the NVIQ of subjects, which is in the [31–123] range. If the performance of OCC trained on male subjects with ASD (leading to AUC = 0.74 on the male population) is evaluated separately on the subsamples of subjects with NVIQ $\geq$ 70 and NVIQ $<$ 70, the values of AUC = 0.81 and AUC = 0.64 were obtained, respectively. A similar trend holds for the OCC trained on the female subjects with ASD (leading on AUC = 0.68 on the female population). In this case AUC = 0.72 and AUC = 0.65 were obtained on the subsamples of subjects with NVIQ $\geq$ 70 and NVIQ $<$ 70, respectively.

Maps of Discriminant Brain Regions

To understand which of the 314 characteristics (i.e., which brain regions and which of the five computed features) are the most relevant to the single-class SVM boundary definition, we trained a single-class SVM with RBF kernel using all the ASD patient group as the target class (with $\nu = 0.1$ and heuristic γ) and we applied the algorithm proposed in Schölkopf et al. (1999) to generate the *preimage* vector $\boldsymbol{z}$. We used the Statistical Pattern Recognition Toolbox for Matlab (STPRTool) (http://cmp.felk.cvut.cz/cmp/software/stprtool/index.html) to generate the *preimage*.

To obtain the null distribution of the preimage $\boldsymbol{z}$, we carried out a permutation test in the training phase by permuting the group labels 10000 times, as described above. Each "artificial" ASD dataset generated a decision function and a corresponding preimage vector $\boldsymbol{z}$. Since each component of $\boldsymbol{z}$ corresponds to one of the 314 characteristics, we obtained a null distribution associated with every characteristic. We counted the number of times the so-generated components of $\boldsymbol{z}$ exceeded (comparing the absolute values) the corresponding values in the $\boldsymbol{z}$ map obtained for the real ASD cases; dividing this value by the number of permutations provided a statistical significance map. Then, we retained only the characteristics with $p < 0.05$. The relevant characteristics (features and regions) resulting from the permutation test applied to male and female data groups are shown in **Tables 3, 4**. As stated before, in case of linear-kernel SVM, the separating hyperplane $\mathbf{w}$ can be represented as an image showing which brain regional features are more relevant for the classification problem. Additionally, the sign of each element of $\mathbf{w}$ directly identifies whether the corresponding feature is greater either in the case or in the control group. This information is inaccessible when using RBF, as the linear problem is solved in the space defined by the non-linear transformation $\mathbf{w} = \Phi(\boldsymbol{z})$, thus the signs of the elements of the z vector (i.e., the *preimage*) do not indicate whether a relevant feature in the classification problem is greater in the case or in the control group. To foresee this information, which is important to compare the result we obtain with those presented in other studies, we simply analyzed the distributions of each feature and reported the trend of the sign of the case-control difference. We indicate in **Tables 3, 4** with arrows pointing up/down the features significantly contributing to the OCC boundary definition whose individual trend is toward increased/decreased values in the group of male subjects with ASD with respect to matched controls.

We show in **Figures 2, 3** the brain regions contributing most to the definition of the OCC boundary, as reported in **Tables 3, 4** for male and female subsets, respectively. For the male population the main regions are: left (L) and right (R) medial orbito frontal cortices, L pars triangularis and R pars opercularis of the inferior frontal gyrus, middle temporal cortex and R insula. For the female population the main regions are: L and R caudate anterior cingulate, pars opercularis, posterior cingulated, cuneus; R pars triangularis postcentral gyrus, superior temporal cortex and superior parietal cortex. They are mostly among the network of structural brain alterations widely reported in the population with ASD, including frontal and temporal areas. Thus, despite the phenotypical heterogeneity in ASD, a common neuroanatomical profile of core features could be detected with the OCC SVM approach.

DISCUSSION

We analyzed the brain structural MRI features of patients with ASD with OCC SVM, starting with the estimation of the OCC performance in the ASD vs. controls discrimination task. Then, we investigated whether the distribution of patterns of brain structures in control subjects is homogeneous enough to enable the definition of a robust boundary, in relation to which the patients with ASD would be classified as outliers. This approach is consistent with previously proposed methods where OCC were implemented on fMRI features to build multivariate normative rules on the healthy control population, which would allow recognizing abnormal cases as outliers (Mourão-Miranda et al., 2011; Sato et al., 2012a,b). In the specific case of the population of young children with ASD we analyzed, we found out that an OCC boundary enclosing the controls, built upon structural MRI brain features, will allow most ASD cases to fall within the boundary. By contrast, a consistent pattern among the patients with ASD could be identified by the OCC approach, which provided a boundary in relation to which most controls were classified as outliers. In other words, we found out evidence that the control group is the more heterogeneous one and therefore the hypersphere or decision boundary enclosing most of the controls contains data in the ASD range. Vice versa, the ASD group showed a common structure that the SVM OCC could capture. This apparently counterintuitive result might be understood in the light of the following considerations. First, we performed a priori heterogeneity reduction of the ASD sample by excluding subjects with ASD secondary to known causes and/or with dysmorphic features (see Exclusion criteria in Section Participants and MRI Data Acquisition). Conversely, the control group was highly heterogeneous, since it comprises children who span the full range of cognitive ability (NVIQ score range: 31–123). This selection is motivated by the our primary choice of including within the cases all ASD children who performed MRI, since focusing just on those who are high-functioning would be non-representative of ASD population comprising about 55% of subjects in the intellectual disability range (Charman et al., 2011). As a necessary consequence, subjects with idiopathic developmental delay (DD) were included within the control group in order to obtain a match on NVIQ and thus a reliable MRI data interpretation (Crone et al., 2010). Therefore, the heterogeneity of MRI structural features within the control sample could be ascribed not only to the normal inter-individual brain variability that occurs among individuals with typical development (Wilke and Holland, 2003; Kanai and Rees, 2011), but also to the heterogeneous subsample of individuals with DD. In fact, by definition, idiopathic DD appears to be a highly heterogeneous disorder in terms of etiopathogenesis and clinical features: it is therefore plausible that also its neuroanatomical substrate is heterogeneous and hence contributes to amplify the cerebral differences detected in our control population. Moreover, we restricted our analysis to an early and relatively narrow age-range (2–6 years), a time-period in which structural MRI findings of ASD patients are more consistent and less heterogeneous across studies (Wolff and Piven, 2013). Specifically, a overgrowth of WM and GM before 2 years of age followed by a growth rate reduction that lead to brain volumes similar to typical children by approximately the school-age period was frequently reported (Lenroot and Yeung, 2013). In addition, by focusing on preschoolers only, we captured the pattern of brain alterations taking place near the clinical onset of the disorder and therefore we minimized the influence of different post-natal variables (e.g., environmental factors, psychiatric comorbidities, rehabilitative intervention) on brain structure. In other words, it is possible that a common altered brain presentation is more frequent in the early stage of the ASD disorder and that inter-subject variability in ASD populations progressively increases with age.

The present work is a proof of concept that the OCC framework can be applied to neuroimaging data to investigate if consistent patterns of alterations do exist even in heterogeneous populations such as ASD. Despite the results we found need to be confirmed against a larger population, the approach we present here is a preliminary step aiming to set up a strategy to identify common altered features in specific disorders.

Analogously, a common brain endophenotype in ASD individuals was detected with different methods of data acquisition, including electroencephalogram (EEG) spectral coherence (Duffy and Als, 2012), voxel based morphometry (Uddin et al., 2011), functional MRI (White et al., 2014), functional connectivity (Murdaugh et al., 2012), and diffusion tensor imaging (Ingalhalikar et al., 2011). These findings did not support the extreme variability of cerebral structure and function in ASD patients, as suggested by other investigations (Alexander et al., 2007; Nordahl et al., 2012; Hahamy et al., 2015).

TABLE 3 | Relevant brain regions and features for the male group ($p < 0.05$).

Male subset		Feature				
Hemisphere	**Region**	**Area**	**Mean curvature**	**Thickness**	**Thickness standard deviation**	**Volume**
lh	Medial orbitofrontal cortex		↑			
	Middle temporal gyrus	↑				
	Pars triangularis	↑	↓			
	Posterior cingulate cortex	↑				↑
	Transverse temporal gyrus	↑				
rh	Insula	↑	↑			
	Medial orbitofrontal cortex		↑			
	Pars opercularis	↑				↑

Arrows pointing up/down indicate the features significantly contributing to the OCC boundary definition, whose individual trend is toward increased/decreased values in the group of male subjects with ASD with respect to matched controls.

TABLE 4 | Relevant brain regions and features for the female group ($p < 0.05$).

Female subset		Feature				
Hemisphere	**Region**	**Area**	**Mean curvature**	**Thickness**	**Thickness standard deviation**	**Volume**
lh	Caudal anterior cingulate cortex			↑		↑
	Cuneus	↓				↑
	Enthorinal cortex				↑	
	Inferior temporal lobe	↓				
	Lateral orbitofrontal cortex				↑	
	Pars opercularis			↓		
	Posterior cingulate				↑	
	Precuneus	↑				↑
	Rostral anterior cingulate cortex		↓			
	Transverse temporal gyrus					↑
rh	Caudal middle frontal gyrus	↑				
	Cuneus				↓	
	Enthorinal cortex				↑	
	Pars opercularis		↓			↑
	Pars triangularis			↓	↓	
	Postcentral gyrus	↑				↑
	Precuneus	↓				
	Rostral anterior cingulate cortex		↑			↑
	Superior parietal cortex		↓			
	Superior temporal gyrus		↓			

Arrows pointing up/down indicate the features significantly contributing to the OCC boundary definition, whose individual trend is toward increased/decreased values in the group of female subjects with ASD with respect to matched controls.

Since we found the rather limited maximum AUC value of 0.74 for the male subset, it is important to highlight that among control subjects we included patients with DD that from a clinical point of view can frequently be considered in the ASD differential diagnosis. Therefore, it is possible that not only at the behavioral level, but also at the neuroanatomical level individuals with ASD and individuals with DD share some features that make the brain-based distinction between each other more difficult. This interpretation of our results is further supported by the fact that the AUC values reported on the subgroups of subjects with high NVIQ values are systematically higher than those obtained on the subgroups with low NVIQ values (see **Table 2**), whereas the performances obtained on the entire samples are positioned in between, as expected. It happens in the analysis of the male and the female subsamples and of the entire data sample. According to this view, the capability to differentiate participants into patient and control groups improved when we restricted the analysis to ASD patients with NVIQ ≥ 70 and therefore we

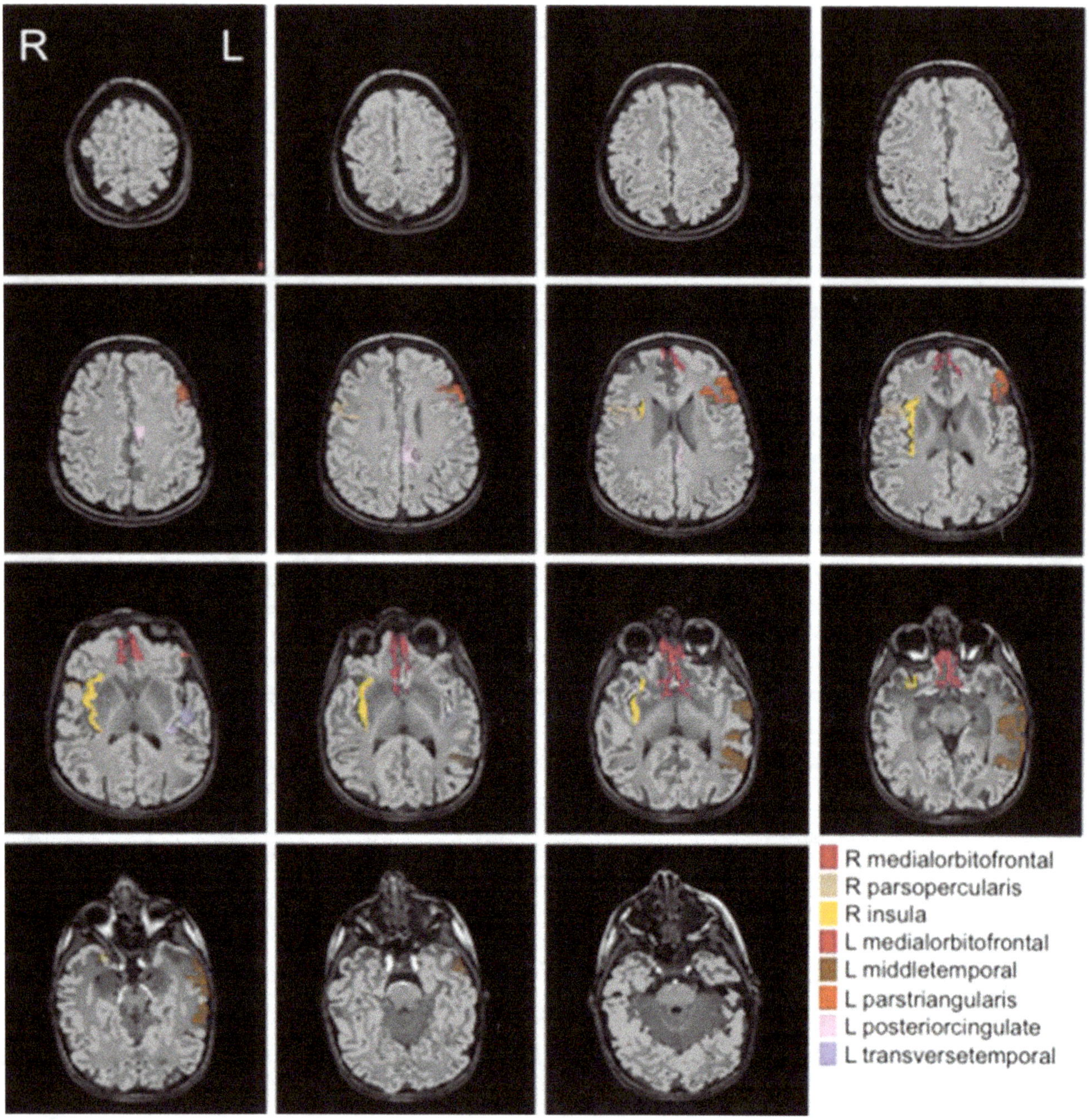

FIGURE 2 | Brain regions most contributing to the definition of the OCC boundary for the male group.

included among control subjects only individuals without DD (AUC = 0.81 and AUC = 0.72 for female and male subsamples, respectively).

The features which had the highest discriminative ability between the cases (both males and females) and the controls belong to four cerebral regions -posterior cingulate cortex (PCC), pars opercularis, and pars triangularis of inferior frontal gyrus, transverse temporal gyrus- all of which would represent a neuroanatomical signature of pre-schoolers with ASD. Specifically, we detected increased left PCC volume in ASD patients. Notably, this region has been included in the default mode network as one of the highest baseline energy consuming regions (Raichle et al., 2001) and has been implicated in arousal and awareness (Vogt and Laureys, 2005), autobiographical memory retrieval (Maddock et al., 2001), as well as in cognitive flexibility and in the ability to regulate the breadth of attention (Leech and Sharp, 2014), functions frequently impaired in patients with ASD (Bruck et al., 2007; Leung and Zakzanis, 2014; Orekhova and Stroganova, 2014).

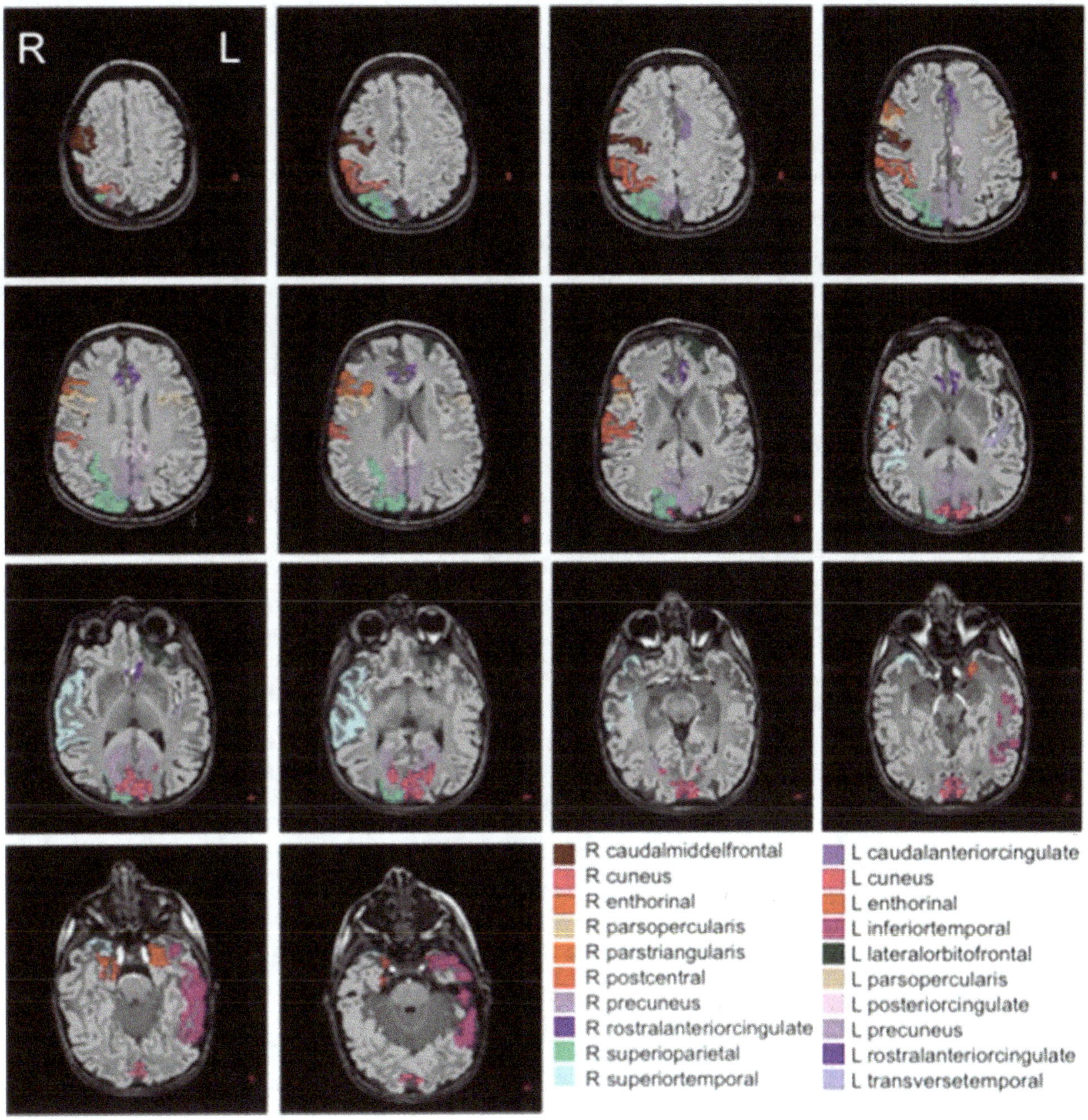

FIGURE 3 | Brain regions most contributing to the definition of the OCC boundary for the female group.

In addition, we identified a significant alteration of pars opercularis and pars triangularis in patients with ASD. These inferior frontal regions together comprise Broca's area, which is primarily involved in higher-order abilities such as expressive language, action imitation, attribution of mental states, and empathy (Iacoboni and Dapretto, 2006). Disruption of this area may therefore lead to core ASD symptoms (Dapretto et al., 2006). In particular, our finding of reduced cortical thickness (CT) in the pars opercularis is in line with results of Zielinski et al. (2014) in children and adolescents with ASD and of Hadjikhani et al. (2006), who reported a local decreases of CT in the pars opercularis of 14 high-functioning adults with ASD compared with matched control subjects. Also, decreased CT in the pars triangularis is in concordance with a previous study demonstrating focal patterns of cortical dysmaturation in children with ASD (Jiao et al., 2010). At the volumetric level, an increase in pars opercularis and pars triangularis was identified in children with ASD compared to controls (Knaus et al., 2009) while an opposite finding characterized adults with high-functioning ASD (Yamasaki et al., 2010), supporting an altered trajectory of neurodevelopment in the autistic disorder. Interestingly, a highly localized structural alteration consisting in a significant reduction of the sulcus maximum depth was recently detected in the Broca's area of young children with ASD (Brun et al., 2016), suggesting its possible role in facilitating early ASD identification.

Our individuals with ASD showed increased volumes (females) and area (males) of the left transverse temporal (Heschl's) gyrus relative to controls. The transverse gyrus of Heschl includes the primary auditory cortex and is critically implicated in early auditory processing (Galaburda and Sanides, 1980). Several ASD symptoms, including altered auditory responsiveness (O'Connor, 2012), language perception and acquisition, are strictly related to this cerebral region. Previous cross-sectional investigations on older patients with ASD failed to observe any volumetric alteration in Heschl's gyrus (Gage et al., 2009; Knaus et al., 2009): it is possible that neuroanatomical differences in this area are age-related, and therefore detectable in our sample of ASD preschoolers, but not more during childhood and adolescence.

Crucially, a longitudinal investigation reported a reduced growth of Heschl's gyrus white matter in the left hemisphere as well as in the right Heschl's gyrus gray matter of children with ASD (Prigge et al., 2013), supporting an abnormality in the trajectory of cerebral development in the ASD group.

It is worth mentioning that the most discriminative brain features that characterize young children with ASD in the current investigation are largely overlapping with those identified in a resting-state connectivity analysis of brain lateralization in 447 high-functioning individuals with ASD (Nielsen et al., 2014). Therefore, a consistent finding was detected in these two studies, despite they do present substantial differences not only as to the numerosity, IQ sample and imaging modalities, but also as to the age of participants (preschoolers in our study vs. individuals across a wide range of ages starting from 6 years in the paper by Nielsen and colleagues), and sites of MRI acquisition (single site in our study vs. multiple sites in Nielsen's report). Hence, this replicated result would open the door to speculation that, irrespective of demographic and clinical features, selective alteration in language and default mode areas is a universal cerebral endophenotype of ASD.

In conclusion, results from the present study suggest that a distinctive neuroanatomical profile could be identified in preschoolers with ASD, independently of their gender, age, and NVIQ. In fact, beside the well-known heterogeneity of the ASD condition, patients seem to share common neuroanatomical substrates that appear to comprise language and default mode regions and could represent the core brain alterations of the disorder in the preschool age.

Several limitations of the current work and directions for future studies should be highlighted. First, the classification performances obtained are quite modest and, in some specific cases, the performances of the OCC classifiers are not significantly different from the chance level, as it happens for example on the sub group of male subjects with low NVIQ values (see **Table 2**). More populated data samples would be necessary to understand whether with improved statistical sensitivity the two overlapping classes can be effectively disentangled. Second, the relatively limited sample size prevented us from reliably subgrouping ASD patients on the basis of gender and NVIQ for investigating possible brain correlates of phenotypic differences. Third, we did not implement in our classification model any feature selection technique. Due to the large number of features (314) with respect to the data sample size we are working with a high risk of overfitting the models. As we are interested most in the discrimination maps generated by the OCC than in the classification performance by itself, the overfitting problem does not seem a major issue. However, to investigate in depth the separability of the ASD and control samples, and to understand whether the modest AUC values we obtained on cross validation are due to the lack of generalization abilities due to model overfitting, a feature selection technique should be implemented. Finally, since patients with ASD were recruited from an ASD Unit in a large tertiary hospital and research university that evaluates patients under 18 years of age from all over Italy, we may not have been fully able to capture children at the less severe end of the spectrum.

Future investigations will involve: (i) analyzing whether a distinct clinical symptoms or behavior profile characterized the outliers within the ASD cohort; (ii) evaluating whether the brain ASD endophenotype detected in the first years of life remains stable over time, or vice-versa developmental changes in ASD symptom profiles impact also on brain structure; (iii) including analysis of patients with other neurodevelopmental disorders which display overlapping clinical features with ASD [e.g., language disorder, social (pragmatic) communication disorder, attention-deficit/hyperactivity disorder, stereotypic movement disorder] in order to verify the specificity of the discriminative brain pattern here identified in ASD patients.

AUTHOR CONTRIBUTIONS

AR and SC designed the study; IG, AG, and AR carried out data processing and analysis; SC and FM interpreted the results; AR, IG, and SC drafted the manuscript; AG edited the manuscript; FM critically revised the manuscript for important intellectual content.

ACKNOWLEDGMENTS

This work has been partially founded by the Italian Ministry of Health and the Tuscany Government (GR2317873, PI: SC), by Sviluppo Toscana (Bando FAS Salute, ARIANNA Project), and by the National Institute of Nuclear Physics (nextMR project).

REFERENCES

Alexander, A. L., Lee, J. E., Lazar, M., Boudos, R., DuBray, M. B., Oakes, T. R., et al. (2007). Diffusion tensor imaging of the corpus callosum in Autism. *Neuroimage* 34, 61–73. doi: 10.1016/j.neuroimage.2006.08.032

American Psychiatric Association (2000). *DSM-IV-TR, Diagnostic and Statistical Manual of Mental Disorders, 4th Edn, Text Revision.* Washington, DC: American Psychiatric Association.

American Psychiatric Association (2013). *Diagnostic and Statistical Manual of Mental Disorders (DSM-5), 5th Edn.* Washington, DC: American Psychiatric Publishing.

Ben-Hur, A., and Weston, J. (2010). User's guide to support vector machines. *Methods Mol. Biol.* 609, 223–239. doi: 10.1007/978-1-60327-241-4_13

Bruck, M., London, K., Landa, R., and Goodman, J. (2007). Autobiographical memory and suggestibility in children with autism spectrum disorder. *Dev. Psychopathol.* 19, 73–95. doi: 10.1017/S0954579407070058

Brun, L., Auzias, G., Viellard, M., Villeneuve, N., Girard, N., Poinso, F., et al. (2016). Localized misfolding within Broca's area as a distinctive feature of autistic disorder. *Biol. Psychiatry Cogn. Neurosci. Neuroimaging* 1, 160–168. doi: 10.1016/j.bpsc.2015.11.003

Calderoni, S., Retico, A., Biagi, L., Tancredi, R., Muratori, F., and Tosetti, M. (2012). Female children with autism spectrum disorder: an insight from mass-univariate and pattern classification analyses. *Neuroimage* 59, 1013–1022. doi: 10.1016/j.neuroimage.2011.08.070

Centers for Disease Control and Prevention (2014). *Prevalence of ASD. MMWR* 63, 1–22.

Charman, T., Pickles, A., Simonoff, E., Chandler, S., Loucas, T., and Baird, G. (2011). IQ in children with autism spectrum disorders: data from the Special Needs and Autism Project (SNAP). *Psychol. Med.* 41, 619–627. doi: 10.1017/S0033291710000991

Crone, E. A., Poldrack, R. A., and Durston, S. (2010). Challenges and methods in developmental neuroimaging. *Hum. Brain Mapp.* 31, 835–837. doi: 10.1002/hbm.21053

Dapretto, M., Davies, M. S., Pfeifer, J. H., Scott, A. A., Sigman, M., Bookheimer, S. Y., et al. (2006). Understanding emotions in others: mirror neuron dysfunction in children with autism spectrum disorders. *Nat. Neurosci.* 9, 28–30. doi: 10.1038/nn1611

De Rubeis, S., and Buxbaum, J. D. (2015). Genetics and genomics of autism spectrum disorder: embracing complexity. *Hum. Mol. Genet.* 24, R24–R31. doi: 10.1093/hmg/ddv273

Duffy, F. H., and Als, H. (2012). A stable pattern of EEG spectral coherence distinguishes children with autism from neuro-typical controls - a large case control study. *BMC Med.* 10:64. doi: 10.1186/1741-7015-10-64

Ecker, C., Marquand, A., Mourão-Miranda, J., Johnston, P., Daly, E. M., Brammer, M. J., et al. (2010a). Describing the brain in autism in five dimensions-magnetic resonance imaging-assisted diagnosis of autism spectrum disorder using a multiparameter classification approach. *J. Neurosci.* 30, 10612–10623. doi: 10.1523/JNEUROSCI.5413-09.2010

Ecker, C., Rocha-Rego, V., Johnston, P., Mourao-Miranda, J., Marquand, A., Daly, E. M., et al. (2010b). Investigating the predictive value of whole-brain structural MR scans in autism: a pattern classification approach. *Neuroimage* 49, 44–56. doi: 10.1016/j.neuroimage.2009.08.024

Fischl, B., Sereno, M. I., and Dale, A. (1999). Cortical surface-based analysis. II: inflation, flattening, and a surface-based coordinate system. *Neuroimage* 9, 195–207. doi: 10.1006/nimg.1998.0396

Fischl, B., van der Kouwe, A., Destrieux, C., Halgren, E., Ségonne, F., Salat, D. H., et al. (2004). Automatically parcellating the human cerebral cortex. *Cereb. Cortex* 14, 11–22. doi: 10.1093/cercor/bhg087

Gage, N. M., Juranek, J., Filipek, P. A., Osann, K., Flodman, P., Isenberg, A. L., et al. (2009). Rightward hemispheric asymmetries in auditory language cortex in children with autistic disorder: an MRI investigation. *J. Neurodev. Disord.* 1, 205–214. doi: 10.1007/s11689-009-9010-2

Galaburda, A., and Sanides, F. (1980). Cytoarchitectonic organization of the human auditory cortex. *J. Comp. Neurol.* 190, 597–610. doi: 10.1002/cne.901900312

Gaonkar, B., and Davatzikos, C. (2013). Analytic estimation of statistical significance maps for support vector machine based multi-variate image analysis and classification. *Neuroimage* 78, 270–283. doi: 10.1016/j.neuroimage.2013.03.066

Gori, I., Giuliano, A., Muratori, F., Saviozzi, I., Oliva, P., Tancredi, R., et al. (2015). Gray matter alterations in young children with autism spectrum disorders: comparing morphometry at the voxel and regional level. *J. Neuroimaging* 25, 866–874. doi: 10.1111/jon.12280

Grzadzinski, R., Huerta, M., and Lord, C. (2013). DSM-5 and autism spectrum disorders (ASDs): an opportunity for identifying ASD subtypes. *Mol. Autism.* 4:12. doi: 10.1186/2040-2392-4-12

Hadjikhani, N., Joseph, R. M., Snyder, J., and Tager-Flusberg, H. (2006). Anatomical differences in the mirror neuron system and social cognition network in autism. *Cereb. Cortex* 16, 1276–1282. doi: 10.1093/cercor/bhj069

Hahamy, A., Behrmann, M., and Malach, R. (2015). The idiosyncratic brain: distortion of spontaneous connectivity patterns in autism spectrum disorder. *Nat. Neurosci.* 18, 302–309. doi: 10.1038/nn.3919

Hanley, J. A., and McNeil, B. J. (1982). The meaning and use of the area under a receiver operating charactertic (ROC) curve. *Radiology* 143, 29–36. doi: 10.1148/radiology.143.1.7063747

Hernandez, L. M., Rudie, J. D., Green, S. A., Bookheimer, S., and Dapretto, M. (2015). Neural signatures of autism spectrum disorders: insights into brain network dynamics. *Neuropsychopharmacology* 40, 171–189. doi: 10.1038/npp.2014.172

Iacoboni, M., and Dapretto, M. (2006). The mirror neuron system and the consequences of its dysfunction. *Nat. Rev. Neurosci.* 7, 942–951. doi: 10.1038/nrn2024

Ingalhalikar, M., Parker, D., Bloy, L., Roberts, T. P., and Verma, R. (2011). Diffusion based abnormality markers of pathology: toward learned diagnostic prediction of ASD. *Neuroimage* 57, 918–927. doi: 10.1016/j.neuroimage.2011.05.023

Jiao, Y., Chen, R., Ke, X., Chu, K., Lu, Z., and Herskovits, E. H. (2010). Predictive models of autism spectrum disorder based on brain regional cortical thickness. *Neuroimage* 50, 89–599. doi: 10.1016/j.neuroimage.2009.12.047

Kanai, R., and Rees, G. (2011). The structural basis of inter-individual differences in human behaviour and cognition. *Nat. Rev. Neurosci.* 12, 231–242. doi: 10.1038/nrn3000

Klein, A., and Tourville, J. (2012). 101 labeled brain images and a consistent human cortical labeling protocol. *Front. Neurosci.* 6:171. doi: 10.3389/fnins.2012.00171

Knaus, T. A., Silver, A. M., Dominick, K. C., Schuring, M. D., Shaffer, N., Lindgren, K. A., et al. (2009). Age-related changes in the anatomy of language regions in autism spectrum disorder. *Brain Imaging Behav.* 3, 51–63. doi: 10.1007/s11682-008-9048-x

Krawczyk, B., and Woźniak, M. (2015). Hypertension type classification using hierarchical ensemble of one-class classifiers for imbalanced data. *ICT Innov. Adv. Intell. Syst. Comput.* 311, 341–349. doi: 10.1007/978-3-319-09879-1_34

Leech, R., and Sharp, D. J. (2014). The role of the posterior cingulate cortex in cognition and disease. *Brain* 137(Pt 1), 12–32. doi: 10.1093/brain/awt162

Lenroot, R. K., and Yeung, P. K. (2013). Heterogeneity within autism spectrum disorders: what have we learned from neuroimaging studies? *Front. Hum. Neurosci.* 7:733. doi: 10.3389/fnhum.2013.00733

Leung, R. C., and Zakzanis, K. K. (2014). Brief report: cognitive flexibility in autism spectrum disorders: a quantitative review. *J. Autism Dev. Dis.* 44, 2628–2645. doi: 10.1007/s10803-014-2136-4

Lord, C., Risi, S., Lambrecht, L., Cook, E. H. Jr., Leventhal, B. L., DiLavore, P. C., et al. (2000). The autism diagnostic observation schedule-generic: a standard measure of social and communication deficits associated with the spectrum of autism. *J. Autism Dev. Disord.* 30, 205–223. doi: 10.1023/A:1005592401947

Maddock, R. J., Garrett, A. S., and Buonocore, M. H. (2001). Remembering familiar people: the posterior cingulate cortex and autobiographical memory retrieval. *Neuroscience* 104, 667–676. doi: 10.1016/S0306-4522(01)00108-7

Metz, C. E. (2006). Receiver operating characteristics analysis: a tool for the quantitative evaluation of observer performance and imaging systems. *J. Am. Coll. Radiol.* 3, 413–422. doi: 10.1016/j.jacr.2006.02.021

Mourão-Miranda, J., Bokde, A. L., Born, C., Hampel, H., and Stetter, M. (2005). Classifying brain states and determining the discriminating activation patterns: support vector machine on functional MRI data. *Neuroimage* 28, 980–995. doi: 10.1016/j.neuroimage.2005.06.070

Mourão-Miranda, J., Hardoon, D. R., Hahn, T., Marquand, A. F., Williams, S. C. R., Shawe-Taylor, J., et al. (2011). Patient classification as an outlier detection problem: an application of the one-class support vector machine. *Neuroimage* 58, 793–804. doi: 10.1016/j.neuroimage.2011.06.042

Moya, M. M., Koch, M. W., and Hostetler, L. D. (1993). *One-Class Classifier Networks for Target Recognition Applications.* NASA STI/Recon Technical Report N, Vol. 93, 24043. Available online at: http://adsabs.harvard.edu/abs/1993STIN...9324043M

Murdaugh, D. L., Shinkareva, S. V., Deshpande, H. R., Wang, J., Pennick, M. R., and Kana, R. K. (2012). Differential deactivation during mentalizing and classification of autism based on default mode connectivity. *PLoS ONE* 7:e50064. doi: 10.1371/journal.pone.0050064

Nielsen, J. A., Zielinski, B. A., Fletcher, P. T., Alexander, A. L., Lange, N., Bigler, E. D., et al. (2014). Abnormal lateralization of functional connectivity between language and default mode regions in autism. *Mol. Autism* 5, 8. doi: 10.1186/2040-2392-5-8

Nordahl, C. W., Scholz, R., Yang, X., Buonocore, M. H., Simon, T., Rogers, S., et al. (2012). Increased rate of amygdala growth in children aged 2 to 4 years with autism spectrum disorders: a longitudinal study. *Arch. Gen. Psychiatry* 69, 53–61. doi: 10.1001/archgenpsychiatry.2011.145

O'Connor, K. (2012). Auditory processing in autism spectrum disorder: a review. *Neurosci. Biobehav. Rev.* 36, 836–854. doi: 10.1016/j.neubiorev.2011.11.008

Orekhova, E. V., and Stroganova, T. A. (2014). Arousal and Attention re-orienting in autism spectrum disorders: evidence from auditory event-related potentials. *Front. Hum. Neurosci.* 8:34. doi: 10.3389/fnhum.2014.00034

Orrù, G., Pettersson-Yeo, W., Marquand, A. F., Sartori, G., and Mechelli, A. (2012). Using support vector machine to identify imaging biomarkers of neurological and psychiatric disease: a critical review. *Neurosci. Biobehav. Rev.* 36, 1140–1152. doi: 10.1016/j.neubiorev.2012.01.004

Pontil, M., and Verri, A. (1997). *Properties of Support Vector Machines.* Available online at: ftp://publications.ai.mit.edu/ai-publications/pdf/AIM-1612.pdf

Prigge, M. D., Bigler, E. D., Fletcher, P. T., Zielinski, B. A., Ravichandran, C., Anderson, J., et al. (2013). Longitudinal Heschl's gyrus growth during childhood and adolescence in typical development and autism. *Autism Res.* 6, 78–90. doi: 10.1002/aur.1265

Raichle, M. E., MacLeod, A. M., Snyder, A. Z., Powers, W. J., Gusnard, D. A., and Shulman, G. L. (2001). A default mode of brain function. *Proc. Natl. Acad. Sci. U.S.A.* 98, 676–682. doi: 10.1073/pnas.98.2.676

Retico, A., Giuliano, A., Tancredi, R., Cosenza, A., Apicella, F., Narzisi, A., et al. (2016). The effect of gender on the neuroanatomy of children with autism spectrum disorders: a support vector machine case-control study. *Mol. Autism* 7, 5. doi: 10.1186/s13229-015-0067-3

Retico, A., Tosetti, M., Muratori, F., and Calderoni, S. (2014). Neuroimaging-based methods for autism identification: a possible translational application? *Funct. Neurol.* 29, 231–239. doi: 10.11138/fneur/2014.29.4.231

Sato, J. R., Hoexter, M. Q., Castellanos, X. F., and Rohde, L. A. (2012b). Abnormal brain connectivity patterns in adults with ADHD: a coherence study. *PLoS ONE* 7:e45671. doi: 10.1371/journal.pone.0045671

Sato, J. R., Rondina, J. M., and Mourão-Miranda, J. (2012a). Measuring abnormal brains: building normative rules in neuroimaging using one-class support vector machines. *Front. Neurosci.* 6:178. doi: 10.3389/fnins.2012.00178

Schölkopf, B., Mika, S., Burges, C. C., Knirsch, P., Müller, K. R., Rätsch, G., et al. (1999). Input space versus feature space in kernel-based methods. *IEEE Trans. Neural Netw.* 10, 1000–1017. doi: 10.1109/72.788641

Schölkopf, B., Platt, J. C., Shawe-Taylor, J., Smola, A. J., and Williamson, R. C. (2001). Estimating the support of a high-dimensional distribution. *Neural Comput.* 13, 1443–1471. doi: 10.1162/089976601750264965

Schölkopf, B., and Smola, A. (2002). *Learning with Kernels.* Cambridge, MA: MIT Press.

Schölkopf, B., Smola, A., J., Williamson, R., and Bartlett, P. L. (2000). New Support vector algorithms. *Neural Comput.* 12, 1207–1245. doi: 10.1162/089976600300015565

Shawe-Taylor, J., and Cristianini, N. (2004). *Kernel Methods for Pattern Analysis.* Cambridge, MA: Cambridge University Press.

Tax, D. M. J., and Duin, R. P. W. (2004). Support vector data description. *Mach. Learn.* 54, 45–66. doi: 10.1023/B:MACH.0000008084.60811.49

Uddin, L., Vinod, M., Young, C. B., Ryali, S., Chen, T., Khouzam, A., et al. (2011). Multivariate searchlight classification of structural magnetic resonance imaging in children and adolescents with autism. *Biol. Psychiatry* 70, 833–841. doi: 10.1016/j.biopsych.2011.07.014

Vapnik, V. (1995). *The Nature of Statistical Learning Theory.* Boston, MA: Kluwer Academic Publishers.

Vogt, B. A., and Laureys, S. (2005). Posterior cingulate, precuneal and retrosplenial cortices: cytology and components of the neural network correlates of consciousness. *Prog. Brain Res.* 150, 205–217. doi: 10.1016/S0079-6123(05)50015-3

Wanh, Z., Childress, A. R., Wang, J., and Detre, J. A. (2007). Support vector machine learning-based fMRI data group analysis. *Neuroimage* 36, 1139–1151. doi: 10.1016/j.neuroimage.2007.03.072

Wee, C. Y., Wang, L., Shi, F., Yap, P. T., and Shen, D. (2014). Diagnosis of autism spectrum disorders using regional and interregional morphological features. *Hum. Brain Mapp.* 35, 3414–3430. doi: 10.1002/hbm.22411

White, S. J., Frith, U., Rellecke, J., Al-Noor, Z., and Gilbert, S. J. (2014). Autistic adolescents show atypical activation of the brain's mentalizing system even without a prior history of mentalizing problems. *Neuropsychologia* 56, 17–25. doi: 10.1016/j.neuropsychologia.2013.12.013

Wilke, M., and Holland, S. K. (2003). Variability of gray and white matter during normal development: a voxel-based MRI analysis. *Neuroreport.* 14, 1887–1890. doi: 10.1097/00001756-200310270-00001

Wolfers, T., Buitelar, J. K., Beckmann, C. F., Franke, B., and Marquand, A. F. (2015). From estimating activation locality to predicting disorder: a review of pattern recognition for neuroimaging-based psychiatric diagnostics. *Neurosci. Biobehav. Rev.* 57, 328–349. doi: 10.1016/j.neubiorev.2015.08.001

Wolff, J. J., and Piven, J. (2013). On the emergence of autism: neuroimaging findings from birth to preschool. *Neuropsychiatry* 3, 209–222. doi: 10.2217/npy.13.11

Yamasaki, S., Yamasue, H., Abe, O., Suga, M., Yamada, H., Inoue, H., et al. (2010). Reduced gray matter volume of pars opercularis is associated with impaired social communication in high-functioning autism spectrum disorders. *Biol. Psychiatry* 68, 1141–1147. doi: 10.1016/j.biopsych.2010.07.012

Zhang, Y., Zhang, B., Coenen, F., Xiao, J., and Lu, W. (2014). One-class kernel subspace ensemble for medical image classification. *EURASIP J. Adv. Signal Process.* 2014, 1–13. doi: 10.1186/1687-6180-2014-17

Zhou, Y., Yu, F., and Duong, T. (2014). Multiparametric MRI characterization and prediction in autism spectrum disorder using graph theory and machine learning. *PLoS ONE* 9:e90405. doi: 10.1371/journal.pone.0090405

Zielinski, B. A., Prigge, M. B., Nielsen, J. A., Froehlich, A. L., Abildskov, T. J., Anderson, J. S., et al. (2014). Longitudinal changes in cortical thickness in autism and typical development. Brain 137(Pt 6), 1799–1812. doi: 10.1093/brain/awu083

6

Atypical Brain Mechanisms of Prediction According to Uncertainty in Autism

Alix Thillay[1*], *Mathieu Lemaire*[1,2], *Sylvie Roux*[1], *Emmanuelle Houy-Durand*[1,2], *Catherine Barthélémy*[1,2], *Robert T. Knight*[3], *Aurélie Bidet-Caulet*[4] and *Frédérique Bonnet-Brilhault*[1,2]

[1] *UMR Institut National de la Santé et de la Recherche Médicale U930, Université François-Rabelais de Tours, Tours, France,* [2] *Centre Universitaire de Pédopsychiatrie, CHRU de Tours, Tours, France,* [3] *Helen Wills Neuroscience Institute and the Department of Psychology, University of California, Berkeley, CA, USA,* [4] *Institut National de la Santé et de la Recherche Médicale U1028, Centre National de la Recherche Scientifique UMR S5292, Centre de Recherche en Neurosciences de Lyon, Bron, France*

Edited by:
Benjamin Gesundheit, Cell El Ltd, Israel

Reviewed by:
Alka Anand Subramanyam, Topiwala National Medical College & BYL Nair Charitable Hospital, India
Alexandra Key, Vanderbilt University, USA

***Correspondence:**
Alix Thillay
alix.thillay@gmail.com

Resistance to change is often reported in autism and may arise from an inability to predict events in uncertain contexts. Using EEG recorded in 12 adults with autism and age-matched controls performing a visual target detection task, we characterized the influence of a certain context (targets preceded by a predictive sequence of three distinct stimuli) or an uncertain context (random targets) on behavior and electrophysiological markers of predictive processing. During an uncertain context, adults with autism were faster than controls to detect targets. They also had an enhancement in CNV amplitude preceding all random stimuli—indexing enhanced preparatory mechanisms, and an earlier N2 to targets—reflecting faster information processing—compared to controls. During a certain context, both controls and adults with autism presented an increase in P3 amplitude to predictive stimuli—indexing information encoding of the predictive sequence, an enhancement in CNV amplitude preceding predictable targets—corresponding to the deployment of preparatory mechanisms, and an earlier P3 to predictable targets—reflecting efficient prediction building and implementation. These results suggest an efficient extraction of predictive information to generate predictions in both controls and adults with autism during a certain context. However, adults with autism displayed a failure to decrease mu power during motor preparation accompanied by a reduced benefit in reaction times to predictable targets. The data reveal that patients with autism over-anticipate stimuli occurring in an uncertain context, in accord with their sense of being overwhelmed by incoming information. These results suggest that adults with autism cannot flexibly modulate cortical activity according to changing levels of uncertainty.

Keywords: autism, prediction, uncertainty, ERP, mu oscillations

INTRODUCTION

Autism Spectrum Disorder (ASD) is a pervasive neurodevelopmental disorder characterized by difficulties in social communication and interaction, associated with restricted, repetitive patterns of behavior, interests, or activities (American Psychiatric Association, 2013). The insistence on sameness is a fundamental feature of ASD and is incorporated into diagnostic criteria. Clinical reports of individuals with ASD show that they react in an unusual way (they may feel stressed and anxious) to unpredictable change occurring in their environment. Such a crucial need for stability in individuals with ASD might arise from a dysfunction in the ability to predict events especially in an ever-changing world (Gomot and Wicker, 2012; Pellicano and Burr, 2012; Palmer et al., 2013; Lawson et al., 2014; Van de Cruys et al., 2014). Pathological restricted and repetitive behaviors and interests, rituals, and routines could represent attempts to regulate uncertainty by imposing sameness and order (Gomot and Wicker, 2012; Pellicano and Burr, 2012; Lawson et al., 2014). In addition, social-communication impairments in ASD could be the consequence of difficulties in adapting quickly to the unpredictable social world (Gomot and Wicker, 2012; Lawson et al., 2014; Van de Cruys et al., 2014; Robic et al., 2015). However, to our knowledge, no study has investigated the brain mechanisms of predictive processing in adults with ASD.

Predictive coding formulations of perception propose that expectations in higher brain areas generate top-down predictions that meet bottom-up stimulus signals in lower hierarchical areas (e.g., Friston, 2005). This prediction capacity is essential to efficiently adapt behaviors in an ever-changing world (Bubic et al., 2010). Predictive processing comprises several processes such as the generation of prediction based on encoding of predictive information, and the implementation of prediction via the deployment of both attentional and motor preparatory mechanisms, resulting in facilitated processing of upcoming events, and optimized behaviors indexed by reduced reaction times. In a previous study using a detection task manipulating target predictability (Bidet-Caulet et al., 2012), we defined electrophysiological (EEG) markers of these different stages in typically developing adults. The P3 amplitude to predictive stimuli was found to index predictive information encoding, increase in the Contingent Negative Variation (CNV; pre-stimulus slow ERP) amplitude to reflect the deployment of preparatory mechanisms, decrease in mu power to reflect motor cortex activation, and the P3 latency to predicted target to serve as a measure of the prediction building and implementation (Bidet-Caulet et al., 2012).

While the encoding of explicit predictive non-social cues has not been examined in ASD, some electrophysiological studies have found inconsistent findings, with evidence for atypical preparation in 8–13 year old children (indexed by an increase in CNV amplitude; Tye et al., 2014) or for a preserved preparation in adults (no significant difference in CNV amplitude compared to controls; Strandburg et al., 1993) with ASD without intellectual disability. Reduced motor anticipation has been clinically reported in ASD since the Kanner initial case reports (Kanner, 1943) and recently from a retrospective study (Brisson et al., 2012). Electromyographic studies found substantial anticipation difficulties, reinforcing these clinical observations (Schmitz et al., 2003; Cattaneo et al., 2007). More precisely, an electrophysiological study investigating the theta frequency band in children (which corresponds to the classic mu rhythm recorded in adults) using a bimanual load-lifting task revealed a lack of increased cortical activity of the motor areas before voluntary unloading in the ASD group (Martineau et al., 2004).

Using EEG recorded in 12 adults with autism and age-matched controls performing a visual target detection task, we characterized the influence of a certain context (targets preceded by a 100% predictive sequence of three distinct stimuli), or an uncertain context (random targets) on behavior and electrophysiological markers of predictive processing. Thus, based on this paradigm, we wanted to answer the following questions: (1) do adults with ASD benefit from the predictive information behaviorally (indexed by reduced reaction times)? (2) do the brain mechanisms involved in predictive processing in a certain context are atypical in adults with ASD? (3) do the brain mechanisms involved in predictive processing in an uncertain context are atypical in adults with ASD (4) what steps involved in prediction, such as extraction of predictive information (indexed by an increase in P3 amplitude) required to generate prediction, attentional, and motor preparation mechanisms (reflected by an increase in CNV amplitude and a decrease in mu power) corresponding to the implementation of prediction (indexed by a reduced target-P3 latency) are specifically affected in adults with ASD?

MATERIALS AND METHODS

Subjects

Twelve adults with ASD without intellectual disability (10 males and 2 females, 1 left-handed), aged from 18 to 27 years (mean ± Standard Error of the Mean = 21 years, 4 ± 10 months) were recruited from the Child Psychiatry Department specialized in autism, University Hospital of Tours, France. They were diagnosed by expert clinicians according to DSM-IV-TR criteria (American Psychiatric Association, 2000) and using the Autism Diagnostic Observation Schedule-Generic (ADOS-G; Lord et al., 2000) and/or the Autism Diagnostic Interview-Revised (ADI-R; Lord et al., 1994). ASD participants did not present any comorbidity at the time of the study. Intelligence quotients (IQ) were assessed by the Wechsler intelligence scales according to the subjects' ages and developmental levels (Wechsler, 1997, 2005). Intelligence scales provided overall intellectual (mean ± SEM = 101 ± 5), verbal (mean ± SEM = 100 ± 3), and performance quotients (mean ± SEM = 104 ± 7).

Twelve healthy volunteers (mean ± SEM = 21 years, 7 ± 11 months; 10 males and 2 females, 1 left-handed) also participated in the study as control (CTRL) subjects. None of these healthy adults had a previous history of psychiatric or neurological problems and they were not taking any drug. The two groups were matched in age, gender, and handedness. While a full Wechsler was administered to the adults with ASD, two non-verbal subtests (block design and matrix reasoning) of Wechsler intelligence scales were used in the CTRL group. Block design standard scores ranged from 1 to 16 (ASD: 10.8 ± 1.2; CTRL: 11.8 ± 0.8), and matrix reasoning standard scores ranged from 6 to 14 (ASD: 10.1 ± 0.8; CTRL: 10.7 ± 0.4). No significant difference between groups was found on the standard scores obtained from these 2 subtests using randomization tests ($p > 0.45$).

All participants had normal or corrected-to-normal vision. The local ethical committee board (Comité de Protection des Personnes de Tours Ouest-1, France) approved the protocol. Written informed consent was obtained from all participants.

Stimuli and Tasks

Subjects sat in a chair in a sound-attenuated room, 94 cm in front of a 19-inch PC screen. The experimenters and computers delivering the visual stimuli and recording the EEG were located in a separate room. We used a paradigm designed to investigate predictive context processing adopted from Fogelson et al. (2009). Stimuli were presented centrally on a computer screen and subtended 3° of visual angle (**Figure 1**).

Stimuli consisted of 15% of targets (downward-facing triangle) and 85% of equal amounts of three types of standards: Triangles facing left, upward, or right. A target could be a random target (randT) preceded by an uncertain context (random sequence of stimuli) or a predictable target (predT) preceded by a certain context, i.e., a three-stimulus predictive sequence (leftward-, upward-, and rightward-facing triangles). Triangles of the predictive sequence are labeled as predS1, predS2, and predS3 stimuli, whereas the corresponding triangles outside the predictive sequence are labeled as randS1, randS2, and randS3, for leftward-, upward-, and rightward-facing triangles, respectively. Participants were instructed to press a button with the dominant-hand index finger in response to target stimuli (downward-facing triangles) and to look for the predictive sequence. Before the recording began, subjects performed a first training session to ensure they were able to detect the target accurately. In a second training session, subjects were introduced to the predictive sequence and were aware that it would be 100% predictive of a target, but that targets would also appear randomly throughout the block. Especially for the adults with ASD, training sessions were repeated as many times as necessary to ensure full understanding of the instructions.

In each block (~2.3 min long), a total of 127 stimuli (11 randTs, 28 randS1, 28 randS2, 28 randS3, 8 predTs, 8 predS1, 8 predS2, and 8 predS3) were presented each for 150 ms with an inter-stimulus interval of 1 s. 17 subjects performed 15 blocks, one subject performed 12 blocks, 2 subjects performed 10 blocks, and 4 subjects performed 4–8 blocks due to fatigue. The stimulus presentation and response recordings were controlled using Presentation software (Neurobehavioral Systems, Albany, CA, USA).

Electroencephalography Recording and Analysis

EEG was recorded from 64 electrodes using Active Two system (Biosemi, The Netherlands). Vertical eye movements were monitored using electrodes placed above and below the left eye. The signal was recorded with a sampling frequency of 512 Hz and filtered at 0–104 Hz. Data were re-referenced offline to the average potential of the two earlobe electrodes.

EEG analyses were based on results from a previous study (Bidet-Caulet et al., 2012). They were performed on standard and target visual stimuli embedded or not embedded in the predictive sequence. We excluded from further analysis: Trials corresponding to standards after a target, standards before or after a button press, a randS2 standard preceded by a randS1 standard but not followed by a randS3 standard (as it is a potential predS2 standard), missed targets, and targets preceded by less than three standards. Eye-movement artifacts were detected using independent component analysis (ICA) and were selectively removed via the inverse ICA transformation. Only 1 or 2 independent components were removed in each subject to clean the data. In five subjects, the flat or excessively noisy signals at one or two electrodes were replaced by their values interpolated from the remaining electrodes using spherical spline interpolation (Perrin et al., 1989). Trials contaminated with excessive muscular activity in the (−700; 700 ms) time-window relative to stimulus onset were also excluded.

As the number of trials for stimuli embedded in the predictive sequence was lower than for the other stimuli, we equalized the number of trials within each pair of to-be-compared stimuli by random selection, for each participant. On average across participants, we obtained mean ± SEM: 68 ± 4, 83 ± 5, 83 ± 5, and 72 ± 5 clean trials for randS1/predS1, randS2/predS2, randS3/predS3, and randT/predT pairs, respectively, for each participant.

Event-Related Potential (ERP) Analysis

We averaged single trials, locked to stimulus onset, separately for each of the eight stimulus categories (randS1, randS2, randS3, randT, predS1, predS2, predS3, predT). The resulting

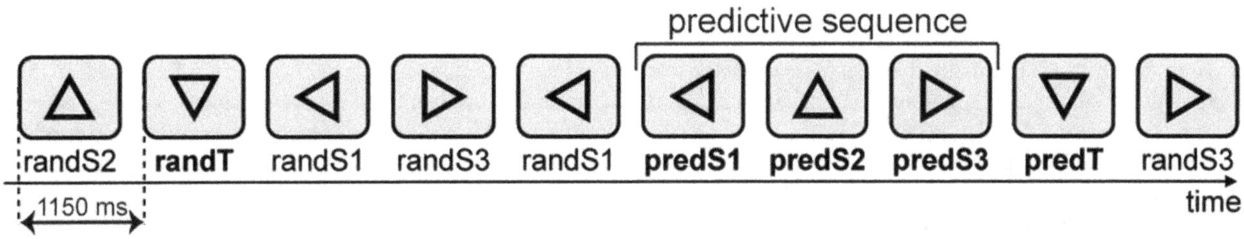

FIGURE 1 | Stimuli. A sequence of triangles was centrally presented on a screen. A target could be a random target (randT) preceded by a non-informative context (random sequence of stimuli) or a predictable target (predT) preceded by an informative context, i.e., a three-stimulus predictive sequence (leftward-, upward-, and rightward-facing triangles). Triangles of the predictive sequence are labeled as predS1, predS2, and predS3 stimuli, whereas the corresponding triangles outside the predictive sequence are labeled as randS1, randS2, and randS3, for leftward-, upward-, and rightward-facing triangles, respectively.

event-related potentials (ERPs) were digitally band-pass filtered between 0.5 and 30 Hz to analyze slower components, or between 4 and 30 Hz to extract early and transient responses by filtering out slow and large components (such as the Continent Negative Variation or CNV and P3) that can overlap fast and small responses (Bidet-Caulet et al., 2012). For post-stimulus analysis, ERPs were corrected with a −100 to 0 ms baseline before stimulus onset. For pre-stimulus analysis, ERPs were not baseline corrected. ERP scalp topographies were computed using spherical spline interpolation (Perrin et al., 1989).

Time-Frequency (TF) Analysis

We analyzed oscillatory activities by means of a Gaussian Morlet's wavelet decomposition (for details, see Tallon-Baudry and Bertrand, 1999). This method led to a power estimate of both evoked (phase-locked to stimulus onset) and induced (jittering in latency) activities in the TF domain. To distinguish induced from evoked activities (reflecting the frequency content of ERPs), we computed, at each point of the TF domain, the stimulus phase-locking factor from the single-trial TF analysis (Tallon-Baudry et al., 1996). This factor ranges from 0 (uniform phase distribution, i.e., high-latency jitter) to 1 (strict phase-locking to the stimulus). The Rayleigh statistic was used to test for the non-uniformity of phase distribution (Jervis et al., 1983), with a threshold of 0.25 to test non-uniformity with $\alpha = 0.05$: A phase-locking factor superior to 0.25 indicated a non-uniform phase distribution and the underlying oscillations were considered to be phase-locked to the stimulus. To assess the deployment of oscillatory activities around the stimuli, we analyzed the oscillation on a large time-window (−500; 500 ms) around each type of stimulus. In each group, we applied the same baseline correction to all stimuli by subtracting the mean power between −500 and −250 ms before all S1 onset, in each frequency band. We focused our analysis on the alpha frequency band (8–14 Hz). Since mu rhythm is recorded over the sensorimotor cortex (central electrodes) at the same frequency range than alpha rhythm (Pineda, 2005), we deliberately distinguished mu and alpha oscillations based on the topography. Importantly, no difference was observed between CTRL and ASD on the mean power in the 8–14 Hz band in the −500 to 500 ms time-window around S1.

Statistical Analysis

To assess statistical differences between groups and conditions, we used a repeated-measure analysis of variance (rmANOVA) with group (ASD vs. CTRL) as the between-subject factor and predictability (predictable vs. random) as the within-subject factor.

Post-hoc analyses were performed with statistical tests based on permutation or randomization for intra- or inter-group comparisons, respectively (Edgington, 1995). Permutation tests consisted of (1) the random permutation of the 12 pairs (corresponding to the 12 subjects) of values, (2) the sum of squared sums of values in the two obtained samples, and (3) the computation of the difference between these two statistic values. We performed all possible permutations (4096) to obtain an estimate of the distribution of this difference under the null hypothesis. This distribution was then compared to the actual difference between the values in the two conditions. Randomization tests consisted of (1) the random constitution of the two samples to compare, (2) the sum of squared sums of values in the two obtained samples, and (3) the computation of the difference between these two statistic values. We performed 10,000 such randomizations to obtain an estimate of the distribution of this difference under the null hypothesis. This distribution was then compared to the actual difference between the values in the two conditions.

Statistical Analysis of Behavioral Data

A button press within the interval of 100–1100 ms after a target onset was considered as a correct response, and a press after a standard was counted as a false alarm (FA). Reaction times (RTs) were computed for correct trials, only. We investigated the benefit in RTs with the predictive context independently of RT to randTs by calculating a RT prediction index [(RT randT-RT predT)/RT randT].

The effect of predictability on the % of hits and RTs was assessed using rmANOVAs. The differences between groups on the % of FAs and the RT prediction index were assessed using randomization tests.

Statistical Analysis of Event-Related Potentials and Oscillatory Activities

To investigate predictive processing in adults with ASD, we compared ERPs and oscillatory activities to the same physical stimuli embedded (predictive stimuli) or not embedded (non-predictive stimuli) in the predictive sequence. No difference was predicted and none was observed between predS1 and randS1 as participants did not know at that time if the stimulus was part of the predictive sequence or not.

For statistical analysis, we computed the rmANOVA on the latencies of N1 (105; 230 ms) and P2 (205; 310 ms) peaks at PO4, and on the latencies of P2 (155; 255 ms) and N2 (215; 350 ms) peaks at FCz. For the P3 to targets, we also analyzed the latency and amplitude of the P3 maximum peak at Pz in the (250; 750 ms) time-window.

To go further and beyond peaks and components, we also performed rmANOVAs for each of the 64 electrodes on specific time-windows based on results in previous EEG studies (Fogelson et al., 2009; Bidet-Caulet et al., 2012). To correct for multiple tests, we first calculated a corrected p-value across time (e.g., 0.05 divided by the number of tested time-windows) and then an effect was deemed significant if a p-value inferior to this threshold was found on at least 4 adjacent electrodes.

To analyze early and transient ERPs, we computed the rmANOVA on the 4–30 Hz band-pass-filtered ERP (pre-stimulus baseline-corrected) amplitude within successive 10 ms time-windows of the (0; 400 ms) time-window relative to stimulus onset. The p-value threshold for significance was set to 0.00125.

To analyze pre-stimulus activity, we computed the rmANOVA on the 0.5–30 Hz band-pass-filtered ERP (not baseline-corrected) mean amplitude in the (−150; 0 ms) time-window, corresponding to the CNV (pre-stimulus slow ERP) latencies. We also computed a randomization test on the pre-stimulus activity before all standards (randS) on the mean amplitude in the (−50; 0 ms) time-window to analyze predictive processing within the uncertain context. For ease of reading, we will refer to the CNV component.

We also computed the rmANOVA on the 0.5–30 Hz band-pass-filtered ERP (pre-stimulus baseline-corrected) mean amplitude in the (200; 600 ms) analysis window, corresponding to the P3 latencies. For ease of reading, we will refer to the P3 component.

For oscillatory activities, the rmANOVA was applied to the mean TF energy values within successive 200 ms time-windows regularly shifted by 100 ms to cover the entire analysis time-window (−500; 500 ms). To correct for multiple tests in the time dimension, the p-value threshold for significance was set to 0.005. To avoid a possible confound due to inclusion of left-handed participants, time-frequency analysis was run with a sample of right-handed participants only (n = 11 for CTRL and ASD). Relation between the RT prediction index and electrophysiological values was assessed using the Spearman rank correlation coefficient.

Results of the rmANOVAs are illustrated on topographical views at a typical latency (usually at the maximum of the difference between conditions). As examples, corresponding ERP or TF time-courses are depicted for a typical electrode showing a significant effect.

The ELAN software package was used for visualization and analysis of EEG, ERP, and TF (Aguera et al., 2011). Custom MATLAB R2010b (MathWorks, Inc) programs were used for rmANOVAs on ERP and TF measures and for the randomization tests. STATISTICA v10 (StatSoft, Inc) software was used for rmANOVAs.

RESULTS

Behavioral Results

All subjects correctly performed the task (CTRL: 97.0 ± 1.3 and 95.6 ± 1.1%, ASD: 93.3 ± 3.1 and 95.3 ± 1.8%, to randTs and predTs, respectively). No effect of group [$F_{(1, 22)} = 0.76$, $p = 0.391$], nor effect of predictability [$F_{(1, 22)} = 0.04$, $p = 0.848$], nor predictability × group interaction [$F_{(1, 22)} = 1.13$, $p = 0.300$] were found significant for the % of hits. Controls made less FAs (0.24 ± 0.05%) than adults with ASD (0.70 ± 0.19%; $p = 0.003$).

Reaction times (RTs) to targets displayed a significant main effect of predictability [$F_{(1, 22)} = 42.15$, $p < 0.001$], a significant predictability × group interaction [$F_{(1, 22)} = 7.58$, $p = 0.012$], but no effect of group [$F_{(1, 22)} = 2.15$, $p = 0.156$; **Figure 2**]. *Post-hoc* tests showed that, in both groups, RTs to predTs were shorter than those to randTs ($p \leq 0.001$). Importantly, RTs to randTs were longer in CTRL than in ASD ($p = 0.012$) while no difference was found to predTs ($p = 0.748$). The RT prediction index was also larger in CTRL compared to ASD ($p = 0.020$; **Figure 2**). In summary, controls present a larger benefit in RTs with the predictive context but are slower to detect randTs than adults with ASD.

Event-Related Potential Results

Early and Transient ERPs

No effect was significant on the amplitude of early and transient ERPs in response to targets, S3 or S2, nor on the N1 and P2 latencies at PO4, the P2, and N2 latencies at FCz to S3 or S2 ($p > 0.061$), the target-N1 latency at PO4 ($p > 0.050$), the target-P2 latency at FCz ($p > 0.068$).

A main effect of predictability was found on the target-P2 latency at PO4 [$F_{(1, 22)} = 6.91$, $p = 0.015$], but no predictability ×

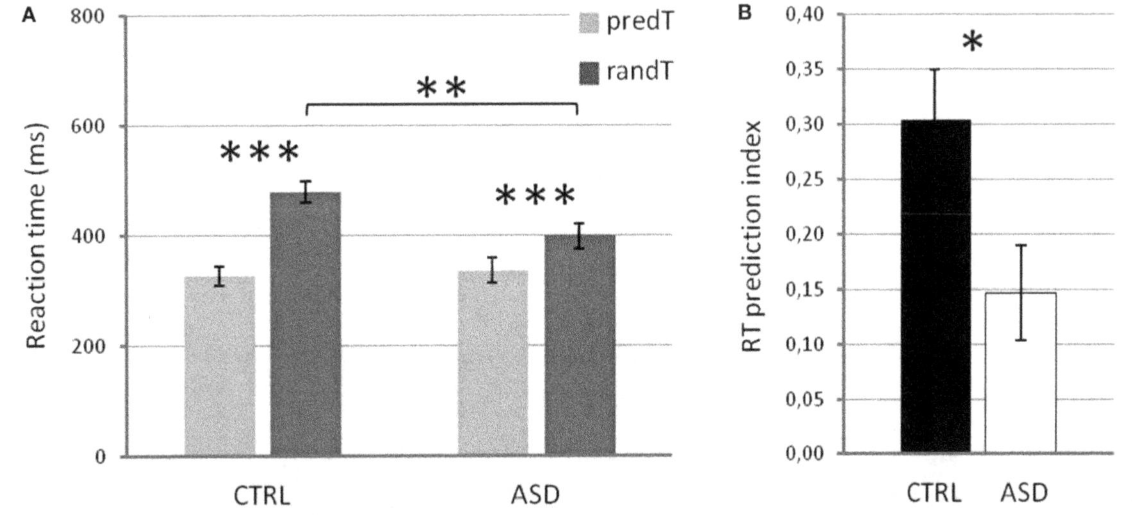

FIGURE 2 | Reaction times in ms (A) for predictable and random targets, and RT prediction index (B) in controls (CTRL) and adults with ASD. Error bars: Standard errors of the mean. Significant differences are indicated by asterisks: *$p \leq 0.05$, **$p \leq 0.01$, ***$p \leq 0.001$.

group interaction [$F_{(1, 22)} = 0.07$, $p = 0.789$], nor group effect [$F_{(1, 22)} = 3.44$, $p = 0.077$], with earlier target-P2 latency to randTs than to predTs.

A predictability × group interaction was found on the target-N2 latency at FCz [$F_{(1, 22)} = 7.40$, $p = 0.012$], but no predictability effect [$F_{(1, 22)} = 2.52$, $p = 0.127$], nor group effect [$F_{(1, 22)} = 1.21$, $p = 0.283$; **Figure 3**]. The N2 to predTs was earlier in latency than to randTs in controls only (CTRL: $p < 0.001$; ASD: $p = 0.440$). A reduced target-N2 latency to randTs ($p = 0.010$) but not to predTs ($p = 0.333$; **Figure 3C**) was found in ASD compared to CTRL.

Only controls displayed a reduction of the target-N2 latency to predTs; whereas adults with ASD showed a reduced target-N2 latency to randTs compared to controls.

CNV

No effect was significant on CNV amplitude preceding S2. A predictability effect, only, was found on CNV amplitude preceding S3, with larger amplitude at parietal electrodes to predS3 [e.g., Pz: $F_{(1, 22)} = 8.34$, $p = 0.008$; **Figure 4**]. CNV amplitude preceding targets (−150 and 0 ms) displayed a predictability × group interaction at left centro-parietal electrodes [e.g., PO3: $F_{(1, 22)} = 6.98$, $p = 0.015$], an effect of predictability on a large fronto-centro-parietal group of electrodes [e.g., Fz: $F_{(1, 22)} = 30.05$, $p < 0.001$], but no effect of group.

At left centro-parietal electrodes, *post-hoc* tests showed an increased CNV before predTs in comparison to randTs in controls only (e.g., at PO3, CTRL: $p = 0.022$; ASD: $p = 0.639$). Moreover, CNV amplitude to randTs was found larger in ASD than in CTRL (e.g., at PO3, randTs: $p = 0.014$; predTs: $p = 0.482$). Furthermore, randomization test showed an increased CNV before randS at parietal electrodes in ASD compared to CTRL (e.g., at PO3, randS: $p = 0.018$).

In summary, at frontal electrodes, both groups displayed an enhancement of the CNV amplitude before targets with increased predictability. At left centro-parietal electrodes, only controls displayed an enhancement of the CNV amplitude before predTs;

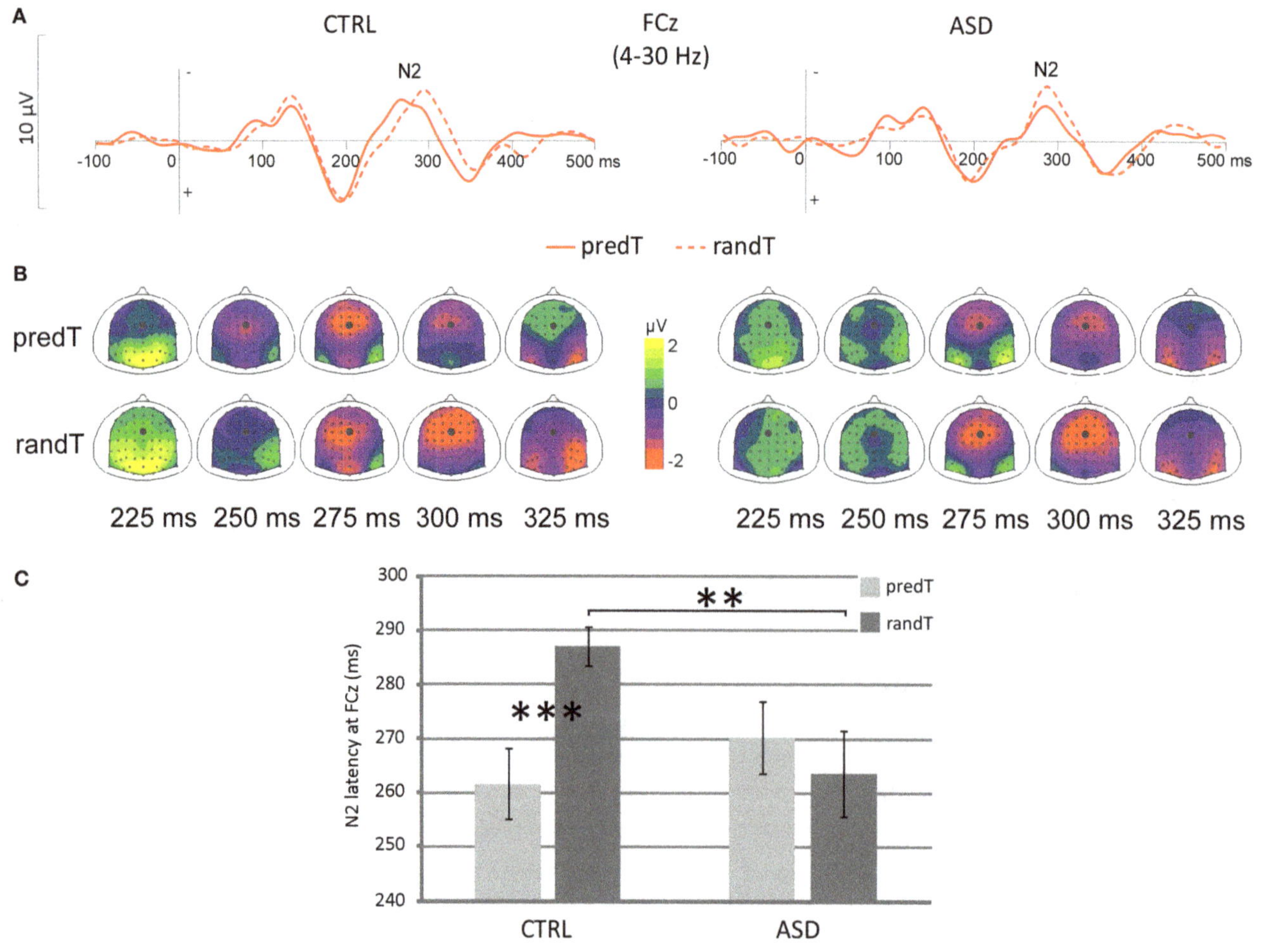

FIGURE 3 | Effect of predictive context on N2 in controls (CTRL) and adults with ASD. (A) Grand-average ERP waveforms band-pass filtered between 4 and 30 Hz to predTs and randTs (solid and dashed red lines, respectively), at the FCz electrode. **(B)** Scalp topographies (top views) of the N2 to predTs and randTs for controls (CTRL) and adults with ASD. The dots indicate the position of FCz electrode. **(C)** Target-N2 latency at FCz in ms for predTs and randTs in controls (CTRL) and adults with ASD. Error bars = standard errors of the mean. Significant differences are indicated by asterisks: **$p \leq 0.01$ ***$p \leq 0.001$.

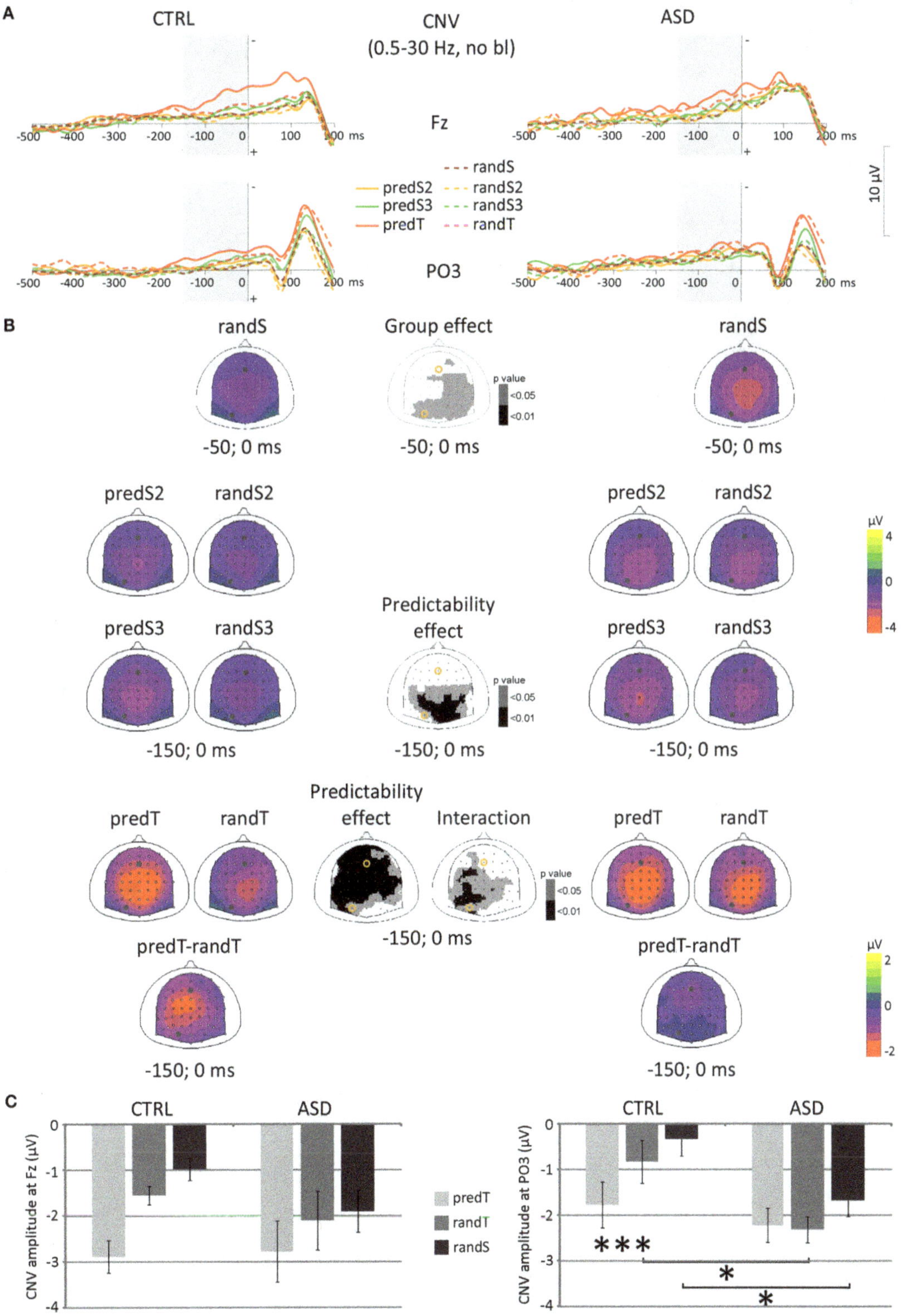

FIGURE 4 | Effect of predictive context on CNV amplitudes in controls (CTRL) and adults with ASD. (A) Grand-average non-baseline-corrected ERP waveforms band-pass filtered between 0.5 and 30 Hz, at the Fz and PO3 electrodes. **(B)** Scalp topographies (top views) of the mean CNV amplitude for each pair of predictive stimulus and its non-predictive analog, and for the difference between predTs and randTs in the −150–0 ms time-window, and for randS in the −50–0 ms time-window for controls (CTRL) and adults with ASD, and scalp topographies of the *p*-value resulting from the ANOVA. The dots and circles indicate the position of Fz and PO3 electrodes. **(C)** CNV mean amplitude between −150 and 0 ms at Fz and PO3 in µV for predTs, randTs, and between −50 and 0 ms for randS in controls (CTRL) and adults with ASD. Error bars = standard errors of the mean. Significant differences are indicated by asterisks: *$p \leq 0.05$, ***$p \leq 0.001$.

whereas adults with ASD showed an increased CNV preceding randTs and randS compared to controls.

P3

P3 amplitude to S2 and S3 displayed a predictability effect, only, at centro-parietal electrodes [e.g., Pz: $F_{(1, 22)} = 10.28, p = 0.004$; and $F_{(1, 22)} = 25.73, p < 0.001$, respectively; **Figure 5**]. These effects corresponded to an enhancement of the P3 amplitude to standard stimuli with predictive value in both groups.

No effect was found significant on the maximum P3 amplitude at Pz to targets.

A predictability effect was found on the target-P3 latency [$F_{(1, 22)} = 13.37, p = 0.001$]. The P3 to predTs was found earlier than to randTs at Pz.

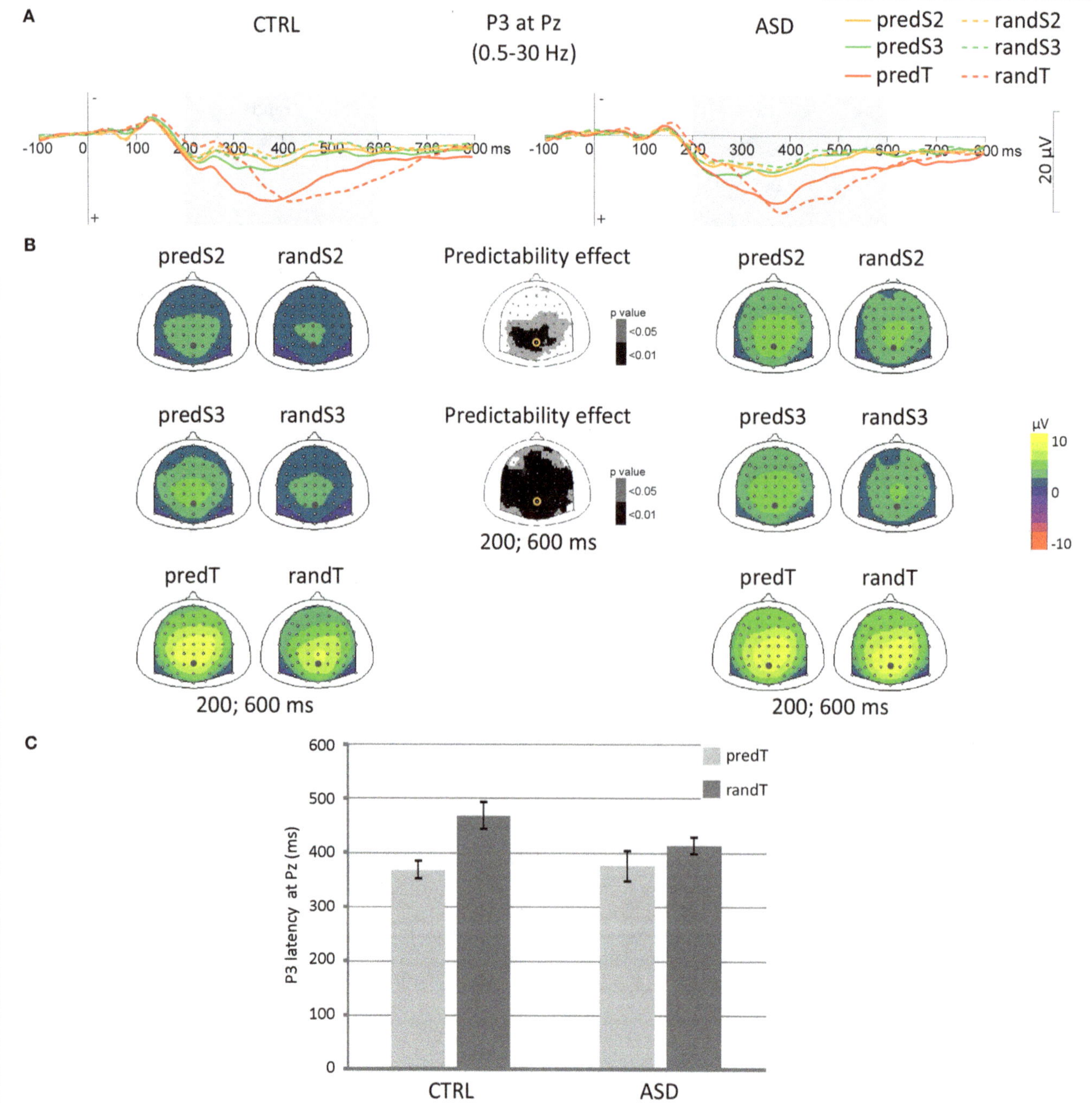

FIGURE 5 | Effect of predictive context on P3 in controls (CTRL) and adults with ASD. (A) Grand-average ERP waveforms band-pass filtered between 0.5 and 30 Hz, at the Pz electrode. **(B)** Scalp topographies (top views) of the mean P3 ERP for each pair of predictive stimulus and its non-predictive analog in the 200–600 ms time-window for controls (CTRL) and adults with ASD, and scalp topographies of the p-value resulting from the ANOVA. The dots and circles indicate the position of the Pz electrode. **(C)** Latency of the P3 maximum in ms at Pz for predicted and random targets in controls (CTRL) and adults with ASD. Error bars = standard errors of the mean.

In both groups, P3 amplitude increased throughout the predictive sequence and P3 latency was shortened to predTs.

Time-Frequency Results

No effect was found on the 8–14 Hz power before S3 or S2.

Left Central Electrodes

A predictability × group interaction was found on the mu power preceding targets between −400 and −200 ms at left central electrodes [e.g., C5: $F_{(1, 20)} = 10.68$, $p = 0.004$; **Figure 6**]. *Post-hoc* tests showed that only controls displayed a decrease in mu power between −400 and −200 ms before predTs compared to randTs (e.g., C5, CTRL: $p = 0.015$; ASD: $p = 0.256$). Moreover, the decrease in mu power was found larger in CTRL than in ASD between −400 and −200 ms before predTs (e.g., C5: $p = 0.002$), but not before randTs (e.g., C5: $p = 0.247$).

Predictability effect on mu power to targets (difference in mu power between randTs and predTs) at C5 was found correlated with the RT prediction index ($r = 0.627$, $p = 0.002$; **Figure 6D**). The larger the power reduction, the larger the benefit in reaction time.

Fronto-Central Electrodes

A predictability × group interaction was found on the alpha power preceding targets between −400 and −100 ms at fronto-central electrodes [e.g., FCz: $F_{(1, 20)} = 11.90$, $p = 0.002$; **Figure 6**]. Controls displayed a decrease in alpha power between −400 and −100 ms before predTs compared to randTs (e.g., FCz: $p = 0.002$); whereas adults with ASD showed a trend for a pre-stimulus alpha increase before predTs compared to randTs (e.g., FCz: $p = 0.054$). The decrease in alpha power was larger in CTRL than in ASD between −400 and −200 ms before predTs (e.g., FCz: ASD > CTRL, $p = 0.047$), but not before randTs (e.g., FCz: $p = 0.394$).

Moreover, a group effect was found on the alpha power between 0 and 300 ms [e.g., FCz: $F_{(1, 20)} = 14.39$, $p = 0.001$]. Controls presented a decrease in alpha power after target onset; whereas adults with ASD showed an increase in alpha power. Analysis of the phase-locking factor indicated an increase in phase-locking to target onset in the alpha band in the same latency range at frontal electrodes in both groups (**Figure 7**). This increase in phase-locking factor corresponds to the alpha content of the P2 and N2 frontal ERP components.

In summary, adults with ASD did not display a decrease in mu power at left central electrodes before predTs, nor a decrease in alpha power at frontal electrodes after all targets.

DISCUSSION

During an uncertain context, adults with ASD were faster to detect the target, presented an increased CNV amplitude indexing enhanced preparatory mechanisms, and a shortened N2 latency reflecting faster information processing.

During a certain context, both controls and adults with ASD presented an increased P3 amplitude indexing information encoding of the predictive sequence, an enhanced CNV amplitude corresponding to the deployment of preparatory mechanisms and a reduced target-P3 latency reflecting efficient prediction building and implementation. However, adults with ASD displayed a failure to decrease mu power during motor preparation. This physiological deficit was accompanied by a reduced benefit in reaction times to predictable targets in patients with ASD.

Taken together, the present results provide novel evidence indicating an atypical detection and processing of targets in an uncertain context, coupled with an atypical motor preparation to predictable targets despite a preserved extraction of predictive information.

CNV and N2: Target Over-Anticipation within an Uncertain Context

Studies of visual target detection in ASD have reported inconsistent findings, with evidence for equivalent (Tsai et al., 2011) or shorter (Dichter et al., 2009; Maekawa et al., 2011) RTs in response to non-cued target compared to controls. In the present study, adults with ASD were faster than controls to detect the target preceded by a non-informative context with similar overall accuracy. No group differences were found on the visual ERP components, suggesting that targets receive similar degrees of sensory processing in adults with ASD and in controls. Critically, adults with ASD displayed an enhanced CNV before the random standards and targets compared to controls, providing evidence of deployment of atypical increased preparatory mechanisms. In addition, adults with ASD displayed a shortened N2 latency to the random target, suggesting shorter stimulus evaluation (Donchin et al., 1986; Hillyard and Picton, 2011), and response activation time (Smid et al., 1990), supporting faster visual information processing in adults with ASD. The enhanced CNV, the earlier N2 and the shorter reaction times suggest an over-anticipation of stimuli in an uncertain context in adults with ASD. This excessive processing may be counterproductive in daily life and may lead to feelings of sensory overload often reported by individuals with ASD.

CNV and P3: Preserved Extraction and Use of Predictive Contextual Information

P3 amplitude progressively increased throughout the predictive sequence, i.e., as a function of task relevance and confidence (Sawaki and Katayama, 2006) comparably in controls and ASD subjects. In agreement with a role of the P3 in context-updating (Donchin and Coles, 1988), the present results support the notion that adults with ASD are able, as well as controls, to extract predictive information from the stimulus train.

Adults with ASD displayed a benefit in reaction time with predictive context suggesting that they generate prediction and use it in order to anticipate the predictable target. Moreover, target predictability shortens P3 latency (indicating a shortened duration of stimulus evaluation processing; Kutas et al., 1977; Duncan-Johnson and Kopell, 1981) and enhances CNV amplitude before the predictable targets (reflecting the enhanced recruitment of preparatory mechanisms; Brunia and van Boxtel, 2001) in both groups, confirming that prediction has been implemented.

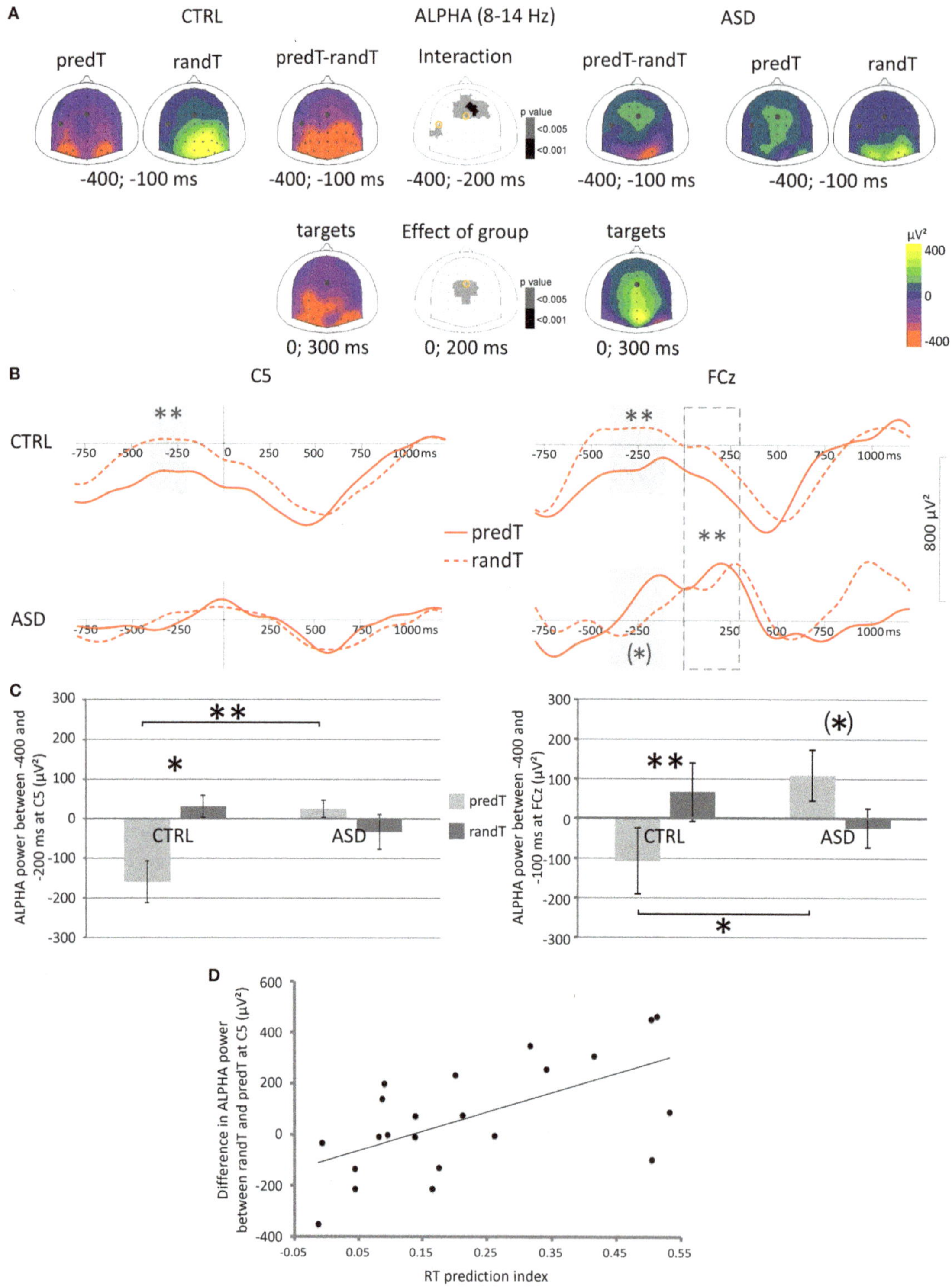

FIGURE 6 | Effect of predictive context on motor and frontal oscillatory activities in the 8–14 Hz frequency band in controls (CTRL) and adults with ASD. (A) Scalp topographies (top views) of the mean TF power value between −400 and −100 ms and 0 and 300 ms, and of the p-value resulting from the ANOVA. The dots and circles indicate the position of the C5 and FCz electrodes. **(B)** Alpha frequency band profiles of TF power at the Fz and C5 electrodes to predTs and randTs (solid and dashed red lines, respectively) in controls (CTRL) and adults with ASD. Time-windows showing a significant difference between the two conditions are indicated by gray bars. Time-window showing a significant difference between the two groups is indicated by dashed gray bar. **(C)** Mean alpha power (μV^2) between −400 and −200 ms at C5 electrode for predTs and randTs in controls (CTRL) and adults with ASD. Mean alpha power (μV^2) between −400 and −100 ms at FCz electrode for predTs and randTs in controls (CTRL) and adults with ASD. Error bars = standard errors of the mean. Significant differences are indicated by asterisks: (*) $p = 0.054$, *$p < 0.05$, **$p \leq 0.01$ **(D)** Difference in mean alpha power (μV^2) between randTs and predTs at C5 plotted against the RT prediction index.

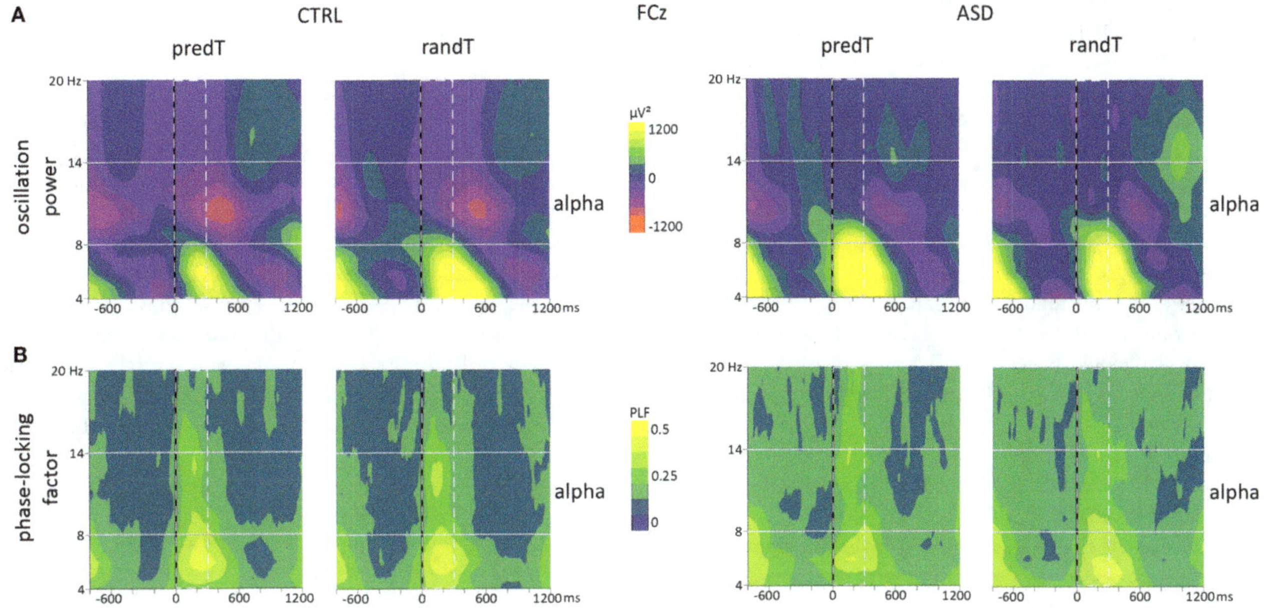

FIGURE 7 | Effect of predictive context on frontal oscillatory activities in controls (CTRL) and adults with ASD. (A) Grand-average TF plots of the oscillation power and **(B)** phase-locking factor (PLF) at the FCz electrode for predTs and randTs. Alpha (8–14 Hz) frequency band is depicted. Time-window showing a significant difference between the two groups is indicated by dashed bar.

Mu Oscillations: Motor Anticipation Failure

In accordance with a previous study (Bidet-Caulet et al., 2012), we observed in controls a decrease in mu power before the predictable target onset at left central electrodes, reflecting motor cortex activation prior to execution of the button press (Pfurtscheller and Lopes da Silva, 1999). However, adults with ASD failed to display this mu decrease before the predictable target, suggesting reduced motor preparation. This motor anticipation failure explain why adults with ASD took less advantage from the predictive information compared to controls (smaller RT prediction index).

This result is in accordance with Kanner's first description (Kanner, 1943), and studies on motor anticipatory functions (Schmitz et al., 2003; Martineau et al., 2004) showing major anticipation difficulties.

Frontal Alpha Oscillations: Atypical Frontal Mechanisms

Electrophysiological results revealed an increased alpha activity in adults with ASD before the predictable targets over fronto-central regions. This alpha increase may reflect frontal compensation strategies to counteract the lack of motor cortex pre-activation for response execution, or an impairment in integrating prediction with behavior, i.e., an executive dysfunction (Luna et al., 2002).

Moreover, after target onset, adults with ASD presented a phase-locked increase in alpha power at fronto-central electrodes (corresponding to the alpha content of the P2 and N2 frontal ERP components); whereas controls showed a large decrease in alpha power overlapping the phase-locked alpha response. Greater alpha power after both random and predictable targets over the fronto-central regions in adults with ASD may reflect an abnormal inhibition of potential frontal processes needed for executive control during predictive processing, which is consistent with previous findings of atypical executive functions associated with frontal hypo-activation in adults with ASD (Luna et al., 2002).

Link with Predictive Coding Model

Predictive models of ASD agree about an imbalance of the weight ascribed to bottom-up sensory signals relative to top-down influence of prior information (Brock, 2012; Pellicano and Burr, 2012; Friston et al., 2013; Lawson et al., 2014; Van de Cruys et al., 2014; Skewes et al., 2015) with ASD perception dominated by sensory input. This would result in a tendency to perceive the world in a more veridical way rather than modulated by prior experience (Gomot and Wicker, 2012; Pellicano and Burr, 2012; Lawson et al., 2014; Skewes et al., 2015; Van de Cruys et al., 2014).

According to predictive models, in typically developing individuals, the changing levels of environmental uncertainty determine the assigned weight to prediction errors (Feldman and Friston, 2010; Van de Cruys et al., 2014). In an optimal system, precision in prediction errors (i.e., brain's degree of confidence in the sensory signal) decreases in contexts with higher uncertainty (i.e., when there are no learnable regularities in the environment). The CNV component has been proposed as a proxy for the precision of prediction errors (Feldman and Friston, 2010; Hesselmann et al., 2010) and its amplitude is enhanced with increasing certainty in normal populations. In agreement with this model, the CNV amplitude increased with enhanced predictability of the upcoming stimulus in typically developing participants in the present and previous studies (Bidet-Caulet et al., 2012). Interestingly, we found that adults with ASD generate a larger CNV, compared to controls, in an uncertain context before all random standards and targets. This result suggests that, in the random context, patients with ASD give a high precision to prediction errors as if they were still looking for learnable regularities; whereas typically developing individuals reduce their precision in prediction errors—they sense that there are no learnable regularities. Adults with ASD resist uncertainty and tend to generate higher levels of sensory precision (Van de Cruys et al., 2014). This finding is in line with an inability to flexibly process prediction errors (Palmer et al., 2013; Van de Cruys et al., 2014), and with a failure to attenuate sensory precision.

A limitation of this study is the relatively small sample size. Further, investigations on bigger sample size are needed in order to confirm our results.

We demonstrate that adults with ASD over-anticipate stimuli occurring in an uncertain context. In a certain context, ASD subjects are able to extract predictive information and to use it in order to anticipate the predictable targets. However, the present results may reflect frontal compensation strategies to counteract the lack of automatic motor cortex pre-activation for execution of the motor response. There is a cost to this excessive processing that may be counterproductive in unpredictable and fluctuating situations, such as the social world, leading to stressful reactions, and a sense of overwhelming. Taken together, these results provide evidence that adults with ASD cannot flexibly modulate cortical activity according to changing levels of uncertainty. Moreover, these findings could ultimately contribute to the treatment of adults with ASD without intellectual disability. Further, research is needed in order to build cognitive remediation programs to provide strategies to patients with ASD so that they overcome prediction weaknesses.

AUTHOR CONTRIBUTIONS

AT has made a substantial contribution to the conception and design, to the acquisition, analysis and interpretation of the data; ML, ED, and CB have made a substantial contribution to the interpretation of the data; SR has made a substantial contribution to the conception and design, and to the acquisition and analysis of data; RK, AC, and FB have made a substantial contribution to the conception and design, and to the analysis and interpretation of the data. All authors have made a substantial contribution to drafting the article or reviewing it critically, have given final approval of the version of the article to be published and have agreed to be accountable for all aspects of the work in ensuring that questions related to the accuracy of integrity of any part of the work are appropriately investigated and resolved.

FUNDING

This work was supported by the Fondation Orange (AT), NINDS grant R37NS21135, and the Nielson Corporation (RK). This work was performed within the framework of the LABEX CORTEX (ANR-11-LABX-0042) of Université de Lyon, within the program "Investissements d'Avenir" (ANR-11-IDEX-0007) operated by the French National Research Agency (ANR).

ACKNOWLEDGMENTS

We thank all the volunteers for their time and effort spent participating in this study, as well as C. Schmitz for her helpful discussions, and L. Corneau for her help during EEG recordings.

REFERENCES

American Psychiatric Association (2000). *Diagnostic and Statistical Manual of Mental Disorders, 4th Edn, Text revision (DSM-IV-TR)*. Washington, DC: American Psychiatric Publishing.

American Psychiatric Association (2013). *Diagnostic and Statistical Manual of Mental Disorders, 5th Edn (DSM-5)*. Washington, DC: American Psychiatric Publishing.

Aguera, P. E., Jerbi, K., Caclin, A., and Bertrand, O. (2011). ELAN: a software package for analysis and visualization of MEG, EEG, and LFP signals. *Comput. Intell. Neurosci.* 2011:158970. doi: 10.1155/2011/158970

Bidet-Caulet, A., Barbe, P. G., Roux, S., Viswanath, H., Barthelemy, C., Bruneau, N., et al. (2012). Dynamics of anticipatory mechanisms during predictive context processing. *Eur. J. Neurosci.* 36, 2996–3004. doi: 10.1111/j.1460-9568.2012.08223.x

Brisson, J., Warreyn, P., Serres, J., Foussier, S., and Adrien-Louis, J. (2012). Motor anticipation failure in infants with autism: a retrospective analysis of feeding situations. *Autism* 16, 420–429. doi: 10.1177/1362361311423385

Brock, J. (2012). Alternative Bayesian accounts of autistic perception: comment on Pellicano and Burr. *Trends Cogn. Sci.* 16, 573–574. doi: 10.1016/j.tics.2012.10.005

Brunia, C. H., and van Boxtel, G. J. (2001). Wait and see. *Int. J. Psychophysiol.* 43, 59–75. doi: 10.1016/S0167-8760(01)00179-9

Bubic, A., von Cramon, D. Y., and Schubotz, R. I. (2010). Prediction, cognition and the brain. *Front. Hum. Neurosci.* 4:25. doi: 10.3389/fnhum.2010.00025

Cattaneo, L., Fabbri-Destro, M., Boria, S., Pieraccini, C., Monti, A., Cossu, G., et al. (2007). Impairment of actions chains in autism and its possible role in intention understanding. *Proc. Natl. Acad. Sci. U.S.A.* 104, 17825–17830. doi: 10.1073/pnas.0706273104

Dichter, G. S., Felder, J. N., and Bodfish, J. W. (2009). Autism is characterized by dorsal anterior cingulate hyperactivation during social target detection. *Soc. Cogn. Affect. Neurosci.* 4, 215–226. doi: 10.1093/scan/nsp017

Donchin, E., and Coles, M. G. H. (1988). Is the P300 component a manifestation of context updating? *Behav. Brain Sci.* 11, 357–374.

Donchin, E., Karis, D., Bashore, T., and Coles, M. (1986). "Cognitive psychophysiology and human information processing," in *Psychophysiology Systems Processes and Applications* (NewYork, NY: Guilford Press). Available online at: http://scholarcommons.usf.edu/psy_facpub/281.

Duncan-Johnson, C. C., and Kopell, B. S. (1981). The Stroop effect: brain potentials localize the source of interference. *Science* 214, 938–940. doi: 10.1126/science.7302571

Edgington, E. S. (1995). *Randomization Tests*. NewYork, NY: Marcel Dekker.

Feldman, H., and Friston, K. J. (2010). Attention, Uncertainty, and Free-Energy. *Front. Hum. Neurosci.* 4:215. doi: 10.3389/fnhum.2010.00215

Fogelson, N., Wang, X., Lewis, J., Kishiyama, M., Ding, M., and Knight, R. (2009). Multi-modal effects of local context on target detection: evidence from P3b. *J. Cogn. Neurosci.* 21, 1680–1692. doi: 10.1162/jocn.2009.21071

Friston, K. (2005). A theory of cortical responses. *Philos. Trans. R. Soc. Lond. B. Biol. Sci.* 360, 815–836. doi: 10.1098/rstb.2005.1622

Friston, K. J., Lawson, R., and Frith, C. D. (2013). On hyperpriors and hypopriors: comment on Pellicano and Burr. *Trends Cogn. Sci.* 17:1. doi: 10.1016/j.tics.2012.11.003

Gomot, M., and Wicker, B. (2012). A challenging, unpredictable world for people with autism spectrum disorder. *Int. J. Psychophysiol.* 83, 240–247. doi: 10.1016/j.ijpsycho.2011.09.017

Hesselmann, G., Sadaghiani, S., Friston, K. J., and Kleinschmidt, A. (2010). Predictive coding or evidence accumulation? false inference and neuronal fluctuations. *PLoS ONE* 5:e9926. doi: 10.1371/journal.pone.0009926

Hillyard, S. A., and Picton, T. W. (2011). "Electrophysiology of cognition," in *Comprehensive Physiology* (John Wiley & Sons, Inc.). Available online at: http://onlinelibrary.wiley.com/doi/10.1002/cphy.cp010513/abstract (Accessed June 10, 2015).

Jervis, B. W., Nichols, M. J., Johnson, T. E., Allen, E., and Hudson, N. R. (1983). A fundamental investigation of the composition of auditory evoked potentials. *IEEE Trans. Biomed. Eng.* 30, 43–50.

Kanner, L. (1943). Autistic disturbances of affective contact. *Nerv. Child* 2, 217–250.

Kutas, M., McCarthy, G., and Donchin, E. (1977). Augmenting mental chronometry: the P300 as a measure of stimulus evaluation time. *Science* 197, 792–795. doi: 10.1126/science.887923

Lawson, R. P., Rees, G., and Friston, K. J. (2014). An aberrant precision account of autism. *Front. Hum. Neurosci.* 8:302. doi: 10.3389/fnhum.2014.00302

Lord, C., Risi, S., Lambrecht, L., Cook, Jr. E. H., Leventhal, B. L., DiLavore, P. C., et al. (2000). The autism diagnostic observation schedule—generic: a standard measure of social and communication deficits associated with the spectrum of autism. *J. Autism Dev. Disord.* 30, 205–223. doi: 10.1023/A:1005592401947

Lord, C., Rutter, M., and Le Couteur, A. (1994). Autism diagnostic interview-revised: a revised version of a diagnostic interview for caregivers of individuals with possible pervasive developmental disorders. *J. Autism Dev. Disord.* 24, 659–685.

Luna, B., Minshew, N. J., Garver, K. E., Lazar, N. A., Thulborn, K. R., Eddy, W. F., et al. (2002). Neocortical system abnormalities in autism: an fMRI study of spatial working memory. *Neurology* 59, 834–840. doi: 10.1212/WNL.59.6.834

Maekawa, T., Tobimatsu, S., Inada, N., Oribe, N., Onitsuka, T., Kanba, S., et al. (2011). Top-down and bottom-up visual information processing of non-social stimuli in high-functioning autism spectrum disorder. *Res. Autism Spectr. Disord.* 5, 201–209. doi: 10.1016/j.rasd.2010.03.012

Martineau, J., Schmitz, C., Assaiante, C., Blanc, R., and Barthélémy, C. (2004). Impairment of a cortical event-related desynchronisation during a bimanual load-lifting task in children with autistic disorder. *Neurosci. Lett.* 367, 298–303. doi: 10.1016/j.neulet.2004.06.018

Palmer, C. J., Paton, B., Hohwy, J., and Enticott, P. G. (2013). Movement under uncertainty: the effects of the rubber-hand illusion vary along the nonclinical autism spectrum. *Neuropsychologia* 51, 1942–1951. doi: 10.1016/j.neuropsychologia.2013.06.020

Pellicano, E., and Burr, D. (2012). When the world becomes "too real": a Bayesian explanation of autistic perception. *Trends Cogn. Sci.* 16, 504–510. doi: 10.1016/j.tics.2012.08.009

Perrin, F., Pernier, J., Bertrand, O., and Echallier, J. F. (1989). Spherical splines for scalp potential and current density mapping. *Electroencephalogr. Clin. Neurophysiol.* 72, 184–187. doi: 10.1016/0013-4694(89)90180-6

Pfurtscheller, G., and Lopes da Silva, F. H. (1999). Event-related EEG/MEG synchronization and desynchronization: basic principles. *Clin. Neurophysiol.* 110, 1842–1857.

Pineda, J. A. (2005). The functional significance of mu rhythms: translating "seeing" and "hearing" into "doing." *Brain Res. Brain Res. Rev.* 50, 57–68. doi: 10.1016/j.brainresrev.2005.04.005

Robic, S., Sonié, S., Fonlupt, P., Henaff, M.-A., Touil, N., Coricelli, G., et al. (2015). Decision-making in a changing world: a study in autism spectrum disorders. *J. Autism Dev. Disord.* 45, 1603–1613. doi: 10.1007/s10803-014-2311-7

Sawaki, R., and Katayama, J. (2006). Stimulus context determines whether non-target stimuli are processed as task-relevant or distractor information. *Clin. Neurophysiol.* 117, 2532–2539. doi: 10.1016/j.clinph.2006.06.755

Schmitz, C., Martineau, J., Barthélémy, C., and Assaiante, C. (2003). Motor control and children with autism: deficit of anticipatory function? *Neurosci. Lett.* 348, 17–20. doi: 10.1016/S0304-3940(03)00644-X

Skewes, J. C., Jegindø, E.-M., and Gebauer, L. (2015). Perceptual inference and autistic traits. *Autism Int. J. Res. Pract.* 19, 301–307. doi: 10.1177/1362361313519872

Smid, H. G. O. M., Mulder, G., and Mulder, L. J. M. (1990). Selective response activation can begin before stimulus recognition is complete: a psychophysiological and error analysis of continuous flow. *Acta Psychol.* 74, 169–210. doi: 10.1016/0001-6918(90)90005-Z

Strandburg, R. J., Marsh, J. T., Brown, W. S., Asarnow, R. F., Guthrie, D., and Higa, J. (1993). Event-related potentials in high-functioning adult autistics: linguistic and nonlinguistic visual information processing tasks. *Neuropsychologia* 31, 413–434.

Tallon-Baudry, C., and Bertrand, O. (1999). Oscillatory gamma activity in humans and its role in object representation. *Trends Cogn. Sci.* 3, 151–162.

Tallon-Baudry, C., Bertrand, O., Delpuech, C., and Pernier, J. (1996). Stimulus specificity of phase-locked and non-phase-locked 40 Hz visual responses in human. *J. Neurosci.* 16, 4240–4249.

Tsai, C.-L., Pan, C.-Y., Wang, C.-H., Tseng, Y.-T., and Hsieh, K.-W. (2011). An event-related potential and behavioral study of impaired inhibitory control in children with autism spectrum disorder. *Res. Autism Spectr. Disord.* 5, 1092–1102. doi: 10.1016/j.rasd.2010.12.004

Tye, C., Asherson, P., Ashwood, K. L., Azadi, B., Bolton, P., McLoughlin, G., et al. (2014). Attention and inhibition in children with ASD, ADHD and co-morbid ASD + ADHD: an event-related potential study. *Psychol. Med.* 44, 1101–1116. doi: 10.1017/S0033291713001049

Van de Cruys, S., Evers, K., Van der Hallen, R., Van Eylen, L., Boets, B., de-Wit, L., et al. (2014). Precise minds in uncertain worlds: predictive coding in autism. *Psychol. Rev.* 121, 649–675. doi: 10.1037/a0037665

Wechsler, D. (1997). *Wechsler Adult Intelligence Scale, 3rd Edn.* San Antonio, TX: The Psychological Corporation.

Wechsler, D. (2005). *Wechsler Intelligence Scale for Children (WISC IV) - Translated.* Paris: ECPA.

7

Impact of Sensory Sensitivity on Physiological Stress Response and Novel Peer Interaction in Children with and without Autism Spectrum Disorder

***Blythe A. Corbett*[1, 2*], *Rachael A. Muscatello*[2] and *Scott D. Blain*[3]**

[1] Department of Psychiatry and Behavioral Sciences, Vanderbilt University, Nashville, TN, USA, [2] Vanderbilt Brain Institute, Neuroscience Graduate Program, Vanderbilt University, Nashville, TN, USA, [3] Department of Psychology and Human Development, Vanderbilt University, Nashville, TN, USA

Edited by:
Benjamin Gesundheit, Cell El Ltd., Israel

Reviewed by:
Alka Anand Subramanyam, Topiwala National Medical College & BYL Nair Charitable Hospital, India
Om Sai Ramesh Vallamkonda, Lady Hardinge Medical College, India

****Correspondence:***
Blythe A. Corbett
blythe.corbett@vanderbilt.edu

Background: For many children with Autism Spectrum Disorder (ASD), social interactions can be stressful. Previous research shows that youth with ASD exhibit greater physiological stress response during peer interaction, compared to typically developing (TD) peers. Heightened sensory sensitivity may contribute to maladaptive patterns of stress and anxiety. The current study investigated between-group differences in stress response to peer interaction, as well as the role of sensory sensitivity.

Methods: Participants included 80 children (40 ASD) between 8 and 12 years. Children participated in the peer interaction paradigm (PIP), an ecologically valid protocol that simulates real-world social interaction. Salivary cortisol was collected before and after the 20 min PIP. Parents completed questionnaires pertaining to child stress (*Stress Survey Schedule*) and sensory sensitivity (*Short Sensory Profile*). Statistical analyses included *t*-tests and ANCOVA models to examine between-group differences in cortisol and play; Pearson correlations to determine relations between cortisol, play, and questionnaire scores; and moderation analyses to investigate interactions among variables.

Results: Controlling for baseline cortisol values, children with ASD showed significantly higher cortisol levels than TD peers, in response to the PIP [$F_{(1, 77)} = 5.77$, $p = 0.02$]. Cortisol during play was negatively correlated with scores on the SSP ($r = -0.242$, $p = 0.03$), and positively correlated with SSS ($r = 0.273$, $p = 0.02$) indicating that higher cortisol was associated with greater sensory sensitivity (lower SSP reflects more impairment) and enhanced stress in various contexts (higher SSS reflects more stress). Furthermore, diagnosis was a significant moderator of the relation between cortisol and SSP, at multiple time points during the PIP ($p < 0.05$).

Conclusions: The current study extends previous findings by showing that higher physiological arousal during play is associated with heightened sensory sensitivity and a pattern of increased stress in various contexts. Results are discussed in a broader context, emphasizing the need to examine relationships between social, behavioral, and physiological profiles in ASD to enhance understanding and improve treatments aimed at ameliorating stress and sensory dysfunction, while enhancing social skills.

Keywords: autism, stress, cortisol, sensory, peer interaction, social, auditory

INTRODUCTION

Impaired social communication is a primary characteristic of Autism Spectrum Disorder (ASD) (American Psychiatric Association, 2013) and may be the result of limitations in social cognition (e.g., Baron-Cohen, 1995) or social motivation (Chevallier et al., 2012). Underlying physiological factors may also impact the extent to which individuals with ASD engage with others in social situations. For example, there is considerable evidence that social interactions are highly stressful for children with ASD (Lopata et al., 2008; Corbett et al., 2010). It may be this exaggerated stress response that drives, in part, reductions in social engagement. There is also significant prevalence of sensory dysfunction in ASD (Rogers et al., 2003; Kern et al., 2006; Tomchek and Dunn, 2007; Ben-Sasson et al., 2009), and these hyper- and/or hypo- sensory sensitivities may further contribute to atypical patterns of social interaction.

Compared to typically developing (TD) peers, children with ASD tend to interact less with other children (Corbett et al., 2010, 2012) and engage in less cooperative play (Corbett et al., 2014b), instead showing a preference to engage in self-play (Humphrey and Symes, 2011). There is also evidence that individuals with ASD have abnormal preferences for interpersonal distance (IPD), including both standing too close or preferring more distance relative to TD peers (Kennedy and Adolphs, 2014; Lough et al., 2015; Perry et al., 2015). As children with ASD become more aware of their limitations in social skills with age (Knott et al., 2006), later peer interactions may be characterized by exacerbated social stress (Schupp et al., 2013). As a result of this stress, these children may display increased avoidance behaviors characterized by decreased social motivation to interact with peers. This notion is supported by research showing that higher cortisol response to a novel social interaction was associated with reduced social communication among children with ASD (Corbett et al., 2014b).

The hypothalamic-pituitary-adrenal (HPA) axis is a highly regulated system that is responsible for maintaining homeostasis via maintenance of a diurnal rhythm, activation in response to stress or threat, and restoration of basal activity via negative feedback mechanisms. Cortisol, an important stress hormone, serves as a measurable indicator of HPA regulation, increasing in concentration after exposure to stressors (Herman and Cullinan, 1997). Cortisol also shows a diurnal rhythm of fluctuating concentration, throughout the day. Typically, diurnal cortisol values are at peak levels in the morning and slowly decline to lowest levels in the evening. In ASD, the diurnal rhythm appears to be altered, such that children with ASD have lower morning cortisol and higher evening cortisol values relative to TD children (Corbett et al., 2008, 2009). Further, many children with ASD show an increased response to stress, as indicated by higher cortisol levels, when interacting with unfamiliar peers (Lopata et al., 2008; Corbett et al., 2010). This stress response appears to be tied to level of social cognition, as those with highest cortisol values tend to show less social motivation (Corbett et al., 2014b). It is important to note, however, that this response is considerably variable within the ASD population (Lopata et al., 2008; Schupp et al., 2013). This suggests the possibility of interactions with other characteristics, which may explain part of the high variability in psychosocial stress response as seen in ASD.

Sensory processing abnormalities are now considered a core symptom of ASD under the Restrictive and Stereotypic Behaviors criteria of the DSM-5 (American Psychiatric Association, 2013). Sensory behaviors have historically been divided into four patterns, including sensory hypo-reactivity, hyper-reactivity, sensory seeking, and sensory avoidance (Dunn, 2001; Ben-Sasson et al., 2009). Complexity arises from the fact that many individuals with ASD will show several of these patterns at one time, with mixed patterns being displayed across sensory domains (Baranek et al., 2006; Tomchek and Dunn, 2007; Lidstone et al., 2014). Recent conceptualizations, therefore, have attempted to classify sensory processing abnormalities in ASD into specific subtypes (Lane et al., 2011, 2014; Uljarević et al., 2016), such as sensory adaptive, sensory moderate, and sensory severe (Uljarević et al., 2016).

Emerging research demonstrates a relationship between sensory sensitivities and arousal/anxiety in ASD. In one study, children with ASD showed lower morning cortisol relative to TD peers, which was associated with higher parent-reported stress as measured by the Stress Survey Schedule (SSS) (Corbett et al., 2009). Similarly, morning cortisol was associated with various domains of sensory functioning derived from the Short Sensory Profile—a parent-reported indicator of sensory sensitivities—(SSP; Dunn, 1999) painting a complex picture based on individual profiles (Corbett et al., 2009). Other studies investigating sensory profiles in ASD have also found relationships between sensory responsivity and anxiety (Green et al., 2012; Lidstone et al., 2014; Wigham et al., 2015; Uljarević et al., 2016), repetitive behaviors and stereotyped movements (Gabriels et al., 2008; Gal et al., 2010; Lidstone et al., 2014), and intolerance of uncertainty (Chamberlain et al., 2013; Wigham et al., 2015). Furthermore, a sample of TD young adults showed a correlation between sensory sensitivity and increased interpersonal distance (Perry et al., 2016), suggesting some role of sensory processing in social behavior. Currently, however, there is limited research that attempts to elucidate the impact of sensory dysfunction on social motivation and communication, especially in a naturalistic play setting.

The current study sought to investigate between-group differences in biobehavioral profiles of psychosocial stress following play with unfamiliar peers, in conjunction with sensory profiles. In order to elucidate the impact of sensory dysfunction on stress and social interaction, the current study sought to measure social engagement during a Peer Interaction Paradigm (PIP) (Corbett et al., 2010) and then to compare social behavior to stress and sensory profiles, as indicated by measures of cortisol and parent reports of stress and sensory sensitivity. It was hypothesized that children with ASD would have greater cortisol in response to play, relative to TD peers. Furthermore, it was hypothesized that cortisol response would be positively correlated with both increased parent-reported stress and sensory sensitivity.

MATERIALS AND METHODS

Participants

The sample included 80 un-medicated, pre-pubertal, children between the ages of 8-to 12 years, including 40 with ASD (mean = 9.65 years) and 40 TD (mean = 9.79 years). The gender composition included 14 females (6 = ASD, 8 = TD) and 66 males (34 = ASD, 32 = TD). ASD diagnosis was based on the Diagnostic and Statistical Manual (DSM-5) criteria (American Psychiatric Association, 2013) and established by all of the following: (1) a previous diagnosis by a psychologist, psychiatrist, or behavioral pediatrician with ASD expertise; (2) current clinical judgment; and (3) corroborated by the ADOS (Lord et al., 2000), administered by research-reliable personnel. For inclusion in the study all participants were required to have an estimated IQ of 80 or above, as measured by the Wechsler Abbreviated Scale of Intelligence (Wechsler, 1999). In addition, pubertal status was determined by the Pubertal Development Scale (Petersen et al., 1988) to confirm that the child had not yet entered puberty.

The Vanderbilt University Institutional Review Board approved the study. The investigation was performed in accordance with the Helsinki Declaration for research involving human subjects. Prior to inclusion in the study, informed written consent from parents and verbal assent from research participants were obtained. Participants were recruited by IRB approved flyers and several recruitment systems via clinics, subject tracking systems, resource centers, support groups, schools, and recreational facilities.

As described below, the study also included children who served as confederates (actor that participates in the study), who were of the same age and gender as the ASD and TD children. Parents of the confederates provided informed consent for them to train for and participate in the study. Confederates were selected based on demonstrated strong social skills, genuine desire to play and interact with children with and without disabilities, and an ability to follow research personnel instructions and translate them into age appropriate play behaviors. All confederates underwent several training procedures, including reading an instruction manual, direct skills modeling, and playground practice. The majority of the confederates had previously participated in research or served as a peer helper for children with disabilities.

Peer Interaction Playground Paradigm

The Peer Interaction Paradigm examines social exchanges between children with and without ASD within a naturalistic playground environment (Corbett et al., 2010). The playground is a 130 by 120 ft. fenced in play area that is part of the Susan Gray Preschool. The 20-min paradigm consisted of periods of free play and opportunities for cooperative play, which was facilitated by an age- and gender-match TD confederate. The trained confederate followed cues provided by research personnel through an earpiece with a remote transmitter, in order to provide structure to play by simultaneously soliciting play with both research participants. Use of a confederate permitted each interactive sequence of free or solicited play to occur within an otherwise natural setting, while also maintaining an even level of play to prevent increased aerobic activity, which could affect cortisol levels. In addition to the confederate, the paradigm involved one child with ASD and one TD child, all three of whom were unfamiliar with each other prior to the interaction. Each participant only took part in one 20-min session, such that the exposure represented a novel social experience. During the protocol, research personnel remained in the building in order to facilitate more natural play behavior.

The paradigm was divided into four 5-min time (T) periods of intermittent free play and solicited play (see **Figure 1**). The first period (T1) consisted of unsolicited free play. During the second period (T2), the confederate was instructed to solicit interaction for cooperative play on the playground equipment. During the third period (T3), the confederate returned to unsolicited free play. During the fourth period (T4), the confederate was instructed to once again solicit the two participants to engage in a cooperative game involving toys.

Interactions were recorded using state-of-the-art video equipment, including four professional Sony EVI D70 (Sony, New York, NY, USA) remotely operated cameras housed in glass cases, which were affixed to the four corners of the playground's fence. The cameras contain pan, tilt, and zoom features allowing full capture of the playground. To record remote audio communication, Motorola MC22OR GMRS-FRS (Motorola, Libertyville, IL, USA) and Audio-Technica (Audio-Technica, Stow, Ohio, USA) transmitters and receivers functioning as battery-operated microphones were clipped to each child's shirt. Audio was recorded using an eight-channel mixing board.

Behavior Coding

The Observer XT Version 8.0 software was used for the collection and analysis of the observational social interaction data (Noldus, 2008). Data were analyzed based on a predefined list of operationalized behaviors (Corbett et al., 2010; Schupp et al., 2013) by research-reliable raters who were unaware of the current study aims. Behaviors were analyzed using a transactional approach (i.e., *who does what to whom*) based on predefined operationalized behaviors (Mendoza and Mason, 1989; Lyons et al., 1990, 1992; Mason et al., 1993). Inter-rater reliability was calculated using Cohen's Kappa at $K = 0.80$, while test-retest reliability was $K = 0.89$. Cooperative play interactions were calculated as percentage of time engaged (verbal 90% and $K = 0.85$; group play 91% and $K = 0.89$). Variables such as cooperative play and verbal interaction were operationalized based upon previously described definitions and as part of a larger study (Corbett et al., 2014b). For the purpose of this study, cooperative play was defined as the percentage of time engaged in a reciprocal activity for enjoyment that involved and relied on the participation of two or more

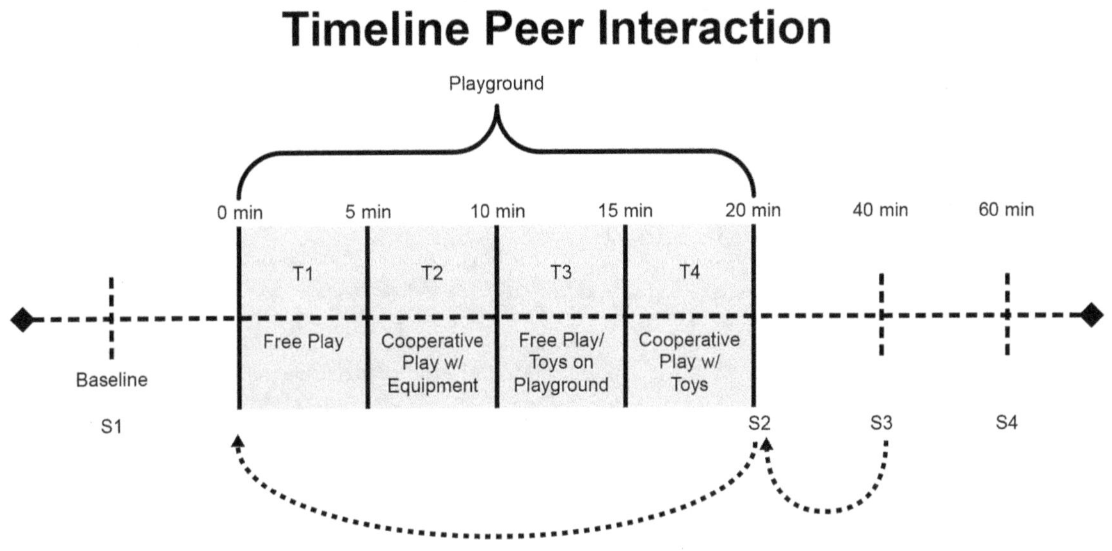

FIGURE 1 | Peer interaction paradigm timeline of events. The 20-min paradigm consists of four 5-min periods of free play (T1), solicited play with equipment (T2), free, unsolicited play (T3), and solicited cooperative play with toys (T4). Salivary cortisol measures were taken at baseline (S1), immediately after the paradigm (S2), 20-min after the paradigm (S3), and 40-min after (S4).

children (e.g., hide and seek). For an expanded description of the behavior coding protocol and operationalized variables, see previous studies (Corbett et al., 2010, 2014b; Schupp et al., 2013).

Salivary Cortisol Sampling

Basal levels of salivary cortisol were collected from home to ascertain the child's afternoon baseline over 3 days, using established methods, as part of a larger study (Corbett et al., 2008). For the purpose of this study, only playground cortisol levels were analyzed.

It is important to note that there is an approximate 20-min time lag between when an event occurs and when a related change in cortisol can be detected in saliva (Kirschbaum and Hellhammer, 1989). The peer interaction included four salivary cortisol samples taken 20 min apart for each subject: S1–(baseline), S2–(immediately post-play), S3–(20 min post-play), and S4–(40 min post play). The S2 measurement taken immediately after the peer interaction represents circulating cortisol levels at the start of the paradigm, while the S3 measurement is representative of levels at the end of the peer interaction (see **Figure 1**). All peer interactions were held in the afternoon between 13:00 and 16:00, for comparison to afternoon baseline values.

Immediately before and following the playground paradigm, the ASD and TD participants were each assigned to an individual room and sat with a research assistant for cortisol sampling. A similar bag of toys and activities was provided to each child in order to maintain consistency in experience across all participants. Samples were collected following the standardized drool procedures outlined in previous studies (Corbett et al., 2008, 2010).

Cortisol Assay

The salivary cortisol assay was performed using a Coat-A-Count® radioimmunoassay kit (Siemens Medical Solutions Diagnostics, Los Angeles, CA) modified to accommodate lower levels of cortisol in human saliva relative to plasma. Saliva samples, which had been stored at −20°C, were thawed and centrifuged at 3460 rpm for 15 min to separate the aqueous component from mucins and other suspended particles. The coated tube from the kit was substituted with a glass tube into which 100 μl of saliva, 100 μl of cortisol antibody (courtesy of Wendell Nicholson, Vanderbilt University, Nashville, TN), and 100 μl of ^{125}I-cortisol were mixed. After incubation at 4°C for 24 h 100 μl of normal rat serum in 0.1% PO4/EDTA buffer (1:50) and precipitating reagent (PR81) were added. The mixture was centrifuged at 3460 rpm for 30 min, decanted, and counted. Serial dilution of samples indicated a linearity of 0.99. Interassay coefficient of variation was 10.4%.

Dependent Measures

Short Sensory Profile (SSP; Dunn, 1999)

The SSP is a parent-report questionnaire designed to assess sensory sensitivity across seven sensory domains, such as auditory sensitivity, tactile sensitivity, and underresponsive/seeks sensation. Parents are asked to rate the frequency with which their child engages in behaviors related to sensory sensitivity in each domain. Possible scores range from 5 points to 1 point, ranging from "never responds in this manner" (5 points) to "always responds in this manner" (1 points). High raw scores indicate typical performance, while lower scores on the SSP are indicative of greater sensory dysfunction. The primary variable of interest for analysis was total raw score.

Stress Survey Schedule (SSS; Groden et al., 2001)

The SSS is a 60-item, parent-report survey designed to measure the daily stress of individuals with ASD and other developmental disabilities. The survey addresses eight domains of stress: Anticipation/Uncertainty, Changes and Threats, Unpleasant Events, Pleasant Events, Sensory/Personal Contact, Food Related Activity, Social/Environmental Interactions, and Ritual Related Stress. Parents are asked to rate intensity of stress for each item on a five-point Likert scale, ranging from none to mild stress (1) to severe stress (5). Internal consistency correlations range from 0.70 to 0.87. Higher total scores are indicative of enhanced stress, and total raw score was used for analysis.

Salivary Cortisol

The primary outcome variable of interest for characterizing the stress response was salivary cortisol. Samples were analyzed for S1–S4, as described above. Because salivary cortisol measurements are positive and skewed toward large values, a log transformation was performed to achieve approximate normality. Log-transformed values were used in all analyses.

Social Behavior

The primary outcome variable for social behavior was percent time spent in cooperative play during solicited play at T4 of the PIP.

Statistical Analysis

Descriptive statistics were calculated for demographic information, as well as parent-report measures of sensory functioning (SSP) and child stress (SSS); possible group differences in these variables were examined using independent samples t-tests. Analysis of covariance (ANCOVA) models were utilized to examine group differences in salivary cortisol response, controlling for baseline cortisol values. Pearson product moment correlations were conducted to examine associations between the sensory and stress measures. Moderation analyses were conducted to determine whether diagnosis was a moderator of the relation between SSP and cortisol response.

All statistical analyses were conducted using SPSS Version 22.0 (IBM Corp, 2013). The PROCESS application for SPSS was used to conduct moderation analyses (Hayes, 2013).

RESULTS

Demographic information for each group is presented in **Table 1**, including age, cognitive, and diagnostic information. Descriptive statistics for SSP, SSS, and cooperative play (separated by group) are listed in **Table 2**. Using independent samples t-tests, there were significant between-group differences on the SSP [$t_{(78)} = 140.44$, $p < 0.0001$] and the SSS [$t_{(77)} = 109.32$, $p < 0.0001$], showing greater parent-reported stress and sensory sensitivity in the ASD group, compared to the TD group.

In order to assess group differences in social behavior, the percent duration of cooperative play during the solicited play period T4 of the PIP was compared between groups, using independent samples t-tests. Results revealed a significant difference between groups in percent duration of cooperative play [$t_{(83)} = 8.349$, $p = 0.005$], showing that children with ASD engage in significantly less cooperative play than TD peers.

Descriptive statistics for cortisol at baseline, during play, and after play are shown in **Table 3**. Analysis of covariance (ANCOVA) was conducted to examine the effect of group on stress (cortisol levels during cooperative play with peers), while controlling for baseline values. Results indicate a significant group difference in cortisol during play (S3) with peers [$F_{(1, 77)} = 5.77$, $p = 0.02$]. There was also a significant group difference in cortisol after play (S4) [$F_{(1, 77)} = 4.78$, $p = 0.03$].

In consideration of these group differences, Pearson product correlations were calculated to assess the relations between physiological stress (cortisol), sensory functioning (SSP), and parent-report stress (SSS). Cortisol during play was negatively correlated with scores on the SSP ($r = -0.24$, $p = 0.03$) and positively correlated with scores on the SSS ($r = 0.27$, $p = 0.02$). Therefore, as cortisol levels increased during the PIP, SSP scores decreased (indicating greater sensory dysfunction) and global stress as measured by the SSS increased.

Moderation analysis was conducted to examine the impact of diagnosis on the relation between stress (cortisol) and sensory (SSP) functioning. Results show that diagnosis was a significant moderator of the association between SSP and cortisol at baseline (S1) [$\Delta R^2 = 0.01$, $F_{(1, 76)} = 8.46$, $p = 0.0047$], the beginning

TABLE 1 | Demographics.

Variable	ASD mean (SD)	TD mean (SD)	*P*-value
Age	9.65 (1.485)	9.79 (1.631)	0.699
SCQ total	20.72 (7.229)	2.37 (2.123)	<0.0001
Performance IQ	111.03 (53.394)	112.45 (12.831)	0.973
Verbal IQ	108.72 (62.858)	112.16 (13.997)	0.240
WASI estimated IQ	101.22 (22.505)	119.47 (13.123)	<0.001

ASD, Autism spectrum disorder; IQ, intelligence quotient; TD, typical development; SCQ, social communication questionnaire; WASI, Weschler abbreviated scale of intelligence.

TABLE 2 | Descriptive statistics for parent-report measures and play.

Variable	ASD mean (SD)	TD mean (SD)	*P*-value
TOTAL SCORES			
Short sensory profile	122.28 (21.393)	172.82 (16.629)	<0.0001
Stress survey schedule	122.02 (30.243)	62.59 (18.823)	<0.0001
PERCENT TIME INTERACTING			
Cooperative play	55.15 (36.08)	74.54 (24.13)	0.005

TABLE 3 | Descriptive statistics for log cortisol at baseline, in response to the PIP, and after the PIP.

Cortisol value	ASD mean (SD)	TD mean (SD)
Baseline cortisol (S1)	−0.1515 (0.333)	−0.1034 (0.267)
Cortisol during play (S3)	−0.1284 (0.303)	−0.2730 (0.373)
Cortisol after play (S4)	−0.2190 (0.293)	−0.3148 (0.266)

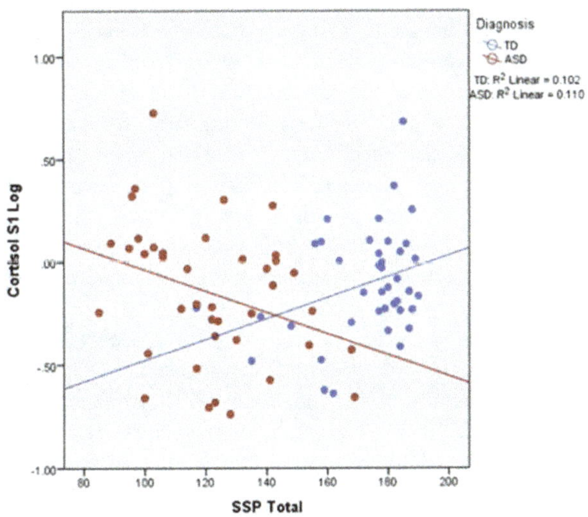

FIGURE 2 | Relationship between cortisol and sensory profile in children with ASD and TD peers.

of play (S2) [$\Delta R^2 = 0.06$, $F_{(1, 76)} = 4.85$, $p = 0.03$], during play (S3) [$\Delta R^2 = 0.02$, $F_{(1, 76)} = 3.94$, $p = 0.05$], and after play (S4) [$\Delta R^2 = 0.05$, $F_{(1, 76)} = 3.95$, $p = 0.05$]. **Figure 2** shows the moderating effect of diagnosis on the relation between SSP and cortisol, indicating that the negative correlation observed between cortisol and sensory functioning in the total sample is driven by the ASD group, whereas the opposite trend appears to hold true for the TD group.

In order to examine the impact of sensory sensitivity on play, we examined the association between SSP score and percent duration spent in cooperative play during the solicited play period, T4. There was a trend level positive association between cooperative play and total SSP ($r = 0.197$, $p = 0.07$). This association suggests that more sensory impairment was associated with less time spent in cooperative play (lower scores on the SSP are indicative of greater sensory dysfunction).

In an effort to further assess the impact of sensory sensitivity on play, *post-hoc* correlational analyses were conducted for individual domains of the SSP along with time spent in cooperative play. Scores on the Auditory domain were significantly positively correlated with cooperative play ($r = 0.218$, $p = 0.04$), while Underresponsive/Seeks Sensation correlated with play at a trend level ($r = 0.196$, $p = 0.07$).

DISCUSSION

While challenges in reciprocal social interaction are synonymous with ASD, sensory dysfunction and heightened stress are often found as well. Thus, the current study sought to examine the impact of sensory dysfunction on stress and social engagement with unfamiliar peers in children with and without ASD. The study utilized measures of social interaction (cooperative play) and physiological arousal (cortisol) during peer play using the PIP (Corbett et al., 2010) to assess the associations of social behavior and physiological stress with parent reports of stress and sensory sensitivity. It was hypothesized that children with ASD would show greater levels of salivary cortisol in response to play, relative to TD peers. Furthermore, it was hypothesized that cortisol response would be positively correlated with both increased parent-reported stress and sensory sensitivity. Therefore, the current study sought to further investigate biobehavioral profiles following play with unfamiliar peers with an emphasis on the impact of sensory sensitivity.

Autism is characterized by prevalence of sensory dysfunction (Rogers et al., 2003; Kern et al., 2006; Tomchek and Dunn, 2007; Ben-Sasson et al., 2009) and increased stress, especially during social interactions (Lopata et al., 2008; Corbett et al., 2010). In the current study, children with ASD showed both increased sensory dysfunction and parent-reported stress, relative to their TD peers. Research has shown that both altered sensory sensitivity and stress have deleterious effects on the overall functioning of children with ASD, especially given their potential associations with a variety of challenges, such as poor response to change (e.g., Chamberlain et al., 2013; Wigham et al., 2015) and anxiety (Green et al., 2012; Lidstone et al., 2014; Wigham et al., 2015; Uljarević et al., 2016).

In addition to group differences in sensory sensitivity and parent-reported stress, differences in salivary cortisol response were observed. Consistent with previous reports (Corbett et al., 2010, 2012, 2014b; Schupp et al., 2013), the ASD group had significantly greater physiological arousal in response to social interaction relative to the TD group, as indicated by higher cortisol levels both during and after the PIP. The increased arousal suggests that children with ASD may perceive social interaction with peers to be more stressful, compared to TD peers. Moreover, cortisol response was significantly correlated with parent-reported stress suggesting that heightened physiological reactions to peer interaction are also associated with a global pattern of elevated stress. Findings add to a growing body of work showing dysregulated patterns of stress in youth with ASD, both in terms of global and diurnal stress (Corbett et al., 2008, 2009), as well as stress in response to social interaction (e.g., Corbett et al., 2014b).

In light of observing group differences for both physiological stress and sensory sensitivity, we explored correlations between these variables. Significant associations were found between cortisol and SSP, such that higher cortisol in response to play was associated with greater sensory impairment. Moderation analyses were conducted to determine whether the correlation was driven by group status. Results showed that ASD diagnosis was a significant moderator of this relation, such that sensory dysfunction was associated with increased salivary cortisol response to peer interaction in the ASD group only. Moreover, this relationship held for cortisol levels at each time point of collection, including baseline cortisol as well as before, during, and after play. Interestingly, the TD group appeared to have the opposite relationship between cortisol and sensory functioning (**Figure 2**), implying that the negative impact of sensory sensitivity on stress reactivity during play is unique to ASD. In other words, greater levels of sensory dysfunction in ASD may lead to increased physiological stress. Thus, it appears that the symptom profile of ASD ostensibly contributes to enhanced reactivity to the environment, which can be manifested in both sensory and physiological functioning. The question still remains whether or not these relationships between stress and sensory sensitivity are bi-directional or whether a uni-directional model exists, such that one symptom precedes and drives the other.

When assessing group differences in cooperative play, the ASD group engaged in significantly less cooperative play, relative to the TD group. This is in line with previous findings that children with ASD tend to engage less than their TD peers during the PIP (e.g., Corbett et al., 2014b). While factors such as social cognition (Baron-Cohen, 1995; Corbett et al., 2014a) and social motivation (Chevallier et al., 2012; Corbett et al., 2014b) appear to play a significant role in explaining group differences in social engagement, sensory dysfunction may also have an impact on social behavior. For example, sensory sensitivity was recently shown to associate with interpersonal distance in TD individuals (Perry et al., 2016). In order to better understand the potential impact of sensory sensitivity on play behavior in ASD, duration spent in cooperative play was analyzed along with sensory processing scores. While overall sensory dysfunction was not associated with play behavior, auditory sensitivity was significantly correlated with play.

Adults with ASD have shown impairments in auditory localization through an inability to use prior perceptual experience to locate sounds (Skewes and Gebauer, 2016). Difficulties in auditory processing and orienting to a stimulus may be linked to emergence of impairments in social and communication behaviors early in development (Osterling et al., 2002). As such, children with ASD fail to orient to stimuli, especially critical social stimuli such as response to their own name (Dawson et al., 1998). It is possible that the inability to attend to stimuli is due, in part, to altered auditory processing, resulting in reduced early social interactions through a lack of joint attention with the caregiver. According to the Enactive Mind hypothesis (Klin et al., 2003), limited early social experiences may contribute to the social communication deficits that characterize ASD. Therefore, if sensory sensitivity alters one's experience in the physical world, interactions in the social world may be absent, incomplete, or unpredictable among children with ASD, thus leading to difficulties in social communication and cognition. While this is an intriguing theory for connecting the sensory and social symptoms of ASD, a great deal of empirical evidence is needed to test for direct links between sensory and social functioning in ASD.

Limitations and Future Directions

The study had several strengths, including a relatively large sample size and use of a validated protocol for observing play behavior in a naturalistic playground setting. Some limitations do exist. Although parent-reports are the most commonly used measure of sensory profile in ASD and provide a useful representation of sensory dysfunction, future studies would benefit from more objective tests of sensory sensitivity such as assessment of various sensory domains (e.g., auditory, tactile) or through clinician-based observations. Furthermore, this study assessed only one novel exposure, representing everyday experiences of interacting with new people. A limitation of the current study is the lack of repeated exposure, which would allow for assessing stress response across several repeat social encounters. The study was also limited to one measure of physiological arousal (i.e., cortisol). Use of other measures such as respiratory sinus arrhythmia (e.g., Benevides and Lane, 2013) could provide a more detailed, continuous assessment of regulation and arousal throughout the protocol.

Novel social experiences are only one aspect of daily social interactions. The current study focused on these novel experiences. Results were consistent with previous reports (Corbett et al., 2010, 2012, 2014b; Schupp et al., 2013) suggesting that when exposed to new peers for the first time, children with ASD experience greater physiological stress and tend to engage in less cooperative play with those new people, relative to their TD peers. However, social interactions are not solely reliant on single interactions with new people. Children interact with the same peers on a daily basis at school, and physiological stress or sensory sensitivity could have significant effects on how children with ASD interact with familiar peers in a setting such as the classroom. Therefore, future studies should investigate the role of sensory sensitivity and physiological stress during repeat exposure.

The findings that sensory dysfunction may negatively impact social behavior is notable and warrants further investigation. It would be helpful to discern whether targeting sensory symptoms via treatment could indirectly improve social motivation in individuals with ASD. While results show several interactions are present between physiological stress, sensory sensitivity, and parent-report stress, the directionality among these variables remains unclear. Future studies are needed to determine the extent to which change in one variable leads to change in another. The findings that the association between cortisol and sensory sensitivity was driven by the ASD group requires further investigation to enhance understanding of the mechanisms behind the purported link, which appears specific to ASD. Finally, while auditory sensitivity and cooperative play were correlated, further research is needed to determine any possible causal impact of sensory sensitivity on social motivation.

Summary

The primary objective of the current study was to examine the impact of sensory sensitivity on stress response and peer interaction in children with and without ASD. Results show that cortisol response to play is elevated in children with ASD and that higher physiological arousal during play is associated with greater sensory sensitivity and parent-reported stress. Additionally, ASD diagnosis confers risk for atypical sensory and stress reactivity, which may further contribute to the core social deficits. Taken together, results provide evidence for important interactions among social, sensory, and physiological profiles in ASD. Characterizing and assessing such profiles may better predict global outcomes, while also serving to inform more effective methods for intervention.

AUTHOR CONTRIBUTIONS

The named authors made significant contributions to the investigation and manuscript. Specifically, BC conceptualized the study design, outlined the organization of the manuscript, guided the literature search, ran data analysis, provided interpretation to the findings, and made significant contributions to the final manuscript. RM read the extant literature, synthesized the results, contributed to interpretation of the findings, and co-wrote the initial draft of the manuscript. SB participated in the acquisition, analysis, and interpretation of the physiological and behavioral data, and contributed to the writing of the manuscript. All authors read and approved the content of the work.

FUNDING

This work was supported by National Institute of Mental Health R01 MH085717 awarded to BC.

REFERENCES

American Psychiatric Association (2013). *Diagnostic and Statistical Manual of Mental Disorders, 5th Edn (DSM-5)*. Washington, DC: American Psychiatric Association. doi: 10.1176/appi.books.9780890425596

Baranek, G. T., David, F. J., Poe, M. D., Stone, W. L., and Watson, L. R. (2006). Sensory Experiences Questionnaire: discriminating sensory features in young children with autism, developmental delays, and typical development. *J. Child Psychol. Psychiatry* 47, 591–601. doi: 10.1111/j.1469-7610.2005.01546.x

Baron-Cohen, S. (1995). *Mindblindness: An Essay on Autism and Theory of Mind*. Cambridge, MA: MIT Press.

Benevides, T. W., and Lane, S. J. (2013). A review of cardiac autonomic measures: considerations for examination of physiological response in children with autism spectrum disorder. *J. Autism Dev. Disord.* 45, 560–575. doi: 10.1007/s10803-013-1971-z

Ben-Sasson, A., Hen, L., Fluss, R., Cermak, S. A., Engel-Yeger, B., and Gal, E. (2009). A meta-analysis of sensory modulation symptoms in individuals with autism spectrum disorders. *J. Autism Dev. Disord.* 39, 1–11. doi: 10.1007/s10803-008-0593-3

Chamberlain, P. D., Rodgers, J., Crowley, M. J., White, S. E., Freeston, M. H., and South, M. (2013). A potentiated startle study of uncertainty and contextual anxiety in adolescents diagnosed with autism spectrum disorder. *Mol. Autism* 4, 31. doi: 10.1186/2040-2392-4-31

Chevallier, C., Kohls, G., Troiani, V., Brodkin, E. S., and Schultz, R. T. (2012). The social motivation theory of autism. *Trends Cogn. Sci.* 16, 231–239. doi: 10.1016/j.tics.2012.02.007

Corbett, B. A., Mendoza, S., Wegelin, J. A., Carmean, V., and Levine, S. (2008). Variable cortisol circadian rhythms in children with autism and anticipatory stress. *J. Psychiatry Neurosci.* 33, 227–234.

Corbett, B. A., Newsom, C., Key, A. P., Qualls, L. R., and Edmiston, E. K. (2014a). Examining the relationship between face processing and social interaction behavior in children with and without autism spectrum disorder. *J. Neurodev. Disord.* 6, 1. doi: 10.1186/1866-1955-6-35

Corbett, B. A., Schupp, C. W., and Lanni, K. E. (2012). Comparing biobehavioral profiles across two social stress paradigms in children with and without autism spectrum disorders. *Mol. Autism* 3, 13. doi: 10.1186/2040-2392-3-13

Corbett, B. A., Schupp, C. W., Levine, S., and Mendoza, S. (2009). Comparing cortisol, stress, and sensory sensitivity in children with autism. *Autism Res.* 2, 39–49. doi: 10.1002/aur.64

Corbett, B. A., Schupp, C. W., Simon, D., Ryan, N., and Mendoza, S. (2010). Elevated cortisol during play is associated with age and social engagement in children with autism. *Mol. Autism* 1, 13. doi: 10.1186/2040-2392-1-13

Corbett, B. A., Swain, D. M., Newsom, C., Wang, L., Song, Y., and Edgerton, D. (2014b). Biobehavioral profiles of arousal and social motivation in autism spectrum disorders. *J. Child Psychol. Psychiatry* 55, 924–934. doi: 10.1111/jcpp.12184

Dawson, G., Meltzoff, A. N., Osterling, J., Rinaldi, J., and Brown, E. (1998). Children with autism fail to orient to naturally occurring social stimuli. *J. Autism Dev. Disord.* 28, 479–485. doi: 10.1023/A:1026043926488

Dunn, W. (1999). *Short Sensory Profile*. San Antonio, TX: Psychological Corporation.

Dunn, W. (2001). The sensations of everyday life: empirical, theoretical, and pragmatic considerations. *Am. J. Occup. Ther.* 55, 608–620. doi: 10.5014/ajot.55.6.608

Gabriels, R. L., Agnew, J. A., Miller, L. J., Gralla, J., Pan, Z., Goldson, E., et al. (2008). Is there a relationship between restricted, repetitive, stereotyped behaviors and interests and abnormal sensory response in children with autism spectrum disorders? *Res. Autism Spectr. Disord.* 2, 660–670. doi: 10.1016/j.rasd.2008.02.002

Gal, E., Dyck, M. J., and Passmore, A. (2010). Relationships between stereotyped movements and sensory processing disorders in children with and without developmental or sensory disorders. *Am. J. Occup. Ther.* 64, 453–461. doi: 10.5014/ajot.2010.09075

Green, S. A., Ben-Sasson, A., Soto, T. W., and Carter, A. S. (2012). Anxiety and sensory over-responsivity in toddlers with autism spectrum disorders: bidirectional effects across time. *J. Autism Dev. Disord.* 42, 1112–1119. doi: 10.1007/s10803-011-1361-3

Groden, J., Diller, A., Bausman, M., Velicer, W., Norman, G., and Cautela, J. (2001). The development of a stress survey schedule for persons with autism and other developmental disabilities. *J. Autism Dev. Disord.* 31, 207–217. doi: 10.1023/A:1010755300436

Hayes, A. F. (2013). *Introduction to Mediation, Moderation, and Conditional Process Analysis*. New York, NY: Guilford Press.

Herman, J. P., and Cullinan, W. E. (1997). Neurocircuitry of stress: central control of the hypothalamo-pituitary-adrenocortical axis. *Trends Neurosci.* 20, 78–84. doi: 10.1016/S0166-2236(96)10069-2

Humphrey, N., and Symes, W. (2011). Peer interaction patterns among adolescents with autistic spectrum disorders (ASDs) in mainstream school settings. *Autism* 15, 397–419. doi: 10.1177/1362361310387804

IBM Corp. (2013). *IBM SPSS Statistics for Windows, Version 22.0*. Armonk, NY: IBM Corp.

Kennedy, D. P., and Adolphs, R. (2014). Violations of personal space by individuals with autism spectrum disorder. *PLoS ONE* 9:e103369. doi: 10.1371/journal.pone.0103369

Kern, J. K., Trivedi, M. H., Garver, C. R., Grannemann, B. D., Andrews, A. A., Savla, J. S., et al. (2006). The pattern of sensory processing abnormalities in autism. *Autism* 10, 480–494. doi: 10.1177/1362361306066564

Kirschbaum, C., and Hellhammer, D. H. (1989). Salivary cortisol in psychobiological research: an overview. *Neuropsychobiology* 22, 150–169. doi: 10.1159/000118611

Klin, A., Jones, W., Schultz, R., and Volkmar, F. (2003). The enactive mind, or from actions to cognition: lessons from autism. *Philos. Trans. R. Soc. Lond. B Biol. Sci.* 358, 345–360. doi: 10.1098/rstb.2002.1202

Knott, F., Dunlop, A.-W., and Mackay, T. (2006). Living with ASD: how do children and their parents assess their difficulties with social interaction and understanding? *Autism* 10, 609–617. doi: 10.1177/1362361306068510

Lane, A. E., Dennis, S. J., and Geraghty, M. E. (2011). Brief report: further evidence of sensory subtypes in autism. *J. Autism Dev. Disord.* 41, 826–831. doi: 10.1007/s10803-010-1103-y

Lane, A. E., Molloy, C. A., and Bishop, S. L. (2014). Classification of children with autism spectrum disorder by sensory subtype: a case for sensory-based phenotypes. *Autism Res.* 7, 322–333. doi: 10.1002/aur.1368

Lidstone, J., Uljarević, M., Sullivan, J., Rodgers, J., McConachie, H., Freeston, M., et al. (2014). Relations among restricted and repetitive behaviors, anxiety and sensory features in children with autism spectrum disorders. *Res. Autism Spectr. Disord.* 8, 82–92. doi: 10.1016/j.rasd.2013.10.001

Lopata, C., Volker, M. A., Putnam, S. K., Thomeer, M. L., and Nida, R. E. (2008). Effect of social familiarity on salivary cortisol and self-reports of social anxiety and stress in children with high functioning autism spectrum disorders. *J. Autism Dev. Disord.* 38, 1866–1877. doi: 10.1007/s10803-008-0575-5

Lord, C., Risi, S., Lambrecht, L., Cook, E. H. Jr., Leventhal, B. L., DiLavore, P. C., et al. (2000). The Autism diagnostic observation schedule—generic: a standard measure of social and communication deficits associated with the spectrum of autism. *J. Autism Dev. Disord.* 30, 205–223. doi: 10.1023/A:1005592401947

Lough, E., Hanley, M., Rodgers, J., South, M., Kirk, H., Kennedy, D. P., et al. (2015). Violations of personal space in young people with autism spectrum disorders and williams syndrome: insights from the social responsiveness scale. *J. Autism Dev. Disord.* 45, 4101–4108. doi: 10.1007/s10803-015-2536-0

Lyons, D., Mason, W. A., and Mendoza, S. P. (1990). Beyond the ethogram: transactional analysis of behavior in primate social interchanges. *Am. J. Primatol.* 20, 209.

Lyons, D. M., Mendoza, S. P., and Mason, W. A. (1992). Sexual segregation in squirrel monkeys (*Saimiri sciureus*): a transactional analysis of adult social dynamics. *J. Comp. Psychol.* 106, 323–330. doi: 10.1037/0735-7036.106.4.323

Mason, W. A., Long, D. D., and Mendoza, S. P. (1993). "Temperament and mother–infant conflict in macaques: a transactional analysis," in *Primate Social Conflict*, ed W. M. S. Mendoza (Albany, NY: State University of New York Press), 205–227.

Mendoza, S. P., and Mason, W. A. (1989). Behavioral and endocrine consequences of heterosexual pair formation in squirrel monkeys. *Physiol. Behav.* 46, 597–603. doi: 10.1016/0031-9384(89)90338-7

Noldus (2008). *The Observer XT*. Vol. 10.5. Wageningen: Noldus Information Technology.

Osterling, J. A., Dawson, G., and Munson, J. A. (2002). Early recognition of 1-year-old infants with autism spectrum disorder versus mental retardation. *Dev. Psychopathol.* 14, 239–251. doi: 10.1017/S0954579402002031

Perry, A., Levy-Gigi, E., Richter-Levin, G., and Shamay-Tsoory, S. G. (2015). Interpersonal distance and social anxiety in autistic spectrum disorders: a behavioral and ERP study. *Soc. Neurosci.* 10, 354–365. doi: 10.1080/17470919.2015.1010740

Perry, A., Nichiporuk, N., and Knight, R. T. (2016). Where does one stand: a biological account of preferred interpersonal distance. *Soc. Cogn. Affect. Neurosci.* 11, 317–326. doi: 10.1093/scan/nsv115

Petersen, A. C., Crockett, L., Richards, M., and Boxer, A. (1988). A self-report measure of pubertal status: reliability, validity, and initial norms. *J. Youth Adolescence* 17, 117–133. doi: 10.1007/BF01537962

Rogers, S. J., Hepburn, S., and Wehner, E. (2003). Parent reports of sensory symptoms in toddlers with autism and those with other developmental disorders. *J. Autism Dev. Disord.* 33, 631–642. doi: 10.1023/B:JADD.0000006000.38991.a7

Schupp, C. W., Simon, D., and Corbett, B. A. (2013). Cortisol responsivity differences in children with autism spectrum disorders during free and cooperative play. *J. Autism Dev. Disord.* 43, 2405–2417. doi: 10.1007/s10803-013-1790-2

Skewes, J. C., and Gebauer, L. (2016). Brief report: suboptimal auditory localization in autism spectrum disorder: support for the bayesian account of sensory symptoms. *J. Autism Dev. Disord.* 46, 2539–2547. doi: 10.1007/s10803-016-2774-9

Tomchek, S. D., and Dunn, W. (2007). Sensory processing in children with and without autism: a comparative study using the short sensory profile. *Am. J. Occup. Ther.* 61, 190–200. doi: 10.5014/ajot.61.2.190

Uljarević, M., Lane, A., Kelly, A., and Leekam, S. (2016). Sensory subtypes and anxiety in older children and adolescents with autism spectrum disorder. *Autism Res.* doi: 10.1002/aur.1602. [Epub ahead of print].

Wechsler, D. (1999). *Wechsler Abbreviated Scale of Intelligence*. San Antonio, TX: Psychological Corporation.

Wigham, S., Rodgers, J., South, M., McConachie, H., and Freeston, M. (2015). The interplay between sensory processing abnormalities, intolerance of uncertainty, anxiety and restricted and repetitive behaviours in autism spectrum disorder. *J. Autism Dev. Disord.* 45, 943–952. doi: 10.1007/s10803-014-2248-x

8

ANOCVA in R: A Software to Compare Clusters between Groups and its Application to the Study of Autism Spectrum Disorder

*Maciel C. Vidal[1], João R. Sato[2], Joana B. Balardin[3], Daniel Y. Takahashi[4] and André Fujita[1]**

[1] *Department of Computer Science, Institute of Mathematics and Statistics, University of São Paulo, São Paulo, Brazil,* [2] *Center of Mathematics, Computation, and Cognition, Universidade Federal do ABC, Santo André, Brazil,* [3] *Hospital Israelita Albert Einstein, São Paulo, Brazil,* [4] *Deparment of Psychology and Princeton Neuroscience Institute, Princeton University, Princeton, NJ, USA*

Edited by:
Alessandro Grecucci, University of Trento, Italy

Reviewed by:
Munis Dundar, Erciyes University, Turkey
Baxter P. Rogers, Vanderbilt University, USA
Sydney Moirangthem, National Institute of Mental Health and Neurosciences, India

***Correspondence:**
André Fujita
fujita@ime.usp.br

Understanding how brain activities cluster can help in the diagnosis of neuropsychological disorders. Thus, it is important to be able to identify alterations in the clustering structure of functional brain networks. Here, we provide an R implementation of Analysis of Cluster Variability (ANOCVA), which statistically tests (1) whether a set of brain regions of interest (ROI) are equally clustered between two or more populations and (2) whether the contribution of each ROI to the differences in clustering is significant. To illustrate the usefulness of our method and software, we apply the R package in a large functional magnetic resonance imaging (fMRI) dataset composed of 896 individuals (529 controls and 285 diagnosed with ASD—autism spectrum disorder) collected by the ABIDE (The Autism Brain Imaging Data Exchange) Consortium. Our analysis show that the clustering structure of controls and ASD subjects are different ($p < 0.001$) and that specific brain regions distributed in the frontotemporal, sensorimotor, visual, cerebellar, and brainstem systems significantly contributed ($p < 0.05$) to this differential clustering. These findings suggest an atypical organization of domain-specific function brain modules in ASD.

Keywords: Analysis of Cluster Variability, silhouette statistic, functional brain network, ABIDE, fMRI

INTRODUCTION

The brain activity is organized in clusters/modules that have different roles in our behavior (Tononi et al., 1999). Alterations in the clustering pattern can be associated with neurologic disorders (Grossberg, 2000; Sato et al., 2016). Thus, it is important to systematically discriminate the clustering structures among different populations. This leads to the problem of how to statistically test the equality of clustering structures of two or more populations and how to identify the features that contribute to the differential clustering structure. These statistical problems were recently solved for a large class of clustering algorithms by using the Analysis of Cluster Variability—ANOCVA (Fujita et al., 2014a).

Here, we provide an implementation of ANOCVA in R for a better dissemination of this technique in the scientific community. ANOCVA was designed to test whether the clustering structures of several populations are equal. Briefly, ANOCVA uses the silhouette statistic

(Rousseeuw, 1987) as a measure of variability of the clustering structure of each population and then compares the variability among populations using an idea similar to the classical analysis of variance (ANOVA). To calculate the statistical significance value, we use a bootstrap procedure that was previously shown to control the type I error.

We illustrate the step-by-step application of ANOCVA by analyzing a large functional magnetic resonance imaging (fMRI) data acquired under a resting-state protocol (ABIDE—The Autism Brain Imaging Data Exchange Consortium) composed of 529 controls and 285 patients diagnosed with autism. Subjects with Autism Spectrum Disorders (ASD) have significant differences in the resting state functional connectivity when compared to healthy subjects (for review, see Kana et al., 2011), suggesting that ASD is as a neural systems disorder with disruptions in several distributed neurocognitive networks of brain regions (Ecker et al., 2015). However, most studies describe integration (Washington et al., 2014; Sporns and Betzel, 2016) and segregation (Assaf et al., 2013) as separate processes. Instead, in this study we consider both processes simultaneously using the idea of clusters, where structures within are integrated and structures between are segregated.

MATERIALS AND METHODS

To formalize ANOCVA, we will first describe the silhouette statistic to define "clustering variability" and then we introduce the ANOCVA. Finally, we describe its implementation and application to ABIDE dataset.

The Silhouette Statistic

The silhouette statistic is a measure of how well an item (regions of interest—ROI in fMRI data) is clustered given a clustering algorithm. In other words, it can also be interpreted as a measure of clustering variability (Rousseeuw, 1987). Formally, let $\chi = \{x_1, .., x_N\}$ be the N ROIs of one subject that are clustered into $C = \{C_1, \ldots, C_r\}$ clusters by a clustering algorithm. Denote the dissimilarity between ROIs x and y by $d(x, y)$. Let $|C|$ be the number of ROIs of C. Then, define $d(x, C) = \frac{1}{|C|} \sum_{y \in C} d(x, y)$ as the average dissimilarity of x to all ROIs of cluster C. Denote $D_q \in C$ as the cluster to which x_q has been assigned by the clustering algorithm. Define $a_q = d(x_q, D_q)$ (the within dissimilarity of x_q) and $b_q = \min_{C_p \neq D_q} d(x_q, C_p)$ (the smallest between dissimilarity of x_q), for $q = 1, \ldots, N$. Then, we can measure how well each ROI x_q has been clustered by analyzing the silhouette statistic given by

$$s_q = \begin{cases} \frac{b_q - a_q}{\max\{b_q, a_q\}}, & if\ |D_q| > 1, \\ 0, & if\ |D_q| = 1. \end{cases}$$

The silhouette statistic s_q assumes values from -1 to $+1$ and its interpretation given by Rousseeuw (1987) is as follows. If $s_q \approx 1$, it means $a_q \ll b_q$, i.e., the ROI x_q has been assigned to an appropriate cluster because the second-best choice cluster is not as close as the actual cluster. If $s_q \approx 0$, then $a_q \approx b_q$. In this case, it is not clear whether ROI x_q should have been assigned to the actual cluster or to the second-best choice cluster because it is equally far away from both. If $s_q \approx -1$, then $a_q \gg b_q$. In other words, the ROI x_q should be assigned to the second-best choice cluster because it lies much closer to it than to the actual cluster. In summary, s_q is a measure of how well the clustering algorithm labeled ROI x_q.

ANOCVA

In the present section, we briefly describe the ANOCVA. For further details, refer to Fujita et al. (2014a). Let $T_1, T_2, \ldots, T_k$ be k types of populations (e.g., controls and ASD). For the j th population, n_j subjects are collected, for $j = 1, \ldots, k$. The items (e.g., ROIs) of the i th subject taken from the j th population are represented by the matrix $X_{i,j} = (x_{i,j,1}, \ldots, x_{i,j,N})$, where each ROI $x_{i,j,q}$ $(q = 1, .., N)$ is a vector containing a time series (the blood-oxygen-level dependent signal).

First, define the $(N \times N)$ matrix of dissimilarities among ROIs of each matrix $X_{i,j}$ by $A_{i,j} = \{d(x_{i,j,q}, x_{i,j,q'})\}$, for $i = 1, \ldots, n_j$, $j = 1, \ldots, k$. Second, let $n = \sum_{j=1}^{k} n_j$, then define the following average matrices of dissimilarities:

$$\bar{A}_j = \frac{1}{n_j} \sum_{i=1}^{n_j} A_{i,j} = \frac{1}{n_j} \sum_{i=1}^{n_j} \{d(x_{i,j,q}, x_{i,j,q'})\} \text{ and}$$

$$\bar{\bar{A}} = \frac{1}{n} \sum_{j=1}^{k} n_j \bar{A}_j, \text{ where } q, q' = 1, \ldots, N.$$

Next, apply a clustering algorithm on the matrix of dissimilarities $\bar{\bar{A}}$, to determine the clustering labels $l_{\bar{\bar{A}}}$. Finally, compute the following silhouette statistics: $s_q^{(\bar{\bar{A}}, l_{\bar{\bar{A}}})}$ (the silhouette statistic of the qth ROI based on the dissimilarity matrix $\bar{\bar{A}}$ and the labeling $l_{\bar{\bar{A}}}$) and $s_q^{(\bar{A}_j, l_{\bar{\bar{A}}})}$ (the silhouette statistic of the qth ROI based on the dissimilarity matrix $\bar{A}_j$ and the labeling $l_{\bar{\bar{A}}}$), for $q = 1, \ldots, N$. The statistical test consists in verifying whether all k populations are equally clustered (present the same clustering structure) or if at least one is clustered in a different manner. If the ROIs from all populations $T_1, \ldots, T_k$ are equally clustered, then the quantities $s_q^{(\bar{\bar{A}}, l_{\bar{\bar{A}}})}$ and $s_q^{(\bar{A}_j, l_{\bar{\bar{A}}})}$ must be close for all $j = 1, \ldots, k$ and $q = 1, \ldots, N$.

Given a clustering algorithm and a distance metric, define the following vectors:

$$S = \left(s_1^{(\bar{\bar{A}}, l_{\bar{\bar{A}}})}, \ldots, s_N^{(\bar{\bar{A}}, l_{\bar{\bar{A}}})}\right)^{\mathrm{T}} \text{ and } S_j = \left(s_1^{(\bar{A}_j, l_{\bar{\bar{A}}})}, \ldots, s_N^{(\bar{A}_j, l_{\bar{\bar{A}}})}\right)^{\mathrm{T}}.$$

Define $\delta S_j = S - S_j$. We will use the statistic $\Delta S = \sum_{j=1}^{k} \delta S_j^{\mathrm{T}} \delta S_j$ to build the test statistic. Notice that under the null hypothesis, all N ROIs are equally clustered along the k populations, i.e., $s_q^{(\bar{\bar{A}}, l_{\bar{\bar{A}}})} \approx s_{q'}^{(\bar{\bar{A}}, l_{\bar{\bar{A}}})}$ for all $q = 1, \ldots, N$ and thus, we expect small ΔS. On the other hand, large ΔS suggests a rejection of the null hypothesis.

To test the contribution of each ROI for the differential clustering, define $\delta s_q = s_q^{(\bar{\bar{A}}, l_{\bar{\bar{A}}})} - \frac{1}{k} \sum_{j=1}^{k} s_q^{(\bar{A}_j, l_{\bar{\bar{A}}})}$, for $q = 1, \ldots, N$.

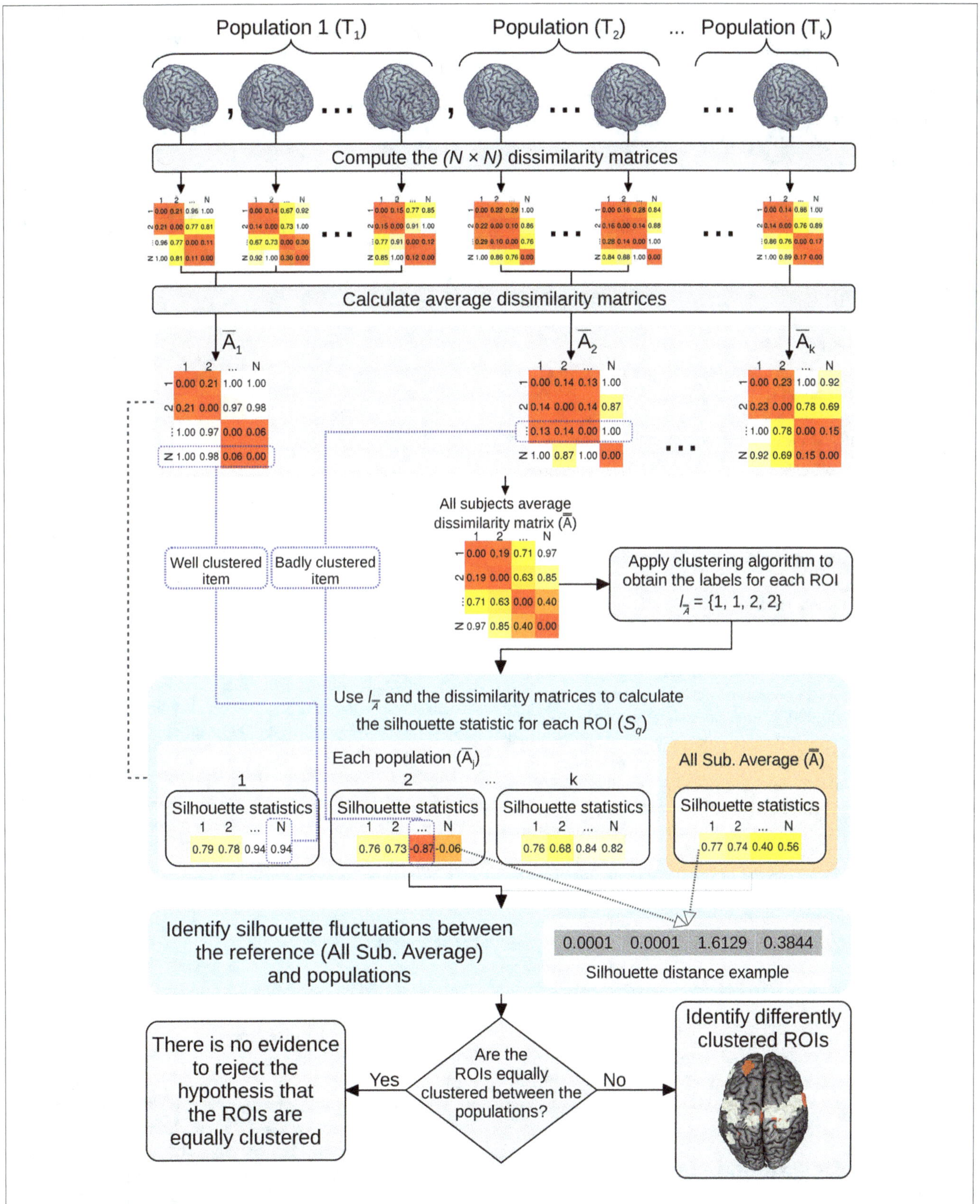

FIGURE 1 | Pipeline schema of the ANOCVA analysis.

This test consists in verifying whether the qth ROI ($q = 1,\ldots, N$) is equally clustered among populations. We will use the statistic $\Delta s_q = \delta s_q^2$, for $q = 1,\ldots,N$ to build the test statistic. Under the null hypothesis, we expect small Δs_q. On the other hand, large Δs_q suggests a rejection of the null hypothesis.

To compute distributions of ΔS and Δs_q under the null hypothesis, Fujita et al. (2014a) proposed a bootstrap procedure described as follows:

1. Resample with replacement n_j subjects from the entire dataset $\{T_1, T_2,\ldots, T_k\}$ in order to construct bootstrap samples T_j^*, for $j = 1,\ldots,k$.
2. Calculate $\bar{A}_j^*$, $\bar{\bar{A}}^*$, $s_q^{\left(\bar{A},l=_{A}\right)*}$ and $s_q^{\left(\bar{A},l=_{A}\right)*}$, for $q = 1,\ldots,N$, using the bootstrap samples T_j^*.
3. Calculate $\widehat{\Delta S}^*$ and $\widehat{\Delta s_q}^*$.
4. Repeat steps 1 to 3 until the desired number of bootstrap replications is obtained.
5. The p-values from the bootstrap tests based on the observed statistics ΔS and Δs_q are the fraction of replicates of $\widehat{\Delta S}^*$ and $\widehat{\Delta s_q}^*$ on the bootstrap dataset T_j^*, respectively, that are at least as large as the observed statistics on the original dataset.

R Implementation

ANOCVA is implemented in R and is freely available at the R project website[1] (package "anocva").

This implementation requires as input, the functional brain networks (ROIs dissimilarity matrices), a vector of labels describing which individual belongs to which group, the number of clusters, and the number of bootstrap samples.

ANOCVA uses the spectral clustering algorithm to cluster the ROIs (Ng et al., 2002). Internal to the spectral clustering algorithm, we use the k -medoids procedure instead of the usual k -means because the former is more robust to outliers than the latter (Aggarwal and Reddy, 2013). If the number of clusters is not known a priori, the ANOCVA R package provides the option to estimate it by using the silhouette or the slope statistic (Fujita et al., 2014b). The slope criterion is the difference of the silhouette statistic as a function of the number of clusters. The difference between the slope and silhouette is the fact that by maximizing the silhouette statistic as described by Rousseeuw (1987) the number of clusters is estimated correctly only when the within-cluster variances are equal. The slope criterion is more robust than the silhouette when the within-cluster variances are unequal.

The output consists in one p-value, which represents whether there is at least one group that clusters in a different manner and a vector of p-values representing which ROI is differentially clustered among groups. The entire ANOCVA analysis pipeline can be visualized in **Figure 1**.

ABIDE Data Description and Pre-processing

The ABIDE Consortium dataset is a large resting state fMRI dataset that includes controls and ASD subjects. It can be downloaded from the ABIDE website[2]. This data was collected in 17 sites that compose the ABIDE Consortium. Data collection was conducted with local internal review board approval, and also in accordance with local internal review board protocols. For further details regarding this dataset, refer to the ABIDE Consortium website.

Data pre-processing and network construction (dissimilarity matrices) were carried out as our previous works (Sato et al., 2015, 2016) using the ABIDE dataset. The final dataset used here is composed of 529 controls (430 males, mean age ± standard deviation of 17.47 ± 7.81 years) and 285 autistic patients (255 males, 17.53 ± 7.13 years).

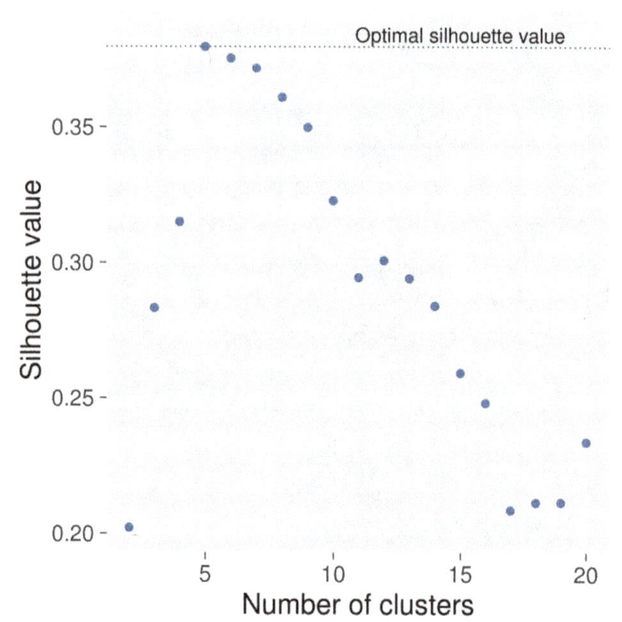

FIGURE 2 | Selection of the number of clusters. The number of clusters was selected by using the silhouette criterion. The number of clusters that presented the highest silhouette statistic is five. In other words, the silhouette criterion suggests that this dataset can be split into five sub-networks.

RESULTS

The problem that we want to solve is the following. Given k populations $T_1, T_2,\ldots, T_k$ where each population T_j ($j = 1,\ldots, k$) is composed of n_j subjects, and each subject has N items that are clustered, we would like to verify whether the clustering structures of the brain networks of the k populations are equal and, if not, which ROIs are differently clustered. In our case, we have $k = 2$ populations with T_1 and T_2 as controls and ASD, respectively. The number of subjects in each population is $n_1 = 529$ and $n_2 = 285$, for T_1 and T_2, respectively. The number of ROIs (items) to be clustered is $N = 316$. Since head movement during magnetic resonance scanning may affect statistical analysis, ANOCVA was

[1] www.r-project.org

[2] http://fcon_1000.projects.nitrc.org/indi/abide/

applied to both "scrubbed" and "not scrubbed" data (Power et al., 2012) with the number of bootstrap samples set to 1000.

The first step in ANOCVA analysis is the construction of the average dissimilarity matrix $\bar{\bar{A}}$ and its clustering. The estimated number of clusters by the silhouette criterion was five as depicted in **Figure 2**. Notice that the highest silhouette statistic was obtained when the number of clusters is five. The sub-networks obtained by applying the spectral clustering on the dissimilarity matrix $\bar{\bar{A}}$ can be visualized in **Figure 3** where each color represents one sub-network (cluster).

Then, ANOCVA calculates the silhouette statistic for each ROI by using the labels obtained by clustering the dissimilarity matrix $\bar{\bar{A}}$ and performs the test. We verified that in fact the entire clustering structure of subjects diagnosed with ASD differs from controls ($p < 0.001$). Next, we tested each ROI to identify which ones significantly contribute to the differential clustering between controls and subjects diagnosed with ASD. ROIs that presented a difference in $p > 5\%$ between "scrubbed" and "not scrubbed" datasets were excluded for subsequent analysis. Remaining p-values were corrected for multiple comparisons by the Bonferroni method. **Figure 4** illustrates the statistically significant ROIs at a p-value threshold of 0.05 after Bonferroni correction. The highlighted regions include portions of the cerebellum and middle frontal gyrus, pre- and post-central gyri, inferior temporal gyrus, and lateral occipital cortex.

DISCUSSION

In the current study, we combined spectral clustering analysis with ANOCVA implemented in R to investigate which brain regions are clustered in a different way between controls and ASD groups. Our results suggest that several regions distributed across different neurocognitive systems significantly contributed to the different clustering network structure observed in ASD. First we demonstrated that the spectral clustering method yielded partitions that were well-characterized as functional modules of the brain that have been consistently identified in previous studies using different approaches (Damoiseaux et al., 2006; Power et al., 2011), including the fronto-temporal, sensorimotor, visual, and cerebellar systems. This is consistent with the hypothesis that the spectral clustering algorithm groups anatomically contiguous and also spatially distributed areas with common brain functionalities in the same cluster. Then, using ANOCVA we showed that the superior division of the lateral parietal cortex, precentral, and postcentral gyri, anterior dorsal middle frontal gyrus, and a medial portion of the cerebellum and of the brainstem have a distinct cluster organization between ASD and controls. All these brain regions have been previously identified as presenting ASD-related differences in studies using functional MRI. For example, the recruitment of portions of the precentral and postcentral gyri as well as the cerebellum across sensorimotor tasks are atypical in ASD, and may underlie deficits in fine motor sequencing and visual motor learning observed in autistic individuals (Müller et al., 2001; Mostofsky et al., 2009).

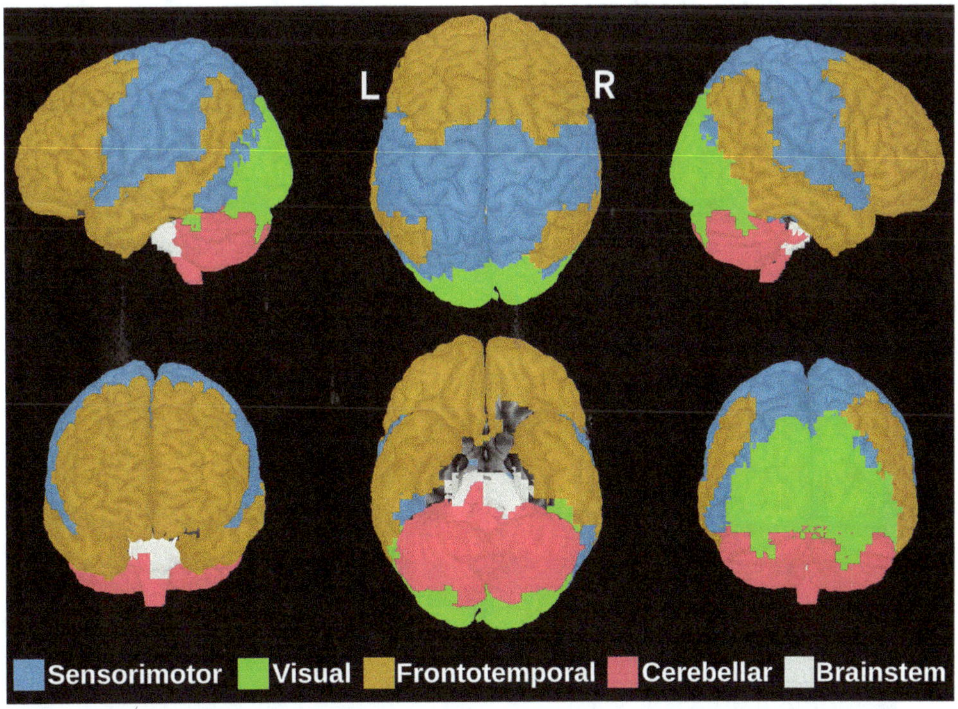

FIGURE 3 | The five brain sub-networks obtained by the spectral clustering algorithm on the dissimilarity matrix $\bar{\bar{A}}$. Each color represents one functional sub-network: sensorimotor (blue), visual (green), frontotemporal (orange), cerebellar (pink), and brainstem (white). R, right; L, Left.

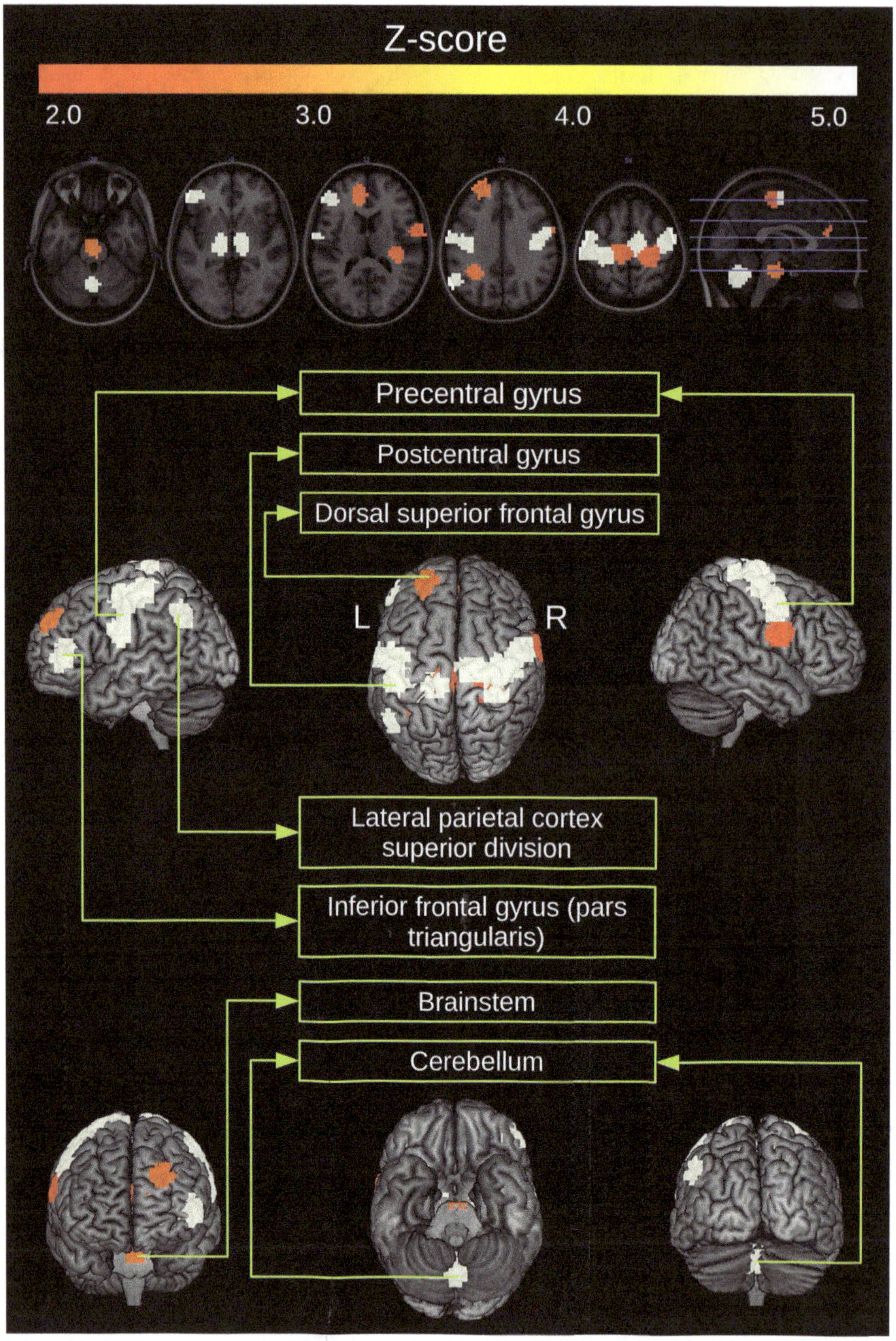

FIGURE 4 | ROIs clustered in a different manner between controls and ASD. ROIs that present a *p*-value (obtained by ANOCVA) lower than 5% after Bonferroni correction were converted to z-scores and highlighted.

Interestingly, these regions have also been implicated in cognitive process crucial for interpersonal interactions such as theory-of-mind (Martineau et al., 2010; Wang et al., 2014). This suggests that these areas are involved in the social communication deficits that are a core clinical feature of ASD. Moreover, the lateral parietal cortex is an important node of the default-mode network, and abnormalities in the connectivity between nodes of this network have been widely investigated in ASD (Kennedy and

Courchesne, 2008; Assaf et al., 2010; Weng et al., 2010) giving its associations with social cognition (Buckner et al., 2008). The identification of these regions by our study therefore confirms that they are key brain structures in ASD that may have a role in the development of sub-networks organization in this population.

Head motion is one of the most challenging obstacles in functional connectivity studies involving clinical populations, which usually present high levels of movement. Our attempt to handle this problem was to apply the scrubbing method proposed by Power et al. (2012), which discards scans acquired under excessive head motion. However, although this approach may reduce the influence of movement artifacts, they may still be present in the scrubbed data. Thus, we opted for a more conservative approach, which consisted in excluding the regions where the p-values were more sensitive to scrubbing. We assumed that the analyses of these regions were more vulnerable to artifacts and thus they were removed. This approach is also helpful to reduce the number of multiple comparisons, by excluding the less reliable tests. Another important limitation to be mentioned is that the ABIDE data is multicentric with heterogeneous acquisition parameters across sites. We minimized the site effect by removing it in the pre-processing stage of the data. Finally, all analyses are based on the CC400 atlas (Craddock et al., 2012), obtained by using a functional parcellation. Since other atlases are different on ROIs size, number of ROIs and spatial location, the parcellation choice is expected to influence our findings. However, this variability does not invalidate the results obtained with CC400 because the procedures adopted here are conservative (regarding type I error control). Finally, an important future question for the presented results is whether the contribution of these specific brain regions to a differential network clustering in ASD is static or may exhibit dynamic changes during rest (Hutchison et al., 2013).

AUTHOR CONTRIBUTIONS

MV, JS, DT, and AF designed the work. MV pre-processed and analyzed the data. JS and JB interpreted the results. All authors drafted the work, read, and approved the final version of the manuscript.

FUNDING

MV was supported by CAPES and CNPq Fellowships. JS was supported by State of São Paulo Research Foundation—FAPESP (#2013/10498-6). DT was partially supported by Pew Latin American Fellowship and Ciência sem Fronteiras Fellowship (CNPq #246778/2012-1). AF was partially supported by FAPESP (#2014/09576-5, #2013/01715-3, #2015/01587-0, #2016/13422-9, and #2013/03447-6), CNPq (#304020/2013-3 and #473063/2013-1), and NAP eScience—PRP—USP.

ACKNOWLEDGMENTS

The authors would like to thank the ABIDE Consortium for providing publicly available the fMRI database.

REFERENCES

Aggarwal, C. C., and Reddy C. K. (eds.). (2013). *Data Clustering: Algorithms and Applications*. Boca Raton, FL: CRC Press.

Assaf, M., Hyatt, C. J., Wong, C. G., Johnson, M. R., Schultz, R. T., Hendler, T., et al. (2013). Mentalizing and motivation neural function during social interactions in autism spectrum disorders. *Neuroimage Clin.* 3, 321–31. doi: 10.1016/j.nicl.2013.09.005

Assaf, M., Jagannathan, K., Calhoun, V. D., Miller, L., Stevens, M. C., Sahl, R., et al. (2010). Abnormal functional connectivity of default mode subnetworks in autism spectrum disorder patients. *NeuroImage* 53, 247–256. doi: 10.1016/j.neuroimage.2010.05.067

Buckner, R. L., Andrews-Hanna, J. R., Schacter, D. L. (2008). The brain's default network: anatomy, function, and relevance to disease. *Ann. N. Y. Acad. Sci.* 1124, 1–38. doi: 10.1196/annals.1440.011

Craddock, R. C., James, G. A., Holtzheimer, P. E., Hu, X. P., Mayberg, H. S. (2012). A whole brain fMRI Atlas generated via spatial constrained spectral clustering. *Hum. Brain Mapp.* 33, 1914–1928. doi: 10.1002/hbm.21333

Damoiseaux, J. S., Rombouts, S. A., Barkhof, F., Scheltens, P., Stam, C. J., Smith, S. M., et al. (2006). Consistent resting-state networks across healthy subjects. *Proc. Natl. Acad. Sci. U.S.A.* 103, 13848–13853. doi: 10.1073/pnas.0601417103

Ecker, C., Bookheimer, S. Y., Murphy, D. G. (2015). Neuroimaging in autism spectrum disorder: brain structure and function across the lifespan. *Lancet Neurol.* 14, 1121–1134. doi: 10.1016/S1474-4422(15)00050-2

Fujita, A., Takahashi, D. Y., Patriota, A. G. (2014b). A non-parametric method to estimate the number of clusters. *Comput. Stat. Data Anal.* 73, 27–39. doi: 10.1016/j.csda.2013.11.012

Fujita, A., Takahashi, D. Y., Patriota, A. G., Sato, J. R. (2014a). A non-parametric statistical test to compare clusters with applications in functional magnetic resonance imaging data. *Stat. Med.* 33, 4949–4962.

Grossberg, S. (2000). The complementary brain: unifying brain dynamics and modularity. *Trends Cogn. Sci.* 4, 233–246. doi: 10.1016/S1364-6613(00)01464-9

Hutchison, R. M., Womelsdorf, T., Allen, E. A., Bandettini, P. A., Calhoun, V. D., Corbetta, M., et al. (2013). Dynamic functional connectivity: promise, issues, and interpretations. *NeuroImage* 80, 360–378. doi: 10.1016/j.neuroimage.2013.05.079

Kana, R. K., Libero, L. E., Moore, M. S. (2011). Disrupted cortical connectivity theory as an explanatory model for autism spectrum disorders. *Phys. Life Rev.* 8, 410–437. doi: 10.1016/j.plrev.2011.10.001

Kennedy, D. P., and Courchesne, E. (2008). Functional abnormalities of the default network during self- and other-reflection in autism. *Soc. Cogn. Affect. Neurosci.* 3, 177–190. doi: 10.1093/scan/nsn011

Martineau, J., Andersson, F., Barthélémy, C., Cottier, J. P., and Destrieux, C. (2010). Atypical activation of the mirror neuron system during perception of hand motion in autism. *Brain Res.* 1320, 168–75. doi: 10.1016/j.brainres.2010.01.035

Mostofsky, S. H., Powell, S. K., Simmonds, D. J., Goldberg, M. C., Caffo, B., and Pekar, J. J. (2009). Decreased connectivity and cerebellar activity in autism during motor task performance. *Brain* 132, 2413–2425. doi: 10.1093/brain/awp088

Müller, R. A., Pierce, K., Ambrose, J. B., Allen, G., and Courchesne, E. (2001). Atypical patterns of cerebral motor activation in autism: a functional magnetic resonance study. *Biol. Psychiatry* 49, 665–676. doi: 10.1016/S0006-3223(00)01004-0

Ng, A., Jordan, M., and Weiss, Y. (2002). "On spectral clustering: analysis and an algorithm," in *Advances in Neural Information Processing Systems*, Vol. 14, eds T. Dietterich, S. Becker, and Z. Ghahramani (London: MIT Press), 849–856.

Power, J. D., Barnes, K. A., Snyder, A. Z., Schlaggar, B. L., Petersen, S. E. (2012). Spurious but systematic correlations in functional connectivity MRI networks arise from subject motion. *NeuroImage* 59, 2142–2154. doi: 10.1016/j.neuroimage.2011.10.018

Power, J. D., Cohen, A. L., Nelson, S. M., Wig, G. S., Barnes, K. A., Church, J. A., et al. (2011). Functional network organization of the human brain. *Neuron* 72, 665–78. doi: 10.1016/j.neuron.2011.09.006

Rousseeuw, P. (1987). Silhouettes: a graphical aid to the interpretation and validation of cluster analysis. *J. Comput. Appl. Math.* 20, 53–65. doi: 10.1016/0377-0427(87)90125-7

Sato, J. R., Balardin, J. B., Vidal, M. C., and Fujita, A. (2016). Identification of segregated regions in the functional brain connectome of autistic patients by a combination of fuzzy spectral clustering and entropy analysis. *J. Psychiatry Neurosci.* 41, 124–132. doi: 10.1503/jpn.140364

Sato, J. R., Vidal, M. C., de Siqueira Santos, S., Massirer, K. B., and Fujita, A. (2015). Complex networks measures in autism spectrum disorders. *IEEE/ACM Trans. Comput. Biol. Bioinform.* doi: 10.1109/TCBB.2015.2476787. [Epub ahead of print].

Sporns, O., and Betzel, R. (2016). Modular brain networks. *Annu. Rev. Psychol.* 67, 613–640. doi: 10.1146/annurev-psych-122414-033634

Tononi, G., Sporns, O., and Edelman, G. M. (1999). Measures of degeneracy and redundancy in biological networks. *Proc. Natl. Acad. Sci. U.S.A.* 96, 3257–3262. doi: 10.1073/pnas.96.6.3257

Wang, S. S., Kloth, A. D., and Badura, A. (2014). The cerebellum, sensitive periods, and autism. *Neuron* 83, 518–532. doi: 10.1016/j.neuron.2014.07.016

Washington, S. D., Gordon, E. M., Brar, J., Warburton, S., Sawyer, A. T., Wolfe, A., et al. (2014). Dysmaturation of the default mode network in autism. *Hum. Brain Mapp.* 35, 1284–1296. doi: 10.1002/hbm.22252

Weng, S. J., Wiggins, J. L., Peltier, S. J., Carrasco, M., Risi, S., Lord, C., et al. (2010). Alterations of resting state functional connectivity in the default network in adolescents with autism spectrum disorders. *Brain Res.* 1313, 202–14. doi: 10.1016/j.brainres.2009.11.057

9

Restriction Spectrum Imaging as a Potential Measure of Cortical Neurite Density in Autism

Ruth A. Carper[1], Jeffrey M. Treiber[2], Nathan S. White[3], Jiwandeep S. Kohli[1] and Ralph-Axel Müller[1]*

[1] Brain Development Imaging Laboratory, Department of Psychology, San Diego State University, San Diego, CA, USA, [2] School of Medicine, University of California San Diego, La Jolla, CA, USA, [3] Multimodal Imaging Laboratory, Department of Radiology, University of California San Diego, La Jolla, CA, USA

Edited by:
Roma Siugzdaite, Ghent University, Belgium

Reviewed by:
Pew-Thian Yap, University of North Carolina at Chapel Hill, USA
Ben Jeurissen, University of Antwerp, Belgium

****Correspondence:***
Ruth A. Carper
rcarper@mail.sdsu.edu

Autism postmortem studies have shown various cytoarchitectural anomalies in cortical and limbic areas including increased cell packing density, laminar disorganization, and narrowed minicolumns. However, there is little evidence on dendritic and axonal organization in ASD. Recent imaging techniques have the potential for non-invasive, *in vivo* studies of small-scale structure in the human brain, including gray matter. Here, Restriction Spectrum Imaging (RSI), a multi-shell diffusion-weighted imaging technique, was used to examine gray matter microstructure in 24 children with ASD (5 female) and 20 matched typically developing (TD) participants (2 female), ages 7–17 years. RSI extends the spherical deconvolution model to multiple length scales to characterize neurite density (ND) and organization. Measures were examined in 48 cortical regions of interest per hemisphere. To our knowledge, this is the first time that a multi-compartmental diffusion model has been applied to cortical gray matter in ASD. The ND measure detected robust age effects showing a significant positive relationship to age in all lobes except left temporal when groups were combined. Results were also suggestive of group differences (ASD<TD) in anterior cingulate, right superior temporal lobe and much of the parietal lobes, but these fell short of statistical significance. For MD, significant group differences (ASD>TD) in bilateral parietal regions as well as widespread age effects were detected. Our findings support the value of multi-shell diffusion imaging for assays of cortical gray matter. This approach has the potential to add to postmortem literature, examining intracortical organization, intracortical axonal content, myelination, or caliber. Robust age effects further support the validity of the ND metric for *in vivo* examination of gray matter microstructure in ASD and across development. While diffusion MRI does not approach the precision of histological studies, *in vivo* imaging measures of microstructure can complement postmortem studies, by allowing access to large sample sizes, a whole-brain field of view, longitudinal designs, and combination with behavioral and functional assays. This makes multi-shell diffusion imaging a promising technique for understanding the underlying cytoarchitecture of the disorder.

Keywords: autism, diffusion, MRI, cerebral cortex, neurite, DTI, gray matter, connectivity

INTRODUCTION

By general consensus, autism spectrum disorder (ASD) is a neurobiological disorder, likely of complex genetic, epigenetic, and possibly environmental origin, with brain development deviating from the typical path beginning in the prenatal period (Bailey et al., 1998; Palmen et al., 2004; Bauman and Kemper, 2005; Hutsler and and Casanova, 2016). Post-mortem studies are indispensible to our understanding of the underlying cellular anomalies. A reduction in the number of cerebellar Purkinje cells was among the earliest histologic reports (Bauman and Kemper, 1985), and a report of patchy neocortical thickening and laminar disorganization followed (Bailey et al., 1998). Increased cell packing density has been found in anterior cingulate, hippocampus and amygdala (Kemper and Bauman, 1998; Schumann and Amaral, 2006), and in prefrontal cortex by some (Bailey et al., 1998; Courchesne et al., 2011), but not all (Bauman and Kemper, 2005) research groups, while decreased density was found in fusiform gyrus (van Kooten et al., 2008). Increases in cortical cell packing density may relate to narrowed mini-columns in dorsolateral prefrontal cortex and superior temporal gyrus (Casanova et al., 2002, 2006; Buxhoeveden et al., 2006), suggesting a reduction in the amount of neuropil space surrounding neurons, which may reflect a decrease in inhibitory neurites in the affected regions. Ectopias (Bailey et al., 1998; Wegiel et al., 2010) and increased dendritic spine densities (Hutsler and Zhang, 2010) have also been reported. These neurostructural findings suggest altered rates of neurogenesis, delayed or reduced apoptosis or pruning or local failures of migration.

The postmortem literature is also quite variable, however, due to limitations which may be addressed through MRI and other *in vivo* imaging techniques. Some postmortem neuropathology is described as "patchy" at the individual case level (Bailey et al., 1998; Hutsler et al., 2007), and some findings are inconsistent across research groups or methods (Bailey et al., 1998; Bauman and Kemper, 2005; Hutsler et al., 2007). Furthermore, it is quite likely that histological differences that can be detected vary with the age of the case, particularly over the course of childhood, as indicated by *in vivo* MRI studies (Courchesne et al., 2001; Carper et al., 2002; Schumann et al., 2010; Hazlett et al., 2011). Such variability is difficult to overcome in postmortem studies, which are usually limited to small samples (averaging about 5 cases per study; Schumann and Nordahl, 2011) across wide age spans, with most cases in the adolescent or adult range. In addition, since histologic studies are extremely time consuming, studies are often limited to samples of only a few anatomical regions rather than whole-brain surveys. Longitudinal studies are furthermore impossible, limiting any developmental interpretations of post-mortem findings. *In vivo* imaging techniques may overcome many of these issues, allowing large sample sizes, whole-brain assessment, and longitudinal studies. However, examination of sub-voxel features such as dendritic or axonal organization and cortical cytoarchitecture has remained beyond the reach of *in vivo* imaging studies on ASD published to date.

The ability to describe cytoarchitecture and neuronal connectivity at the sub-millimeter level in living subjects would be a tremendous boon to research of neurodevelopmental and other neurologic disorders. Continuing improvements in system hardware and advances in acquisition techniques and sequence programming continue to push back the limits on spatial resolution. At the same time, new models for analysis of diffusion MRI allow examination of separate compartments within a single voxel. The combination of multi-shell diffusion acquisitions and multi-compartmental analysis approaches permits estimates of neurite (both axon and dendrite) content and organization within clinically manageable acquisition times (Jensen et al., 2005; Lu et al., 2006; Zhang et al., 2012; White et al., 2013). *Multi-shell* diffusion imaging (i.e., acquisition at multiple b-values and multiple diffusion directions), allows classification of diffusion at multiple length scales, disambiguating restricted (slow) diffusion from hindered (fast) diffusion. Inclusion of high b-values allows insight into micro-scale structures such as the organization and density of dendritic and axonal processes (neurites; Barazany et al., 2009; Raffelt et al., 2012; Assaf et al., 2013; Dell'Acqua et al., 2013). Here we used Restriction Spectrum Imaging (RSI, White et al., 2013), one such analysis approach, for *in vivo* examination of neurite organization within cerebral cortex in an ASD population.

RSI extends the spherical deconvolution model (Tournier et al., 2004) across these multiple length scales to characterize neurite density and organization at each imaged voxel. Analogous models have been used to examine white matter in one study of young adults with ASD (Lazar et al., 2014) but, to our knowledge, this is the first time that a multi-compartmental model has been applied to cortical gray matter in this population and the first time this age group has been addressed. We examined 48 cortical regions of interest per hemisphere in a population of 24 ASD and 20 TD children and adolescents.

MATERIALS AND METHODS

Participants

Participants ranged between 7 and 17 years of age and included both males and females. All potential ASD participants were administered the Autism Diagnostic Observation Schedule (ADOS, Lord et al., 2001), and their parents completed the Autism Diagnostic Interview-Revised (ADI-R, Rutter et al., 1995). Final diagnosis of Autism Spectrum Disorder was determined by a trained clinical psychologist according to DSM-V criteria (American Psychiatric Association, 2013) and with reference to ADOS and ADI-R scores. Children with known history of neurological disorders other than ASD (e.g., Fragile X syndrome, epilepsy) were excluded. Typically developing (TD) participants were recruited from the community, excluding anyone with a personal or family history of autism or a personal history of other neurologic or psychiatric conditions. Participants were also administered the Wechsler Abbreviated Scale of Intelligence (WASI, Wechsler, 1999), the Social Responsiveness Scale (SRS, Constantino and Gruber, 2005), and the Edinburgh Handedness Inventory (Oldfield, 1971). The study was approved by the University of California, San Diego, and San Diego State University Institutional Review Boards, with written informed consent and assent provided by all participants and caregivers.

MRI Data Acquisition and Preprocessing

MRI data were collected on a GE Discovery MR 750 3.0T system using an 8-channel head coil. Diffusion was measured with a multi-shell EPI sequence encoded for 45 non-collinear diffusion directions, (15 unique directions at each of 3 b-values: 500, 1500, and 4000 s/mm^2) and 2 at b = 0 s/mm^2 (in-plane resolution=1.875 × 1.875 mm, thickness = 2.5 mm, TR = 7 s, TE = 87.4 ms, flip = 90°). An anatomical T1-weighted fast spoiled gradient echo (FSPGR) scan (1 mm^3, TR = 8.108 s, TE = 3.172 ms, flip = 8°) was also acquired. Preprocessing of diffusion data was performed using in-house software and included eddy current correction (Zhuang et al., 2006), rigid body correction for motion with corresponding adjustments to the vector matrix, correction of susceptibility-induced field distortions (Holland et al., 2010), and correction for gradient non-linearities (Jovicich et al., 2006).

Quality Assessment and Motion Quantification

Multi-shell diffusion images were initially collected from 33 ASD and 24 TD children and adolescents. Average translation and rotation between acquisitions was calculated for each participant and considered for group matching. All image data, including each diffusion direction and b-value, were also visually inspected for motion-related signal dropout and other artifacts. The high b-value shell is particularly sensitive to motion-related dropout leading to a high exclusion rate. Seven subjects were excluded for excessive dropout (5 ASD, 2 TD) and an additional six for translation >1 mm or rotation >.01 radians (0.6 degrees, 4 ASD, 2 TD). Participants who were excluded did not differ significantly from those who were included with regard to age, IQ, or symptom severity (ADOS, ADI, SRS), for either subject group.

Restriction Spectrum Imaging

The RSI model is based on the compartmentalization of water in brain tissue. Diffusion of water molecules within brain tissue is constrained by cell membranes and other structures and thus ranges from *restricted diffusion,* as in intra-cellular spaces where water is (on time scales examined here) unable to diffuse beyond the cellular or axonal membrane, to *free diffusion,* found in fluid spaces where diffusion is unencumbered by barriers such as membranes or large proteins (Le Bihan, 2012). Between these extremes, diffusion is *hindered*, e.g., in extracellular spaces where water must follow a tortuous path to pass around cell membranes or other obstacles, but is not enclosed by such barriers (Assaf and Basser, 2005). RSI applies a mathematical model (White et al., 2013, 2014) to determine the proportion of a voxel (*volume fraction*) and signal (*signal fraction*) stemming from hindered, restricted, or free water compartments and the geometry of diffusion within each of these compartments (isotropic or anisotropic). The algorithm is described in detail in the original validation study (White et al., 2013) and represents an extension of the linear spherical deconvolution model (Tournier et al., 2004; Dell'Acqua et al., 2007; Jian and Vemuri, 2007; Kaden et al., 2007) to multiple diffusion length scales. In the current application we used five diffusion length scales. The volume fraction of anisotropic restricted diffusion (the shortest length scale examined) is believed to reflect the relative density of neuronal processes (neurite density, ND; White et al., 2013). ND was calculated for each voxel, as were the fractional anisotropy (FA) and mean diffusivity (MD) derived from the diffusion tensor. The ND volume fraction was standardized to a 1–1000 range; FA ranged 0–1.

Analysis of Anatomical Images and Extraction of ROIs

Preprocessing of anatomical T1 scans included correction for gradient non-linearities (Jovicich et al., 2006) and brain extraction (Smith, 2002). A gray matter mask was derived for each subject (Avants et al., 2011b) and affine registration was used to align each participant's T1 to the corresponding RSI image and to a sample-specific template in MNI space which had been derived using Advanced Normalization Tools (ANTS, Avants et al., 2010, 2011a). This allowed backward transformation of the Harvard-Oxford cortical atlas (http://fsl.fmrib.ox.ac.uk/fsl/fslwiki/Atlases) from MNI space to each individual's native diffusion space, providing 48 gyral-level ROIs for each hemisphere. Average ND, FA, and MD within gray matter were calculated for each of these ROIs and for the overall cerebral lobes (see Supplementary Table 1 for ROIs and their lobar designations).

RESULTS

The final sample included 24 ASD participants (5 female) aged 7–17 years, and 20 TD participants (2 female) aged 8–17 years. Groups were well matched for age, non-verbal IQ, and motion measures with all $p > 0.5$ (**Table 1**). The ASD group had lower verbal IQ as is frequently found in this socio-communicative disorder.

Linear regressions were performed on ND, FA, and MD measures separately for each lobe and hemisphere with age, group, group-by-age interaction, and a constant included in each model. The false discovery rate (FDR, Benjamini and Hochberg, 1995) was used to correct for multiple comparisons. All regressions performed on a single dependent variable (ND, FA, or MD) were included within a statistical family with the significance of each overall F-test included in that correction. Coefficients were corrected in a similar fashion.

Lobar Effects

Regressions were significant for ND in all lobes in the right hemisphere and for frontal, parietal, and occipital lobes in the left hemisphere (**Table 2**). The effects of age were significant and positive (increasing with age) in all of these. Rates ranged from 1.38 per year (left occipital lobe) to 4.11 per year (right frontal lobe) with the volume fraction standardized to a 1–1000 scale (**Figures 1A,B**). Group differences showed reduced ND in left parietal and left occipital lobes in ASD compared to TD participants (**Figure 2**) with moderate effect sizes ranging

TABLE 1 | Demographics.

	ASD (n = 24) mean ± *SD* [range]	TD (n = 20) mean ± *SD* [range]	p-value
Age (years)	13.41 ± 3.30 [7.43–17.98]	13.72 ± 2.91 [8.19–17.69]	0.693
WASI_VIQ	91.83 ± 17.25 [56–118]	104.45 ± 10.28 [73–126]	0.005
WASI_NVIQ	98.54 ± 19.33 [53–140]	101.65 ± 15.06 [62–123]	0.552
Avg. Translation	0.61 ± 0.11 [0.41–0.86]	0.62 ± 0.12 [0.33–0.85]	0.791
Avg. Rotation	0.003 ± 0.0021 [0.0012–0.0081]	0.0029 ± 0.0025 [0.0011–0.0098]	0.893
SRS Total	84.13 ± 8.53 [62–100]	43.15 ± 5.61 [35–52]	<0.001
ADOS-2 SA	12.26 ± 3.86 [6–20]		
ADOS-2 RRB	3.44 ± 2.33 [1–12]		
ADOS-2 Severity	8.32 ± 1.70 [4–10]		
ADI Soc	18.50 ± 4.08 [13–28]		
ADI Comm	13.25 ± 4.40 [6–24]		
ADI Rep	5.96 ± 2.48 [1–12]		
Female	n = 5	n = 2	
Left Handed	n = 5	n = 2	

ASD, Autism Spectrum Disorder; TD, Typically Developing; WASI, Wechsler Abbreviated Scales of Intelligence; VIQ, Verbal IQ; NVIQ, Non-verbal IQ; SRS, Social Responsiveness Scale; ADOS-2, Autism Diagnostic Observation Schedule-2nd edition; SA, Social Affect; RRB, Restricted and Repetitive Behavior; ADI-R, Autism Diagnostic Interview, Revised; Soc, Social interaction subscale; Comm, Communication subscale; Rep, Restricted and Repetitive Behaviors subscale.

TABLE 2 | Linear regression results (p-values) for neurite density, fractional anisotropy, and mean diffusivity by lobe.

	Lobe		Group	Age	Age X Group	Overall F-test
ND	Left	Frontal	0.290	0.003*	0.425	0.011*
		Parietal	0.018	0.002*	0.471	0.001*
		Temporal	0.215	0.197	0.622	0.270
		Occipital	0.043	<0.001*	0.657	<0.001*
	Right	Frontal	0.237	<0.001*	0.281	<0.001*
		Parietal	0.051	0.015*	0.397	0.011*
		Temporal	0.106	0.005*	0.995	0.013*
		Occipital	0.121	0.003*	0.269	0.004*
FA	Left	Frontal	0.678	0.807	0.275	0.709
		Parietal	0.751	0.418	0.045	0.147
		Temporal	0.393	0.748	0.159	0.470
		Occipital	0.312	0.659	0.663	0.726
	Right	Frontal	0.984	0.090	0.417	0.284
		Parietal	0.640	0.083	0.035	0.037
		Temporal	0.656	0.147	0.698	0.438
		Occipital	0.368	0.561	0.453	0.664
MD	Left	Frontal	0.091	0.001*	0.788	0.002*
		Parietal	0.011	<0.001*	0.760	<0.001*
		Temporal	0.115	0.091	0.665	0.137
		Occipital	0.027	<0.001*	0.840	<0.001*
	Right	Frontal	0.080	<0.001*	0.547	<0.001*
		Parietal	0.020	<0.001*	0.864	<0.001*
		Temporal	0.088	0.025*	0.509	0.044
		Occipital	0.041	<0.001*	0.601	<0.001*

*Uncorrected p-values of each coefficient shown. *Significant following FDR correction for multiple comparisons. Tests of each coefficient and dependent variable (ND, FA, MD) treated as a statistical family for FDR.*

from 0.37 to 0.75, but these did not survive correction for multiple comparisons. Interactions between group and age were not significant.

On the MD measure, regressions were significant bilaterally in frontal, parietal and occipital lobes, but not temporal lobes. All of these showed significant negative effects of age (decreasing with age) with rates ranging from -2.445×10^{-6} mm^2/s per year (left frontal lobe) to -3.875×10^{-6} mm^2/s per year (left parietal lobe). MD was higher in ASD in the parietal and occipital lobes bilaterally (**Figure 2**) again with medium effect sizes (0.49 to 0.67). However, these did not survive correction for multiple comparisons. There were no significant interactions. By contrast, similar linear regression analyses for FA values did not reach significance after correction for multiple comparisons.

Localized Effects

Individual ROIs were also examined for a more localized understanding of effects in MD and ND (see Supplementary Table 1 for list of ROIs examined), using similar linear regression models. For each dependent variable, all regions were included bilaterally to correct each coefficient for multiple comparisons (48 regions x 2 hemispheres).

Regressions on ND were significant for all regions on the dorsolateral aspect of the right frontal lobe as well as the right anterior cingulate, paracingulate, operculum and insula (Supplementary Table 2, **Figures 1C,D**). Left frontal effects were restricted to anterior cingulate, paracingulate, central operculum, and posterior portions of the dorsal surface. Regressions were also significant for all subregions of parietal lobes (except bilateral superior parietal lobule, right precuneus, and right postcentral),

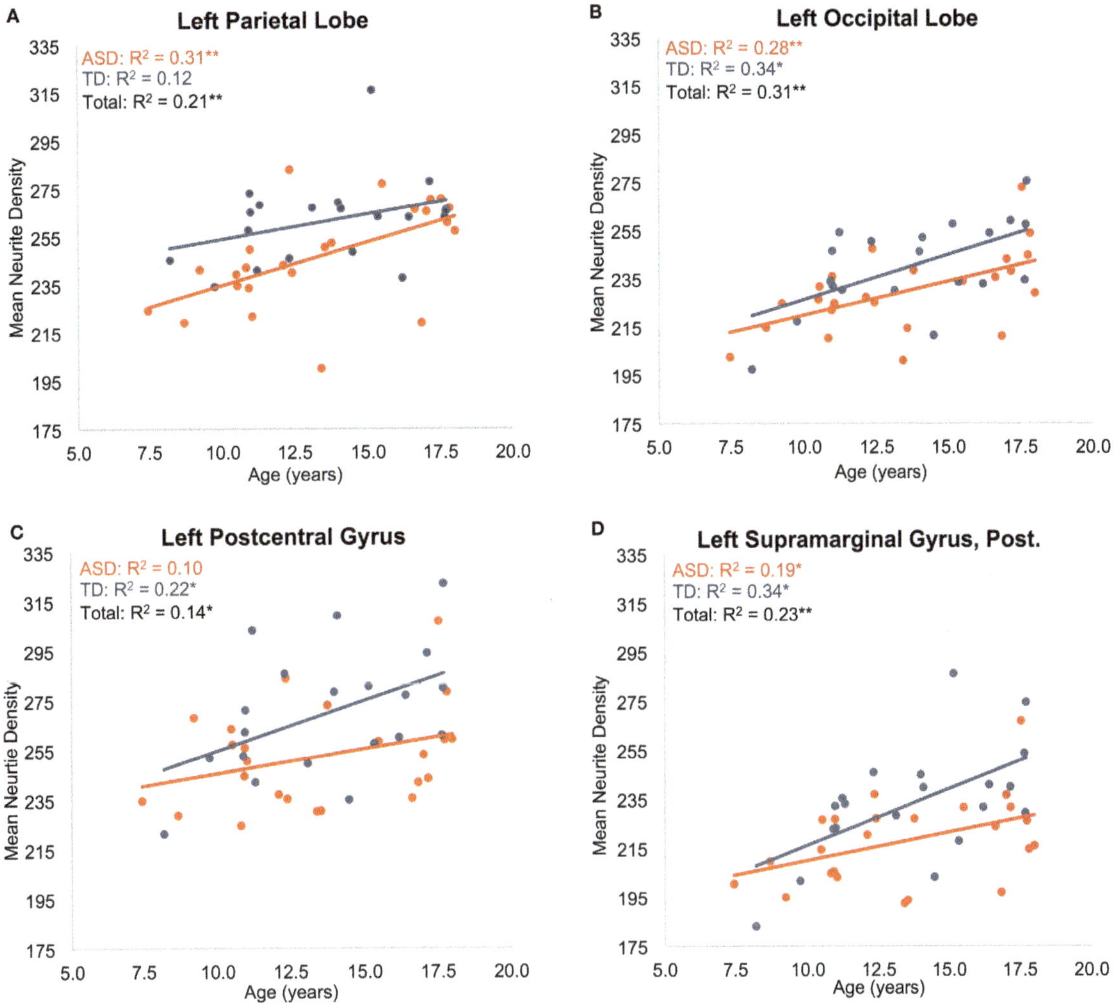

FIGURE 1 | Effects of age on neurite density. Mean ND is shown as a function of subject age for: **(A)** left parietal lobe, **(B)** left occipital lobe, **(C)** left postcentral gyrus, **(D)** posterior division of left supramarginal gyrus. ASD indicated in red, TD indicated in blue. Neurite density standardized to a 0–1000 range. $^*p < 0.05$, $^{**}p < 0.005$.

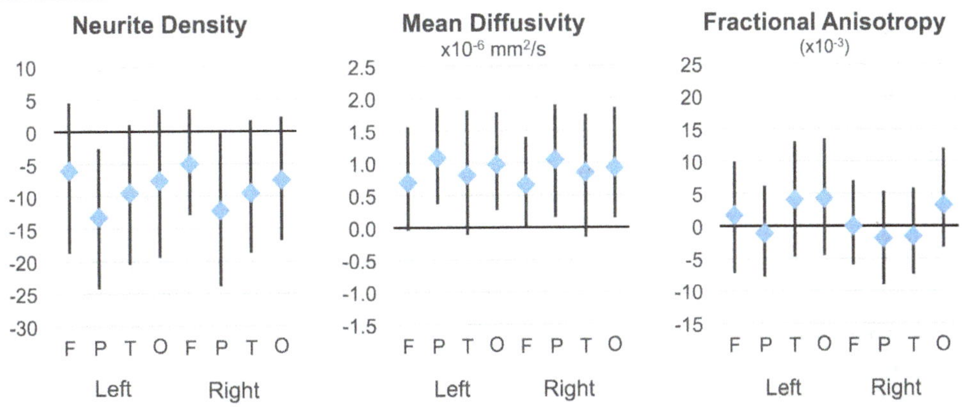

FIGURE 2 | Group differences in ND, MD, and FA. Group differences and 95% confidence intervals are shown for each cortical lobe. Positive values indicate ASD >TD. Neurite density standardized to a 0–1000 range.

a few bilateral temporal regions including posterolateral regions, planum temporale, Heschl's gyrus, and right temporal occipital fusiform gyrus, and portions of occipital lobe including bilateral posterior cingulate. All of these except left Heschl's gyrus exhibited significantly greater ND with increasing age.

Group effects (see Supplementary Figure 1 for group differences and confidence intervals) suggested that ND was reduced in ASD in a number of regions (e.g., anterior cingulate, precentral and supramarginal gyri bilaterally, parts of superior temporal gyrus, fusiform, and planum temporale on the right), but only left temporal occipital fusiform cortex survived correction for multiple comparisons (and overall regression was not significant). The only significant group-by-age interaction was in right anterior cingulate with ND increasing more rapidly with age in ASD.

With only one exception (right temporal occipital fusiform), all regions that showed significant positive age effects on ND also showed significant negative effects on the MD measure (Supplementary Figure 2, Supplementary Table 3). In addition, left superior parietal lobule was affected, and more of left frontal lobes (left middle frontal, subcallosal gyri), and occipital lobes (bilateral intracalcarine cortex and pole, right lateral occipital gyrus, left supracalcarine, cuneal, and lingual regions) showed age effects.

Group differences on MD did not survive correction, but the tendency was toward higher MD in ASD than TD particularly in parietal regions and in several frontal and occipital regions (see Supplementary Figure 2 for group differences and confidence intervals). Interactions were not significant.

DISCUSSION

The present study is—to our knowledge—the first to apply a multi-compartmental diffusion model using multishell MRI to the study of *cortical gray matter* microstructure in ASD. We found robust age effects for both ND (increasing) and MD (decreasing), but not FA, a measure more suited to tissues with well-aligned microstructure such as in the deep white matter. Trends toward decreased ND and increased MD in ASD did not survive correction for multiple comparisons when examined at the lobar level. More localized examination again showed robust age effects in the ND and MD measures, and a significant group difference was found on ND (ASD<TD) in the left temporal occipital fusiform gyrus. While other ND differences did not survive correction for multiple comparisons, examination of confidence intervals (Supplementary Figures 1, 2) suggests that larger sample sizes or improvements in signal-to-noise and motion control (see Limitations) may support such differences.

Our findings indicate that multi-shell, multi-compartmental approaches may provide a valuable addition to our ability to examine gray matter microstructure in ASD and other disorders. While the RSI derived ND measure may not be as sensitive as the tensor-derived MD measure, it offers greater interpretability and specificity as discussed below.

Neurite Density and Mean Diffusivity

The ND measure is likely driven primarily by axons, and particularly myelinated axons, rather than dendrites within cerebral cortex. At the diffusion time-scales examined here, unmyelinated neurites allow some amount of water exchange across the cellular membrane. Since the ND measure is derived from elements with cylindrical symmetry, wherein diffusion is restricted in the direction transverse to the cylinder, but relatively unencumbered along the long axis, unmyelinated elements will contribute less overall signal to the neurite water compartment due to greater water exchange. Hence, lower ND such as that seen in younger participants likely reflects: (1) lower density of myelinated axons, (2) thinner myelin (allowing greater average water exchange), or possibly (3) smaller average caliber of myelinated axons which would be associated with less water in the restricted cylindrical pool.

Cortical MD may be driven by the same factors (but in the opposite direction) since ND and MD measures will tend to correlate inversely with each other. MD is highest where diffusion is free and lowest where it is restricted (e.g., areas of high ND). However, MD is derived from a tensor model and does not distinguish intracellular from extracellular compartments as do RSI derived measures. Other possible causes of MD effects therefore cannot be excluded in regions where ND effects were not detected. Inflammatory responses also lead to increased MD due to increased tissue water (Alexander et al., 2007) but would not be expected to alter intracellular measures such as ND. Signs of inflammation have been reported in ASD (Vargas et al., 2005; Zimmerman et al., 2005; Morgan et al., 2010; Suzuki et al., 2013) so this potential contributor must be considered. Alternatively, MD may simply be a more robust measure than ND when examining gray matter. With only about 25% of the cortical diffusion volume fraction being restricted, ND signal-to-noise will be lower than in the composite MD measure. The relative simplicity of the tensor model may also make measures such as MD more robust than those derived from the more complex RSI model. However, since effect sizes for ND ranged from medium to large (0.37 to 0.75) the lack of more significant findings may have been due to limited sample size, accompanied by expected variability due to the known etiological heterogeneity in ASD (Geschwind and State, 2015).

Age Effects

The validity of the ND metric was supported by robust maturational effects detected in our study. ND increased significantly with age in all lobes except left temporal when groups were combined, showing clear sensitivity to developmental change. At first glance, the direction of change may appear unexpected: The number of cortical synapses, and presumably the complexity of dendritic branches, begins to decrease prior to age 8 years (Huttenlocher and Dabholkar, 1997), while cortical gray matter volume stabilizes (Courchesne et al., 2000), so that a measure of "neurite density" might be expected to decline during this period. However, as described above, the ND measure is probably particularly sensitive to the degree of axonal myelination, which continues well into adulthood. This is supported by multi-shell diffusion studies on neurotypical white matter development that also found age related increases in intraneurite compartments using compartmental diffusion models other than RSI. In a recent abstract, Chang et al. (2015) reported increasing intra-axonal volume fractions across childhood and adolescence using neurite orientation dispersion and density imaging (NODDI). Significant age related increases were also reported by Jelescu et al. (2015) in infants and toddlers, and by Billiet et al. (2015) in adults, with both of these using both NODDI and diffusion kurtosis imaging. These latter studies concluded that the age effects must be at least partially reflective of ongoing myelination, rather than strictly of intra-axonal volume fractions. Indeed, the same NODDI measure was found to correlate with direct staining of myelin in a rat model (Jespersen et al., 2007).

Localization of Group Trends

While group differences on ND were only marginal,—surviving correction for multiple comparisons in only a single region—and therefore must be viewed with substantial caution, the localization of these results deserves some consideration in context of the postmortem literature. ND tended to be lower in ASD than TD in bilateral anterior cingulate gyri, for which increased cell packing density has been reported in several ASD post-mortem cases (Kemper and Bauman, 1998; Schumann and Amaral, 2006). This region also showed the only group-by-age interaction surviving correction, with the ASD group showing a greater increase in ND with age than TD. One of these postmortem studies also examined axons just beneath the cortex (Zikopoulos and Barbas, 2010). In that study, axons were sampled from white matter beneath four areas of frontal lobe in five adult ASD postmortem cases, finding a relative shift from larger to smaller caliber axons exiting the anterior cingulate cortex. As discussed above, smaller myelinated axons are one potential source of ND reductions, which would be consistent with our findings. Zikopoulos and Barbas (2010) also found decreased myelin thickness in axons exiting orbital frontal cortex compared to controls. But, while myelin thickness is another potential source of ND changes, we found little evidence of a group difference in orbital cortex. Other areas where shifts in cell packing density have been reported in ASD include the hippocampus and amygdala, which were not examined here, the prefrontal cortex (though not consistently), and potentially the superior temporal gyrus given findings of narrowed minicolumns. In our sample, ND did tend to be lower in the ASD group in the superior temporal gyrus and its superior aspect (Heschl's gyrus, planum temporale) primarily in the right hemisphere. We found no evidence of prefrontal differences. One group has reported *decreased* cell density in fusiform cortex, whereas we found lower ND that was limited to the posterior aspect of the gyrus.

LIMITATIONS

The absence of significant group differences in RSI may partly reflect the inter-case variability of cytoarchitectonic abnormalities in ASD, commonly found in the literature (Bailey et al., 1998; Hutsler et al., 2007; Wegiel et al., 2010). Additionally, some neuropathologies may not affect the same regions of cortex across all ASD cases, such as laminar differences that have been described as "patchy" (Hutsler et al., 2007). Group-wise analyses such as those used here would not be sensitive to such subject-specific anomalies. Notably, one recent study demonstrated the utility of a multi-compartment diffusion approach for identification of focal cortical dysplasias, not unlike those reported in ASD cases, on a case-wise basis (Winston et al., 2014). Intracellular volume fraction, their marker of neurite density, highlighted focal dysplasias more prominently than traditional diffusion or structural imaging. With a large normative sample, it might be possible to detect focal dysplasias *in vivo* on a case-wise basis in ASD and other disorders using RSI or other compartmental diffusion models.

As with all MRI methodologies, subject motion during scanning can be an issue, particularly when comparing groups that may differ in their likelihood of motion. We thoroughly screened all scans for subject motion resulting in well-matched subject groups. However, better protection of multi-shell diffusion sequences from motion may be possible. Our highest *b*-value shell ($b = 4000$ s/mm^2) was particularly susceptible to motion-related slice dropout, forcing us to exclude c. 27% of ASD participants. This could be improved either by reducing the maximum gradient strength while losing sensitivity to the shortest diffusion distances or, more simply, by repeating the acquisition of this highest shell to allow signal averaging.

Although RSI provides insight to subvoxel neural content in the form of separate intra and extracellular compartments, partial volume effects are still relevant. Voxel size was large (8.8 mm^3) leading to inclusion of both gray and white matter within voxels and averaging across lamina. Higher resolutions may be possible with accelerated imaging techniques, but are unlikely to reach sublaminar resolution in the near future.

RSI is not sensitive to all types of cytoarchitectonic anomalies reported in the ASD literature, such as dysmorphology of specific cell types, ectopias, and abnormal dendritic spine density.

The sample examined here spanned a broad and developmentally complex age range, from 7 to 17 years. After controlling for subject motion, sample sizes of 24 and 20 participants per group were somewhat limited for such a broad range. We were also limited to participants who were relatively high functioning in order to maximize subject cooperation during scanning. Results derived here may not, therefore, generalize to lower-functioning ASD populations or to populations outside of the examined age range.

CONCLUSION

DWI methods are typically restricted to examination of white matter. However, RSI shows substantial promise for microstructural examination of gray matter in ASD. The method is sensitive to effects of age, suggests that group differences may be detected with larger sample sizes, and offers greater interpretability than the traditional diffusion tensor measures FA and MD. The robust age effects that were found for ND support the validity and sensitivity of multi-shell, multi-compartment DWI for *in vivo* examination of gray matter in developmental populations. While RSI is not sensitive to all types of cytoarchitectonic anomalies reported in the ASD literature, measures are likely to reflect intracortical axonal content, myelination, and caliber, which have received limited attention in postmortem studies and can thus complement these in important ways. In the context of fundamental advantages of *in vivo* studies, which can be combined with functional (functional imaging or behavioral) assays, provide a whole brain field of view, and can be administered in longitudinal designs, the first findings reported here suggest that multishell diffusion imaging may be a promising complement to postmortem neurohistology in ASD.

AUTHOR CONTRIBUTIONS

RC, NW, and RM contributed to the conception and design of the work; RC, JT, and JK contributed to the processing, analysis, and presentation of data; all authors contributed to the manuscript itself.

FUNDING

This study was supported by National Institutes of Health grants R01-MH081023 and K01-MH097972, and by National Science Foundation Grant No. 1430082.

ACKNOWLEDGMENTS

Our sincere thanks to our participants and their families for sharing their time with us. Additional thanks to Dr. Qidi Peng and Miss Afrooz Jahedi for statistical consultation.

REFERENCES

Alexander, A. L., Lee, J. E., Lazar, M., and Field, A. S. (2007). Diffusion tensor imaging of the brain. *Neurotherapeutics* 4, 316–329. doi: 10.1016/j.nurt.2007.05.011

Assaf, Y., Alexander, D. C., Jones, D. K., Bizzi, A., Behrens, T. E., Clark, C. A., et al. (2013). The CONNECT project: combining macro- and micro-structure. *Neuroimage* 80, 273–282. doi: 10.1016/j.neuroimage.2013.05.055

American Psychiatric Association (2013). *Diagnostic and Statistical Manual of Mental Disorders, 5th Edn.* Washington, DC: American Psychiatric Association.

Assaf, Y., and Basser, P. J. (2005). Composite hindered and restricted model of diffusion (CHARMED) MR imaging of the human brain. *Neuroimage* 27, 48–58. doi: 10.1016/j.neuroimage.2005.03.042

Avants, B. B., Tustison, N. J., Song, G., Cook, P. A., Klein, A., and Gee, J. C. (2011a). A reproducible evaluation of ANTs similarity metric performance in brain image registration. *Neuroimage* 54, 2033–2044. doi: 10.1016/j.neuroimage.2010.09.025

Avants, B. B., Tustison, N. J., Wu, J., Cook, P. A., and Gee, J., C. (2011b). An open source multivariate framework for n-tissue segmentation with evaluation on public data. *Neuroinformatics* 9, 381–400. doi: 10.1007/s12021-011-9109-y

Avants, B. B., Yushkevich, P., Pluta, J., Minkoff, D., Korczykowski, M., Detre, J., et al. (2010). The optimal template effect in hippocampus studies of diseased populations. *Neuroimage* 49, 2457–2466. doi: 10.1016/j.neuroimage.2009.09.062

Bailey, A., Luthert, P., Dean, A., Harding, B., Janota, I., Montgomery, M., et al. (1998). A clinicopathological study of autism. *Brain* 121 (Pt 5), 889–905.

Barazany, D., Basser, P. J., and Assaf, Y. (2009). *In vivo* measurement of axon diameter distribution in the corpus callosum of rat brain. *Brain* 132, 1210–1220. doi: 10.1093/brain/awp042

Bauman, M. L., and Kemper, T. L. (1985). Histoanatomic observations of the brain in early infantile autism. *Neurology* 35, 866–874.

Bauman, M. L., and Kemper, T. L. (2005). Neuroanatomic observations of the brain in autism: a review and future directions. *Int. J. Dev. Neurosci.* 23, 183–187. doi: 10.1016/j.ijdevneu.2004.09.006

Benjamini, Y., and Hochberg, Y. (1995). Controlling the false discovery rate - a practical and powerful approach to multiple testing. *J. R. Stat. Soc. Ser. B Methodol.* 57, 289–300.

Billiet, T., Vandenbulcke, M., Madler, B., Peeters, R., Dhollander, T., Zhang, H., et al. (2015). Age-related microstructural differences quantified using myelin water imaging and advanced diffusion MRI. *Neurobiol. Aging* 36, 2107–2121. doi: 10.1016/j.neurobiolaging.2015.02.029

Buxhoeveden, D. P., Semendeferi, K., Buckwalter, J., Schenker, N., Switzer, R., and Courchesne, E. (2006). Reduced minicolumns in the frontal cortex of patients with autism. *Neuropathol. Appl. Neurobiol.* 32, 483–491. doi: 10.1111/j.1365-2990.2006.00745.x

Carper, R. A., Moses, P., Tigue, Z. D., and Courchesne, E. (2002). Cerebral lobes in autism: early hyperplasia and abnormal age effects. *Neuroimage* 16, 1038–1051. doi: 10.1006/nimg.2002.1099

Casanova, M. F., Buxhoeveden, D. P., Switala, A. E., and Roy, E. (2002). Minicolumnar pathology in autism. *Neurology* 58, 428–432. doi: 10.1212/WNL.58.3.428

Casanova, M. F., van Kooten, I. A., Switala, A. E., van Engeland, H., Heinsen, H., Steinbusch, H. W., et al. (2006). Minicolumnar abnormalities in autism. *Acta Neuropathol.* 112, 287–303. doi: 10.1007/s00401-006-0085-5

Chang, Y.-S., Owen, J. P., Pojman, N. J., Thieu, T., Bukshpun, P., Wakahiro, M. L. J., et al. (2015). *White Matter Changes of Neurite Density and Orientation Dispersion during Human Brain Maturation (Abstract).* Honolulu, HI: Organization for Human Brain Mapping.

Constantino, J. N., and Gruber, C. P. (2005). *Social Responsiveness Scale.* Los Angeles, CA: Western Psychological Services.

Courchesne, E., Chisum, H. J., Townsend, J., Cowles, A., Covington, J., Egaas, B., et al. (2000). Normal brain development and aging: quantitative analysis at *in vivo* MR imaging in healthy volunteers. *Radiology* 216, 672–682. doi: 10.1148/radiology.216.3.r00au37672

Courchesne, E., Karns, C. M., Davis, H. R., Ziccardi, R., Carper, R. A., Tigue, Z. D., et al. (2001). Unusual brain growth patterns in early life in patients with autistic disorder: an MRI study. *Neurology* 57, 245–254. doi: 10.1212/WNL.57.2.245

Courchesne, E., Mouton, P. R., Calhoun, M. E., Semendeferi, K., Ahrens-Barbeau, C., Hallet, M. J., et al. (2011). Neuron number and size in prefrontal cortex of children with autism. *JAMA* 306, 2001–2010. doi: 10.1001/jama.2011.1638

Dell'Acqua, F., Rizzo, G., Scifo, P., Clarke, R. A., Scotti, G., and Fazio, F. (2007). A model-based deconvolution approach to solve fiber crossing in diffusion-weighted MR imaging. *IEEE Trans. Biomed. Eng.* 54, 462–472. doi: 10.1109/TBME.2006.888830

Dell'Acqua, F., Simmons, A., Williams, S. C., and Catani, M. (2013). Can spherical deconvolution provide more information than fiber orientations? Hindrance modulated orientational anisotropy, a true-tract specific index to characterize white matter diffusion. *Hum. Brain Mapp.* 34, 2464–2483. doi: 10.1002/hbm.22080

Geschwind, D. H., and State, M. W. (2015). Gene hunting in autism spectrum disorder: on the path to precision medicine. *Lancet Neurol.* 14, 1109–1120. doi: 10.1016/S1474-4422(15)00044-7

Hazlett, H. C., Poe, M. D., Gerig, G., Styner, M., Chappell, C., Smith, R. G., et al. (2011). Early brain overgrowth in autism associated with an increase in cortical surface area before age 2 years. *Arch. Gen. Psychiatry* 68, 467–476. doi: 10.1001/archgenpsychiatry.2011.39

Holland, D., Kuperman, J. M., and Dale, A. M. (2010). Efficient correction of inhomogeneous static magnetic field-induced distortion in Echo Planar Imaging. *Neuroimage* 50, 175–183. doi: 10.1016/j.neuroimage.2009.11.044

Hutsler, J. J., and Casanova, M. F. (2016). Review: cortical construction in autism spectrum disorder: columns, connectivity and the subplate. *Neuropathol. Appl. Neurobiol.* 42, 115–134. doi: 10.1111/nan.12227

Hutsler, J. J., Love, T., and Zhang, H. (2007). Histological and magnetic resonance imaging assessment of cortical layering and thickness in autism spectrum disorders. *Biol. Psychiatry* 61, 449–457. doi: 10.1016/j.biopsych.2006.01.015

Hutsler, J. J., and Zhang, H. (2010). Increased dendritic spine densities on cortical projection neurons in autism spectrum disorders. *Brain Res.* 1309, 83–94. doi: 10.1016/j.brainres.2009.09.120

Huttenlocher, P. R., and Dabholkar, A. S. (1997). Regional differences in synaptogenesis in human cerebral cortex. *J. Comp. Neurol.* 387, 167–178.

Jelescu, I. O., Veraart, J., Adisetiyo, V., Milla, S. S., Novikov, D. S., and Fieremans, E. (2015). One diffusion acquisition and different white matter models: how does microstructure change in human early development based on WMTI and NODDI? *Neuroimage* 107, 242–256. doi: 10.1016/j.neuroimage.2014.12.009

Jensen, J. H., Helpern, J. A., Ramani, A., Lu, H., and Kaczynski, K. (2005). Diffusional kurtosis imaging: the quantification of non-gaussian water diffusion by means of magnetic resonance imaging. *Magn. Reson. Med.* 53, 1432–1440. doi: 10.1002/mrm.20508

Jespersen, S. N., Kroenke, C. D., Østergaard, L., Ackerman, J. J. H., and Yablonskiy, D. A (2007). Modeling dendrite density from magnetic resonance diffusion measurements. *Neuroimage* 34, 1473–1486. doi: 10.1016/j.neuroimage.2006.10.037

Jian, B., and Vemuri, B. C. (2007). A unified computational framework for deconvolution to reconstruct multiple fibers from diffusion weighted MRI. *IEEE Trans. Med. Imaging* 26, 1464–1471. doi: 10.1109/TMI.2007.907552

Jovicich, J., Czanner, S., Greve, D., Haley, E., van der Kouwe, A., Gollub, R., et al. (2006). Reliability in multi-site structural MRI studies: effects of gradient non-linearity correction on phantom and human data. *Neuroimage* 30, 436–443. doi: 10.1016/j.neuroimage.2005.09.046

Kaden, E., Knosche, T. R., and Anwander, A. (2007). Parametric spherical deconvolution: inferring anatomical connectivity using diffusion MR imaging. *Neuroimage* 37, 474–488. doi: 10.1016/j.neuroimage.2007.05.012

Kemper, T. L., and Bauman, M. (1998). Neuropathology of infantile autism. *J. Neuropathol. Exp. Neurol.* 57, 645–652.

Lazar, M., Miles, L. M., Babb, J. S., and Donaldson, J. B. (2014). Axonal deficits in young adults with High Functioning Autism and their impact on processing speed. *Neuroimage Clin.* 4, 417–425. doi: 10.1016/j.nicl.2014.01.014

Le Bihan, D. (2012). Diffusion, confusion and functional MRI. *Neuroimage* 62, 1131–1136. doi: 10.1016/j.neuroimage.2011.09.058

Lord, C., Rutter, M., DiLavore, P., and Risi, S. (2001). *Autism Diagnostic Observation Schedule.* Los Angeles, CA: Western Psychological Services.

Lu, H., Jensen, J. H., Ramani, A., and Helpern, J. A. (2006). Three-dimensional characterization of non-gaussian water diffusion in humans using diffusion kurtosis imaging. *NMR Biomed.* 19, 236–247. doi: 10.1002/nbm.1020

Morgan, J. T., Chana, G., Pardo, C. A., Achim, C., Semendeferi, K., Buckwalter, J., et al. (2010). Microglial activation and increased microglial density observed in the dorsolateral prefrontal cortex in autism. *Biol. Psychiatry* 68, 368–376. doi: 10.1016/j.biopsych.2010.05.024

Oldfield, R. C. (1971). The assessment and analysis of handedness: the Edinburgh inventory. *Neuropsychologia* 9, 97–113.

Palmen, S. J. M. C., van Engeland, H., Hof, P. R., and Schmitz, C. (2004). Neuropathological findings in autism. *Brain* 127, 2572–2583. doi: 10.1093/brain/awh287

Raffelt, D., Tournier, J. D., Rose, S., Ridgway, G. R., Henderson, R., Crozier, S., et al. (2012). Apparent Fibre Density: a novel measure for the analysis of diffusion-weighted magnetic resonance images. *Neuroimage* 59, 3976–3994. doi: 10.1016/j.neuroimage.2011.10.045

Rutter, M., Lord, C., and LeCouteur, A. (1995). *Autism Diagnostic Interview - R.* Chicago, IL: Department of Psychiatry, University of Chicago.

Schumann, C. M., and Amaral, D. G. (2006). Stereological analysis of amygdala neuron number in autism. *J. Neurosci.* 26, 7674–7679. doi: 10.1523/JNEUROSCI.1285-06.2006

Schumann, C. M., Bloss, C. S., Barnes, C. C., Wideman, G. M., Carper, R. A., Akshoomoff, N., et al. (2010). Longitudinal magnetic resonance imaging study of cortical development through early childhood in autism. *J. Neurosci.* 30, 4419–4427. doi: 10.1523/JNEUROSCI.5714-09.2010

Schumann, C. M., and Nordahl, C. W. (2011). Bridging the gap between MRI and postmortem research in autism. *Brain Res.* 1380, 175–186. doi: 10.1016/j.brainres.2010.09.061

Smith, S. M. (2002). Fast robust automated brain extraction. *Hum. Brain Mapp.* 17, 143–155. doi: 10.1002/hbm.10062

Suzuki, K., Sugihara, G., Ouchi, Y., Nakamura, K., Futatsubashi, M., Takebayashi, K., et al. (2013). Microglial activation in young adults with autism spectrum disorder. *JAMA Psychiatry* 70, 49–58. doi: 10.1001/jamapsychiatry.2013.272

Tournier, J. D., Calamante, F., Gadian, D. G., and Connelly, A. (2004). Direct estimation of the fiber orientation density function from diffusion-weighted MRI data using spherical deconvolution. *Neuroimage* 23, 1176–1185. doi: 10.1016/j.neuroimage.2004.07.037

van Kooten, I. A., Palmen, S. J., von Cappeln, P., Steinbusch, H. W., Korr, H., Heinsen, H., et al. (2008). Neurons in the fusiform gyrus are fewer and smaller in autism. *Brain* 131, 987–999. doi: 10.1093/brain/awn033

Vargas, D. L., Nascimbene, C., Krishnan, C., Zimmerman, A. W., and Pardo, C. A. (2005). Neuroglial activation and neuroinflammation in the brain of patients with autism. *Ann. Neurol.* 57, 67–81. doi: 10.1002/ana.20315

Wechsler, D. (1999). *Wechsler Abbreviated Scale of Intelligence.* San Antonio, TX: Psychological Corporation.

Wegiel, J., Kuchna, I., Nowicki, K., Imaki, H., Wegiel, J., Marchi, E., et al. (2010). The neuropathology of autism: defects of neurogenesis and neuronal migration, and dysplastic changes. *Acta Neuropathol.* 119, 755–770. doi: 10.1007/s00401-010-0655-4

White, N. S., Leergaard, T. B., D'Arceuil, H., Bjaalie, J. G., and Dale, A. M. (2013). Probing tissue microstructure with restriction spectrum imaging: Histological and theoretical validation. *Hum. Brain Mapp.* 34, 327–346.

White, N. S., Mcdonald, C. R., Farid, N., Kuperman, J., Karow, D., Schenker-Ahmed, N. M., et al. (2014). Diffusion-weighted imaging in cancer: physical foundations and applications of restriction spectrum imaging. *Cancer Res.* 74, 4638–4652. doi: 10.1158/0008-5472.CAN-13-3534

Winston, G. P., Micallef, C., Symms, M. R., Alexander, D. C., Duncan, J. S., and Zhang, H. (2014). Advanced diffusion imaging sequences could aid assessing patients with focal cortical dysplasia and epilepsy. *Epilepsy Res.* 108, 336–339. doi: 10.1016/j.eplepsyres.2013.11.004

Zhang, H., Schneider, T., Wheeler-Kingshott, C. A., and Alexander, D. C. (2012). NODDI: practical *in vivo* neurite orientation dispersion and density imaging of the human brain. *Neuroimage* 61, 1000–1016. doi: 10.1016/j.neuroimage.2012.03.072

Zhuang, J., Hrabe, J., Kangarlu, A., Xu, D., Bansal, R., Branch, C. A., et al. (2006). Correction of eddy-current distortions in diffusion tensor images using the known directions and strengths of diffusion gradients. *J. Magn. Reson. Imaging* 24, 1188–1193. doi: 10.1002/jmri.20727

Zikopoulos, B., and Barbas, H. (2010). Changes in prefrontal axons may disrupt the network in autism. *J. Neurosci.* 30, 14595–14609. doi: 10.1523/JNEUROSCI.2257-10.2010

Zimmerman, A. W., Jyonouchi, H., Comi, A. M., Connors, S. L., Milstien, S., Varsou, A., et al. (2005). Cerebrospinal fluid and serum markers of inflammation in autism. *Pediatr. Neurol.* 33, 195–201. doi: 10.1016/j.pediatrneurol.2005.03.014

10

Neuropathological Mechanisms of Seizures in Autism Spectrum Disorder

Richard E. Frye[1,2], Manuel F. Casanova[3], S. Hossein Fatemi[4], Timothy D. Folsom[4], Teri J. Reutiman[4], Gregory L. Brown[5], Stephen M. Edelson[6], John C. Slattery[1,2] and James B. Adams[7]*

[1] Autism Research Program, Arkansas Children's Research Institute, Little Rock, AR, USA, [2] Department of Pediatrics, University of Arkansas for Medical Sciences, Little Rock, AR, USA, [3] Department of Biomedical Sciences, University of South Carolina School of Medicine Greenville, Greenville, SC, USA, [4] Department of Psychiatry, University of Minnesota Medical School, Minneapolis, MN, USA, [5] Serenity Health Care Center, Waukesha, WI, USA, [6] Autism Research Institute, San Diego, CA, USA, [7] School for Engineering of Matter, Transport, and Energy, Arizona State University, Tempe, AZ, USA

Edited by:
Joshua Pesach Rosenzweig, Cell-El, Israel

Reviewed by:
Bashkim Kadriu, Albert Einstein College of Medicine at Bronx-Lebanon Hospital Center, USA
Andrew Walter Zimmerman, UMass Medical School, USA

***Correspondence:**
Richard E. Frye
refrye@uams.edu

This manuscript reviews biological abnormalities shared by autism spectrum disorder (ASD) and epilepsy. Two neuropathological findings are shared by ASD and epilepsy: abnormalities in minicolumn architecture and γ-aminobutyric acid (GABA) neurotransmission. The peripheral neuropil, which is the region that contains the inhibition circuits of the minicolumns, has been found to be decreased in the post-mortem ASD brain. ASD and epilepsy are associated with inhibitory GABA neurotransmission abnormalities including reduced $GABA_A$ and $GABA_B$ subunit expression. These abnormalities can elevate the excitation-to-inhibition balance, resulting in hyperexcitablity of the cortex and, in turn, increase the risk of seizures. Medical abnormalities associated with both epilepsy and ASD are discussed. These include specific genetic syndromes, specific metabolic disorders including disorders of energy metabolism and GABA and glutamate neurotransmission, mineral and vitamin deficiencies, heavy metal exposures and immune dysfunction. Many of these medical abnormalities can result in an elevation of the excitatory-to-inhibitory balance. Fragile X is linked to dysfunction of the mGluR5 receptor and Fragile X, Angelman and Rett syndromes are linked to a reduction in $GABA_A$ receptor expression. Defects in energy metabolism can reduce GABA interneuron function. Both pyridoxine dependent seizures and succinic semialdehyde dehydrogenase deficiency cause GABA deficiencies while urea cycle defects and phenylketonuria cause abnormalities in glutamate neurotransmission. Mineral deficiencies can cause glutamate and GABA neurotransmission abnormalities and heavy metals can cause mitochondrial dysfunction which disrupts GABA metabolism. Thus, both ASD and epilepsy are associated with similar abnormalities that may alter the excitatory-to-inhibitory balance of the cortex. These parallels may explain the high prevalence of epilepsy in ASD and the elevated prevalence of ASD features in individuals with epilepsy.

Keywords: autism spectrum disorder, seizures, epilepsy, genetic syndrome, metabolic disorders, excitatory-to-inhibitory cortical balance, gamma-aminobutyric acid

INTRODUCTION

Autism spectrum disorders (ASD) is a behaviorally defined disorder that has recently been estimated to affect as many as 1 out of 45 individuals (Zablotsky et al., 2015). Although, ASD is defined by behavioral features, it is associated with co-occurring medical conditions. For example, epilepsy is more prevalent in ASD than in the typically developing children with a prevalence ranging from 5 to 38% (Deykin and Macmahon, 1979; Volkmar and Nelson, 1990; Tuchman and Rapin, 2002; Danielsson et al., 2005; Hara, 2007). Data from surveys performed by the Autism Research Institute on over 1200 participants suggests that the prevalence is between 15 and 19%. Epilepsy is one of the most disabling ASD co-morbidities as children with ASD and epilepsy are more likely to have intellectual disability (Tuchman, 2013) and increased mortality (Shavelle et al., 2001; Pickett et al., 2011) as compared to children with ASD without epilepsy. In addition, epilepsy in ASD tends to be more treatment-resistant as compared to epilepsy in typically developing children (Sansa et al., 2011).

One of the major questions in ASD research is its etiology. Much ASD research concentrates on genetic causes (Rossignol and Frye, 2012b) even though inherited single gene and chromosomal defects only account for a minority of ASD cases (Schaefer et al., 2013). However, genetic etiologies may be overrepresented in children with ASD and epilepsy as many genetic syndromes and gene mutations associated with ASD include epilepsy as a common feature (Murdoch and State, 2013; Tuchman et al., 2013).

Although some have suggested that clinical seizures do not have any special causative significance in ASD (Tuchman and Rapin, 1997), ASD coexists with epilepsy in several disorders (see Section Specific Medical Disorders Associated with Both ASD and Epilepsy) suggesting that the same neuropathology may result in both ASD and epilepsy. Thus, this manuscript reviews the shared biological abnormalities in ASD and epilepsy in two sections. The section called Basic Neuropathological Mechanisms of Seizures in ASD discusses two neuropathological mechanisms that have been described in ASD that can also cause epilepsy. Both mechanisms involve an abnormal reduction in inhibitory mechanisms of the brain, thereby resulting in an increase in the excitatory-to-inhibitory balance. The section called Specific Medical Disorders Associated with Both ASD and Epilepsy will review specific clinical disorders that have been described in both ASD and epilepsy with special reference to underlying neuropathological mechanisms that can cause seizures.

Overall, our review finds that many disorders associated with ASD increase the excitatory-to-inhibitory balance by either (1) reducing inhibitory circuits in the brain through a decrease in the inhibitory neurotransmitter γ-aminobutyric acid (GABA), or (2) increasing excitatory circuits in the brain through an increase in glutamate neurotransmission. Elevation in the excitatory-to-inhibitory balance in the brain can lead to seizures. By carefully outlining these disorders, insight into the etiologies that underlie ASD may be better understood.

BASIC NEUROPATHOLOGICAL MECHANISMS OF SEIZURES IN ASD

Several neuropathological processes associated with ASD are also associated with epilepsy. Here we review two such neuropathological processes: (1) minicolumn architecture and (2) GABA neurotransmission.

Minicolumn Architecture

The minicolumn is a radially-oriented assembly of neurons and cellular elements considered to be an elemental modular microcircuit of the neocortex (Buxhoeveden and Casanova, 2002; Casanova et al., 2006). The minicolumn core contains pyramidal cell arrays surrounded by a peripheral neuropil space that contains GABAergic inhibitory interneurons and other cells such as the double-bouquet cell (Mountcastle, 1997; Buxhoeveden and Casanova, 2002; Defelipe, 2005). Double-bouquet cells feature axonal bundles which provide a vertical stream of inhibition (Mountcastle, 1997). This inhibitory stream insulates the minicolumn core from the excitation from other surrounding minicolumns (Defelipe et al., 1990; Favorov and Kelly, 1994; Defelipe, 1999).

The peripheral neuropil space has been shown to be reduced in post-mortem brain tissue from ASD individuals (Buxhoeveden and Casanova, 2002), with this reduction most prominent over the prefrontal cortex (Casanova et al., 2006). The neuropil space is reduced within the region that contains the inhibition circuits of minicolumns (Defelipe et al., 1990; Favorov and Kelly, 1994; Defelipe, 1999). These architectural changes should, theoretically, disrupt the normal balance between excitation and inhibition influences within the columnar organization of the cortex (Casanova et al., 2003). A reduction of GABAergic inhibitory activity has been proposed to result in hyperexcitability of minicolumn circuits and can explain some of the symptomatology observed in ASD, including the high incidence of seizures and auditory-tactile hypersensitivity (Rubenstein and Merzenich, 2003). Networks of inhibitory interneurons acting as GABA gated pacemakers are also critically involved in gamma oscillations (Grothe and Klump, 2000). Abnormalities in gamma oscillations are associated with problems with binding and the coactivation of neural assemblies. A deficit in binding and gamma oscillations has been proposed to explain many of the symptoms related to ASD (e.g., visuoperceptual defects, understanding and using context; Grice et al., 2001; Brock et al., 2002; Brown et al., 2005; Rippon et al., 2007; Tommerdahl et al., 2007).

GABA Transmission

GABA is the major inhibitory neurotransmitter of the central nervous system (CNS). Abnormalities in GABA neurotransmission have been associated with epilepsy. GABBR1A, GABBR1B, and GABBR2 receptor subunits are reduced in the hippocampi of patients with temporal lobe epilepsy (Princivalle et al., 2003), and animal models have also

Abbreviations: AMPA, α-amino-3-hydroxy-5-methyl-4-isoxazolepropionic acid; NMDA, N-methyl-D-aspartate; ASD, autism spectrum disorder; ATP, adenosine-5′-triphosphate; CNS, central nervous system; GABA, γ-aminobutyric acid.

shown a link between GABA receptor expression and epilepsy (Schuler et al., 2001; Han et al., 2006). Individuals with ASD have been shown to have abnormalities in GABAergic brain systems (Blatt et al., 2001; Dhossche et al., 2002; Fatemi, 2008), as well as a reduction in $GABA_A$(Fatemi et al., 2009) and $GABA_B$ (Fatemi et al., 2009) receptor subunits in both the frontal and parietal cortices, as compared to controls, with the ASD group also demonstrating a markedly higher rate of epilepsy than the controls. In addition, the GABA subunits found to be reduced in individuals with ASD (i.e., GABRα1 and GABBR1) have been associated with childhood absence epilepsy, juvenile myoclonic epilepsy, and atypical absence seizures (Delgado-Escueta, 2007; Kang et al., 2009).

SPECIFIC MEDICAL DISORDERS ASSOCIATED WITH BOTH ASD AND EPILEPSY

Genetic Disorders

The neurobiological mechanisms leading to seizures in genetic syndromes that are associated with ASD are diverse and complex. Imbalances in GABA and glutamate have been suggested to underlie CNS dysfunction in several of these genetic syndromes. Defects in $GABA_A$ function has been implicated in Fragile X (D'hulst and Kooy, 2007) and recent studies on Fragile X suggest that mGluR5 dysfunction results in heightened excitability and secondary alterations in GABA function (Frye, 2014). Dysfunction in $GABA_A$ receptor function has also been implicated in Angelman syndrome (Pelc et al., 2008). Indeed, a cluster of genes coding for three $GABA_A$ receptor subunits lie adjacent to the critical Angelman region (i.e., UBE3A). Mutations within the Rett syndrome gene (i.e., MECP2) decreases expression of GABRB3, a gene responsible for encoding the $beta_3$ subunit of the $GABA_A$ receptor, and DLX5, a gene which regulates the production of enzymes responsible for GABA production.

Some genetic syndromes associated with epilepsy and ASD are associated with metabolic abnormalities. For example, mouse models of both Angelman and Rett syndromes demonstrate mitochondrial dysfunction (Kriaucionis et al., 2006; Su et al., 2011) and mitochondrial dysfunction is reported in a Rett syndrome case (Condie et al., 2010). Phelan-McDermid Syndrome (PMS) and duplication of the 22q13 region are both associated with ASD and mitochondrial dysfunction (Frye, 2012b; Frye et al., 2016a). As mentioned below, disruption of mitochondrial metabolism can result in changes to the excitatory-to-inhibitory balance.

Single gene disorders associated with both ASD and epilepsy have been associated with abnormalities in the excitatory- to-inhibitory balance (Srivastava and Schwartz, 2014). Mutations in CNTNAP2 (Peñagarikano et al., 2011) or CNTNAP4 (Karayannis et al., 2014) result in reduced GABAergic neurotransmission. The SYNGAP1 haploinsufficiency animal model shows an increase in neuronal excitability and an increase in seizure susceptibility (Clement et al., 2012). Other genes are associated with a relative decrease in the excitatory-to-inhibitory balance. Animal model with NLGN3 mutations demonstrates increased inhibitory neurotransmission (Tabuchi et al., 2007). Cellular (Shcheglovitov et al., 2013) and animal models (Bangash et al., 2011; Wang et al., 2011b) demonstrate a reduction in excitatory neurotransmission when SHANK3 is disrupted. Animal models with decreased synapsin I (SYN1) demonstrate reduced glutamate release (Li et al., 1995).

Metabolic Disorders

Disorders of Energy Metabolism

Disorders of energy metabolism have been associated with ASD (Giulivi et al., 2010; Frye and Naviaux, 2011; Frye, 2012c; Rose et al., 2014a,b) and epilepsy (Frye, 2015). Some children with ASD have mitochondrial dysfunction that is different than classic mitochondrial disease (Frye and Rossignol, 2011; Rossignol and Frye, 2012a; Frye, 2012a). Of children with mitochondrial disease and ASD, 41% have seizures (Rossignol and Frye, 2012a).

Other disorders of energy metabolism are associated with ASD and epilepsy, including disorders of creatine metabolism (Póo-Argúelles et al., 2006; Longo et al., 2011) and adenylosuccinate lyase deficiency (Spiegel et al., 2006; Jurecka et al., 2008). Creatine and phosphocreatine play important roles in energy storage and transmission of high-energy phosphates. Adenylosuccinate lyase deficiency is a rare autosomal disorder of *de novo* purine synthesis (Spiegel et al., 2006; Jurecka et al., 2008). The purine nucleotide cycle regulates cellular metabolism by controlling levels of fumarate, a citric acid cycle intermediate, and adenosine, the precursor to adenosine-5′-triphosphate (ATP) (Spiegel et al., 2006).

An energy deficiency can result in seizures. Neurons with high firing rates, such as inhibitory GABA interneurons (Anderson et al., 2008), are disproportionally affected by an energy deficit. In addition, processes critically involved in the release and reuptake of neurotransmitters and maintenance of the neuronal resting potential, such as calcium homeostasis, are critically dependent on mitochondrial function (Li et al., 2004; Quiroz et al., 2008; Chen and Chan, 2009).

Disorders of GABA Neurotransmission

Several metabolic disorders directly lead to GABA metabolism abnormalities. Pyridoxine and its primary biologically active form, pyridoxal-5-phosphate, are essential cofactors for over 110 enzymes, including glutamic acid decarboxylase (GAD), the enzyme that produces GABA from glutamate. Pyridoxal-5-phosphate depletion reduces GAD activity which, in turn, increases glutamate, decreases GABA synthesis and decreases cortical inhibition (Gospe et al., 1994; Gospe, 2002; Mills et al., 2006). This occurs in pyridoxine dependent seizures.

Succinic semialdehyde dehydrogenase deficiency is an autosomal recessive disorder of GABA metabolism. It results from a defect in the aldehyde dehydrogenase gene (ALDH5A1; Jakobs et al., 1981). Aldehyde dehydrogenase is partially responsible for the degradation of GABA and when this enzyme is deficient GABA is degraded through an alternative pathway, resulting in the formation of gamma-hydroxybutyric acid and GABA elevations in the brain. Positron emission tomography studies suggest that chronic elevation in GABA down-regulates

$GABA_A$ receptors, leading to a deficit in cortical inhibition and an elevation in the excitatory-to-inhibitory balance (Pearl et al., 2009a,b).

Disorders of Glutamate Neurotransmission

Two types of metabolic disorders (urea cycle defects and phenylketonuria) may result in dysfunction of glutamate neurotransmission. Glutamate is the major excitatory cortical neurotransmitter and excess glutamate results in an elevation in the excitatory-to-inhibitory balance, leading to seizures.

Urea cycle defects result in ammonia elevations. Astrocytes exposed to ammonia do not express glutamate reuptake transporters that normally reduce extracellular glutamate (Rose, 2006). Thus, increased ammonia levels in the brain can result in elevated extracellular glutamate.

Neurological consequences of phenylketonuria are usually avoided by dietary treatment starting at birth (Williams et al., 2008). However, epilepsy and ASD may develop in untreated children and in those noncompliant to the prescribed diet (Baieli et al., 2003). Such children demonstrate high levels of phenylalanine in the brain. Phenylalanine antagonizes both N-methyl-D-aspartate (NMDA) and non-NMDA glutamate receptors (i.e., α-amino-3-hydroxy-5-methyl-4-isoxazolepropionic acid (AMPA) receptors; Glushakov et al., 2003). Chronic elevation in phenylalanine leads to an upregulation of several NMDA and AMPA receptor subunits (Glushakov et al., 2005), increased glutamate receptor density and increased glutamate release (Martynyuk et al., 2005). Such changes in glutamate neurotransmission predispose the brain to heightened excitability and seizures, especially if the phenylalanine level is transiently lowered (Martynyuk et al., 2005).

Mineral Deficiencies

Magnesium is essential in neurotransmitter metabolism and in modulating neurotransmitter receptor function. Ionized magnesium is important in seizure control. Ionized magnesium is a NMDA antagonist (Ault et al., 1980; Hallak, 1998) and may be a factor in some epilepsies (Hallak et al., 1992; Mathern et al., 1998; Mikuni et al., 1999). NMDA receptor activation by glutamate results in calcium influx (Macdermott et al., 1986; Delorenzo and Limbrick, 1996), which is pro-epileptogenic (Delorenzo, 1986; Heinemann and Hamon, 1986). Low ionized magnesium or altered balance between ionized magnesium and ionized calcium may precipitate seizures (Chaistitwanich et al., 1987). Patients with epilepsy have been shown to have significantly lower mean ionized magnesium levels and an increase in the ionized calcium to ionized magnesium ratio in spite of normal total serum magnesium levels (Sinert et al., 2007).

The role of zinc in epilepsy is not clear. Low zinc levels has been associated with seizures in children (Ganesh and Janakiraman, 2008; Mollah et al., 2008) and in the EL epileptic mouse (Fukahori and Itoh, 1990). Zinc acts as an anticonvulsant (Williamson and Spencer, 1995; Cole et al., 2000) and decreases seizure susceptibility (Fukahori and Itoh, 1990). However, zinc has been shown to be proconvulsant in a mouse model (Pei et al., 1983). Zinc co-localizes with glutamate where it inhibits the reuptake of synaptic GABA, thereby increasing the cortical inhibitory tone (Cohen-Kfir et al., 2005). Thus, a zinc deficiency could increase the relative excitatory-to-inhibitory balance.

Vitamin Deficiencies

Children with ASD have been shown to have abnormalities in cobalamin dependent pathways (Frye and James, 2014), and cobalamin supplementation improves metabolites in these pathways (James et al., 2009a; Adams et al., 2011; Frye et al., 2013a; Hendren et al., 2016) and behavior (Adams et al., 2011; Frye et al., 2013a,b; Hendren et al., 2016). The exact mechanism in which cobalamin deficiency causes seizures is unclear but infants with cobalamin deficiency manifest seizures (Benbir et al., 2007; Erol et al., 2007). Cobalamin is essential for myelin synthesis and methylation (Kumar, 2004). Neurons with damaged myelin sheaths are more susceptible to the excitatory effects of glutamate (Akaike et al., 1993).

Cerebral folate deficiency (CFD) is characterized by low 5-methyltetrahydrofolate in the CNS and is associated with ASD and seizures (Ramaekers et al., 2002; Ramaekers and Blau, 2004). Children with idiopathic ASD have a high prevalence of folate receptor alpha autoantibodies that causes CFD (Frye et al., 2013c, 2016b). Folate is essential in a wide range of metabolic processes, including redox and homocysteine metabolism and gene methylation (Obeid et al., 2007). Disruption in these processes could disrupted redox metabolism, thereby depleting glutathione which, in turn, can decreased glutamate degradation, leading to increased cortical excitability (Deepmala et al., 2015).

Heavy Metals

Several epidemiologic studies support a relationship between ASD and exposure to mercury or other heavy metals (Rossignol et al., 2014). Epilepsy has been associated with exposure to toxic levels of heavy metals including lead (Silbergeld et al., 1979; Swartzwelder, 1985; Lockitch et al., 1991; Arrieta et al., 2005) and mercury (Torres et al., 2000). Heavy metals may have toxic effects on the brain by reducing mitochondrial function (James et al., 2009b; Belyaeva et al., 2011; Wang et al., 2011a; Rose et al., 2015), causing apoptosis (Wang et al., 2011a; Pal et al., 2012), and increasing levels of reactive oxygen species (James et al., 2009b; Furieri et al., 2011; Wang et al., 2011a). Although the mechanism(s) by which heavy metals cause epilepsy are not clear, both mitochondrial dysfunction (Rossignol and Frye, 2012a) and high levels of reactive oxygen species (Riazi et al., 2010; Specchio et al., 2010; Waldbaum and Patel, 2010), have been linked to epilepsy.

Immune Dysregulation

Multiple studies have demonstrated evidence of abnormal immune system activation in individuals with ASD. Unusually high levels of proinflammatory cytokines have been found in the cerebrospinal fluid of individuals with ASD (Vargas et al., 2005). Abnormal activation of the intrinsic immune system in the cerebral cortex, white matter, and cerebellum has been demonstrated in individuals with ASD at autopsy (Vargas et al., 2005).

Children with ASD manifest autoantibodies implicated in childhood epilepsy syndromes associated with language regression (Connolly et al., 2006) and cognitive and behavioral changes (Ganor et al., 2004; Vincent et al., 2004) and drug-resistant epilepsy (Majoie et al., 2006) as well as autoantibodies to critical brain elements, such as myelin basic protein, brain derived neurotrophic factor and endothelial cells (Connolly et al., 1999). GAD65 autoantibodies are associated with several neurological disorders including drug-resistant epilepsy (Blanc et al., 2009). One study found GAD65 autoantibodies in 15% of children with ASD (Rout et al., 2012) but other studies have failed to find these autoantibodies in ASD children (Kalra et al., 2015).

Certain autoantibodies, such as the folate receptor alpha autoantibody, could result in specific syndromes like CFD and a recent study suggests that the folate receptor alpha autoantibody may also interfere with cobalamin metabolism (Frye et al., 2016b). Autoantibodies associated with specific seizure syndromes could also result in the dysfunction of specific neural elements. Autoantibodies can also be an epiphenomenon of underlying immune dysregulation.

SUMMARY

Many of these disorders associated with both seizures and ASD increase the excitatory-to-inhibitory balance. Some disorders reduce brain inhibition by reducing the inhibitory neurotransmitter GABA by a reduction in GABA production, metabolic failure of inhibitory GABA neurons or dysfunction of GABA receptors. Other disorders increase brain excitation by increasing the excitatory neurotransmitter glutamate through increased production, alterations in degradation, or altering glutamate receptors. Independent of these disorders, neuropathological research on ASD points to abnormalities in inhibitory GABA pathways.

A few studies suggest that some gene mutations are associated with a reduction in the excitatory-to-inhibitory balance. This appears to contradict the classic association of seizures with cortical excitability. It may be that these changes cause instability in neuronal networks or compensatory changes at the neuronal level that may create abnormalities in neural excitability. For example, although brain GABA is increased in patients with succinic semialdehyde dehydrogenase deficiency, GABA receptors are down regulated, leading to an elevation in the excitatory-to-inhibitory balance (Pearl et al., 2009a,b).

Clearly further research examining these pathways in more detail could help guide the development of targeted treatments and improve our understanding of the clinical implication of these changes. This review suggests that neurological dysfunction in at least a subset of children with ASD is based on alterations in the excitatory-to inhibitory balance in the brain.

AUTHOR CONTRIBUTIONS

This manuscript was developed as part of the Elias Tembenis Seizure Think Tanks at the Autism One Meeting in Chicago in May of 2009 and 2010 and at the Autism Canada Meeting in Toronto, Canada in October of 2009. These Think Tanks included scientists and clinicians with expertise in seizures related to ASD. The participants represented a wide variety of researchers and practitioners who treat ASD. Individual participants who provided written text for the supplement or contributed in the editing of the document are recognized as authors. Dr. Fatemi's research fellows assisted with the writing despite not attending the Think Tank so they are recognized as authors.

ACKNOWLEDGMENTS

This research has been supported by a National Institute of Child Health and Development grant to SF. This manuscript was supported by the Elias Tembenis Seizure Think Tanks conducted at the Autism One Meetings, the Autism International Association and the Autism Research Foundation.

REFERENCES

Adams, J. B., Audhya, T., McDonough-Means, S., Rubin, R. A., Quig, D., Geis, E., et al. (2011). Effect of a vitamin/mineral supplement on children and adults with autism. *BMC Pediatr.* 11:111. doi: 10.1186/1471-2431-11-111

Akaike, A., Tamura, Y., Sato, Y., and Yokota, T. (1993). Protective effects of a vitamin B12 analog, methylcobalamin, against glutamate cytotoxicity in cultured cortical neurons. *Eur. J. Pharmacol.* 241, 1–6. doi: 10.1016/0014-2999(93)90925-8

Anderson, M. P., Hooker, B. S., and Herbert, M. R. (2008). Bridging from cells to cognition in autism pathophysiology: biological pathways to defective brain function and plasticity *Am. J. Biochem. Biotechnol.* 4, 167–176. doi: 10.3844/ajbbsp.2008.167.176

Arrieta, O., Palencia, G., García-Arenas, G., Morales-Espinosa, D., Hernández-Pedro, N., and Sotelo, J. (2005). Prolonged exposure to lead lowers the threshold of pentylenetetrazole-induced seizures in rats. *Epilepsia* 46, 1599–1602. doi: 10.1111/j.1528-1167.2005.00267.x

Ault, B., Evans, R. H., Francis, A. A., Oakes, D. J., and Watkins, J. C. (1980). Selective depression of excitatory amino acid induced depolarizations by magnesium ions in isolated spinal cord preparations. *J. Physiol.* 307, 413–428. doi: 10.1113/jphysiol.1980.sp013443

Baieli, S., Pavone, L., Meli, C., Fiumara, A., and Coleman, M. (2003). Autism and phenylketonuria. *J. Autism Dev. Disord.* 33, 201–204. doi: 10.1023/A:1022999712639

Bangash, M. A., Park, J. M., Melnikova, T., Wang, D., Jeon, S. K., Lee, D., et al. (2011). Enhanced polyubiquitination of Shank3 and NMDA receptor in a mouse model of autism. *Cell* 145, 758–772. doi: 10.1016/j.cell.2011.03.052

Belyaeva, E. A., Korotkov, S. M., and Saris, N. E. (2011). In vitro modulation of heavy metal-induced rat liver mitochondria dysfunction: a comparison of copper and mercury with cadmium. *J. Trace Elem. Med. Biol.* 25(Suppl. 1), S63–S73. doi: 10.1016/j.jtemb.2010.10.007

Benbir, G., Uysal, S., Saltik, S., Zeybek, C. A., Aydin, A., Dervent, A., et al. (2007). Seizures during treatment of Vitamin B12 deficiency. *Seizure* 16, 69–73. doi: 10.1016/j.seizure.2006.10.016

Blanc, F., Ruppert, E., Kleitz, C., Valenti, M. P., Cretin, B., Humbel, R. L., et al. (2009). Acute limbic encephalitis and glutamic acid decarboxylase antibodies: a reality? *J. Neurol. Sci.* 287, 69–71. doi: 10.1016/j.jns.2009.09.004

Blatt, G. J., Fitzgerald, C. M., Guptill, J. T., Booker, A. B., Kemper, T. L., and Bauman, M. L. (2001). Density and distribution of hippocampal neurotransmitter receptors in autism: an autoradiographic study. *J. Autism Dev. Disord.* 31, 537–543. doi: 10.1023/A:1013238809666

Brock, J., Brown, C. C., Boucher, J., and Rippon, G. (2002). The temporal binding deficit hypothesis of autism. *Dev. Psychopathol.* 14, 209–224. doi: 10.1017/S0954579402002018

Brown, C., Gruber, T., Boucher, J., Rippon, G., and Brock, J. (2005). Gamma abnormalities during perception of illusory figures in autism. *Cortex* 41, 364–376. doi: 10.1016/S0010-9452(08)70273-9

Buxhoeveden, D. P., and Casanova, M. F. (2002). The minicolumn hypothesis in neuroscience. *Brain* 125, 935–951. doi: 10.1093/brain/awf110

Casanova, M. F., Buxhoeveden, D., and Gomez, J. (2003). Disruption in the inhibitory architecture of the cell minicolumn: implications for autism. *Neuroscientist* 9, 496–507. doi: 10.1177/1073858403253552

Casanova, M., Van Kooten, I., Switala, A., Van Engeland, H., Heinsen, H., Steinbusch, H., et al. (2006). Abnormalities of cortical minicolumnar organization in the prefrontal lobes of autistic patients. *Clin. Neurosci. Res.* 6, 127–133. doi: 10.1016/j.cnr.2006.06.003

Chaistitwanich, R., Mahoney, A. W., Hendricks, D. G., and Sisson, D. V. (1987). Dietary calcium and phosphorus and seizure susceptibility of magnesium deficient rats. *Pharmacol. Biochem. Behav.* 27, 443–449. doi: 10.1016/0091-3057(87)90347-9

Chen, H., and Chan, D. C. (2009). Mitochondrial dynamics–fusion, fission, movement, and mitophagy–in neurodegenerative diseases. *Hum. Mol. Genet.* 18, R169–R176. doi: 10.1093/hmg/ddp326

Clement, J. P., Aceti, M., Creson, T. K., Ozkan, E. D., Shi, Y., Reish, N. J., et al. (2012). Pathogenic SYNGAP1 mutations impair cognitive development by disrupting maturation of dendritic spine synapses. *Cell* 151, 709–723. doi: 10.1016/j.cell.2012.08.045

Cohen-Kfir, E., Lee, W., Eskandari, S., and Nelson, N. (2005). Zinc inhibition of gamma-aminobutyric acid transporter 4 (GAT4) reveals a link between excitatory and inhibitory neurotransmission. *Proc. Natl. Acad. Sci. U.S.A.* 102, 6154–6159. doi: 10.1073/pnas.0501431102

Cole, T. B., Robbins, C. A., Wenzel, H. J., Schwartzkroin, P. A., and Palmiter, R. D. (2000). Seizures and neuronal damage in mice lacking vesicular zinc. *Epilepsy Res.* 39, 153–169. doi: 10.1016/S0920-1211(99)00121-7

Condie, J., Goldstein, J., and Wainwright, M. S. (2010). Acquired microcephaly, regression of milestones, mitochondrial dysfunction, and episodic rigidity in a 46,XY male with a de novo MECP2 gene mutation. *J. Child Neurol.* 25, 633–636. doi: 10.1177/0883073809342004

Connolly, A. M., Chez, M. G., Pestronk, A., Arnold, S. T., Mehta, S., and Deuel, R. K. (1999). Serum autoantibodies to brain in Landau-Kleffner variant, autism, and other neurologic disorders. *J. Pediatr.* 134, 607–613. doi: 10.1016/S0022-3476(99)70248-9

Connolly, A. M., Chez, M., Streif, E. M., Keeling, R. M., Golumbek, P. T., Kwon, J. M., et al. (2006). Brain-derived neurotrophic factor and autoantibodies to neural antigens in sera of children with autistic spectrum disorders, Landau-Kleffner syndrome, and epilepsy. *Biol. Psychiatry* 59, 354–363. doi: 10.1016/j.biopsych.2005.07.004

Danielsson, S., Gillberg, I. C., Billstedt, E., Gillberg, C., and Olsson, I. (2005). Epilepsy in young adults with autism: a prospective population-based follow-up study of 120 individuals diagnosed in childhood. *Epilepsia* 46, 918–923. doi: 10.1111/j.1528-1167.2005.57504.x

Deepmala, Slattery, J., Kumar, N., Delhey, L., Berk, M., Dean, O., et al. (2015). Clinical trials of N-acetylcysteine in psychiatry and neurology: a systematic review. *Neurosci. Biobehav. Rev.* 55, 294–321. doi: 10.1016/j.neubiorev.2015.04.015

Defelipe, J. (1999). Chandelier cells and epilepsy. *Brain* 122(Pt 10), 1807–1822. doi: 10.1093/brain/122.10.1807

Defelipe, J. (2005). "Reflections on the structure of the cortical minicolumn," in *Neocortical Modularity and the Cell Minicolumn*, ed M. F. Casanova (New York, NY: Nova Biomedical), 57–92.

Defelipe, J., Hendry, S. H., Hashikawa, T., Molinari, M., and Jones, E. G. (1990). A microcolumnar structure of monkey cerebral cortex revealed by immunocytochemical studies of double bouquet cell axons. *Neuroscience* 37, 655–673. doi: 10.1016/0306-4522(90)90097-N

Delgado-Escueta, A. V. (2007). Advances in genetics of juvenile myoclonic epilepsies. *Epilepsy Curr.* 7, 61–67. doi: 10.1111/j.1535-7511.2007.00171.x

Delorenzo, R. J. (1986). A molecular approach to the calcium signal in brain: relationship to synaptic modulation and seizure discharge. *Adv. Neurol.* 44, 435–464.

Delorenzo, R. J., and Limbrick, D. D. Jr. (1996). Effects of glutamate on calcium influx and sequestration/extrusion mechanisms in hippocampal neurons. *Adv. Neurol.* 71, 37–46.

Deykin, E. Y., and Macmahon, B. (1979). The incidence of seizures among children with autistic symptoms. *Am. J. Psychiatry* 136, 1310–1312. doi: 10.1176/ajp.136.10.1310

Dhossche, D., Applegate, H., Abraham, A., Maertens, P., Bland, L., Bencsath, A., et al. (2002). Elevated plasma gamma-aminobutyric acid (GABA) levels in autistic youngsters: stimulus for a GABA hypothesis of autism. *Med. Sci. Monit.* 8, PR1–PR6.

D'hulst, C., and Kooy, R. F. (2007). The GABAA receptor: a novel target for treatment of fragile X? *Trends Neurosci.* 30, 425–431. doi: 10.1016/j.tins.2007.06.003

Erol, I., Alehan, F., and Gümüs, A. (2007). West syndrome in an infant with vitamin B12 deficiency in the absence of macrocytic anaemia. *Dev. Med. Child Neurol.* 49, 774–776. doi: 10.1111/j.1469-8749.2007.00774.x

Fatemi, S. H. (2008). The hyperglutamatergic hypothesis of autism. *Prog. Neuropsychopharmacol. Biol. Psychiatry.* 32, 911. author reply: 912–913.

Fatemi, S. H., Reutiman, T. J., Folsom, T. D., and Thuras, P. D. (2009). GABA(A) receptor downregulation in brains of subjects with autism. *J. Autism Dev. Disord.* 39, 223–230. doi: 10.1007/s10803-008-0646-7

Favorov, O. V., and Kelly, D. G. (1994). Minicolumnar organization within somatosensory cortical segregates: II. Emergent functional properties. *Cereb. Cortex* 4, 428–442. doi: 10.1093/cercor/4.4.428

Frye, R. E. (2012a). Biomarker of abnormal energy metabolism in children with autism spectrum disorder. *North Am. J. Med. Sci.* 5, 141–147. doi: 10.7156/v5i3p141

Frye, R. E. (2012b). Mitochondrial disease in 22q13 duplication syndrome. *J. Child Neurol.* 27, 942–949. doi: 10.1177/0883073811429858

Frye, R. E. (2012c). Novel mitochondrial Cytochrome B gene polymorphisms associated with autism. *J. Pediatr. Neurol.* 10, 35–40. doi: 10.3233/JPN-2012-0530

Frye, R. E. (2014). Clinical potential, safety, and tolerability of arbaclofen in the treatment of autism spectrum disorder. *Drug Healthc. Patient Saf.* 6, 69–76. doi: 10.2147/DHPS.S39595

Frye, R. E. (2015). Metabolic and mitochondrial disorders associated with epilepsy in children with autism spectrum disorder. *Epilepsy Behav.* 47, 147–157. doi: 10.1016/j.yebeh.2014.08.134

Frye, R. E., Cox, D., Slattery, J., Tippett, M., Kahler, S., Granpeesheh, D., et al. (2016a). Mitochondrial Dysfunction may explain symptom variation in Phelan-McDermid Syndrome. *Sci. Rep.* 6, 19544. doi: 10.1038/srep19544

Frye, R. E., Delatorre, R., Taylor, H. B., Slattery, J., Melnyk, S., Chowdhury, N., et al. (2013a). Metabolic effects of sapropterin treatment in autism spectrum disorder: a preliminary study. *Transl. Psychiatry* 3:e237. doi: 10.1038/tp.2013.14

Frye, R. E., Delhey, L., Slattery, J., Tippett, M., Wynne, R., Rose, S., et al. (2016b). Blocking and binding folate receptor alpha autoantibodies identify novel autism spectrum disorder subgroups. *Front. Neurosci.* 10:80. doi: 10.3389/fnins.2016.00080

Frye, R. E., and James, S. J. (2014). Metabolic pathology of autism in relation to redox metabolism. *Biomark. Med.* 8, 321–330. doi: 10.2217/bmm.13.158

Frye, R. E., Melnyk, S., Fuchs, G., Reid, T., Jernigan, S., Pavliv, O., et al. (2013b). Effectiveness of methylcobalamin and folinic Acid treatment on adaptive behavior in children with autistic disorder is related to glutathione redox status. *Autism Res. Treat.* 2013, 609705. doi: 10.1155/2013/609705

Frye, R. E., and Naviaux, R. K. (2011). Autistic disorder with complex IV overactivity: a new mitochondrial syndrome. *J. Pediatr. Neurol.* 9, 427–434. doi: 10.3233/JPN-2011-0507

Frye, R. E., and Rossignol, D. A. (2011). Mitochondrial dysfunction can connect the diverse medical symptoms associated with autism spectrum disorders. *Pediatr. Res.* 69, 41R–47R. doi: 10.1203/pdr.0b013e318212f16b

Frye, R. E., Sequeira, J. M., Quadros, E. V., James, S. J., and Rossignol, D. A. (2013c). Cerebral folate receptor autoantibodies in autism spectrum disorder. *Mol. Psychiatry* 18, 369–381. doi: 10.1038/mp.2011.175

Fukahori, M., and Itoh, M. (1990). Effects of dietary zinc status on seizure susceptibility and hippocampal zinc content in the El (epilepsy) mouse. *Brain Res.* 529, 16–22. doi: 10.1016/0006-8993(90)90806-M

Furieri, L. B., Galán, M., Avendaño, M. S., García-Redondo, A. B., Aguado, A., Martínez, S., et al. (2011). Endothelial dysfunction of rat coronary arteries after exposure to low concentrations of mercury is dependent on reactive oxygen species. *Br. J. Pharmacol.* 162, 1819–1831. doi: 10.1111/j.1476-5381.2011.01203.x

Ganesh, R., and Janakiraman, L. (2008). Serum zinc levels in children with simple febrile seizure. *Clin. Pediatr.* 47, 164–166. doi: 10.1177/0009922807306165

Ganor, Y., Goldberg-Stern, H., Amrom, D., Lerman-Sagie, T., Teichberg, V. I., Pelled, D., et al. (2004). Autoimmune epilepsy: some epilepsy patients harbor autoantibodies to glutamate receptors and dsDNA on both sides of the blood-brain barrier, which may kill neurons and decrease in brain fluids after hemispherotomy. *Clin. Dev. Immunol.* 11, 241–252. doi: 10.1080/17402520400001736

Giulivi, C., Zhang, Y. F., Omanska-Klusek, A., Ross-Inta, C., Wong, S., Hertz-Picciotto, I., et al. (2010). Mitochondrial dysfunction in autism. *JAMA* 304, 2389–2396. doi: 10.1001/jama.2010.1706

Glushakov, A. V., Dennis, D. M., Sumners, C., Seubert, C. N., and Martynyuk, A. E. (2003). L-phenylalanine selectively depresses currents at glutamatergic excitatory synapses. *J. Neurosci. Res.* 72, 116–124. doi: 10.1002/jnr.10569

Glushakov, A. V., Glushakova, O., Varshney, M., Bajpai, L. K., Sumners, C., Laipis, P. J., et al. (2005). Long-term changes in glutamatergic synaptic transmission in phenylketonuria. *Brain* 128, 300–307. doi: 10.1093/brain/awh354

Gospe, S. M. (2002). Pyridoxine-dependent seizures: findings from recent studies pose new questions. *Pediatr. Neurol.* 26, 181–185. doi: 10.1016/S0887-8994(01)00407-6

Gospe, S. M. Jr., Olin, K. L., and Keen, C. L. (1994). Reduced GABA synthesis in pyridoxine-dependent seizures. *Lancet* 343, 1133–1134. doi: 10.1016/S0140-6736(94)90236-4

Grice, S. J., Spratling, M. W., Karmiloff-Smith, A., Halit, H., Csibra, G., De Haan, M., et al. (2001). Disordered visual processing and oscillatory brain activity in autism and Williams syndrome. *Neuroreport* 12, 2697–2700. doi: 10.1097/00001756-200108280-00021

Grothe, B., and Klump, G. M. (2000). Temporal processing in sensory systems. *Curr. Opin. Neurobiol.* 10, 467–473. doi: 10.1016/S0959-4388(00)00115-X

Hallak, M. (1998). Effect of parenteral magnesium sulfate administration on excitatory amino acid receptors in the rat brain. *Magnes. Res.* 11, 117–131.

Hallak, M., Berman, R. F., Irtenkauf, S. M., Evans, M. I., and Cotton, D. B. (1992). Peripheral magnesium sulfate enters the brain and increases the threshold for hippocampal seizures in rats. *Am. J. Obstet. Gynecol.* 167, 1605–1610. doi: 10.1016/0002-9378(92)91749-Z

Han, Y., Qin, J., Bu, D. F., Chang, X. Z., and Yang, Z. X. (2006). Successive alterations of hippocampal gamma-aminobutyric acid B receptor subunits in a rat model of febrile seizure. *Life Sci.* 78, 2944–2952. doi: 10.1016/j.lfs.2005.11.023

Hara, H. (2007). Autism and epilepsy: a retrospective follow-up study. *Brain Dev.* 29, 486–490. doi: 10.1016/j.braindev.2006.12.012

Heinemann, U., and Hamon, B. (1986). Calcium and epileptogenesis. *Exp. Brain Res.* 65, 1–10. doi: 10.1007/BF00243826

Hendren, R. L., James, S. J., Widjaja, F., Lawton, B., Rosenblatt, A., and Bent, S. (2016). Randomized, placebo-controlled trial of Methyl B12 for children with autism. *J. Child Adolesc. Psychopharmacol.* doi: 10.1089/cap.2015.0159. [Epub ahead of print].

Jakobs, C., Bojasch, M., Mönch, E., Rating, D., Siemes, H., and Hanefeld, F. (1981). Urinary excretion of gamma-hydroxybutyric acid in a patient with neurological abnormalities. The probability of a new inborn error of metabolism. *Clin. Chim. Acta* 111, 169–178. doi: 10.1016/0009-8981(81)90184-4

James, S. J., Melnyk, S., Fuchs, G., Reid, T., Jernigan, S., Pavliv, O., et al. (2009a). Efficacy of methylcobalamin and folinic acid treatment on glutathione redox status in children with autism. *Am. J. Clin. Nutr.* 89, 425–430. doi: 10.3945/ajcn.2008.26615

James, S. J., Rose, S., Melnyk, S., Jernigan, S., Blossom, S., Pavliv, O., et al. (2009b). Cellular and mitochondrial glutathione redox imbalance in lymphoblastoid cells derived from children with autism. *FASEB J.* 23, 2374–2383. doi: 10.1096/fj.08-128926

Jurecka, A., Zikanova, M., Tylki-Szymanska, A., Krijt, J., Bogdanska, A., Gradowska, W., et al. (2008). Clinical, biochemical and molecular findings in seven Polish patients with adenylosuccinate lyase deficiency. *Mol. Genet. Metab.* 94, 435–442. doi: 10.1016/j.ymgme.2008.04.013

Kalra, S., Burbelo, P. D., Bayat, A., Ching, K. H., Thurm, A., Iadarola, M. J., et al. (2015). No evidence of antibodies against GAD65 and other specific antigens in children with autism. *BBA Clin.* 4, 81–84. doi: 10.1016/j.bbacli.2015.08.001

Kang, J. Q., Shen, W., and Macdonald, R. L. (2009). Two molecular pathways (NMD and ERAD) contribute to a genetic epilepsy associated with the GABA(A) receptor GABRA1 PTC mutation, 975delC, S326fs328X. *J. Neurosci.* 29, 2833–2844. doi: 10.1523/JNEUROSCI.4512-08.2009

Karayannis, T., Au, E., Patel, J. C., Kruglikov, I., Markx, S., Delorme, R., et al. (2014). Cntnap4 differentially contributes to GABAergic and dopaminergic synaptic transmission. *Nature* 511, 236–240. doi: 10.1038/nature13248

Kriaucionis, S., Paterson, A., Curtis, J., Guy, J., Macleod, N., and Bird, A. (2006). Gene expression analysis exposes mitochondrial abnormalities in a mouse model of Rett syndrome. *Mol. Cell. Biol.* 26, 5033–5042. doi: 10.1128/MCB.01665-05

Kumar, S. (2004). Recurrent seizures: an unusual manifestation of vitamin B12 deficiency. *Neurol. India* 52, 122–123.

Li, L., Chin, L. S., Shupliakov, O., Brodin, L., Sihra, T. S., Hvalby, O., et al. (1995). Impairment of synaptic vesicle clustering and of synaptic transmission, and increased seizure propensity, in synapsin I-deficient mice. *Proc. Natl. Acad. Sci. U.S.A.* 92, 9235–9239. doi: 10.1073/pnas.92.20.9235

Li, Z., Okamoto, K., Hayashi, Y., and Sheng, M. (2004). The importance of dendritic mitochondria in the morphogenesis and plasticity of spines and synapses. *Cell* 119, 873–887. doi: 10.1016/j.cell.2004.11.003

Lockitch, G., Berry, B., Roland, E., Wadsworth, L., Kaikov, Y., and Mirhady, F. (1991). Seizures in a 10-week-old infant: lead poisoning from an unexpected source. *CMAJ* 145, 1465–1468.

Longo, N., Ardon, O., Vanzo, R., Schwartz, E., and Pasquali, M. (2011). Disorders of creatine transport and metabolism. *Am. J. Med. Genet. C Semin. Med. Genet.* 157C, 72–78. doi: 10.1002/ajmg.c.30292

Macdermott, A. B., Mayer, M. L., Westbrook, G. L., Smith, S. J., and Barker, J. L. (1986). NMDA-receptor activation increases cytoplasmic calcium concentration in cultured spinal cord neurones. *Nature* 321, 519–522. doi: 10.1038/321519a0

Majoie, H. J., De Baets, M., Renier, W., Lang, B., and Vincent, A. (2006). Antibodies to voltage-gated potassium and calcium channels in epilepsy. *Epilepsy Res.* 71, 135–141. doi: 10.1016/j.eplepsyres.2006.06.003

Martynyuk, A. E., Glushakov, A. V., Sumners, C., Laipis, P. J., Dennis, D. M., and Seubert, C. N. (2005). Impaired glutamatergic synaptic transmission in the PKU brain. *Mol. Genet. Metab.* 86(Suppl. 1), S34–S42. doi: 10.1016/j.ymgme.2005.06.014

Mathern, G. W., Pretorius, J. K., Mendoza, D., Lozada, A., Leite, J. P., Chimelli, L., et al. (1998). Increased hippocampal AMPA and NMDA receptor subunit immunoreactivity in temporal lobe epilepsy patients. *J. Neuropathol. Exp. Neurol.* 57, 615–634. doi: 10.1097/00005072-199806000-00008

Mikuni, N., Babb, T. L., Ying, Z., Najm, I., Nishiyama, K., Wylie, C., et al. (1999). NMDA-receptors 1 and 2A/B coassembly increased in human epileptic focal cortical dysplasia. *Epilepsia* 40, 1683–1687. doi: 10.1111/j.1528-1157.1999.tb01584.x

Mills, P. B., Struys, E., Jakobs, C., Plecko, B., Baxter, P., Baumgartner, M., et al. (2006). Mutations in antiquitin in individuals with pyridoxine-dependent seizures. *Nat. Med.* 12, 307–309. doi: 10.1038/nm1366

Mollah, M. A., Rakshit, S. C., Anwar, K. S., Arslan, M. I., Saha, N., Ahmed, S., et al. (2008). Zinc concentration in serum and cerebrospinal fluid simultaneously decrease in children with febrile seizure: findings from a prospective study in Bangladesh. *Acta Paediatr.* 97, 1707–1711. doi: 10.1111/j.1651-2227.2008.01001.x

Mountcastle, V. B. (1997). The columnar organization of the neocortex. *Brain* 120(Pt 4), 701–722. doi: 10.1093/brain/120.4.701

Murdoch, J. D., and State, M. W. (2013). Recent developments in the genetics of autism spectrum disorders. *Curr. Opin. Genet. Dev.* 23, 310–315. doi: 10.1016/j.gde.2013.02.003

Obeid, R., Mccaddon, A., and Herrmann, W. (2007). The role of hyperhomocysteinemia and B-vitamin deficiency in neurological and psychiatric diseases. *Clin. Chem. Lab. Med.* 45, 1590–1606. doi: 10.1515/CCLM.2007.356

Pal, P. B., Pal, S., Das, J., and Sil, P. C. (2012). Modulation of mercury-induced mitochondria-dependent apoptosis by glycine in hepatocytes. *Amino Acids* 42, 1669–1683. doi: 10.1007/s00726-011-0869-3

Pearl, P. L., Gibson, K. M., Cortez, M. A., Wu, Y., Carter Snead, O. 3rd., Knerr, I., et al. (2009a). Succinic semialdehyde dehydrogenase deficiency: lessons from mice and men. *J. Inherit. Metab. Dis.* 32, 343–352. doi: 10.1007/s10545-009-1034-y

Pearl, P. L., Gibson, K. M., Quezado, Z., Dustin, I., Taylor, J., Trzcinski, S., et al. (2009b). Decreased GABA-A binding on FMZ-PET in succinic semialdehyde dehydrogenase deficiency. *Neurology* 73, 423–429. doi: 10.1212/WNL.0b013e3181b163a5

Pei, Y., Zhao, D., Huang, J., and Cao, L. (1983). Zinc-induced seizures: a new experimental model of epilepsy. *Epilepsia* 24, 169–176. doi: 10.1111/j.1528-1157.1983.tb04876.x

Pelc, K., Boyd, S. G., Cheron, G., and Dan, B. (2008). Epilepsy in Angelman syndrome. *Seizure* 17, 211–217. doi: 10.1016/j.seizure.2007.08.004

Peñagarikano, O., Abrahams, B. S., Herman, E. I., Winden, K. D., Gdalyahu, A., Dong, H., et al. (2011). Absence of CNTNAP2 leads to epilepsy, neuronal migration abnormalities, and core autism-related deficits. *Cell* 147, 235–246. doi: 10.1016/j.cell.2011.08.040

Pickett, J., Xiu, E., Tuchman, R., Dawson, G., and Lajonchere, C. (2011). Mortality in individuals with autism, with and without epilepsy. *J. Child Neurol.* 26, 932–939. doi: 10.1177/0883073811402203

Póo-Argüelles, P., Arias, A., Vilaseca, M. A., Ribes, A., Artuch, R., Sans-Fito, A., et al. (2006). X-Linked creatine transporter deficiency in two patients with severe mental retardation and autism. *J. Inherit. Metab. Dis.* 29, 220–223. doi: 10.1007/s10545-006-0212-4

Princivalle, A. P., Richards, D. A., Duncan, J. S., Spreafico, R., and Bowery, N. G. (2003). Modification of GABA(B1) and GABA(B2) receptor subunits in the somatosensory cerebral cortex and thalamus of rats with absence seizures (GAERS). *Epilepsy Res.* 55, 39–51. doi: 10.1016/S0920-1211(03)00090-1

Quiroz, J. A., Gray, N. A., Kato, T., and Manji, H. K. (2008). Mitochondrially mediated plasticity in the pathophysiology and treatment of bipolar disorder. *Neuropsychopharmacology* 33, 2551–2565. doi: 10.1038/sj.npp.1301671

Ramaekers, V. T., and Blau, N. (2004). Cerebral folate deficiency. *Dev. Med. Child Neurol.* 46, 843–851. doi: 10.1111/j.1469-8749.2004.tb00451.x

Ramaekers, V. T., Häusler, M., Opladen, T., Heimann, G., and Blau, N. (2002). Psychomotor retardation, spastic paraplegia, cerebellar ataxia and dyskinesia associated with low 5-methyltetrahydrofolate in cerebrospinal fluid: a novel neurometabolic condition responding to folinic acid substitution. *Neuropediatrics* 33, 301–308. doi: 10.1055/s-2002-37082

Riazi, K., Galic, M. A., and Pittman, Q. J. (2010). Contributions of peripheral inflammation to seizure susceptibility: cytokines and brain excitability. *Epilepsy Res.* 89, 34–42. doi: 10.1016/j.eplepsyres.2009.09.004

Rippon, G., Brock, J., Brown, C., and Boucher, J. (2007). Disordered connectivity in the autistic brain: challenges for the 'new psychophysiology'. *Int. J. Psychophysiol.* 63, 164–172. doi: 10.1016/j.ijpsycho.2006.03.012

Rose, C. (2006). Effect of ammonia on astrocytic glutamate uptake/release mechanisms. *J. Neurochem.* 97(Suppl. 1), 11–15. doi: 10.1111/j.1471-4159.2006.03796.x

Rose, S., Frye, R. E., Slattery, J., Wynne, R., Tippett, M., Melnyk, S., et al. (2014a). Oxidative stress induces mitochondrial dysfunction in a subset of autistic lymphoblastoid cell lines. *Transl. Psychiatry* 4:e377. doi: 10.1038/tp.2014.15

Rose, S., Frye, R. E., Slattery, J., Wynne, R., Tippett, M., Pavliv, O., et al. (2014b). Oxidative stress induces mitochondrial dysfunction in a subset of autism lymphoblastoid cell lines in a well-matched case control cohort. *PLoS ONE* 9:e85436. doi: 10.1371/journal.pone.0085436

Rose, S., Wynne, R., Frye, R. E., Melnyk, S., and James, S. J. (2015). Increased susceptibility to ethylmercury-induced mitochondrial dysfunction in a subset of autism lymphoblastoid cell lines. *J. Toxicol.* 2015, 573701. doi: 10.1155/2015/573701

Rossignol, D. A., and Frye, R. E. (2012a). Mitochondrial dysfunction in autism spectrum disorders: a systematic review and meta-analysis. *Mol. Psychiatry* 17, 290–314. doi: 10.1038/mp.2010.136

Rossignol, D. A., and Frye, R. E. (2012b). A review of research trends in physiological abnormalities in autism spectrum disorders: immune dysregulation, inflammation, oxidative stress, mitochondrial dysfunction and environmental toxicant exposures. *Mol. Psychiatry* 17, 389–401. doi: 10.1038/mp.2011.165

Rossignol, D. A., Genuis, S. J., and Frye, R. E. (2014). Environmental toxicants and autism spectrum disorders: a systematic review. *Transl. Psychiatry* 4:e360. doi: 10.1038/tp.2014.4

Rout, U. K., Mungan, N. K., and Dhossche, D. M. (2012). Presence of GAD65 autoantibodies in the serum of children with autism or ADHD. *Eur. Child Adolesc. Psychiatry* 21, 141–147. doi: 10.1007/s00787-012-0245-1

Rubenstein, J. L., and Merzenich, M. M. (2003). Model of autism: increased ratio of excitation/inhibition in key neural systems. *Genes Brain Behav.* 2, 255–267. doi: 10.1034/j.1601-183X.2003.00037.x

Sansa, G., Carlson, C., Doyle, W., Weiner, H. L., Bluvstein, J., Barr, W., et al. (2011). Medically refractory epilepsy in autism. *Epilepsia* 52, 1071–1075. doi: 10.1111/j.1528-1167.2011.03069.x

Schaefer, G. B., Mendelsohn, N. J., Professional, P., and Guidelines, C. (2013). Clinical genetics evaluation in identifying the etiology of autism spectrum disorders: 2013 guideline revisions. *Genet. Med.* 15, 399–407. doi: 10.1038/gim.2013.32

Schuler, V., Lüscher, C., Blanchet, C., Klíx, N., Sansig, G., Klebs, K., et al. (2001). Epilepsy, hyperalgesia, impaired memory, and loss of pre- and postsynaptic GABA(B) responses in mice lacking GABA(B(1)). *Neuron* 31, 47–58. doi: 10.1016/S0896-6273(01)00345-2

Shavelle, R. M., Strauss, D. J., and Pickett, J. (2001). Causes of death in autism. *J. Autism Dev. Disord.* 31, 569–576. doi: 10.1023/A:1013247011483

Shcheglovitov, A., Shcheglovitova, O., Yazawa, M., Portmann, T., Shu, R., Sebastiano, V., et al. (2013). SHANK3 and IGF1 restore synaptic deficits in neurons from 22q13 deletion syndrome patients. *Nature* 503, 267–271. doi: 10.1038/nature12618

Silbergeld, E. K., Miller, L. P., Kennedy, S., and Eng, N. (1979). Lead, GABA, and seizures: effects of subencephalopathic lead exposure on seizure sensitivity and GABAergic function. *Environ. Res.* 19, 371–382. doi: 10.1016/0013-9351(79)90062-8

Sinert, R., Zehtabchi, S., Desai, S., Peacock, P., Altura, B. T., and Altura, B. M. (2007). Serum ionized magnesium and calcium levels in adult patients with seizures. *Scand. J. Clin. Lab. Invest.* 67, 317–326. doi: 10.1080/00365510601051441

Specchio, N., Fusco, L., Claps, D., and Vigevano, F. (2010). Epileptic encephalopathy in children possibly related to immune-mediated pathogenesis. *Brain Dev.* 32, 51–56. doi: 10.1016/j.braindev.2009.09.017

Spiegel, E. K., Colman, R. F., and Patterson, D. (2006). Adenylosuccinate lyase deficiency. *Mol. Genet. Metab.* 89, 19–31. doi: 10.1016/j.ymgme.2006.04.018

Srivastava, A. K., and Schwartz, C. E. (2014). Intellectual disability and autism spectrum disorders: causal genes and molecular mechanisms. *Neurosci. Biobehav. Rev.* 46(Pt 2), 161–174. doi: 10.1016/j.neubiorev.2014.02.015

Su, H., Fan, W., Coskun, P. E., Vesa, J., Gold, J. A., Jiang, Y. H., et al. (2011). Mitochondrial dysfunction in CA1 hippocampal neurons of the UBE3A deficient mouse model for Angelman syndrome. *Neurosci. Lett.* 487, 129–133. doi: 10.1016/j.neulet.2009.06.079

Swartzwelder, H. S. (1985). Central neurotoxicity after exposure to organic lead: susceptibility to seizures. *Neurosci. Lett.* 58, 225–228. doi: 10.1016/0304-3940(85)90168-5

Tabuchi, K., Blundell, J., Etherton, M. R., Hammer, R. E., Liu, X., Powell, C. M., et al. (2007). A neuroligin-3 mutation implicated in autism increases inhibitory synaptic transmission in mice. *Science* 318, 71–76. doi: 10.1126/science.1146221

Tommerdahl, M., Tannan, V., Cascio, C. J., Baranek, G. T., and Whitsel, B. L. (2007). Vibrotactile adaptation fails to enhance spatial localization in adults with autism. *Brain Res.* 1154, 116–123. doi: 10.1016/j.brainres.2007.04.032

Torres, A. D., Rai, A. N., and Hardiek, M. L. (2000). Mercury intoxication and arterial hypertension: report of two patients and review of the literature. *Pediatrics* 105:E34. doi: 10.1542/peds.105.3.e34

Tuchman, R. (2013). Autism and social cognition in epilepsy: implications for comprehensive epilepsy care. *Curr. Opin. Neurol.* 26, 214–218. doi: 10.1097/WCO.0b013e32835ee64f

Tuchman, R. F., and Rapin, I. (1997). Regression in pervasive developmental disorders: seizures and epileptiform electroencephalogram correlates. *Pediatrics* 99, 560–566. doi: 10.1542/peds.99.4.560

Tuchman, R., Hirtz, D., and Mamounas, L. A. (2013). NINDS epilepsy and autism spectrum disorders workshop report. *Neurology* 81, 1630–1636. doi: 10.1212/WNL.0b013e3182a9f482

Tuchman, R., and Rapin, I. (2002). Epilepsy in autism. *Lancet Neurol.* 1, 352–358. doi: 10.1016/S1474-4422(02)00160-6

Vargas, D. L., Nascimbene, C., Krishnan, C., Zimmerman, A. W., and Pardo, C. A. (2005). Neuroglial activation and neuroinflammation in the brain of patients with autism. *Ann. Neurol.* 57, 67–81. doi: 10.1002/ana.20315

Vincent, A., Buckley, C., Schott, J. M., Baker, I., Dewar, B. K., Detert, N., et al. (2004). Potassium channel antibody-associated encephalopathy: a potentially immunotherapy-responsive form of limbic encephalitis. *Brain* 127, 701–712. doi: 10.1093/brain/awh077

Volkmar, F. R., and Nelson, D. S. (1990). Seizure disorders in autism. *J. Am. Acad. Child Adolesc. Psychiatry* 29, 127–129. doi: 10.1097/00004583-199001000-00020

Waldbaum, S., and Patel, M. (2010). Mitochondria, oxidative stress, and temporal lobe epilepsy. *Epilepsy Res.* 88, 23–45. doi: 10.1016/j.eplepsyres.2009.09.020

Wang, L., Wang, H., Li, J., Chen, D., and Liu, Z. (2011a). Simultaneous effects of lead and cadmium on primary cultures of rat proximal tubular cells: interaction of apoptosis and oxidative stress. *Arch. Environ. Contam. Toxicol.* 61, 500–511. doi: 10.1007/s00244-011-9644-4

Wang, X., Mccoy, P. A., Rodriguiz, R. M., Pan, Y., Je, H. S., Roberts, A. C., et al. (2011b). Synaptic dysfunction and abnormal behaviors in mice lacking major isoforms of Shank3. *Hum. Mol. Genet.* 20, 3093–3108. doi: 10.1093/hmg/ddr212

Williams, R. A., Mamotte, C. D., and Burnett, J. R. (2008). Phenylketonuria: an inborn error of phenylalanine metabolism. *Clin. Biochem. Rev.* 29, 31–41.

Williamson, A., and Spencer, D. (1995). Zinc reduces dentate granule cell hyperexcitability in epileptic humans. *Neuroreport* 6, 1562–1564. doi: 10.1097/00001756-199507310-00024

Zablotsky, B., Black, L. I., Maenner, M. J., Schieve, L. A., and Blumberg, S. J. (2015). *Estimated Prevalence of Autism and Other Developmental Disabilities Following Questionnaire Changes in the 2014 National Health Interview Survey.* Hyattsville, MD: National Center for Health Statistics. National Health Statistics Reports No. 87.

11

Rehabilitative Interventions and Brain Plasticity in Autism Spectrum Disorders: Focus on MRI-Based Studies

Sara Calderoni[1], Lucia Billeci[2], Antonio Narzisi[1], Paolo Brambilla[3,4], Alessandra Retico[5] and Filippo Muratori[1,2]*

[1] IRCCS Stella Maris Foundation, Pisa, Italy, [2] Department of Clinical and Experimental Medicine, University of Pisa, Pisa, Italy, [3] Department of Neurosciences and Mental Health, Fondazione IRCCS Ca' Granda Ospedale Maggiore Policlinico, University of Milan, Milan, Italy, [4] Department of Psychiatry and Behavioral Sciences, University of Texas Health Science Center at Houston, Houston, TX, USA, [5] Pisa Section of National Institute of Nuclear Physics, Pisa, Italy

Edited by:
Remo Job,
University of Trento, Italy

Reviewed by:
Rajshekhar Bipeta,
Gandhi Medical College and Hospital, India
Stephanie Ameis,
University of Toronto, Canada

***Correspondence:**
Sara Calderoni
sara.calderoni@fsm.unipi.it

Clinical and research evidence supports the efficacy of rehabilitative intervention for improving targeted skills or global outcomes in individuals with autism spectrum disorder (ASD). However, putative mechanisms of structural and functional brain changes are poorly understood. This review aims to investigate the research literature on the neural circuit modifications after non-pharmacological intervention. For this purpose, longitudinal studies that used magnetic resonance imaging (MRI)-based techniques at the start and at the end of the trial to evaluate the neural effects of rehabilitative treatment in subjects with ASD were identified. The six included studies involved a limited number of patients in the active group (from 2 to 16), and differed by acquisition method (task-related and resting-state functional MRI) as well as by functional MRI tasks. Overall, the results produced by the selected investigations demonstrated brain plasticity during the treatment interval that results in an activation/functional connectivity more similar to those of subjects with typical development (TD). Repeated MRI evaluation may represent a promising tool for the detection of neural changes in response to treatment in patients with ASD. However, large-scale randomized controlled trials after standardized rehabilitative intervention are required before translating these preliminary results into clinical use.

Keywords: autism spectrum disorder, brain plasticity, magnetic resonance imaging, treatment effects, outcome

INTRODUCTION

Autism spectrum disorders (ASD) are a heterogeneous group of neurodevelopmental conditions characterized by persistent deficits in social communication and interaction across multiple contexts, in addition to restricted, repetitive patterns of behavior, interests, or activities, all of which significantly impact on adaptive functioning (American Psychiatric Association, 2013). Although the exact etiology of ASD remains elusive, a combination of genetic and environmental factors during critical periods of development has been implicated (Hallmayer et al., 2011), possibly leading to altered brain architecture beginning early in life (Wolff and Piven, 2013; Conti et al., 2015), or even in prenatal developmental stages (Stoner et al., 2014). Specifically, brain underpinnings revealed by magnetic resonance imaging (MRI) include an early altered developmental trajectory of global and regional brain structures (see Chen et al., 2011 and Bellani et al., 2013 for reviews of structural MRI studies in ASD), with an atypical growing of white matter tracts (see Ameis and Catani, 2015 for a review of diffusion tensor imaging -DTI- studies in ASD), altered task-dependent cerebral response (see Dickstein et al., 2013 for a review of functional MRI -fMRI- studies in ASD), and abnormal neuronal activity in the absence of stimulation (see Uddin et al., 2013 for a review of resting-state fMRI -rs-fMRI- studies in ASD). Notably, abnormalities in brain correlates of ASD are likely to be influenced by study design characteristics and a wide range of clinical and demographic features (Lenroot and Yeung, 2013). In particular, an age-dependency of brain volume differences between ASD patients and controls with typical development (TD) has been repeatedly detected: in fact, while an increased total brain volume is noted in infants and toddlers with ASD compared to TD, an absence of group differences later in childhood is frequently reported (Courchesne et al., 2007; Amaral et al., 2008). The deviation from the normal brain growth trajectory described in young subjects with ASD can lead to atypical organization of structural and functional cerebral connectivity (Lewis and Elman, 2008).Indeed, an excess of short-distance with diminished long-range connectivity has been proposed (Just et al., 2007), producing a brain profile ineffective for processing and integrating "higher-order" information that ultimately leads to several of the most common ASD neuropsychological characteristics (Wass, 2011; Narzisi et al., 2013). In this framework, a rehabilitative intervention for patients with ASD is considered a treatment able to enhance neuroplasticity (Dawson, 2008), i.e., the capacity of cerebral neurons and neural circuits to structurally and functionally change in response to external stimuli, environmental modifications, or injuries (Pascual-Leone et al., 2005). However, neural substrates underlying observed clinical improvement after early interventions are not yet fully elucidate (Sullivan et al., 2014). In this view, the introduction of advanced MRI techniques, such as fMRI, rs-fMRI, and DTI, have been recently used to investigate brain plasticity by monitoring the effects of rehabilitative therapy in ASD patients. Specifically, longitudinal studies that include pre- and post-treatment MRI acquisition have provided new insights on the neural mechanisms targeted in rehabilitative therapy and, in addition, an objective measure of response to treatment.

Therefore, the goal of the current review is to summarize the existing MRI-based evidences of functional and structural plasticity induced by rehabilitation therapy in patients with ASD. To this aim, longitudinal studies that use MRI-based techniques pre- and post- rehabilitative intervention to explore the impact of treatment on neural substrates in ASD patients were analyzed. To our knowledge, no review article exists addressing the question of whether and how non-psychopharmacological interventions shape the brain of patients with ASD.

METHODS

Studies in which functional or structural MRI was used to evaluate rehabilitative treatment response in patients with ASD were eligible for inclusion. Relevant articles were identified from searches in two electronic databases (Pubmed and Scopus). Search terms included the following: "autis*," "neuroimaging," "MRI," "magnetic resonance," "fMRI," "rs-fMRI," "DTI," "diffusion tensor," "training," "treatment," and "rehabilitation" both in isolation and in combination. We further limited the results to "English" and "Humans." No article type limitations or time period restrictions were applied, and the latest search was undertaken in September 2015. We identified longitudinal studies that examined MRI-based differences in brain structure and function between pre- and post- rehabilitative treatment in individuals with ASD. This paper reports a selective narrative description of the identified investigations.

RESULTS

We found six studies published between 2006 and 2015 that investigated whether rehabilitation strategies enhance brain plasticity, as evaluated by either rs-fMRI ($n = 1$) (Murdaugh et al., 2015), or task-related fMRI ($n = 5$; Bölte et al., 2006, 2015; Voos et al., 2013; Ventola et al., 2015; Murdaugh et al., 2016). A list of these studies and their characteristics are detailed in **Table 1**.

The first attempt to demonstrate the presence of brain plasticity in ASD following a specific rehabilitation treatment was performed by Bölte et al. (2006) who selected (with randomization) 10 adult patients. Of them, five received a 5-weeks computer-based facial affect training program (2-h per week), while the remaining five ASD patients did not undergo any special training. The effects of training program have been demonstrated on both behavioral and neurobiological level.

However, an atypical pattern of increased activation in the right superior parietal lobule post-training in ASD subjects, rather than the activation of the fusiform face area usually found in participants with TD, was detected. Therefore, the authors concluded that the intervention group learned to recognize emotions by using compensatory mechanisms involving the recruitment of different brain regions.

More recently, a similar study was conducted by the same group (Bölte et al., 2015) to explore the neural effects of the same computer based training (1 h/week for 8 weeks) aimed at improving facial affect recognition. The investigation focused on 32 adolescent with high-functioning ASD: half of them received the specific training plus standard care, whereas the other half received standard care only. Each ASD group was scanned twice, pre and post-training, using task-related fMRI consisting of facial affect recognition. A control group of 25 subjects with TD was also enrolled to compare the behavioral assessment and the brain activations to that of patients with ASD at baseline. As expected, reduced ability to recognize facial expressions coupled with reduced social brain activity was found in individuals with ASD. After training was completed, a relevant improvement in facial recognition characterized the active group and was associated with an increased activity in the social brain areas.

To investigate the possibility that early rehabilitative treatment induces activation changes of brain regions involved in social perception in young children with ASD, Voos et al.

TABLE 1 | Summary of studies utilizing MRI pre- and post-rehabilitative treatment of ASD patients.

	Bölte et al., 2006	Voos et al., 2013	Ventola et al., 2015	Murdaugh et al., 2015	Bölte et al., 2015	Murdaugh et al., 2016
Study type	Randomized cross-over trial	Case series	Uncontrolled pre-post trial	Randomized cross-over trial	Non-randomized parallel group trial	Randomized cross-over trial
Center	Frankfurt University, Germany	Yale University, USA	Yale University, USA	University of Alabama at Birmingham, USA	Frankfurt University, Germany	University of Alabama at Birmingham, USA
Number of ASD patients in the active group	5 males	2 (1 male and 1 female)	10 (8 males)	16 (12 males)	16 males	13 (11 males)
Controls	5 ASD males	No	5 TD (2 males)	15 ASD (12 males) and 22 TD (16 males)	16 ASD (14 males) and 25 TD (21 males)	13 ASD (10 males) and 19 TD (14 males)
Mean age of ASD patients	29.4 years	~5 years	~5 years	10.3 years	19.3 years	10.9 years
ID in ASD patients	No	No	No	No	No	No
MRI technique	fMRI (facial affect recognition task)	fMRI (social perception task)	fMRI (social perception task)	rs-fMRI	fMRI (facial affect recognition task)	fMRI (sentence comprehension task) and rs-fMRI
Type of treatment	Computer-based facial affect recognition training	PRT	PRT	Reading intervention	Computer-based facial affect recognition training	Reading intervention
Duration of treatment	2 h per week for 5 weeks	8–10 h per week for 4 months	7 h per week for 16 weeks	20 h per week for 10 weeks	1 h per week for 8 weeks	20 h per week for 10 weeks
Clinical outcome(s) in the active group	Improvements in facial affect recognition	Improvement on ADOS, CELF-4, and Vineland-II scores	Improvement on SRS-2 and ADOS scores	Improvement in reading comprehension, as measured by the GORT-4 Comprehension subtest	Improvements in facial affect recognition	Improvement in reading comprehension, as measured by the GORT-4 Comprehension subtest
MRI outcome(s) in the active group	Increased activation in the R superior parietal lobule and maintained activation in the R medial occipital gyrus	Different increased activation in the two patients: L dorsolateral prefrontal cortex and L fusiform gyrus in one subject, R posterior superior temporal sulcus, L ventrolateral prefrontal cortex and bilateral fusiform gyri in the other patient	5 ASD patients showed significant increased activation in R posterior superior temporal sulcus, ventral striatum, and putamen; 5 ASD patients showed significant decreased activation in R posterior superior temporal sulcus, thalamus, amygdala, and hippocampus	Enhanced connectivity of Broca's area with R middle frontal gyrus, R superior temporal gyrus, L supramarginal gyrus, and R caudate; reduced connectivity of Broca's area with R middle occipital gyrus and R posterior cingulate cortex	Increased activation in amygdala, fusiform gyrus, and temporal pole bilaterally, medial prefrontal cortex, and L posterior superior temporal sulcus	Increased activation in brain regions underlying language and visuospatial processing, bilateral insula, R postcentral gyrus, and compensatory recruitment of R-hemisphere and subcortical regions
						Increased functional connectivity between L middle temporal gyrus and L frontal regions
					Enhanced connectivity of Wernicke's area with R anterior cingulate, L middle orbital gyrus, bilateral inferior frontal gyrus, R middle frontal gyrus, R middle cingulate, R precentral gyrus	
Follow-up period	No	No	No	No	No	No

ASD, Autism Spectrum Disorders; MRI, Magnetic Resonance Imaging; DTI, Diffusion Tensor Imaging; fMRI, functional Magnetic Resonance Imaging; rs-fMRI, resting-state functional Magnetic Resonance Imaging; ID, intellectual disability; TD, controls with typical developing; PRT, Pivotal Response Treatment; CELF-4, Clinical Evaluation of Language Fundamentals—Fourth Edition; ADOS, Autism Diagnostic Observation Schedule; SRS-2, Social Responsiveness Scale-Second Edition; GORT-4, Gray Oral Reading Tests-4th Edition; R, right; L, left.

(2013) included two ASD preschoolers to receive 8–10 h per week for 4 months of Pivotal Response Treatment (PRT), a well-known empirically validated behavioral treatment for children with ASD (Koegel et al., 1987). After rehabilitation, significant behavioral improvements in core ASD deficits, adaptive skills, and language were signaled and, at the neural level, a modification in the processing of biological motion. Interestingly, the effects of the same treatment on brain activation are different in the two children, in line with the heterogeneity of the response to therapy in the ASD condition (Kim et al., 2015).

The same group performed a subsequent work based on an enlarged sample size of 10 preschoolers with ASD (Ventola et al., 2015). Before treatment, two groups of ASD children could be distinguished based on their activation profiles– reduced or increased- in posterior superior temporal sulcus (pSTS) in comparison with TD controls. Following a 16-week PRT treatment (7-h per week) a significant improvement of clinical ASD manifestations emerged, coupled with an activation in pSTS more similar to that of TD children. Therefore, treatment modifications are reached through two different neural modalities: a decrease in activation following treatment for ASD subjects who exhibited hyper-activation in the pSTS at baseline and *vice-versa*.

A randomized clinical trial (Murdaugh et al., 2015) was designed to explore modifications in functional connectivity after the intensive reading intervention "Visualizing and Verbalizing for Language Comprehension and Thinking" (Lindamood and Bell, 1997) in children with ASD. A total of 31 ASD patients were randomized either to a 10-week reading intervention (active group) or to receive the same intervention after the two imaging sessions were completed (wait-list control group). An additional control group of TD children served as a baseline comparison for brain activation and did not participate in the intervention protocol. Rs-fMRI revealed that after the training the active group had an increased connectivity using Broca's and Wernicke's area as seeding points. In order to verify whether functional connectivity changes in the active group were specifically related to the targeted training, a comparison between post-intervention connectivity in active and control ASD participants was conducted. After rehabilitation, increased rs-fMRI within the reading network was found in the active group, as well as an additional recruitment of frontal regions (left superior frontal gyrus and middle frontal gyrus), interpreted as compensatory mechanisms for language comprehension.

Some subjects originally enrolled in this latter study also underwent fMRI (Murdaugh et al., 2016), in order to investigate changes in brain activation following the reading intervention (Lindamood and Bell, 1997). Pre- and post-training task-related fMRI (sentence comprehension) revealed increased activation in visual and posterior language regions, bilateral insula and right postcentral gyrus, with an additional recruitment of right-hemisphere and subcortical regions as possible compensatory mechanisms for language comprehension. Moreover, an increased functional connectivity between left middle temporal gyrus and left frontal regions has been found after training in the active group. Intriguingly, the intervention-induced brain modifications positively correlated with the improvements in individual reading comprehension. Compared to ASD wait-list control group at the second imaging session, patients in the active group showed an increased activation in some areas of frontal, parietal, and temporal cortices.

DISCUSSION

Designing studies able to measure neural change in response to therapy is thought to be an important goal for autism research (McPartland and Pelphrey, 2012). According to this view, the current review investigated studies that applied MRI-based neuroimaging techniques pre- and post-rehabilitative treatment in ASD. Results from the six included investigations (Bölte et al., 2006, 2015; Voos et al., 2013; Murdaugh et al., 2015, 2016; Ventola et al., 2015) suggested that training-induced behavioral changes were accompanied by significant modifications in neural activity and/or functional connectivity that varied as a function of the specific training intervention. Preliminary evidence suggests that early intervention can mitigate the severity of core and associated features of autism (Warren et al., 2011), improve the long-term outcome of treated patients (Estes et al., 2015), and even reverse some of the ASD symptoms (Rogers et al., 2014). These behavioral improvements are supposed to result from changes in brain structure and function that are particularly achievable in critical period plasticity in early life. At these specific time windows, environmental stimuli most potently shape cortical brain circuitries responsible for the acquisition of different types of skills and abilities (Bardin, 2012). However, results from the studies included in this review reflect that brain plasticity, also in ASD patients, is not limited to early developmental stage (Voos et al., 2013; Ventola et al., 2015), but includes also the school-age period (Murdaugh et al., 2015, 2016), and adulthood (Bölte et al., 2006, 2015).

Notably, the six included studies pertained to three research group, each of whom performed two investigations to evaluate the effects of a specific rehabilitative treatment. In this context, rehabilitation treatments received by patients with ASD are highly heterogeneous in terms of targeted impairments. In particular, the group coordinated by Ventola focused on the neural effects of a comprehensive intervention program specifically developed to target the core social and communication deficits of children with ASD (Voos et al., 2013; Ventola et al., 2015); Bölte and colleagues utilized a computer-based program to target specific impairment in facial affect recognition (Bölte et al., 2006, 2015), while Murdaugh et al. administered a protocol to improve reading comprehension, an ancillary deficit in ASD individuals (Murdaugh et al., 2015, 2016).

In spite of the encouraging results on behavioral and brain plasticity, the studies examined in this review suffer from several drawbacks. In fact, reports generally comprised of a limited number of subjects (ranging from 2 to 16 ASD individuals in the active group), and the relatively small sample size makes it difficult to homogeneously subgroup ASD patients based on their clinical profile (e.g., level of intelligence quotient and language, core ASD symptom severity, adaptive functioning, psychiatric comorbidities). Therefore, it is difficult to identify baseline clinical characteristics that influence behavioral and brain outcome of examined patients. Moreover, the lack of MRI follow-up data after the second scan hampered testing for stability of brain modifications obtained following rehabilitative treatment. In fact, it remains to investigate whether such improvements in brain functions are sustained without further intervention or whether maintenance training is necessary.

In addition, the studies included in the current review had different design. Two investigations (Voos et al., 2013; Ventola et al., 2015) lacked of a non-active control group of ASD subjects, whereas the others included as control group subjects in the waitlist (Bölte et al., 2006; Murdaugh et al., 2015, 2016), or patients receiving standard care only (Bölte et al., 2015). The presence of a non-active control group of ASD individuals is essential to discern whether an hypothesized biomarker for the prediction of treatment response is really predictive of response to a specific intervention, or rather is predictive of prognosis, independent from the type of rehabilitative treatment or even in the absence of it. Four studies included TD controls who underwent one MRI session (Bölte et al., 2015; Murdaugh et al., 2015, 2016; Ventola et al., 2015) in order to compare brain profiles of ASD patients and controls at baseline. Unfortunately, no study included MRI measures of TD subjects after the treatment under investigation: the lack of these data do not allow to provide evidence that neural changes are ascribable to effects of treatment rather than to normal brain maturation.

Despite their heterogeneity, all the six included studies reported significant modifications in task-related brain activation or in functional connectivity following rehabilitative intervention: crucially, the absence of negative or inconclusive results suggests the risk of publication bias. Instead, it could be useful the clinical and neural characterization of "non-responders" to a specific rehabilitative treatment in order to redirect these patients toward different intervention strategies.

Of particular interest, participants in these studies are generally highly selected individuals (e.g., exclusion of younger patients, and/or subjects with intellectual disability), who differ from patients seen in the clinical practice. Even if this choice is surely motivated by the necessity of patient compliance with the MRI examination (capacity of lying still in a confined space for a long time, as well as of tolerating the acoustic noise and of understanding task instructions), it limited information about brain plasticity in the full range of the autistic spectrum. Future naturalistic studies in larger samples could contribute to identifying biomarkers sensitive to rehabilitative treatment in the conventional clinical population. In this context, the use of sleep MRI (Pierce, 2011), and of task-free MRI techniques (DTI, rs-fMRI) would aid inclusion of non-collaborative ASD patients.

Future Directions

Prognostic factors of effective rehabilitative intervention in ASD are to date poorly clarified and generally based on patient's clinical characteristics and family profile only (Vivanti et al., 2014). The inclusion of MRI-based measures pre- and post-treatment will be crucial for understanding the neural mechanisms underlying different patient outcome. In other words, specific brain regions/network as putative biomarkers for treatment response would be identified, contributing to the knowledge on "what works for whom and why," and thus paving the way for the individualization of treatment in ASD. In order to overcome this limitation, future randomized control trials should incorporate pre and post-treatment neuroimaging protocols and compare the effects of distinct therapeutic treatments on patient's baseline neural biomarker.

Future investigations would also benefit from machine learning classification techniques to predict response to rehabilitative treatment at an individual level. In these studies, subjects are split into responders and non-responders after treatment, and machine-learning techniques are used to allocate patients to either category based on their pretreatment brain profile. However, the accuracy of these methods is currently not sufficiently satisfactory to suggest their use in clinical practice (Retico et al., 2014; Wolfers et al., 2015).

Finally, it will be crucial the use of multimodal neuroimaging techniques for detecting brain change between baseline and post-training in ASD. In this perspective, some recent studies have investigated connectivity in ASD using simultaneous structural -DTI- and functional -fcMRI- methods (Kana et al., 2012; Delmonte et al., 2013; Deshpande et al., 2013; Mueller et al., 2013; Nair et al., 2013): the integration of these data with neurophysiological approaches (electroencephalography–EEG- and magnetoencephalography–MEG-) may significantly enhance their temporal resolution. Moreover, the combination of both structural (MRI/DTI) and functional (fMRI/EEG) neuroimaging techniques could provide new insights on the timecourse by which the neural changes occur after rehabilitation: preliminary results on healthy older adults suggest that functional change may precede structural and cognitive change (Lampit et al., 2015), but the temporal dynamics of training-induced neural modifications have not been investigated yet in ASD subjects. In this perspective, the detection of functional changes could suggest that the rehabilitative intervention is effective, even if clinical modifications are not yet perceptible in the ASD patient. Thus, it would be possible to prevent dropout from a potentially beneficial intervention and consequently to reduce waste of resources as well as of valuable time for improving ASD prognosis.

AUTHOR CONTRIBUTIONS

SC wrote the paper with contributions from LB, AN, PB, AR, and FM. All authors read and approved the final manuscript.

ACKNOWLEDGMENTS

This work was *partly* supported by grant from the IRCCS Stella Maris Foundation (Ricerca Corrente, and the "5 × 1000" voluntary contributions, Italian Ministry of Health to FM). SC and AR were partly supported by the Italian Ministry of Health and by Tuscany Region with the grant (GR-2010-2317873). PB was partly supported by the Italian Ministry of Health (GR-2010-2316745), and by the BIAL Foundation to Dr. Brambilla (Fellowship #262/12).

REFERENCES

Amaral, D. G., Schumann, C. M., and Nordahl, C. W. (2008). Neuroanatomy of autism. *Trends Neurosci.* 31, 137–145. doi: 10.1016/j.tins.2007.12.005

Ameis, S. H., and Catani, M. (2015). Altered white matter connectivity as a neural substrate for social impairment in Autism Spectrum Disorder. *Cortex* 62, 158–181. doi: 10.1016/j.cortex.2014.10.014

American Psychiatric Association (2013). *Diagnostic and Statistical Manual of Mental Disorders (DSM-5), 5th Edn.* Washington, DC: American Psychiatric Publishing.

Bardin, J. (2012). Neurodevelopment: unlocking the brain. *Nature* 487, 24–26. doi: 10.1038/487024a

Bellani, M., Calderoni, S., Muratori, F., and Brambilla, P. (2013). Brain anatomy of autism spectrum disorders II. Focus on amygdala. *Epidemiol. Psychiatr. Sci.* 22, 309–312. doi: 10.1017/S2045796013000346

Bölte, S., Ciaramidaro, A., Schlitt, S., Hainz, D., Kliemann, D., Beyer, A., et al. (2015). Training-induced plasticity of the social brain in autism spectrum disorder. *Br. J. Psychiatry* 207, 149–157. doi: 10.1192/bjp.bp.113.143784

Bölte, S., Hubl, D., Feineis-Matthews, S., Prvulovic, D., Dierks, T., and Poustka, F. (2006). Facial affect recognition training in autism: can we animate the fusiform gyrus? *Behav. Neurosci.* 120, 211–216. doi: 10.1037/0735-7044.120.1.211

Chen, R., Jiao, Y., and Herskovits, E. H. (2011). Structural MRI in autism spectrum disorder. *Pediatr. Res.* 69, 63R–68R. doi: 10.1203/PDR.0b013e318212c2b3

Conti, E., Calderoni, S., Marchi, V., Muratori, F., Cioni, G., and Guzzetta, A. (2015). The first 1000 days of the autistic brain: a systematic review of diffusion imaging studies. *Front. Hum. Neurosci.* 9:159. doi: 10.3389/fnhum.2015.00159

Courchesne, E., Pierce, K., Schumann, C. M., Redcay, E., Buckwalter, J. A., Kennedy, D. P., et al. (2007). Mapping early brain development in autism. *Neuron* 56, 399–413. doi: 10.1016/j.neuron.2007.10.016

Dawson, G. (2008). Early behavioral intervention, brain plasticity, and the prevention of autism. *Dev. Psychopathol.* 20, 775–803. doi: 10.1017/S0954579408000370

Delmonte, S., Gallagher, L., O'Hanlon, E., McGrath, J., and Balsters, J. H. (2013). Functional and structural connectivity of frontostriatal circuitry in Autism Spectrum Disorder. *Front. Hum. Neurosci.* 7:430. doi: 10.3389/fnhum.2013.00430

Deshpande, G., Libero, L. E., Sreenivasan, K. R., Deshpande, H. D., and Kana, R. K. (2013). Identification of neural connectivity signatures of autism using machine learning. *Front. Hum. Neurosci.* 7:670. doi: 10.3389/fnhum.2013.00670

Dickstein, D. P., Pescosolido, M. F., Reidy, B. L., Galvan, T., Kim, K. L., Seymour, K. E., et al. (2013). Developmental meta-analysis of the functional neural correlates of autism spectrum disorders. *J. Am. Acad. Child Adolesc. Psychiatry* 52, 279–289. doi: 10.1016/j.jaac.2012.12.012

Estes, A., Munson, J., Rogers, S. J., Greenson, J., Winter, J., and Dawson, G. (2015). Long-term outcomes of early intervention in 6-year-old children with autism spectrum disorder. *J. Am. Acad. Child Adolesc. Psychiatry* 54, 580–587. doi: 10.1016/j.jaac.2015.04.005

Hallmayer, J., Cleveland, S., Torres, A., Phillips, J., Cohen, B., Torigoe, T., et al. (2011). Genetic heritability and shared environmental factors among twin pairs with autism. *Arch. Gen. Psychiatry* 68, 1095–1102. doi: 10.1001/archgenpsychiatry.2011.76

Just, M. A., Cherkassky, V. L., Keller, T. A., Kana, R. K., and Minshew, N. J. (2007). Functional and anatomical cortical underconnectivity in autism: evidence from an fMRI study of an executive function task and corpus callosum morphometry. *Cereb. Cortex* 17, 951–961. doi: 10.1093/cercor/bhl006

Kana, R. K., Libero, L. E., Hu, C. P., Deshpande, H. D., and Colburn, J. S. (2012). Functional brain networks and white matter underlying theory-of-mind in autism. *Soc. Cogn. Affect. Neurosci.* 9, 98–105. doi: 10.1093/scan/nss106

Kim, S. H., Macari, S., Koller, J., and Chawarska, K. (2015). Examining the phenotypic heterogeneity of early Autism Spectrum Disorder: subtypes and short-term outcomes. *J Child Psychol Psychiatry.* doi: 10.1111/jcpp.12448. [Epub ahead of print].

Koegel, R. L., O'Dell, M. C., and Koegel, L. K. (1987). A natural language paradigm for nonverbal autistic children. *J. Autism Dev. Disord.* 17, 187–200.

Lampit, A., Hallock, H., Suo, C., Naismith, S. L., and Valenzuela, M. (2015). Cognitive training-induced short-term functional and long-term structural plastic change is related to gains in global cognition in healthy older adults: a pilot study. *Front. Aging Neurosci.* 7:14. doi: 10.3389/fnagi.2015.00014

Lenroot, R. K., and Yeung, P. K. (2013). Heterogeneity within Autism Spectrum Disorders: what have we learned from neuroimaging studies? *Front. Hum. Neurosci.* 7:733. doi: 10.3389/fnhum.2013.00733

Lewis, J. D., and Elman, J. L. (2008). Growth-related neural reorganization and the autism phenotype: a test of the hypothesis that altered brain growth leads to altered connectivity. *Dev. Sci.* 11, 135–155. doi: 10.1111/j.1467-7687.2007.00634.x

Lindamood, P., and Bell, N. (1997). Sensory-cognitive factors in the controversy over reading instruction. *J. Dev. Learn. Dis.* 1, 143–182.

McPartland, J. C., and Pelphrey, K. A. (2012). The implications of social neuroscience for social disability. *J. Autism Dev. Disord.* 42, 1256–1262. doi: 10.1007/s10803-012-1514-z

Mueller, S., Keeser, D., Samson, A. C., Kirsch, V., Blautzik, J., Grothe, M., et al. (2013). Convergent findings of altered functional and structural brain connectivity in individuals with high functioning autism: a multimodal MRI study. *PLoS ONE* 8:e67329. doi: 10.1371/journal.pone.0067329

Murdaugh, D. L., Deshpande, H. D., and Kana, R. K. (2016). The impact of reading intervention on brain responses underlying language in children with autism. *Autism Res.* 9, 141–154. doi: 10.1002/aur.1503

Murdaugh, D. L., Maximo, J. O., and Kana, R. K. (2015). Changes in intrinsic connectivity of the brain's reading network following intervention in children with autism. *Hum. Brain Mapp.* 36, 2965–2979. doi: 10.1002/hbm.22821

Nair, A., Treiber, J. M., Shukla, D. K., Shih, P., and Müller, R. A. (2013). Thalamocortical connectivity in autism spectrum disorder: a study of functional and anatomical connectivity. *Brain* 136, 1942–1955. doi: 10.1093/brain/awt079

Narzisi, A., Muratori, F., Calderoni, S., Fabbro, F., and Urgesi, C. (2013). Neuropsychological profile in high functioning autism spectrum disorders. *J. Autism Dev. Disord.* 43, 1895–1909. doi: 10.1007/s10803-012-1736-0

Pascual-Leone, A., Amedi, A., Fregni, F., and Merabet, L. B. (2005). The plastic human brain cortex. *Annu. Rev. Neurosci.* 28, 377–401. doi: 10.1146/annurev.neuro.27.070203.144216

Pierce, K. (2011). Early functional brain development in autism and the promise of sleep fMRI. *Brain Res.* 1380, 162–174. doi: 10.1016/j.brainres.2010.09.028

Retico, A., Tosetti, M., Muratori, F., and Calderoni, S. (2014). Neuroimaging-based methods for autism identification: a possible translational application? *Funct. Neurol.* 29, 231–239. doi: 10.11138/fneur/2014.29.4.231

Rogers, S. J., Vismara, L., Wagner, A. L., McCormick, C., Young, G., and Ozonoff, S. (2014). Autism treatment in the first year of life: a pilot study of infant start, a parent-implemented intervention for symptomatic infants. *J. Autism Dev. Disord.* 44, 2981–2995. doi: 10.1007/s10803-014-2202-y

Stoner, R., Chow, M. L., Boyle, M. P., Sunkin, S. M., Mouton, P. R., Roy, S., et al. (2014). Patches of disorganization in the neocortex of children with autism. *N. Engl. J. Med.* 370, 1209–1219. doi: 10.1056/NEJMoa1307491

Sullivan, K., Stone, W. L., and Dawson, G. (2014). Potential neural mechanisms underlying the effectiveness of early intervention for children with autism spectrum disorder. *Res. Dev. Disabil.* 35, 2921–2932. doi: 10.1016/j.ridd.2014.07.027

Uddin, L. Q., Supekar, K., and Menon, V. (2013). Reconceptualizing functional brain connectivity in autism from a developmental perspective. *Front. Hum. Neurosci.* 7:458. doi: 10.3389/fnhum.2013.00458

Ventola, P., Yang, D. Y., Friedman, H. E., Oosting, D., Wolf, J., Sukhodolsky, D. G., et al. (2015). Heterogeneity of neural mechanisms of response to pivotal response treatment. *Brain Imaging Behav.* 9, 74–88. doi: 10.1007/s11682-014-9331-y

Vivanti, G., Prior, M., Williams, K., and Dissanayake, C. (2014). Predictors of outcomes in autism early intervention: why don't we know more? *Front. Pediatr.* 2:58. doi: 10.3389/fped.2014.00058

Voos, A. C., Pelphrey, K. A., Tirrell, J., Bolling, D. Z., Vander Wyk, B., Kaiser, M. D., et al. (2013). Neural mechanisms of improvements in social motivation after pivotal response treatment: two case studies. *J. Autism Dev. Disord.* 43, 1–10. doi: 10.1007/s10803-012-1683-9

Warren, Z., McPheeters, M. L., Sathe, N., Foss-Feig, J. H., Glasser, A., and Veenstra-Vanderweele, J. (2011). A systematic review of early intensive intervention for autism spectrum disorders. *Pediatrics* 127, e1303–e1311. doi: 10.1542/peds.2011-0426

Wass, S. (2011). Distortions and disconnections: disrupted brain connectivity in autism. *Brain Cogn.* 75, 18–28. doi: 10.1016/j.bandc.2010.10.005

Wolfers, T., Buitelaar, J. K., Beckmann, C., Franke, B., and Marquand, A. F. (2015). From estimating activation locality to predicting disorder: a review of pattern recognition for neuroimaging-based psychiatric diagnostics. *Neurosci. Biobehav. Rev.* 57, 328–349. doi: 10.1016/j.neubiorev.2015.08.001

Wolff, J. J., and Piven, J. (2013). On the emergence of autism: neuroimaging findings from birth to preschool. *Neuropsychiatry* 3, 209–222. doi: 10.2217/npy.13.11

12

Neuroanatomical Alterations in High-Functioning Adults with Autism Spectrum Disorder

Tehila Eilam-Stock[1,2,3], *Tingting Wu*[2], *Alfredo Spagna*[1,2], *Laura J. Egan*[1,2] *and Jin Fan*[1,2,3,4,5*]

[1] Department of Psychiatry, Icahn School of Medicine at Mount Sinai, New York, NY, USA, [2] Department of Psychology, Queens College, City University of New York, Flushing, NY, USA, [3] The Graduate Center, City University of New York, New York, NY, USA, [4] Department of Neuroscience, Icahn School of Medicine at Mount Sinai, New York, NY, USA, [5] Friedman Brain Institute, Icahn School of Medicine at Mount Sinai, New York, NY, USA

Edited by:
Alessandro Grecucci,
University of Trento, Italy

Reviewed by:
Vivek Agarwal,
King George's Medical University, India
Alka Anand Subramanyam,
TNMC & BYL Nair Ch. Hospital, India

***Correspondence:**
Jin Fan
jin.fan@qc.cuny.edu

Autism spectrum disorder (ASD) is a pervasive neurodevelopmental condition, affecting cognition and behavior throughout the life span. With recent advances in neuroimaging techniques and analytical approaches, a considerable effort has been directed toward identifying the neuroanatomical underpinnings of ASD. While gray-matter abnormalities have been found throughout cortical, subcortical, and cerebellar regions of affected individuals, there is currently little consistency across findings, partly due to small sample-sizes and great heterogeneity among participants in previous studies. Here, we report voxel-based morphometry of structural magnetic resonance images in a relatively large sample of high-functioning adults with ASD ($n = 66$) and matched typically-developing controls ($n = 66$) drawn from multiple studies. We found decreased gray-matter volume in posterior brain regions, including the posterior hippocampus and cuneus, as well as increased gray-matter volume in frontal brain regions, including the medial prefrontal cortex, superior and inferior frontal gyri, and middle temporal gyrus in individuals with ASD. We discuss our results in relation to findings obtained in previous studies, as well as their potential clinical implications.

Keywords: autism, voxel-based morphometry, gray matter volume, autism brain imaging data exchange, ABIDE

INTRODUCTION

Autism spectrum disorder (ASD) is a neurodevelopmental condition characterized by abnormal social interactions and communication, repetitive behaviors, restricted interests, and atypical sensory processing (American Psychiatric Association, 2013). Advances in neuroimaging techniques and analyses over the past two decades have led to a burgeoning of structural studies aimed toward identifying the neuroanatomical underpinnings of ASD. Overall, findings suggest a complex neurodevelopmental trajectory, characterized by an early brain overgrowth (Courchesne et al., 2003; Zielinski et al., 2014; Zwaigenbaum et al., 2014), followed by arrested growth later in childhood and early adolescence (Courchesne et al., 2001; Mak-Fan et al., 2012), and accelerated neural atrophy later in adulthood (Courchesne et al., 2011; Lange et al., 2015). While studies were able to localize the neuroanatomical alterations in ASD to specific brain regions (Carper and Courchesne, 2005; Schumann et al., 2010; Scheel et al., 2011; Zielinski et al., 2014; Dierker et al., 2015; Libero et al., 2015), structures (Stanfield et al., 2008; Schumann et al., 2009; Via et al., 2011; Nickl-Jockschat et al., 2012; Maier et al., 2015) and networks (Ameis et al., 2011; Barttfeld et al., 2011; Solso et al., 2015), reports have been largely inconsistent.

The inconsistency in neuroanatomical findings of previous studies may have stemmed from several factors, including differences in methodology, data acquisition, analytical approaches, clinical and demographic characteristics of the samples, as well as small sample-sizes. As ASD is a complex condition with multiple etiologies, risk factors, and diverse clinical manifestations (Amaral et al., 2008; Ecker et al., 2013b; Chen et al., 2015), there is an inherent variability among individuals with ASD that is likely related to variations in neuroanatomical abnormalities. Indeed, ASD is linked to a great variety of gene mutations, each of which has the potential to affect neural development through different pathways and in different ways, including gene transcription, expression and regulation, protein synthesis and translation, synaptic formation and function, as well as cell migration (Persico and Bourgeron, 2006; Sahin and Sur, 2015). The clinical manifestation of ASD symptoms can also vary between affected individuals (Amaral et al., 2008), and there is an ongoing debate among scientists and clinicians regarding the inclusion of previously diagnostically-segregated groups (e.g., Asperger's syndrome vs. autism) under the unifying umbrella of the new guidelines for ASD diagnosis (Mcalonan et al., 2008; Toal et al., 2010; Mandy et al., 2012). In addition, intelligence quotient (IQ) scores vary significantly between individuals with ASD, with intellectual disability in the majority of affected individuals, but average or above-average scores in the high-functioning end of the spectrum (Toal et al., 2010).

In order to address the inconsistency in neuroanatomical reports of ASD, recent studies have used meta-analytic approaches (Cauda et al., 2011; Duerden et al., 2012; DeRamus and Kana, 2015), larger sample-sizes (Toal et al., 2010; Ecker et al., 2012; Haar et al., 2014; Itahashi et al., 2015; Sussman et al., 2015), and stricter inclusion criteria according to age (Raznahan et al., 2009; Toal et al., 2010; Greimel et al., 2013), gender (Ecker et al., 2012; Itahashi et al., 2015), IQ (Ecker et al., 2012; Itahashi et al., 2015; Maier et al., 2015), and diagnosis (Mcalonan et al., 2008; Toal et al., 2010; Via et al., 2011). Multivariate classification techniques were also used in an attempt to better characterize the complex patterns of neuroanatomical alterations in ASD (Ecker et al., 2010a,b; Jiao et al., 2010; Uddin et al., 2011; Haar et al., 2014). Only a few studies, however, investigated brain anatomy in large, matched samples of high-functioning adults with ASD and typically-developing controls (TDC) (e.g., Ecker et al., 2012).

To mitigate issues of sample variability and inconsistent findings, we conducted a neuromorphometric study in a relatively large sample of high-functioning adults with ASD ($n = 66$) and gender, age, and IQ-matched TDC ($n = 66$). The samples were selected from the Autism Brain Imaging Data Exchange (ABIDE) database (Di Martino et al., 2014), and included data from ASD and TDC participants collected in a previous study from our lab as well. We used voxel-based morphometry (VBM) (Ashburner and Friston, 2000), an automated, unbiased, and conservative approach, to investigate alterations in regional gray-matter (GM) volume of individuals with ASD. We also examined the possible contributions of gender, age, and ASD symptom severity by including them as regressors in our model.

MATERIALS AND METHODS

Participants

The samples were selected from the ABIDE database (Di Martino et al., 2014), which is a multicenter database containing anatomical MRI scans, clinical measures, and demographic data from approximately 1000 participants, with age range of 6–65 years. The ABIDE database offers a non-precedent opportunity for investigating neuroanatomical alterations in large samples of individuals with ASD. The MRI data selected for this study were collected from ASD and TDC adult participants in three different sites: New York University Langone Medical Center (NYU), Social Brain Lab at the Research School of Behavioral and Cognitive Neurosciences, NeuroImaging Center, University Medical Center Groeningen and Netherlands Institute for Neurosciences (SBL), and Katholieke Universiteit Leuven (KUL). Only participants with T1 images and sites that provided a relatively large number of adult participants (at least 12 in each group) were included. Participants who could not be matched according to their demographic data were excluded. MRI data from a previous study conducted in our lab at the Icahn School of Medicine at Mount Sinai (ISMMS; Eilam-Stock et al., 2014) were also used. The total number of participants was 66 in the ASD group and 66 in the TDC group (NYU $n = 19$; SBL $n = 15$; KUL $n = 14$; ISMMS $n = 18$). Demographic information for the combined samples are shown in **Table 1**.

Selected participants with ASD were all in the high-functioning end of the spectrum (IQ > 80), and received a DSM-IV-TR diagnosis of Autistic Disorder, Asperger's Disorder, or Pervasive Developmental Disorder Not-Otherwise-Specified. Detailed information regarding the diagnostic protocols for the ABIDE database at each site are publicly available on the ABIDE website (http://fcon_1000.projects.nitrc.org/indi/abide). After matching for gender, the ASD and TDC groups were matched on age across sites [$t_{(130)} = 0.2$; $p = 0.99$] and within each site separately [NYU $t_{(36)} = 0.23$; $p = 0.81$; SBL $t_{(28)} = 0.40$; $p = 0.69$; KUL $t_{(26)} = -1.10$; $p = 0.28$; ISMMS $t_{(34)} = 0.18$; $p = 0.86$]. The ASD and TDC groups were also matched on full score IQ (FSIQ) across sites [$t_{(113)} = 1.7$; $p = 0.9$] and within each site [NYU $t_{(36)} = -1.16$; $p = 0.25$; KUL $t_{(26)} = -0.72$; $p = 0.48$; ISMMS $t_{(34)} = 1.25$; $p = 0.22$], with the exception of participants from the SBL dataset for whom FSIQ scores were not available. Of note, however, all ASD and TDC participants from the SBL dataset were tested for FSIQ, and their scores were all within the normal range (http://fcon_1000.projects.nitrc.org/indi/abide/).

All sites contributing to the ABIDE database received approval from their local Institutional Review Boards for the acquisition of their data. In addition, all data retrieved from the ABIDE database are completely anonymous with no inclusion of protected health information, as required by the HIPAA guidelines (http://fcon_1000.projects.nitrc.org/indi/abide/). For the data acquired at ISMMS, all participants provided written informed consent, approved by the Institutional Review Board.

TABLE 1 | Demographic information.

Group	n	Age (years)				Gender		Full Scale IQ			
		Mean	SD	Max	Min	M	F	Mean	SD	Max	Min
TDC											
Total	66	27	7	43	18	60	6	114	12	143	89
SBL	15	34	7	42	20	15		–	–	–	–
KUL	14	23	3	29	18	14		113	10	134	98
NYU	19	25	5	32	18	15	4	113	12	139	91
ISMMS	18	28	7	43	20	16	2	117	15	143	89
ASD											
Total	66	27	8	64	18	60	6	110	14	143	80
SBL	15	35	10	64	22	15		–	–	–	–
KUL	14	22	4	32	18	14		109	13	128	89
NYU	19	25	6	39	18	15	4	108	13	137	80
ISMMS	18	28	6	42	19	16	2	111	17	143	87

TDC, typically-developed controls; ASD, autism spectrum disorder; SD, standard deviation; the two samples (TDC, ASD) did not differ in age [$t_{(130)} = 0.20$; $p = 0.99$] and in IQ [$t_{(113)} = 1.70$; $p = 0.90$].

Voxel-Based Morphometry Analysis

To measure differences in GM volume between the ASD and TDC groups, we conducted VBM analyses using the VBM8 toolbox (http://dbm.neuro.uni-jena.de/vbm) and Statistical Parametric Mapping (SPM8, Welcome Trust Centre for Neuroimaging, University College London, UK) in MATLAB R2012b (Mathworks Inc., Sherborn, MA). First, all T1-weighted images were manually reoriented to the anterior commissure—posterior commissure plane to improve the coregistration of T1 images to the template. Then, each image was segmented into six tissue classes (i.e., GM, white matter, cerebrospinal fluid, bone, non-brain soft tissue, and air outside of the head and in nose, sinus, and ears) using the SPM standard tissue probability map (Mazziotta et al., 1995) with default parameters. Segmented GM images were spatially normalized to the "IXI500_MNI152" template, using the DARTEL algorithm (Ashburner, 2007) with default parameters. Non-linear warping for the effect of spatial normalization was corrected to generate these modulated normalized images, which represent relative volume after correcting for brain size. Each image was then smoothed using an 8-mm full width at half maximum Gaussian kernel.

A two-sample *t*-test was conducted for smoothed GM volume images from the ASD and TDC groups using a random-effect general linear model (GLM), with gender and age as nuisance regressors. Because the scans were taken at multiple sites which may have different MRI scanners and scanning protocols, an inherent variability may exist within the data. Therefore, we included an equal number of ASD and TDC participants within each site. We also used the locations as a dummy variable in our model. As suggested by the VBM8 manual, an absolute threshold mask of 0.1 was used for all the second-level analyses. To test the relationship between autism symptom severity and GM volume, we conducted an additional second-level GLM analysis for ASD participants, using their Autism Diagnostic Observation Schedule (ADOS) scores (Lord et al., 2000) as a regressor. Higher ADOS scores are indicative of increased ASD severity. Forty ASD participants for whom the ADOS scores were available (ABIDE $n = 27$; ISMMS $n = 13$) were selected from the original sample for this analysis. The significance level for the height of each voxel was set to $p < 0.005$ (uncorrected), with a contiguous-voxel extent threshold $k > 17$ voxels, to correct for multiple voxel comparisons. This threshold was estimated by using 10,000 Monte Carlo simulations with a customized Matlab program (Slotnick et al., 2003). The corrected a priori height threshold was $p < 0.05$.

RESULTS

Between-Group Differences in Gray-Matter Volume

A between-group comparison of GM volume revealed increased volume in frontal, temporal, and cerebellar brain regions in the ASD group, compared to the TDC group. These regions included the medial prefrontal cortex (extending to the right), left superior frontal gyrus, left inferior frontal gyrus—pars opercularis (Broca's area), left inferior frontal gyrus—pars orbitalis, left middle temporal gyrus, and left cerebellum VIIb (**Figure 1** and **Table 2**). In addition, compared to the TDC group, decreased GM volume in posterior brain regions in the ASD group was found, including the left posterior hippocampus and the cuneus bilaterally (**Figure 1** and **Table 2**). These results remained consistent following an additional GLM analyses with age, gender, and site as nuisance regressors.

Neuroanatomical Correlations with ASD Symptom Severity

To assess the relationship between ASD symptom severity and GM volume, ADOS scores of 40 participants with ASD were used as a regressor in our GLM model. Results revealed negative correlations between symptom severity and GM volume in the right superior frontal gyrus, left middle frontal gyrus, inferior frontal gyri—pars orbitalis bilaterally, restrosplenial

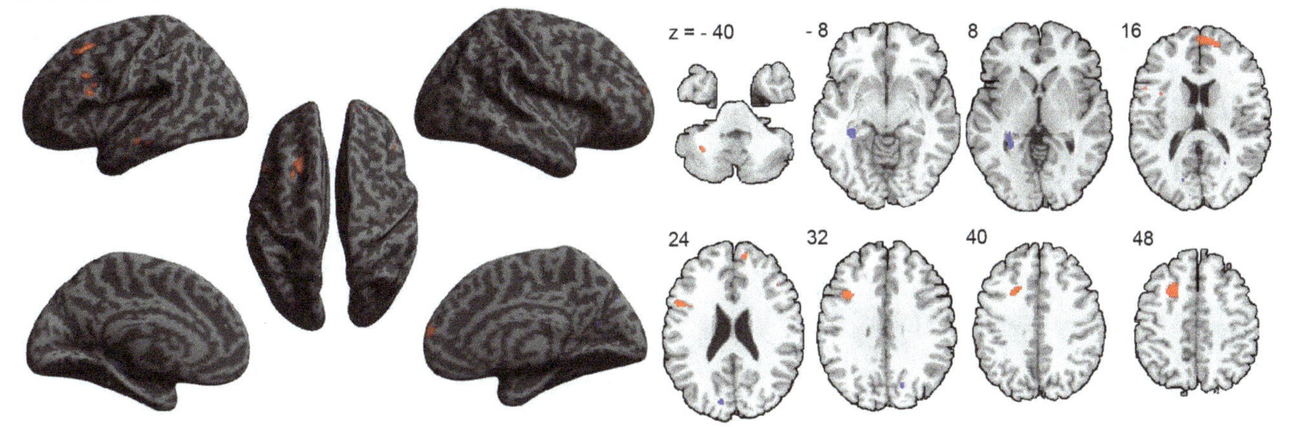

FIGURE 1 | Differences in gray-matter volume between the ASD and TDC groups. Red indicates areas of increased gray-matter volume in ASD (ASD > TDC). Blue indicates areas of decreased gray-matter volume in ASD (ASD < TDC).

TABLE 2 | Brain regions with abnormal gray-matter volume in ASD.

Region	L/R	BA	*x*	*y*	*z*	T	Z	K
ASD < TDC								
Posterior Hippocampus	L	36	−35	−36	−3	3.53	3.44	283
Cuneus	L	18/19	−12	−83	23	3.48	3.40	83
Cuneus	R	18	17	−72	32	2.82	2.77	31
ASD > TDC								
Superior frontal gyrus	L	8	−21	12	44	3.85	3.74	455
Superior frontal gyrus (medial)	R	10	2	54	11	3.50	3.41	634
Inferior frontal gyrus	L	44	−39	15	32	3.37	3.29	91
Inferior frontal gyrus	L	44	−51	11	26	3.35	3.27	196
Middle temporal gyrus	L	21	−62	−12	−14	3.12	3.06	86
Middle temporal gyrus	L	21	−59	−27	−12	3.06	3.00	35
Superior frontal gyrus (medial)	L	10	−18	62	21	2.97	2.91	28
Inferior frontal gyrus	R	45	44	29	26	2.92	2.87	18
Cerebellum VIIb	L		−33	−57	−41	2.91	2.86	24
Inferior frontal gyrus	L	47	−50	39	−15	2.87	2.82	34

Height threshold: $T = 2.72$, $p < 0.005$, Extent threshold: $k > 17$.

cortex bilaterally, supplementary motor area bilaterally, right middle cingulate cortex, thalamus bilaterally, and putamen bilaterally (**Figure 2** and **Table 3**), indicating that decreased GM volume in these regions is associated with more severe ASD symptoms. No significant positive correlations between symptom severity and GM volume were found.

DISCUSSION

Gray-Matter Volume Abnormalities along the Anterior-Posterior Axis

Our results show a general pattern of increased GM volume in anterior brain regions and decreased GM volume in posterior brain regions in the ASD group, relative to TDC. A few theoretical accounts for the lobular specificity of neuroanatomical abnormalities in ASD across development have emerged, and may shed light on the differences in GM volume found in our study. Research on brain development in ASD across the lifespan has demonstrated a complex neurodevelopmental trajectory in affected individuals, characterized by an early brain overgrowth (Courchesne et al., 2003; Zielinski et al., 2014; Zwaigenbaum et al., 2014), followed by arrested growth later in childhood and early adolescence (Courchesne et al., 2001; Mak-Fan et al., 2012), and accelerated neural atrophy in adulthood (Courchesne et al., 2011; Lange et al., 2015). Studies in very young individuals with ASD (i.e., 2–4 years old) observed an increase of 5–12% in brain volume that was specifically localized to the frontal and temporal lobes (Carper et al., 2002; Redcay and Courchesne, 2005; Courchesne et al., 2007). This significant enlargement in anterior brain regions is reduced in older ages, though

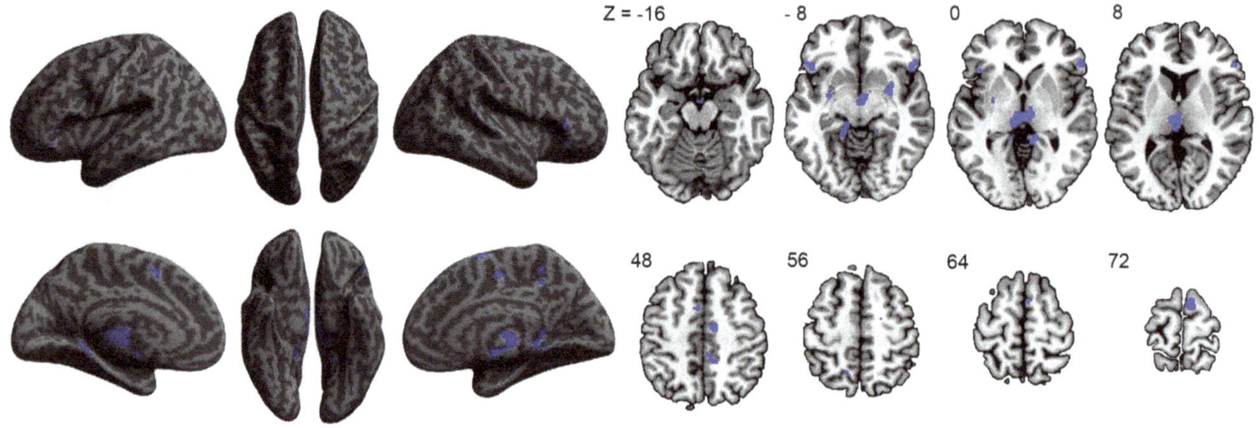

FIGURE 2 | Correlations between gray-matter volume and ASD symptom severity as indicated by the ADOS scores of each participant (n = 40). All significant correlations found were negative and are indicated in blue.

TABLE 3 | Correlations between gray-matter volume and ASD symptom severity.

Region	L/R	BA	*x*	*y*	*z*	T	Z	K
NEGATIVE								
Inferior frontal gyrus	R	47	54	24	−9	4.35	3.88	301
Inferior frontal gyrus	R	45	54	32	3	3.18	2.97	
Corpus mamillare	R		3	−12	−12	4.27	3.82	1342
Restrosplenial cortex	L	30	−15	−41	−6	3.67	3.36	
Thalamus	R		9	−18	−3	3.54	3.26	
Thalamus	L		6	−19	−3	3.33	3.09	
Mid cingulate cortex	R	6	14	−11	50	4.26	3.81	77
Restrosplenial cortex	R	30	8	−42	0	4.04	3.65	193
Inferior frontal gyrus	L	47	−47	23	−6	3.70	3.39	178
Supplementary motor area	R	6	6	0	74	3.69	3.38	198
Mid cingulate cortex	R	23	8	−39	48	3.24	3.02	139
Precuneus	L	7	−14	−59	56	3.22	3.00	19
Putamen	R		30	2	−9	3.10	2.90	143
Middle frontal gyrus	L	8/9	−32	36	44	3.07	2.87	20
Putamen	L		−30	−6	−6	2.97	2.79	95
Supplementary motor area	L	6	−9	9	51	2.96	2.78	79
Superior frontal gyrus	R	6	21	−6	59	2.90	2.73	25

n = 40, Height threshold: $T = 2.72$, $p < 0.005$, Extent threshold: $k > 17$. Structures listed below clusters with a K-value were within that same cluster with different local maxima.

GM volume in these regions continues to be greater in ASD participants relative to TDC throughout development (1–3% increase) (Redcay and Courchesne, 2005; Courchesne et al., 2007). By contrast, the occipital lobe is not enlarged in young children with ASD (Carper et al., 2002; Courchesne et al., 2007). The occipital lobe is phylogenetically older than the frontal and temporal lobes, and its maturation occurs earlier in development (Ecker et al., 2013b); while the frontal and temporal lobes continue to develop throughout the first years of life, the occipital lobe does not change dramatically across the life span in typically developing individuals (Gogtay and Thompson, 2010).

Models of ASD suggest that the frontal and temporal enlargements that characterize early brain development in ASD may be a result of increased numbers of excitatory pyramidal neurons in these regions (Courchesne and Pierce, 2005a; Courchesne et al., 2007, 2011; Santos et al., 2011). This localized overgrowth may damage the local connectivity patterns within these regions, as well as the large-scale connectivity between these regions and the rest of the brain (Courchesne and Pierce, 2005b; Courchesne et al., 2007; Geschwind and Levitt, 2007; Ecker et al., 2013b; Chen et al., 2015). In the typically-developing brain, the connectivity patterns that develop throughout the first years of life allow for the higher-level cognitive skills that develop at the same time, including socio-emotional skills, language, and executive functions (Akshoomoff et al., 2002; Courchesne et al., 2007). Thus, it is reasonable to hypothesize that the aberrant connectivity patterns in ASD within the overgrowing frontal and temporal lobes, as well as between these regions and the rest of the brain, are at the core of the cognitive and behavioral deficits in ASD (Akshoomoff et al., 2002; Geschwind and Levitt, 2007). As individuals with ASD reach adulthood, processes of accelerated neuronal atrophy take place throughout the brain (Courchesne et al., 2011; Lange et al., 2015), perhaps to compensate for the early overgrowth in these individuals. The early localized enlargement of the anterior brain in ASD, together with the later broader neuronal atrophy in these individuals may, therefore, account for both our and others (e.g., Ecker et al., 2012) findings in adult ASD samples. The accelerated atrophy in adulthood may cause a GM volume decrease in both anterior parts of the brain, which are still greater relative to TDC though to a lesser extent, as well as in the posterior brain (mainly in the occipital cortex), which is now reduced relative to TDC.

Gray-Matter Volume Abnormalities in Cortical and Sub-Cortical Brain Regions

ASD is a complex disorder with multiple symptoms affecting both high-level (e.g., socio-emotional processing, self-referential processing, language) and low-level (e.g., sensory processing) functions. It is not surprising, therefore, that the extent of neuroanatomical alterations found in our study, as well as in previous empirical investigations, encompasses regions, structures, and neural networks throughout the brain. A hallmark of ASD is abnormal socio-emotional processing, including deficits in theory of mind (i.e., the ability to understand other's beliefs, intentions and perspectives; Baron-Cohen et al., 1985; Baron-Cohen, 2000; Pilowsky et al., 2000), affective evaluations (Hill et al., 2004; Dapretto et al., 2006), and empathy (Minio-Paluello et al., 2009; Fan et al., 2013; Hadjikhani et al., 2014; Gu et al., 2015). Theory of mind relies on several neural regions, including the medial prefrontal cortex, lateral orbitofrontal cortex, middle frontal gyrus, superior temporal gyrus, temporal pole, temporoparietal junction, and cuneus (Frith and Frith, 1999; Gallagher and Frith, 2003; Saxe and Kanwisher, 2003; Amodio and Frith, 2006; Völlm et al., 2006). In our study we found GM abnormalities in the medial prefrontal cortex (increased GM volume) and cuneus (decreased GM volume). We also found negative correlations between GM volume in the middle frontal gyrus and ASD symptom severity. These structural abnormalities may be related, therefore, to the commonly seen theory of mind deficits in individuals with ASD. Our finding of increased GM volume in the medial prefrontal cortex in ASD may also explain the emotional evaluation difficulties commonly seen in this disorder, as this region plays a role in that domain as well (Phan et al., 2002; Harris et al., 2007; Etkin et al., 2011).

Our results of GM abnormalities in the inferior frontal gyrus, but not the ventromedial prefrontal cortex, may be related to a specific deficit in emotional empathy (e.g., feeling another person's pain) but preserved cognitive empathy (e.g., understanding that another person is in pain) in ASD (Minio-Paluello et al., 2009; Fan et al., 2013; Hadjikhani et al., 2014). Indeed, a recent lesion study demonstrated an anatomical dissociation between the cognitive and emotional components of empathy, such that the ventromedial prefrontal cortex is necessary for cognitive empathy, while the inferior frontal gyrus is essential for emotional empathy (Shamay-Tsoory et al., 2009). Additionally, in a functional MRI study investigating brain regions associated with empathy for pain, we found abnormal brain activation in the inferior frontal gyrus in ASD, with no group differences in ventromedial prefrontal cortex activation (Gu et al., 2015).

Our findings also point to several GM abnormalities in ASD that may be related to limited self-referential processing (Lombardo et al., 2007, 2010; Uddin, 2011) and autobiographical memory (Bowler et al., 2000; Crane and Goddard, 2008; Lind and Bowler, 2010) in this disorder. Studies that investigated the neural substrates of self-referential processing in typically-developing samples found that these processes activate a set of regions along the medial axis of the brain, commonly termed cortical midline structures (Northoff et al., 2006), including the medial prefrontal cortex/pregenual anterior cingulate cortex, the dorsomedial prefrontal cortex/middle cingulate cortex, and the precuneus/posterior cingulate cortex (Kelley et al., 2002; Northoff et al., 2006; Lombardo et al., 2010). The left inferior frontal gyrus was also found to be activated during self-related judgments (Kelley et al., 2002). In addition, the posterior hippocampus is involved in the storage and retrieval of autobiographical memories (Fernández et al., 1998; Kim, 2015). Our results of increased GM volume in the medial prefrontal cortex and the left inferior frontal gyrus, decreased GM volume in the posterior hippocampus, and negative correlations between GM volume in the middle cingulate cortex and precuneus and ASD symptom severity, may be related, therefore, to aberrant self-referential processing and autobiographical memory in individuals with ASD.

The increased GM volume in the left inferior frontal gyrus and left middle temporal gyrus in the ASD group in the present study may be related to altered language functions in affected individuals, especially in the semantics domain. Although language abilities vary greatly across the ASD spectrum, ranging from a severe language delay to normal language development, there is empirical evidence suggesting that semantic processing is compromised even in high-functioning individuals with ASD who do not exhibit any language delay (Harris et al., 2006; Kamio et al., 2007). High-functioning adults with ASD also showed significantly reduced activation in the left inferior frontal gyrus (Broca's area) during semantic processing (Harris et al., 2006). Indeed, the left inferior frontal gyrus, together with the left middle temporal gyrus, is involved in semantic processing in the typically-developing brain (Goel and Dolan, 2001; Visser et al., 2012). In our study, both of these regions were identified as areas of increased GM volume in ASD, which may serve as neuroanatomical substrates for the abnormal semantic processing in this disorder.

Although we did not find GM alterations in the thalamus in ASD, we did find a significant negative correlation between thalamic GM volume and ASD symptom severity. In addition, we observed decreased GM volume in the cuneus in the ASD group. The thalamus is a main hub for sensory processing across modalities, and it can affect sensory perception by integrating and relaying feedforward and feedback information between the sensory cortices and higher-order cortical regions (e.g., frontal lobe; Alitto and Usrey, 2003; Cudeiro and Sillito, 2006; Briggs and Usrey, 2008). The cuneus is a secondary visual area which may play a role in modulation of visual processing (Vanni et al., 2001). Abnormal sensory processing (both hyper-and-hypo-sensitivity) have been extensively documented in the ASD literature, especially in the visual modality (Behrmann et al., 2006; Vandenbroucke et al., 2008), and are now included in the ASD diagnostic criteria in the diagnostic and statistical manual of mental disorders (DSM-5) (American Psychiatric Association, 2013). Together, these findings may be related to the abnormal sensory processing commonly seen in individuals with ASD.

LIMITATIONS

Although our results are consistent with some previous reports, they did not replicate other findings of GM alterations in adults with ASD. For example, in a study that specifically examined between-group differences in the amygdala and hippocampus in 30 high-functioning (IQ > 100) adults with ASD and gender, age, and IQ matched control participants (Maier et al., 2015), increased hippocampal volume bilaterally was found in ASD, opposite to our results. Yet, other studies failed to find any significant differences in GM volume between adults with ASD and TDC (Haar et al., 2014; Riedel et al., 2014; Riddle et al., 2016). This variability in structural findings may be due to relatively small sample sizes (Riedel et al., 2014; Maier et al., 2015) or differences in methodology and sample characteristics (Haar et al., 2014; Riddle et al., 2016). Thus, large-sample studies of different sub-groups within the ASD spectrum will likely promote a better characterization of neuroanatomical alterations that contribute to ASD symptomatology.

The current study took advantage of the relatively large sample of participants with ASD provided by the ABIDE database, and limited the inclusion criteria (i.e., high-functioning adults) to increase statistical power and reduce variability. However, as ASD is a complex condition with multiple contributing factors and etiologies, it is possible that our sample was not sufficiently homogeneous. While we attempted to control for different variables that may have contributed to the previously reported inconsistent findings, such as age and IQ, there are many other factors we did not take into account, such as genetic factors or clinical presentations. On the other hand, when using stricter inclusion criteria, the generalizability of the data is inevitably reduced. For example, it is possible that our findings represent neuroanatomical alterations in high-functioning adults with ASD only, and are less applicable to the majority of the ASD population, which has lower level of functioning and greater symptom severity. Studies with more individuals across the spectrum and higher severity of autism may shed a different light on the matter entirely. Future studies that continue to investigate neuroanatomy in large samples of affected individuals from different clinical and demographic subgroups, will, therefore, significantly contribute to our understanding of neuroanatomical alterations in individuals with ASD.

We measured GM volume using voxel-based morphometry, as this is one of the most informative and commonly used measures in the study of neuroanatomical abnormalities in clinical populations. However, other neuroanatomical measures were used in previous studies of ASD, which may also be useful indicators of structural abnormalities. These include measures of cortical folding and sulcal depth (Nordahl et al., 2007), cortical thickness (Hyde et al., 2010), cortical surface area (Ecker et al., 2013a), local gyrification index (Wallace et al., 2013), as well as diffusion tensor imaging for white-matter tract (Ameis et al., 2011; see Ecker et al., 2015 for review). Multivariate classification techniques were also recently used as a viable method for identifying complex patterns of neuroanatomical alterations in ASD (Ecker et al., 2010a,b; Jiao et al., 2010; Uddin et al., 2011; Haar et al., 2014). It would be valuable, therefore, to conduct studies with large samples that look at other structural measures as well.

CLINICAL IMPLICATIONS

Our study adds to the growing literature investigating neuroanatomical abnormalities in ASD. The research endeavor to characterize the profile of brain anatomy in ASD across development may have clinical implications, as it may facilitate identification of biomarkers for different subgroups within the ASD spectrum (Ecker et al., 2013b, 2015). While the behavioral markers of ASD have been extensively investigated and are relatively defined and agreed upon by researchers and clinicians, the neuroanatomical, neurofunctional and genetic profiles of ASD still warrant rigorous research. Once our knowledge of the different markers of ASD has been sufficiently advanced, the different pieces of the puzzle will come together to create a clear picture of this currently ill-understood disorder. This will allow for better diagnosis and treatment for ASD, which may be more specific to individuals or subgroups within the spectrum.

AUTHOR CONTRIBUTIONS

All authors (TE, TW, AS, LE, and JF) contributed to data analysis and report writing.

FUNDING

JF and AS were supported by the grant from Simons Foundation Autism Research Initiative (SFARI) 330704. JF was also supported by the National Institute of Mental Health of the National Institutes of Health under Award Number of and R21 MH083164. The content is solely the responsibility of the authors. The funders had no role in study design, data collection and analysis, decision to publish, or preparation of the manuscript.

ACKNOWLEDGMENTS

We thank the numerous contributors to the ABIDE database for their effort in the collection, organization and sharing of their datasets, the NITRC (http://www.nitrc.org) for providing the data sharing platform for the ABIDE initiative, and the other informatics databases for providing additional platforms (see http://fcon_1000.projects.nitrc.org/indi/abide).

REFERENCES

Akshoomoff, N., Pierce, K., and Courchesne, E. (2002). The neurobiological basis of autism from a developmental perspective. *Dev. Psychopathol.* 14, 613–634. doi: 10.1017/S0954579402003115

Alitto, H. J., and Usrey, W. M. (2003). Corticothalamic feedback and sensory processing. *Curr. Opin. Neurobiol.* 13, 440–445. doi: 10.1016/S0959-4388(03)00096-5

Amaral, D. G., Schumann, C. M., and Nordahl, C. W. (2008). Neuroanatomy of autism. *Trends Neurosci.* 31, 137–145. doi: 10.1016/j.tins.2007.12.005

Ameis, S. H., Fan, J., Rockel, C., Voineskos, A. N., Lobaugh, N. J., Soorya, L., et al. (2011). Impaired structural connectivity of socio-emotional circuits in autism spectrum disorders: a diffusion tensor imaging study. *PLoS ONE* 6:e28044. doi: 10.1371/journal.pone.0028044

American Psychiatric Association (2013). *Diagnostic and Statistical Manual of Mental Disorders: DSM-5.* Arlington: American Psychiatric Association.

Amodio, D. M., and Frith, C. D. (2006). Meeting of minds: the medial frontal cortex and social cognition. *Nat. Rev. Neurosci.* 7, 268–277. doi: 10.1038/nrn1884

Ashburner, J. (2007). A fast diffeomorphic image registration algorithm. *Neuroimage* 38, 95–113. doi: 10.1016/j.neuroimage.2007.07.007

Ashburner, J., and Friston, K. J. (2000). Voxel-based morphometry-the methods. *Neuroimage* 11, 805–821. doi: 10.1006/nimg.2000.0582

Baron-Cohen, S. (2000). *Theory of Mind and Autism: A Fifteen Year Review.* New York, NY: Oxford University Press.

Baron-Cohen, S., Leslie, A. M., and Frith, U. (1985). Does the autistic child have a "theory of mind"? *Cognition* 21, 37–46. doi: 10.1016/0010-0277(85)90022-8

Barttfeld, P., Wicker, B., Cukier, S., Navarta, S., Lew, S., and Sigman, M. (2011). A big-world network in ASD: dynamical connectivity analysis reflects a deficit in long-range connections and an excess of short-range connections. *Neuropsychologia* 49, 254–263. doi: 10.1016/j.neuropsychologia.2010.11.024

Behrmann, M., Thomas, C., and Humphreys, K. (2006). Seeing it differently: visual processing in autism. *Trends Cogn. Sci.* 10, 258–264. doi: 10.1016/j.tics.2006.05.001

Bowler, D. M., Gardiner, J. M., and Grice, S. J. (2000). Episodic memory and remembering in adults with asperger syndrome. *J. Autism Dev. Disord.* 30, 295–304. doi: 10.1023/A:1005575216176

Briggs, F., and Usrey, W. M. (2008). Emerging views of corticothalamic function. *Curr. Opin. Neurobiol.* 18, 403–407. doi: 10.1016/j.conb.2008.09.002

Carper, R. A., and Courchesne, E. (2005). Localized enlargement of the frontal cortex in early autism. *Biol. Psychiatry* 57, 126–133. doi: 10.1016/j.biopsych.2004.11.005

Carper, R. A., Moses, P., Tigue, Z. D., and Courchesne, E. (2002). Cerebral lobes in autism: early hyperplasia and abnormal age effects. *Neuroimage* 16, 1038–1051. doi: 10.1006/nimg.2002.1099

Cauda, F., Geda, E., Sacco, K., D'agata, F., Duca, S., Geminiani, G., et al. (2011). Grey matter abnormality in autism spectrum disorder: an activation likelihood estimation meta-analysis study. *J. Neurol. Neurosurg. Psychiatry* 82, 1304–1313. doi: 10.1136/jnnp.2010.239111

Chen, J. A., Peñagarikano, O., Belgard, T. G., Swarup, V., and Geschwind, D. H. (2015). The Emerging Picture of Autism Spectrum Disorder: genetics and pathology. *Annu. Rev. Pathol. Mech. Dis.* 10, 111–144. doi: 10.1146/annurev-pathol-012414-040405

Courchesne, E., Campbell, K., and Solso, S. (2011). Brain growth across the life span in autism: age-specific changes in anatomical pathology. *Brain Res.* 1380, 138–145. doi: 10.1016/j.brainres.2010.09.101

Courchesne, E., Carper, R., and Akshoomoff, N. (2003). Evidence of brain overgrowth in the first year of life in autism. *JAMA* 290, 337–344. doi: 10.1001/jama.290.3.337

Courchesne, E., Karns, C., Davis, H., Ziccardi, R., Carper, R., Tigue, Z., et al. (2001). Unusual brain growth patterns in early life in patients with autistic disorder an MRI study. *Neurology* 57, 245–254. doi: 10.1212/WNL.57.2.245

Courchesne, E., and Pierce, K. (2005a). Brain overgrowth in autism during a critical time in development: implications for frontal pyramidal neuron and interneuron development and connectivity. *Int. J. Dev. Neurosci.* 23, 153–170. doi: 10.1016/j.ijdevneu.2005.01.003

Courchesne, E., and Pierce, K. (2005b). Why the frontal cortex in autism might be talking only to itself: local over-connectivity but long-distance disconnection. *Curr. Opin. Neurobiol.* 15, 225–230. doi: 10.1016/j.conb.2005.03.001

Courchesne, E., Pierce, K., Schumann, C. M., Redcay, E., Buckwalter, J. A., Kennedy, D. P., et al. (2007). Mapping early brain development in autism. *Neuron* 56, 399–413. doi: 10.1016/j.neuron.2007.10.016

Crane, L., and Goddard, L. (2008). Episodic and semantic autobiographical memory in adults with autism spectrum disorders. *J. Autism Dev. Disord.* 38, 498–506. doi: 10.1007/s10803-007-0420-2

Cudeiro, J., and Sillito, A. M. (2006). Looking back: corticothalamic feedback and early visual processing. *Trends Neurosci.* 29, 298–306. doi: 10.1016/j.tins.2006.05.002

Dapretto, M., Davies, M. S., Pfeifer, J. H., Scott, A. A., Sigman, M., Bookheimer, S. Y., et al. (2006). Understanding emotions in others: mirror neuron dysfunction in children with autism spectrum disorders. *Nat. Neurosci.* 9, 28–30. doi: 10.1038/nn1611

DeRamus, T. P., and Kana, R. K. (2015). Anatomical likelihood estimation meta-analysis of grey and white matter anomalies in autism spectrum disorders. *Neuroimage Clin.* 7, 525–536. doi: 10.1016/j.nicl.2014.11.004

Dierker, D. L., Feczko, E., Pruett, J. R., Petersen, S. E., Schlaggar, B. L., Constantino, J. N., et al. (2015). Analysis of cortical shape in children with simplex autism. *Cereb. Cortex* 25, 1042–1051. doi: 10.1093/cercor/bht294

Di Martino, A., Yan, C.-G., Li, Q., Denio, E., Castellanos, F. X., Alaerts, K., et al. (2014). The autism brain imaging data exchange: towards a large-scale evaluation of the intrinsic brain architecture in autism. *Mol. Psychiatry* 19, 659–667. doi: 10.1038/mp.2013.78

Duerden, E. G., Mak-Fan, K. M., Taylor, M. J., and Roberts, S. W. (2012). Regional differences in grey and white matter in children and adults with autism spectrum disorders: an activation likelihood estimate (ALE) meta-analysis. *Autism Res.* 5, 49–66. doi: 10.1002/aur.235

Ecker, C., Bookheimer, S. Y., and Murphy, D. G. (2015). Neuroimaging in autism spectrum disorder: brain structure and function across the lifespan. *Lancet Neurol.* 14, 1121–1134. doi: 10.1016/S1474-4422(15)00050-2

Ecker, C., Ginestet, C., Feng, Y., Johnston, P., Lombardo, M. V., Lai, M. C., et al. (2013a). Brain surface anatomy in adults with autism: the relationship between surface area, cortical thickness, and autistic symptoms. *JAMA Psychiatry* 70, 59–70. doi: 10.1001/jamapsychiatry.2013.265

Ecker, C., Marquand, A., Mourao-Miranda, J., Johnston, P., Daly, E. M., Brammer, M. J., et al. (2010a). Describing the brain in autism in five dimensions-magnetic resonance imaging-assisted diagnosis of autism spectrum disorder using a multiparameter classification approach. *J. Neurosci.* 30, 10612–10623. doi: 10.1523/JNEUROSCI.5413-09.2010

Ecker, C., Rocha-Rego, V., Johnston, P., Mourao-Miranda, J., Marquand, A., Daly, E. M., et al. (2010b). Investigating the predictive value of whole-brain structural MR scans in autism: a pattern classification approach. *Neuroimage* 49, 44–56. doi: 10.1016/j.neuroimage.2009.08.024

Ecker, C., Spooren, W., and Murphy, D. G. (2013b). Translational approaches to the biology of autism: false dawn or a new era? *Mol. Psychiatry* 18, 435–442. doi: 10.1038/mp.2012.102

Ecker, C., Suckling, J., Deoni, S. C., Lombardo, M. V., Bullmore, E. T., Baron-Cohen, S., et al. (2012). Brain anatomy and its relationship to behavior in adults with autism spectrum disorder: a multicenter magnetic resonance imaging study. *Arch. Gen. Psychiatry* 69, 195–209. doi: 10.1001/archgenpsychiatry.2011.1251

Eilam-Stock, T., Xu, P., Cao, M., Gu, X., Van Dam, N. T., Anagnostou, E., et al. (2014). Abnormal autonomic and associated brain activities during rest in autism spectrum disorder. *Brain* 137, 153–171. doi: 10.1093/brain/awt294

Etkin, A., Egner, T., and Kalisch, R. (2011). Emotional processing in anterior cingulate and medial prefrontal cortex. *Trends Cogn. Sci.* 15, 85–93. doi: 10.1016/j.tics.2010.11.004

Fan, Y. T., Chen, C., Chen, S. C., Decety, J., and Cheng, Y. (2013). Empathic arousal and social understanding in individuals with autism: evidence from fMRI and ERP measurements. *Soc. Cogn. Affect Neurosci.* 9, 1203–1213. doi: 10.1093/scan/nst101

Fernández, G., Weyerts, H., Schrader-Bolsche, M., Tendolkar, I., Smid, H. G., Tempelmann, C., et al. (1998). Successful verbal encoding into episodic memory engages the posterior hippocampus: a parametrically analyzed functional magnetic resonance imaging study. *J. Neurosci.* 18, 1841–1847.

Frith, C. D., and Frith, U. (1999). Interacting minds–a biological basis. *Science* 286, 1692–1695. doi: 10.1126/science.286.5445.1692

Gallagher, H. L., and Frith, C. D. (2003). Functional imaging of 'theory of mind'. *Trends Cogn. Sci.* 7, 77–83. doi: 10.1016/S1364-6613(02)00025-6

Geschwind, D. H., and Levitt, P. (2007). Autism spectrum disorders: developmental disconnection syndromes. *Curr. Opin. Neurobiol.* 17, 103–111. doi: 10.1016/j.conb.2007.01.009

Goel, V., and Dolan, R. J. (2001). The functional anatomy of humor: segregating cognitive and affective components. *Nat. Neurosci.* 4, 237–238. doi: 10.1038/85076

Gogtay, N., and Thompson, P. M. (2010). Mapping gray matter development: implications for typical development and vulnerability to psychopathology. *Brain Cogn.* 72, 6–15. doi: 10.1016/j.bandc.2009.08.009

Greimel, E., Nehrkorn, B., Schulte-Rüther, M., Fink, G. R., Nickl-Jockschat, T., Herpertz-Dahlmann, B., et al. (2013). Changes in grey matter development in autism spectrum disorder. *Brain Struct. Funct.* 218, 929–942. doi: 10.1007/s00429-012-0439-9

Gu, X., Eilam-Stock, T., Zhou, T., Anagnostou, E., Kolevzon, A., Soorya, L., et al. (2015). Autonomic and brain responses associated with empathy deficits in autism spectrum disorder. *Hum. Brain Mapp.* 36, 3323–3338. doi: 10.1002/hbm.22840

Haar, S., Berman, S., Behrmann, M., and Dinstein, I. (2014). Anatomical abnormalities in autism? *Cereb. Cortex* 26, 1440–1452. doi: 10.1093/cercor/bhu242

Hadjikhani, N., Zürcher, N. R., Rogier, O., Hippolyte, L., Lemonnier, E., Ruest, T., et al. (2014). Emotional contagion for pain is intact in autism spectrum disorders. *Transl. Psychiatry* 4, e343. doi: 10.1038/tp.2013.113

Harris, G. J., Chabris, C. F., Clark, J., Urban, T., Aharon, I., Steele, S., et al. (2006). Brain activation during semantic processing in autism spectrum disorders via functional magnetic resonance imaging. *Brain Cogn.* 61, 54–68. doi: 10.1016/j.bandc.2005.12.015

Harris, L. T., Mcclure, S. M., Van Den Bos, W., Cohen, J. D., and Fiske, S. T. (2007). Regions of the MPFC differentially tuned to social and nonsocial affective evaluation. *Cogn. Affect. Behav. Neurosci.* 7, 309–316. doi: 10.3758/CABN.7.4.309

Hill, E., Berthoz, S., and Frith, U. (2004). Brief report: cognitive processing of own emotions in individuals with autistic spectrum disorder and in their relatives. *J. Autism Dev. Disord.* 34, 229–235. doi: 10.1023/B:JADD.0000022613.41399.14

Hyde, K. L., Samson, F., Evans, A. C., and Mottron, L. (2010). Neuroanatomical differences in brain areas implicated in perceptual and other core features of autism revealed by cortical thickness analysis and voxel-based morphometry. *Hum. Brain Mapp.* 31, 556–566. doi: 10.1002/hbm.20887

Itahashi, T., Yamada, T., Nakamura, M., Watanabe, H., Yamagata, B., Jimbo, D., et al. (2015). Linked alterations in gray and white matter morphology in adults with high-functioning autism spectrum disorder: a multimodal brain imaging study. *Neuroimage Clin.* 7, 155–169. doi: 10.1016/j.nicl.2014.11.019

Jiao, Y., Chen, R., Ke, X., Chu, K., Lu, Z., and Herskovits, E. H. (2010). Predictive models of autism spectrum disorder based on brain regional cortical thickness. *Neuroimage* 50, 589–599. doi: 10.1016/j.neuroimage.2009.12.047

Kamio, Y., Robins, D., Kelley, E., Swainson, B., and Fein, D. (2007). Atypical lexical/semantic processing in high-functioning autism spectrum disorders without early language delay. *J. Autism Dev. Disord.* 37, 1116–1122. doi: 10.1007/s10803-006-0254-3

Kelley, W. M., Macrae, C. N., Wyland, C. L., Caglar, S., Inati, S., and Heatherton, T. F. (2002). Finding the self? An event-related fMRI study. *J. Cogn. Neurosci.* 14, 785–794. doi: 10.1162/08989290260138672

Kim, H. (2015). Encoding and retrieval along the long axis of the hippocampus and their relationships with dorsal attention and default mode networks: the HERNET model. *Hippocampus* 25, 500–510. doi: 10.1002/hipo.22387

Lange, N., Travers, B. G., Bigler, E. D., Prigge, M. B., Froehlich, A. L., Nielsen, J. A., et al. (2015). Longitudinal volumetric brain changes in autism spectrum disorder ages 6–35 years. *Autism Res.* 8, 82–93. doi: 10.1002/aur.1427

Libero, L. E., Deramus, T. P., Lahti, A. C., Deshpande, G., and Kana, R. K. (2015). Multimodal neuroimaging based classification of autism spectrum disorder using anatomical, neurochemical, and white matter correlates. *Cortex* 66, 46–59. doi: 10.1016/j.cortex.2015.02.008

Lind, S. E., and Bowler, D. M. (2010). Episodic memory and episodic future thinking in adults with autism. *J. Abnorm. Psychol.* 119, 896–905. doi: 10.1037/a0020631

Lombardo, M. V., Barnes, J. L., Wheelwright, S. J., and Baron-Cohen, S. (2007). Self-referential cognition and empathy in autism. *PLoS ONE* 2:e883. doi: 10.1371/journal.pone.0000883

Lombardo, M. V., Chakrabarti, B., Bullmore, E. T., Sadek, S. A., Pasco, G., Wheelwright, S. J., et al. (2010). Atypical neural self-representation in autism. *Brain* 133, 611–624. doi: 10.1093/brain/awp306

Lord, C., Risi, S., Lambrecht, L., Cook E. H., Jr, Leventhal, B. L., Dilavore, P. C., et al. (2000). The autism diagnostic observation schedule—generic: a standard measure of social and communication deficits associated with the spectrum of autism. *J. Autism Dev. Disord.* 30, 205–223. doi: 10.1023/A:1005592401947

Maier, S., Van Elst, L. T., Beier, D., Ebert, D., Fangmeier, T., Radtke, M., et al. (2015). Increased hippocampal volumes in adults with high functioning autism spectrum disorder and an IQ> 100: a manual morphometric study. *Psychiatry Res.* 234, 152–155. doi: 10.1016/j.pscychresns.2015.08.002

Mak-Fan, K. M., Taylor, M. J., Roberts, W., and Lerch, J. P. (2012). Measures of cortical grey matter structure and development in children with autism spectrum disorder. *J. Autism Dev. Disord.* 42, 419–427. doi: 10.1007/s10803-011-1261-6

Mandy, W. P., Charman, T., and Skuse, D. H. (2012). Testing the construct validity of proposed criteria for DSM-5 autism spectrum disorder. *J. Am. Acad. Child Adolesc. Psychiatry* 51, 41–50. doi: 10.1016/j.jaac.2011.10.013

Mazziotta, J. C., Toga, A. W., Evans, A., Fox, P., and Lancaster, J. (1995). A probabilistic atlas of the human brain: theory and rationale for Its development. *Neuroimage* 2, 89–101. doi: 10.1006/nimg.1995.1012

Mcalonan, G. M., Suckling, J., Wong, N., Cheung, V., Lienenkaemper, N., Cheung, C., et al. (2008). Distinct patterns of grey matter abnormality in high-functioning autism and Asperger's syndrome. *J. Child Psychol. Psychiatry* 49, 1287–1295. doi: 10.1111/j.1469-7610.2008.01933.x

Minio-Paluello, I., Baron-Cohen, S., Avenanti, A., Walsh, V., and Aglioti, S. M. (2009). Absence of embodied empathy during pain observation in Asperger syndrome. *Biol. Psychiatry* 65, 55–62. doi: 10.1016/j.biopsych.2008.08.006

Nickl-Jockschat, T., Habel, U., Maria Michel, T., Manning, J., Laird, A. R., Fox, P. T., et al. (2012). Brain structure anomalies in autism spectrum disorder—a meta–analysis of VBM studies using anatomic likelihood estimation. *Hum. Brain Mapp.* 33, 1470–1489. doi: 10.1002/hbm.21299

Nordahl, C. W., Dierker, D., Mostafavi, I., Schumann, C. M., Rivera, S. M., Amaral, D. G., et al. (2007). Cortical folding abnormalities in autism revealed by surface-based morphometry. *J. Neurosci.* 27, 11725–11735. doi: 10.1523/JNEUROSCI.0777-07.2007

Northoff, G., Heinzel, A., De Greck, M., Bermpohl, F., Dobrowolny, H., and Panksepp, J. (2006). Self-referential processing in our brain–a meta-analysis of imaging studies on the self. *Neuroimage* 31, 440–457. doi: 10.1016/j.neuroimage.2005.12.002

Persico, A. M., and Bourgeron, T. (2006). Searching for ways out of the autism maze: genetic, epigenetic and environmental clues. *Trends Neurosci.* 29, 349–358. doi: 10.1016/j.tins.2006.05.010

Phan, K. L., Wager, T., Taylor, S. F., and Liberzon, I. (2002). Functional neuroanatomy of emotion: a meta-analysis of emotion activation studies in PET and fMRI. *Neuroimage* 16, 331–348. doi: 10.1006/nimg.2002.1087

Pilowsky, T., Yirmiya, N., Arbelle, S., and Mozes, T. (2000). Theory of mind abilities of children with schizophrenia, children with autism, and normally developing children. *Schizophr. Res.* 42, 145–155. doi: 10.1016/S0920-9964(99)00101-2

Raznahan, A., Toro, R., Daly, E., Robertson, D., Murphy, C., Deeley, Q., et al. (2009). Cortical anatomy in autism spectrum disorder: an *in vivo* MRI study on the effect of age. *Cereb. Cortex* 20, 1332–1340. doi: 10.1093/cercor/bhp198

Redcay, E., and Courchesne, E. (2005). When is the brain enlarged in autism? A meta-analysis of all brain size reports. *Biol. Psychiatry* 58, 1–9. doi: 10.1016/j.biopsych.2005.03.026

Riddle, K., Cascio, C. J., and Woodward, N. D. (2016). Brain structure in autism: a voxel-based morphometry analysis of the Autism Brain Imaging Database Exchange (ABIDE). *Brain Imaging Behav.* doi: 10.1007/s11682-016-9534-5. [Epub ahead of print].

Riedel, A., Maier, S., Ulbrich, M., Biscaldi, M., Ebert, D., Fangmeier, T., et al. (2014). No significant brain volume decreases or increases in adults with high-functioning autism spectrum disorder and above average intelligence: a voxel-based morphometric study. *Psychiatry Res.* 223, 67–74. doi: 10.1016/j.pscychresns.2014.05.013

Sahin, M., and Sur, M. (2015). Genes, circuits, and precision therapies for autism and related neurodevelopmental disorders. *Science* 350:aab3897. doi: 10.1126/science.aab3897

Santos, M., Uppal, N., Butti, C., Wicinski, B., Schmeidler, J., Giannakopoulos, P., et al. (2011). Von Economo neurons in autism: a stereologic study of the frontoinsular cortex in children. *Brain Res.* 1380, 206–217. doi: 10.1016/j.brainres.2010.08.067

Saxe, R., and Kanwisher, N. (2003). People thinking about thinking people. the role of the temporo-parietal junction in "theory of mind". *Neuroimage* 19, 1835–1842. doi: 10.1016/S1053-8119(03)00230-1

Scheel, C., Rotarska-Jagiela, A., Schilbach, L., Lehnhardt, F. G., Krug, B., Vogeley, K., et al. (2011). Imaging derived cortical thickness reduction in high-functioning autism: key regions and temporal slope. *Neuroimage* 58, 391–400. doi: 10.1016/j.neuroimage.2011.06.040

Schumann, C. M., Barnes, C. C., Lord, C., and Courchesne, E. (2009). Amygdala enlargement in toddlers with autism related to severity of social and communication impairments. *Biol. Psychiatry* 66, 942–949. doi: 10.1016/j.biopsych.2009.07.007

Schumann, C. M., Bloss, C. S., Barnes, C. C., Wideman, G. M., Carper, R. A., Akshoomoff, N., et al. (2010). Longitudinal magnetic resonance imaging study of cortical development through early childhood in autism. *J. Neurosci.* 30, 4419–4427. doi: 10.1523/JNEUROSCI.5714-09.2010

Shamay-Tsoory, S. G., Aharon-Peretz, J., and Perry, D. (2009). Two systems for empathy: a double dissociation between emotional and cognitive empathy in inferior frontal gyrus versus ventromedial prefrontal lesions. *Brain* 132, 617–627. doi: 10.1093/brain/awn279

Slotnick, S. D., Moo, L. R., Segal, J. B., and Hart, J. (2003). Distinct prefrontal cortex activity associated with item memory and source memory for visual shapes. *Cogn. Brain Res.* 17, 75–82. doi: 10.1016/S0926-6410(03)00082-X

Solso, S., Xu, R., Proudfoot, J., Hagler, D. J. Jr, Campbell, K., Venkatraman, V., et al. (2015). Diffusion tensor imaging provides evidence of possible axonal overconnectivity in frontal lobes in autism spectrum disorder toddlers. *Biol. Psychiatry* 79, 676–684. doi: 10.1016/j.biopsych.2015.06.029

Stanfield, A. C., Mcintosh, A. M., Spencer, M. D., Philip, R., Gaur, S., and Lawrie, S. M. (2008). Towards a neuroanatomy of autism: a systematic review and meta-analysis of structural magnetic resonance imaging studies. *Eur. Psychiatry* 23, 289–299. doi: 10.1016/j.eurpsy.2007.05.006

Sussman, D., Leung, R., Vogan, V., Lee, W., Trelle, S., Lin, S., et al. (2015). The autism puzzle: diffuse but not pervasive neuroanatomical abnormalities in children with ASD. *Neuroimage Clin.* 8, 170–179. doi: 10.1016/j.nicl.2015.04.008

Toal, F., Daly, E. M., Page, L., Deeley, Q., Hallahan, B., Bloemen, O., et al. (2010). Clinical and anatomical heterogeneity in autistic spectrum disorder: a structural MRI study. *Psychol. Med.* 40, 1171–1181. doi: 10.1017/S0033291709991541

Uddin, L. Q. (2011). The self in autism: an emerging view from neuroimaging. *Neurocase* 17, 201–208. doi: 10.1080/13554794.2010.509320

Uddin, L. Q., Menon, V., Young, C. B., Ryali, S., Chen, T., Khouzam, A., et al. (2011). Multivariate searchlight classification of structural magnetic resonance imaging in children and adolescents with autism. *Biol. Psychiatry* 70, 833–841. doi: 10.1016/j.biopsych.2011.07.014

Vandenbroucke, M. W., Scholte, H. S., Van Engeland, H., Lamme, V. A., and Kemner, C. (2008). A neural substrate for atypical low-level visual processing in autism spectrum disorder. *Brain* 131, 1013–1024. doi: 10.1093/brain/awm321

Vanni, S., Tanskanen, T., Seppä, M., Uutela, K., and Hari, R. (2001). Coinciding early activation of the human primary visual cortex and anteromedial cuneus. *Proc. Natl. Acad. Sci. U.S.A.* 98, 2776–2780. doi: 10.1073/pnas.041600898

Via, E., Radua, J., Cardoner, N., Happé, F., and Mataix-Cols, D. (2011). Meta-analysis of gray matter abnormalities in autism spectrum disorder: should Asperger disorder be subsumed under a broader umbrella of autistic spectrum disorder? *Arch. Gen. Psychiatry* 68, 409–418. doi: 10.1001/archgenpsychiatry.2011.27

Visser, M., Jefferies, E., Embleton, K. V., and Lambon Ralph, M. A. (2012). Both the middle temporal gyrus and the ventral anterior temporal area are crucial for multimodal semantic processing: distortion-corrected fMRI evidence for a double gradient of information convergence in the temporal lobes. *J. Cogn. Neurosci.* 24, 1766–1778. doi: 10.1162/jocn_a_00244

Völlm, B. A., Taylor, A. N., Richardson, P., Corcoran, R., Stirling, J., Mckie, S., et al. (2006). Neuronal correlates of theory of mind and empathy: a functional magnetic resonance imaging study in a nonverbal task. *Neuroimage* 29, 90–98. doi: 10.1016/j.neuroimage.2005.07.022

Wallace, G. L., Robustelli, B., Dankner, N., Kenworthy, L., Giedd, J. N., and Martin, A. (2013). Increased gyrification, but comparable surface area in adolescents with autism spectrum disorders. *Brain* 136, 1956–1967. doi: 10.1093/brain/awt106

Zielinski, B. A., Prigge, M. B., Nielsen, J. A., Froehlich, A. L., Abildskov, T. J., Anderson, J. S., et al. (2014). Longitudinal changes in cortical thickness in autism and typical development. *Brain* 137, 1799–1812. doi: 10.1093/brain/awu083

Zwaigenbaum, L., Young, G. S., Stone, W. L., Dobkins, K., Ozonoff, S., Brian, J., et al. (2014). Early head growth in infants at risk of autism: a baby siblings research consortium study. *J. Am. Acad. Child Adolesc. Psychiatry* 53, 1053–1062. doi: 10.1016/j.jaac.2014.07.007

13

Autism as a Disorder of High Intelligence

Bernard J. Crespi *

Department of Biological Sciences and Human Evolutionary Studies Program, Simon Fraser University, Burnaby, BC, Canada

Edited by:
Joshua Pesach Rosenzweig, Cell-El Therapeutics Ltd., Israel

Reviewed by:
Kerstin Jessica Plessen, University of Copenhagen, Denmark
Rex Eugene Jung, University of New Mexico, USA

***Correspondence:**
Bernard J. Crespi
crespi@sfu.ca

A suite of recent studies has reported positive genetic correlations between autism risk and measures of mental ability. These findings indicate that alleles for autism overlap broadly with alleles for high intelligence, which appears paradoxical given that autism is characterized, overall, by below-average IQ. This paradox can be resolved under the hypothesis that autism etiology commonly involves enhanced, but imbalanced, components of intelligence. This hypothesis is supported by convergent evidence showing that autism and high IQ share a diverse set of convergent correlates, including large brain size, fast brain growth, increased sensory and visual-spatial abilities, enhanced synaptic functions, increased attentional focus, high socioeconomic status, more deliberative decision-making, profession and occupational interests in engineering and physical sciences, and high levels of positive assortative mating. These findings help to provide an evolutionary basis to understanding autism risk as underlain in part by dysregulation of intelligence, a core human-specific adaptation. In turn, integration of studies on intelligence with studies of autism should provide novel insights into the neurological and genetic causes of high mental abilities, with important implications for cognitive enhancement, artificial intelligence, the relationship of autism with schizophrenia, and the treatment of both autism and intellectual disability.

Keywords: intelligence, autism, schizophrenia, genetic correlation, pleiotropy, evolution

INTRODUCTION

> *'How wonderful that we have met with a paradox. Now we have some hope of making progress.'*
> *Niels Bohr*

Autism is conventionally regarded as a neurodevelopmental disorder that involves deficits in social interaction and social communication, combined with restricted or repetitive patterns of behavior and interests. However useful this definition may be for practical purposes, it also represents a reified, more or less arbitrary, historical and societal construction that fits neither with Kanner's (1943) original description (Evans, 2013) nor with the standard medical model of disease whereby maladaptive phenotypes must be understood in terms of alteration to specific adaptive systems (Nesse and Stein, 2012; Crespi, 2016).

Autism may, alternatively, be regarded as a syndrome, a constellation of phenotypes, sets of which tend to be found together relatively often, or sets of which when found together cause particular problems for children, families, and communities (Happé et al., 2006). Any given individual "with" autism will exhibit some more or less unique collection of such phenotypes (e.g., van Os, 2009), which is due to their more or less unique genomic makeup and early developmental environment. By this simple logic, any diagnoses of autism should be regarded not as any sort of endpoint, but as a rough, initial signpost toward eventual determination of the genetic, developmental, hormonal, neurological, psychological, and/or environmental causes of each individual's altered autism-related cognition, affect and behavior.

The finding that autism has many causes (Happé and Ronald, 2008) should direct attention to improved means of differentially diagnosing its personalized bases. This process, in turn, centers on determining what adaptive neural and psychological systems has been altered, and how, to result in some set of autistic traits in some individual. Autistic phenotypes have been linked, for example, to increased protein synthesis at synapses (Bourgeron, 2009), higher excitatory to inhibitory neurotransmission (Rubenstein and Merzenich, 2003), enhanced local compared to global processing and connectivity (Happé and Frith, 2006), a bias toward systemizing over empathizing (Baron-Cohen, 2009), and enhanced perceptual functioning (Mottron et al., 2006). These patterns and theories are not mutually exclusive, but none of them includes an explicit evolutionary dimension, such that their proximate causes remain ungrounded in the one discipline that unites across all biological-psychological levels in the context of ultimate, long-term determinants of psychological adaptation and maladaptation (Crespi, 2016).

Risks for autism, like risks of cancer, diabetes, or arthritis, have evolved along the human lineage (Crespi and Leach, 2016). As such, evolutionary biology becomes a valuable conceptual and analytic tool for connecting adaptive brain systems with the ways in which they can become altered and maladaptive in psychiatric disorders (Fjell et al., 2015). So what adaptive, evolved human brain systems are changed, in what different ways, to produce the phenotypes characteristic of autism? The most prominent neurological change along the human lineage is, of course, the tripling of brain size and associated changes in brain organization and functions, and our concomitant tremendous increase in intelligence compared to other great apes (Roth and Dicke, 2005). A notable set of "brain size genes" has been demonstrated to have been subject to natural selection in humans and other mammals (Montgomery and Mundy, 2014), and variation among extant humans in intelligence is now known to be highly polygenic, underlain by hundreds to thousands of alleles each of small effect (e. g., Davies et al., 2011; Benyamin et al., 2014; Plomin and Deary, 2015).

The genetical evolution of high intelligence in humans has increased scope for two main forms of dysregulation. First, the developmental and neural systems that connect genetic variation and environments with intelligence may be subject to maladaptive alterations by purely deleterious mutations, maladapted genotypes, or harmful environments, that degrade the "intelligence development" system. This route generally leads to what we call intellectual disability (Vissers et al., 2016), with overall reductions in intelligence and the functioning of its physiological and neural subsystems. Second, the development of intelligence can be affected, by genes or environments, in the opposite direction, toward higher levels of functioning. If this change results in balanced enhancements in all of the components of high intellect, general intelligence will be increased. However, if some, or most, but not all inter-dependent general cognitive-intellectual functions are enhanced, what would we observe?

Autism has long been characterized by relatively low intelligence as measured by most standard tests (e. g., Hoekstra et al., 2009). However, a suite of recent studies, described in more detail below, has demonstrated that alleles "for" autism, that is, common alleles that each contributes slightly to its risk, overlap substantially and significantly with alleles "for" high intelligence (Bulik-Sullivan et al., 2015; Clarke et al., 2015; Hill et al., 2015; Hagenaars et al., 2016). To a notable, and well-replicated, degree, then, many "autism" alleles are "high intelligence" alleles. How can these paradoxical observations be reconciled?

In this article I describe and evaluate the hypothesis that a substantial proportion of "autism risk" is underlain by high, but more or less imbalanced, components of intelligence. First, I provide a brief overview of the genetic, developmental and neurological bases and correlates of human intelligence, from research within this particular domain, and relate the structure of intelligence in neurotypical individuals to the differences between autistic individuals and neurotypical individuals. Second, I compare the best-validated correlates of variation among humans in intelligence with established characteristics of autistic individuals, compared to controls. These two areas of study, intelligence and autism, have thus far developed virtually independently from one another; I thus integrate and synthesize them in the context of testing the hypothesis addressed here. In doing so, I also compare results for autism with those for schizophrenia, the other primary human neurodevelopmental disorder, in light of theories for how these two conditions are related to one another (Crespi and Badcock, 2008; Crespi, 2016). Finally, I develop a framework for consilience of these findings with previous theory on autism, and describe the implications of the results, with regard to the causes, treatments, and understanding of autism, and the structure and study of human intelligence. The primary novelty and usefulness of this synthesis is that it provides the first comprehensive connections of the causes and symptoms of autism with alterations to a specific human-elaborated adaptive system, intelligence, and thereby generates new insights and research questions into the natures and inter-relationships of intelligence, autism, and schizophrenia.

THE ARCHITECTURE AND CORRELATES OF HUMAN INTELLIGENCE

Human intelligence has been studied predominantly from psychometric, genetic, neurological, and psychological perspectives. Psychometric studies tracing back to Spearman (1904) have demonstrated that virtually all measures of human mental abilities are moderately to highly positively correlated with one another, such that a common factor, typically called "*g*," underlies their joint co-variation. Between the general, primary *g* factor, and the diverse, specific measures of mental abilities, is a small set of secondary factors that each statistically accounts for covariation among a larger set of functionally-similar abilities. The Verbal-Perceptual-Rotational (VPR) model of Johnson and Bouchard (2005a,b, 2007; **Figure 1**), with three such secondary factors, represents the currently best-supported psychometric description of human intelligence structure. Under this model, "Verbal" refers to verbal fluency and knowledge, "Perceptual" refers to perceptual speed and mechanical and spatial abilities other than mental rotation, and "Rotational" refers to mental rotation, which involves mental movements of imagined objects or persons, as in the classic Mental Rotation test from Vandenberg and Kruse (1978; Johnson and Bouchard, 2005b; Major et al., 2012). The components of the VPR model correspond on a broad scale with brain structural organization in that verbal skills are relatively left-hemispheric, spatial and non-verbal abilities are relatively right-hemispheric, and mental rotation depends, in part, on strongly bihemispheric functions associated with corpus callosum size (Johnson and Bouchard, 2005b; Karadi et al., 2006; Schoenemann, 2006).

In addition to its success in describing patterns of co-variation among aspects of human intelligence, the VPR model also demonstrates evidence of tradeoffs between sets of cognitive abilities: when controlling for variation in *g*, image rotation ability is inversely associated with verbal ability, and scores on tests indicative of a strong focus of attention are inversely associated with scores indicating diffuse focus (Johnson and Bouchard, 2007; **Figure 2**). These two tradeoffs also exhibit sex differences, with males over-represented at the high rotational-strong focus pole, and more females at the pole with higher verbal abilities and more-diffuse focus (Johnson and Bouchard, 2007). Such sex differences and negative correlations are important given the strong male biases found in autism (Fombonne, 2009; Baron-Cohen et al., 2011), the extensive data showing that autism involves reductions in verbal skills but (1) increases in focus of attention (e. g., Ploog, 2010; Sabatos-DeVito et al., 2016), (2) enhanced perceptual and spatial abilities [as reflected in prowess, for example, in Block Design and the Embedded Figures test (EFT); Mottron et al., 2006; Muth et al., 2014], and (3) superior ability in non-rotational (though not rotational) aspects of the mental rotation task (Zapf et al., 2015). Considered together, these findings provide evidence that the cognitive structure of autism dovetails with the structure of the independently derived best-supported model for the psychometric architecture of human intelligence, but that it is characterized by increases in some, specific, components of intelligence and decreases in others, leading to a profile that is imbalanced and reflects extremes of typical variation. As such, autism-related differences in VPR-model structured intelligence appear to reflect its evolutionary bases in altered expression of adaptive cognitive variation (Crespi, 2016), with autistic cognition mediated by

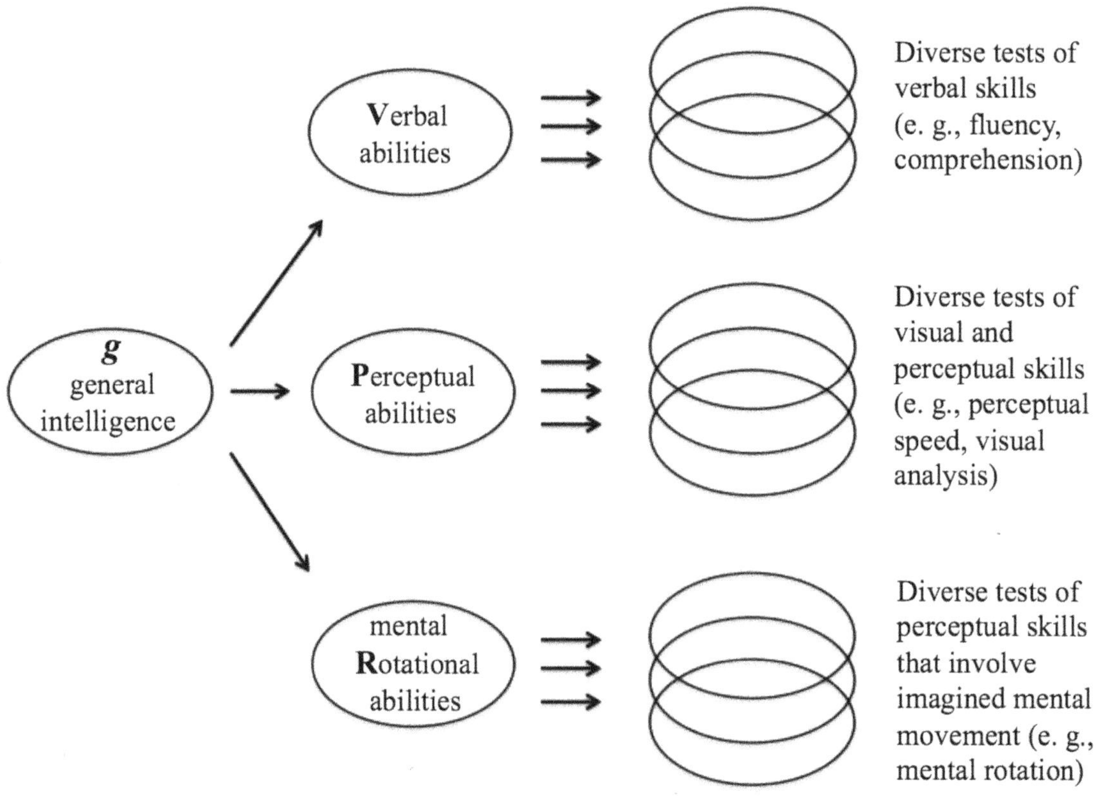

FIGURE 1 | The VPR model of intelligence. Under this model, the higher-level architecture of human intelligence, as indicated by diverse mental-ability tasks, involves one general factor, *g*, and three mid-level factors, Verbal, Perceptual, and image Rotation, that reflect variation among individuals in large-scale neural structure and processing. Adapted from Johnson et al. (2007).

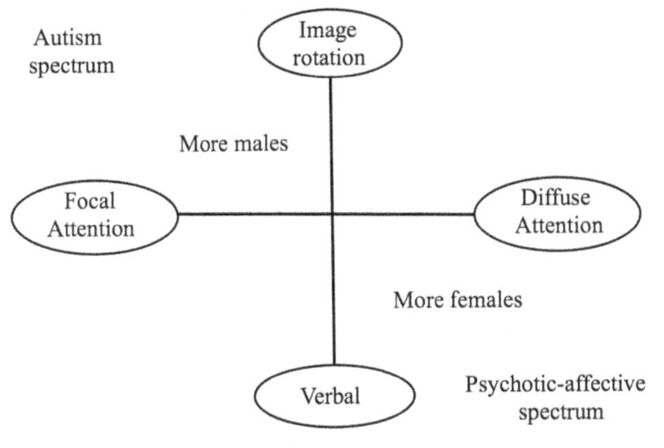

FIGURE 2 | Two orthogonal dimensions of intelligence, which emerge after the general factor *g* is statistically removed. Poles of each of the two dimensions demonstrate inverse associations with one another, indicative of neurally-based cognitive trade-offs. The psychotic-affective spectrum includes mainly schizophrenia, bipolar disorder, depression, and borderline personality disorder. Adapted from Johnson et al. (2007).

relative extremes of tradeoffs (Johnson and Bouchard, 2007, 2008). In contrast to autism, schizophrenia is characterized by a focus of attention decreased relative to controls (e.g., Morris et al., 2013), notably-poor visual-spatial relative to verbal abilities (Kravariti et al., 2006), and reduced ability in non-rotational (though not in rotational) aspects of mental rotation tasks (Thakkar and Park, 2010; Benson and Park, 2013). These patterns of findings derive directly from the VPR model, and indicate that its further application and extension will help to clarify the psychometric structure of autistic, neurotypical, and schizophrenia-associated cognition.

A second model for the higher-level psychometric structure of intelligence is its division into a "fluid" component, reflecting ability to solve novel problems, use logic, and identify patterns, in ways that are independent of acquired and cultural knowledge, and a "crystallized" component, indicative of ability to utilize acquired and learned knowledge and experience (e. g., Nisbett et al., 2012). This subdivision of intelligence fits less well than the VPR model to patterns of covariation across mental ability tests (Johnson and Bouchard, 2005a,b), but its validity and usefulness are supported by the underpinning of fluid vs. crystallized intelligence by distinct sets of genes (Christoforou et al., 2014), their different patterns of change with age (with fluid changing like physical traits, but crystallized showing little age-related decline; Deary et al., 2010), and the primacy of social learning in human cultural adaptation (Henrich, 2015). As for the VPR model, the structure of intelligence in autism reflects the fluid-crystallized dichotomy, in that fluid intelligence is relatively or absolutely enhanced in autism, but crystallized intelligence is reduced, compared to controls (Dawson et al., 2007; Hayashi et al., 2008; see also Nader et al., 2016). This pattern again indicates imbalance, and elevation, in components of intelligence in autism that correspond to its evolved and psychometrically characterized structure.

Intelligence, usually measured by strong correlates of *g*, has a clear polygenic basis, as well as established connections with neurological variation. Recent GWA studies have provided evidence that many hundreds or thousands of alleles, each of very small effect, underlie variation among individuals in *g*, although only a fraction of its high heritability can be accounted for at this point (Plomin and Deary, 2015). By contrast, data from studies of the genetic basis of intellectual disability show that it is due mainly to moderate or large effect *de novo* deleterious alleles, rather than a concentration of weakly-deleterious, small-effect, segregating alleles; these findings indicate that "high intelligence requires that everything work right, including most of the positive alleles and few of the negative alleles associated with intelligence" (Plomin and Deary, 2015, p. 103; Franić et al., 2015; Hill et al., 2015). Plomin and Deary (2015, p. 103) also point out an important question regarding such "positive genetics" of intelligence, for psychiatric disorders: if individuals at the positive end of the polygenic distribution of "risk" simply have low risk, or if they "have special powers." In this article, I am evaluating the hypothesis that such "special powers" indeed exist, in the contexts of autism and intelligence, and in comparison to schizophrenia. Finally, Plomin and Deary (2015) point out that assortative mating is notably stronger (~0.40) for intelligence than for most other human traits, which maintains additive genetic variation for this trait as well as generating more "extreme" intelligence phenotypes than otherwise expected. Increased autism risk has been attributed by Baron-Cohen et al. (2006) to assortative mating between two individuals high in "systemizing," and assortative mating is much high among individuals diagnosed with ASD than other disorders (Nordsletten et al., 2016); how might intelligence variation play a role in this process and its sequelae?

As described in detail below, the neurological basis of intelligence has been well established for a suite of phenotypes, including large brain size and high numbers of neurons, large hippocampus size, high efficacy of working memory, fast neuronal processing speed, neural efficiency, fast rates of brain growth and pruning, and specific patterns of gray matter and white matter distributions. Most broadly, high intelligence appears to reflect high functionality, speed, and integration of a fronto-parietal brain network that subserves the sensory acquisition, abstraction, alternative model-testing, and deployment of information (the Parieto-Frontal Integration Theory; Jung and Haier, 2007; Colom et al., 2010; **Figure 3**). This "intelligence network" overlaps substantially with the "task-positive network," whose activation is inversely associated with that of the "default mode" or "task-negative" network (e.g., Uddin et al., 2009), as might be expected given that mental abilities and intelligence are measured in the context of particular tasks. The general and specific functioning of this distributed, fronto-parietal network are highly compatible with the VPR psychometric model described above (Deary et al., 2010), with genetic bases to VPR abilities and fronto-parietal structure and function (Johnson et al., 2007).

In addition to its substantial psychometric and genetic basis, and neurological underpinnings, intelligence is also notably associated with two additional factors that are relevant to the autism spectrum: sensory abilities and socioeconomic status. Positive correlations of *g* with sensory abilities in the auditory,

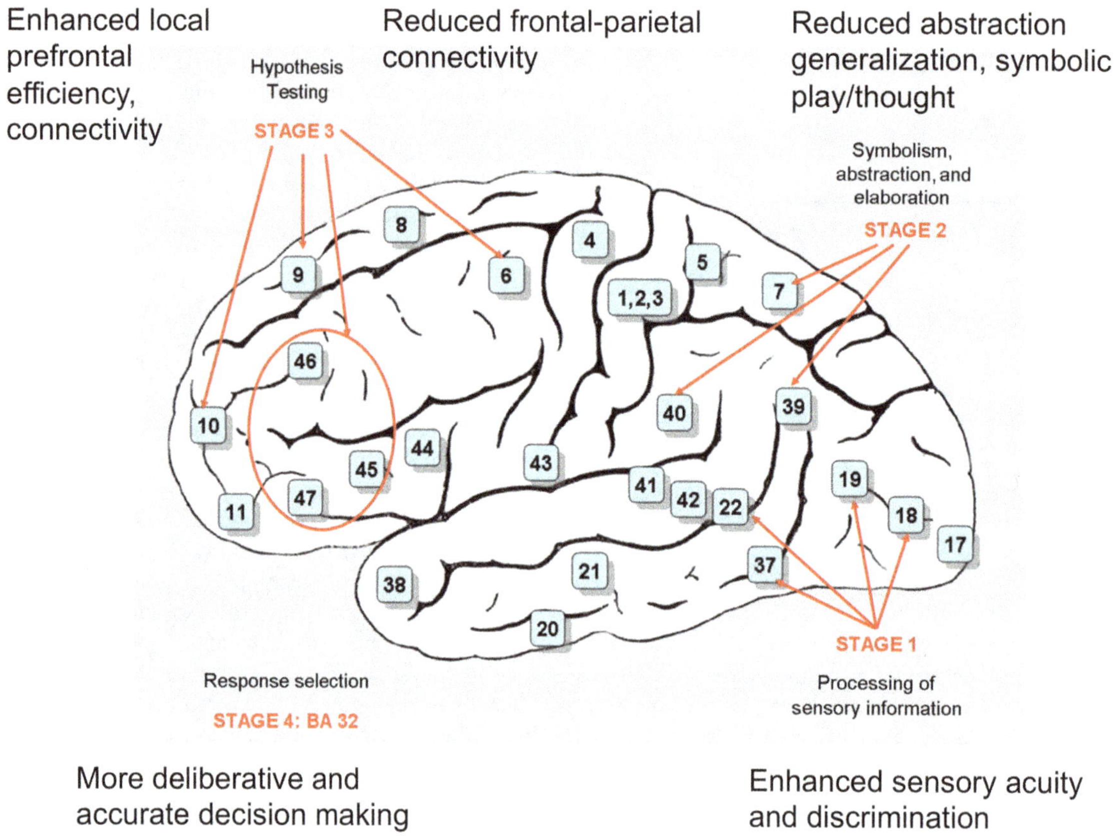

FIGURE 3 | Brain regions, and temporal stages, representing the P-FIT (Parietal Frontal Integration Theory) model of intelligence. Postulated alterations in autism, compared to control individuals, are shown along the periphery, and described in the text. Adapted from Colom et al. (2010).

visual, and tactile domains have been well documented and replicated, across over a century of testing (Deary et al., 2004). Such sensory tests include, for example, ability to discriminate closely-similar stimuli, temporal information processing skill, or sensitivity in stimulus detection, that apparently reflect aspects of processing speed, focal-attentional abilities, and ability to suppress irrelevant stimuli. As described further below, Galton (1883) and Spearman (1904, pp. 268–272) indeed virtually equated higher cognitive abilities with more-accurate sensory discrimination, and postulated "general discrimination" skills that underpinned sensory abilities across different modalities and correlated near unity with general intelligence. Genetically-based positive associations of intelligence with socioeconomic status, as well as with education levels and occupational status, have also been well documented (Marioni et al., 2014; Trzaskowski et al., 2014; Krapohl and Plomin, 2016; review in Plomin and Deary, 2015). These findings indicate that the same alleles pleiotropically mediate high intelligence and high socioeconomic status (vs. low levels of both), again through many alleles of small effect that account for a small, though statistically significant, proportion of the variance in both traits.

The upshot of these considerations from psychometrics, genetics, neuroscience, psychology, and sociology is that high intelligence involves many beneficial alleles of small effect, an absence of *de novo* deleterious mutations, high performance with balanced integration of neural subsystems (as well as large brain size and more neurons), enhanced sensory abilities, high socioeconomic status, and a notable degree of assortative mating. How, then, do these genetic and phenotypic correlates of intelligence, and associated ones, relate to the genetic basis and phenotypic correlates of autism?

GENETIC OVERLAP OF AUTISM WITH INTELLIGENCE

Recent increases in sample sizes, extensions of target phenotypes analyzed, and developments in analytic methods for genome-wide association studies, have allowed the first robust tests of the sign and magnitude of genetic correlations, due to pleiotropy and linkage disequilibrium, between intelligence and other traits including risk of psychiatric conditions. Four studies have used data from the Psychiatric Genetics Consortium (PGC) on polygenic risk for autism (Cross-Disorder Group of the Psychiatric Genomics Consortium, 2013) to assess overlap of autism risk alleles (identified from over 5000 cases) with alleles for aspects of cognitive ability and intelligence. All four of these studies, which used diverse, independent populations and tests (or correlates) of cognitive abilities, have reported significant, substantial genetically-based positive associations of autism risk with intelligence, notably including full-scale IQ and a PCA-based measure of *g* (Clarke et al., 2015), childhood IQ, college attendance, and years of education (Bulik-Sullivan et al., 2015), cognitive function in childhood and educational attainment (Hill et al., 2015), and verbal-numerical reasoning and educational level reached (Hagenaars et al., 2016). These studies indicate that polygenic, small-effect size alleles that increased risk of autism are also associated with increased intelligence (and strong correlates of intelligence, such as education level; Davies et al., 2016) among neurotypical individuals.

In direct contrast to these findings for autism, genetic risk for schizophrenia has been demonstrated to be negatively associated with measures of cognitive ability and intelligence, across a broad suite of studies (McIntosh et al., 2013; Lencz et al., 2014; Bulik-Sullivan et al., 2015; Hill et al., 2015; Hagenaars et al., 2016; Hubbard et al., 2016). These results indicate that a substantial proportion of schizophrenia risk alleles also represent alleles "for" lower intelligence. Such findings for schizophrenia accord well with large bodies of research on cognitive deficits in first-degree relatives of individuals with schizophrenia (Snitz et al., 2006), and among children who are premorbid for schizophrenia (and thus will develop it at or after adolescence; Woodberry et al., 2008).

The question of whether intelligence, or any of its components, are elevated, compared to controls, among parents, siblings, or higher-order relatives of individuals with autism has yet to be investigated systematically, although this pattern is predicted by the positive genetic correlations of autism risk with measures of IQ. Tests conducted thus far have yielded diverse results, but individuals with autism clearly exhibit a similar cognitive profile to their sibs across WAIS subtests, with high scores on Block Design and Object Assembly, and low scores on Comprehension and Coding, relative to controls (Gizzonio et al., 2014). Similarly, siblings of individuals with autism have shown better working memory (for non-social targets) than control individuals (Noland et al., 2010) and higher visual-motion sensitivity (McCleery et al., 2007), and parents of individuals with autism are faster than controls at the EFT (Baron-Cohen and Hammer, 1997). Kanner (1943) and Rimland (1964, pp. 29–30) believed that parents of individuals with autism were of higher intelligence than control parents (see Levine and Olson, 1968), but their hypotheses have apparently not been subject to robust empirical testing, with most such studies of parents focusing on social deficits and alterations. By contrast, as described above, there is clear evidence for relatively low IQ, on average, among individuals with autism, at least as measured by most standardized tests.

How can this paradox of low IQ, but positive genetic correlations of autism risk with intelligence, be resolved? None of the papers on genetic correlations of autism with intelligence discuss possible explanations, or ways to investigate the conundrum further. I have proposed here the hypothesis that autism involves high but imbalanced intelligence, such that some or many genetically-based components of intelligence are enhanced, but imbalance across components increases risk and patterns of expression for autistic phenotypes, and for diagnoses. By this hypothesis, higher intelligence may co-occur with higher risk for imbalance and cognitive and affective consequences from it, given that the components of cognitive ability are expected to interact strongly and may do so to a greater degree at the higher end of ability. The "high intelligence imbalance" hypothesis is useful because it makes clear predictions, and thus directs attention toward specific forms of existing data and new, informative future data to collect.

AUTISM AND THE CORRELATES OF INTELLIGENCE

The "high intelligence imbalance" hypothesis predicts that autism should be associated, at a phenotypic level, with substantiated correlates of intelligence. I elaborate here on the most-notable joint correlates of intelligence and autism, focusing on phenotypes that are associated with intelligence and that are over-developed or over-expressed in autism.

Brain Size and Growth

Large brain size and head circumference, especially in childhood but also adulthood, represent some of the best-substantiated phenotypic correlates of autism (e.g., Fukumoto et al., 2011; Foster et al., 2015; meta-analysis in Sacco et al., 2015). Autism-linked increases in brain size have been shown to involve higher numbers of neurons (Courchesne et al., 2013), a thicker cortex (Hardan et al., 2006; Karama et al., 2011; Ecker et al., 2013; Smith et al., 2016), increased hippocampus volume (Barnea-Goraly et al., 2014; Maier et al., 2015), increased brain growth rates in early childhood (Campbell et al., 2014), increased rate of cortical thinning in adolescence (Hardan et al., 2009; Mak-Fan et al., 2012), a combination of "accelerated expansion in early childhood" with "accelerated thinning in in later childhood and adolescence" (Zielinski et al., 2014), and increased processing of more-local, detailed information (White et al., 2009).

Faster increase in cortical thickness between ages 6 and 12, followed by faster cortical thickness deceleration between ages 12 and 18 (indicative of neuronal and synaptic pruning), has been linked with higher intelligence in typically-developing children (Shaw et al., 2006). These findings provide evidence that trajectories of brain growth rate during middle childhood to adolescence are notably associated with IQ, with an overall pattern of accelerated growth and accelerated pruning that matches trajectories reported in autism, though with different timings of growth in early childhood. Within humans (e.g., Ivanovic et al., 2004; Witelson et al., 2006; Menary et al., 2013), and among non-human primates (Deaner et al., 2007) species, brain size (and cortical thickness, for humans) are also positively correlated with measures of intelligence, an effect that appears to be mediated predominantly by numbers of neurons (Roth and Dicke, 2005; Dicke and Roth, 2016).

In contrast to these patterns in autism, brain size, hippocampus size, and cortical thickness are reduced among individuals with schizophrenia, including at first episode (e.g., Steen et al., 2006; Rais et al., 2012; Rimol et al., 2012;

Oertel-Knöchel et al., 2013). These reductions appear to be associated with reduced brain growth rates in late childhood and early adolescence (Gogtay et al., 2008), followed by increased gray matter loss in adolescence and early adulthood (e.g., Pantelis et al., 2005; Rapoport and Gogtay, 2011).

The genetic bases of brain size and growth, and intelligence, in relation to autism and schizophrenia, remain largely unknown. However, as one example of such inter-relations, numbers of repeat units of a protein domain referred to as *DUF1220* have been positively associated with a suite of characters including: (1) brain size (within humans, and across species of anthropoid primates; Dumas et al., 2012; Keeney et al., 2014), (2) IQ and mathematical aptitude (Davis et al., 2015), and (3) the severity of autism (Davis et al., 2014); by contrast, *DUF1220* repeat numbers are inversely associated with positive-symptom (though not negative-symptom) severity in schizophrenia (Quick et al., 2015). These findings indicate strongly pleiotropic effects of this molecular domain on brain size, intelligence, autism, and schizophrenia, whereby autism is linked with large brain size and high IQ, but positive symptom schizophrenia shows a diametric result.

Brain Connectivity

Low global, relative to local, structural and functional connectivity of the brain has been demonstrated in autism by a large suite of studies (reviews in Courchesne and Pierce, 2005; Maximo et al., 2014), and it follows in part, presumably, from increased brain size itself. Under the P-FIT model of intelligence (**Figure 3**), effective long-range connectivity is required for the integration of parietal and frontal brain regions that underlies IQ (Jung and Haier, 2007); "efficient" patterns of brain connectivity involving small-world network-level organization (with an optimal mix of short and long-rage connections) have thus, for example, been positively associated with measures of intelligence (van den Heuvel et al., 2009; Koenis et al., 2015; Kim et al., 2016). These findings suggest that relative reductions in long-range connectivity may represent an important constraint on general intelligence among individuals with autism, contributing to imbalances between its constituent parts. Testing of this hypothesis will, however, require analyses of local and global brain connectivity patterns in relation to both autism (compared to controls) and variation in intelligence (in each group) using the same methodology, to determine the degree to which the long-range connectivity pathways central to the P-FIT model (e.g., the arcuate fasciculus, and connections to the lateral prefrontal cortex; Jung and Haier, 2007; Cole et al., 2012) are differentially reduced in efficiency among individuals with autism.

In contrast to reduced long-range brain connectivity, increased local connectivity has been linked with enhanced ability in some domains, such as auditory pitch perception (Loui et al., 2011), which shows a notable association with the autism spectrum (Stanutz et al., 2014). Increased local connectivity, especially of the prefrontal cortex, also characterizes the valproic acid animal model of autism (Rinaldi et al., 2008) and the "intense world" theory of autism etiology (Markram and Markram, 2010), which involves perception, attention, and memory that are enhanced to levels that interfere with social functioning.

Higher local connectivity in sensory regions of the brain has been suggested as the basis for sensory hyper-sensitivities in autism (Belmonte et al., 2004) as well as hyper-developed attention to detail and systemizing (Baron-Cohen et al., 2009). Considered together, these findings suggest that increased local brain connectivity in autism is linked with specific enhanced abilities or interests, such that components or facets of general intelligence are increased whereas *g* itself is reduced. These brain network alterations in autism can be described most simply as involving increased brain modularity and parallel processing, which may enhance region-specific functions (such as sensory abilities and visual-spatial skills) but also lead to reduced general intelligence due to under-developed long-range connectivities.

Decreased local and increased long-range connectivity have been described in childhood-onset schizophrenia (Baribeau and Anagnostou, 2013), and increased connectivity has also been found within the default mode in schizophrenia across multiple studies (Whitfield-Gabrieli et al., 2009; Tang et al., 2013), with several reviews pointing out the opposite nature of this pattern compared to that found in autism (Broyd et al., 2009; Karbasforoushan and Woodward, 2012). However, robust tests of this hypothesis require joint connectivity analysis of individuals with autism and schizophrenia using the same protocols.

Neuronal Function

Synaptic plasticity represents a core component of brain function, and, in principle, it underlies on a neuronal scale the long-term macroscopic changes in cortical thickness across childhood and adolescence that have been linked with intelligence (e.g., Shaw et al., 2006). Protein synthesis in dendritic spines mediates synaptic plasticity, and has been associated with diverse aspects of cognition, learning and memory (Sutton and Schuman, 2006; Kasai et al., 2010). Evidence of exaggerated protein synthesis at dendrites has been reported in human syndromic autism and in multiple animal models of autism (Kelleher and Bear, 2008; Bourgeron, 2009; Gkogkas et al., 2013; Santini et al., 2013; Santini and Klann, 2014; review in Mottron et al., 2014), indicating that gains of function or expression in key molecular mediators of cognition may characterize the autism spectrum (e.g., Figure 1 in Kulkarni and Firestein, 2012). Increased levels of neuronal plasticity and synaptic remodeling likewise characterize some theory for autism and animal models (Markram and Markram, 2010; Isshiki et al., 2014; Oberman and Pascual-Leone, 2014).

The degree to which neuronal functions such as synaptic plasticity, dendritic spine protein synthesis levels, and dendrite dynamics including flexibility and stability influence variation in general intelligence remains unclear. However, a recent GWA study found that the strongest functional enrichment for genes linked with fluid intelligence was synaptic "efficiency," whereas for crystallized intelligence it was synaptic depression and LTD (long-term depression; Christoforou et al., 2014). These findings suggest strong associations of neuronal and synaptic function with intelligence, such that autism may commonly involve dysregulation of intelligence-associated neuronal processes toward hyper-functional dynamics. The gene *CYFIP1* represents an apparent example of a locus that mediates such effects: high expression of this gene, which coordinates mRNA translation at dendrites, has been associated with autism (Oguro-Ando et al., 2015; Wang et al., 2015); by contrast, deletions that reduce its expression have been strongly linked with risk of schizophrenia, as well as with aspects of impaired cognition (especially dyslexia and dyscalculia) among otherwise-neurotypical individuals (Stefansson et al., 2008, 2014; Tam et al., 2010).

Sensory Functions, Attention, and Special Abilities

As noted above, Galton (1883) and Spearman (1904) first described hypotheses and psychometric evidence that sensory abilities and sensory discrimination skills were strongly positively associated with high intelligence. A resurgence of interest in this phenomenon has led to consistent and diverse evidence for small to moderate links of specific sensory discrimination abilities with intelligence, but strong correlations (e.g., 0.68 and 0.92 in Deary et al., 2004) of intelligence with latent factors that integrate sensory ability variation across domains (Meyer et al., 2010). The causes of correlations between general intelligence and sensory discrimination abilities remain largely unknown, but they appear to be related to: (a) ability to focus intensely while ignoring irrelevant stimuli (Melnick et al., 2013); (b) a strong positive genetic correlation between intelligence and sensory-neural processing speed (Lee et al., 2012); (c) speed of neural oscillations, which may underlie both sensory discrimination skills and intelligence (Troche and Rammsayer, 2009a,b; Troche et al., 2009); (d) white matter structure and integrity, which are positively associated with neural processing speed (e.g., Turken et al., 2008; Kerchner et al., 2012); (e) regional or global increases in gray matter (e.g., Deary et al., 2010; Hyde et al., 2010), and (f) the role of sensory input as a limiting step in general cognitive ability, upon which all further neurological components of intelligence depend. Further evaluation of these hypotheses, through GWAS-based tests for genetic correlation and neurological studies that jointly address sensory discrimination and intelligence, are required to evaluate their robustness and generality.

A large body of evidence has shown that sensory discrimination and sensory acuity abilities are commonly enhanced in autism compared to controls, across auditory (O'Riordan and Passetti, 2006; Heaton et al., 2008; Eigsti and Fein, 2013; Stanutz et al., 2014), visual (Ashwin et al., 2009; Brosnan et al., 2012; Falter et al., 2012), and tactile (Blakemore et al., 2006; Cascio et al., 2008; Nakano et al., 2012) domains. As for the links with IQ, causation remains largely obscure. However, Blaser et al. (2014) demonstrate that the autism-associated advantage in visual search is associated with stronger phasic pupillary response, which is indicative of stronger attentional focus and implicates the locus coeruleus-norepinephrine system in (at least) visual discrimination proficiency. This finding is of especially notable interest given that autism is characterized, on a general diagnostic basis, by increased attention to detail, difficulties in switching of attention, and attentional stimulus "overselectivity" on specific aspects of the physical environment (Murray et al., 2005; Ploog, 2010). High attention to detail on the Autism Quotient test, high intelligence, and high rates of autism in family members have also been reported among child prodigies (children who display highly-advanced abilities in fields such as music, mathematics, chess, or art; Ruthsatz and Urbach, 2012). Baron-Cohen et al. (2009) describe evidence that such high attention to detail in autism is a consequence of enhanced sensory abilities, and also leads to high levels of an analytical, "systemizing" cognition. Finally, Sabatos-DeVito et al. (2016) describe experiments that link atypical sensory processing in autism to attentional engagement, suggesting that these two facets of autism share neurological and psychological links.

One visual-spatial test, the embedded-figures test (EFT), represents a paradigmatic task showing superiority in autism for speed, accuracy, or both (Happé and Frith, 2006; Muth et al., 2014; Horlin et al., 2016). This test has traditionally been considered as indicative of a local cognitive "style," but three sets of findings: (a) high positive correlations of EFT performance with measures of fluid intelligence (e, g., McKenna et al., 1986; McKenna, 1990), (b) demonstration by Khodadady and Tafaghodi (2013) that EFT performance is strongly, positively linked with intelligence, and (c) the visual-spatial search and discrimination nature of the task, suggest that it can also be interpreted as a metric of visual sensory ability and discrimination that is, like other such metrics, highly associated with intelligence, especially fluid intelligence that is often not matched in autism-control comparison studies. In contrast to the patterns of EFT enhancement found for autism, meta-analysis indicates that EFT performance is significantly and substantially reduced in schizophrenia (Panton et al., 2016). Indeed, more generally, sensory discrimination and abilities are consistently reduced in schizophrenia (Bates, 2005; Force et al., 2008; Javitt, 2009a,b), as expected under the hypothesis that they represent psychologically-diametric conditions (Crespi and Badcock, 2008; Crespi, 2016).

Considered together, these findings suggest that increased sensory discrimination ability in autism represents a component or strong correlate of intelligence that is frequently enhanced to the point of imbalance with other aspects of IQ. Indeed, under the P-FIT model (**Figure 3**), sensory abilities are represented by the first, sensory processing stage of intelligence circuitry: data acquisition and coding mainly via occipital and parietal regions of the brain. Hyper-functioning of these regions may thus result in imbalanced intelligence, whereby efficient integration with downstream regions, especially parietal regions that subserve symbolism, abstraction and categorization of sensory information, becomes dysregulated (e.g., Froehlich et al., 2012; Church et al., 2015; Eduardo Mercado et al., 2015; **Figure 3**). The gene *GABRB3*, which codes for a GABA receptor, represents a possible example of a locus that is pleiotropically linked to sensory sensitivity, autism risk, and components of intelligence, given that SNPs in this gene have been linked with tactile sensitivity, risk of Asperger syndrome, and scores on the embedded figures and mental rotation tests (Tavassoli et al., 2012; Warrier et al., 2013).

Finally, autism is the only psychiatric condition characterized by notable rates of savant skills, which in this context represent highly-structured, rule-based abilities largely restricted to a few spheres of mental ability: calendar calculating, rote memory, mathematical computation, musical memory, and realistic drawing (Howlin et al., 2009; Snyder, 2009; Treffert, 2014; Meilleur et al., 2015). Savantism appears to represent an extreme of imbalanced components of mental ability in autism, given its highly limited range of enhancements and apparent negative associations of special skills with verbal and social abilities (Crespi and Leach, 2016).

Decision-Making

Decision making, or "response selection," mediated by the anterior cingulate cortex, represents the fourth stage in the P-FIT model of intelligence (Jung and Haier, 2007; **Figure 3**). Autism has been characterized, in a recent suite of studies, by more "deliberative" decision making (compared to controls), that tends to reduce biases and errors associated with fast and intuitive, but often "irrational," decision-making (De Martino et al., 2008; Brosnan et al., 2014, 2016; South et al., 2014). Given that susceptibilities to cognitive biases are negatively associated with measures of intelligence, weakly though significantly (e.g., Teovanović et al., 2015), these findings suggest that this component of intelligence is enhanced in autism, at least in some contexts. More-deliberative decision making in autism may be associated, and underpinned, by enhanced explanatory drive to seek information in ambiguous circumstances, with regard to physical (rather than social) problems (Rutherford and Subiaul, 2015).

In contrast to these results for autism, some cognitive biases, such as "jumping to conclusions," and "bias against disconfirmatory evidence" are increased in schizophrenia compared to controls (Woodward et al., 2006; Dudley et al., 2016). Similarly, performance on the Iowa Gambling task of decision-making ability is reduced in schizophrenia (Sevy et al., 2007; Adida et al., 2011) but increased in autism (South et al., 2014), in each case compared to controls. Despite such findings, the degree to which more-deliberative or enhanced decision-making is more intelligent *per se*, and does not itself entail costs, remains unclear; for example, faster, more-intuitive decision-making may be favored in many social situations (South et al., 2014), and rationality appears to be at least partially dissociable from intelligence (Stanovich and West, 2014).

Socioeconomic Status

Socioeconomic status, intelligence, and education level achieved have been demonstrated to exhibit strong positive correlations amongst themselves, although the reasons for these associations have remained unspecified (Deary and Johnson, 2010). A recent suite of studies has shown that such links are substantially genetically based, indicating that a large number of alleles pleiotropically affect socioeconomic status, intelligence, and educational achievement (Marioni et al., 2014; Trzaskowski et al., 2014; Krapohl and Plomin, 2016). These findings are of interest in the context of autism because autism also shows significant, positive genetic correlations with educational attainment, which is strongly positively associated with socioeconomic status as well (Bulik-Sullivan et al., 2015; Hill et al., 2015; Hagenaars et al., 2016).

The hypothesis that autism risk in offspring is positively associated with high parental intelligence, and high socioeconomic status, traces to Kanner (1943, p. 248), who stated, referring to autistic children, that "they all come of highly intelligent families," at high levels of educational, socioeconomic and occupational achievement (Kanner and Lesser, 1958; Rimland, 1964). King (1975) reviewed a set of demographic studies motivated by these findings, and reported strong support for the pattern of high socioeconomic status linked with autism, including support from studies (e.g., Lotter, 1966, 1967) that checked all young children (of 8–10 years) in a given geographic area for infantile autism, and thus should be largely independent of confounding ascertainment or help-seeking biases, variation in access to relevant health care, or variation in parental awareness.

Recent studies of socioeconomic correlates of autism have generated variable results, most of which, however, find that autism is positively related to indicators or strong correlates of high socioeconomic status (Durkin et al., 2010; Van Meter et al., 2010; King and Bearman, 2011; Leonard et al., 2011; Thomas et al., 2012; Bakian et al., 2015); other studies report links with low socioeconomic conditions, or no associations (Rai et al., 2012; Sun et al., 2014). The degree to which biases and confounding factors mediate the positive associations remains largely unknown, although it is noteworthy that both mild to moderate intellectual disability, and schizophrenia, show notable patterns of association with measures of low socioeconomic status (Werner et al., 2007; Leonard et al., 2011; Emerson, 2012; Zheng et al., 2012).

Given that autism risk shows strong genetic correlations with intelligence and years of education, and that these two variables are strongly linked with higher socioeconomic status in a demographic context, the findings described above suggest that autism risk and high socioeconomic status are also expected to show a basis in pleiotropy as demonstrated by positive genetic correlation. However, this hypothesis requires direct genetic tests that take account of known confounding factors and inter-correlated traits (King and Bearman, 2011), as well as analyzing hypotheses for the causal underpinnings of the genetic and phenotypic associations.

Profession

Profession, occupation, and vocational interests have been associated with autism in the context of Baron-Cohen's theory that the autism spectrum is mediated by high "systemizing" (drive to understand non-social, mechanistic and rule-based systems) combined with low "empathizing" (drive to understand and connect with people, socially and emotionally; Baron-Cohen, 2009). Under this systemizing-empathizing theory, persons expressing high levels of autism spectrum psychological traits are predicted to engage in, or plan to enter, professions that involve systemizing, especially engineering and the physical, mathematical and technical sciences. This prediction of the theory has received considerable, though not fully unequivocal, support (Baron-Cohen et al., 1997, 1998, 2007; Windham et al., 2009; Campbell and Wang, 2012; Roelfsema et al., 2012; Spek and Velderman, 2013; Wei et al., 2013). In contrast to these results, schizophrenia and mood disorders are associated with professions in the arts and humanities, across a diverse array of studies (Nettle, 2006; Kyaga et al., 2011; Campbell and Wang, 2012; Crespi et al., 2016).

Associations of autism with technical professions, in the context of autism's links with intelligence, raise the issue of whether intelligence, as measured by tests of IQ, varies in relation to profession. This controversial topic has been addressed in a suite of studies, all of which report that more-technical professions or occupational plans, especially in engineering, the physical sciences, and mathematics, are associated with relatively high IQs or strong correlates of IQ (Wolfle and Oxtoby, 1952; Hauser, 2002; Wai et al., 2009; Eysenck, 2012 p. xi). The psychological, sociological, and economic causes of these findings are ambiguous, but the results, taken at face value and in conjunction with the vocational correlates of autism, support the hypothesis that the autism spectrum is associated in some manner with relatively high intelligence.

In the context of Baron-Cohen's systemizing-empathizing hypothesis, these findings appear somewhat problematic, because systemizing, as measured by the Systemizing Quotient questionnaire, appears to be uncorrelated with IQ (Ling et al., 2009). Given the diversity of causes of autism, this condition may, however, certainly be associated with both systemizing and high, imbalanced intelligence, even if the two are not connected in simple or direct and causal ways.

Assortative Mating

Positive assortative mating, the mating between individuals who are relatively-similar for a given phenotype or genotype, results in a disproportionate concentration of the relevant alleles among offspring, an increase in additive genetic variance for the trait, and a concomitant rise in heritability (Plomin and Deary, 2015). Humans mate positively assortatively for a wide variety of phenotypes, with intelligence as one of the traits exhibiting the highest correlation between mates, on the order of 0.40–0.60 (Escorial and Martín-Buro, 2012; Plomin and Deary, 2015). To the extent that high intelligence potentiates imbalance in the components of intelligence due to either increases or reductions in its parts, strong assortative mating for intelligence is expected to intensify its effects.

Is there also assortative mating for autism or autism spectrum traits? Baron-Cohen et al. (2006) describe evidence of assortative mating between couples who are both high in the autism-associated psychological trait of systemizing. This hypothesis is supported, for example, by findings that both fathers and mothers of children with ASD exhibit elevated rates of systemizing-related occupations in their fathers (Baron-Cohen et al., 1997), as well as both showing high performance on the EFT (Baron-Cohen and Hammer, 1997). The most direct evidence for assortative mating for autistic phenotypes comes from Nordsletten et al. (2016), who reported much higher rates of assortative mating by psychiatric diagnosis for adults with ASDs (0.45–0.48), than for any other of a large set of disorders. To the extent that autism is genetically correlated with metrics of high intelligence (as described above), these findings indicate that humans mate positively assortatively not just for intelligence, but also for the autism-associated genetic underpinnings of intelligence. Genetic consequences for offspring would thus include both high intelligence and elevated risk of autism, provided that, under the intelligence-imbalance hypothesis addressed here, this process also involved dysregulation of one or more of its components. Further evaluation of this hypothesis would benefit from determining the degree to which positive assortative mating also occurs for autism-related cognitive phenotypes in non-clinical populations, data which would indicate the generality and strength of any such effects.

DISCUSSION

Risk and expression of autism is mediated by alterations to adaptive, evolved cognitive systems, and human intelligence represents one of the most important and pervasive changes along the human lineage and a principal source of cognitive variation among individuals. In this article, I have described the novel paradox that autism is positively genetically correlated with high intelligence, even though individuals with autism tend to have substantially lower IQs than controls. I then evaluated the idea that the paradox can be resolved under the hypothesis that autism involves high yet imbalanced intelligence, such that some or most components of intelligence are increased, but in such a way that overall performance is often reduced. This hypothesis extends previous studies of intelligence in relation to autism (e.g., Dawson et al., 2007; Hayashi et al., 2008; Nader et al., 2016) by providing the first comprehensive integration of the study of intelligence with the study of this condition, in the context of a novel "high and imbalanced intelligence" model that provides specific predictions and guidance for future work. The primary conclusions and implications from testing the hypothesis are four-fold.

First, the psychometric structure of human intelligence, as encompassed by the VPR model and the fluid/crystallized dichotomy, corresponds well with the differences in cognitive profiles between individual with autism and controls. Autism thus involves absolutely or relatively enhanced abilities in the Perceptual domain, but reduced or preserved Verbal and Rotation skills, and absolutely or relatively enhanced fluid intelligence, but reduced or preserved crystallized intelligence. Given that Perceptual domain tasks and tests quantify visual-spatial, sensory discrimination, mechanistic, scientific, and attentional abilities and motivations (Johnson and Deary, 2011), such enhancements are consistent with a large body of previous work on autism but can serve to unify and connect such skills with their neurological and genetic bases. The VPR model can also help to explain the male bias in autism as related to increased focus of attention, reduced verbal skills, and enhanced image rotation ability (or components thereof), given that these patterns emerge from the VPR model once the effects of g are controlled. Considered together, these results imply that although major aspects of intelligence differ between individuals with autism and controls, the differences align with the evolved, neurologically-based axes of cognitive architecture that underlie human mental abilities. Finally, this model may help to frame hypotheses for the autism-related co-variation in perceptual abilities described by Meilleur et al. (2014), perhaps as a manifestation of the increased importance of this facet of intelligence in autistic cognition.

The main implications of these results are that they provide a non-arbitrary, well-validated context (the theory of intelligence) for the interpretation of differences between individuals with and without autism, and they should motivate novel and comprehensive integration of the study of intelligence with the study of autism. With regard to treatments for autism, such integration is useful because it indicates that imbalances in components of intelligence, and their neural underpinnings, may represent novel and malleable targets for individualized therapies that seek to increase the degree of balance, thereby reducing autism symptoms and enhancing everyday social and non-social functioning and well-being. In both phenotypic and genetic contexts, future studies of intelligence in autism might usefully focus on individuals with autism that is apparently mediated by polygenic (rather than monogenic, oligogenic, or syndromic) effects, given that only such causes of autism are expected to be directly relevant to its positive genetic correlation with intelligence. Do such individuals have "too many," or a biased neurological-associated set, of alleles for high intelligence? What developmental and molecular pathways are affected by such sets of genes, and can they also serve as foci for therapies?

Second, a broad swath of correlates of autism, including large brain size, fast brain growth, increased sensory and visual-spatial abilities, enhanced synaptic functions, increased attentional focus, high socioeconomic status, more deliberative decision-making, profession and occupational interests in engineering and physical sciences, and high levels of positive assortative mating, also represent strong correlates of intelligence (**Figure 4**). These findings broadly support the high, imbalanced intelligence hypothesis, although targeted tests are required for more-robust evaluation. Future studies can usefully focus on how these joint correlates of autism and intelligence are related to one another, especially across levels from genes to neurobiology and psychological traits.

Third, the theory and results described here are largely consilient with three of the major psychological theories of autism, systemizing-empathizing bias (Baron-Cohen, 2009), enhanced perceptual function (Mottron et al., 2006), and the intense world (Markram and Markram, 2010), although they ground the patterns supporting each theory in a specific domain of human adaptation, intelligence. This compatibility of theories need not imply that autism has one or few specific causes at the genetic, neurological, and psychological levels—it has many—but it focuses attention on what information will be most useful to collect, to differentially diagnose the causes of autism for each specific individual. What alleles are related to what components of intelligence under the VPR model, and what is their overlap with alleles underlying different phenotypes

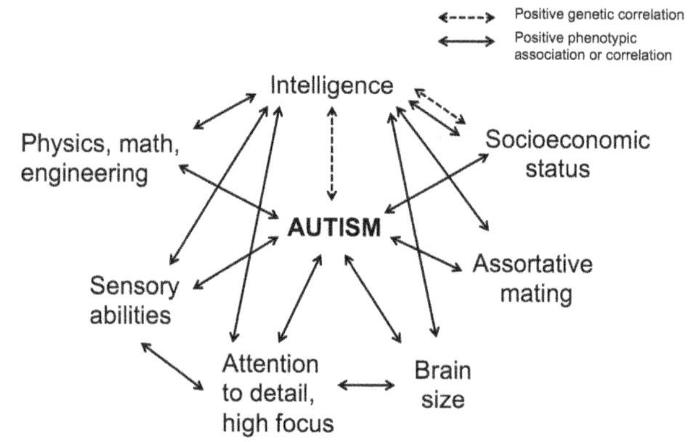

FIGURE 4 | Autism and intelligence are genetically correlated with one another, indicative of a shared genetic basis, and they share phenotypic correlations or associations with a broad suite of traits. These patterns suggest that autism risk is mediated in part by high, but imbalanced, components of intelligence.

found in autism? What neurological processes underlie negative associations between focal and diffuse attention, and verbal vs. rotational abilities (Johnson et al., 2008), and how do they relate to neurological differences among individuals with autism? More generally, what developmental and neurological components of intelligence are altered in autism, and how? And how can the genes, neurodevelopment, and psychology of each individual with autism, or subsets of individuals, be fit within these frameworks?

Fourth, comparisons of autism with schizophrenia for the genetic and phenotypic correlates of intelligence described here support the hypothesis that these two sets of conditions can be regarded as psychiatric, psychological, neurological and genetic "opposites," especially as evidenced by consistent negative genetic correlations of schizophrenia risk with measures of intelligence. Jung (2014) indeed contrasts intelligence and the autism spectrum as diametric to creativity and the schizophrenia spectrum (see also Figure 1 in Crespi et al., 2016; Krapohl and Plomin, 2016), as two major, inversely-associated domains of human cognition. Inverse associations of intelligence with personality correlates of imagination (Openness and apophenia, defined as seeing pattern where none exists) are also supported by factor-analytic studies of personality structure, and by studies that relate working memory, white matter tract integrity, and dopaminergic neurotransmission to both intelligence and imagination (DeYoung et al., 2012). To the extent that autism represents most broadly a disorder of high intelligence (and low imagination), and schizophrenia a disorder of high imagination (and low intelligence), studying these psychiatric conditions will also provide novel insights into variation among neurotypical individuals, and human cognitive architecture, at their largest and smallest scales, with important implications for such fields as artificial intelligence and cognitive enhancement (e.g., Minzenberg et al., 2008; Blaser et al., 2014).

The primary limitations of the hypotheses and predictions evaluated here are that intelligence, as measured in most standardized tests, does not quantify aspects of social and emotional phenotypes that are also highly relevant to disorders such as autism and schizophrenia. Moreover, some key questions remain unresolved, such as how and why especially-high intelligence in one domain would tend to reduce intelligence test scores overall, how and why systemizing and empathizing are related to intelligence and its components (as well as genetic underpinnings), and how autism risk is mediated by polygenic effects, many of which apparently involve alleles for high intelligence, as well as by monogenic or oligogenic effects, which are expected to be deleterious and cause dysfunctions. Addressing these and other questions will require integration of data from evolutionary biology, genetics, the study of intelligence, and autism, and testing of hypotheses that involves spanning across these levels of analysis and theory.

AUTHOR CONTRIBUTIONS

BC conceived and wrote the paper.

FUNDING

I am grateful to NSERC for financial support.

ACKNOWLEDGMENTS

I thank Drs Benjamin Gesundheit, Joshua Pesach Rosenzweig, and Yehuda Julyus Shoenfeld for inviting me to prepare this article, the Human Evolutionary Studies Group at Simon Fraser University for helpful discussions, and S. Read for expert technical assistance.

REFERENCES

Adida, M., Maurel, M., Kaladjian, A., Fakra, E., Lazerges, P., Da Fonseca, D., et al. (2011). Decision-making and schizophrenia. *Encephale* 37(Suppl. 2), S110–S116. doi: 10.1016/S0013-7006(11)70036-7

Ashwin, E., Ashwin, C., Rhydderch, D., Howells, J., and Baron-Cohen, S. (2009). Eagle-eyed visual acuity: an experimental investigation of enhanced perception in autism. *Biol. Psychiatry* 65, 17–21. doi: 10.1016/j.biopsych.2008.06.012

Bakian, A. V., Bilder, D. A., Carbone, P. S., Hunt, T. D., Petersen, B., and Rice, C. E. (2015). Brief report: independent validation of Autism Spectrum Disorder case status in the Utah Autism and Developmental Disabilities Monitoring (ADDM) network site. *J. Autism Dev. Disord.* 45, 873–880. doi: 10.1007/s10803-014-2187-6

Baribeau, D. A., and Anagnostou, E. (2013). A comparison of neuroimaging findings in childhood onset schizophrenia and autism spectrum disorder: a review of the literature. *Front. Psychiatry* 4:175. doi: 10.3389/fpsyt.2013.00175

Barnea-Goraly, N., Frazier, T. W., Piacenza, L., Minshew, N. J., Keshavan, M. S., Reiss, A. L., et al. (2014). A preliminary longitudinal volumetric MRI study of amygdala and hippocampal volumes in autism. *Prog. Neuropsychopharmacol. Biol. Psychiatry* 48, 124–128. doi: 10.1016/j.pnpbp.2013.09.010

Baron-Cohen, S. (2006). The hyper-systemizing, assortative mating theory of autism. *Prog. Neuropsychopharmacol. Biol. Psychiatry* 30, 865–872. doi: 10.1016/j.pnpbp.2006.01.010

Baron-Cohen, S. (2009). Autism: the Empathizing–Systemizing (E-S) theory. *Ann. N.Y. Acad. Sci.* 1156, 68–80. doi: 10.1111/j.1749-6632.2009.04467.x

Baron-Cohen, S., Ashwin, E., Ashwin, C., Tavassoli, T., and Chakrabarti, B. (2009). Talent in autism: hyper-systemizing, hyper-attention to detail and sensory hypersensitivity. *Philos. Trans. R. Soc. Lond. B Biol. Sci.* 364, 1377–1383. doi: 10.1098/rstb.2008.0337

Baron-Cohen, S., Bolton, P., Wheelwright, S., Scahill, V., Short, L., Mead, G., et al. (1998). Autism occurs more often in families of physicists, engineers, and mathematicians. *Autism* 2, 296–301. doi: 10.1177/1362361398023008

Baron-Cohen, S., and Hammer, J. (1997). Parents of children with Asperger syndrome: what is the cognitive phenotype? *J. Cogn. Neurosci.* 9, 548–554. doi: 10.1162/jocn.1997.9.4.548

Baron-Cohen, S., Lombardo, M. V., Auyeung, B., Ashwin, E., Chakrabarti, B., and Knickmeyer, R. (2011). Why are autism spectrum conditions more prevalent in males? *PLoS Biol.* 9:e1001081. doi: 10.1371/journal.pbio.1001081

Baron-Cohen, S., Wheelwright, S., Burtenshaw, A., and Hobson, E. (2007). Mathematical talent is linked to autism. *Hum. Nat.* 18, 125–131. doi: 10.1007/s12110-007-9014-0

Baron-Cohen, S., Wheelwright, S., Stott, C., Bolton, P., and Goodyer, I. (1997). Is there a link between engineering and autism? *Autism* 1, 101–109. doi: 10.1177/1362361397011010

Bates, T. C. (2005). The panmodal sensory imprecision hypothesis of schizophrenia: reduced auditory precision in schizotypy. *Pers. Indiv. Diff.* 38, 437–449. doi: 10.1016/j.paid.2004.04.021

Belmonte, M. K., Allen, G., Beckel-Mitchener, A., Boulanger, L. M., Carper, R. A., and Webb, S. J. (2004). Autism and abnormal development of brain connectivity. *J. Neurosci.* 24, 9228–9231. doi: 10.1523/JNEUROSCI.3340-04.2004

Benson, T. L., and Park, S. (2013). Exceptional visuospatial imagery in schizophrenia; implications for madness and creativity. *Front. Hum. Neurosci.* 7:756. doi: 10.3389/fnhum.2013.00756

Benyamin, B., Pourcain, B., Davis, O. S., Davies, G., Hansell, N. K., Brion, M. J., et al. (2014). Childhood intelligence is heritable, highly polygenic and associated with FNBP1L. *Mol. Psychiatry* 19, 253–258. doi: 10.1038/mp.2012.184

Blakemore, S. J., Tavassoli, T., Calò, S., Thomas, R. M., Catmur, C., Frith, U., et al. (2006). Tactile sensitivity in Asperger syndrome. *Brain Cogn.* 61, 5–13. doi: 10.1016/j.bandc.2005.12.013

Blaser, E., Eglington, L., Carter, A. S., and Kaldy, Z. (2014). Pupillometry reveals a mechanism for the Autism Spectrum Disorder (ASD) advantage in visual tasks. *Sci. Rep.* 4:4301. doi: 10.1038/srep04301

Bourgeron, T. (2009). A synaptic trek to autism. *Curr. Opin. Neurobiol.* 19, 231–234. doi: 10.1016/j.conb.2009.06.003

Brosnan, M., Chapman, E., and Ashwin, C. (2014). Adolescents with autism spectrum disorder show a circumspect reasoning bias rather than 'jumping-to-conclusions.' *J. Autism Dev. Disord.* 44, 513–520. doi: 10.1007/s10803-013-1897-5

Brosnan, M. J., Gwilliam, L. R., and Walker, I. (2012). Brief report: the relationship between visual acuity, the embedded figures test and systemizing in autism spectrum disorders. *J. Autism Dev. Disord.* 42, 2491–2497. doi: 10.1007/s10803-012-1505-0

Brosnan, M., Lewton, M., and Ashwin, C. (2016). Reasoning on the Autism Spectrum: a dual process theory account. *J. Autism Dev. Disord.* 46, 2115–2125. doi: 10.1007/s10803-016-2742-4

Broyd, S. J., Demanuele, C., Debener, S., Helps, S. K., James, C. J., and Sonuga-Barke, E. J. (2009). Default-mode brain dysfunction in mental disorders: a systematic review. *Neurosci. Biobehav. Rev.* 33, 279–296. doi: 10.1016/j.neubiorev.2008.09.002

Bulik-Sullivan, B., Finucane, H. K., Anttila, V., Gusev, A., Day, F. R., Loh, P. R., et al. (2015). An atlas of genetic correlations across human diseases and traits. *Nat. Genet.* 47, 1236–1241. doi: 10.1038/ng.3406

Campbell, B. C., and Wang, S. S. H. (2012). Familial linkage between neuropsychiatric disorders and intellectual interests. *PLoS ONE* 7:e30405. doi: 10.1371/journal.pone.0030405

Campbell, D. J., Chang, J., and Chawarska, K. (2014). Early generalized overgrowth in autism spectrum disorder: prevalence rates, gender effects, and clinical outcomes. *J. Am. Acad. Child Adolesc. Psychiatry* 53, 1063–1073. doi: 10.1016/j.jaac.2014.07.008

Cascio, C., McGlone, F., Folger, S., Tannan, V., Baranek, G., Pelphrey, K. A., et al. (2008). Tactile perception in adults with autism: a multidimensional psychophysical study. *J. Autism Dev. Disord.* 38, 127–137. doi: 10.1007/s10803-007-0370-8

Christoforou, A., Espeseth, T., Davies, G., Fernandes, C. P., Giddaluru, S., Mattheisen, M., et al. (2014). GWAS-based pathway analysis differentiates between fluid and crystallized intelligence. *Genes Brain Behav.* 13, 663–674. doi: 10.1111/gbb.12152

Church, B. A., Rice, C. L., Dovgopoly, A., Lopata, C. J., Thomeer, M. L., Nelson, A., et al. (2015). Learning, plasticity, and atypical generalization in children with autism. *Psychon. Bull. Rev.* 22, 1342–1348. doi: 10.3758/s13423-014-0797-9

Clarke, T. K., Lupton, M. K., Fernandez-Pujals, A. M., Starr, J., Davies, G., Cox, S., et al. (2015). Common polygenic risk for autism spectrum disorder (ASD) is associated with cognitive ability in the general population. *Mol. Psychiatry* 21, 419–425. doi: 10.1038/mp.2015.12

Cole, M. W., Yarkoni, T., Repovš, G., Anticevic, A., and Braver, T. S. (2012). Global connectivity of prefrontal cortex predicts cognitive control and intelligence. *J. Neurosci.* 32, 8988–8999. doi: 10.1523/JNEUROSCI.0536-12.2012

Colom, R., Karama, S., Jung, R. E., and Haier, R. J. (2010). Human intelligence and brain networks. *Dialogues Clin. Neurosci.* 12, 489–501.

Courchesne, E., Mouton, P. R., Calhoun, M. E., Ahrens-Barbeau, C., Hallet, M. J., Carter Barnes, C., et al. (2013). "An overabundance of prefrontal cortex neurons underlies early brain overgrowth in autism," in *Neurostereology: Unbiased Stereology of Neural Systems*, ed P. R. Mouton (Hoboken, NJ: Wiley-Blackwell), 73–83.

Courchesne, E., and Pierce, K. (2005). Why the frontal cortex in autism might be talking only to itself: local over-connectivity but long-distance disconnection. *Curr. Opin. Neurobiol.* 15, 225–230. doi: 10.1016/j.conb.2005.03.001

Crespi, B., and Badcock, C. (2008). Psychosis and autism as diametrical disorders of the social brain. *Behav. Brain Sci.* 31, 241–261; discussion 261–320. doi: 10.1017/s0140525x08004214

Crespi, B. J. (2016). "The evolutionary etiologies of autism spectrum and psychotic-affective spectrum disorders," in *Evolutionary Thinking in Medicine: From Research to Policy and Practice*, eds A. Alvergne, C. Jenkinson, and C. Faurie (New York, NY: Oxford University Press), 299–327.

Crespi, B., and Leach, E. (2016). "The evolutionary biology of human neurodevelopment: evo-neuro-devo comes of age," in *Evolutionary Developmental Anthropology*, eds J. Boughner and C. Rolian (Hoboken, NJ: Wiley), 205–229.

Crespi, B., Leach, E., Dinsdale, N., Mokkonen, M., and Hurd, P. (2016). Imagination in human social cognition, autism, and psychotic-affective conditions. *Cognition* 150, 181–199. doi: 10.1016/j.cognition.2016.02.001

Davies, G., Marioni, R. E., Liewald, D. C., Hill, W. D., Hagenaars, S. P., Harris, S. E., et al. (2016). Genome-wide association study of cognitive functions and educational attainment in UK Biobank (N = 112 151). *Mol. Psychiatry* 21, 758–767. doi: 10.1038/mp.2016.45

Davies, G., Tenesa, A., Payton, A., Yang, J., Harris, S. E., Liewald, D., et al. (2011). Genome-wide association studies establish that human intelligence is highly heritable and polygenic. *Mol. Psychiatry* 16, 996–1005. doi: 10.1038/mp.2011.85

Davis, J. M., Searles, V. B., Anderson, N., Keeney, J., Dumas, L., and Sikela, J. M. (2014). DUF1220 dosage is linearly associated with increasing severity of the three primary symptoms of autism. *PLoS Genet.* 10:e1004241. doi: 10.1371/journal.pgen.1004241

Davis, J. M., Searles, V. B., Anderson, N., Keeney, J., Raznahan, A., Horwood, L. J., et al. (2015). DUF1220 copy number is linearly associated with increased cognitive function as measured by total IQ and mathematical aptitude scores. *Hum. Genet.* 134, 67–75. doi: 10.1007/s00439-014-1489-2

Dawson, M., Soulières, I., Gernsbacher, M. A., and Mottron, L. (2007). The level and nature of autistic intelligence. *Psychol. Sci.* 18, 657–662. doi: 10.1111/j.1467-9280.2007.01954.x

Deaner, R. O., Isler, K., Burkart, J., and Van Schaik, C. (2007). Overall brain size, and not encephalization quotient, best predicts cognitive ability across non-human primates. *Brain Behav. Evol.* 70, 115–124. doi: 10.1159/000102973

Deary, I. J., Bell, P. J., Bell, A. J., Campbell, M. L., and Fazal, N. D. (2004). Sensory discrimination and intelligence: testing Spearman's other hypothesis. *Am. J. Psychol.* 117, 1–18. doi: 10.2307/1423593

Deary, I. J., and Johnson, W. (2010). Intelligence and education: causal perceptions drive analytic processes and therefore conclusions. *Int. J. Epidemiol.* 39, 1362–1369. doi: 10.1093/ije/dyq072

Deary, I. J., Penke, L., and Johnson, W. (2010). The neuroscience of human intelligence differences. *Nat. Rev. Neurosci.* 11, 201–211. doi: 10.1038/nrn2793

De Martino, B., Harrison, N. A., Knafo, S., Bird, G., and Dolan, R. J. (2008). Explaining enhanced logical consistency during decision making in autism. *J. Neurosci.* 28, 10746–10750. doi: 10.1523/JNEUROSCI.2895-08.2008

DeYoung, C. G., Grazioplene, R. G., and Peterson, J. B. (2012). From madness to genius: the Openness/Intellect trait domain as a paradoxical simplex. *J. Res. Pers.* 46, 63–78. doi: 10.1016/j.jrp.2011.12.003

Dicke, U., and Roth, G. (2016). Neuronal factors determining high intelligence. *Phil. Trans. R. Soc. B Biol. Sci.* 371:20150180. doi: 10.1098/rstb.2015.0180

Dudley, R., Taylor, P., Wickham, S., and Hutton, P. (2016). Psychosis, delusions and the "jumping to conclusions" reasoning bias: a systematic review and meta-analysis. *Schizophr. Bull.* 42, 652–665. doi: 10.1093/schbul/sbv150

Dumas, L. J., O'Bleness, M. S., Davis, J. M., Dickens, C. M., Anderson, N., Keeney, J. G., et al. (2012). DUF1220-domain copy number implicated in human brain-size pathology and evolution. *Am. J. Hum. Genet.* 91, 444–454. doi: 10.1016/j.ajhg.2012.07.016

Durkin, M. S., Maenner, M. J., Meaney, F. J., Levy, S. E., DiGuiseppi, C., Nicholas, J. S., et al. (2010). Socioeconomic inequality in the prevalence of autism spectrum disorder: evidence from a US cross-sectional study. *PLoS ONE* 5:e11551. doi: 10.1371/journal.pone.0011551

Ecker, C., Ginestet, C., Feng, Y., Johnston, P., Lombardo, M. V., Lai, M. C., et al. (2013). Brain surface anatomy in adults with autism: the relationship between surface area, cortical thickness, and autistic symptoms. *JAMA Psychiatry* 70, 59–70. doi: 10.1001/jamapsychiatry.2013.265

Eduardo Mercado, B. A. C. III, Coutinho, M. V., Dovgopoly, A., Lopata, C. J., Toomey, J. A., and Thomeer, M. L. (2015). Heterogeneity in perceptual category learning by high functioning children with autism spectrum disorder. *Front. Integrative Neurosci.* 9:42. doi: 10.3389/fnint.2015.00042

Eigsti, I. M., and Fein, D. A. (2013). More is less: pitch discrimination and language delays in children with optimal outcomes from autism. *Autism Res.* 6, 605–613. doi: 10.1002/aur.1324

Emerson, E. (2012). Deprivation, ethnicity and the prevalence of intellectual and developmental disabilities. *J. Epidemiol. Commun. Health.* 66, 218–224. doi: 10.1136/jech.2010.111773

Escorial, S., and Martín-Buro, C. (2012). The role of personality and intelligence in assortative mating. *Spanish J. Psychol.* 15, 680–687. doi: 10.5209/rev_SJOP.2012.v15.n2.38879

Evans, B. (2013). How autism became autism: the radical transformation of a central concept of child development in Britain. *Hist. Human Sci.* 26, 3–31. doi: 10.1177/0952695113484320

Eysenck (2012). *The Measurement of Intelligence*. Berlin: Springer Science and Business Media.

Falter, C. M., Elliott, M. A., and Bailey, A. J. (2012). Enhanced visual temporal resolution in autism spectrum disorders. *PLoS ONE* 7:e32774. doi: 10.1371/journal.pone.0032774

Fjell, A. M., Westlye, L. T., Amlien, I., Tamnes, C. K., Grydeland, H., Engvig, A., et al. (2015). High-expanding cortical regions in human development and evolution are related to higher intellectual abilities. *Cereb. Cortex* 25, 26–34. doi: 10.1093/cercor/bht201

Fombonne, E. (2009). Epidemiology of pervasive developmental disorders. *Pediatr. Res.* 65, 591–598. doi: 10.1203/PDR.0b013e31819e7203

Force, R. B., Venables, N. C., and Sponheim, S. R. (2008). An auditory processing abnormality specific to liability for schizophrenia. *Schizophr. Res.* 103, 298–310. doi: 10.1016/j.schres.2008.04.038

Foster, N. E., Doyle-Thomas, K. A., Tryfon, A., Ouimet, T., Anagnostou, E., Evans, A. C., et al. (2015). Structural gray matter differences during childhood development in autism spectrum disorder: a multimetric approach. *Pediatr. Neurol.* 53, 350–359. doi: 10.1016/j.pediatrneurol.2015.06.013

Franić, S., Dolan, C. V., Broxholme, J., Hu, H., Zemojtel, T., Davies, G. E., et al. (2015). Mendelian and polygenic inheritance of intelligence: a common set of causal genes? Using next-generation sequencing to examine the effects of 168 intellectual disability genes on normal-range intelligence. *Intelligence* 49, 10–22. doi: 10.1016/j.intell.2014.12.001

Froehlich, A. L., Anderson, J. S., Bigler, E. D., Miller, J. S., Lange, N. T., DuBray, M. B., et al. (2012). Intact prototype formation but impaired generalization in autism. *Res. Autism Spectr. Disord.* 6, 921–930. doi: 10.1016/j.rasd.2011.12.006

Fukumoto, A., Hashimoto, T., Mori, K., Tsuda, Y., Arisawa, K., and Kagami, S. (2011). Head circumference and body growth in autism spectrum disorders. *Brain Dev.* 33, 569–575. doi: 10.1016/j.braindev.2010.09.004

Galton, F. (1883). *Inquiries into the Human Faculty & Its Development.* London: JM Dent and Company.

Cross-Disorder Group of the Psychiatric Genomics Consortium (2013). Genetic relationship between five psychiatric disorders estimated from genome-wide SNPs. *Nat. Genet.* 45, 984–994. doi: 10.1038/ng.2711

Gizzonio, V., Avanzini, P., Fabbri-Destro, M., Campi, C., and Rizzolatti, G. (2014). Cognitive abilities in siblings of children with autism spectrum disorders. *Exp. Brain Res.* 232, 2381–2390. doi: 10.1007/s00221-014-3935-8

Gkogkas, C. G., Khoutorsky, A., Ran, I., Rampakakis, E., Nevarko, T., Weatherill, D. B., et al. (2013). Autism-related deficits via dysregulated eIF4E-dependent translational control. *Nature* 493, 371–377. doi: 10.1038/nature11628

Gogtay, N., Lu, A., Leow, A. D., Klunder, A. D., Lee, A. D., Chavez, A., et al. (2008). Three-dimensional brain growth abnormalities in childhood-onset schizophrenia visualized by using tensor-based morphometry. *Proc. Natl. Acad. Sci. U.S.A.* 105, 15979–15984. doi: 10.1073/pnas.0806485105

Hagenaars, S. P., Harris, S. E., Davies, G., Hill, W. D., Liewald, D. C., Ritchie, S. J., et al. (2016). Shared genetic aetiology between cognitive functions and physical and mental health in UK Biobank ($N = 112\ 151$) and 24 GWAS consortia. *Mol. Psychiatry.* doi: 10.1038/mp.2015.225. [Epub ahead of print].

Happé, F., and Frith, U. (2006). The weak coherence account: detail-focused cognitive style in autism spectrum disorders. *J. Autism Dev. Disord.* 36, 5–25. doi: 10.1007/s10803-005-0039-0

Happé, F., and Ronald, A. (2008). The 'fractionable autism triad': a review of evidence from behavioural, genetic, cognitive and neural research. *Neuropsychol. Rev.* 18, 287–304. doi: 10.1007/s11065-008-9076-8

Happé, F., Ronald, A., and Plomin, R. (2006). Time to give up on a single explanation for autism. *Nat. Neurosci.* 9, 1218–1220. doi: 10.1038/nn1770

Hardan, A. Y., Libove, R. A., Keshavan, M. S., Melhem, N. M., and Minshew, N. J. (2009). A preliminary longitudinal magnetic resonance imaging study of brain volume and cortical thickness in autism. *Biol. Psychiatry* 66, 320–326. doi: 10.1016/j.biopsych.2009.04.024

Hardan, A. Y., Muddasani, S., Vemulapalli, M., Keshavan, M. S., and Minshew, N. J. (2006). An MRI study of increased cortical thickness in autism. *Am. J. Psychiatry* 163, 1290–1292. doi: 10.1176/ajp.2006.163.7.1290

Hauser, R. M. (2002). *Meritocracy, Cognitive Ability, and the Sources of Occupational Success.* Madison, WI: Center for Demography and Ecology, University of Wisconsin.

Hayashi, M., Kato, M., Igarashi, K., and Kashima, H. (2008). Superior fluid intelligence in children with Asperger's disorder. *Brain Cogn.* 66, 306–310. doi: 10.1016/j.bandc.2007.09.008

Heaton, P., Hudry, K., Ludlow, A., and Hill, E. (2008). Superior discrimination of speech pitch and its relationship to verbal ability in autism spectrum disorders. *Cogn. Neuropsychol.* 25, 771–782. doi: 10.1080/02643290802336277

Henrich, J. (2015). *The Secret of Our Success: How Culture Is Driving Human Evolution, Domesticating Our Species, and Making Us Smarter.* Princeton, NJ: Princeton University Press.

Hill, W. D., Davies, G., CHARGE Cognitive Working Group, Liewald, D. C., McIntosh, A. M., and Deary, I. J. (2015). Age-dependent pleiotropy between general cognitive function and major psychiatric disorders. *Biol. Psychiatry.* doi: 10.1016/j.biopsych.2015.08.033. [Epub ahead of print].

Hoekstra, R. A., Happé, F., Baron-Cohen, S., and Ronald, A. (2009). Association between extreme autistic traits and intellectual disability: insights from a general population twin study. *Br. J. Psychiatry* 195, 531–536. doi: 10.1192/bjp.bp.108.060889

Horlin, C., Black, M., Falkmer, M., and Falkmer, T. (2016). Proficiency of individuals with autism spectrum disorder at disembedding figures: a systematic review. *Dev. Neurorehabil.* 19, 54–63. doi: 10.3109/17518423.2014.888102

Howlin, P., Goode, S., Hutton, J., and Rutter, M. (2009). Savant skills in autism: psychometric approaches and parental reports. *Philos. Trans. R. Soc. Lond. B Biol. Sci.* 364, 1359–1367. doi: 10.1098/rstb.2008.0328

Hubbard, L., Tansey, K. E., Rai, D., Jones, P., Ripke, S., Chambert, K. D., et al. (2016). Evidence of common genetic overlap between schizophrenia and cognition. *Schizophr. Bull.* 42, 832–842. doi: 10.1093/schbul/sbv168

Hyde, K. L., Samson, F., Evans, A. C., and Mottron, L. (2010). Neuroanatomical differences in brain areas implicated in perceptual and other core features of autism revealed by cortical thickness analysis and voxel-based morphometry. *Hum. Brain Mapp.* 31, 556–566. doi: 10.1002/hbm.20887

Isshiki, M., Tanaka, S., Kuriu, T., Tabuchi, K., Takumi, T., and Okabe, S. (2014). Enhanced synapse remodelling as a common phenotype in mouse models of autism. *Nat. Commun.* 5. doi: 10.1038/ncomms5742

Ivanovic, D. M., Leiva, B. P., Castro, C. G., Olivares, M. G., Jansana, J. M. M., Castro, V. G., et al. (2004). Brain development parameters and intelligence in Chilean high school graduates. *Intelligence* 32, 461–479. doi: 10.1016/j.intell.2004.07.001

Javitt, D. C. (2009a). Sensory processing in schizophrenia: neither simple nor intact. *Schizophr. Bull.* 35, 1059–1064. doi: 10.1093/schbul/sbp110

Javitt, D. C. (2009b). When doors of perception close: bottom-up models of disrupted cognition in schizophrenia. *Annu. Rev. Clin. Psychol.* 5, 249–275. doi: 10.1146/annurev.clinpsy.032408.153502

Johnson, W., and Bouchard, T. J. (2005a). Constructive replication of the visual–perceptual-image rotation model in Thurstone's (1941) battery of 60 tests of mental ability. *Intelligence* 33, 417–430. doi: 10.1016/j.intell.2004.12.001

Johnson, W., and Bouchard, T. J. (2005b). The structure of human intelligence: it is verbal, perceptual, and image rotation (VPR), not fluid and crystallized. *Intelligence* 33, 393–416. doi: 10.1016/j.intell.2004.12.002

Johnson, W., and Bouchard, T. J. (2007). Sex differences in mental abilities: g masks the dimensions on which they lie. *Intelligence* 35, 23–39. doi: 10.1016/j.intell.2006.03.012

Johnson, W., and Bouchard, T. J. (2008). Linking abilities, interests, and sex via latent class analysis. *J. Career Assess.* 17, 3–38. doi: 10.1177/1069072708325738

Johnson, W., Bouchard, T. J., McGue, M., Segal, N. L., Tellegen, A., Keyes, M., et al. (2007). Genetic and environmental influences on the Verbal-Perceptual-Image Rotation (VPR) model of the structure of mental abilities in the Minnesota study of twins reared apart. *Intelligence* 35, 542–562. doi: 10.1016/j.intell.2006.10.003

Johnson, W., and Deary, I. J. (2011). Placing inspection time, reaction time, and perceptual speed in the broader context of cognitive ability: the VPR model in the Lothian Birth Cohort 1936. *Intelligence* 39, 405–417. doi: 10.1016/j.intell.2011.07.003

Johnson, W., Jung, R. E., Colom, R., and Haier, R. J. (2008). Cognitive abilities independent of IQ correlate with regional brain structure. *Intelligence* 36, 18–28. doi: 10.1016/j.intell.2007.01.005

Jung, R. E. (2014). Evolution, creativity, intelligence, and madness: "Here Be Dragons". *Front. Psychol.* 5:784. doi: 10.3389/fpsyg.2014.00784

Jung, R. E., and Haier, R. J. (2007). The Parieto-Frontal Integration Theory (P-FIT) of intelligence: converging neuroimaging evidence. *Behav. Brain Sci.* 30, 135–154. doi: 10.1017/S0140525X07001185

Kanner, L. (1943). Autistic disturbances of affective contact. *Nervous Child. Acta Paedopsychiatr.* 35, 100–136.

Kanner, L., and Lesser, L. I. (1958). Early infantile autism. *Pediatr. Clin. North Am.* 5, 711.

Karadi, K., Kallai, J., Kover, F., Nemes, J., Makany, T., and Nagy, F. (2006). Endogenous testosterone concentration, mental rotation, and size of the corpus callosum in a sample of young Hungarian women. *Percept. Mot. Skills* 102, 445–453. doi: 10.2466/pms.102.2.445-453

Karama, S., Colom, R., Johnson, W., Deary, I. J., Haier, R., Waber, D. P., et al. (2011). Cortical thickness correlates of specific cognitive performance accounted for by the general factor of intelligence in healthy children aged 6 to 18. *Neuroimage* 55, 1443–1453. doi: 10.1016/j.neuroimage.2011.01.016

Karbasforoushan, H., and Woodward, N. D. (2012). Resting-state networks in schizophrenia. *Curr. Top. Med. Chem.* 12, 2404–2414. doi: 10.2174/156802612805289863

Kasai, H., Fukuda, M., Watanabe, S., Hayashi-Takagi, A., and Noguchi, J. (2010). Structural dynamics of dendritic spines in memory and cognition. *Trends Neurosci.* 33, 121–129. doi: 10.1016/j.tins.2010.01.001

Keeney, J. G., Dumas, L., and Sikela, J. M. (2014). The case for DUF1220 domain dosage as a primary contributor to anthropoid brain expansion. *Front. Hum. Neurosci.* 8:427. doi: 10.3389/fnhum.2014.00427

Kelleher, R. J., and Bear, M. F. (2008). The autistic neuron: troubled translation? *Cell* 135, 401–406. doi: 10.1016/j.cell.2008.10.017

Kerchner, G. A., Racine, C. A., Hale, S., Wilheim, R., Laluz, V., Miller, B. L., et al. (2012). Cognitive processing speed in older adults: relationship with white matter integrity. *PLoS ONE* 7:e50425. doi: 10.1371/journal.pone.0050425

Khodadady, E., and Tafaghodi, A. (2013). Cognitive styles and fluid intelligence: are they related? *J. Stud. Soc. Sci.* 3, 138–150.

Kim, D. J., Davis, E. P., Sandman, C. A., Sporns, O., O'Donnell, B. F., Buss, C., et al. (2016). Children's intellectual ability is associated with structural network integrity. *Neuroimage* 124, 550–556. doi: 10.1016/j.neuroimage.2015.09.012

King, M. D., and Bearman, P. S. (2011). Socioeconomic status and the increased prevalence of autism in California. *Am. Sociol. Rev.* 76, 320–346. doi: 10.1177/0003122411399389

King, P. D. (1975). Early infantile autism: relation to schizophrenia. *J. Am. Acad. Child Psychiatry* 14, 666–682. doi: 10.1016/S0002-7138(09)61465-5

Koenis, M. M., Brouwer, R. M., van den Heuvel, M. P., Mandl, R. C., van Soelen, I. L., Kahn, R. S., et al. (2015). Development of the brain's structural network efficiency in early adolescence: a longitudinal DTI twin study. *Hum. Brain Mapp.* 36, 4938–4953. doi: 10.1002/hbm.22988

Krapohl, E., and Plomin, R. (2016). Genetic link between family socioeconomic status and children's educational achievement estimated from genome-wide SNPs. *Mol. Psychiatry* 21, 437–443. doi: 10.1038/mp.2015.2

Kravariti, E., Toulopoulou, T., Mapua-Filbey, F., Schulze, K., Walshe, M., Sham, P., et al. (2006). Intellectual asymmetry and genetic liability in first-degree relatives of probands with schizophrenia. *Br. J. Psychiatry* 188, 186–187. doi: 10.1192/bjp.bp.104.008177

Kulkarni, V. A., and Firestein, B. L. (2012). The dendritic tree and brain disorders. *Mol. Cell. Neurosci.* 50, 10–20. doi: 10.1016/j.mcn.2012.03.005

Kyaga, S., Lichtenstein, P., Boman, M., Hultman, C., Långström, N., and Landén, M. (2011). Creativity and mental disorder: family study of 300 000 people with severe mental disorder. *Br. J. Psychiatry* 199, 373–379. doi: 10.1192/bjp.bp.110.085316

Lee, T., Mosing, M. A., Henry, J. D., Trollor, J. N., Lammel, A., Ames, D., et al. (2012). Genetic influences on five measures of processing speed and their covariation with general cognitive ability in the elderly: the older Australian twins study. *Behav. Genet.* 42, 96–106. doi: 10.1007/s10519-011-9474-1

Lencz, T., Knowles, E., Davies, G., Guha, S., Liewald, D. C., Starr, J. M., et al. (2014). Molecular genetic evidence for overlap between general cognitive ability and risk for schizophrenia: a report from the Cognitive Genomics consorTium (COGENT). *Mol. Psychiatry* 19, 168–174. doi: 10.1038/mp.2013.166

Leonard, H., Glasson, E., Nassar, N., Whitehouse, A., Bebbington, A., Bourke, J., et al. (2011). Autism and intellectual disability are differentially related to sociodemographic background at birth. *PLoS ONE* 6:e17875. doi: 10.1371/journal.pone.0017875

Levine, M., and Olson, R. P. (1968). Intelligence of parents of autistic children. *J. Abnorm. Psychol.* 73, 215. doi: 10.1037/h0020120

Ling, J., Burton, T. C., Salt, J. L., and Muncer, S. J. (2009). Psychometric analysis of the systemizing quotient (SQ) scale. *Br. J. Psychol.* 100, 539–552. doi: 10.1348/000712608X368261

Lotter, V. (1966). Epidemiology of autistic conditions in young children. Part I: prevalence. *Soc. Psychiatry* 1, 124–135. doi: 10.1007/bf00584048

Lotter, V. (1967). Epidemiology of autistic conditions in young children. Part II: some characteristics of the parents and children. *Soc. Psychiatry* 1, 163–173. doi: 10.1007/BF00578950

Loui, P., Li, H. C., Hohmann, A., and Schlaug, G. (2011). Enhanced cortical connectivity in absolute pitch musicians: a model for local hyperconnectivity. *J. Cogn. Neurosci.* 23, 1015–1026. doi: 10.1162/jocn.2010.21500

Maier, S., van Elst, L. T., Beier, D., Ebert, D., Fangmeier, T., Radtke, M., et al. (2015). Increased hippocampal volumes in adults with high functioning autism spectrum disorder and an IQ> 100: a manual morphometric study. *Psychiatry Res. Neuroimaging* 234, 152–155. doi: 10.1016/j.pscychresns.2015.08.002

Major, J. T., Johnson, W., and Deary, I. J. (2012). Comparing models of intelligence in Project TALENT: the VPR model fits better than the CHC and extended Gf-Gc models. *Intellig* 40, 543–559. doi: 10.1016/j.intell.2012.07.006

Mak-Fan, K. M., Taylor, M. J., Roberts, W., and Lerch, J. P. (2012). Measures of cortical grey matter structure and development in children with autism spectrum disorder. *J. Autism Dev. Disord.* 42, 419–427. doi: 10.1007/s10803-011-1261-6

Marioni, R. E., Davies, G., Hayward, C., Liewald, D., Kerr, S. M., Campbell, A., et al. (2014). Molecular genetic contributions to socioeconomic status and intelligence. *Intelligence* 44, 26–32. doi: 10.1016/j.intell.2014.02.006

Markram, K., and Markram, H. (2010). The intense world theory–a unifying theory of the neurobiology of autism. *Front. Hum. Neurosci.* 4:224. doi: 10.3389/fnhum.2010.00224

Maximo, J. O., Cadena, E. J., and Kana, R. K. (2014). The implications of brain connectivity in the neuropsychology of autism. *Neuropsychol. Rev.* 24, 16–31. doi: 10.1007/s11065-014-9250-0

McCleery, J. P., Allman, E., Carver, L. J., and Dobkins, K. R. (2007). Abnormal magnocellular pathway visual processing in infants at risk for autism. *Biol. Psychiatry* 62, 1007–1014. doi: 10.1016/j.biopsych.2007.02.009

McIntosh, A. M., Gow, A., Luciano, M., Davies, G., Liewald, D. C., Harris, S. E., et al. (2013). Polygenic risk for schizophrenia is associated with cognitive change between childhood and old age. *Biol. Psychiatry* 73, 938–943. doi: 10.1016/j.biopsych.2013.01.011

McKenna, F. P. (1990). Learning implications of field dependence-independence: cognitive style versus cognitive ability. *Appl. Cogn. Psychol.* 4, 425–437. doi: 10.1002/acp.2350040602

McKenna, F. P., Duncan, J., and Brown, I. D. (1986). Cognitive abilities and safety on the road: a re-examination of individual differences in dichotic listening and search for embedded figures. *Ergonomics* 29, 649–663. doi: 10.1080/00140138608968300

Meilleur, A. A. S., Berthiaume, C., Bertone, A., and Mottron, L. (2014). Autism-specific covariation in perceptual performances: "g" or "p" factor? *PLoS ONE* 9:e103781. doi: 10.1371/journal.pone.0103781

Meilleur, A. A. S., Jelenic, P., and Mottron, L. (2015). Prevalence of clinically and empirically defined talents and strengths in autism. *J. Autism Dev. Disord.* 45, 1354–1367. doi: 10.1007/s10803-014-2296-2

Melnick, M. D., Harrison, B. R., Park, S., Bennetto, L., and Tadin, D. (2013). A strong interactive link between sensory discriminations and intelligence. *Curr. Biol.* 23, 1013–1017. doi: 10.1016/j.cub.2013.04.053

Menary, K., Collins, P. F., Porter, J. N., Muetzel, R., Olson, E. A., Kumar, V., et al. (2013). Associations between cortical thickness and general intelligence in children, adolescents and young adults. *Intelligence* 41, 597–606. doi: 10.1016/j.intell.2013.07.010

Meyer, C. S., Hagmann-von Arx, P., Lemola, S., and Grob, A. (2010). Correspondence between the general ability to discriminate sensory stimuli and general intelligence. *J. Indiv. Diff.* 31, 46–56. doi: 10.1027/1614-0001/a000006

Minzenberg, M. J., Watrous, A. J., Yoon, J. H., Ursu, S., and Carter, C. S. (2008). Modafinil shifts human locus coeruleus to low-tonic, high-phasic activity during functional MRI. *Science* 322, 1700–1702. doi: 10.1126/science.1164908

Montgomery, S. H., and Mundy, N. I. (2014). Microcephaly genes evolved adaptively throughout the evolution of eutherian mammals. *BMC Evol. Biol.* 14:120. doi: 10.1186/1471-2148-14-120

Morris, R., Griffiths, O., Le Pelley, M. E., and Weickert, T. W. (2013). Attention to irrelevant cues is related to positive symptoms in schizophrenia. *Schiz. Bull.* 39, 575–582. doi: 10.1093/schbul/sbr192

Mottron, L., Belleville, S., Rouleau, G. A., and Collignon, O. (2014). Linking neocortical, cognitive, and genetic variability in autism with alterations of brain plasticity: the Trigger-Threshold-Target model. *Neurosci. Biobehav. Rev.* 47, 735–752. doi: 10.1016/j.neubiorev.2014.07.012

Mottron, L., Dawson, M., Soulieres, I., Hubert, B., and Burack, J. (2006). Enhanced perceptual functioning in autism: an update, and eight principles of autistic perception. *J. Autism Dev. Disord.* 36, 27–43. doi: 10.1007/s10803-005-0040-7

Murray, D., Lesser, M., and Lawson, W. (2005). Attention, monotropism and the diagnostic criteria for autism. *Autism* 9, 139–156. doi: 10.1177/1362361305051398

Muth, A., Hönekopp, J., and Falter, C. M. (2014). Visuo-spatial performance in autism: a meta-analysis. *J. Autism Dev. Disord.* 44, 3245–3263. doi: 10.1007/s10803-014-2188-5

Nader, A. M., Courchesne, V., Dawson, M., and Soulières, I. (2016). Does WISC-IV underestimate the intelligence of autistic children? *J. Autism Dev. Disord.* 46, 1582–1589. doi: 10.1007/s10803-014-2270-z

Nakano, T., Kato, N., and Kitazawa, S. (2012). Superior haptic-to-visual shape matching in autism spectrum disorders. *Neuropsychologia* 50, 696–703. doi: 10.1016/j.neuropsychologia.2011.12.024

Nesse, R. M., and Stein, D. J. (2012). Towards a genuinely medical model for psychiatric nosology. *BMC Med.* 10:5. doi: 10.1186/1741-7015-10-5

Nettle, D. (2006). Schizotypy and mental health amongst poets, visual artists, and mathematicians. *J. Res. Pers.* 40, 876–890. doi: 10.1016/j.jrp.2005.09.004

Nisbett, R. E., Aronson, J., Blair, C., Dickens, W., Flynn, J., Halpern, D. F., et al. (2012). Intelligence: new findings and theoretical developments. *Am. Psychol.* 67, 130. doi: 10.1037/a0026699

Noland, J. S., Reznick, J. S., Stone, W. L., Walden, T., and Sheridan, E. H. (2010). Better working memory for non-social targets in infant siblings of children with Autism Spectrum Disorder. *Dev. Sci.* 13, 244–251. doi: 10.1111/j.1467-7687.2009.00882.x

Nordsletten, A. E., Larsson, H., Crowley, J. J., Almqvist, C., Lichtenstein, P., and Mataix-Cols, D. (2016). Patterns of nonrandom mating within and across 11 major psychiatric disorders. *JAMA Psychiatry* 73, 354–361. doi: 10.1001/jamapsychiatry.2015.3192

O'Riordan, M., and Passetti, F. (2006). Discrimination in autism within different sensory modalities. *J. Autism Dev. Disord.* 36, 665–675. doi: 10.1007/s10803-006-0106-1

Oberman, L. M., and Pascual-Leone, A. (2014). Hyperplasticity in Autism Spectrum Disorder confers protection from Alzheimer's disease. *Med. Hypotheses* 83, 337–342. doi: 10.1016/j.mehy.2014.06.008

Oertel-Knöchel, V., Knöchel, C., Rotarska-Jagiela, A., Reinke, B., Prvulovic, D., Haenschel, C., et al. (2013). Association between psychotic symptoms and cortical thickness reduction across the schizophrenia spectrum. *Cereb. Cortex* 23, 61–70. doi: 10.1093/cercor/bhr380

Oguro-Ando, A., Rosensweig, C., Herman, E., Nishimura, Y., Werling, D., Bill, B. R., et al. (2015). Increased CYFIP1 dosage alters cellular and dendritic morphology and dysregulates mTOR. *Mol. Psychiatry* 20, 1069–1078. doi: 10.1038/mp.2014.124

Pantelis, C., Yücel, M., Wood, S. J., Velakoulis, D., Sun, D., Berger, G., et al. (2005). Structural brain imaging evidence for multiple pathological processes at different stages of brain development in schizophrenia. *Schizophr. Bull.* 31, 672–696. doi: 10.1093/schbul/sbi034

Panton, K. R., Badcock, D. R., and Badcock, J. C. (2016). A metaanalysis of perceptual organization in schizophrenia, schizotypy, and other high-risk groups based on variants of the embedded figures task. *Front. Psychol.* 7:237. doi: 10.3389/fpsyg.2016.00237

Plomin, R., and Deary, I. J. (2015). Genetics and intelligence differences: five special findings. *Mol. Psychiatry* 20, 98–108. doi: 10.1038/mp.2014.105

Ploog, B. O. (2010). Stimulus overselectivity four decades later: a review of the literature and its implications for current research in autism spectrum disorder. *J. Autism Dev. Disord.* 40, 1332–1349. doi: 10.1007/s10803-010-0990-2

Quick, V. S., Davis, J. M., Olincy, A., and Sikela, J. M. (2015). DUF1220 copy number is associated with schizophrenia risk and severity: implications for understanding autism and schizophrenia as related diseases. *Transl. Psychiatry* 5, e697. doi: 10.1038/tp.2015.192

Rai, D., Lewis, G., Lundberg, M., Araya, R., Svensson, A., Dalman, C., et al. (2012). Parental socioeconomic status and risk of offspring autism spectrum disorders in a Swedish population-based study. *J. Am. Acad. Child Adolesc. Psychiatry* 51, 467–476. doi: 10.1016/j.jaac.2012.02.012

Rais, M., Cahn, W., Schnack, H. G., Pol, H. H., Kahn, R. S., and van Haren, N. E. M. (2012). Brain volume reductions in medication-naive patients with schizophrenia in relation to intelligence quotient. *Psychol. Med.* 42, 1847–1856. doi: 10.1017/S0033291712000098

Rapoport, J. L., and Gogtay, N. (2011). Childhood onset schizophrenia: support for a progressive neurodevelopmental disorder. *Int. J. Dev. Neurosci.* 29, 251–258. doi: 10.1016/j.ijdevneu.2010.10.003

Rimland, B. (1964). *Infantile Autism: The Syndrome and Its Implications for a Neural Theory of Behavior*. New York, NY: Appleton-Century-Crofts.

Rimol, L. M., Nesvåg, R., Hagler, D. J., Bergmann, Ø., Fennema-Notestine, C., Hartberg, C. B., et al. (2012). Cortical volume, surface area, and thickness in schizophrenia and bipolar disorder. *Biol. Psychiatry* 71, 552–560. doi: 10.1016/j.biopsych.2011.11.026

Rinaldi, T., Perrodin, C., and Markram, H. (2008). Hyper-connectivity and hyper-plasticity in the medial prefrontal cortex in the valproic acid animal model of autism. *Front. Neural Circuits* 2:4. doi: 10.3389/neuro.04.004.2008

Roelfsema, M. T., Hoekstra, R. A., Allison, C., Wheelwright, S., Brayne, C., Matthews, F. E., et al. (2012). Are autism spectrum conditions more prevalent in an information-technology region? A school-based study of three regions in the Netherlands. *J. Autism Dev. Disord.* 42, 734–739. doi: 10.1007/s10803-011-1302-1

Roth, G., and Dicke, U. (2005). Evolution of the brain and intelligence. *Trends Cogn. Sci.* 9, 250–257. doi: 10.1016/j.tics.2005.03.005

Rubenstein, J. L. R., and Merzenich, M. M. (2003). Model of autism: increased ratio of excitation/inhibition in key neural systems. *Genes Brain Behav.* 2, 255–267. doi: 10.1034/j.1601-183X.2003.00037.x

Rutherford, M. D., and Subiaul, F. (2015). Children with autism spectrum disorder have an exceptional explanatory drive. *Autism.* doi: 10.1177/13623613156 05973. [Epub ahead of print].

Ruthsatz, J., and Urbach, J. B. (2012). Child prodigy: a novel cognitive profile places elevated general intelligence, exceptional working memory and attention to detail at the root of prodigiousness. *Intelligence* 40, 419–426. doi: 10.1016/j.intell.2012.06.002

Sabatos-DeVito, M., Schipul, S. E., Bulluck, J. C., Belger, A., and Baranek, G. T. (2016). Eye tracking reveals impaired attentional disengagement associated with sensory response patterns in children with autism. *J. Autism Dev. Disord.* 46, 1319–1333. doi: 10.1007/s10803-015-2681-5

Sacco, R., Gabriele, S., and Persico, A. M. (2015). Head circumference and brain size in autism spectrum disorder: a systematic review and meta-analysis. *Psychiatry Res.* 234, 239–251. doi: 10.1016/j.pscychresns.2015.08.016

Santini, E., Huynh, T. N., MacAskill, A. F., Carter, A. G., Pierre, P., et al. (2013). Exaggerated translation causes synaptic and behavioural aberrations associated with autism. *Nature* 493, 411–415. doi: 10.1038/nature11782

Santini, E., and Klann, E. (2014). Reciprocal signaling between translational control pathways and synaptic proteins in autism spectrum disorders. *Sci. Signal.* 7, re10. doi: 10.1126/scisignal.2005832

Schoenemann, P. T. (2006). Evolution of the size and functional areas of the human brain. *Annu. Rev. Anthropol.* 35, 379–406. doi: 10.1146/annurev.anthro.35.081705.123210

Sevy, S., Burdick, K. E., Visweswaraiah, H., Abdelmessih, S., Lukin, M., et al. (2007). Iowa gambling task in schizophrenia: a review and new data in patients with schizophrenia and co-occurring cannabis use disorders. *Schizophr. Res.* 92, 74–84. doi: 10.1016/j.schres.2007.01.005

Shaw, P., Greenstein, D., Lerch, J., Clasen, L., Lenroot, R., Gogtay, N. E. E. A., et al. (2006). Intellectual ability and cortical development in children and adolescents. *Nature* 440, 676–679. doi: 10.1038/nature04513

Smith, E., Thurm, A., Greenstein, D., Farmer, C., Swedo, S., Giedd, J., et al. (2016). Cortical thickness change in autism during early childhood. *Hum. Brain Mapp.* 37, 2616–2629. doi: 10.1002/hbm.23195

Snitz, B. E., MacDonald, A. W., and Carter, C. S. (2006). Cognitive deficits in unaffected first-degree relatives of schizophrenia patients: a meta-analytic review of putative endophenotypes. *Schizophr. Bull.* 32, 179–194. doi: 10.1093/schbul/sbi048

Snyder, A. (2009). Explaining and inducing savant skills: privileged access to lower level, less-processed information. *Philos. Trans. R. Soc. Lond. B Biol. Sci.* 364, 1399–1405. doi: 10.1098/rstb.2008.0290

South, M., Chamberlain, P. D., Wigham, S., Newton, T., Le Couteur, A., McConachie, H., et al. (2014). Enhanced decision making and risk avoidance in high-functioning autism spectrum disorder. *Neuropsychol.* 28, 222. doi: 10.1037/neu0000016

Spearman, C. (1904). "General Intelligence," objectively determined and measured. *Am. J. Psychol.* 15, 201–292. doi: 10.2307/1412107

Spek, A. A., and Velderman, E. (2013). Examining the relationship between autism spectrum disorders and technical professions in high functioning adults. *Res. Autism Spectr. Disord.* 7, 606–612. doi: 10.1016/j.rasd.2013.02.002

Stanovich, K. E., and West, R. F. (2014). What intelligence tests miss. *Psychologist* 27, 80–83.

Stanutz, S., Wapnick, J., and Burack, J. A. (2014). Pitch discrimination and melodic memory in children with autism spectrum disorders. *Autism* 18, 137–147. doi: 10.1177/1362361312462905

Steen, R. G., Mull, C., McClure, R., Hamer, R. M., and Lieberman, J. A. (2006). Brain volume in first-episode schizophrenia. *Br. J. Psychiatry* 188, 510–518. doi: 10.1192/bjp.188.6.510

Stefansson, H., Meyer-Lindenberg, A., Steinberg, S., Magnusdottir, B., Morgen, K., Arnarsdottir, S., et al. (2014). CNVs conferring risk of autism or schizophrenia affect cognition in controls. *Nature* 505, 361–366. doi: 10.1038/nature12818

Stefansson, H., Rujescu, D., Cichon, S., Pietiläinen, O. P., Ingason, A., Steinberg, S., et al. (2008). Large recurrent microdeletions associated with schizophrenia. *Nature* 455, 232–236. doi: 10.1038/nature07229

Sun, X., Allison, C., Auyeung, B., Matthews, F. E., Zhang, Z., Baron-Cohen, S., et al. (2014). Comparison between a mandarin Chinese version of the childhood autism spectrum test and the Clancy autism behaviour scale in mainland China. *Res. Dev. Disabil.* 35, 1599–1608. doi: 10.1016/j.ridd.2014.02.005

Sutton, M. A., and Schuman, E. M. (2006). Dendritic protein synthesis, synaptic plasticity, and memory. *Cell* 127, 49–58. doi: 10.1016/j.cell.2006.09.014

Tam, G. W., van de Lagemaat, L. N., Redon, R., Strathdee, K. E., Croning, M. D., Malloy, M. P., et al. (2010). Confirmed rare copy number variants implicate novel genes in schizophrenia. *Biochem. Soc. Trans.* 38, 445–451. doi: 10.1042/BST0380445

Tang, J., Liao, Y., Song, M., Gao, J. H., Zhou, B., Tan, C., et al. (2013). Aberrant default mode functional connectivity in early onset schizophrenia. *PLoS ONE* 8:e71061. doi: 10.1371/journal.pone.0071061

Tavassoli, T., Auyeung, B., Murphy, L. C., Baron-Cohen, S., and Chakrabarti, B. (2012). Variation in the autism candidate gene GABRB3 modulates tactile sensitivity in typically developing children. *Mol. Autism* 3, 1. doi: 10.1186/2040-2392-3-6

Teovanović, P., Knežević, G., and Stankov, L. (2015). Individual differences in cognitive biases: evidence against one-factor theory of rationality. *Intelligence* 50, 75–86. doi: 10.1016/j.intell.2015.02.008

Thakkar, K. N., and Park, S. (2010). Empathy, schizotypy, and visuospatial transformations. *Cog. Neuropsych.* 15, 477–500. doi: 10.1080/13546801003711350

Thomas, P., Zahorodny, W., Peng, B., Kim, S., Jani, N., Halperin, W., et al. (2012). The association of autism diagnosis with socioeconomic status. *Autism* 16, 201–213. doi: 10.1177/1362361311413397

Treffert, D. A. (2014). Savant syndrome: realities, myths and misconceptions. *J. Autism Dev. Disord.* 44, 564–571. doi: 10.1007/s10803-013-1906-8

Troche, S. J., Houlihan, M. E., Stelmack, R. M., and Rammsayer, T. H. (2009). Mental ability, P300, and mismatch negativity: analysis of frequency and duration discrimination. *Intelligence* 37, 365–373. doi: 10.1016/j.intell.2009.03.002

Troche, S. J., and Rammsayer, T. H. (2009a). "Neural oscillations and intelligence: the temporal resolution power hypothesis," in *Chronobiology and Chronopsychology*, eds T. G. Baudson, A. Seemüller, and M. Dresler (Lengerich: Pabst Press), 62–76.

Troche, S. J., and Rammsayer, T. H. (2009b). The influence of temporal resolution power and working memory capacity on psychometric intelligence. *Intelligence* 37, 479–486. doi: 10.1016/j.intell.2009.06.001

Trzaskowski, M., Harlaar, N., Arden, R., Krapohl, E., Rimfeld, K., McMillan, A., et al. (2014). Genetic influence on family socioeconomic status and children's intelligence. *Intelligence* 42, 83–88. doi: 10.1016/j.intell.2013.11.002

Turken, U., Whitfield-Gabrieli, S., Bammer, R., Baldo, J. V., Dronkers, N. F., and Gabrieli, J. D. (2008). Cognitive processing speed and the structure of white matter pathways: convergent evidence from normal variation and lesion studies. *Neuroimage* 42, 1032–1044. doi: 10.1016/j.neuroimage.2008.03.057

Uddin, L. Q., Clare Kelly, A. M., Biswal, B. B., Xavier Castellanos, F., and Milham, M. P. (2009). Functional connectivity of default mode network components: correlation, anticorrelation, and causality. *Hum. Brain Mapp.* 30, 625–637. doi: 10.1002/hbm.20531

Vandenberg, S. G., and Kruse, A. R. (1978). Mental rotations, a group test of three-dimensional spatial visualization. *Percept. Mot. Skills* 47, 599–604. doi: 10.2466/pms.1978.47.2.599

van den Heuvel, M. P., Stam, C. J., Kahn, R. S., and Pol, H. E. H. (2009). Efficiency of functional brain networks and intellectual performance. *J. Neurosci.* 29, 7619–7624. doi: 10.1523/JNEUROSCI.1443-09.2009

Van Meter, K. C., Christiansen, L. E., Delwiche, L. D., Azari, R., Carpenter, T. E., and Hertz-Picciotto, I. (2010). Geographic distribution of autism in California: a retrospective birth cohort analysis. *Autism Res.* 3, 19–29. doi: 10.1002/aur.110

van Os, J. (2009). 'Salience syndrome' replaces 'schizophrenia' in DSM-V and ICD-11: psychiatry's evidence-based entry into the 21st century? *Acta Psychiatr. Scand.* 120, 363–372. doi: 10.1111/j.1600-0447.2009.01456.x

Vissers, L. E., Gilissen, C., and Veltman, J. A. (2016). Genetic studies in intellectual disability and related disorders. *Nat. Rev. Genet.* 17, 9–18. doi: 10.1038/nrg3999

Wai, J., Lubinski, D., and Benbow, C. P. (2009). Spatial ability for STEM domains: aligning over 50 years of cumulative psychological knowledge solidifies its importance. *J. Edu. Psychol.* 101, 817. doi: 10.1037/a0016127

Wang, J., Tao, Y., Song, F., Sun, Y., Ott, J., and Saffen, D. (2015). Common regulatory variants of CYFIP1 contribute to susceptibility for Autism Spectrum Disorder (ASD) and classical autism. *Annals Hum. Genet.* 79, 329–340. doi: 10.1111/ahg.12121

Warrier, V., Baron-Cohen, S., and Chakrabarti, B. (2013). Genetic variation in GABRB3 is associated with Asperger syndrome and multiple endophenotypes relevant to autism. *Mol. Autism* 4, 1. doi: 10.1186/2040-2392-4-48

Wei, X., Jennifer, W. Y., Shattuck, P., McCracken, M., and Blackorby, J. (2013). Science, technology, engineering, and mathematics (STEM) participation among college students with an autism spectrum disorder. *J. Autism Dev. Disord.* 43, 1539–1546. doi: 10.1007/s10803-012-1700-z

Werner, S., Malaspina, D., and Rabinowitz, J. (2007). Socioeconomic status at birth is associated with risk of schizophrenia: population-based multilevel study. *Schizophr. Bull.* 33, 1373–1378. doi: 10.1093/schbul/sbm032

White, S., O'Reilly, H., and Frith, U. (2009). Big heads, small details and autism. *Neuropsychologia* 47, 1274–1281. doi: 10.1016/j.neuropsychologia.2009.01.012

Whitfield-Gabrieli, S., Thermenos, H. W., Milanovic, S., Tsuang, M. T., Faraone, S. V., McCarley, R. W., et al. (2009). Hyperactivity and hyperconnectivity of the default network in schizophrenia and in first-degree relatives of persons with schizophrenia. *Proc. Natl. Acad. Sci. U.S.A.* 106, 1279–1284. doi: 10.1073/pnas.0809141106

Windham, G. C., Fessel, K., and Grether, J. K. (2009). Autism spectrum disorders in relation to parental occupation in technical fields. *Autism Res.* 2, 183–191. doi: 10.1002/aur.84

Witelson, S. F., Beresh, H., and Kigar, D. L. (2006). Intelligence and brain size in 100 postmortem brains: sex, lateralization and age factors. *Brain* 129, 386–398. doi: 10.1093/brain/awh696

Wolfle, D., and Oxtoby, T. (1952). Distributions of ability of students specializing in different fields. *Science* 116, 311.

Woodberry, K. A., Giuliano, A. J., and Seidman, L. J. (2008). Premorbid IQ in schizophrenia: a meta-analytic review. *Am. J. Psychiatry* 165, 579–587. doi: 10.1176/appi.ajp.2008.07081242

Woodward, T. S., Moritz, S., Cuttler, C., and Whitman, J. C. (2006). The contribution of a cognitive bias against disconfirmatory evidence (BADE) to delusions in schizophrenia. *J. Clin. Exp. Neuropsychol.* 28, 605–617. doi: 10.1080/13803390590949511

Zapf, A. C., Glindemann, L. A., Vogeley, K., and Falter, C. M. (2015). Sex differences in mental rotation and how they add to the understanding of autism. *PLoS ONE* 10:e0124628. doi: 10.1371/journal.pone.0124628

Zheng, X., Chen, R., Li, N., Du, W., Pei, L., Zhang, J., et al. (2012). Socioeconomic status and children with intellectual disability in China. *J. Intellect. Disabil. Res.* 56, 212–220. doi: 10.1111/j.1365-2788.2011.01470.x

Zielinski, B. A., Prigge, M. B., Nielsen, J. A., Froehlich, A. L., Abildskov, T. J., Anderson, J. S., et al. (2014). Longitudinal changes in cortical thickness in autism and typical development. *Brain* 137, 1799–1812. doi: 10.1093/brain/awu083

14

Noise Reduction in Arterial Spin Labeling Based Functional Connectivity Using Nuisance Variables

Kay Jann [1], Robert X. Smith [1], Edgar A. Rios Piedra [1], Mirella Dapretto [2] and Danny J. J. Wang [1]*

[1] *Laboratory of FMRI Technology, Department of Neurology, University of California Los Angeles, Los Angeles, CA, USA,*
[2] *Department of Psychiatry and Biobehavioral Sciences, University of California Los Angeles, Los Angeles, CA, USA*

Edited by:
Alessandro Grecucci, University of Trento, Italy

Reviewed by:
Roberto Viviani, University of Innsbruck, Austria
Weiying Dai, Binghamton University, USA

***Correspondence:**
Kay Jann
kay.jann@loni.usc.edu

Arterial Spin Labeling (ASL) perfusion image series have recently been utilized for functional connectivity (FC) analysis in healthy volunteers and children with autism spectrum disorders (ASD). Noise reduction by using nuisance variables has been shown to be necessary to minimize potential confounding effects of head motion and physiological signals on BOLD based FC analysis. The purpose of the present study is to systematically evaluate the effectiveness of different noise reduction strategies (NRS) using nuisance variables to improve perfusion based FC analysis in two cohorts of healthy adults using state of the art 3D background-suppressed (BS) GRASE pseudo-continuous ASL (pCASL) and dual-echo 2D-EPI pCASL sequences. Five different NRS were performed in healthy volunteers to compare their performance. We then compared seed-based FC analysis using 3D BS GRASE pCASL in a cohort of 12 children with ASD (3f/9m, age 12.8 $\pm$ 1.3 years) and 13 typically developing (TD) children (1f/12m; age 13.9 $\pm$ 3 years) in conjunction with NRS. Regression of different combinations of nuisance variables affected FC analysis from a seed in the posterior cingulate cortex (PCC) to other areas of the default mode network (DMN) in both BOLD and pCASL data sets. Consistent with existing literature on BOLD-FC, we observed improved spatial specificity after physiological noise reduction and improved long-range connectivity using head movement related regressors. Furthermore, 3D BS GRASE pCASL shows much higher temporal SNR compared to dual-echo 2D-EPI pCASL and similar effects of noise reduction as those observed for BOLD. Seed-based FC analysis using 3D BS GRASE pCASL in children with ASD and TD children showed that noise reduction including physiological and motion related signals as nuisance variables is crucial for identifying altered long-range connectivity from PCC to frontal brain areas associated with ASD. This is the first study that systematically evaluated the effects of different NRS on ASL based FC analysis. 3D BS GRASE pCASL is the preferred ASL sequence for FC analysis due to its superior temporal SNR. Removing physiological noise and motion parameters is critical for detecting altered FC in neurodevelopmental disorders such as ASD.

Keywords: functional connectivity (FC), noise reduction, default mode network (DMN), arterial spin labeling (ASL), blood oxygenation level dependent (BOLD), cerebral blood flow (CBF)

INTRODUCTION

Functional connectivity (FC) analysis to compute functionally connected networks (FCNs) has become a major imaging approach to investigate the brain's organization and function. Moreover, comparing different cohorts such as elderly subjects to young adults, or healthy control groups to psychiatric populations, have identified patterns of altered connectivity within specific FCNs. In the past few years, however, it has become evident that there are several potential confounding factors that may lead to spurious findings when not properly addressed. Physiological noise such as fluctuations in respiratory and cardiac cycles or head movements can influence BOLD signal intensities in fMRI. This is particularly relevant since different study cohorts could exhibit different patterns or amounts of such confounding factors (e.g., children, elderly, and psychiatric patients tend to have more difficulties to lay motionless inside the MR scanner). Accordingly, using nuisance variables to account for noise related signal fluctuations in BOLD-fMRI based FC analysis has been shown to be imperative to minimize or avoid potential confounding effects of motion or other physiological factors (e.g., respiration and heart rate) on network connectivity measures (Murphy et al., 2013).

Physiological fluctuations or changes in cardiac pulsation and respiratory cycles can cause changes in blood CO_2 pressure (Wise et al., 2004), which in turn influences the BOLD signal. Hence variability in respiration and cardiac pulsation could give rise to spuriously correlated signals in distributed brain areas (Birn, 2012). Furthermore, the set of brain areas affected by these physiological fluctuations could resemble the patterns associated with certain FCNs (Birn et al., 2008). Accordingly, separating physiological noise from BOLD signal fluctuations increases sensitivity for detecting neuronal related FCNs. While these variations in physiological parameters are ideally measured by concurrent recordings with pulse oximetry and respiration belt (Chang and Glover, 2009b), data driven techniques have been proposed to estimate nuisance regressors from the fMRI data itself. Furthermore, regions that are unlikely to exhibit neuronal related BOLD signal changes such as in cerebro-spinal fluid (CSF) or white matter (WM) have been used to efficiently remove these physiological variations (Birn et al., 2008; Weissenbacher et al., 2009).

In addition to physiological noise, recent observations indicate also that head movements during the MR acquisition can have detrimental effects on FC measures (Power et al., 2012; Satterthwaite et al., 2012; Van Dijk et al., 2012). Head motion in the magnetic field perturbs the spin history and can introduce spurious signal variances that tend to be more similar locally than between distant brain areas. This biases FC analyses toward increased local correlations and reduced long-range correlations, a critical issue when comparing subject cohorts that might differ in their ability to lie still (e.g., children or psychiatric patients). Indeed children and psychiatric cohorts have displayed this pattern of increased local but reduced long-range FC, raising the critical question as to whether and to what extent these findings reflect motion effects. A variety of approaches to deal with motion effects in FC analyses have since been proposed, most of which include nuisance variables to regress out potential signal fluctuations related to head movements by using motion parameters estimated from rigid body volume alignments (for review see Power et al., 2015). In summary, in BOLD fcMRI several confounding factors have been identified and strategies have been proposed to minimize their influences.

Besides BOLD fcMRI, Arterial Spin Labeling (ASL) datasets have been recently used to compute FCNs (Viviani et al., 2011; Liang et al., 2012; Jann et al., 2015a) (review Chen et al., 2015).This approach was made feasible by technical advances in state-of-the-art ASL pulse sequences resulting in improved signal-to-noise ratio (SNR) and temporal stability (Chen et al., 2011; Vidorreta et al., 2013). These technical advances include pseudo-continuous ASL (pCASL) (Wu et al., 2007; Dai et al., 2008), background suppression and three-dimensional (3D) fast imaging sequences such as GRASE (a hybrid of gradient and spin echo) or stack of spirals. In addition to improved acquisition techniques, physiological noise regression in ASL has been shown to increase temporal SNR (Wang, 2012). To date, however, no study has systematically investigated the effect of noise reduction, using the same nuisance variables as proposed for BOLD, on ASL based FC. Therefore, the primary purpose of this study was to investigate the effect of motion and physiological noise reduction on ASL based FC. A second goal of this study was to apply the optimal noise-reduction strategy for ASL based FC analysis in a cohort of children with autism spectrum disorders (ASD) and typically developing children.

METHODS

All adult neurotypical participants in this study gave written informed consent according to a research protocol approved by the UCLA Institutional Review Board. Inclusion criteria of healthy volunteers included no history of psychiatric or neurological disorders, and no contraindications to MRI scan. Scans were performed on a 3T Siemens TIM Trio scanner, using body coil as the transmitter and 12-ch head coil as the receiver. We acquired ASL and BOLD data in 10 healthy young participants (6f/4m; age [mean $\pm$ sd] = 22 $\pm$ 3 years) with a 3D background-suppressed (BS: 85% suppression) GRASE pCASL sequence (60 label/control pairs, TR/TE/τ/PLD = 4000/22/1200/1000 ms; 26 slices, 64 $\times$ 64 matrix, voxel-size 3.44 $\times$ 3.44 $\times$ 5 mm^3) and a standard 2D EPI BOLD sequence (240 Volumes, TR/TE = 2000/30 ms, 30 slices, 64 $\times$ 64 matrix, slice thickness = 4 mm with 1 mm gap). For comparison, a separate cohort of 10 healthy volunteers (7f/3m; age [mean $\pm$ sd] = 25.7 $\pm$ 8 years) underwent resting state fMRI scans using a dual-echo 2D EPI pCASL sequence (128 label/control pairs, TR/TE1/TE2/τ/PLD = 4000/10/25/1200/1500 ms; 18 slices, 64 $\times$ 64 matrix, voxel-size 3.44 $\times$ 3.44 $\times$ 6 mm^3) to simultaneously acquire ASL and BOLD data. All datasets were first realigned to account for spatial motion displacements (for ASL separately for label and control images). Five different regression models using different sets of nuisance variables [here termed Noise Reduction Strategies (NRS)] were then performed:

- *NRS1*: no nuisance variables for noise reduction.
- *NRS2*: 6 motion parameters (3 translations x, y, z and 3 rotations α, β, γ) and their 1st derivatives.
- *NRS3*: same as NRS2 plus additional regressor for Framewise Displacement (FD). FD was computed following the procedure described by Power et al. (2012). Rotational displacements were recomputed to millimeters of displacement on a sphere with 5 cm radius. The volume by volume (framewise) head displacement in translational and recomputed rotational parameters were then calculated and summed up. Mean FD ($\pm$SD) in mm for the groups in each dataset were: 3D GRASE pCASL 0.244 ($\pm$0.065), standard BOLD 0.192 ($\pm$0.060), 2D dual-echo pCASL 0.179 ($\pm$0.066) and dual-echo BOLD 0.153 ($\pm$0.049). *T*-tests did not reveal a significant difference between ASL and BOLD within the groups ($t_{3D} = 1.81; p = 0.086/t_{2D} = 0.996; p = 0.333$), nor between groups for BOLD ($t = 1.612$; $p = 0.124$). There was a small difference showing slightly higher motion in 3D pCASL than 2D pCASL ($t = -2.194$; $p = 0.042$).
- *NRS4*: White matter and CSF fluctuations (mean signal fluctuations within brain segmentation tissue probability masks thresholded at 0.95 for WM and 0.85 for CSF and coregistered/resampled to functional images).
- *NRS5*: NRS3 + NRS4.

CBF images were computed for all NRSs (one compartment model, pair-wise subtraction of Label/Control images) (Alsop et al., 2015). BOLD and CBF images were coregistered to individual anatomical scans, normalized to MNI template and smoothed with an 8 mm FWHM Gaussian kernel.

Connectivity Analysis

FC analysis was performed with Seed Based Correlation Analysis (SBA) using the posterior cingulate cortex (PCC) as a seed (template seed from Shirer et al., 2012) to identify the Default Mode Network (DMN). DMN maps for each NRS in all four datasets as well as overall DMNs for the four datasets were calculated by one-sample *t*-tests to identify all areas with correlations significantly greater than zero across all subjects. We determined the similarity of the DMN maps derived using different NRSs between each other as well as to a template BOLD-DMN (Shirer et al., 2012) and template ASL-DMN (Jann et al., 2015a) using Dice Similarity Coefficients (Dice, 1945; Jann et al., 2015a), which compares the number of common voxels between two maps based on the formula DSC (A,B) = $2(A \cap B)/(A + B)$, where A and B are the two maps.

To investigate the effect of NRS on the often-discussed long-range connectivity between PCC and anterior cingulate/medial prefrontal cortex (ACC/mPFC) (Power et al., 2012, 2015; Satterthwaite et al., 2012; Van Dijk et al., 2012), we calculated the correlation between those two ROIs based on the template DMN nodes (Shirer et al., 2012) using different NRSs. FC changes due to different NRSs were further investigated by a voxel-wise analysis on the individual subjects' SBA connectivity maps for each NRS by computing voxel-wise repeated-measures ANOVA and *post-hoc* ROI based paired *t*-tests.

Distance Related Effects of Motion

We further investigated the relationship between spatial distance, the use of head motion related nuisance variables and FC changes in BOLD and pCASL data, respectively. Specifically, we parcellated the brain into 264 spherical ROIs defined by the Power-Atlas (Power et al., 2012). For the parcellated data we then computed the cross-correlation matrix using data processed with NRS4 (WM/CSF regression only) and NRS5 (WM/CSF regression + motion regression), respectively. Subtraction of the two cross-correlation matrices provides the difference in connectivity between any two ROIs (ΔFC) between NRS5 and NRS4. Plotting these ΔFC values against the Euclidean distance between the respective ROIs and fitting a linear equation to these plots examined the presence of a relation between ΔFC and spatial distance (Power et al., 2014, 2015).

Effects on Temporal SNR and Global-CBF Quantification

Finally, we estimated tSNR within gray matter and performed an ANOVA on these values to test for significant improvements in tSNR following noise reduction. Global mean CBF was also compared to test whether NRS affects mean CBF quantification between the two pCASL sequences.

Application of NRS in Children with ASD

To investigate the effects of NRS on seed-based FC analysis in a clinical cohort, we compared FC differences between a group of 12 children with ASD (3f/9m, age 12.8 $\pm$ 1.3 years; IQ = 107.0 $\pm$ 14.9) and an age and IQ matched group of 13 typically developing (TD) children (1f/12m; age 13.9 $\pm$ 3 years; IQ = 104.8 $\pm$ 14.4). Subjects and parents provided written consent according to the guidelines specified by the UCLA Institutional Review Board. Clinical diagnosis of ASD was confirmed with the Autism Diagnostic Observation Schedule (ADOS; Lord et al., 2000), Autism Diagnostic Interview-Revised (ADI-R; Lord et al., 1994) and best clinical judgment. Mean ADOS severity score was 7.6 (range 6–10). Statistical tests to compare group characteristics were not significant: Mann-Whitney *U*-Test for age ($U = 44$, $z = 1.822$, $p = 0.068$) and IQ ($U = 73.5$, $z = -0.2178$, $p = 0.826$) and Chi-square test with Yates correction for small samples for gender (0.401, $p = 0.527$).

We used the 3D BS GRASE pCASL sequence to acquire CBF data in these two groups given its favorable temporal characteristics shown in the above analyses. Preprocessing was identical as described above and NRS4 and NRS5 were compared to NRS1 in these cohorts. FC from the PCC-seed was computed for each subject and NRS. Within group analyses included comparisons between NRSs using voxel-wise paired-sample *t*-tests. In addition, between-group comparisons were performed by voxel-wise two-sample *t*-tests (correction for multiple comparison at $\alpha < 0.05$ was done by cluster-size estimation, CSE for NRS0 = 133 voxels, NRS4 = 115 voxels and NRS5 = 114 voxels). This analysis will reveal the effects of different NRSs on the outcome of ASL-FC differences between

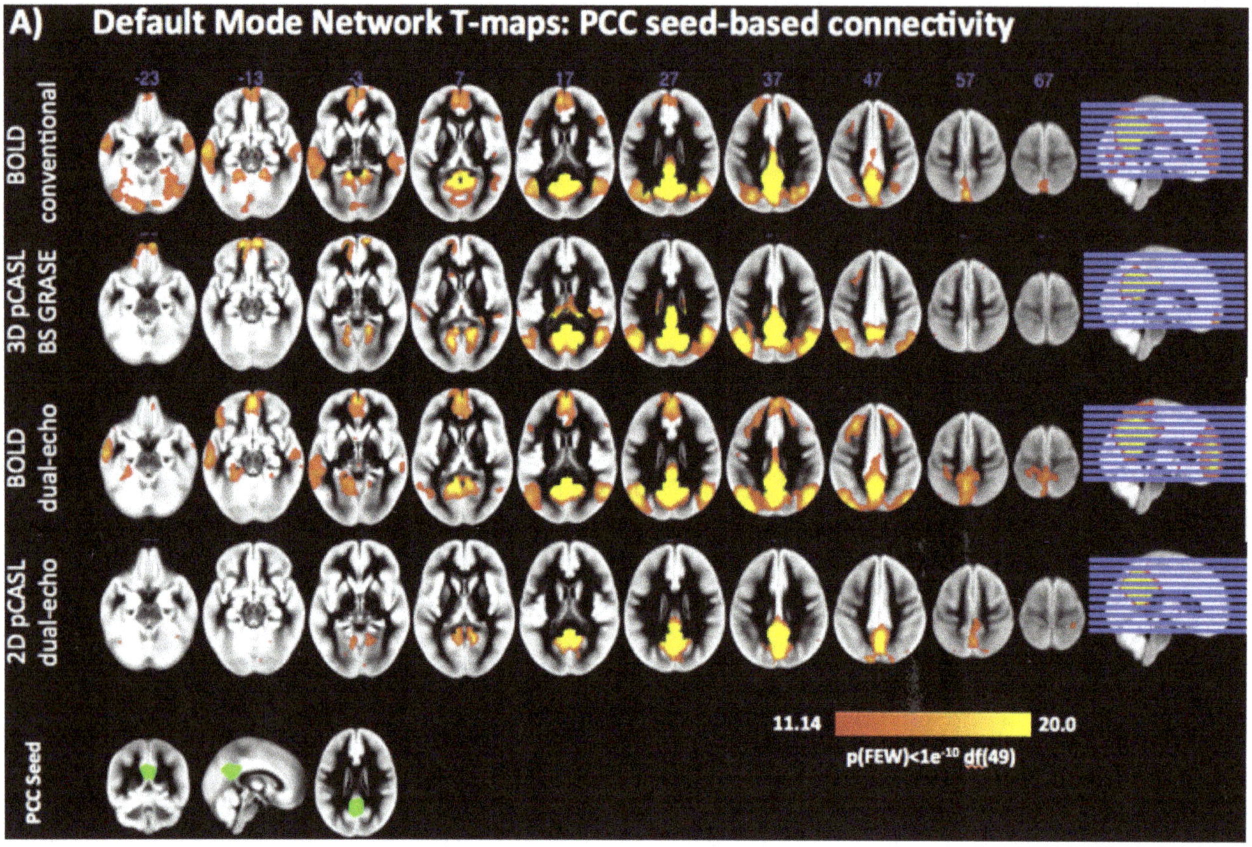

FIGURE 1 | Statistical t-maps displaying the spatial pattern of the DMNs as identified by Seed based Correlation analysis from a PCC seed (Lower left, green) on pCASL and BOLD datasets.

ASD and TD. To minimize the effects of differences in head motion between the groups, the ASD and TD groups were also matched for the amount of motion: mean frame-wise displacement (FD) for ASD was 0.453 ± 0.238 and TD 0.392 ± 0.241 (t-test $t = -0.641$, $p = 0.528$).

RESULTS

Both pCASL and BOLD data showed correlation maps using the PCC as the seed that resemble the DMN. **Figure 1** displays the PCC-Seed and the DMNs computed as t-maps across all NRSs for each dataset thresholded at family wise corrected $p < 1e^{-10}$. Dice Similarity Coefficients (DSCs) to the template BOLD-DMN (Shirer et al., 2012) and the template ASL-DMN (Jann et al., 2015a), respectively, are listed in **Table 1**. NRS1–3 showed low similarity while NRS4&5 showed greater overlap with the DMN templates. Furthermore, 2D pCASL showed the lowest DSC values, especially to the template ASL-DMN. **Figure 2** displays the cross-comparison of NRSs within each dataset to the template BOLD-DMN. Notably, DSC values between the separate NRS-DMNs showed that the DMN-maps without WM/CSF correction (NRS1–3) were highly similar to each other, while the DMNs with WM/CSF correction (NRS4, 5) showed high similarity to each other.

TABLE 1 | Dice Similarity Coefficients (DSCs) for all NRS in each condition to a template BOLD-DMN (Shirer et al., 2012) and a template ASL-DMN (Jann et al., 2015a), respectively.

	NRS1	NRS2	NRS3	NRS4	NRS5	Combined
TEMPLATE BOLD-DMN						
BOLD conventional	0.10	0.12	0.12	0.18	0.19	0.25
3D BS GRASE pCASL	0.12	0.11	0.11	0.19	0.19	0.17
BOLD dual-echo	0.09	0.09	0.09	0.28	0.39	0.39
2D pCASL	0.09	0.08	0.08	0.19	0.21	0.19
TEMPLATE ASL-DMN						
BOLD conventional	0.24	0.27	0.27	0.40	0.43	0.51
3D BS GRASE pCASL	0.36	0.40	0.40	0.51	0.49	0.55
BOLD dual-echo	0.24	0.23	0.23	0.51	0.55	0.58
2D pCASL	0.29	0.26	0.26	0.33	0.32	0.35

*The column termed combined represents the DMN t-maps across all subjects and NRSs as displayed in **Figure 1**.*

Effects of NRS on FC

Analysis of the connectivity between PCC and ACC/mPFC ROIs in both BOLD datasets showed a general decrease of FC after WM/CSF regression [$F_{BOLDconv(4,\ 9)} = 25.53$, $p < 1e\text{-}10$, $t_{NRS0vsNRS4} = 5.34$, $p = 0.0005$; $F_{BOLDdual-echo(4,\ 9)} = 12.49$,

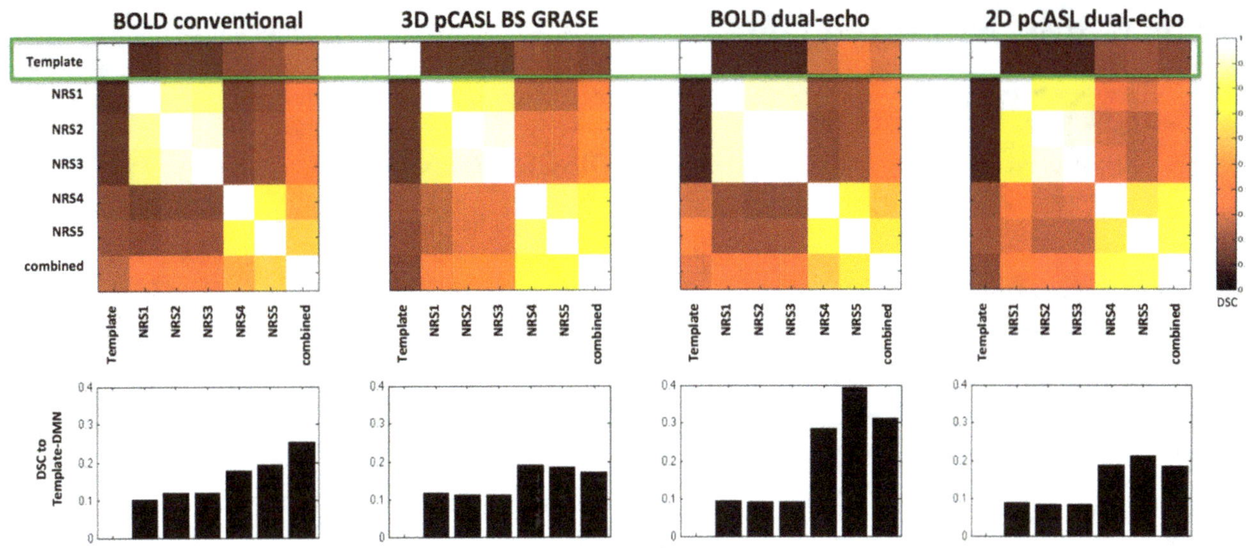

FIGURE 2 | Dice Similarity Coefficients (DSCs) between the spatial maps of the DMNs after different stages of noise reduction (NRS1–5). Template DMN derived from Shirer et al. (2012). Combined DMN computed as one-sample *t*-test across spatial correlation maps of all subjects and NRS. Clusters along the diagonal indicate that WM/CSF regression has large effect on similarity. Specifically after WM/CSF correction (NRS4/5) DSC values to the template DMN are increased (green rectangle and also bar-plots below cluster-plots), indicating increased spatial specificity of the DMN.

$p < 1e^{-10}$, $t_{NRS0vsNRS4} = 2.69$, $p = 0.025$], while motion parameter regression showed a tendency to slightly increase FC (*t*-test between NRS5 and NRS4 = $t_{BOLDconv} = 1.55$, $p = 0.155$; $t_{BOLDde} = 1.14$, $p = 0.284$). The same trend was observed for 3D GRASE pCASL [$F_{3DpCASL(4,\ 9)} = 75.5$, $p < 1e^{-10}$; $t_{NRS0vsNRS4} = 14.19$, $p < 0.0001$ and *t*-test NRS5 vs. NRS4: $t_{3DpCASL} = 1.51$, $p = 0.165$]; however, FC values were overall lower. For 2D pCASL there was little to no correlation between the two ROIs and no significant effect in the ANOVA ($F_{2DpCASL} = 1.4$, $p = 0.254$). Mean values of correlation coefficient across subjects for all NRSs and datasets are displayed in **Figure 3**.

A more detailed analysis of NRS effects throughout the DMN was performed by voxel-wise repeated-measures ANOVA (**Figure 4**). Results revealed that FC between PCC and mPFC/ACC were modified by NRS. Details for all ROIs including the results of the repeated-measures ANOVAs are listed in **Table 2**. For every ROI showing an effect of NRS, the boxplots represent the FC values (median and 75% interval across subjects) after different NRSs, revealing the directions of FC changes (i.e., increases or decreases). Moreover, the horizontal lines above the boxplots indicate the significance of *post-hoc* paired *t*-tests ($p < 0.05$) between any NRSs (*t* and *p* values for all *post-hoc t*-tests can be found in **Supplemental Table 1**). Similar to the analysis of connectivity between the PCC and ACC/mPFC ROIs, the voxel-wise ANOVA and *post-hoc t*-tests indicated that WM/CSF signal regression significantly reduces FC throughout the DMN. Furthermore, using head movement related nuisance variables in addition to WM/CSF (comparison between NRS5 and NRS4) tended to increase long-range FC from PCC to frontal areas while reducing local (within PCC) FC (**Table 2**). This distance-related effect was further investigated in a highly parcellated seed based approach.

Distance Dependence of Motion-Regression Effects

The scatter plots in **Figure 5** suggest a relationship between motion correction effects (after WM/CSF signal regression) and the distance between the connected ROIs. Specifically, ΔFC was increasingly positive the farther apart any two areas, thus yielding increased long-range connectivity and reduced or constant local short-range connectivity.

NRS Effects on Temporal SNR and Global CBF

Global tSNR in BOLD was expectedly higher than that of pCASL; furthermore, 3D pCASL showed 4.4 ± 0.4 times higher global tSNR than 2D pCASL. Differences in tSNR after NRS were observed for all modalities and with a similar behavior suggesting that motion regression increases tSNR and combining motion regression with WM/CSF regression results in highest increase in tSNR (**Figure 6**). This observation is supported by repeated-measures ANOVA analyses for both BOLD and 3D GRASE pCASL sequences: $F_{(4,\ 9)BOLD-S} = 7.5$, $p < 0.001$, $F_{BOLD-DE} = 21.92$, $p < 5e^{-10}$, $F_{ASL-3D-BS} = 7.78$, $p < 7.5e^{-5}$, whereas there was no significant effect for 2D dual-echo pCASL: $F_{ASL-2D-DE} = 0.73$, $p = 0.58$.

Along with the increase in temporal SNR for 3D GRASE pCASL, global mean CBF was also slightly higher for NRS4&5 than those observed for NRS1-3 [$F_{(4,\ 9)} = 63.36$, $p < 0.00001$]. An opposite effect was observed for 2D dual-echo pCASL where regression of WM/CSF signals (NRS4&5) slightly reduced global mean CBF [$F_{(4,\ 9)} = 3.36$, $p < 0.02$], as shown in **Table 3**.

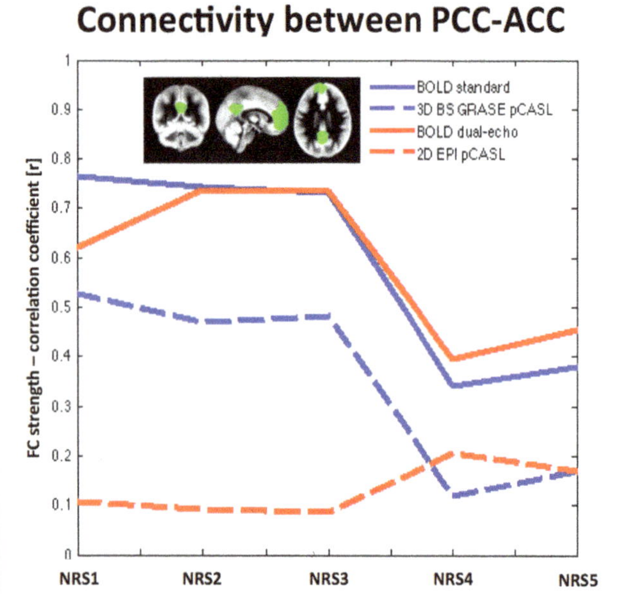

FIGURE 3 | Region-to-Region correlation between two template areas of the DMN: the PCC and the ACC/mPFC (shown in green in the small inlet figure). Overall BOLD exhibits stronger correlation values than ASL. Noise reduction shows similar behavior in FC changes for both BOLD datasets (solid lines) as well as the 3D BS GRASE pCASL data (blue dashed line), while showing little effect for 2D pCASL. A more regionally detailed analysis of these effects is displayed in **Figure 4**.

Results of NRS in Children with ASD vs. TD Children

Within-group

Comparing correlation maps seeded from the PCC revealed differences in long-range connections to the frontal cortex after noise reduction in both groups (TD and ASD children). Specifically, differences between NRS4 and NRS5 revealed increased long-range and decreased local correlations within the DMN, which are in accordance with the general observations of motion-regression effects (**Supplemental Figure 1**). In TD children, we found increased correlation to superior frontal gyri and to the hippocampi, as well as reduced local connectivity in PCC. In ASD children, we observed increased correlations with the orbitofrontal cortex (OFC) and similarly reductions in FC in PCC. Furthermore, we observed increases in anti-correlation to areas associated to other large-scale networks in autism: from PCC to the dorsal ACC, part of salience network, as well as regions of the motor network. Hence, in addition to within network effects (DMN), noise reduction might also increase the separation between networks.

Between-group

Direct comparisons between the TD and ASD groups revealed evidence highlighting the importance of noise reduction (**Figure 7**). While group differences without any noise-reduction (NRS1) showed decreased local FC in the precuneus and increased FC to lateral temporal areas bilaterally in the ASD group as compared to the TD group, group differences after noise regression (NRS4&5) revealed areas with reduced long-range FC from PCC to the dorsal portion of the prefrontal cortex and parahippocampal gyri in the ASD vs. the TD group. The areas showing reduced connectivity with the lateral temporal lobes in the ASD group were no longer evident.

DISCUSSION

FC analysis has become a major tool to assess the functional organization of brain networks as well as their integrity or alterations in clinical populations. However, to be clinically applicable, possible confounding factors for FC analysis need to be identified, understood and accounted for. For BOLD based FC such effects include physiological noise related to pulsatile fluctuations of the blood flow caused by heart beat (Shmueli et al., 2007; Chang et al., 2009) as well as changes in BOLD signal due to variations in rate and depth of respiration (Birn et al., 2006; Birn, 2012). More recently, it has been shown that even slight head movements can affect FC analysis outcomes (Power et al., 2012; Van Dijk et al., 2012).

By using different sets of nuisance variables (here termed Noise Reduction Strategies: NRS) representing noise from physiological noise sources and head movements in two separate BOLD and pCASL implementations, our study showed that accounting for physiological noise and motion-induced effects could indeed alter the connectivity strength and hence spatial maps of the DMN. For BOLD rs-fMRI, these effects have been described and were replicated in our study. For ASL, so far little has been known regarding how noise reduction affects ASL signal and ASL based FC analysis.

Noise Reduction Effects in Bold Based FC

Our findings generally align well with what has been described with regard to noise reduction effects in BOLD based FC analysis. First, regression of physiological noise related nuisance variables from WM and CSF signal fluctuations (Dagli et al., 1999; Windischberger et al., 2002; Birn et al., 2008; Weissenbacher et al., 2009; Jo et al., 2010) reduces connectivity in several brain areas but at the same time increases the spatial specificity of FC maps (Chang and Glover, 2009a; Birn, 2012; Power et al., 2015). The correlation maps generated by NRS4 and NRS5 are highly restricted to areas of the DMN while NRS1–3 display more widespread correlation maps that comprise areas affected by respiratory and heart rate pulsatility (Birn et al., 2008). Statistical comparisons using DCSs further demonstrated that the spatial maps for NRSs including physiological noise regression improved their similarity to the template DMN. A decrease in connectivity strength after removing physiological fluctuations is expected since noise induced spurious correlations are removed from the signal (Weissenbacher et al., 2009). Furthermore, temporal SNR was improved by noise reduction indicating reduced signal variance.

Using head motion nuisance regressors showed less pronounced effects. For conventional BOLD and dual-echo BOLD, frontal regions showed a trend of FC increases between NRS4 and NRS5 as well as FC decreases in the medial posterior cortex and PCC. Significant increases were only observed in ACC for the conventional BOLD dataset and the right angular gyrus for dual-echo BOLD (**Table 2**). However, the data overall

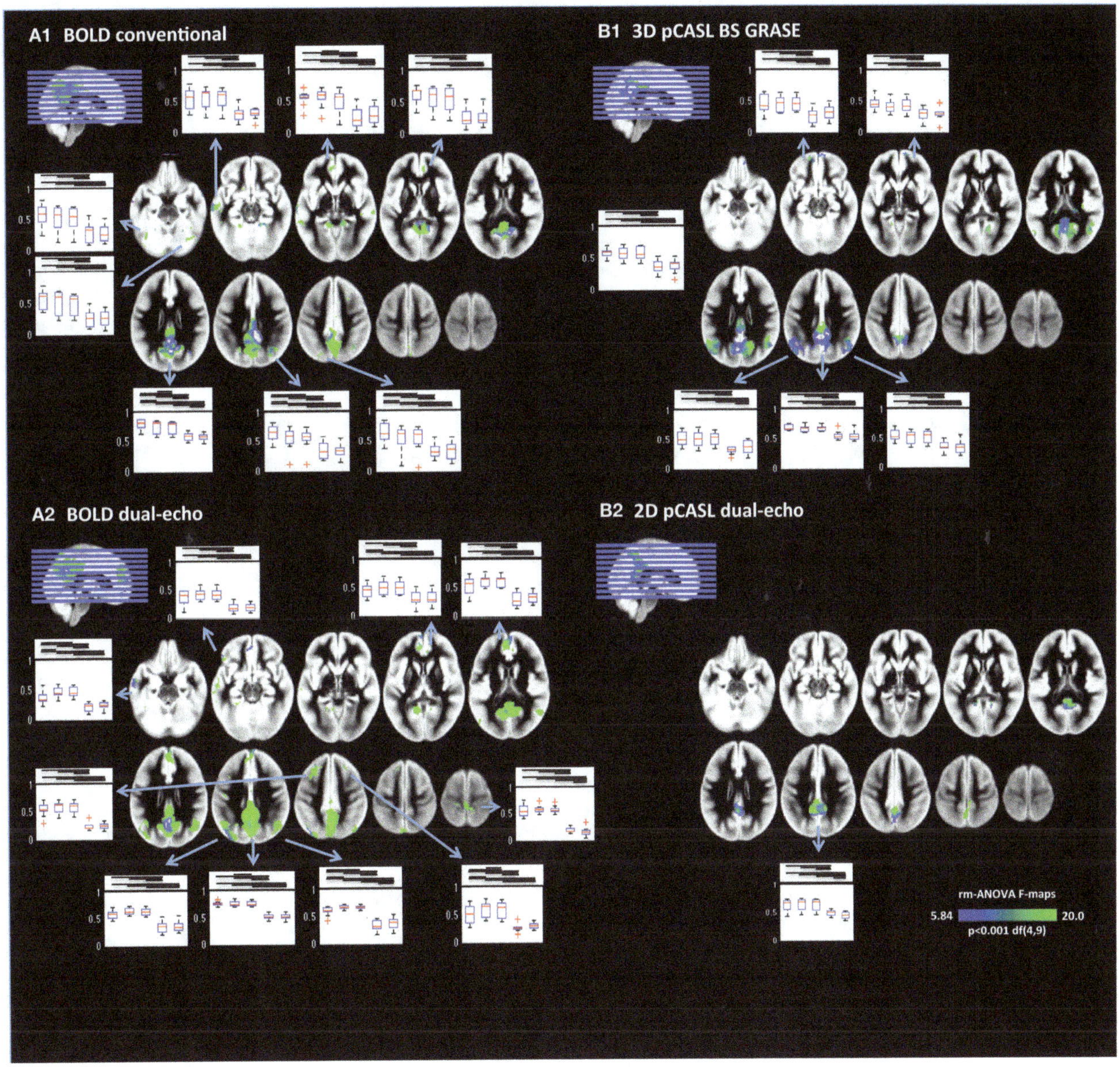

FIGURE 4 | Voxel-wise repeated-measures ANOVA F-maps highlighting the areas with significant FC changes after NRS. Results are limited to areas within the DMNs as displayed in **Figure 1**. Box plots display the regional FC values for NRS1–5. Generally physiological noise reduction (WM and CSF fluctuations) reduced FC significantly (bars above box plots indicate significance between NRS-FC values). Motion correction had more subtle effects on FC but nevertheless significant increases can be seen in several areas mainly in the frontal cortex.

suggest that reduction of head movement related signals improves FC strength between anterior and posterior areas. This effect has attracted wide interest in recent years since the head movement effects are subtle and can cause group differences between cohorts with different movement profiles (e.g., patient populations or children Van Dijk et al., 2010; Satterthwaite et al., 2012). Notably, in this study, there were no head movement differences within the neurotypical adult groups nor between the ASD and TD groups as evidenced by mean framewise displacement. Moreover, the spatial extent of DMN and regional effects of NRS onto FC within the DMN were compared within datasets separately (except for the between-group comparison of ASD vs. TD discussed below). Our participants further showed only small amount of motion hence changes were expected to be subtle. In a further analysis, we segregated the cortex into 264 regions and computed the distance dependence of FC due to reduction of head motion effects. This confirmed that long-range connections show proportionally larger increase in FC than connections between more proximal areas. This finding is in line with prior evidence that motion affects long- and short-range connections differently (Power et al., 2012, 2014; Van Dijk et al., 2012). Comparing our linear fitting results to recent work by Power et al. (2012, 2015) confirms that the distance dependency effects are in the same order of magnitude.

TABLE 2 | Clusters showing a change in functional connectivity across noise reduction strategies (NRS).

	Cluster size	Peak MNI coordinate			peak F	Anatomical area	BA	rm-ANOVA		Effects of motion regression	
Cluster	#voxels	*x*	*y*	*z*				$F_{(4, 9)}$	*P*	*Post-hoc t*-test NRS5-NRS4	*p*
3D BOLD											
1	91	34.0	−70.1	−23.9	47.3898	Fusiform_R	19	6.02	8.10E-04	−0.40	0.6996
2	329	−52.0	−14.1	−9.9	61.1242	Temporal_Mid_L	21	4.45	0.005	−0.01	0.9912
3	5290	0.0	−60.1	56.1	97.9045	Precuneus/posterior cingulate	(7/31)	15.95	1.34E-07	−1.20	0.2598
4	54	−18.0	−44.1	−11.9	38.5708	Fusiform_L	19	13.77	6.60E-07	−1.22	0.2534
5	53	−6.0	41.9	2.1	29.5438	Cingulum_Ant_L	32/10	4.03	0.0084	2.42	0.0386*
6	52	10.0	43.9	8.1	46.4137	Cingulum_Ant_R	32	11.14	5.56E-06	0.08	0.9390
7	259	28.0	−76.1	40.1	28.0085	Occipital_Sup_R	19	7.67	1.41E-04	−0.59	0.5716
8	86	−20.0	−62.1	38.1	42.1778	Parietal_Sup_L	7	4.37	0.0055	−0.72	0.4925
3D ASL											
1	129	14.0	63.9	6.1	23.8028	Frontal_Sup_Medial_R	(11/10)	6.67	4.03E-04	0.54	0.6032
2	184	−10.0	45.9	−3.9	44.5863	Cingulum_Ant_L	32	6.29	6.03E-04	3.34	0.0087*
3	4003	4.0	−44.1	46.1	37.23	Precuneus/posterior cingulate	7,31	3.17	0.0248	−0.61	0.5562
4	864	50.0	−46.1	28.1	28.0536	SupraMarginal_R	39	11.67	3.55E-06	0.11	0.9122
5	70	28.0	−34.1	12.1	33.0022	sub lobar		4.31	0.0059	−0.05	0.9604
6	1338	−56.0	−54.1	28.1	27.4496	SupraMarginal_L	39	6.06	7.78E-04	2.00	0.0770
2D BOLD											
1	333	−60.0	−24.1	−5.9	40.2981	Temporal_Mid_L	21	0.86	0.499	1.35	0.2113
2	81	−46.0	25.9	−9.9	50.8921	Frontal_Inf_Orb_L	47	4.32	0.0059	0.13	0.8987
3	91	−6.0	43.9	−3.9	19.2798	Cingulum_Ant_L	10.11	2.27	0.0805	0.59	0.5717
4	5609	4.0	−28.1	44.1	243.5297	Cingulum_Mid_R	31	0.85	0.5048	−1.46	0.1791
5	975	8.0	31.9	24.1	85.5258	Cingulum_Ant_R	10,32,9	2.74	0.0435	1.56	0.1521
6	833	48.0	−56.1	40.1	97.0885	Angular_R	39	2.97	0.0321	2.64	0.0268*
7	1014	−40.0	−54.1	34.1	66.9547	Angular_L	19,39	2.91	0.0347	0.99	0.3491
8	314	−22.0	15.9	44.1	251.0319	Frontal_Mid_L	8	4.41	0.0053	−0.15	0.8875
9	74	26.0	23.9	52.1	55.824	Frontal_Sup_R	8	3.12	0.0265	2.03	0.0735
10	188	8.0	−44.1	64.1	154.553	Paracentral_Lobule_R	6	0.49	0.745	−2.46	0.0363*
2D ASL											
1	2273	4.0	−36.1	58.1	72.8902	Posterior Cingulate	31,7	6.14	7.11E-04	−3.26	0.0099*

*Listed are cluster coordinates, size, and anatomical location as well as statistical test results for repeated measures ANOVA and post-hoc T-test between NRS5 vs. NRS4 (FC changes due to motion regression). *Indicate significant differences between NRS5 vs NRS4.*

TABLE 3 | Mean global CBF for both pCASL sequences and all NRSs.

Global CBF [ml/100g/min]	NRS1	NRS2	NRS3	NRS4	NRS5
2D EPI pCASL	59.66 ± 11.45	59.79 ± 11.45	59.79 ± 11.45	58.21 ± 9.77	58.17 ± 9.88
3D BS GRASE pCASL	59.99 ± 9.70	59.98 ± 9.68	59.99 ± 9.69	64.37 ± 10.78	64.37 ± 10.78

No differences were observed.

In summary, in both BOLD datasets the observed effects of noise reduction are in agreement with previous work, highlighting the importance of taking into account the effect of physiological and motion related confounds in FC analyses.

Noise Reduction Effects in ASL based FC

ASL based FC has recently gained interest in the research community (Chuang et al., 2008; Zou et al., 2009; Viviani et al., 2011; Jann et al., 2013; Dai et al., 2015; Jann et al., 2015a, for recent review see Chen et al., 2015) and in clinical studies (Orosz et al., 2012; Kindler et al., 2013; Jann et al., 2015b), since it provides not only assessments of functional brain networks but also a surrogate measure of metabolism, cerebral blood flow (CBF). Moreover, there appears to be a relation between connectivity strength and local CBF suggesting that increased connectivity of a region is more energy demanding (Liang et al., 2013; Tomasi et al., 2013; Jann et al., 2015a). While the feasibility of ASL based FC and the similarity of the identified networks to BOLD networks has been previously demonstrated (Chuang et al., 2008; Zou et al., 2009; Viviani et al., 2011; Jann et al., 2013, 2015a; Dai et al., 2015), it remains unknown how noise regression in ASL could benefit these analyses. Our results show that 3D GRASE pCASL with background suppression (BS) benefits from noise reduction as temporal SNR (tSNR) significantly increases in a similar manner as for BOLD (**Figure 6**). For 2D pCASL without BS there was a minor gain in tSNR (Wang et al., 2008; Wang, 2012) although this did not reach significance. Furthermore, we observed that 3D BS GRASE pCASL offers a four-times higher

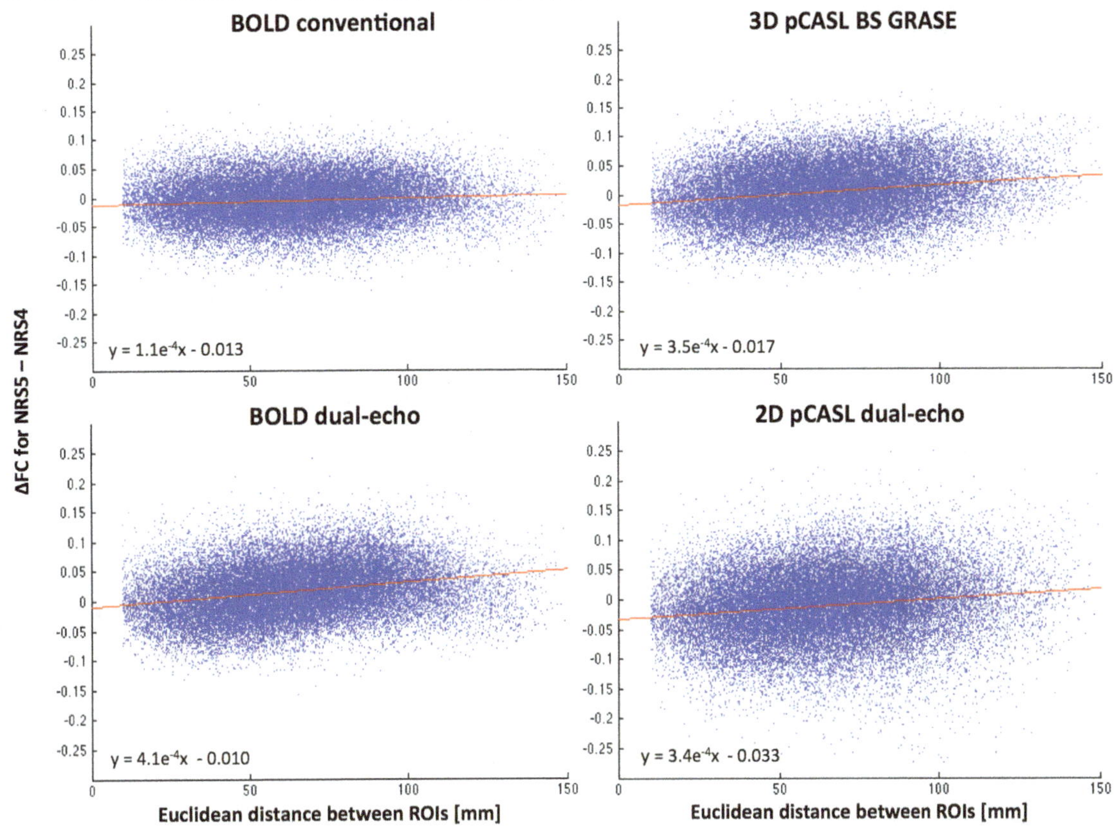

FIGURE 5 | Distance dependence of FC changes between NRS4 and NRS5 (indicating motion correction effects only, after correction for physiological noise). Scatter plots reveal that FC between more distant areas is increased more than for proximal areas. Red lines represent the linear fit between distance and ΔFC (see also equations).

tSNR than that of 2D pCASL. This higher tSNR across all NRSs can mainly be attributed to the background suppression (brain tissue signal suppressed by 85%), while the 3D readout mainly contributes to improved spatial SNR (Vidorreta et al., 2013; Chen et al., 2015; Wang et al., 2015). Based on tSNR measurements, 3D BS GRASE pCASL should be more suitable for CBF based FC analyses than 2D pCASL without BS.

The FC analysis on the CBF datasets demonstrated that the DMN can be detected in both pCASL implementations, albeit with less statistical power in the 2D pCASL due to lower tSNR and/or small sample size of this study. Removing WM and CSF fluctuations to minimize cardiac and respiration related noise prior to FC analysis resulted in reduced FC between PCC and ACC in the ROI based analysis for 3D BS GRASE pCASL whereas no significant effect was found for 2D pCASL. Notably, at the selected statistical threshold, 2D dual-echo pCASL did not show significant correlations between CBF signals in the seed area in the PCC and the anterior part of the DMN (i.e., the mPFC/ACC). It remains to be determined whether using larger samples or lower statistical thresholds will make 2D ASL based FC analysis feasible. Furthermore, as discussed above, the BOLD images acquired at the second echo of the dual echo ASL sequence used in our study showed highly similar network maps, correlation strength and behavior to NRS as the conventional BOLD sequence. On the other hand, the FC strength decrease between PCC and the frontal ROI in 3D BS GRASE pCASL mirrors the effects observed for BOLD. Not surprisingly, the CBF-FC was generally lower than that of BOLD in both ASL implementations, in agreement with other studies comparing ASL and BOLD FC (Viviani et al., 2011; Jann et al., 2015a). This globally decreased FC strength is a consequence of intrinsically lower tSNR in ASL and due to the subtraction of label and control images that generates shorter timeseries for FC analysis in CBF data. However, while FC strength is lower, comparison of the spatial maps using DSC analysis revealed that the DMNs were similar between CBF and BOLD datasets. Similar to BOLD rs-fMRI, physiological noise reduction by using WM and CSF derived nuisance variables in 3D BS GRASE pCASL also resulted in improved spatial specificity when compared to a template DMN. Including head movement related nuisance variables into the preprocessing pipeline resulted in slight improvements of FC in anterior-posterior connections in 3D BS GRASE pCASL. This effect again was similar to the effect observed in the BOLD data (Van Dijk et al., 2010, 2012; Power et al., 2012, 2015). The voxel-wise repeated-measures ANOVA across NRSs confirmed the template-ROI based analyses between PCC and frontal areas and revealed additional areas in the inferior parietal lobes (IPL) where noise reduction had effects on FC. Voxel-wise maps were dominated by effects from physiological noise reduction that generally reduced FC in all DMN areas. Furthermore, the two

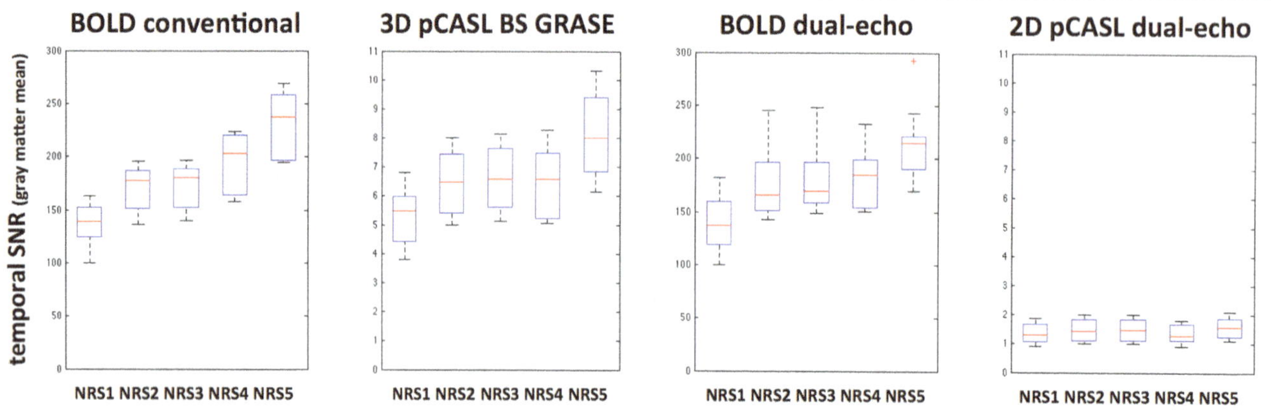

FIGURE 6 | Boxplots indicating tSNR increases after different noise reduction strategies (NRS1–5) in all analyzed MRI sequences. Significant effects were found for all but the 2D dual-echo pCASL datasets.

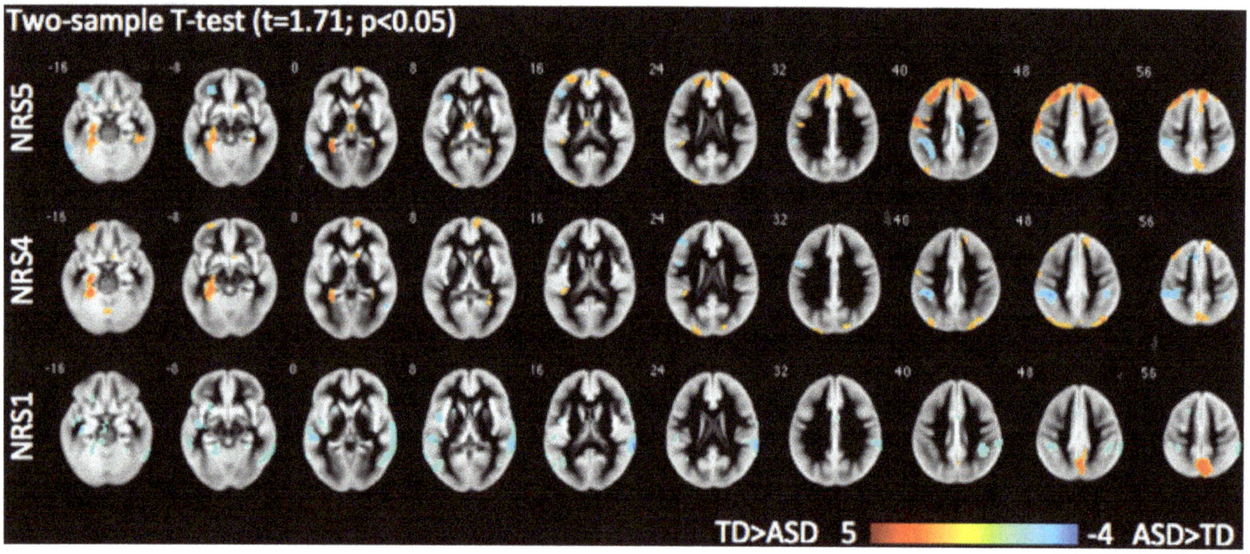

FIGURE 7 | Group differences between typically developing (TD) children and children with autism spectrum disorder (ASD) for different NRS in 3D BS GRASE pCASL data: NRS1 no noise reduction, NRS4 WM/CSF fluctuations removed, NRS5 WM/CSF and motion regression. While seed based FC (from PCC) in NRS1 did not reveal differences in frontal areas, NRS5 clearly delineates reduced long-range connections in ASD compared to TD.

frontal areas in 3D BS GRASE pCASL showed an increase in FC after motion correction although only the right mPFC ROI reached significance (**Figure 4B1**). The IPLs showed minor increases in FC whereas the PCC exhibited a minor reduction of local FC (**Table 1**). In 2D pCASL only the PCC was above the threshold for defining the DMN (compared to **Figure 1**). It showed significant decrease of local connectivity strength following motion regression in addition to physiological noise removal, and thus results are in agreement with the general observations of this study.

Finally, the whole brain parcellated connectivity analysis showed a similar motion related distance dependence of FC changes (**Figure 5**), with effects more pronounced for long-range than short-range connections. Notably, since this analysis was not limited to the DMN areas, the effect was observed in both the 3D BS GRASE and 2D dual-echo pCASL datasets. This suggests that although 2D pCASL shows low connectivity overall, on a less stringent threshold for connectivity results, it could still benefit from motion regression prior to FC analysis in the same fashion as the other datasets.

In summary, 3D BS GRASE pCASL revealed similar DMN maps at the same statistical threshold as BOLD, albeit with generally reduced FC strength. Moreover, 3D BS GRASE pCASL displayed similar FC changes as a function of different sets of nuisance variables used in the preprocessing, showing improved spatial specificity after physiological noise reduction and improved long-range connectivity with motion correction. In contrast, 2D dual-echo pCASL showed weak connectivity overall, which did not survive the same statistical threshold set for this study. This is most likely a problem of low tSNR for this

ASL implementation that has no background suppression or the small sample size.

Results for Clinical Cohort: Children with ASD vs. Matched TD Children

In both ASD and TD groups, motion regression reduced local connectivity in posterior DMN areas while it significantly increased connectivity with superior frontal areas in the TD group and with orbitofrontal areas in the ASD group. Furthermore, in ASD we observed an increased anti-correlation between PCC and areas of the anterior salience network as well as areas of the somatomotor network. This suggests that noise reduction might affect not only within network effects (DMN), it may also benefit the separation between functional networks in autism. These alterations in FC due to noise reduction were also observed in direct group comparisons, leading to marked changes in observed group differences, both in terms of hyper- and hypoconnectivity. While all NRS (NRS 1,4,5) yielded altered connectivity in somatomotor network in ASD, NRS4&5 revealed reduced long-range FC from PCC to the dorsal portion of the prefrontal cortex and parahippocampal gyri, with suppression of hyperconnectivity with lateral-temporal areas. Overall, noise reduction altered the pattern of temporal lobe hyperconnectivity highlighting instead long-range hypoconnections to frontal areas and the medial temporal lobes (i.e., parahippocampal gyri). Similar motion related effects on FC were found in a study using independent component analysis to identify BOLD-DMN subnetworks in ASD (Starck et al., 2013). They reported that after accounting for motion effects, group differences between posterior and anterior DMN subnetworks, as well as in a ventral subnetwork including the parahippocampal gyrus were accentuated. Moreover, altered connectivity from PCC to superior frontal and the parahippocampal gyri in ASD have also been related to deficits in social functioning (Monk et al., 2009; Weng et al., 2010).

Recently, an anterior-posterior gradient of hyper- and hypoconnectivity received considerable attention in neuroimaging studies of ASD (Keown et al., 2013; Rudie and Dapretto, 2013; Di Martino et al., 2014) and is discussed in the context of improved selective cognitive abilities (local hyperconnectivity) and impaired social functioning (long-range hypoconnectivity between frontal and posterior cortices) (Jann et al., 2015b).

CONCLUSION

Noise reduction affected FC analysis from a seed in the PCC to other brain areas of the DMN in all datasets (BOLD and pCASL). First, changes in FC strength and spatial maps of the DMN with regard to physiological nuisance variables (WM/CSF signals) and head movement related nuisance variables were replicated in two separate BOLD datasets, one with a conventional EPI implementation and another based on data acquired in a 2D dual-echo pCASL sequence. Second, analysis of NRS effects on FC analysis of CBF data demonstrated that 3D BS GRASE pCASL shows similar behavior as that observed for BOLD. The favorable noise properties of 3D BS GRASE pCASL as compared to 2D dual-echo pCASL and the improved tSNR after noise reduction render this pCASL implementation more suitable for CBF based FC analyses showing similar networks (Dai et al., 2015; Jann et al., 2015a) and dependence on noise reduction as BOLD. The dual-echo 2D pCASL used here provides perfusion and BOLD images with optimal contrasts, hence can provide proper BOLD based FC results and quantitative CBF (Zhu et al., 2013). FC analysis on the CBF timeseries of 2D pCASL should be treated with caution due to intrinsically low tSNRin conjunction with small sample size. However, a potential advantage of dual-echo ASL, that was not investigated here, is that the TE dependence of signal relaxation might be utilized to separate BOLD and non-BOLD signals (Kundu et al., 2012, 2013). The sensitivity of 2D pCASL can be improved in the future with optimized background suppression strategies in conjunction with multiband acquisitions (Shao et al., 2016).

Finally, applying the full spectrum of NRS in a cohort of children with ASD and typically developing controls we observed that 3D BS GRASE pCASL based FC analysis yielded results that are in accordance with effects of head motion and group differences between ASD and TD children observed in BOLD-DMNs. These findings underline the complex changes in functional organization in ASD and the impact that different preprocessing steps could have on the research findings (Nair et al., 2014).

AUTHOR CONTRIBUTIONS

KJ designed the experiment, performed the analyses and wrote the manuscript. ER analyzed the data and RS designed the experiment and contributed analysis tools. MD wrote the manuscript. DW conceptualized the study and wrote the manuscript.

ACKNOWLEDGMENTS

This work was supported by grants from NICHD (P50 HD055784), NIMH (1R01- MH080892), 5P50HD055784-07 sub#: 5845, R01-NS081077, R01-EB014922, the Garen and Shari Staglin and the International Mental Health Research Organization. KJ holds a fellowship of the Swiss National Science Foundation (SNF)/Swiss Foundation for Grants in Biology and Medicine (SFGBM) grant no.s142743 and 155345.

SUPPLEMENTARY MATERIAL

Supplemental Table 1 | This table lists all *post-hoc t*-test (after ANOVA) *t* and *p*-values between all NRS in each brain area and for all 4 examined modalities.

Supplemental Figure 1 | Differences in group wise FC seeded from the PCC after motion regression. (A) Connectivity in Children with ASD for NRS4 and NRS5. **(B)** Difference between NRS4 and NRS5 in ASD. **(C)** Connectivity in TD children for NRS4 and NRS5. **(D)** Difference between NRS4 and NRS5 in TD.

REFERENCES

Alsop, D. C., Detre, J. A., Golay, X., Günther, M., Jeroen, H., Hernandez-Garcia, L., et al. (2015). Recommended Implementation of Arterial Spin Labeled Perfusion MRI for clinical applications: a consensus of the ISMRM Perfusion Study Group and the European Consortium for ASL in Dementia. *Magn. Reson. Med.* 73, 102–116. doi: 10.1002/mrm.25197

Birn, R. M. (2012). The role of physiological noise in resting-state functional connectivity. *Neuroimage* 62, 864–870. doi: 10.1016/j.neuroimage.2012.01.016

Birn, R. M., Diamond, J. B., Smith, M. A., and Bandettini, P. A. (2006). Separating respiratory-variation-related fluctuations from neuronal-activity-related fluctuations in fMRI. *Neuroimage* 31, 1536–1548. doi: 10.1016/j.neuroimage.2006.02.048

Birn, R. M., Murphy, K., and Bandettini, P. A. (2008). The effect of respiration variations on independent component analysis results of resting state functional connectivity. *Hum. Brain Mapp.* 29, 740–750. doi: 10.1002/hbm.20577

Chang, C., Cunningham, J. P., and Glover, G. H. (2009). Influence of heart rate on the BOLD signal: the cardiac response function. *Neuroimage* 44, 857–869. doi: 10.1016/j.neuroimage.2008.09.029

Chang, C., and Glover, G. H. (2009a). Effects of model-based physiological noise correction on default mode network anti-correlations and correlations. *Neuroimage* 47, 1448–1459. doi: 10.1016/j.neuroimage.2009.05.012

Chang, C., and Glover, G. H. (2009b). Relationship between respiration, end-tidal CO_2, and BOLD signals in resting-state fMRI. *Neuroimage* 47, 1381–1393. doi: 10.1016/j.neuroimage.2009.04.048

Chen, J. J., Jann, K., and Wang, D. J. (2015). Characterizing resting-state Brain function using Arterial Spin Labeling. *Brain Connect.* 5, 527–542. doi: 10.1089/brain.2015.0344

Chen, Y., Wang, D. J., and Detre, J. A. (2011). Test-retest reliability of arterial spin labeling with common labeling strategies. *J. Magn. Reson. Imaging* 33, 940–949. doi: 10.1002/jmri.22345

Chuang, K. H., van Gelderen, P., Merkle, H., Bodurka, J., Ikonomidou, V. N., Koretsky, A. P., et al. (2008). Mapping resting-state functional connectivity using perfusion MRI. *Neuroimage* 40, 1595–1605. doi: 10.1016/j.neuroimage.2008.01.006

Dagli, M. S., Ingeholm, J. E., and Haxby, J. V. (1999). Localization of cardiac-induced signal change in fMRI. *Neuroimage* 9, 407–415. doi: 10.1006/nimg.1998.0424

Dai, W., Garcia, D., de Bazelaire, C., and Alsop, D. (2008). Continuous flow-driven inversion for arterial spin labeling using pulsed radio frequency and gradient fields. *Magn. Reson. Med.* 60, 1488–1497. doi: 10.1002/mrm.21790

Dai, W., Varma, G., Scheidegger, R., and Alsop, D. C. (2015). Quantifying fluctuations of resting state networks using arterial spin labeling perfusion MRI. *J. Cereb. Blood Flow Metab.* 36, 463–473. doi: 10.1177/0271678X156 15339

Dice, L. R. (1945). Measurment of the amount of ecologic association between species. *Ecology* 26, 297–302. doi: 10.2307/1932409

Di Martino, A., Yan, C. G., Li, Q., Denio, E., Castellanos, F. X., Alaerts, K., et al. (2014). The autism brain imaging data exchange: towards a large-scale evaluation of the intrinsic brain architecture in autism. *Mol. Psychiatry* 19, 659–667. doi: 10.1038/mp.2013.78

Jann, K., Gee, D. G., Kilroy, E., Schwab, S., Cannon, T. D., and Wang, D. J. (2015a). Functional connectivity in BOLD and CBF data: similarity and reliability of Resting Brain Networks. *Neuroimage* 106, 111–122. doi: 10.1016/j.neuroimage.2014.11.028

Jann, K., Hernandez, L. M., Beck-Pancer, D., McCarron, R., Smith, R. X., Dapretto, M., et al. (2015b). Altered resting perfusion and functional connectivity of default mode network in youth with autism spectrum disorder. *Brain Behav.* 5:e00358. doi: 10.1002/brb3.358

Jann, K., Orosz, A., Dierks, T., Wang, D. J., Wiest, R., and Federspiel, A. (2013). Quantification of network perfusion in ASL cerebral blood flow data with seed based and ICA approaches. *Brain Topogr.* 26, 569–580. doi: 10.1007/s10548-013-0280-3

Jo, H. J., Saad, Z. S., Simmons, W. K., Milbury, L. A., and Cox, R. W. (2010). Mapping sources of correlation in resting state FMRI, with artifact detection and removal. *Neuroimage* 52, 571–582. doi: 10.1016/j.neuroimage.2010.04.246

Keown, C. L., Shih, P., Nair, A., Peterson, N., Mulvey, M. E., and Muller, R. A. (2013). Local functional overconnectivity in posterior brain regions is associated with symptom severity in autism spectrum disorders. *Cell Rep.* 5, 567–572. doi: 10.1016/j.celrep.2013.10.003

Kindler, J., Jann, K., Homan, P., Hauf, M., Walther, S., Strik, W., et al. (2013). Static and dynamic characteristics of cerebral blood flow during the resting state in Schizophrenia. *Schizophr. Bull.* 41, 163–170. doi: 10.1093/schbul/sbt180

Kundu, P., Brenowitz, N. D., Voon, V., Worbe, Y., Vertes, P. E., Inati, S. J., et al. (2013). Integrated strategy for improving functional connectivity mapping using multiecho fMRI. *Proc. Natl. Acad. Sci. U.S.A.* 110, 16187–16192. doi: 10.1073/pnas.1301725110

Kundu, P., Inati, S. J., Evans, J. W., Luh, W. M., and Bandettini, P. A. (2012). Differentiating BOLD and non-BOLD signals in fMRI time series using multi-echo EPI. *Neuroimage* 60, 1759–1770. doi: 10.1016/j.neuroimage.2011.12.028

Liang, X. Y., Tournier, J. D., Masterton, R., Connelly, A., and Calamante, F. (2012). A k-space sharing 3D GRASE pseudocontinuous ASL method for whole-brain resting-state functional connectivity. *Int. J. Imaging Syst. Technol.* 22, 37–43. doi: 10.1002/ima.22006

Liang, X., Zou, Q., He, Y., and Yang, Y. (2013). Coupling of functional connectivity and regional cerebral blood flow reveals a physiological basis for network hubs of the human brain. *Proc. Natl. Acad. Sci. U.S.A.* 110, 1929–1934. doi: 10.1073/pnas.1214900110

Lord, C., Risi, S., Lambrecht, L., Cook, E. H. Jr., Leventhal, B. L., DiLavore, P. C., et al. (2000). The autism diagnostic observation schedule-generic: a standard measure of social and communication deficits associated with the spectrum of autism. *J. Autism Dev. Disord.* 30, 205–223. doi: 10.1023/A:1005592401947

Lord, C., Rutter, M., and Le Couteur, A. (1994). Autism Diagnostic Interview-Revised: a revised version of a diagnostic interview for caregivers of individuals with possible pervasive developmental disorders. *J. Autism Dev. Disord.* 24, 659–685. doi: 10.1007/BF02172145

Monk, C. S., Peltier, S. J., Wiggins, J. L., Weng, S. J., Carrasco, M., Risi, S., et al. (2009). Abnormalities of intrinsic functional connectivity in autism spectrum disorders. *Neuroimage* 47, 764–772. doi: 10.1016/j.neuroimage.2009.04.069

Murphy, K., Birn, R. M., and Bandettini, P. A. (2013). Resting-state fMRI confounds and cleanup. *Neuroimage* 80, 349–359. doi: 10.1016/j.neuroimage.2013.04.001

Nair, A., Keown, C. L., Datko, M., Shih, P., Keehn, B., and Muller, R. A. (2014). Impact of methodological variables on functional connectivity findings in autism spectrum disorders. *Hum. Brain Mapp.* 35, 4035–4048. doi: 10.1002/hbm.22456

Orosz, A., Jann, K., Federspiel, A., Horn, H., Hofle, O., Dierks, T., et al. (2012). Reduced cerebral blood flow within the default-mode network and within total gray matter in major depression. *Brain Connect.* 2, 303–310. doi: 10.1089/brain.20 12.0101

Power, J. D., Barnes, K. A., Snyder, A. Z., Schlaggar, B. L., and Petersen, S. E. (2012). Spurious but systematic correlations in functional connectivity MRI networks arise from subject motion. *Neuroimage* 59, 2142–2154. doi: 10.1016/j.neuroimage.2011.10.018

Power, J. D., Mitra, A., Laumann, T. O., Snyder, A. Z., Schlaggar, B. L., and Petersen, S. E. (2014). Methods to detect, characterize, and remove motion artifact in resting state fMRI. *Neuroimage* 84, 32–341. doi: 10.1016/j.neuroimage.2013.08.048

Power, J. D., Schlaggar, B. L., and Petersen, S. E. (2015). Recent progress and outstanding issues in motion correction in resting state fMRI. *Neuroimage* 105, 536–551. doi: 10.1016/j.neuroimage.2014.10.044

Rudie, J. D., and Dapretto, M. (2013). Convergent evidence of brain overconnectivity in children with autism? *Cell Rep.* 5, 565–566. doi: 10.1016/j.celrep.2013.10.043

Satterthwaite, T. D., Wolf, D. H., Loughead, J., Ruparel, K., Elliott, M. A., Hakonarson, H., et al. (2012). Impact of in-scanner head motion on multiple measures of functional connectivity: relevance for studies of neurodevelopment in youth. *Neuroimage* 60, 623–632. doi: 10.1016/j.neuroimage.2011.12.063

Shao, X., Wang, Y., and Wang, D. J. (2016). "A constrained slice-dependent background suppression scheme for simultaneous multi-slice pseudo-continuous arterial spin labeling," in *International Society for Magnetic Resonance in Medicine, Program No 0286* (Singapore).

Shirer, W. R., Ryali, S., Rykhlevskaia, E., Menon, V., and Greicius, M. D. (2012). Decoding subject-driven cognitive states with whole-brain connectivity patterns. *Cereb. Cortex* 22, 158–165. doi: 10.1093/cercor/bhr099

Shmueli, K., van Gelderen, P., de Zwart, J. A., Horovitz, S. G., Fukunaga, M., Jansma, J. M., et al. (2007). Low-frequency fluctuations in the cardiac rate as a source of variance in the resting-state fMRI BOLD signal. *Neuroimage* 38, 306–320. doi: 10.1016/j.neuroimage.2007.07.037

Starck, T., Nikkinen, J., Rahko, J., Remes, J., Hurtig, T., Haapsamo, H., et al. (2013). Resting state fMRI reveals a default mode dissociation between retrosplenial and medial prefrontal subnetworks in ASD despite motion scrubbing. *Front. Hum. Neurosci.* 7:802. doi: 10.3389/fnhum.2013.00802

Tomasi, D., Wang, G. J., and Volkow, N. D. (2013). Energetic cost of brain functional connectivity. *Proc. Natl. Acad. Sci. U.S.A.* 110, 13642–13647. doi: 10.1073/pnas.1303346110

Van Dijk, K. R., Hedden, T., Venkataraman, A., Evans, K. C., Lazar, S. W., and Buckner, R. L. (2010). Intrinsic functional connectivity as a tool for human connectomics: theory, properties, and optimization. *J. Neurophysiol.* 103, 297–321. doi: 10.1152/jn.00783.2009

Van Dijk, K. R., Sabuncu, M. R., and Buckner, R. L. (2012). The influence of head motion on intrinsic functional connectivity MRI. *Neuroimage* 59, 431–438. doi: 10.1016/j.neuroimage.2011.07.044

Vidorreta, M., Wang, Z., Rodriguez, I., Pastor, M. A., Detre, J. A., and Fernandez-Seara, M. A. (2013). Comparison of 2D and 3D single-shot ASL perfusion fMRI sequences. *Neuroimage* 66, 662–671. doi: 10.1016/j.neuroimage.2012.10.087

Viviani, R., Messina, I., and Walter, M. (2011). Resting state functional connectivity in perfusion imaging: correlation maps with BOLD connectivity and resting state perfusion. *PLoS ONE* 6:e27050. doi: 10.1371/journal.pone.0027050

Wang, Y., Moeller, S., Li, X., Vu, A. T., Krasileva, K., Ugurbil, K., et al. (2015). Simultaneous multi-slice Turbo-FLASH imaging with CAIPIRINHA for whole brain distortion-free pseudo-continuous arterial spin labeling at 3 and 7 T. *Neuroimage* 113, 279–288. doi: 10.1016/j.neuroimage.2015.03.060

Wang, Z. (2012). Improving cerebral blood flow quantification for arterial spin labeled perfusion MRI by removing residual motion artifacts and global signal fluctuations. *Magn. Reson. Imaging* 30, 1409–1415. doi: 10.1016/j.mri.2012.05.004

Wang, Z., Aguirre, G. K., Rao, H., Wang, J., Fernandez-Seara, M. A., Childress, A. R., et al. (2008). Empirical optimization of ASL data analysis using an ASL data processing toolbox: *ASLtbx*. *Magn. Reson. Imaging* 26, 261–269. doi: 10.1016/j.mri.2007.07.003

Weissenbacher, A., Kasess, C., Gerstl, F., Lanzenberger, R., Moser, E., and Windischberger, C. (2009). Correlations and anticorrelations in resting-state functional connectivity MRI: a quantitative comparison of preprocessing strategies. *Neuroimage* 47, 1408–1416. doi: 10.1016/j.neuroimage.2009.05.005

Weng, S. J., Wiggins, J. L., Peltier, S. J., Carrasco, M., Risi, S., Lord, C., et al. (2010). Alterations of resting state functional connectivity in the default network in adolescents with autism spectrum disorders. *Brain Res.* 1313, 202–214. doi: 10.1016/j.brainres.2009.11.057

Windischberger, C., Langenberger, H., Sycha, T., Tschernko, E. M., Fuchsjager-Mayerl, G., Schmetterer, L., et al. (2002). On the origin of respiratory artifacts in BOLD-EPI of the human brain. *Magn. Reson. Imaging* 20, 575–582. doi: 10.1016/S0730-725X(02)00563-5

Wise, R. G., Ide, K., Poulin, M. J., and Tracey, I. (2004). Resting fluctuations in arterial carbon dioxide induce significant low frequency variations in BOLD signal. *Neuroimage* 21, 1652–1664. doi: 10.1016/j.neuroimage.2003.11.025

Wu, W.-C., Fernández-Seara, M., Detre, J. A., Wehrli, F. W., and Wang, J. (2007). A theoretical and experimental investigation of the tagging efficiency of pseudocontinuous arterial spin labeling. *Magn. Reson. Med.* 58, 1020–1027. doi: 10.1002/mrm.21403

Zhu, S., Fang, Z., Hu, S., Wang, Z., and Rao, H. (2013). Resting state brain function analysis using concurrent BOLD in ASL perfusion fMRI. *PLoS ONE* 8:e65884. doi: 10.1371/journal.pone.0065884

Zou, Q., Wu, C. W., Stein, E. A., Zang, Y., and Yang, Y. (2009). Static and dynamic characteristics of cerebral blood flow during the resting state. *Neuroimage* 48, 515–524. doi: 10.1016/j.neuroimage.2009.07.006

15

Aberrant Development of Speech Processing in Young Children with Autism: New Insights from Neuroimaging Biomarkers

Holger F. Sperdin[1]* *and Marie Schaer*[1,2]

[1] *Office Médico-Pédagogique, Department of Psychiatry, University of Geneva School of Medicine, Geneva, Switzerland,*
[2] *Stanford Cognitive & Systems Neuroscience Laboratory, Stanford University School of Medicine, Palo Alto, CA, USA*

Edited by:
Roma Siugzdaite,
Ghent University, Belgium

Reviewed by:
Nandini Chatterjee Singh,
National Brain Research Centre, India
Bart Boets,
KU Leuven, Belgium

***Correspondence:**
Holger F. Sperdin
holger.sperdin@unige.ch

From the time of birth, a newborn is continuously exposed and naturally attracted to human voices, and as he grows, he becomes increasingly responsive to these speech stimuli, which are strong drivers for his language development and knowledge acquisition about the world. In contrast, young children with autism spectrum disorder (ASD) are often insensitive to human voices, failing to orient and respond to them. Failure to attend to speech in turn results in altered development of language and social-communication skills. Here, we review the critical role of orienting to speech in ASD, as well as the neural substrates of human voice processing. Recent functional neuroimaging and electroencephalography studies demonstrate that aberrant voice processing could be a promising marker to identify ASD very early on. With the advent of refined brain imaging methods, coupled with the possibility of screening infants and toddlers, predictive brain function biomarkers are actively being examined and are starting to emerge. Their timely identification might not only help to differentiate between phenotypes, but also guide the clinicians in setting up appropriate therapies, and better predicting or quantifying long-term outcome.

Keywords: ASD, MRI, EEG, language development, voice, auditory processing, toddler, infant

INTRODUCTION

Autism, a term initially introduced by Kanner (1943) and almost at the same period by Asperger (1944), is a pervasive disorder of neurodevelopment with an early onset. According to the most recent census, autism affects up to 1 in 68 children (1.5%) in the United States (Baio, 2014). ASD is characterized by impairments in core areas of cognitive and adaptive function, social interactions, and communication (American Psychiatric Association and American Psychiatric Association. Dsm-5 Task Force, 2013). Individuals with ASD show a reduced interest in socially relevant stimuli (McPartland et al., 2011; Pelphrey et al., 2011; Chevallier et al., 2012; Kohls et al., 2012), tend to avoid eye-contact with their immediate surrounding (Senju and Johnson, 2009; Elsabbagh et al., 2012; Jones and Klin, 2013), and show repetitive behaviors and restricted interests (Turner, 1999; Watt et al., 2008; Arnott et al., 2010). Moreover, affected children often present language delay, with deficits in expressive and receptive language skills (Hudry et al., 2010; Eigsti et al., 2011; Mody et al., 2013; Simms and Jin, 2015). Multiple causes are implicated in autism and recent accounts indicate the presence of abnormal development occurring at the cellular and molecular levels during prenatal life (Stoner et al., 2014; Baron-Cohen et al., 2015), with a clear impact of genetic, neurobiological, environmental factors, and combinations thereof (Geschwind and Levitt, 2007; Abrahams and Geschwind, 2010; Betancur, 2011; Zhubi et al., 2014; Robinson et al., 2015). One of the core domains that is particularly impaired and that constitutes a hallmark feature in autism is language. Behaviorally, children with autism do not orient naturally to vocal stimuli as typically developing (TD) children do (Dawson et al., 2004; Kuhl et al., 2005). They often show a reduced sensitivity to human voices, but are responsive to other non-vocal stimuli (Klin, 1991, 1992). This would suggest that the neural mechanisms underlying the orientation to voices and their processing might not develop in the same way as in TD individuals. Currently, the exact time when the developmental trajectory of the brain systems implicated in human voice processing starts to deviate from a normal path is unknown, but recent neuroimaging results that we discuss below suggest the presence of differences already from the age of 2 years (e.g., Lombardo et al., 2015).

Neuroimaging provides an excellent window to better understand the neural bases of speech and language abnormalities in young children with ASD. Differences in brain anatomy have been investigated using structural magnetic resonance imaging (MRI); patterns of changes to structural connectivity have been examined using diffusion tensor imaging (DTI); changes in cortical activity measured using functional MRI (fMRI); and altered spatio-temporal brain dynamics quantified using high-density electroencephalography (EEG). Despite the fact that all these techniques are non-invasive, their use in children involves numerous challenges (de Bie et al., 2010; Raschle et al., 2012). Perhaps the most noteworthy of these challenges is the requirement for the child to remain still for extended periods of time, otherwise creating difficulties for placing the electrode caps on a young child's head in EEG experiments, or leading to movement artifacts in MRI acquisitions. Nonetheless, recent years have seen practical and methodological advancements, which tremendously improved the feasibility of neuroimaging research studies in young children (in particular in the MRI field). For example, mock MRI scanning facilities are increasingly used to prepare preschoolers and school-aged children for a successful real MRI acquisition (Cantlon et al., 2006; Epstein et al., 2007; de Bie et al., 2010; Nordahl et al., 2016). Although initial studies of infants and toddlers used anesthesia or mild sedation (e.g., Boddaert et al., 2004a; Fransson et al., 2007), protocols for obtaining MRI acquisitions during natural sleep have been proposed for young children with ASD (e.g., Nordahl et al., 2008; Ortiz-Mantilla et al., 2010; Eyler et al., 2012; Shen et al., 2013; Lombardo et al., 2015). Scanning during natural sleep allows to study at the functional and structural levels how the brain systems implicated in human speech and language processing are developing in very young infants and toddlers and to detect early biomarkers for ASD. We will discuss how these recent neuroimaging studies performed in very young children with ASD or at risk have begun to reveal impairments at multiple levels in the brain systems implicated in speech and language processing.

In EEG, the experiments are generally performed during wakefulness (see **Figure 1**; e.g., Boersma et al., 2013; Kuhl et al., 2013; Seery et al., 2013, 2014). The EEG field has also seen recent methodological advancement. Modern electrical source estimations of high density EEG now reach an approximation in the whole brain of the 3-D distribution of the neuronal activity at each moment in time (Michel et al., 2004; Brunet et al., 2011; Michel and Murray, 2012; Custo et al., 2014) and have been shown to represent stable and reliable estimates when compared with intracranial recordings, lesions and animal studies and other neuroimaging methods (Pittau et al., 2014 for review). For this reason, EEG studies of infants at risk and toddlers with ASD should provide source estimations when possible as they may add valuable information regarding how they differ in their early brain development compared to their TD peers. Improving the precision of source localization by using individual MRI scans of infants/toddlers or age-appropriate template MRIs is also possible. Their estimation in normally and abnormally developing infants/toddlers (or those at risk) can subsequently be compared with results from available fMRI experiments. This is important as most fMRI experiments are currently being performed in a sleep state while EEG experiments are mostly being conducted in awake participants. Finally, compared to the EEG experiments using a traditional voltage waveform analysis approach and that will be reviewed here, electrical neuroimaging methods are reference-independent and take into account the additional information of multichannel electrodes recordings. As such, they avoid the traditional statistical pitfalls inherent to traditional voltage waveform analysis (see Murray et al., 2008 for discussion). So-called "microstate" analyses are also available, allowing to identify dominant state topographies in spontaneous EEG recordings acquired in young infants and toddlers with ASD (Koenig et al., 2002; Lehmann and Michel, 2011). These methods have been successfully applied on EEG

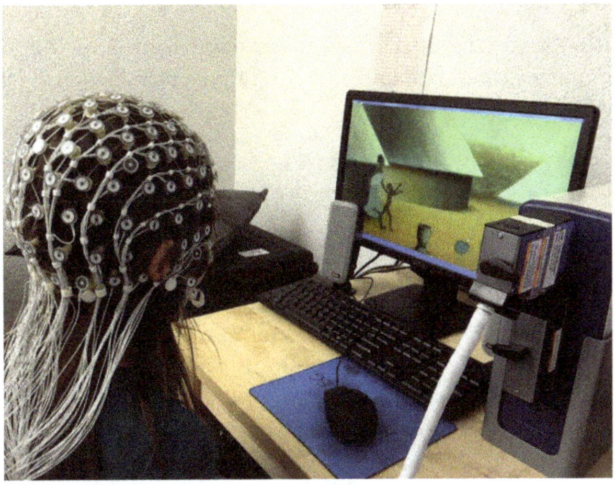

FIGURE 1 | Example of an EEG set-up with a young child. A video is displayed on a standard screen, and the child is wearing a 129 electrodes cap. Sounds are displayed via external speakers.

data acquired in clinical population of children and young adolescents (Rihs et al., 2013; Berchio et al., 2014; Tomescu et al., 2014) and could be used to examine the developmental trajectories of infants/toddlers with ASD and infants at risk for autism.

While other reviews of auditory and speech processing impairments have been published focusing on older children and adults (e.g., Haesen et al., 2011; Kujala et al., 2013), here, we provide an overview of some of the most recent neuroimaging experiments (primarily fMRI and EEG) of very young children (before 4 years of age) with ASD investigating impairments in the brain systems implicated in human vocalizations and henceforth speech and language processing (e.g., Kuhl et al., 2013; Lombardo et al., 2015) and in at-risk populations (before the age of 2) to identify early endophenotypes (Seery et al., 2013, 2014; Blasi et al., 2015). We will principally review recent experiments that have used voice related auditory stimuli (e.g., sentences, words, syllables). After a brief description of the language development in the typically developing individual during the first year, we will summarize part of the clinical body of evidence pointing to altered speech and language development in very young children with ASD and in infants at high-risk for ASD. Afterwards, we describe the neural systems within the superior temporal cortical regions implicated in human voice processing and their development in the TD brain and present functional evidence in adults and young adolescents indicating the presence of an aberrant form of voice processing. Next we focus on the cross-sectional studies using fMRI and EEG which were conducted at specific time points during infancy/toddlerhood. They address group differences in early speech and language-related processing within these voice areas within superior temporal cortical regions along other language related brain neural systems. The results thereof indicate the presence of structural, functional, and connectivity group differences being already present in infancy and/or toddlerhood. We finally highlight recent results from the few existing prospective fMRI and EEG studies which employed a longitudinal design and demonstrated by using voice related auditory stimuli that aberrant voice processing is not only a feature present in older children and adults with ASD but also a promising candidate to identify ASD very early on during the development.

LANGUAGE DEVELOPMENT IN TYPICALLY DEVELOPING INDIVIDUALS

The different steps involved in early speech perception and production have been extensively examined (see **Figure 2**; Kuhl, 2004, 2010 for reviews). TD newborns are rapidly attracted by human voices within the first days of life (Cheng et al., 2012). At 1 month of age, they are already responsive to speech sounds (Eimas et al., 1971). Language-related brain areas are activated in response to human speech sounds to some extent in 3 month old infants, well before the onset of speech production (Dehaene-Lambertz et al., 2002, 2006), while cerebral specialization for the human voice over other sounds emerges over the first 6 months of life (Minagawa-Kawai et al., 2011; Lloyd-Fox et al., 2012). By 4 months, infants know that speech conveys information that relate words to physical objects (Marno et al., 2015). Around 5 months, they can recognize the sound patterns of their own name, and between 6 and 9 months they are capable of correctly directing their gaze to named pictures suggesting the presence of some form of word comprehension (Mandel et al., 1995; Tincoff and Jusczyk, 1999, 2012; Bergelson and Swingley, 2012). With respect to pre-linguistic production skills, between 0 and 2 months, newborns first produce vegetative vocalizations (non-speech sounds such as burps, coughs, and cries). At 3 months, infants start to produce vowel-like sounds followed by the onset around 6 months of a babbling phase that becomes robust by 10 months of age. Canonical babbling is a precursor to the emergence of the first words production, which are generally produced by the end of the first year. During the first year of the infant's development and the following years into toddlerhood, the human voice is a natural driver for the infant's language skills development.

LANGUAGE DEVELOPMENT IN TODDLERS WITH ASD AND INFANTS AT RISK

In individuals with autism, the degree of impairment and delay in language greatly varies from one person to another, with a tremendous heterogeneity in early language development and later clinical outcomes (Mitchell et al., 2006; Geurts and Embrechts, 2008; Luyster et al., 2008; Tager-Flusberg et al., 2009; Lenroot and Yeung, 2013; Lord et al., 2015). Some toddlers present substantial delay or deficits while others have a typical early language development or mild delay and catch up. The former are children that often show the most severe and pertaining symptoms in the long term, compared to those with relatively preserved language abilities (Fein et al., 2013; Kasari et al., 2013; Tager-Flusberg and Kasari, 2013). Converging clinical estimates indicate that more than half of the children with ASD will have persisting language impairments throughout their lifespan (e.g., Anderson et al., 2007; Pickles et al., 2014). So far, the heterogeneity of early language development and the neurodevelopmental basis for this variability in clinical outcomes are not fully understood. In this review, we also discuss how neuroimaging studies examining the neural bases of early human speech and language impairments in autism have started to be used to predict outcome in affected children.

In toddlers with ASD, language difficulties are often present both when they are spoken to (i.e., receptive language) and when they express themselves (i.e., expressive language; Hudry et al., 2010; Simms and Jin, 2015). Indeed, parents of children diagnosed with ASD often sought medical advice because of strong concerns related to language development (Dahlgren and Gillberg, 1989; De Giacomo and Fombonne, 1998; Wetherby et al., 2004; Herlihy et al., 2015). Retrospective interviews with the families, analysis of retrospective video birthday tapes recorded at 12 months of age of children diagnosed with ASD, as well as prospective accounts of infants at risk often report an unresponsiveness to name and a general lack of

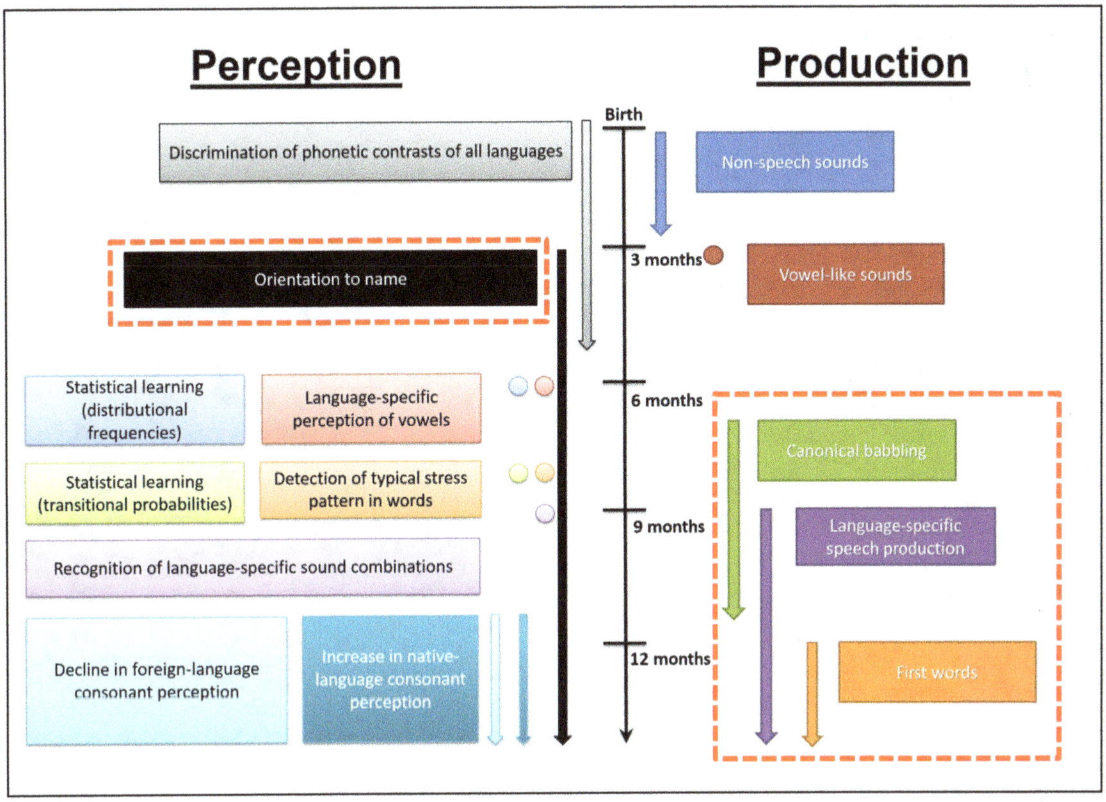

FIGURE 2 | Illustration of the changes occurring in speech perception and production in typically developing human infants during their first year of life (adapted from Kuhl, 2004). Red dashed rectangles indicate early expressive and receptive language delays/impairments (that is, unresponsiveness to name, delayed canonical babbling, increased non-speech productions, decreased speech-like vocalization, delayed occurrence of the first words) known to be sensitive indicators of an increased risk for later being diagnosed with ASD

orientation to human voices (Osterling and Dawson, 1994; Baranek, 1999; Yirmiya et al., 2006; Nadig et al., 2007; Oner et al., 2014; Stenberg et al., 2014). In sum, a large body of clinical studies to date point to expressive and receptive language deficits already in the first year of life for young children who will subsequently develop ASD during toddlerhood, suggesting that the neural systems responsible for orienting to and processing human vocalizations are altered very early on.

Infants at risk for autism are increasingly studied prospectively, to measure whether the abilities to understand language described above are already altered in infants who will develop autism later on. Siblings of a child with ASD have a very high risk to develop ASD, ~20 times higher compared to infants with no family history of ASD (Rogers, 2009; Ozonoff et al., 2011). In a context where early intensive non-pharmacological interventions are critical to improve the long term outcome of affected individuals (Dawson, 2008; Dawson et al., 2010; Klintwall et al., 2013), it is instrumental to detect ASD as early as possible, (see also Schaer et al., 2014 for a review). As such, studies of high-risk infants allow to map the early developmental trajectories of infants who will develop ASD, and to highlight endophenotypes of ASD (Viding and Blakemore, 2007). Numerous studies of high-risk infants focused on early language development as delays in communication and language development become apparent early in life, even before the first year or shortly thereafter. Differences in vocal production (such as consonant inventory, presence of canonical syllables, and non-speech vocalizations), between low-risk and high-risk infants between 9 and 12 months has been associated with later outcomes at 24 months (Paul et al., 2011; Jones et al., 2014 for review). Another prospective study of infants at risk tested at target ages 6, 14, and 24 months and who were followed up and diagnosed with ASD at 24 months indicates that language delays or deficits are already observable at around 14 months of age (Landa and Garrett-Mayer, 2006). A recent retrospective study of toddlers with ASD reported low rates of canonical babbling and vocalization frequency between 9 and 12 months and 15–18 month compared to age-matched TD peers, several months before a diagnosis of ASD was made (Patten et al., 2014). As a result, a delay or deficit in language development very early on has become integral part of the red flags indicating a greater susceptibility for developing autism (Barbaro and Dissanayake, 2009; Zwaigenbaum et al., 2013; see **Figure 2**, red dashed rectangles).

THE VOICE AS A UNIQUE AUDITORY STIMULUS IN THE TYPICALLY DEVELOPING BRAIN

The human voice is clearly one of the most salient and important auditory stimuli in our acoustic environment. It conveys both linguistic and extra-linguistic information. It delivers speech information permitting us as individuals to recognize the others and to attribute emotional states to them (Belin et al., 2000; Ethofer et al., 2009). While language is generally thought to be processed in specialized brain areas such as the inferior frontal gyrus (IFG; also known as Broca's area), the superior and middle temporal gyruses (STG, MTG, also termed Wernicke's area) and angular gyrus, voice selective areas have been located bilaterally in the upper bank of the middle superior temporal sulcus (STS) over the temporal poles (see **Figure 3A**). Their existence has particularly been highlighted by fMRI experiments in the adult brain by comparing the cortical activation patterns induced by vocal vs. non-vocal sounds (Belin et al., 2000, 2004; Kriegstein and Giraud, 2004; Belin, 2006, for review; Latinus and Belin, 2011; Deen et al., 2015; Pernet et al., 2015). When a voice is perceived, the brain begins by a low-level analysis of the acoustic features involving sub-cortical nuclei and primary auditory cortical regions. Subsequently, the voice is processed during a voice-specific stage where its structure is encoded. Three types of vocal information are then extracted and further processed in partially separable but functionally interacting pathways: the speech content, the affective content and the vocal identity (see **Figure 3B**). Early studies of very young infants have shown that voice sensitive cortices within the temporal areas develop as a voice selective brain system between 4 and 7 months of age in the typically developing brain and to become responsive to the quality of the voice during speech (emotional voice prosody) by the age of 7 months with a right hemispheric dominance (Belin and Grosbras, 2010; Grossmann et al., 2010; Blasi et al., 2011; Lloyd-Fox et al., 2012). A recent study of typically developing preschoolers (mean age = 5.8 years) compared voice-specific vs. speech-sound specific functional brain activity and demonstrated that the right STS already works as a specialized temporal voice system (Raschle et al., 2014), similarly to what has been reported in the adult brain (Belin et al., 2002; Belin and Zatorre, 2003; von Kriegstein et al., 2003).

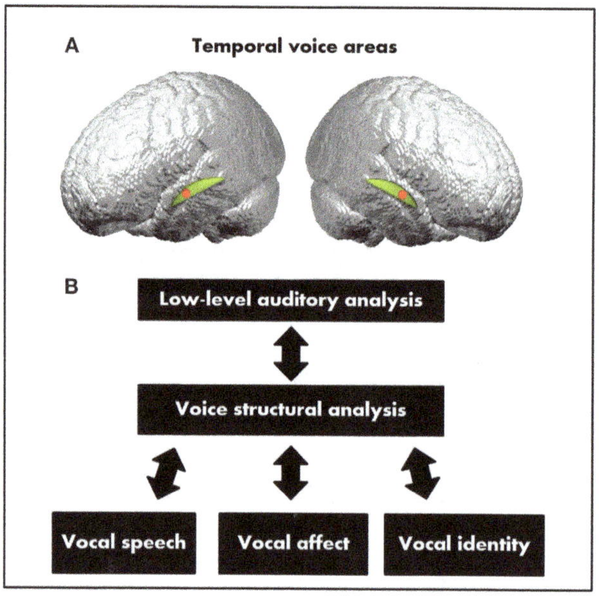

FIGURE 3 | (A) Temporal voice areas (TVA). The TVA (represented here by the red dots) are mostly located along the middle and anterior parts of the superior temporal sulcus (STS) bilaterally over the temporal plan (represented here in green). **(B)** A model of voice perception. After a stage of voice structural encoding constrained to vocal sounds, three partially dissociable functional pathways process the three main types of vocal information: speech, identity, and affect (adapted from Belin et al., 2004).

ABERRANT VOICE PROCESSING IN OLDER CHILDREN AND ADULTS WITH ASD

Difficulties to speak and to interact socially in an appropriate manner are central traits of autism and have been linked to abnormal processing of social information in both the visual and auditory modalities (e.g., Dawson et al., 1998, 2004; Klin et al., 2009; Chevallier et al., 2012 for review). Children and adults with ASD often tend to ignore human vocalizations in their surrounding but are responsive to other non-vocal stimuli indicating a detachment from their social environment (Klin, 1991, 1992; Kuhl et al., 2005). Early acquisition of language capacities is closely intertwined to social function in typically developing children and children on the spectrum (e.g., Goldstein et al., 2003; Kuhl et al., 2003; Norbury et al., 2010). Although, it is still not established why many individuals with ASD are often insensitive to human vocalizations, anomalies within voice selective areas have been highlighted in older children and adults with ASD. Using fMRI, Gervais and colleagues showed in a seminal study that adults on the spectrum (mean age = 25 years) failed to activate voice selective regions of the STS but showed similar activation patterns to the comparison group in response to non-vocal sounds (Gervais et al., 2004). This finding suggested an aberrant form of processing with respect to auditory information having a social content such as a voice does. This would suggest that a sound with a social content might not be adequately processed, most likely due to the abnormal development of cerebral regions implicated in the analysis of the social content of auditory stimuli (Gervais et al., 2004). Decreased gray matter volume in the bilateral voice specific STS have been observed in 10 year old children with ASD (Boddaert et al., 2004b). Abrams and colleagues hypothesized that this may be the consequence of individuals with ASD having impaired function of emotional and reward systems which in turn prevents them from engaging with acoustic information with a high social content such as speech stimuli (Abrams et al., 2013). In order to test their hypothesis, Abrams and colleagues scanned and compared 20 young children with

ASD to age- and intelligence quotient-matched TD controls (mean age = 9.8 years) using a resting-state fMRI protocol. By looking at the intrinsic functional connectivity in the voice-selective posterior STS (pSTS) bilaterally, they found the presence of underconnectivity between the left-hemisphere pSTS and the bilateral ventral tegmental areas in children with ASD. This was also the case for other regions such as the nucleus accumbens, left-hemisphere insula, orbitofrontal, and ventromedial prefrontal cortices. Moreover, diminished connectivity was evident between right-hemisphere pSTS and the orbitofrontal cortex and amygdala.

An important aspect of the study by Abrams and colleagues was that the degree of underconnectivity between voice-selective cortex and reward pathways predicted symptom severity for communication deficits in children with ASD, thus providing a connectivity biomarker for this specific group of patients. The study of the connectivity profile using a resting-state fMRI protocol during infancy and toddlerhood is now needed to further our understanding regarding how the functional connectivity between reward pathways and voice- and speech-related brain areas develops. Several neuroimaging studies performed in high-functioning older children and adults with ASD point to the presence of impairments in the neural basis of language processing in general (e.g., Gaffrey et al., 2007; Knaus et al., 2008; Herringshaw et al., 2016 for recent review). These experiments often including an overt task have revealed the existence of abnormal frontal and/or temporal responses during language processing tasks compared to TD individuals and reversed or reduced laterality within fronto-temporal language regions (e.g., Boddaert et al., 2003; Flagg et al., 2005; Kleinhans et al., 2008; Knaus et al., 2010; Lindell and Hudry, 2013; Herringshaw et al., 2016). In sum, experiments that used language tasks or rest scanning in the awake state indicate the presence of aberrant processing of human vocalizations in older children and adults with ASD.

In the following sections, we summarize the experiments investigating the neuronal underpinnings of human speech and language abnormalities during early periods of development: infancy and toddlerhood. These recent experiments have mostly used auditory speech stimuli which implicitly require analysis of the human voice. Importantly, several studies have included low-functioning toddlers with ASD or studied infants at high-risk for ASD. In contrast to experiments performed with older high-functioning children and adults with ASD and that include a task, scanning of very young infants is performed during natural sleep, at rest in the absence of an overt task or by passively presenting speech-stimuli (e.g., sentences, words, syllables). Overall, findings from these studies indicate that the brain systems implicated in human speech and language processing follow a different developmental pathway in individuals with ASD when compared to TD individuals very early on in the development already. We begin by a summary of the structural and functional differences that have been found in young toddlers with ASD and infants at risk.

STRUCTURAL DIFFERENCES IN TODDLERS WITH ASD AND INFANTS AT RISK

Several studies suggested brain overgrowth during the first year of life in toddlers with ASD (e.g., Courchesne et al., 2001, 2003, 2011; Redcay and Courchesne, 2005; Hazlett et al., 2011; Nordahl et al., 2011; Shen et al., 2013). For example, Sparks and colleagues measured an increased brain volume in toddlers with ASD (aged 3–4 years) compared to aged-matched TD controls and developmentally delayed (DD) children (Sparks et al., 2002). Longitudinal measurements indicate the presence of gray and white matter cerebral overgrowth in toddlers at 2 years (Hazlett et al., 2005). In a longitudinal study, Schumann and colleagues followed up toddlers and school aged children with ASD (1.5 years up to 5 years of age). They found both gray and white matter enlargements by 2.5 years of age in fronto-temporal regions along with cingulate cortices, regions related but not limited to language development (Schumann et al., 2010). A global increase in gray matter volumes in toddlers with ASD aged between 2 and 3 years compared to DD toddlers has recently been reported (Xiao et al., 2014). The locus of this difference manifested regionally in the right STG, a cortical region known to be involved in spoken language comprehension (Lattner et al., 2005). In older children with ASD, this locus has been shown to be enlarged to aged match controls (mean age = 13.5 years; Jou et al., 2010) and to exhibit a different pattern of activation during speech processing compared to TD adolescents (mean age = 12 years; Lai et al., 2011). Other studies indicate the presence of structural anomalies within language-related brain areas in older children and adults (e.g., Prigge et al., 2013; Itahashi et al., 2015; Lai et al., 2015). It is hypothesized that this early brain overgrowth during infancy and toddlerhood in ASD is followed by a period of decline in brain size from childhood to adulthood (Courchesne et al., 2011; Lange et al., 2015).

Diffusion imaging studies have also revealed the presence of widespread disruption of white matter integrity in long-range and short-range connections in toddlers, older children and adults with ASD (see Hoppenbrouwers et al., 2014; Conti et al., 2015 for reviews). For example, accelerated white matter maturation has been reported in a small sample of seven participants aged between 1.8 and 3.3 years (Ben Bashat et al., 2007). Altered white matter integrity has also been found in toddlers with ASD (mean age = 3.2 years; Weinstein et al., 2011). Xiao et al. (2014) showed altered structural brain connectivity in multiple regions that have been related but not limited to language functions such as the posterior cingulate cortex, subregions of the limbic lobes as well as the corpus callosum in toddlers with ASD aged between 2 and 3 years (Xiao et al., 2014). It even appears that white matter anomalies might develop before the first year in infants who are later diagnosed with ASD. Wolff and collegues observed abnormalities in white matter fiber tracts in infants at risk (at 6 months) and who were diagnosed at 24 months (Wolff et al., 2012). In a recent study of infants at high-risk for ASD and diagnosed at 24 months, white matter connectivity abnormalities were present specifically over Broca's area in the frontal lobes, and more generally in the temporal, parietal, occipital lobes as compared to both low-and high-risk infants not classified as ASD (Lewis et al., 2014).

Anatomical data indicate a period of early brain overgrowth (between 1 and 5 years) followed by normalization during adolescence. Structural connectivity experiments also report a developmental shift from greater structural connectivity in very young children with ASD to lower connectivity in older children (see Hoppenbrouwers et al., 2014; Conti et al., 2015 for recent discussions). These alterations impinge on acquiring normal language functions and lead to other higher-order cognitive, social, and communicative functions deficits. However, it is still unclear how those differences relate and can yet reflect the early language development heterogeneity inherent to autism. The field is also currently hampered by the widespread methodology differences in terms of subject inclusion criteria (high vs. low functioning autism), control groups, size of cohorts, age range, neuroimaging methods and parameters. Future cross-sectional and longitudinal experiments spanning early childhood to adulthood are necessary including larger sample size. Only then it will be possible to get a clearer picture within this complex and increasingly expanding field of research.

FUNCTIONAL STUDIES IN TODDLERS WITH ASD USING VOICE-RELATED AUDITORY STIMULI

Brain abnormalities underlying human voice processing during toddlerhood have also been found. A seminal EEG experiment performed by Kuhl et al. (2005) indicated the presence of different event-related potential (ERP) response pattern to speech stimuli in toddlers with ASD compared to TD (mean age = 3.5 years). In this experiment, toddlers were passively presented with standard and deviant phonemes. In individuals with typical development, contrasting the brain responses that are produced by the deviant sound with the ones produced by the standard sound causes a mismatch negativity (MMN). The MMN is a robust index of automatic sound discrimination (MMN, Näätänen, 1995, 2003 for reviews). In toddlers with ASD, there was no evidence for an MMN, whereas in TD the MMN was present. Using an auditory preference test, the group of toddlers with ASD was subdivided between those who preferred human vocalization (i.e., motherese speech sounds) and those who preferred non-speech analogs. An MMN appeared in the group that preferred motherese sounds similarly to what was found in TD toddlers while toddlers with ASD who preferred the non-speech sounds still did not exhibit an MMN. These findings are important as they reveal a link between early social preferences and early language processing skills in toddlers with ASD.

A functional study by Redcay and Courchesne (2008) found that the brain systems of speech perception were responding differently to speech stimuli in toddlers with ASD compared to TD toddlers. In a cross-sectional experiment with a small sample size, the authors scanned toddlers aged between 2 and 3 years using a natural sleep fMRI experimental design. They recorded brain activity when toddlers were asleep and listened to normal speech of a human voice (forward and backward speech stimuli), and the ones from toddlers with ASD. Results indicated the recruitment of different regions and with a different laterality dominance. Specifically, toddlers with ASD exhibited hypoactivation of many regions traditionally recruited during early language acquisition in comparison to those with TD, suggesting that at that age toddlers with ASD are already on a deviant developmental trajectory characterized by a greater recruitment of right hemispheric regions during speech perception (Redcay and Courchesne, 2008). The same research group then performed an fMRI experiment where they increased their sample size and included even younger children (aged between 12 and 48 months; Eyler et al., 2012). Using a prospective, cross-sectional design this time, 80 toddlers listened to a bedtime story during their sleep (speech sound stimuli from a human voice). Toddlers were also followed up to get record of their evolution and to ensure confirmation of later ASD diagnosis. A different brain pattern of brain activation was found between toddlers who were at risk and who were later diagnosed with ASD and the toddlers who followed a normal development path. Specifically, toddlers with ASD had deficient left hemisphere responses to speech sounds with an abnormal right-lateralized temporal cortical response to language; this deficit worsened during growth to become most severe by the age of four. Contrarily, TD toddlers had a reversed pattern of brain activity and lateralization with the presence of more temporal cortical responses and a left lateralized pattern of brain activation that became stronger with development. Two important observations can be made. Firstly, lateralization in response to auditory speech sounds differs between groups. Abnormal lateralization in response to language has also been reported in experiments performed in older children and adults with ASD (e.g., Kleinhans et al., 2008; Minagawa-Kawai et al., 2009). Secondly, weaker brain responses to speech sounds over the temporal pole were present in the ASD group, suggesting the presence of an early specific and abnormal brain response pattern to speech sounds in toddlers with ASD (Eyler et al., 2012).

FUNCTIONAL STUDIES IN INFANTS AT RISK USING VOICE-RELATED AUDITORY STIMULI

In a recent study, Seery et al. (2013) suggested that this atypical lateralization is an ASD endophenotype already observable during the first year of life. Comparing infants at risk for ASD with low-risk infants aged between 6 and 12 months, the authors reported significant group differences in the development of lateralized ERP responses to speech (using consonant-vowel auditory stimuli). More specifically, the low-risk group displayed a lateralized response to the speech sounds whereas the high-risk group did not (Seery et al., 2013). In a subsequent study, the same research group found atypical ERPs to repeated speech sounds in 9 month old infants at risk (Seery et al., 2014). Atypical lateralization of the ERP to words at 2 years of age has also been observed in ASD toddlers with poor social skills (Kuhl et al., 2013). In a very recent sleep fMRI study that also included behavioral assessment of parent-infant interactions, Blasi et al. (2015) compared cortical responses between emotional voices and environmental sound stimuli. They found that high-risk infants for ASD (aged between 4 and 7 months) did not show this early specialization suggesting the presence very early on of atypical neural responses to human voice with and without emotional valence in at-risk populations, at least (Blasi et al., 2015). Taken together, these results indicate that during early development, speech, and language-critical areas over the temporal poles do not show the same brain responses to voice related stimuli as observed in TD young individuals. An absence or atypical lateralization of brain responses and functional hypoactivation in response to speech related content were already reported in infants at risk and toddlers with ASD. Moreover, voice-selective cortices in populations show lesser degree of specialization already in infants at risk. In sum, similarly to the experiments performed in high-functioning older children and despite the use of different experimental conditions, abnormalities in lateralization and aberrant functional activation during voice processing are already found very early on, during infancy and toddlerhood.

DYSFUNCTIONAL CONNECTIVITY IN TODDLERS WITH ASD AND INFANTS AT RISK USING VOICE-RELATED AUDITORY STIMULI

Aside from the differences in functional activation described in the previous section, extant functional connectivity studies using fMRI or EEG with voice-related stimuli have shown altered connectivity between brain regions involved in language processing in young children with autism. Using fMRI, Dinstein and colleagues demonstrated reduced inter-hemispheric synchrony across language brain areas in young toddlers with ASD (Dinstein et al., 2011). They recorded spontaneous brain activity in three groups of toddlers during natural sleep (TD, ASD, and language delay). Seventy-two participants aged between 12 and 46 months (mean age = 29 months for the toddlers with ASD) were presented with auditory stimulation containing words, pseudo words, sentences, tones, or environmental sounds. The aim was to test for differences in synchronization between various brain regions between the three groups and explore a possible relation with the development of early autistic behavioral symptoms within the group of toddlers with ASD. Stimulus-evoked responses were regressed out so as to only keep spontaneous fMRI fluctuations in the data. In doing so, the authors controlled that any differences in synchronization between the groups were not due to differences in auditory-evoked responses between participants. Results indicated the presence of weaker interhemispheric synchronization between the IFG and the STG, two brain areas mediating speech and language processing in the ASD toddler group as compared to the two other groups. Moreover, analyses within the group of toddlers with ASD revealed that the synchronization strength was highest in those with overall good verbal capacities and was weakest in those with impaired verbal capacities. This indicates that, the functional connectivity between regions implicated in language processing has a different pattern compared to TD peers in toddlerhood already (Dinstein et al., 2011).

Using EEG, aberrant reduced functional connectivity has even been reported before the onset of any ASD symptoms, in infants at risk for ASD (Righi et al., 2014). They presented speech sounds (syllables) in the awake state, while EEG was concomitantly acquired in infants at high-risk and infants at low-risk for ASD. Acquisitions were performed at 6 and at 12 months of age. The participants were followed up at 36 months in order to identify which ones would develop ASD or not. By computing the intra-hemispheric linear coherence in the gamma frequency band, (that is, an estimation of synchronization across brain regions) between electrodes of interest located over the frontal and temporo-parietal regions in the left and right hemispheres, the authors found that at 6 months, linear coherence values were similar across groups. At 12 months however, infants at high-risk and later diagnosed with ASD showed reduced functional connectivity (that is, lower linear coherence, and thus less integration) compared to both infants at low-risk and those at high-risk who were not later diagnosed with ASD. In addition, significant differences in functional connectivity between the low-risk and high-risk infants who did not become autistic were found, with lower coherence values in the high-risk infant group. In contrast to what has been previously reported in fMRI with toddlers (Redcay and Courchesne, 2008; Eyler et al., 2012) or with EEG in infants at-risk for ASD (Seery et al., 2013), the study did not reveal any early group differences in hemispheric lateralization. However, as discussed by the authors, the estimation of the linear coherence is an approach less sensitive to stimulus-locked activity whereas fMRI and ERPs are. As such Righi's approach might not have captured existing hemispheric differences. Taken together, published functional connectivity studies examining the early development of language related brain areas demonstrate aberrant brain connectivity patterns in both toddlers with ASD (Dinstein et al., 2011), and in 12 month old infants at risk who later develop autism (Righi et al., 2014). This suggests that aberrant wiring of the cerebral regions responsible for language processing precede the onset of the typical autism phenotype, and might be responsible for the early signs clinically observed in infants who will develop ASD, such as unresponsiveness to name, lack of orientation to human voices and delay in the development of receptive and expressive language skills.

LANGUAGE HETEROGENEITY IN TODDLERS WITH ASD: INSIGHTS FROM EARLY BRAIN BIOMARKERS

Findings reviewed so far indicate early functional differences in speech-related processing within superior temporal cortical regions and other language-critical brain areas. The anatomical and connectivity differences reported above in toddlers with ASD and infants at risk for ASD mostly correspond to group differences. While these results are informative, they do not permit to fully address the critical question of the heterogeneity of early language development in ASD and its relation to later outcome. To successfully tackle the question of heterogeneity, research groups have started using prospective and longitudinal designs with larger sample sizes to examine the hypothesis that different subgroups of individuals with ASD have different phenotypes and developmental pathways (Kuhl et al., 2013; Lombardo et al., 2015). These studies open avenues to better understand predictor of outcomes, as predictive brain biomarkers that can differentiate between these subtle phenotypes emerge (Bölte et al., 2013; Lenroot and Yeung, 2013; Ecker et al., 2015). For instance, in a recent developmental study, Lombardo et al. (2015) searched for early functional neuroimaging biomarkers that would reflect the heterogeneity observed in early language development in ASD. The authors measured early cortical responses to speech using a prospective sleep fMRI paradigm (participants aged between 12 and 48 months). The experiment included four different groups with TD infants, infants with a language/developmental delay (LD/DD), infants with ASD having a good language outcome at 4 years of age ("ASD good") or a bad language development outcome ("ASD Poor"; that is, they measured developmental trajectories of language growth over the first 4 years of life). Pre-diagnosis fMRI brain data in response to three types of speech stimuli (complex forward speech, simple forward speech, and backward speech) were acquired in each participants. The aim was to test whether early functional measures could have a predictive value when combined with clinical-behavioral information. First, they found that in response to speech stimuli, "ASD good" toddlers recruited language-sensitive superior temporal cortices in a very similar way to the control groups (that is, the non-ASD language/developmentally delayed individuals). However, in the "ASD poor" group, language-sensitive superior temporal cortices were found to be hypoactive in response to the same speech stimuli. The multivoxel activation pattern was different to the one observed in the three other control groups indicating a lack of functional differentiation to these speech stimuli in the ASD poor group. Another important finding by Lombardo et al. (2015) was that the brain response patterns to general auditory processing was preserved in the "ASD poor" group (that is, similar to the other control groups), whereas the brain activity specifically related to language and speech was weaker and less specific. For example no engagement of the left hemisphere was found as this was the case in the three other groups. This would suggest on the one hand a general preservation of the neural systems devoted to general auditory processing during infancy and on the other, the presence of a dysfunction of the neural systems at a higher level of processing and implicated in voice-related content leading to the aberrant processing of auditory stimuli containing speech and language related information. Interestingly, the connectivity between primary auditory cortex and the reward and affective brain circuitry seems to be preserved in high-functioning older children with ASD, whereas connectivity between the voice structural module (see **Figure 3B**) described in Belin's model above and the reward system is impaired, preventing the normal processing of speech related content but allowing low-level sensory processing to occur (Abrams et al., 2013).

The results provided by the study by Lombardo et al. are important for several reasons. First, they indicate the presence during toddlerhood already of brain related differences in the neural underpinnings implicated in the processing of early voice related auditory information and this between different subtypes of ASD (that is, differences between ASD poor and ASD good). Second, longitudinal measurements of pre-diagnostic clinical behavioral information and early fMRI language and speech-related brain responses and combination thereof was found to have a strong predictive value in terms of determining later ASD subgroup prognosis.

Other experiments also point to the presence of early brain biomarkers in EEG. Kuhl et al. (2013) found that the response pattern of ERPs to words at the age of 2 year was predictive of later receptive language capacities at ages 4 and 6 years (Kuhl et al., 2013). In comparison to the Lombardo et al. (2015) study where clinical groups were subdivided based on their language skills, Kuhl and colleagues compared the ERPs in response to words in 2 year old children that were subdivided as a function of social symptoms, into "ASD high" (sever social symptoms) and "ASD low" less social symptoms. Results showed only a left lateralized brain response similar to the TD group in the "ASD low" group. Only the single electrode where the time locked response manifested was different between those two groups (T3 for TD and P3 for "ASD low"). For the "ASD high" group on the other hand, the ERP was more diffuse and right lateralized. Then, in a second phase of the study, the authors looked at the predictive power of their P3 effect found in the first phase for all ASD toddlers on linguistic, cognitive, and adaptive functions at ages 4 and 6 years. For the ASD toddlers who had strong negativity in the ERP to known words at P3 measured at enrollment, a better outcome was observed at 6 years of age. In stark contrast, toddlers with ASD who did not show this ERP sensitivity at intake had worse outcomes (that is, they showed less improvement). Interestingly, the ERP measures to words furthermore exceeded the predictive value of cognitive measures performed at intake. Another important finding by this study was that the predictive aspect of the brain response to words at age 2 years of age did not modulate depending on the type of intensive treatments the toddlers received. Adding another control condition with no treatments may perhaps have added valuable information with respect to the effectiveness of the treatments as recent evidences indicate that early behavioral intervention is associated with normalized patterns of EEG brain activity in the visual modality at least (Dawson et al., 2012). Unfortunately and as mentioned by the authors, the source localization of those differences could not be performed. As already discussed, methods for estimating inverse solutions are now available and it will be important in further studies to include those when possible.

PERSPECTIVE AND FUTURE DIRECTIONS

Neuroimaging studies using exciting new approaches that combine early brain measurements with early behavioral data are starting to highlight important differences in the functional and structural wiring of the young autistic brain compared to the TD one using auditory speech and language related stimuli. With time, the field will hopefully see the appearance of other experiments with larger sample sizes combined with longitudinal measurements to subtype ASD infants according to the core impaired dimension of early language development that was the main focus of the present review, and of social interaction and communication deficits that are both central hallmarks of autism. This will help to explore the efficiency of early intervention in correcting the developmental trajectories on the one hand, and to tackle the question of heterogeneity inherent to autism on the other. Ultimately this will lead to the possibility of improving, developing and modifying therapeutic interventions and adapting them depending to the infant's specific needs. Moreover, because autism cannot always be diagnosed with high certainty before the age of 2–3 years (Zwaigenbaum et al., 2009; Jones et al., 2014), additional prospective longitudinal studies of high-risk populations are necessary to provide understanding about how, when and where developmental trajectories that result in ASD deviate from the TD young brain. These later will in turn aid to understand the general heterogeneity observed in early language development in autism as well as allow early identification of toddlers who should receive intensive therapeutic intervention. The few experiments of infants at risk reported here indicate that brain differences in response to human voice and its speech and language related content are already present before the end of the first year in some cases suggesting that aberrant voice processing could be a promising marker to identify ASD very early on.

Achieving a better understanding regarding which neural systems implicated in speech and language-critical processing are impaired very early on is difficult to highlight and this for several reasons. First, scanning individuals aged between 6 months and 3 year implies using scanning conditions with passive presentation of stimuli most of the time. Implementing tasks that need an engagement of the participant at such a young age is difficult to achieve. For example asking what is voice specific vs. speech specific has only been addressed by one study so far, which used a behavioral task in preschool TD children aged around 6 years (Raschle et al., 2014). In the studies discussed in this review, based in infants and toddlers (i.e., before 4 years), the vast majority of experiments used contrast between speech stimuli and rest, reversed speech or other auditory stimuli (words, sentences, and syllables). Yet, contrasting speech stimuli vs. rest activation does not allow to determine what is specifically related to the voice and what is related to the speech content. The question remains open as to whether a voice specific impairment is present in the brain of young children with ASD. Thus, future experiments should include contrasts between voice specific vs. speech specific brain related activity. This would allow to test whether aberrant voice processing that has been reported in older children and young adults is indeed a hallmark in autism very early on leading to impairments in the social-communication language brain. Currently there is only one experiment to our knowledge where the brain responses to human vocalizations alone were contrasted with non-vocal sounds in infants at risk for autism (Blasi et al., 2015). However, the authors reported that their sample had not been assessed for ASD at the age of 3 years yet. Further work is thus needed to resolve this issue.

Some authors have also recently hypothesized that it is not human speech *per se* that is an issue in autism but rather the mode of communication of speech that might be challenging for individuals with ASD. For example, recent results suggest that the mode of presentation of human speech sounds might play a role in speech perception in older children and young adults with autism. In an fMRI experiments, Lai et al. (2012) passively presented familiar human speech stimuli (spoken sentences by parents) or song stimuli containing vocals to children with ASD (including low functioning ones) and aged matched controls. While brain activations were found to be different between the children with ASD and TD during the spoken condition, they turned out to be comparable when speech was delivered in a sung format (Lai et al., 2012). Another study found comparable brain activation patterns and preserved fronto-temporal connections between children with ASD and aged matched controls during perception of sung but not spoken words (Sharda et al., 2015). Most of the experiments reviewed here have shown abnormalities in lateralization and aberrant functional activation during speech processing during infancy and toddlerhood similarly to what has been reported in older children and adults. However, none of them varied the mode of presentation of the speech sounds that were always presented in a spoken format. Interestingly, one experiment found that toddlers with ASD (aged 2 years) who preferred motherese speech signals (that is, a pattern of speech characterized by high-pitch intonations) exhibit similar ERP responses compared to aged match TD controls in a passive syllable discrimination task (Kuhl et al., 2005). In this later, toddlers with ASD who didn't preferred an analog speech signal had different ERP responses compared to TD toddlers. It will be instrumental to detect how early the mode of communication impacts human speech processing in infants and toddlers with ASD and in at risk population as preliminary results now suggest that sung over spoken speech might effectively improve socio-communicative behaviors in toddlers with ASD at least (Paul et al., 2015).

Another final important aspect that has to be considered besides the various impairments in the development of speech processing highlighted by the relevant neuroimaging literature we reviewed here, is that functional and structural anomalies have also been reported at earlier stages of the auditory processing system in autism. Some studies highlight functional abnormalities within low level primary sensory auditory pathways in adults with ASD (Dinstein et al., 2012; Haigh et al., 2015). A recent experiment points toward the presence of maturational differences in the development of primary/secondary auditory areas in children with ASD aged between 6 and 14 years (Edgar et al., 2015). The presence of abnormal auditory brainstem response in newborns/infants (tested between 0 and 3 months) and toddlers (tested between 1.5 and 3.5 years) later diagnosed with ASD has also been demonstrated (Miron et al., 2015). Further work is thus required to understand how these impairments in the early stages of the auditory processing system might impinge on the development of speech and language processing in autism.

AUTHOR CONTRIBUTIONS

HS and MS wrote the paper, read, and approved the final manuscript.

ACKNOWLEDGMENTS

This research review is supported by a grant from the National Center of Competence in Research (NCCR) "SYNAPSY—The Synaptic Bases of Mental Diseases" financed by the Swiss National Science Foundation (SNF, Grant number: 51AU40_125759). MS is further supported by an individual fellowship from the SNF (#158831).

REFERENCES

Abrahams, B. S., and Geschwind, D. H. (2010). Connecting genes to brain in the autism spectrum disorders. *Arch. Neurol.* 67, 395–399. doi: 10.1001/archneurol.2010.47

Abrams, D. A., Lynch, C. J., Cheng, K. M., Phillips, J., Supekar, K., Ryali, S., et al. (2013). Underconnectivity between voice-selective cortex and reward circuitry in children with autism. *Proc. Natl. Acad. Sci. U.S.A.* 110, 12060–12065. doi: 10.1073/pnas.1302982110

American Psychiatric Association and American Psychiatric Association. Dsm-5 Task Force (2013). *Diagnostic and Statistical Manual of Mental Disorders: DSM-5.* Washington, DC: American Psychiatric Association.

Anderson, D. K., Lord, C., Risi, S., Dilavore, P. S., Shulman, C., Thurm, A., et al. (2007). Patterns of growth in verbal abilities among children with autism spectrum disorder. *J. Consult. Clin. Psychol.* 75, 594–604. doi: 10.1037/0022-006X.75.4.594

Arnott, B., McConachie, H., Meins, E., Fernyhough, C., Couteur, A. L., Turner, M., et al. (2010). The frequency of restricted and repetitive behaviors in a community sample of 15-month-old infants. *J. Dev. Behav. Pediatr.* 31, 223–229. doi: 10.1097/DBP.0b013e3181d5a2ad

Asperger, H. (1944). The "autistic psychopathy" in childhood. *Arch. Psychiatrie Nervenkrankheiten* 117, 76–136. doi: 10.1007/BF01837709

Baio, J. (2014). Prevalence of autism spectrum disorder among children aged 8 years - autism and developmental disabilities monitoring network, 11 sites, United States, 2010. *MMWR. Surveill. Summ.* 63, 1–21.

Baranek, G. T. (1999). Autism during infancy: a retrospective video analysis of sensory-motor and social behaviors at 9-12 months of age. *J. Autism Dev. Disord.* 29, 213–224. doi: 10.1023/A:1023080005650

Barbaro, J., and Dissanayake, C. (2009). Autism spectrum disorders in infancy and toddlerhood: a review of the evidence on early signs, early identification tools, and early diagnosis. *J. Dev. Behav. Pediatr.* 30, 447–459. doi: 10.1097/DBP.0b013e3181ba0f9f

Baron-Cohen, S., Auyeung, B., Nørgaard-Pedersen, B., Hougaard, D. M., Abdallah, M. W., Melgaard, L., et al. (2015). Elevated fetal steroidogenic activity in autism. *Mol. Psychiatry* 20, 369–376. doi: 10.1038/mp.2014.48

Belin, P. (2006). Voice processing in human and non-human primates. *Philos. Trans. R. Soc. Lond. B Biol. Sci.* 361, 2091–2107. doi: 10.1098/rstb.2006.1933

Belin, P., Fecteau, S., and Bédard, C. (2004). Thinking the voice: neural correlates of voice perception. *Trends Cogn. Sci.* 8, 129–135. doi: 10.1016/j.tics.2004.01.008

Belin, P., and Grosbras, M. H. (2010). Before speech: cerebral voice processing in infants. *Neuron* 65, 733–735. doi: 10.1016/j.neuron.2010.03.018

Belin, P., and Zatorre, R. J. (2003). Adaptation to speaker's voice in right anterior temporal lobe. *Neuroreport* 14, 2105–2109. doi: 10.1097/00001756-200311140-00019

Belin, P., Zatorre, R. J., and Ahad, P. (2002). Human temporal-lobe response to vocal sounds. *Brain Res. Cogn. Brain Res.* 13, 17–26. doi: 10.1016/S0926-6410(01)00084-2

Belin, P., Zatorre, R. J., Lafaille, P., Ahad, P., and Pike, B. (2000). Voice-selective areas in human auditory cortex. *Nature* 403, 309–312. doi: 10.1038/35002078

Ben Bashat, D., Kronfeld-Duenias, V., Zachor, D. A., Ekstein, P. M., Hendler, T., Tarrasch, R., et al. (2007). Accelerated maturation of white matter in young children with autism: a high b value DWI study. *Neuroimage* 37, 40–47. doi: 10.1016/j.neuroimage.2007.04.060

Berchio, C., Rihs, T. A., Michel, C. M., Brunet, D., Apicella, F., Muratori, F., et al. (2014). Parieto-frontal circuits during observation of hidden and visible motor acts in children. A high-density EEG source imaging study. *Brain Topogr.* 27, 258–270. doi: 10.1007/s10548-013-0314-x

Bergelson, E., and Swingley, D. (2012). At 6-9 months, human infants know the meanings of many common nouns. *Proc. Natl. Acad. Sci. U.S.A.* 109, 3253–3258. doi: 10.1073/pnas.1113380109

Betancur, C. (2011). Etiological heterogeneity in autism spectrum disorders: more than 100 genetic and genomic disorders and still counting. *Brain Res.* 1380, 42–77. doi: 10.1016/j.brainres.2010.11.078

Blasi, A., Lloyd-Fox, S., Sethna, V., Brammer, M. J., Mercure, E., Murray, L., et al. (2015). Atypical processing of voice sounds in infants at risk for autism spectrum disorder. *Cortex* 71, 122–133. doi: 10.1016/j.cortex.2015.06.015

Blasi, A., Mercure, E., Lloyd-Fox, S., Thomson, A., Brammer, M., Sauter, D., et al. (2011). Early specialization for voice and emotion processing in the infant brain. *Curr. Biol.* 21, 1220–1224. doi: 10.1016/j.cub.2011.06.009

Boddaert, N., Belin, P., Chabane, N., Poline, J. B., Barthélémy, C., Mouren-Simeoni, M. C., et al. (2003). Perception of complex sounds: abnormal pattern of cortical activation in autism. *Am. J. Psychiatry* 160, 2057–2060. doi: 10.1176/appi.ajp.160.11.2057

Boddaert, N., Chabane, N., Belin, P., Bourgeois, M., Royer, V., Barthelemy, C., et al. (2004a). Perception of complex sounds in autism: abnormal auditory cortical processing in children. *Am. J. Psychiatry* 161, 2117–2120. doi: 10.1176/appi.ajp.161.11.2117

Boddaert, N., Chabane, N., Gervais, H., Good, C. D., Bourgeois, M., Plumet, M. H., et al. (2004b). Superior temporal sulcus anatomical abnormalities in childhood autism: a voxel-based morphometry MRI study. *Neuroimage* 23, 364–369. doi: 10.1016/j.neuroimage.2004.06.016

Boersma, M., Kemner, C., De Reus, M. A., Collin, G., Snijders, T. M., Hofman, D., et al. (2013). Disrupted functional brain networks in autistic toddlers. *Brain Connect.* 3, 41–49. doi: 10.1089/brain.2012.0127

Bölte, S., Marschik, P. B., Falck-Ytter, T., Charman, T., Roeyers, H., and Elsabbagh, M. (2013). Infants at risk for autism: a European perspective on current status, challenges and opportunities. *Eur. Child Adolesc. Psychiatry* 22, 341–348. doi: 10.1007/s00787-012-0368-4

Brunet, D., Murray, M. M., and Michel, C. M. (2011). Spatiotemporal analysis of multichannel EEG: CARTOOL. *Comput. Intell. Neurosci.* 2011:813870. doi: 10.1155/2011/813870

Cantlon, J. F., Brannon, E. M., Carter, E. J., and Pelphrey, K. A. (2006). Functional imaging of numerical processing in adults and 4-y-old children. *PLoS Biol.* 4:e125. doi: 10.1371/journal.pbio.0040125

Cheng, Y., Lee, S. Y., Chen, H. Y., Wang, P. Y., and Decety, J. (2012). Voice and emotion processing in the human neonatal brain. *J. Cogn. Neurosci.* 24, 1411–1419. doi: 10.1162/jocn_a_00214

Chevallier, C., Kohls, G., Troiani, V., Brodkin, E. S., and Schultz, R. T. (2012). The social motivation theory of autism. *Trends Cogn. Sci.* 16, 231–239. doi: 10.1016/j.tics.2012.02.007

Conti, E., Calderoni, S., Marchi, V., Muratori, F., Cioni, G., and Guzzetta, A. (2015). The first 1000 days of the autistic brain: a systematic review of diffusion imaging studies. *Front. Hum. Neurosci.* 9:159. doi: 10.3389/fnhum.2015.00159

Courchesne, E., Campbell, K., and Solso, S. (2011). Brain growth across the life span in autism: age-specific changes in anatomical pathology. *Brain Res.* 1380, 138–145. doi: 10.1016/j.brainres.2010.09.101

Courchesne, E., Carper, R., and Akshoomoff, N. (2003). Evidence of brain overgrowth in the first year of life in autism. *JAMA* 290, 337–344. doi: 10.1001/jama.290.3.337

Courchesne, E., Karns, C. M., Davis, H. R., Ziccardi, R., Carper, R. A., Tigue, Z. D., et al. (2001). Unusual brain growth patterns in early life in patients with autistic disorder: an MRI study. *Neurology* 57, 245–254. doi: 10.1212/WNL.57.2.245

Custo, A., Vulliemoz, S., Grouiller, F., Van De Ville, D., and Michel, C. (2014). EEG source imaging of brain states using spatiotemporal regression. *Neuroimage* 96, 106–116. doi: 10.1016/j.neuroimage.2014.04.002

Dahlgren, S. O., and Gillberg, C. (1989). Symptoms in the first two years of life. A preliminary population study of infantile autism. *Eur. Arch. Psychiatry Neurol. Sci.* 238, 169–174. doi: 10.1007/BF00451006

Dawson, G. (2008). Early behavioral intervention, brain plasticity, and the prevention of autism spectrum disorder. *Dev. Psychopathol.* 20, 775–803. doi: 10.1017/S0954579408000370

Dawson, G., Jones, E. J., Merkle, K., Venema, K., Lowy, R., Faja, S., et al. (2012). Early behavioral intervention is associated with normalized brain activity in young children with autism. *J. Am. Acad. Child Adolesc. Psychiatry* 51, 1150–1159. doi: 10.1016/j.jaac.2012.08.018

Dawson, G., Meltzoff, A. N., Osterling, J., Rinaldi, J., and Brown, E. (1998). Children with autism fail to orient to naturally occurring social stimuli. *J. Autism Dev. Disord.* 28, 479–485. doi: 10.1023/A:1026043926488

Dawson, G., Rogers, S., Munson, J., Smith, M., Winter, J., Greenson, J., et al. (2010). Randomized, controlled trial of an intervention for toddlers with autism: the Early Start Denver Model. *Pediatrics* 125, e17–23. doi: 10.1542/peds.2009-0958

Dawson, G., Toth, K., Abbott, R., Osterling, J., Munson, J., Estes, A., et al. (2004). Early social attention impairments in autism: social orienting, joint attention, and attention to distress. *Dev. Psychol.* 40, 271–283. doi: 10.1037/0012-1649.40.2.271

de Bie, H. M. A., Boersma, M., Wattjes, M. P., Adriaanse, S., Vermeulen, R. J., Oostrom, K. J., et al. (2010). Preparing children with a mock scanner training protocol results in high quality structural and functional MRI scans. *Eur. J. Pediatr.* 169, 1079–1085. doi: 10.1007/s00431-010-1181-z

Deen, B., Koldewyn, K., Kanwisher, N., and Saxe, R. (2015). Functional organization of social perception and cognition in the superior temporal sulcus. *Cereb. Cortex* 25, 4596–4609. doi: 10.1093/cercor/bhv111

De Giacomo, A., and Fombonne, E. (1998). Parental recognition of developmental abnormalities in autism. *Eur. Child Adolesc. Psychiatry* 7, 131–136. doi: 10.1007/s007870050058

Dehaene-Lambertz, G., Dehaene, S., and Hertz-Pannier, L. (2002). Functional neuroimaging of speech perception in infants. *Science* 298, 2013–2015. doi: 10.1126/science.1077066

Dehaene-Lambertz, G., Hertz-Pannier, L., Dubois, J., Mériaux, S., Roche, A., Sigman, M., et al. (2006). Functional organization of perisylvian activation during presentation of sentences in preverbal infants. *Proc. Natl. Acad. Sci. U.S.A.* 103, 14240–14245. doi: 10.1073/pnas.0606302103

Dinstein, I., Heeger, D. J., Lorenzi, L., Minshew, N. J., Malach, R., and Behrmann, M. (2012). Unreliable evoked responses in autism. *Neuron* 75, 981–991. doi: 10.1016/j.neuron.2012.07.026

Dinstein, I., Pierce, K., Eyler, L., Solso, S., Malach, R., Behrmann, M., et al. (2011). Disrupted neural synchronization in toddlers with autism. *Neuron* 70, 1218–1225. doi: 10.1016/j.neuron.2011.04.018

Ecker, C., Bookheimer, S. Y., and Murphy, D. G. (2015). Neuroimaging in autism spectrum disorder: brain structure and function across the lifespan. *Lancet Neurol.* 14, 1121–1134. doi: 10.1016/S1474-4422(15)00050-2

Edgar, J. C., Fisk Iv, C. L., Berman, J. I., Chudnovskaya, D., Liu, S., Pandey, J., et al. (2015). Auditory encoding abnormalities in children with autism spectrum disorder suggest delayed development of auditory cortex. *Mol. Autism* 6, 69. doi: 10.1186/s13229-015-0065-5

Eigsti, I. M., De Marchena, A. B., Schuh, J. M., and Kelley, E. (2011). Language acquisition in autism spectrum disorders: a developmental review. *Res. Autism Spectr. Disord.* 5, 681–691. doi: 10.1016/j.rasd.2010.09.001

Eimas, P. D., Siqueland, E. R., Jusczyk, P., and Vigorito, J. (1971). Speech perception in infants. *Science* 171, 303–306. doi: 10.1126/science.171.3968.303

Elsabbagh, M., Mercure, E., Hudry, K., Chandler, S., Pasco, G., Charman, T., et al. (2012). Infant neural sensitivity to dynamic eye gaze is associated with later emerging autism. *Curr. Biol.* 22, 338–342. doi: 10.1016/j.cub.2011.12.056

Epstein, J. N., Casey, B. J., Tonev, S. T., Davidson, M., Reiss, A. L., Garrett, A., et al. (2007). Assessment and prevention of head motion during imaging of patients with attention deficit hyperactivity disorder. *Psychiatry Res.* 155, 75–82. doi: 10.1016/j.pscychresns.2006.12.009

Ethofer, T., Van De Ville, D., Scherer, K., and Vuilleumier, P. (2009). Decoding of emotional information in voice-sensitive cortices. *Curr. Biol.* 19, 1028–1033. doi: 10.1016/j.cub.2009.04.054

Eyler, L. T., Pierce, K., and Courchesne, E. (2012). A failure of left temporal cortex to specialize for language is an early emerging and fundamental property of autism. *Brain* 135, 949–960. doi: 10.1093/brain/awr364

Fein, D., Barton, M., Eigsti, I. M., Kelley, E., Naigles, L., Schultz, R. T., et al. (2013). Optimal outcome in individuals with a history of autism. *J. Child Psychol. Psychiatry* 54, 195–205. doi: 10.1111/jcpp.12037

Flagg, E. J., Cardy, J. E., Roberts, W., and Roberts, T. P. (2005). Language lateralization development in children with autism: insights from the late field magnetoencephalogram. *Neurosci. Lett.* 386, 82–87. doi: 10.1016/j.neulet.2005.05.037

Fransson, P., Skiold, B., Horsch, S., Nordell, A., Blennow, M., Lagercrantz, H., et al. (2007). Resting-state networks in the infant brain. *Proc. Natl. Acad. Sci. U.S.A.* 104, 15531–15536. doi: 10.1073/pnas.0704380104

Gaffrey, M. S., Kleinhans, N. M., Haist, F., Akshoomoff, N., Campbell, A., Courchesne, E., et al. (2007). A typical participation of visual cortex during word processing in autism: an fMRI study of semantic decision. *Neuropsychologia* 45, 1672–1684. doi: 10.1016/j.neuropsychologia.2007.01.008

Gervais, H., Belin, P., Boddaert, N., Leboyer, M., Coez, A., Sfaello, I., et al. (2004). Abnormal cortical voice processing in autism. *Nat. Neurosci.* 7, 801–802. doi: 10.1038/nn1291

Geschwind, D. H., and Levitt, P. (2007). Autism spectrum disorders: developmental disconnection syndromes. *Curr. Opin. Neurobiol.* 17, 103–111. doi: 10.1016/j.conb.2007.01.009

Geurts, H. M., and Embrechts, M. (2008). Language profiles in ASD, SLI, and ADHD. *J. Autism Dev. Disord.* 38, 1931–1943. doi: 10.1007/s10803-008-0587-1

Goldstein, M. H., King, A. P., and West, M. J. (2003). Social interaction shapes babbling: testing parallels between birdsong and speech. *Proc. Natl. Acad. Sci. U.S.A.* 100, 8030–8035. doi: 10.1073/pnas.1332441100

Grossmann, T., Oberecker, R., Koch, S. P., and Friederici, A. D. (2010). The developmental origins of voice processing in the human brain. *Neuron* 65, 852–858. doi: 10.1016/j.neuron.2010.03.001

Haesen, B., Boets, B., and Wagemans, J. (2011). A review of behavioural and electrophysiological studies on auditory processing and speech perception in autism spectrum disorders. *Res. Autism Spectr. Disord.* 5, 701–714. doi: 10.1016/j.rasd.2010.11.006

Haigh, S. M., Heeger, D. J., Dinstein, I., Minshew, N., and Behrmann, M. (2015). Cortical variability in the sensory-evoked response in autism. *J. Autism Dev. Disord.* 45, 1176–1190. doi: 10.1007/s10803-014-2276-6

Hazlett, H. C., Poe, M., Gerig, G., Smith, R. G., Provenzale, J., Ross, A., et al. (2005). Magnetic resonance imaging and head circumference study of brain size in autism: birth through age 2 years. *Arch. Gen. Psychiatry* 62, 1366–1376. doi: 10.1001/archpsyc.62.12.1366

Hazlett, H. C., Poe, M. D., Gerig, G., Styner, M., Chappell, C., Smith, R. G., et al. (2011). Early brain overgrowth in autism associated with an increase in cortical surface area before age 2 years. *Arch. Gen. Psychiatry* 68, 467–476. doi: 10.1001/archgenpsychiatry.2011.39

Herlihy, L., Knoch, K., Vibert, B., and Fein, D. (2015). Parents' first concerns about toddlers with autism spectrum disorder: effect of sibling status. *Autism* 19, 20–28. doi: 10.1177/1362361313509731

Herringshaw, A. J., Ammons, C. J., Deramus, T. P., and Kana, R. K. (2016). Hemispheric differences in language processing in autism spectrum disorders: a meta-analysis of neuroimaging studies. *Autism Res.* doi: 10.1002/aur.1599. [Epub ahead of print].

Hoppenbrouwers, M., Vandermosten, M., and Boets, B. (2014). Autism as a disconnection syndrome: a qualitative and quantitative review of diffusion tensor imaging studies. *Res. Autism Spectr. Disord.* 8, 387–412. doi: 10.1016/j.rasd.2013.12.018

Hudry, K., Leadbitter, K., Temple, K., Slonims, V., McConachie, H., Aldred, C., et al. (2010). Preschoolers with autism show greater impairment in receptive compared with expressive language abilities. *Int. J. Lang. Commun. Disord.* 45, 681–690. doi: 10.3109/13682820903461493

Itahashi, T., Yamada, T., Nakamura, M., Watanabe, H., Yamagata, B., Jimbo, D., et al. (2015). Linked alterations in gray and white matter morphology in adults with high-functioning autism spectrum disorder: a multimodal brain imaging study. *Neuroimage Clin.* 7, 155–169. doi: 10.1016/j.nicl.2014.11.019

Jones, E. J., Gliga, T., Bedford, R., Charman, T., and Johnson, M. H. (2014). Developmental pathways to autism: a review of prospective studies of infants at risk. *Neurosci. Biobehav. Rev.* 39, 1–33. doi: 10.1016/j.neubiorev.2013.12.001

Jones, W., and Klin, A. (2013). Attention to eyes is present but in decline in 2-6-month-old infants later diagnosed with autism. *Nature* 504, 427–431. doi: 10.1038/nature12715

Jou, R. J., Minshew, N. J., Keshavan, M. S., Vitale, M. P., and Hardan, A. Y. (2010). Enlarged right superior temporal gyrus in children and adolescents with autism. *Brain Res.* 1360, 205–212. doi: 10.1016/j.brainres.2010.09.005

Kanner, L. (1943). Autistic disturbances of affective contact. *Nervous Child* 2, 217–250.

Kasari, C., Brady, N., Lord, C., and Tager-Flusberg, H. (2013). Assessing the minimally verbal school-aged child with autism spectrum disorder. *Autism Res.* 6, 479–493. doi: 10.1002/aur.1334

Kleinhans, N. M., Müller, R. A., Cohen, D. N., and Courchesne, E. (2008). Atypical functional lateralization of language in autism spectrum disorders. *Brain Res.* 1221, 115–125. doi: 10.1016/j.brainres.2008.04.080

Klin, A. (1991). Young autistic children's listening preferences in regard to speech: a possible characterization of the symptom of social withdrawal. *J. Autism Dev. Disord.* 21, 29–42. doi: 10.1007/BF02206995

Klin, A. (1992). Listening preferences in regard to speech in four children with developmental disabilities. *J. Child Psychol. Psychiatry* 33, 763–769. doi: 10.1111/j.1469-7610.1992.tb00911.x

Klin, A., Lin, D. J., Gorrindo, P., Ramsay, G., and Jones, W. (2009). Two-year-olds with autism orient to non-social contingencies rather than biological motion. *Nature* 459, 257–261. doi: 10.1038/nature07868

Klintwall, L., Eldevik, S., and Eikeseth, S. (2013). Narrowing the gap: effects of intervention on developmental trajectories in autism. *Autism.* 19, 53–63. doi: 10.1177/1362361313510067

Knaus, T. A., Silver, A. M., Kennedy, M., Lindgren, K. A., Dominick, K. C., Siegel, J., et al. (2010). Language laterality in autism spectrum disorder and typical controls: a functional, volumetric, and diffusion tensor MRI study. *Brain Lang.* 112, 113–120. doi: 10.1016/j.bandl.2009.11.005

Knaus, T. A., Silver, A. M., Lindgren, K. A., Hadjikhani, N., and Tager-Flusberg, H. (2008). fMRI activation during a language task in adolescents with ASD. *J. Int. Neuropsychol. Soc.* 14, 967–979. doi: 10.1017/S1355617708081216

Koenig, T., Prichep, L., Lehmann, D., Sosa, P. V., Braeker, E., Kleinlogel, H., et al. (2002). Millisecond by millisecond, year by year: normative EEG microstates and developmental stages. *Neuroimage* 16, 41–48. doi: 10.1006/nimg.2002.1070

Kohls, G., Chevallier, C., Troiani, V., and Schultz, R. T. (2012). Social 'wanting' dysfunction in autism: neurobiological underpinnings and treatment implications. *J. Neurodev. Disord.* 4:10. doi: 10.1186/1866-1955-4-10

Kriegstein, K. V., and Giraud, A. L. (2004). Distinct functional substrates along the right superior temporal sulcus for the processing of voices. *Neuroimage* 22, 948–955. doi: 10.1016/j.neuroimage.2004.02.020

Kuhl, P. K. (2004). Early language acquisition: cracking the speech code. *Nat. Rev. Neurosci.* 5, 831–843. doi: 10.1038/nrn1533

Kuhl, P. K. (2010). Brain mechanisms in early language acquisition. *Neuron* 67, 713–727. doi: 10.1016/j.neuron.2010.08.038

Kuhl, P. K., Coffey-Corina, S., Padden, D., and Dawson, G. (2005). Links between social and linguistic processing of speech in preschool children with autism: behavioral and electrophysiological measures. *Dev. Sci.* 8, F1–F12. doi: 10.1111/j.1467-7687.2004.00384.x

Kuhl, P. K., Coffey-Corina, S., Padden, D., Munson, J., Estes, A., and Dawson, G. (2013). Brain responses to words in 2-year-olds with autism predict developmental outcomes at age 6. *PLoS ONE* 8:e64967. doi: 10.1371/journal.pone.0064967

Kuhl, P. K., Tsao, F. M., and Liu, H. M. (2003). Foreign-language experience in infancy: effects of short-term exposure and social interaction on phonetic learning. *Proc. Natl. Acad. Sci. U.S.A.* 100, 9096–9101. doi: 10.1073/pnas.1532872100

Kujala, T., Lepistö, T., and Näätänen, R. (2013). The neural basis of aberrant speech and audition in autism spectrum disorders. *Neurosci. Biobehav. Rev.* 37, 697–704. doi: 10.1016/j.neubiorev.2013.01.006

Lai, G., Pantazatos, S. P., Schneider, H., and Hirsch, J. (2012). Neural systems for speech and song in autism. *Brain* 135, 961–975. doi: 10.1093/brain/awr335

Lai, G., Schneider, H. D., Schwarzenberger, J. C., and Hirsch, J. (2011). Speech stimulation during functional MR imaging as a potential indicator of autism. *Radiology* 260, 521–530. doi: 10.1148/radiol.11101576

Lai, M. C., Lombardo, M. V., Ecker, C., Chakrabarti, B., Suckling, J., Bullmore, E. T., et al. (2015). Neuroanatomy of individual differences in language in adult males with autism. *Cereb. Cortex* 25, 3613–3628. doi: 10.1093/cercor/bhu211

Landa, R., and Garrett-Mayer, E. (2006). Development in infants with autism spectrum disorders: a prospective study. *J. Child Psychol. Psychiatry* 47, 629–638. doi: 10.1111/j.1469-7610.2006.01531.x

Lange, N., Travers, B. G., Bigler, E. D., Prigge, M. B., Froehlich, A. L., Nielsen, J. A., et al. (2015). Longitudinal volumetric brain changes in autism spectrum disorder ages 6-35 years. *Autism Res.* 8, 82–93. doi: 10.1002/aur.1427

Latinus, M., and Belin, P. (2011). Human voice perception. *Curr. Biol.* 21, R143–R145. doi: 10.1016/j.cub.2010.12.033

Lattner, S., Meyer, M. E., and Friederici, A. D. (2005). Voice perception: sex, pitch, and the right hemisphere. *Hum. Brain Mapp.* 24, 11–20. doi: 10.1002/hbm.20065

Lehmann, D., and Michel, C. M. (2011). EEG-defined functional microstates as basic building blocks of mental processes. *Clin. Neurophysiol.* 122, 1073–1074. doi: 10.1016/j.clinph.2010.11.003

Lenroot, R. K., and Yeung, P. K. (2013). Heterogeneity within autism spectrum disorders: what have we learned from neuroimaging studies? *Front. Hum. Neurosci.* 7:733. doi: 10.3389/fnhum.2013.00733

Lewis, J. D., Evans, A. C., Pruett, J. R., Botteron, K., Zwaigenbaum, L., Estes, A., et al. (2014). Network inefficiencies in autism spectrum disorder at 24 months. *Transl. Psychiatry* 4:e388. doi: 10.1038/tp.2014.24

Lindell, A. K., and Hudry, K. (2013). Atypicalities in cortical structure, handedness, and functional lateralization for language in autism spectrum disorders. *Neuropsychol. Rev.* 23, 257–270. doi: 10.1007/s11065-013-9234-5

Lloyd-Fox, S., Blasi, A., Mercure, E., Elwell, C. E., and Johnson, M. H. (2012). The emergence of cerebral specialization for the human voice over the first months of life. *Soc. Neurosci.* 7, 317–330. doi: 10.1080/17470919.2011.614696

Lombardo, M. V., Pierce, K., Eyler, L. T., Carter Barnes, C., Ahrens-Barbeau, C., Solso, S., et al. (2015). Different functional neural substrates for good and poor language outcome in autism. *Neuron* 86, 567–577. doi: 10.1016/j.neuron.2015.03.023

Lord, C., Bishop, S., and Anderson, D. (2015). Developmental trajectories as autism phenotypes. *Am. J. Med. Genet. C Semin. Med. Genet.* 169, 198–208. doi: 10.1002/ajmg.c.31440

Luyster, R. J., Kadlec, M. B., Carter, A., and Tager-Flusberg, H. (2008). Language assessment and development in toddlers with autism spectrum disorders. *J. Autism Dev. Disord.* 38, 1426–1438. doi: 10.1007/s10803-007-0510-1

Mandel, D. R., Jusczyk, P. W., and Pisoni, D. B. (1995). Infants recognition of the sound patterns of their own names. *Psychol. Sci.* 6, 314–317. doi: 10.1111/j.1467-9280.1995.tb00517.x

Marno, H., Farroni, T., Vidal Dos Santos, Y., Ekramnia, M., Nespor, M., and Mehler, J. (2015). Can you see what I am talking about? Human speech triggers referential expectation in four-month-old infants. *Sci. Rep.* 5:13594. doi: 10.1038/srep13594

McPartland, J. C., Coffman, M., and Pelphrey, K. A. (2011). Recent advances in understanding the neural bases of autism spectrum disorder. *Curr. Opin. Pediatr.* 23, 628–632. doi: 10.1097/MOP.0b013e32834cb9c9

Michel, C. M., and Murray, M. M. (2012). Towards the utilization of EEG as a brain imaging tool. *Neuroimage* 61, 371–385. doi: 10.1016/j.neuroimage.2011.12.039

Michel, C. M., Murray, M. M., Lantz, G., Gonzalez, S., Spinelli, L., and Grave De Peralta, R. (2004). EEG source imaging. *Clin. Neurophysiol.* 115, 2195–2222. doi: 10.1016/j.clinph.2004.06.001

Minagawa-Kawai, Y., Naoi, N., Kikuchi, N., Yamamoto, J., Nakamura, K., and Kojima, S. (2009). Cerebral laterality for phonemic and prosodic cue decoding in children with autism. *Neuroreport* 20, 1219–1224. doi: 10.1097/WNR.0b013e32832fa65f

Minagawa-Kawai, Y., Van Der Lely, H., Ramus, F., Sato, Y., Mazuka, R., and Dupoux, E. (2011). Optical brain imaging reveals general auditory and language-specific processing in early infant development. *Cereb. Cortex* 21, 254–261. doi: 10.1093/cercor/bhq082

Miron, O., Ari-Even Roth, D., Gabis, L. V., Henkin, Y., Shefer, S., Dinstein, I., et al. (2015). Prolonged auditory brainstem responses in infants with autism. *Autism Res.* 9, 689–695. doi: 10.1002/aur.1561

Mitchell, S., Brian, J., Zwaigenbaum, L., Roberts, W., Szatmari, P., Smith, I., et al. (2006). Early language and communication development of infants later diagnosed with autism spectrum disorder. *J. Dev. Behav. Pediatr.* 27, S69–S78. doi: 10.1097/00004703-200604002-00004

Mody, M., Manoach, D. S., Guenther, F. H., Kenet, T., Bruno, K. A., McDougle, C. J., et al. (2013). Speech and language in autism spectrum disorder: a view through the lens of behavior and brain imaging. *Neuropsychiatry* 3, 223–232. doi: 10.2217/npy.13.19

Murray, M. M., Brunet, D., and Michel, C. M. (2008). Topographic ERP analyses: a step-by-step tutorial review. *Brain Topogr.* 20, 249–264. doi: 10.1007/s10548-008-0054-5

Näätänen, R. (1995). The mismatch negativity: a powerful tool for cognitive neuroscience. *Ear Hear.* 16, 6–18. doi: 10.1097/00003446-199502000-00002

Näätänen, R. (2003). Mismatch negativity: clinical research and possible applications. *Int. J. Psychophysiol.* 48, 179–188. doi: 10.1016/S0167-8760(03)00053-9

Nadig, A. S., Ozonoff, S., Young, G. S., Rozga, A., Sigman, M., and Rogers, S. J. (2007). A prospective study of response to name in infants at risk for autism. *Arch. Pediatr. Adolesc. Med.* 161, 378–383. doi: 10.1001/archpedi.161.4.378

Norbury, C. F., Griffiths, H., and Nation, K. (2010). Sound before meaning: word learning in autistic disorders. *Neuropsychologia* 48, 4012–4019. doi: 10.1016/j.neuropsychologia.2010.10.015

Nordahl, C. W., Lange, N., Li, D. D., Barnett, L. A., Lee, A., Buonocore, M. H., et al. (2011). Brain enlargement is associated with regression in preschool-age boys with autism spectrum disorders. *Proc. Natl. Acad. Sci. U.S.A.* 108, 20195–20200. doi: 10.1073/pnas.1107560108

Nordahl, C. W., Mello, M., Shen, A. M., Shen, M. D., Vismara, L. A., Li, D., et al. (2016). Methods for acquiring MRI data in children with autism spectrum disorder and intellectual impairment without the use of sedation. *J. Neurodev. Disord.* 8, 20. doi: 10.1186/s11689-016-9154-9

Nordahl, C. W., Simon, T. J., Zierhut, C., Solomon, M., Rogers, S. J., and Amaral, D. G. (2008). Brief report: methods for acquiring structural MRI data in very young children with autism without the use of sedation. *J. Autism Dev. Disord.* 38, 1581–1590. doi: 10.1007/s10803-007-0514-x

Oner, P., Oner, O., and Munir, K. (2014). Three-item Direct Observation Screen (TIDOS) for autism spectrum disorder. *Autism* 18, 733–742. doi: 10.1177/1362361313487028

Ortiz-Mantilla, S., Choe, M. S., Flax, J., Grant, P. E., and Benasich, A. A. (2010). Associations between the size of the amygdala in infancy and language abilities during the preschool years in normally developing children. *Neuroimage* 49, 2791–2799. doi: 10.1016/j.neuroimage.2009.10.029

Osterling, J., and Dawson, G. (1994). Early recognition of children with autism: a study of first birthday home videotapes. *J. Autism Dev. Disord.* 24, 247–257. doi: 10.1007/BF02172225

Ozonoff, S., Young, G. S., Carter, A., Messinger, D., Yirmiya, N., Zwaigenbaum, L., et al. (2011). Recurrence risk for autism spectrum disorders: a baby siblings research consortium study. *Pediatrics* 128, E488–E495. doi: 10.1542/peds.2010-2825

Patten, E., Belardi, K., Baranek, G. T., Watson, L. R., Labban, J. D., and Oller, D. K. (2014). Vocal patterns in infants with autism spectrum disorder: canonical babbling status and vocalization frequency. *J. Autism Dev. Disord.* 44, 2413–2428. doi: 10.1007/s10803-014-2047-4

Paul, A., Sharda, M., Menon, S., Arora, I., Kansal, N., Arora, K., et al. (2015). The effect of sung speech on socio-communicative responsiveness in children with autism spectrum disorders. *Front. Hum. Neurosci.* 9:555. doi: 10.3389/fnhum.2015.00555

Paul, R., Fuerst, Y., Ramsay, G., Chawarska, K., and Klin, A. (2011). Out of the mouths of babes: vocal production in infant siblings of children with ASD. *J. Child Psychol. Psychiatry* 52, 588–598. doi: 10.1111/j.1469-7610.2010.02332.x

Pelphrey, K. A., Shultz, S., Hudac, C. M., and Vander Wyk, B. C. (2011). Research review: constraining heterogeneity: the social brain and its development in autism spectrum disorder. *J. Child Psychol. Psychiatry* 52, 631–644. doi: 10.1111/j.1469-7610.2010.02349.x

Pernet, C. R., McAleer, P., Latinus, M., Gorgolewski, K. J., Charest, I., Bestelmeyer, P. E., et al. (2015). The human voice areas: spatial organization and inter-individual variability in temporal and extra-temporal cortices. *Neuroimage* 119, 164–174. doi: 10.1016/j.neuroimage.2015.06.050

Pickles, A., Anderson, D. K., and Lord, C. (2014). Heterogeneity and plasticity in the development of language: a 17-year follow-up of children referred early for possible autism. *J. Child Psychol. Psychiatry* 55, 1354–1362. doi: 10.1111/jcpp.12269

Pittau, F., Megevand, P., Sheybani, L., Abela, E., Grouiller, F., Spinelli, L., et al. (2014). Mapping epileptic activity: sources or networks for the clinicians? *Front. Neurol.* 5:218. doi: 10.3389/fneur.2014.00218

Prigge, M. D., Bigler, E. D., Fletcher, P. T., Zielinski, B. A., Ravichandran, C., Anderson, J., et al. (2013). Longitudinal Heschl's gyrus growth during childhood and adolescence in typical development and autism. *Autism Res.* 6, 78–90. doi: 10.1002/aur.1265

Raschle, N., Zuk, J., Ortiz-Mantilla, S., Sliva, D. D., Franceschi, A., Grant, P. E., et al. (2012). Pediatric neuroimaging in early childhood and infancy: challenges and practical guidelines. *Ann. N.Y. Acad. Sci.* 1252, 43–50. doi: 10.1111/j.1749-6632.2012.06457.x

Raschle, N. M., Smith, S. A., Zuk, J., Dauvermann, M. R., Figuccio, M. J., and Gaab, N. (2014). Investigating the neural correlates of voice versus speech-sound directed information in pre-school children. *PLoS ONE* 9:e115549. doi: 10.1371/journal.pone.0115549

Redcay, E., and Courchesne, E. (2005). When is the brain enlarged in autism? A meta-analysis of all brain size reports. *Biol. Psychiatry* 58, 1–9. doi: 10.1016/j.biopsych.2005.03.026

Redcay, E., and Courchesne, E. (2008). Deviant functional magnetic resonance imaging patterns of brain activity to speech in 2-3-year-old children with autism spectrum disorder. *Biol. Psychiatry* 64, 589–598. doi: 10.1016/j.biopsych.2008.05.020

Righi, G., Tierney, A. L., Tager-Flusberg, H., and Nelson, C. A. (2014). Functional connectivity in the first year of life in infants at risk for autism spectrum disorder: an EEG study. *PLoS ONE* 9:e105176. doi: 10.1371/journal.pone.0105176

Rihs, T. A., Tomescu, M. I., Britz, J., Rochas, V., Custo, A., Schneider, M., et al. (2013). Altered auditory processing in frontal and left temporal cortex in 22q11.2 deletion syndrome: a group at high genetic risk for schizophrenia. *Psychiatry Res.* 212, 141–149. doi: 10.1016/j.pscychresns.2012.09.002

Robinson, E. B., Neale, B. M., and Hyman, S. E. (2015). Genetic research in autism spectrum disorders. *Curr. Opin. Pediatr.* 27, 685–691. doi: 10.1097/MOP.0000000000000278

Rogers, S. J. (2009). What are infant siblings teaching us about autism in infancy? *Autism Res.* 2, 125–137. doi: 10.1002/aur.81

Schaer, M., Franchini, M., and Eliez, S. (2014). Latest findings in autism research. *Swiss Arch. Neurol. Psychiatry* 165, 277–289.

Schumann, C. M., Bloss, C. S., Barnes, C. C., Wideman, G. M., Carper, R. A., Akshoomoff, N., et al. (2010). Longitudinal magnetic resonance imaging study of cortical development through early childhood in autism. *J. Neurosci.* 30, 4419–4427. doi: 10.1523/JNEUROSCI.5714-09.2010

Seery, A., Tager-Flusberg, H., and Nelson, C. A. (2014). Event-related potentials to repeated speech in 9-month-old infants at risk for autism spectrum disorder. *J. Neurodev. Disord.* 6:43. doi: 10.1186/1866-1955-6-43

Seery, A. M., Vogel-Farley, V., Tager-Flusberg, H., and Nelson, C. A. (2013). Atypical lateralization of ERP response to native and non-native speech in infants at risk for autism spectrum disorder. *Dev. Cogn. Neurosci.* 5, 10–24. doi: 10.1016/j.dcn.2012.11.007

Senju, A., and Johnson, M. H. (2009). Atypical eye contact in autism: models, mechanisms and development. *Neurosci. Biobehav. Rev.* 33, 1204–1214. doi: 10.1016/j.neubiorev.2009.06.001

Sharda, M., Midha, R., Malik, S., Mukerji, S., and Singh, N. C. (2015). Fronto-temporal connectivity is preserved during sung but not spoken word listening, across the autism spectrum. *Autism Res.* 8, 174–186. doi: 10.1002/aur.1437

Shen, M. D., Nordahl, C. W., Young, G. S., Wootton-Gorges, S. L., Lee, A., Liston, S. E., et al. (2013). Early brain enlargement and elevated extra-axial fluid in infants who develop autism spectrum disorder. *Brain* 136, 2825–2835. doi: 10.1093/brain/awt166

Simms, M. D., and Jin, X. M. (2015). Autism, language disorder, and social (pragmatic) communication disorder: DSM-V and differential diagnoses. *Pediatr Rev.* 36, 355–362. doi: 10.1542/pir.36-8-355

Sparks, B. F., Friedman, S. D., Shaw, D. W., Aylward, E. H., Echelard, D., Artru, A. A., et al. (2002). Brain structural abnormalities in young children with autism spectrum disorder. *Neurology* 59, 184–192. doi: 10.1212/WNL.59.2.184

Stenberg, N., Bresnahan, M., Gunnes, N., Hirtz, D., Hornig, M., Lie, K. K., et al. (2014). Identifying children with autism spectrum disorder at 18 months in a general population sample. *Paediatr. Perinat. Epidemiol.* 28, 255–262. doi: 10.1111/ppe.12114

Stoner, R., Chow, M. L., Boyle, M. P., Sunkin, S. M., Mouton, P. R., Roy, S., et al. (2014). Patches of disorganization in the neocortex of children with autism. *N. Engl. J. Med.* 370, 1209–1219. doi: 10.1056/NEJMoa 1307491

Tager-Flusberg, H., and Kasari, C. (2013). Minimally verbal school-aged children with autism spectrum disorder: the neglected end of the spectrum. *Autism Res.* 6, 468–478. doi: 10.1002/aur.1329

Tager-Flusberg, H., Rogers, S., Cooper, J., Landa, R., Lord, C., Paul, R., et al. (2009). Defining spoken language benchmarks and selecting measures of expressive language development for young children with autism spectrum disorders. *J. Speech Lang. Hear. Res.* 52, 643–652. doi: 10.1044/1092-4388 (2009/08-0136)

Tincoff, R., and Jusczyk, P. W. (1999). Some beginnings of word comprehension in 6-month-olds. *Psychol. Sci.* 10, 172–175. doi: 10.1111/1467-9280.00127

Tincoff, R., and Jusczyk, P. W. (2012). Six-month-olds comprehend words that refer to parts of the body. *Infancy* 17, 432–444. doi: 10.1111/j.1532-7078.2011.00084.x

Tomescu, M. I., Rihs, T. A., Becker, R., Britz, J., Custo, A., Grouiller, F., et al. (2014). Deviant dynamics of EEG resting state pattern in 22q11.2 deletion syndrome adolescents: a vulnerability marker of schizophrenia? *Schizophr. Res.* 157, 175–181. doi: 10.1016/j.schres.2014.05.036

Turner, M. (1999). Annotation: repetitive behaviour in autism: a review of psychological research. *J. Child Psychol. Psychiatry* 40, 839–849. doi: 10.1111/1469-7610.00502

Viding, E., and Blakemore, S. J. (2007). Endophenotype approach to developmental psychopathology: implications for autism research. *Behav. Genet.* 37, 51–60. doi: 10.1007/s10519-006-9105-4

von Kriegstein, K., Eger, E., Kleinschmidt, A., and Giraud, A. L. (2003). Modulation of neural responses to speech by directing attention to voices or verbal content. *Brain Res. Cogn. Brain Res.* 17, 48–55. doi: 10.1016/S0926-6410(03) 00079-X

Watt, N., Wetherby, A. M., Barber, A., and Morgan, L. (2008). Repetitive and stereotyped behaviors in children with autism spectrum disorders in the second year of life. *J. Autism Dev. Disord.* 38, 1518–1533. doi: 10.1007/s10803-007-0532-8

Weinstein, M., Ben-Sira, L., Levy, Y., Zachor, D. A., Ben Itzhak, E., Artzi, M., et al. (2011). Abnormal white matter integrity in young children with autism. *Hum. Brain Mapp.* 32, 534–543. doi: 10.1002/hbm.21042

Wetherby, A. M., Woods, J., Allen, L., Cleary, J., Dickinson, H., and Lord, C. (2004). Early indicators of autism spectrum disorders in the second year of life. *J. Autism Dev. Disord.* 34, 473–493. doi: 10.1007/s10803-004-2544-y

Wolff, J. J., Gu, H., Gerig, G., Elison, J. T., Styner, M., Gouttard, S., et al. (2012). Differences in white matter fiber tract development present from 6 to 24 months in infants with autism. *Am. J. Psychiatry* 169, 589–600. doi: 10.1176/appi.ajp.2011.11091447

Xiao, Z., Qiu, T., Ke, X., Xiao, X., Xiao, T., Liang, F., et al. (2014). Autism spectrum disorder as early neurodevelopmental disorder: evidence from the brain imaging abnormalities in 2-3 years old toddlers. *J. Autism Dev. Disord.* 44, 1633–1640. doi: 10.1007/s10803-014-2033-x

Yirmiya, N., Gamliel, I., Pilowsky, T., Feldman, R., Baron-Cohen, S., and Sigman, M. (2006). The development of siblings of children with autism at 4 and 14 months: social engagement, communication, and cognition. *J. Child Psychol. Psychiatry* 47, 511–523. doi: 10.1111/j.1469-7610.2005.01528.x

Zhubi, A., Cook, E. H., Guidotti, A., and Grayson, D. R. (2014). Epigenetic mechanisms in autism spectrum disorder. *Int. Rev. Neurobiol.* 115, 203–244. doi: 10.1016/B978-0-12-801311-3.00006-8

Zwaigenbaum, L., Bryson, S., and Garon, N. (2013). Early identification of autism spectrum disorders. *Behav. Brain Res.* 251, 133–146. doi: 10.1016/j.bbr.2013.04.004

Zwaigenbaum, L., Bryson, S., Lord, C., Rogers, S., Carter, A., Carver, L., et al. (2009). Clinical assessment and management of toddlers with suspected autism spectrum disorder: insights from studies of high-risk infants. *Pediatrics* 123, 1383–1391. doi: 10.1542/peds.2008-1606

16

Paternal HLA-C and Maternal Killer-Cell Immunoglobulin-Like Receptor Genotypes in the Development of Autism

*Moriya Gamliel[1], Karen L. Anderson[2], Richard P. Ebstein[3], Nurit Yirmiya[4] and David Mankuta[2]**

[1] *Department of Immunology and Cancer Research, Hadassah-Hebrew University Medical Center, Jerusalem, Israel,* [2] *Department of Obstetrics and Gynecology, Hadassah-Hebrew University Medical Center, Jerusalem, Israel,* [3] *Department of Psychology, National University of Singapore, Singapore,* [4] *Department of Psychology, The Hebrew University of Jerusalem, Jerusalem, Israel*

Edited by:
Benjamin Gesundheit, Cell El Ltd., Israel

Reviewed by:
Munis Dundar, Erciyes University, Turkey
Ganesan Venkatasubramanian, National Institute of Mental Health and Neurosciences, India

***Correspondence:**
David Mankuta
mankutad@gmail.com

Killer-cell immunoglobulin-like receptors (KIRs) are a family of cell surface proteins found on natural killer cells, which are components of the innate immune system. KIRs recognize MHC class I proteins, mainly HLA-C and are further divided into two groups: short-tailed 2/3DS activating receptors and long-tailed 2/3DL inhibitory receptors. Based on the Barker Hypothesis, the origins of illness can be traced back to embryonic development in the uterus, and since KIR:HLA interaction figures prominently in the maternal–fetal interface, we investigated whether specific KIR:HLA combinations may be found in autism spectrum disorders (ASD) children compared with their healthy parents. This study enrolled 49 ASD children from different Israeli families, and their healthy parents. Among the parents, a higher frequency of HLA-C2 allotypes was found in the fathers, while its corresponding ligand 2DS1 was found in higher percentage in the maternal group. However, such skewing in KIR:HLA frequencies did not appear in the ASD children. Additionally, analysis of "overall activation" indicated higher activation in maternal than in paternal cohorts.

Keywords: autism, pregnancy, natural killer, KIR, HLA

INTRODUCTION

Autism spectrum disorders (ASD) encompass a range of neurodevelopmental syndromes defined by difficulties in social communication and stereotyped behaviors (1). Recent data indicate a prevalence of up to 1 in 66 children (2). Although studies in families and twins (3) point toward a significant genetic component with a high sibling recurrence risk (4), in only a few cases can a clear genetic component be identified. Various factors – hormonal, immunological, and biochemical – have been implicated in autism's etiology, but their roles in the symptomology of the disease remain undefined (5). Immune system dysregulation reported in ASD patients includes differential cell fractions and reactivity, autoimmune phenomena, altered cytokine and antibody profiles, and genetic correlations (6). These findings partially corroborate the theory that chronic neurological inflammation in fetal or newborn brain underlies the development of ASD. Subsequent dysregulation of the immune system may contribute to ASD development in genetically susceptible children.

Abbreviations: ASD, autism spectrum disorders; HLA, histocompatibility leukocyte antigens; KIR, killer-cell immunoglobulin-like receptor; NK, natural killer.

Altered natural killer (NK) cell activity has been reported in the periphery of ASD patients (7). However, these innate immune cells' function in the pathogenesis of autism is yet unclear. NK cells act specifically against infected or transformed cells, with their actions governed by a balance between activating and inhibitory receptors, each recognizing specific molecules on a given target (8). Killer-cell immunoglobulin-like receptors (KIRs) are a group of cell surface molecules involved in regulating activity of NK (and some T) cells. KIRs are classified as either inhibitory or activating. Their nomenclature is based on the number of extracellular Ig-like domains, and whether the cytoplasmic domain is *long* (L) or *short* (S). The KIR gene family is clustered within the LRC leukocyte receptor complex on chromosome 19q13.4, encoding a total of 14 genes and 2 pseudo genes. KIR genes exhibit allelic and haplotypic variability, while each mature NK cell expresses a specific set of KIRs.

Killer-cell immunoglobulin-like receptor counterparts, the HLA class I ligands, are also extremely polymorphic. This generates an additional level of functional diversity. Both KIRs and their HLA ligands are encoded on different chromosomes (19 and 6, respectively), and therefore segregate independently of each other. This expands the repertoire of possible profiles within any given population (9). Specific KIR–HLA combinations have been suggested as underlying susceptibility as well as resistance to various diseases and conditions (10); the functional implications are less clear. Genetic associations have been reported in infectious diseases (11), autoimmunity (12), inflammatory conditions, reproductive failure, and cancer. Biological models in such studies need to incorporate these receptor:ligand interactions, beyond mere consideration of KIR–HLA genotyping. Indeed, several methods have been proposed to analyze the overall genotyping detected in a specific subject or whole population (13, 14).

The KIR family predominantly recognizes HLA class I molecules. Specifically, HLA-C is recognized by both inhibitory receptors (KIRs 2DL1, 2DL2, and 2DL3) and activating receptors (KIRs 2DS1, 2DS2, and 2DS4) (**Figure 1**). HLA-C group 1 (C1) allotypes have an asparagine residue at position 80 (C1:N^{80}), and serve as ligands for KIRs 2DL2, 2DL3, and 2DS2. HLA-C group 2 (C2) allotypes function as ligands for KIRs 2DL1 and 2DS1; C2 allotypes have a lysine at position 80 (C2:K^{80}). The interactional affinities of these groups may differ. KIR 2DS4 can bind to both HLA-C C1 and C2 allotypes, and certain HLA-A alleles. KIRs 3DL1 and (putatively) 3DS1 interact with HLA-A BW4:I80 as well as HLA-B allotypes [with either isoleucine (BW4:I80) or threonine (BW4:T80) at position 80].

The aim of our research was to genotype the KIR receptors known to interact with HLA ligands in autistic children and their non-autistic parents (mothers and fathers, separately), and to compare KIR receptor: HLA ligand frequencies between these groups. Our hypothesis was that a non-random distribution of these genes profiles should be found if interactions between these two classes of molecules are relevant to autism.

According to the Barker Hypothesis (15), the source of pathologies – including mental disorders such as ASD – can be traced back to embryonic existence in the intrauterine environment (16, 17). KIRs are expressed by maternal NK cells (decidua, uterine lining), which are in close contact with HLA-expressing fetal tissues (placenta). Such prenatal interaction between maternal KIR and the fetal HLA in the uterus may lead to either enhanced NK activation or NK inhibition, which in turn may exert influence upon the placenta and/or developing fetus (18–20). Resulting immune activation and effects upon the central nervous system may lead to neurological and psychiatric disorders in predisposed patients. A mouse model for intrauterine maternal immune activation has already been demonstrated as a possible mechanism for autism- and schizophrenia-related behaviors in offspring (21).

MATERIALS AND METHODS

Participants

This study comprised of 49 ASD-diagnosed children (38 males, 11 females, a male:female ratio of 3.4:1) from Jewish Israeli families, and their parents. Another six sets of parents of ASD-diagnosed children were enrolled, though no DNA samples were available from their children. DNA samples were collected in Israeli special education schools and treatment centers, by the Israeli Society for Autistic Children (ALUT).[1]

Many of the probands had already been diagnosed with ASD by independent clinicians; two trained clinicians confirmed the

[1] http://www.autismaroundtheglobe.org/countries/Israel.asp

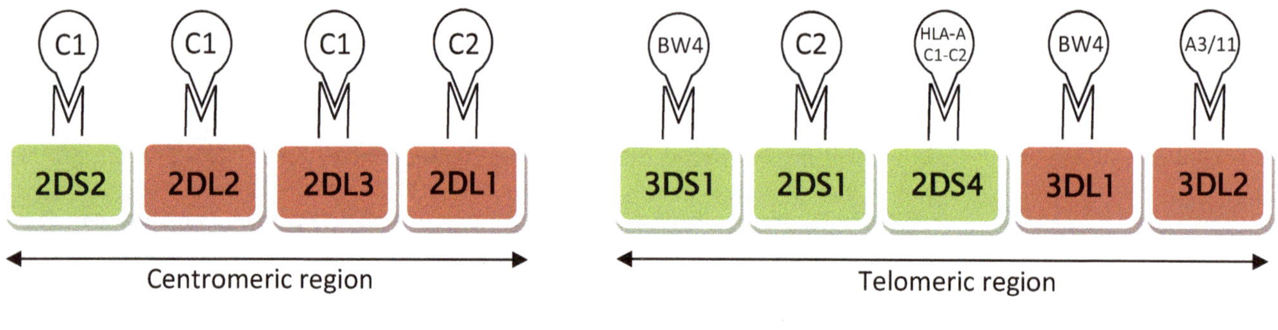

FIGURE 1 | Schematic diagram of activating (green) and inhibitory (red) receptors on natural killer cells, arranged according to centromic/telomeric location. These receptors are known to interact specifically with HLA ligands (HLA Cl or C2, HLA A and B BW4). HLA-C group 1 (Cl) allotypes serve as ligands for KIRs 2DS2, 2DL2, and 2DL3; HLA-C group 2 (C2) functions as ligands for KIRs 2DL1 and 2DS1.

diagnosis for autism or Pervasive Developmental Disorder-Not Otherwise Specified (PDD-NOS). All probands were diagnosed using the Autism Diagnostic Observation Scale-Generic (ADOS-G) and the Autism Diagnostic Interview-Revised (ADI-R). In addition, parents were interviewed using the Vineland Adaptive Behavior Scales-second edition (Vineland™-II) survey interview edition (VABS).

Probands ranged in age between 25 months to 33 years and 8 months. None of the subjects were known, according to parental reports, to have known genetic factors such as chromosomal aberrations, tuberous sclerosis, or other medical complications that could be related to autism. Parents were screened for psychiatric illness (including ASD); all results were found to be negative.

The Ethics Committee of the Israeli Health Ministry approved this study. All participants signed informed consent forms in advance.

Genotyping

DNA was extracted from either peripheral blood or buccal cells using a commercial DNA purification kit (Epicentre's Master Pure™, Madison, WI, USA).

The presence or absence of nine KIR genes known to interact with specific HLA ligands was determined by SSP-PCR (sequence-specific primer polymerase chain reaction), as previously described (22, 23), using nine pairs of primers specific for these KIR genes. This mapping enables verification of presence or absence of a KIR, without discriminating specific heterozygous or homozygote status. A 440/750-bp fragment of the CRP/CAMP, respectively, was included in each PCR as an internal control. The following KIR genes were amplified under identical conditions: 2DL2, 2DL1, 3DL1, 2DS2, 2DS4, and 3DS1. Their PCR thermo-profile comprised 2 min at 92°C; then 25 s at 91°C, 45 s at 65°C, and 45 s at 72°C for 4 cycles; 25 s at 91°C, 45 s at 60°C, and 45 s at 72°C for 26 cycles; 25 s at 91°C, 60 s at 55°C, and 45 s at 72°C for 5 cycles, and 10 min at 72°C (an extension step, in the case of 3DL1 and 3DS1 was set to 2 min). Other KIR amplifications (for 2DL3, 3DL2, and 2DS1) were initiated with denaturation for 2 min at 92°C; then 25 s at 91°C, 45 s at 57°C, and 45 s at 72°C for 4 cycles; 25 s at 91°C, 45 s at 54°C, and 45 s at 72°C for 26 cycles; 25 s at 91°C, 60 s at 50°C, and 45 s at 72°C for 5 cycles, and 10 min at 72°C. All primer sequences, expected PCR products and allelic recoveries are listed in **Table 1**.

The distinction of HLA-C KIR ligand groups C1 (N^{80}) and C2 (K^{80}) was also performed by SSP-PCR. The common HLA-C forward primer was either paired with the C1 (N^{80}) or C2 (K^{80}) reverse primers, leading to an amplification product of 139 bp (**Table 2**). This mapping enables discrimination between heterozygous/homozygous status, i.e., C1–C1, C1–C2, or C2–C2. In each HLA PCR reaction, a 440-bp fragment of the CRP gene was included as an internal PCR control. The thermo-profile comprised an initial denaturation of 3 min at 95°C; then 10 s at 95°C, 30 s at 65°C, and 45 s at 72°C for 10 cycles; 10 s at 95°C, 30 s at 58°C, 45 s at 72°C for 22 cycles, and 10 min at 72°C.

For HLA-C protocol validation, selected samples (n = 30; 10 homozygous C1/C1, 10 homozygous C2/C2 and 10 heterozygous C1/C2) that had previously been typed for HLA-C at high resolution by LIFECODES® HLA SSO Typing Kit (Gen-Probe, Inc.) (Later sequenced by Allele SEQR® HLA PCR/Sequencing Kit, Abbott Molecular) were analyzed by our SSP-PCR.

HLA-A BW4 and HLA-B BW4-I^{80}/T^{80} were identified under the same conditions as HLA-C. Validation for HLA-A and B was also performed by selected samples previously genotyped by high

TABLE 1 | KIR genotyping primers.

KIR	Forward primers (5′–3′) / Reverse primers (5′–3′)	Amplicon (bp)	Annealing temp (°C)	Control gene	Alleles not detected
2DS2	CGGGCCCCACGGTTT GGTCACTCGAGTTTGACCACTCA	240	60	CRP	
2DS4	TAGGCTCCCTGCAGTGCG GAGTTTGACCACTCGTAGGGAGC	129	63	CAMP	2DS4*003 2DS4*004 2DS4*006 2DS4*007 2DS4*009
2DS1	CTTCTCCATCAGTCGCAT AGGGTCACTGGGAGCTGACAA	102	53	CAMP	
3DS1	GCCCAGCGCTGTGGTGCCTCGC CTGCAAGGGCACGCATCATGGA	1958	71	CAMP	3DS1*047
2DL2	CTGGCCCACCCAGGTCG GGACCGATGGAGAAGTTGGCT	173	60	CRP	2DL2*004
2DL1	AACTTCTCCATCAGTCGCATGAC GGTCACTGGGAGCTGACAC	100	60	CRP	
2DL3	CTTCATCGCTGGTGCTG AGGCTCTTGGTCCATTACAA	516	54	CAMP	2DL3*007
3DL1	CTCCATCGGTCCCATGATGCT CGCTCTCTCCTGCCTGAACCT	1725	65	CAMP	
3DL2	CCCATGAACGTAGGCTCCG CACACGCAGGGCAGGG	130	54	CRP	

Expected PCR products, annealing temperature (°C), and allelic specificity are given per pair of primers. Primer reference is (22) for all KIRs except 2DS1, for which the primer reference is (23).

resolution methods. All primer sequences [based on Hong et al. (23)] and expected PCR products for HLA-A, -B, and -C genotyping are listed in **Table 2**.

All amplified SSP-PCR products were visualized by agarose gel electrophoresis using a non-mutagenic fluorescent reagent ("Novel Juice"; GeneDireX, Las Vegas City, NV, USA). Selected sample from each amplified band was sent for sequencing.

Statistical Analysis

The Wilcoxon Signed-Ranks test ($p < 0.05$) was determined using SPSS software. When combination of more than one factor to specific receptor was detected, some different aspects were detected. The first refers to all ligands equally, and compares the sum of all ligands (relevant to specific receptor) found in each person to determine the mean value. This is defined as "Ligand Composite" (**Table 7**). Secondly, an alternative designation of "Ligand One+" compares existence of at least one ligand to this specific receptor. This was the case in C1 + 2DL2/2DL3/2DS2, C2 + 2DL1/2DS1 (**Table 8**). In contrast, for overall signaling (**Table 9**) and in the case of A_BW4 + 3DL1/3DS1 and B_BW4 + 3DL1/3DS1 (**Table 7**) only the first option is shown. All HLAB genotyping analysis is described as "total," meaning having I^{80}/T^{80}.

RESULTS

HLA and KIRs Frequency Comparison

Comparison of the nine different KIR genes and HLA frequencies revealed several main differences between parents of autistic children (**Tables 3–5**).

The most surprising finding is higher frequency of HLA-C2 allotypes in fathers of ASD children (mean 0.73 vs. 0.52, $p = 0.038$), in contrast to C1 frequencies, which were the same in both mothers and fathers (0.88 vs. 0.91) (**Table 5**). On the other hand, 2DS1, which is known to interact specifically with HLA-C2, was found in higher percentage (0.55 vs. 0.34, $p = 0.022$) in the maternal group (**Table 4**). Additionally 3DS1, with its specificity against BW4 allotypes, was found to be higher in mothers than in their ASD children (0.51 vs. 0.36, $p = 0.044$) (**Table 4**). Other KIR frequencies (2DL2, 2DL1, 2DL3, 3DL1, 3DL2, 2DS2, and 2DS4) were similar in both mothers and fathers, and corresponded with values expected in Asian populations.[2] Most KIR and HLA frequencies in ASD children were similar to those detected in parents.

Positive correlation between parent (mother or father) and child, reflecting the likelihood of transferring the gene (**Tables 3–5**) were found relative to most of genes, which may reflect a high probability of homozygous genotyping for these genes.

KIR Signaling Through HLA Molecules

Relevant combinations between KIR receptors and their specific HLA ligands were detected (**Table 6**). ASD children did not exhibit

[2] http://www.allelefrequencies.net/kir6008a.asp

TABLE 2 | PCR primers for human leukocyte antigen (HLA) amplification.

HLA allotype	Direction	Forward primers (5′–3′) / Reverse primers (5′–3′)	Amplicon (bp)
HLA-C	Forward	CGCCGCGAGTCCGAGAGG	139
	Reverse (C1: N^{80})	GTTGTAGTAGCCGCGCAGG	
	Reverse (C2: K^{80})	GTTGTAGTAGCCGCGCAGT	
HLA-A	Forward	CCATTGGGTGTCGGGTTTC	569
BW4:I^{80}	Reverse	CTCTGGTTGTAGTAGCGGAGCGCG	
HLA-B	Forward	ACCCGGACTCAGAATCTCC	366
BW4:I^{80}	Reverse	CTCTGGTTGTAGTAGCGGAGCGCG	
HLA-B	Forward	ACCCGGACTCAGAATCTCC	369
BW4:T^{80}	Reverse	CTCTGGTTGTAGTAGCGGAGCAGG	

Expected PCR product sizes are given. In the case of HLA-C, forward primer was either paired with the C1 (N^{80}) or C2 (K^{80}) reverse primers, leading to an amplification product of 139 bp.
F, forward; R, reverse.

TABLE 3 | Inhibitory KIR frequencies in Israeli families with at least 1 ASD-diagnosed child.

Inhibitory KIR		Child^{ASD}	Father	Child^{ASD}	Mother	Father	Mother
2DL2	Mean	0.59	0.63	0.58	0.66	0.64	0.68
	Z	−0.577		−0.894		−0.408	
	Pearson's *r*	0.487*		0.204		NR	
2DL1	Mean	0.96	0.98	0.96	0.96	0.98	0.95
	Z	−1		0		−1	
	Pearson's *r*	0.7*		−0.039		NR	
2DL3	Mean	0.86	0.84	0.87	0.89	0.84	0.88
	Z	−0.302		−0.333		−0.535	
	Pearson's *r*	0.135		0.212		NR	
3DL1	Mean	0.94	0.94	0.94	0.89	0.93	0.89
	Z	0		−1.342		−0.707	
	Pearson's *r*	0.645*		0.428*		NR	
3DL2	Mean	1	1	1	1	1	1
	Z	0		0		0	
	Pearson's *r*	NR		NR		NR	

Z = Wilcoxon Signed-Ranks Test value.
NR = not relevant.
**p ≤ 0.01.*

TABLE 4 | Activating KIR frequencies in Israeli families with at least 1 ASD-diagnosed child.

Activating KIR		Child^{ASD}	Father	Child^{ASD}	Mother	Father	Mother
2DS2	Mean	0.61	0.63	0.6	0.62	0.64	0.66
	Z	−0.302		−0.209		−0.209	
	Pearson's *r*	0.523**		0.086		NR	
2DS4	Mean	0.96	0.96	0.94	0.89	0.94	0.91
	Z	0		−1.342		−0.707	
	Pearson's *r*	0.478**		0.428**		NR	
2DS1	Mean	0.51	0.37	0.49	0.57	0.34	0.55
	Z	−1.528		−1.069		−2.268*	
	Pearson's *r*	0.154		0.478**		NR	
3DS1	Mean	0.37	0.39	0.36	0.51	0.39	0.5
	Z	−0.728		−2*		−1.279	
	Pearson's *r*	0.281*		0.419**		NR	

Z = Wilcoxon Signed-Ranks Test value.
NR = not relevant.
**p ≤ 0.05.*
***p ≤ 0.01.*

TABLE 5 | HLA ligand frequencies in Israeli families with at least 1 ASD-diagnosed child.

HLA Ligand		Child^{ASD}		Father	Child^{ASD}		Mother	Father		Mother
HLAC1	Mean	0.86		0.9	0.83		0.85	0.88		0.91
	Z		−0.707			−0.333			−0.577	
	Pearson's *r*		0.248			0.371**			NR	
HLAC2	Mean	0.65		0.72	0.68		0.57	0.73		0.52
	Z		−0.535			−1.342			−2.058*	
	Pearson's *r*		0.353**			0.214			NR	
HLA-A-BW4	Mean	0.33		0.37	0.3		0.28	0.36		0.3
	Z		−0.577			−0.229			−0.557	
	Pearson's *r*		0.462**			0.134			NR	
HLA-B-BW4	Mean	0.88		0.86	0.88		0.81	0.87		0.8
	Z		0.33			1.272			1	
	Pearson's *r*		0.203			0.248*			NR	

Z = Wilcoxon Signed-Ranks Test value.
NR = not relevant.
$^{*}p \leq 0.05$.
$^{**}p \leq 0.01$.

TABLE 6 | Frequency of each KIR detected and its corresponding ligand in Israeli ASD families, consisting of both parents and an ASD-diagnosed child.

KIR		Child^{ASD}		Father	Child^{ASD}		Mother	Father		Mother
2DL2 + C1	*Z*		−0.832			−1.342			−1.177	
	Pearson's *r*		0.474**			0.259			NR	
2DL1 + C2	*Z*		−0.535			−1.091			−1.859	
	Pearson's *r*		0.372**			0.176			NR	
2DL3 + C1	*Z*		0			0			−0.426	
	Pearson's *r*		0.227			0.321*			NR	
3DL1 + A_BW4	*Z*		−0.227			−0.243			−0.392	
	Pearson's *r*		0.148			0.156			NR	
3DL1 + B_BW4	*Z*		−0.302			−1.941*			−1.225	
	Pearson's *r*		0.283*			0.359**			NR	
2DS2 + C1	*Z*		−0.577			−0.853			−1	
	Pearson's *r*		0.511**			0.174			NR	
2DS4 + A_BW4	*Z*		−0.577			−0.243			−0.6	
	Pearson's *r*		0.393**			0.156			NR	
2DS4 + B_BW4	*Z*		−0.302			−1.941*			−1.279	
	Pearson's *r*		0.211			0.359**			NR	
2DS1 + C2	*Z*		−0.243			−0.775			−0.784	
	Pearson's *r*		0.132			0.345**			NR	
3DS1 + A_BW4	*Z*		0			−0.577			−0.535	
	Pearson's *r*		0.456**			0.12			NR	
3DS1 + B_BW4	*Z*		−0.728			−1.414			−0.853	
	Pearson's *r*		0.25			0.295*			NR	

Z = Wilcoxon Signed-Ranks Test value.
NR, not relevant.
$^{*}p \leq 0.05$.
$^{**}p \leq 0.01$.

high frequency of the combination HLA-C2 + KIR2DS1, despite elevated paternal HLA-C2 and maternal 2DS1 frequencies.

Correlational analysis between parent (mother or father) and child reflected the likelihood of transferring a gene with its corresponding ligand. Significant values were reported in most cases (**Table 6**). It is important to mention, these gene families are located on different autosomal chromosomes, supporting homozygous status for most of the genes.

The next evaluation involves the examination of particular HLA ligands with presence/absence of all relevant activating/inhibitory KIR genes (**Table 7**). "Ligand Composite" analysis (see Materials and Methods) was compared between ASD children and their parents, as well as "Ligand One+" values (**Table 8**). Significant differences were found between parental groups in the case of C2 + 2DL1/2DS1 "Ligand One+" ($p = 0.040$).

Overall Balance of Activation and Inhibition

Final analysis (**Table 9**) presents a full view of the genotyping. It may allow insight to the overall expected interaction of KIR/HLA in Israeli autistic individuals and their non-autistic parents,

TABLE 7 | Comparison of particular HLA ligands with presence/absence of all relevant activating/inhibitory KIR genes in Israeli ASD families.

Ligand composite		Child^{ASD} Father	Child^{ASD} Mother	Father Mother
C1 + 2DL2/2DL3/2DS2	*Z*	−0.363	−0.779	−1.178
C2 + 2DL1/2DS1	*Z*	−0.213	−0.288	−0.704
A_BW4 + 3DL1/3DS1	*Z*	−0.216	−0.378	−0.429
B_BW4 + 3DL1/3DS1	*Z*	−0.382	−0.177	−0.28

Z = Wilcoxon Signed-Ranks Test value.

TABLE 8 | Interactions of KIR and HLA in autistic Israeli patients and their parents, based on overall genotype mapping.

Ligand one+		Child^{ASD} Father	Child^{ASD} Mother	Father Mother
C1 + 2DL2/2DL3/2DS2	*Z*	−0.707	−0.333	−0.577
C2 + 2DL1/2DS1	*Z*	−0.535	−1.342	−2.058*

Z = Wilcoxon Signed-Ranks Test value.
**p ≤ 0.05.*

TABLE 9 | Overall ligand and interaction summaries.

		Child^{ASD}		Father	Child^{ASD}		Mother	Father		Mother
KIRs: activating	Mean	2.4043		2.3191	2.3962		2.5849	2.2593		2.6667
	Pearson's *r*		0.331*			0.274*			0.104	
	t-Test		0.443			−1.121			−2.015*	
KIRs: inhibitory	Mean	4.3469		4.3878	4.3585		4.3962	4.4		4.3818
	Pearson's *r*		0.229			−0.023			0.153	
	t-Test		−0.362			−0.286			0.155	
Interactions: activating	Mean	1.9149		1.9787	1.9245		2.0377	1.9259		2.1111
	Pearson's *r*		0.216			0.142			−0.119	
	t-Test		−0.308			−0.636			−0.778	
Interactions: inhibitory	Mean	2.6939		2.7959	2.6981		2.6038	2.8214		2.6607
	Pearson's *r*		0.272			0.114			−0.099	
	t-Test		−0.647			0.582			0.903	

**p ≤ 0.05.*
***p ≤ 0.01.*

based on all genotype mapping. Mothers have significantly higher levels of activating signals than their male counterparts ($p = 0.049$).

DISCUSSION

Despite the increased attention garnered by autism research in recent years, the condition is currently diagnosed only after the infant reaches 2 or 3 years of age. Findings in autistic patients indicate multifactorial inheritance, while definitive genetic factors can be diagnosed in only a small percentage of cases. Immunological studies revealed a unique and distinguishing profile in ASD patients compared to controls. In the context of NK cells, altered gene expression, absolute number and function have been reported (7, 24, 25). Reports of modified NK function led us to investigate the highly polymorphic cell surface proteins on NK cells, called KIRs, to search for genetic background underlying the immune abnormalities. By interacting with MHC class I proteins expressed on all cell types, KIRs regulate the killing function of NK.

The most significant finding in this study is the unequal distribution of HLA-C2 (higher in fathers of ASD children) known to interact with KIR 2DS1 (higher in mothers of ASD children) to activate NK function. Analysis of "overall activation" (**Table 9**) signaling pointed to higher activation in maternal than paternal cohorts. Most HLA and KIR frequencies in ASD children ranged between those of their parents, indicating regular independent genetic inheritance from parents to children. This reinforced the importance of the specific HLA–KIR combinations between parents, though the mechanisms involved are still unclear. Our limitation in interpreting these findings lies in the absence of unusual prevalence of these genes or their combination in the ASD children, in comparison to their healthy parents.

Some reports correlated these initial interactions between parental cells as a possible mechanism for subsequent disease development or other complications. Hiby et al. (26) reported an increased HLA-C2 frequency in different cohorts of affected pregnancies: (a) recurrent miscarriage (RM) couples and their conception products, (b) fetal growth restriction (FGR), and (c) preeclampsia. Conversely, lack of activating KIR (in women affected by RM) or increased inhibitory KIR (in women with preeclampsia) (26, 27) has already been reported. Specifically, KIR 2DS1 seemed to be protective because of its significant lack in RM women. We find this plausible, since activating KIR 2DS1 compete with inhibitory KIR 2DL1 in interaction with HLA-C2, such that a predominance of KIR 2DS1 can overcome the strong inhibitory effect mediated by KIR 2DL1. All these findings support the importance of the innate immune system (mediated by maternal uterine NK and fetal trophoblast cells), modulated by KIR–HLA interaction to play a beneficial role in reproductive success.

Some papers have already pointed out differential segregation of KIR–HLA genes in autistic patients. Our study expands upon this by focusing within ASD families. Torres et al. (28) examined a large autistic cohort, revealing a highly significant increase in the activating KIR gene 2DS1 and its cognate HLA-C2 ligand. This increase in activating KIR may explain, at least partially, the high frequency of autoimmune diseases in autism patients. Guerini et al. (29) compared ASD children to their non-ASD mothers and showed both that activating KIR/HLA combinations were increased and inhibitory KIR/HLA were reduced in ASD children. This difference was proposed as having resulted from the genetic influence of the mothers, as these molecules' expression and interaction are relevant in the surrounding uterus.

Ethnic populations are known to differ in KIR genotype frequencies and genotype content (30). To the best of our knowledge, this is the first study to research KIR and HLA combinations in the Israeli Jewish population. As shown in the Allele Frequency Net Database,[3] our geographical location has higher frequency of HLA-C2 (around 0.4–0.7 in Africa and the Middle East). However, we showed here a significant skewing between maternal and paternal C2 frequencies. It raises an interesting question, since HLA clusters map in autosomal chromosomes, leading to independent segregation without respect to gender.

Genotype mapping of this system has certain limitations. While theoretically all gene segments identified by our SSP-PCR system may be expressed on the cell surface (meaning the functional KIR repertoire may depend on the KIR genotype), the transcription and translation processes may lead to different phenotype profiles. Another limitation of the SSP-PCR method in this context is the inability to determine the heterozygous/homozygous status of each of these KIRs. Our future plans are to determine not only genotype, but also RNA and protein levels. Another point to take into account is that NK cell function is a very complicated process determined upon the balance of an array of receptors, of which KIR is only one family. Moreover, the affinity of these interactions may differ (e.g., KIR 2DL3:HLA-C1 interaction is thought to be weak, compared to KIR 2DL2:HLA-C1 or KIR 2DL1:HLA-C2), such that one interaction may wield greater influence than another. It is also becoming increasingly clear that genetic factors, such as promoters and epigenetic mechanisms, are important in controlling NK cell receptor expression and function.

This study comprised a relatively small cohort of ASD-affected families – though statistically verified based on the minor allele frequency (MAF) of C2 (39.5%). In the absence of a control group, our findings were compared with the general population data of our geographical area. Additionally, the clinical patient data have not been thoroughly listed here, places limitations upon the reader in drawing parallels to other patient cohorts. The trends revealed in this preliminary investigation need to be further corroborated in ongoing and expanded research efforts.

Finally, we would like to emphasis another interesting aspect. On the one hand, different pregnancy complications (FGR, spontaneous abortion, placental abruption) are known to stem (at least to some degree) from immunological factors. On the other hand, perinatal factors unrelated to the immunological milieu may also be important in the pathogenesis of ASD. Certain complications during gestation were found to occur with increased frequency in mothers of ASD patients; an immunological basis has been suggested as underlying a portion of these. In some cases, intermediate factors may play a partial role in the association (e.g., reduced birth weight).

CONCLUSION

The aim of our research was to genotype the KIR receptors and their relevant HLA ligands in autistic children and their non-autistic parents, in order to screen for possible unique combinations. The most interesting finding in this study is higher frequency of HLA-C2 allotypes in the paternal group besides higher percentage of KIR 2DS1 in the maternal group. Such interaction may lead to NK activation. An absence of unusual prevalence of these genes or their combination in the ASD children, limited our ability to interpret these findings. Moreover, analysis of "overall activation" signaling pointed to higher activation in maternal than paternal cohorts.

AUTHOR CONTRIBUTIONS

Mrs. MG is a Ph.D. student. She is the major contributor to this manuscript doing the thinking, bench work, and manuscript writing. Mrs. KA contributed to the bench work as well as writing the manuscript. Prof. NY is an initiator of the original study and has performed the clinical diagnosis of all the participants of the study. Prof. RE is the initiator of original study recruited the families and the original head of the lab. Dr. DM is the head of the lab the study was conducted in, supported the study, and contributed to the manuscript writing and editing.

ACKNOWLEDGMENTS

This work was supported by a research grant (#232-12-13B) from the National Institute for Psychobiology in Israel, founded by the Charles E. Smith Family, and the Harris Foundation. The authors wish to thank Mrs. Shoshana Israel, Ph.D., and Mrs. Amal Halabi, M.Sc., for their help with validating HLA primers, and Dr. Lubov Nemanov for her assistance in processing patient samples. MG was supported by the Hoffman Leadership and Responsibility Fund, at the Hebrew University.

[3] http://www.allelefrequencies.net/

REFERENCES

1. Caronna EB, Milunsky JM, Tager-Flusberg H. Autism spectrum disorders: clinical and research frontiers. *Arch Dis Child* (2008) 93:518–23. doi:10.1136/adc.2006.115337
2. Blumberg SJ, Bramlett MD, Kogan MD, Schieve LA, Jones JR, Lu MC. Changes in prevalence of parent-reported autism spectrum disorder in school-aged U.S. children: 2007 to 2011-2012. *Natl Health Stat Report* (2013) 1-11:1following11.
3. Persico AM, Napolioni V. Autism genetics. *Behav Brain Res* (2013) 251:95–112. doi:10.1016/j.bbr.2013.06.012
4. Geschwind DH. Genetics of autism spectrum disorders. *Trends Cogn Sci* (2011) 15:409–16. doi:10.1016/j.tics.2011.07.003
5. Hu VW. From genes to environment: using integrative genomics to build a "systems-level" understanding of autism spectrum disorders. *Child Dev* (2013) 84:89–103. doi:10.1111/j.1467-8624.2012.01759.x
6. Noriega DB, Savelkoul HF. Immune dysregulation in autism spectrum disorder. *Eur J Pediatr* (2014) 173:33–43. doi:10.1007/s00431-013-2183-4
7. Enstrom AM, Lit L, Onore CE, Gregg JP, Hansen RL, Pessah IN, et al. Altered gene expression and function of peripheral blood natural killer cells in children with autism. *Brain Behav Immun* (2009) 23:124–33. doi:10.1016/j.bbi.2008.08.001
8. Biassoni R. Natural killer cell receptors. *Adv Exp Med Biol* (2008) 640:35–52. doi:10.1007/978-0-387-09789-3_4
9. Rajalingam R, Ashouri E. Gene-specific PCR typing of killer cell immunoglobulin-like receptors. *Methods Mol Biol* (2013) 1034:239–55. doi:10.1007/978-1-62703-493-7_12
10. Jamil KM, Khakoo SI. KIR/HLA interactions and pathogen immunity. *J Biomed Biotechnol* (2011) 2011:298348. doi:10.1155/2011/209348
11. De Re V, Caggiari L, De Zorzi M, Toffoli G. KIR molecules: recent patents of interest for the diagnosis and treatment of several autoimmune diseases, chronic inflammation, and B-cell malignancies. *Recent Pat DNA Gene Seq* (2011) 5:169–74. doi:10.2174/187221511797636266
12. Kulkarni S, Martin MP, Carrington M. The Yin and Yang of HLA and KIR in human disease. *Semin Immunol* (2008) 20:343–52. doi:10.1016/j.smim.2008.06.003
13. Holm SJ, Sakuraba K, Mallbris L, Wolk K, Stahle M, Sanchez FO. Distinct HLA-C/KIR genotype profile associates with guttate psoriasis. *J Invest Dermatol* (2005) 125:721–30. doi:10.1111/j.0022-202X.2005.23879.x
14. Zhi D, Sun C, Sedimbi SK, Luo F, Shen S, Sanjeevi CB. Killer cell immunoglobulin-like receptor along with HLA-C ligand genes are associated with type 1 diabetes in Chinese Han population. *Diabetes Metab Res Rev* (2011) 27:872–7. doi:10.1002/dmrr.1264
15. Barker DJ, Osmond C, Golding J, Kuh D, Wadsworth ME. Growth in utero, blood pressure in childhood and adult life, and mortality from cardiovascular disease. *BMJ* (1989) 298:564–7. doi:10.1136/bmj.298.6673.564
16. Gamliel M, Ebstein R, Yirmiya N, Mankuta D. Minor fetal sonographic findings in autism spectrum disorder. *Obstet Gynecol Surv* (2012) 67:176–86. doi:10.1097/OGX.0b013e31824bb5d6
17. Hagberg H, Gressens P, Mallard C. Inflammation during fetal and neonatal life: implications for neurologic and neuropsychiatric disease in children and adults. *Ann Neurol* (2012) 71:444–57. doi:10.1002/ana.22620
18. Bashirova AA, Martin MP, McVicar DW, Carrington M. The killer immunoglobulin-like receptor gene cluster: tuning the genome for defense. *Annu Rev Genomics Hum Genet* (2006) 7:277–300. doi:10.1146/annurev.genom.7.080505.115726
19. Chazara O, Xiong S, Moffett A. Maternal KIR and fetal HLA-C: a fine balance. *J Leukoc Biol* (2011) 90:703–16. doi:10.1189/jlb.0511227
20. Xiong S, Sharkey AM, Kennedy PR, Gardner L, Farrell LE, Chazara O, et al. Maternal uterine NK cell-activating receptor KIR2DS1 enhances placentation. *J Clin Invest* (2013) 123:4264–72. doi:10.1172/JCI68991
21. Patterson PH. Immune involvement in schizophrenia and autism: etiology, pathology and animal models. *Behav Brain Res* (2009) 204:313–21. doi:10.1016/j.bbr.2008.12.016
22. Chainonthee W, Bottcher G, Gagne K, Fussel M, Bignon JD, Wassmuth R. Improved KIR gene and HLA-C KIR ligand sequence-specific primer polymerase chain reaction genotyping using whole genome amplification. *Tissue Antigens* (2010) 76:135–43. doi:10.1111/j.1399-0039.2010.01479.x
23. Hong HA, Loubser AS, de Assis Rosa D, Naranbhai V, Carr W, Paximadis M, et al. Killer-cell immunoglobulin-like receptor genotyping and HLA killer-cell immunoglobulin-like receptor-ligand identification by real-time polymerase chain reaction. *Tissue Antigens* (2011) 78:185–94. doi:10.1111/j.1399-0039.2011.01749.x
24. Ashwood P, Corbett BA, Kantor A, Schulman H, Van de Water J, Amaral DG. In search of cellular immunophenotypes in the blood of children with autism. *PLoS One* (2011) 6:e19299. doi:10.1371/journal.pone.0019299
25. Vojdani A, Mumper E, Granpeesheh D, Mielke L, Traver D, Bock K, et al. Low natural killer cell cytotoxic activity in autism: the role of glutathione, IL-2 and IL-15. *J Neuroimmunol* (2008) 205:148–54. doi:10.1016/j.jneuroim.2008.09.005
26. Hiby SE, Walker JJ, O'Shaughnessy KM, Redman CW, Carrington M, Trowsdale J, et al. Combinations of maternal KIR and fetal HLA-C genes influence the risk of preeclampsia and reproductive success. *J Exp Med* (2004) 200:957–65. doi:10.1084/jem.20041214
27. Flores AC, Marcos CY, Paladino N, Arruvito L, Williams F, Middleton D, et al. KIR receptors and HLA-C in the maintenance of pregnancy. *Tissue Antigens* (2007) 69(Suppl 1):112–3. doi:10.1111/j.1399-0039.2006.762_8.x
28. Torres AR, Westover JB, Givvons C, Johnson RC, Ward DC. Activating killer-cell immunoglobulin-like receptors (KIR) and their cognate HLA ligands are significantly increased in autism. *Brain Behav Immun* (2012) 26:1122–7. doi:10.1016/j.bbi.2012.07.014
29. Guerini FR, Bolognesi E, Chiappedi M, Manca S, Ghezzo A, Agliardi C, et al Activating KIR molecules and their cognate ligands prevail in children with a diagnosis of ASD and in their mothers. *Brain Behav Immun* (2014) 36:54–60. doi:10.1016/j.bbi.2013.10.006
30. Takeshita LY, Gonzalez-Galarza FF, dos Santos EJ, Maia MH, Rahman MM, Zain SM, et al. A database for curating the associations between killer cell immunoglobulin-like receptors and diseases in worldwide populations. *Database (Oxford)* (2013) 2013:bat021. doi:10.1093/database/bat021

17

Uncovering the Social Deficits in the Autistic Brain: A Source-Based Morphometric Study

Alessandro Grecucci[1], Danilo Rubicondo[1,2], Roma Siugzdaite[3], Luca Surian[1] and Remo Job[1]*

[1] Department of Psychology and Cognitive Sciences, University of Trento, Trento, Italy, [2] Center for Mind/Brain Sciences, University of Trento, Trento, Italy, [3] Department of Experimental Psychology, Faculty of Psychological and Pedagogical Sciences, Ghent University, Ghent, Belgium

Edited by:
Ahmet O. Caglayan,
Yale University, USA

Reviewed by:
Munis Dundar,
Erciyes University, Turkey
Chiara Nosarti,
King's College London, UK

***Correspondence:**
Alessandro Grecucci
alessandro.grecucci@unitn.it

Autism is a neurodevelopmental disorder that mainly affects social interaction and communication. Evidence from behavioral and functional MRI studies supports the hypothesis that dysfunctional mechanisms involving social brain structures play a major role in autistic symptomatology. However, the investigation of anatomical abnormalities in the brain of people with autism has led to inconsistent results. We investigated whether specific brain regions, known to display functional abnormalities in autism, may exhibit mutual and peculiar patterns of covariance in their gray-matter concentrations. We analyzed structural MRI images of 32 young men affected by autistic disorder (AD) and 50 healthy controls. Controls were matched for sex, age, handedness. IQ scores were also monitored to avoid confounding. A multivariate Source-Based Morphometry (SBM) was applied for the first time on AD and controls to detect maximally independent networks of gray matter. Group comparison revealed a gray-matter source that showed differences in AD compared to controls. This network includes broad temporal regions involved in social cognition and high-level visual processing, but also motor and executive areas of the frontal lobe. Notably, we found that gray matter differences, as reflected by SBM, significantly correlated with social and behavioral deficits displayed by AD individuals and encoded via the Autism Diagnostic Observation Schedule scores. These findings provide support for current hypotheses about the neural basis of atypical social and mental states information processing in autism.

Keywords: autism, morphometric analysis, social deficits, neuroscience, developmental disabilities

INTRODUCTION

Autism Spectrum Disorder (ASD) is a category of pervasive developmental disorders (PDD) that affect 1 in 150 children (Rapin and Tuchman, 2008). Autistic symptomatology is characterized by severe impairments that mainly affect social interaction, communication, while sparing basic cognitive skills (Misra, 2014), and not implying emotional disturbance (Rapin and Tuchman, 2008). The term ASD was introduced by Allen (1988) and included: autistic disorder (AD), Asperger syndrome (AS), and PDD not otherwise specified (Levy et al., 2009; Pina-Camacho et al., 2012). Recently, the DSM V revised the conceptualization of those disorders and currently diagnostic classifications only include Autism Spectrum Disorders (ASD) (Lord and Bishop, 2015). Nevertheless, the diagnostic criteria adopted in the current study still refer to DSM IV, and we focused primarily on autism disorder (AD). Consequently, we use the words "autism" and "autistic" to specifically refer to AD.

The mind-blindness theory proposed that characteristic problem in social interaction arises because AD have difficulties in mentalizing and understanding psychological dynamics in other people and in oneself (Baron-Cohen et al., 1985; Frith et al., 1991). Support for this model comes from behavioral studies showing that autistics poorly perform on tasks that require theory of mind (ToM) abilities (Baron-Cohen et al., 1985; Misra, 2014). The poor performance of people with autism on ToM task is thought to be due to a conceptual deficit or to processing peculiarities. In normally developing children ToM tasks elicit intuitive social insights into people. In contrast, autistic children treat these tasks as logical-reasoning problems relying on language and non-social cognitive functions (Tager-Flusberg et al., 2009). In line with this hypothesis, functional MRI investigations of AD have highlighted reduced responses in cortical areas related to social interaction (Frith, 2003; Di Martino et al., 2009; Lombardo et al., 2011; Gliga et al., 2014), and the engagement of areas associated with general problem solving abilities (Frith, 2003). Moreover, functional connectivity in a group with autism shows abnormal pattern in areas mediating ToM and in the mirror neuron system (MNS) as well (Fishman et al., 2014; Cheng et al., 2015; Kana et al., 2015).

On the other hand, studies of volumetric changes in the autistic brain resulted in inconsistent brain structures across studies: prefrontal cortex (Courchesne et al., 2011b), cerebellum (Sparks et al., 2002), temporal lobe (Palmen et al., 2006), both the frontal (Herbert et al., 2004; Jiao et al., 2010) and parietal lobes (Courchesne et al., 1993) and amygdala (Schumann et al., 2004). Some inconsistencies in the structural MRI literature may be attributed to differences in methodology, age, heterogeneity of the disorder (Geschwind, 2009), or diffuse structural abnormalities. Diffuse structural abnormalities in autism could reflect impairment of many, if not most, brain networks (Müller, 2007).

Recently, predictive models of autism based on pattern recognition in structural MR images have been successfully developed. Ecker et al. (2010) adopted a support vector machine (SVM) method to discriminate ASD individuals from controls. Brain areas in the temporal lobe, precuneus, hippocampal, and fusiform gyri were crucial for discrimination. Neural abnormalities discovered with such methodologies, however, rarely correlate with clinical criteria, or correlate only with generic total scores, and not with specific subscales (Eliez and Reiss, 2000; Lord et al., 2000; Hardan et al., 2006a,b; Ecker et al., 2010; Griebling et al., 2010). In other words, these correlations may refer more to a general severity of pathology than to specific deficits.

We suggest that neuroanatomical markers of autism disorder may be better understood by studying large-scale anatomical networks (Minshew and Williams, 2007; Schaer et al., 2013). SBM is a data-driven multivariate alternative to the standard Voxel-Based Morphometry (VBM), and it may be particularly suitable to the investigation of anatomical changes in autism. SBM takes into account information across different voxels and identifies unpredicted, naturally occurring patterns of covariance across brain regions (Xu et al., 2009). Notably, such anatomical covariance has been shown to reflect functional connectivity (Evans, 2013). For these reasons, we expect SBM to individuate large anatomical networks of gray-matter which show aberrant patterns of covariance in AD, as compared to control. We also expect those networks to include brain areas that previous studies showed to be anatomically or functionally abnormal.

Given the heterogeneity of AD and the need for large-scale samples of MR and clinical measures, the present study utilizes the ABIDE (Autism Brain Imaging Data Exchange) database.

METHODS

Participants

Structural MRI of 82 participants (32 AD and 50 controls) were extracted from Autism Brain Imaging Data Exchange (ABIDE). Details of acquisition, informed consent, site-specific protocols, specific diagnostic criteria for each data set can be found at http://fcon_1000.projects.nitrc.org/indi/abide/index.html. The following committees approved the protocols of each site: the Human Subjects Protection Committee of the California Institute of Technology (CAL), the Institutional Review Board at the University of Pittsburgh (PBG) and the University of Utah School of Medicine (USM).

From around 3000 subjects available, we carefully selected participants by gender (males), age (range: 18–39 years old), as well as parameters of the MR scanners (image type: T1; magnetic field strength: 3T). This first selection resulted in a dataset composed by structural MRI of 283 subject acquired with 12 different MRI scanners. Next, the 283 subjects were screened on the basis of the DSV-IV for either the absence of any neuropsychiatric disorders (control group), or the diagnosis of Autism (AD) (patients group). Further inclusion criteria were: (a) the indication of the IQ score computed on the basis of Wechsler abbreviated scale of intelligence (WASI); (b) scores on at least three specific subscales of the Autism diagnostic observation schedule (ADOS) for AD participants. Finally, individuals with any other pathology or comorbidity were rejected. An in house made Dori script iteratively sampled the database until controls and AD group were balanced for age and there was no association between groups and a particular scanner.

This procedure yielded a dataset comprising 82 participants (32 AD and 50 controls) tested on one of the two MR scanners, with the same MR sequence (Table 1 in Supplementary Material). The scanners belonged to the same vendor (i.e., Siemens MAGNETOM TrioTim, Siemens MAGNETOM Allegra), and participants were equally distributed between scanners (See Table 1 in Supplementary Material). The two groups did not differed for age [$t_{(31)} = 0.2953$, $p = 0.7728$]. However, there was a difference in IQ scores [$t_{(31)} = 2.9586$, $p = 0.0041$]. See Table 1 in Supplementary Material. This is in line with previous observations for which the prevalence of mental retardation in autism is ~60% groups, and AD naturally differ from normal controls for IQ (Amaral et al., 2008).

Data Analysis

Source-based morphometry (SBM) is a multivariate technique that takes advantage of independent component analysis (ICA) (Lee, 1998; Xu et al., 2009). ICA is a statistical technique that is widely used in many fields of biomedical research for signal analysis. In the field of neuroscience ICA has found important application in EEG/MEG/fMRI data analyses to isolate noisy artifacts.

Pulling images from different MR scanners is known to lead to confounding, even though MR sequences are the same (Han et al., 2006). This is especially true for a massive univariate analysis, such as VBM. However, SBM can decompose the MR signal in several maximally independent sources, or independent components (ICs). In this study, few sources may reflect signal differences among MR scanners, while the majority of ICs individuate networks of gray-matter that share patterns of covariance among subjects (Xu et al., 2009; Kaspárek et al., 2010; Kubera et al., 2014). Artifactual components are usually easy to detect because are asymmetric, do not follow the anatomical organization of the brain, and do not exhibit any coherent patterns. In addition, the distribution of subjects throughout scanners is similar in both controls and AD, and this should guarantee that group differences are not due to artifact components.

The preprocessing of images is identical to the procedure adopted for classical VBM analyses. Brain extraction and robust center estimation was automatically carried out using FSL Brain extraction tool (BET) (Smith, 2002). For normalization and segmentation we used the SPM toolbox VBM8. Images were spatially normalized to the 152 average T1 MNI (Montreal Neurological Institute) template, and segmented into gray-matter (GM), white-matter (WM), and cerebrospinal fluid (CSF). The normalized gray-matter images were smoothed with 8-mm full width at half-maximum (FWHM) Gaussian kernel to establish spatial correspondence between the different brains.

Source-based morphometry analysis was carried out using the GIFT toolbox (http://icatb.sourceforge.net) (Xu et al., 2009). The minimum description length (MDL) principle was used to estimate a number of independent components. MDL found eight reliable ICs. We performed ICA using a neural network algorithm (Infomax) that attempts to minimize the mutual information of the network outputs to identify naturally grouping and maximally independent sources (Bell and Sejnowski, 1995). ICA was repeated 20 times in ICASSO (http://research.ics.aalto.fi/ica/icasso/) and the resulting components were clustered to ensure the consistency and reliability of the results. Reliability is quantified using a quality index Iq, ranging from 0 to 1 and reflecting the difference between intra-cluster and extra-cluster similarity (Himberg et al., 2004). All the 8 components extracted from the GM images were found to be associated with an $Iq > 0.97$ indicating a highly stable ICA decomposition.

SBM involves converting each gray-matter volume into a vector. As a result, we obtained a matrix where the 82 rows represent the 82 subjects (the first 50 rows represent controls, while the other 32 AD), and each column indicates a voxel. This matrix was decomposed into two matrices by ICA. The first matrix is named "mixing matrix" and it is composed by a subject per row and an IC per column. Therefore, the mixing matrix indicates how much a subject expresses a given component. For this reason, values in the mixing matrix are called "loading coefficients." The second matrix is named source matrix and it specifies the relation between the ICs and the voxels. For gray-matter volume component visualization the source matrix was reshaped back to a three-dimensional image, scaled to unit standard deviations (Z maps) and thresholded at $Z > 2.5$.

We used the mixing matrix to verify whether components are differently expressed between controls and AD. A two sample t-test without assuming equal variances (F-test revealed unequal variances) was used to test whether all the ICs are similarity expressed by either of the groups. Similarly, we used the loading coefficients in the mixing matrix to test a linear relation among ADOS scores and the level of components' expression. All the results were thresholded at $p < 0.05$ corrected for Family Wise Error (FWE).

RESULTS

We extracted eight independent components (**Figure 1**). However, only the 7th component was significantly different [$t_{(31)} = 2.9482$, $p_{(FWE)} = 0.0042$] between AD and controls. We call this component "autism-specific structural network" (ASN). Anatomical labels of the regions composing ASN were obtained using the WFU PickAtlas (Tzourio-Mazoyer et al., 2002). Among regions that differ between AD and controls we found: inferior, middle, superior temporal gyri, fusiform gyrus, parahippocampal gyrus, paracentral lobule, precuneus, cerebellar tonsil, and portions of the inferior, middle, and superior frontal gyri (**Figure 2**). All the gray-matter regions of ASN are presented in Table 2 in Supplementary Material, and in **Figure 2**.

To ensure that differences in IQ (see Table 1 in Supplementary Material) did not account for brain differences we correlated ASN loading coefficients (i.e., 7th column of the mixing matrix) against IQ values. The correlation was not significant ($p = 0.6336$), thus excluding the relevance of IQ on this component.

Notably, ASN significantly correlated with the total scores of ADOS, and also with two ADOS subscales measuring highly relevant impairments in AD, i.e., difficulties in social interactions and stereotyped behavior. Both variables show significant correlation with the loading coefficient of ASN, after Bonferroni correction for multiple comparisons. Classic Total ADOS Score: $r = 0.4708$, $p_{(FWE)} = 0.0065$. Social Total subscore: $r = 0.4269$, $p_{(FWE)} = 0.0148$. Stereotyped behaviors and restricted interest: $r = 0.4152$, $p_{(FWE)} = 0.0181$. See **Figure 2**.

DISCUSSION

In this study we presented for the first time a whole brain morphometric method (SBM), based on independent component analysis, which shows alterations in gray-matter between AD individuals and controls. This innovative multivariate procedure was applied to detect brain networks that exhibit abnormal pattern of gray-matter covariance in AD. We showed that morphometric changes in autism, as detected by SBM, are significantly associated with observable social and behavioral deficits (ADOS scores).

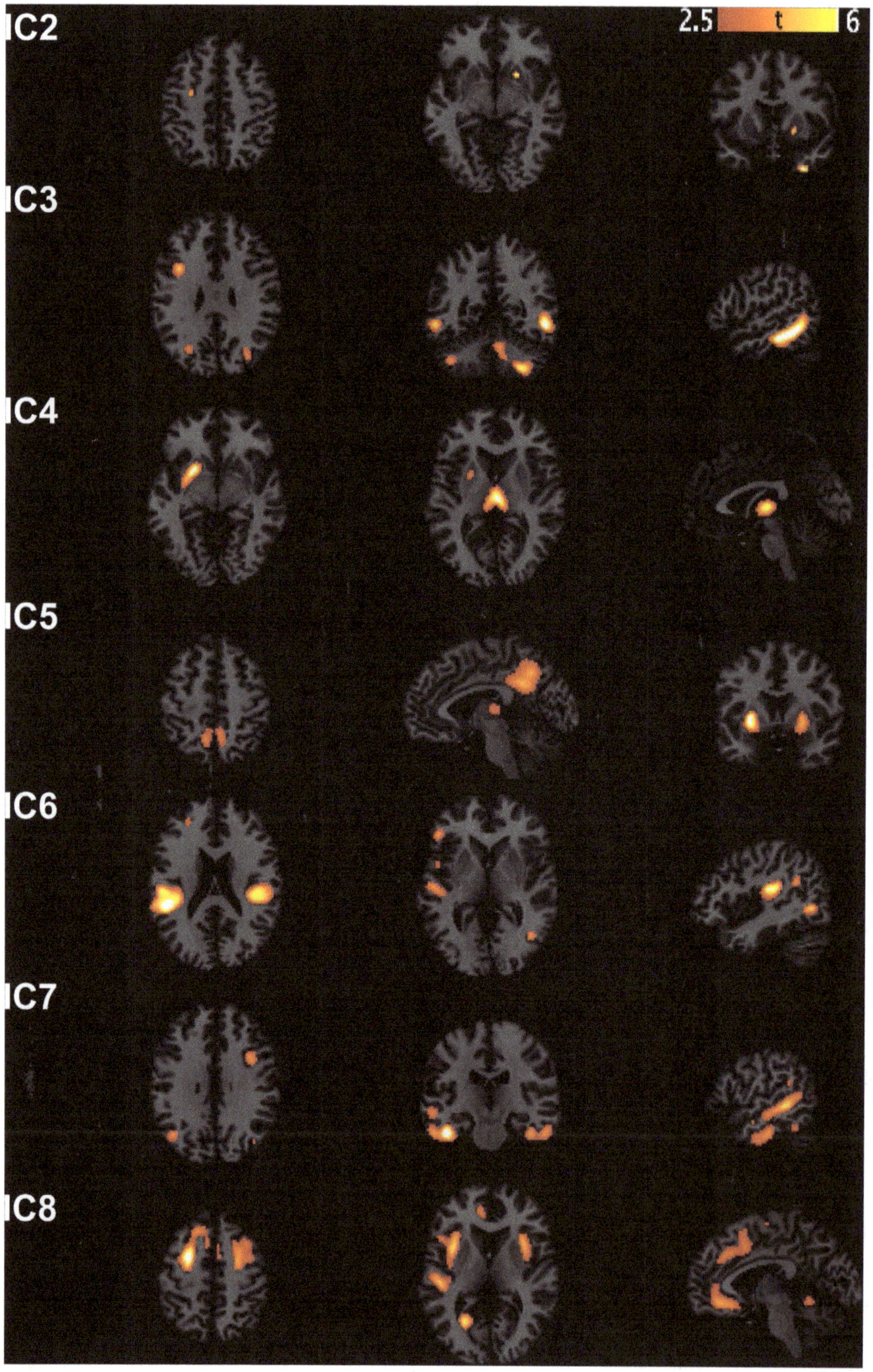

FIGURE 1 | Sources discovered by SBM. According to the estimation of the number of components, eight independent components were extracted. Note that IC1 is not graphically represented because no voxel survived after thresholding for $Z > 2.5$.

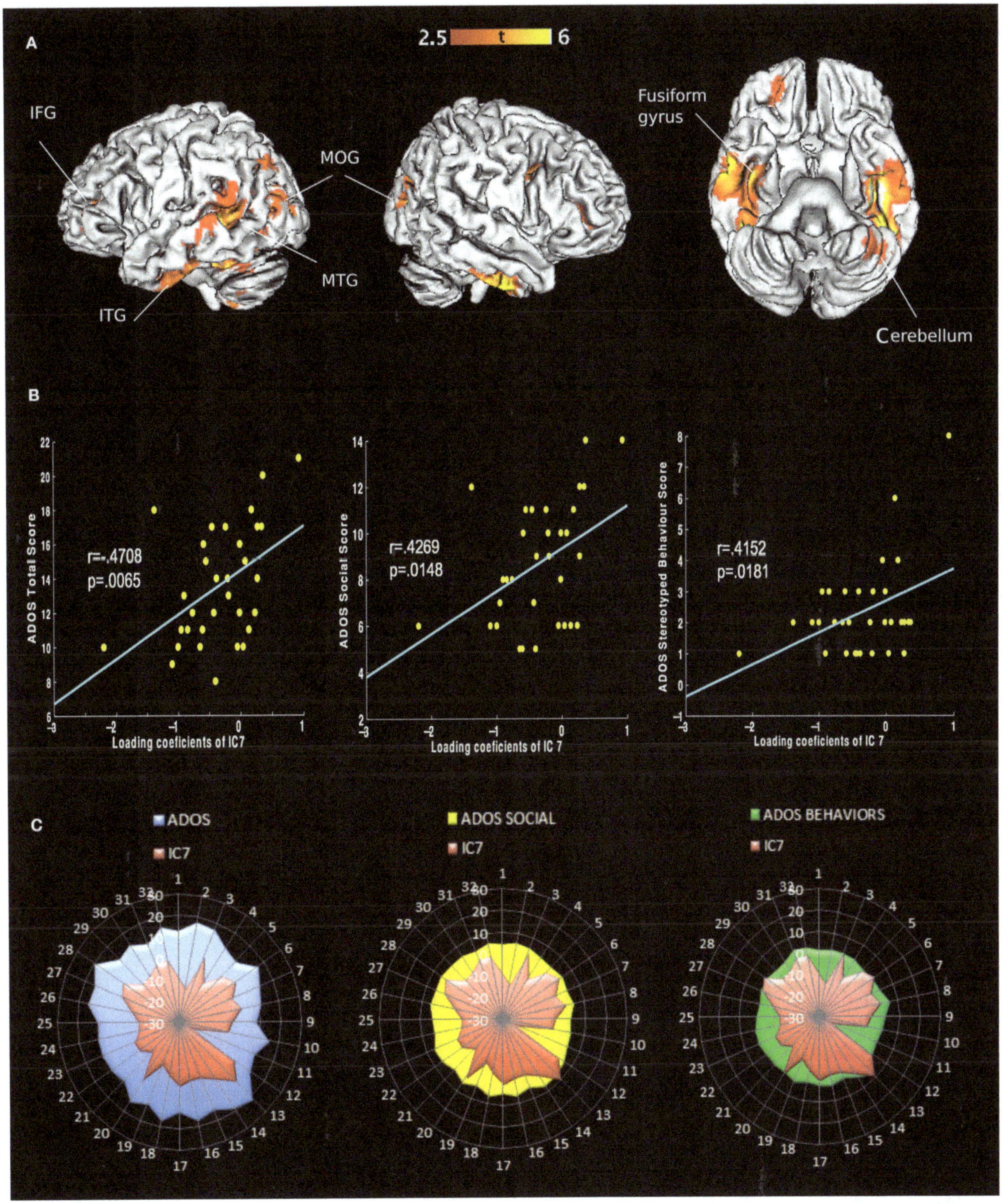

FIGURE 2 | Representation of ASN in the brain and behavior in AD. (A) Only the seventh component shows different loading coefficient between ASD and controls. The regions involved are: inferior frontal gyrus, middle frontal gyrus, superior frontal gyrus, inferior temporal gyrus, middle temporal gyrus and superior temporal gyrus, fusiform gyrus, parahippocampal gyrus, paracentral lobule, precuneus and cerebellar tonsil (Table 2 in Supplementary Material). **(B)** Correlations of behavioral measures with loading coeficients values in IC 7: Classic Total ADOS Score (communication subscore + social interaction subscore); Social Total subscore: Stereotyped behaviors and restricted interest. **(C)** Covariance plots showing each subjects' ADOS scores and individual ASN loading coefficients.

SBM addresses a different question in comparison with massive univariate approaches to morphological changes, as Voxel-Base-Morphometry (VBM) or ROI differences between groups. Univariate approaches detect voxel- or ROI-based changes in gray-matter concentrations, while SBM individuates different levels of expression in maximally independent gray-matter networks. Differences in network expression in turn implicate differences in gray-matter concentrations, distributed along patterns of voxel-covariation. SBM is particularly suitable to study autism as spectrum disorder, since anatomical changes are likely to be distributed along networks of brain regions. In this scenario, such anatomical changes may not be locally detectable by univariate approaches.

In the present study we found an autism-specific structural network (ASN) which covers brain regions found to exhibit functional and structural abnormalities in previous studies compared with controls (Castelli et al., 2002; Saxe and Wexler, 2005; Amaral et al., 2008; Courchesne et al., 2011b; Ecker et al., 2012; Nickl-Jockschat et al., 2012; Pappaianni et al., 2016).

Autism-Specific Structural Network (ASN)

Temporal Lobe

The core of ASN is localized in temporal regions involved in processing and integrating social stimuli, such as faces and intention-related movements.

ASN is centered in vast portions of the temporal lobes, suggesting that the temporal lobe may have particular relevance in the autistic disorder. ASN includes parts of the inferior, medial and superior temporal sulci, the fusiform gyrus, and the parahippocampal gyrus. Temporal lobe regions are implicated in social perception, auditory processing, language, and theory of mind. These abilities were shown to be the most damaged in autism (Gendry Meresse et al., 2005). In the present study inferior temporal and fusiform gyri are the brain regions which disclosed the greatest differences between AD and controls. These are the areas involved in high-level visual processing and object recognition, in particular face recognition (Rossion et al., 2003). Furthermore, the posterior superior temporal sulcus (STS) is a core region for perception of social acts (Zilbovicius et al., 2006). STS appears to respond also to biological motion and to how another person's motion is related to his/her intentions (Vander Wyk et al., 2009). Pelphrey et al. (2007) individuated a functional deficit in ASD regarding neural mechanisms for processing emotional facial expressions and biological motion. This system of regions referring to the deficit includes the amygdala, posterior STS and fusiform gyrus. This evidence provides further support for the idea that autism disorder relates to an impairment in processing social-relevant information (Baron-Cohen et al., 1985).

Frontal Lobe

ASN includes bilateral clusters in both the superior frontal gyrus (BA6) and in the precentral gyrus (BA4). Those areas correspond to premotor, supplementary, and primary motor cortices. Action processing impairments and repetitive movements are commonly observed among subjects affected by autism. Even though motor impairments are not considered one of the main symptoms of ASD, recently increasing attention has been directed to motor aspects aiming to improve a diagnostic process (Torres et al., 2013).

Our results also showed abnormalities in the inferior part of the frontal gyrus, a brain region implied in executive processes and language (Gotts et al., 2012; Libero et al., 2014). Since AD are largely characterized by deficits in imitation, language, ToM and empathy, a theory known as "broken mirror" hypothesis of ASD, has suggested that a dysfunctional MNS is an important factor in AD pathogenesis (Oberman et al., 2005). Sustaining this hypothesis, some recent studies have found abnormal pattern of functional connectivity in networks believed to underlie social abilities, as MNS and ToM systems (Fishman et al., 2014). However, the role of the mirror system in understanding AD symptomatology is still controversial (Grecucci et al., 2013; Hamilton, 2013; Enticott et al., 2014).

Other Areas Implicated in Autism

Cerebellar pathology is usually reported in autism (Courchesne et al., 1994, 2011a; Cauda et al., 2011; Rogers et al., 2013), both at structural and functional level (Fatemi et al., 2012). We also found cerebellum to be a part of the autism-specific structural network. Evidence suggests that the cerebellum supports cognitive functions, including language and executive functions (Becker and Stoodley, 2013), which are typically damaged in autism.

Previous meta-analyses of VBM in ASD have proposed that the amygdala and the insula are two brain regions frequently associated with abnormalities in autism (Cauda et al., 2011). In our study, we did not find structural changes in those regions. Our interpretation is that the amygdala and the insula are likely to play a role in autism, though these areas belong to a broader limbic system that, considered as a whole, may be sufficiently preserved in AD. Therefore, the neurostructural configuration of the limbic system was not markedly different between AD and controls.

Correlations with Behavioral Deficits

Finally, we found that the autism-specific structural network (ASN loading coefficients) significantly correlates with ADOS social and ADOS stereotypic behavior scores. Such evidence further supports the relation between the structural differences in ASN and the behavioral deficits displayed by AD individuals. These findings provide support for current hypotheses about the neural basis of atypical social and mental states information processing in autism.

CONCLUSION

Autism is a behaviorally diagnosed pathology, although evidence of brain abnormalities in AD, such as atypical neural "connectivity" (Ecker et al., 2012), are increasing. MRI investigation is a precious tool for shedding light on both the neurological causes and the neurodevelopment of AD. This knowledge is needed to get fast and objective diagnosis, but also for developing appropriate treatments. The present study, along with increasing evidence (Ecker et al., 2010; Jiao et al., 2010), suggests that structural MRI may become a diagnostic instrument useful to improve the traditional behavior-based diagnosis.

AUTHOR CONTRIBUTIONS

AG: Experimental design, data collection and writing. DR: Experimental design, data collection, analyses and writing. RS: Experimental design, data collection, analyses, and writing. LS: writing of the paper. RJ: writing of the paper.

ACKNOWLEDGMENTS

We would like to thank the Comune of Rovereto and the Neuropsychoanalysis Foundation for grants that supported the present study. Special thanks go to Aidas Aglinskas for precious advice.

REFERENCES

Allen, D. A. (1988). Austistic spectrum disorders: clinical presentation in preschool children. *J. Child Neurol.* 3(Suppl.), S48–S56. doi: 10.1177/088307388800300110

Amaral, D. G., Schumann, C. M., and Nordahl, C. W. (2008). Neuroanatomy of autism. *Trends Neurosci.* 31, 137–145. doi: 10.1016/j.tins.2007.12.005

Baron-Cohen, S., Leslie, A. M., and Frith, U. (1985). Does the autistic child have a "theory of mind"? *Cognition* 21, 37–46.

Becker, E. B. E., and Stoodley, C. J. (2013). Autism spectrum disorder and the cerebellum. *Int. Rev. Neurobiol.* 113, 1–34. doi: 10.1016/B978-0-12-418700-9.00001-0

Bell, A. J., and Sejnowski, T. J. (1995). An information-maximization approach to blind separation and blind deconvolution. *Neural Comput.* 7, 1129–1159.

Castelli, F., Frith, C., Happé, F., and Frith, U. (2002). Autism, Asperger syndrome and brain mechanisms for the attribution of mental states to animated shapes. *Brain* 125(Pt 8), 1839–1849. doi: 10.1093/brain/awf189

Cauda, F., Geda, E., Sacco, K., D'Agata, F., Duca, S., Geminiani, G., et al. (2011). Grey matter abnormality in autism spectrum disorder: an activation likelihood estimation meta-analysis study. *J. Neurol. Neurosurg. Psychiatr.* 82, 1304–1313. doi: 10.1136/jnnp.2010.239111

Cheng, W., Rolls, E. T., Gu, H., Zhang, J., and Feng, J. (2015). Autism: reduced connectivity between cortical areas involved in face expression, theory of mind, and the sense of self. *Brain* 138(Pt 5), 1382–1393. doi: 10.1093/brain/awv051

Courchesne, E., Campbell, K., and Solso, S. (2011a). Brain growth across the life span in autism: age-specific changes in anatomical pathology. *Brain Res.* 1380, 138–145. doi: 10.1016/j.brainres.2010.09.101

Courchesne, E., Mouton, P. R., Calhoun, M. E., Semendeferi, K., Ahrens-Barbeau, C., Hallet, M. J., et al. (2011b). Neuron number and size in prefrontal cortex of children with autism. *JAMA* 306, 2001–2010. doi: 10.1001/jama.2011.1638

Courchesne, E., Press, G. A., and Yeung-Courchesne, R. (1993). Parietal lobe abnormalities detected with MR in patients with infantile autism. *Am. J. Roentgenol.* 160, 387–393. doi: 10.2214/ajr.160.2.8424359

Courchesne, E., Townsend, J., Akshoomoff, N. A., Saitoh, O., Yeung-Courchesne, R., Lincoln, A. J., et al. (1994). Impairment in shifting attention in autistic and cerebellar patients. *Behav. Neurosci.* 108, 848–865. doi: 10.1037/0735-7044.108.5.848

Di Martino, A., Ross, K., Uddin, L. Q., Sklar, A. B., Castellanos, F. X., and Milham, M. P. (2009). Functional brain correlates of social and nonsocial processes in autism spectrum disorders: an activation likelihood estimation meta-analysis. *Biol. Psychiatry* 65, 63–74. doi: 10.1016/j.biopsych.2008.09.022

Ecker, C., Rocha-Rego, V., Johnston, P., Mourao-Miranda, J., Marquand, A., Daly, E. M., et al. (2010). Investigating the predictive value of whole-brain structural MR scans in autism: a pattern classification approach. *Neuroimage* 49, 44–56. doi: 10.1016/j.neuroimage.2009.08.024

Ecker, C., Suckling, J., Deoni, S. C., Lombardo, M. V., Bullmore, E. T., Baron-Cohen, S., et al. (2012). Brain anatomy and its relationship to behavior in adults with autism spectrum disorder: a multicenter magnetic resonance imaging study. *Arch. Gen. Psychiatry* 69, 195–209. doi: 10.1001/archgenpsychiatry.2011.1251

Eliez, S., and Reiss, A. L. (2000). MRI neuroimaging of childhood psychiatric disorders: a selective review. *J. Child Psychol. Psychiatry* 41, 679–694. doi: 10.1111/1469-7610.00656

Enticott, P. G., Kennedy, H. A., Johnston, P. J., Rinehart, N. J., Tonge, B. J., Taffe, J. R., et al. (2014). Emotion recognition of static and dynamic faces in autism spectrum disorder. *Cogn. Emot.* 28, 1110–1118. doi: 10.1080/02699931.2013.867832

Evans, A. C. (2013). Networks of anatomical covariance. *Neuroimage* 80, 489–504. doi: 10.1016/j.neuroimage.2013.05.054

Fatemi, S. H., Aldinger, K. A., Ashwood, P., Bauman, M. L., Blaha, C. D., Blatt, G. J., et al. (2012). Consensus paper: pathological role of the cerebellum in autism. *Cerebellum* 11, 777–807. doi: 10.1007/s12311-012-0355-9

Fishman, I., Keown, C. L., Lincoln, A. J., Pineda, J. A., and Müller, R.-A. (2014). Atypical cross talk between mentalizing and mirror neuron networks in autism spectrum disorder. *JAMA Psychiatry* 71, 751–760. doi: 10.1001/jamapsychiatry.2014.83

Frith, C. (2003). What do imaging studies tell us about the neural basis of autism? *Novartis Found. Symp.* 251, 149–66; discussion 166–76, 281–97.

Frith, U., Morton, J., and Leslie, A. M. (1991). The cognitive basis of a biological disorder: autism. *Trends Neurosci.* 14, 433–438.

Gendry Meresse, I., Zilbovicius, M., Boddaert, N., Robel, L., Philippe, A., Sfaello, I., et al. (2005). Autism severity and temporal lobe functional abnormalities. *Ann. Neurol.* 58, 466–469. doi: 10.1002/ana.20597

Geschwind, D. H. (2009). Advances in autism. *Annu. Rev. Med.* 60, 367–380. doi: 10.1146/annurev.med.60.053107.121225

Gliga, T., Jones, E. J. H., Bedford, R., Charman, T., and Johnson, M. H. (2014). From early markers to neuro-developmental mechanisms of autism. *Dev. Rev.* 34, 189–207. doi: 10.1016/j.dr.2014.05.003

Gotts, S. J., Simmons, W. K., Milbury, L. A., Wallace, G. L., Cox, R. W., and Martin, A. (2012). Fractionation of social brain circuits in autism spectrum disorders. *Brain* 135(Pt 9), 2711–2725. doi: 10.1093/brain/aws160

Grecucci, A., Brambilla, P., Siugzdaite, R., Londero, D., Fabbro, F., and Rumiati, R. I. (2013). Emotional resonance deficits in autistic children. *J. Autism Dev. Disord.* 43, 616–628. doi: 10.1007/s10803-012-1603-z

Griebling, J., Minshew, N. J., Bodner, K., Libove, R., Bansal, R., Konasale, P., et al. (2010). Dorsolateral prefrontal cortex magnetic resonance imaging measurements and cognitive performance in autism. *J. Child Neurol.* 25, 856–863. doi: 10.1177/0883073809351313

Hamilton, A. F. (2013). Reflecting on the mirror neuron system in autism: a systematic review of current theories. *Dev. Cogn. Neurosci.* 3, 91–105. doi: 10.1016/j.dcn.2012.09.008

Han, X., Jovicich, J., Salat, D., van der Kouwe, A., Quinn, B., Czanner, S., et al. (2006). Reliability of MRI-derived measurements of human cerebral cortical thickness: the effects of field strength, scanner upgrade and manufacturer. *Neuroimage* 32, 180–194. doi: 10.1016/j.neuroimage.2006.02.051

Hardan, A. Y., Girgis, R. R., Adams, J., Gilbert, A. R., Keshavan, M. S., and Minshew, N. J. (2006a). Abnormal brain size effect on the thalamus in autism. *Psychiatry Res.* 147, 145–151. doi: 10.1016/j.pscychresns.2005.12.009

Hardan, A. Y., Girgis, R. R., Lacerda, A. L. T., Yorbik, O., Kilpatrick, M., Keshavan, M. S., et al. (2006b). Magnetic resonance imaging study of the orbitofrontal cortex in autism. *J. Child Neurol.* 21, 866–871.

Herbert, M. R., Ziegler, D. A., Makris, N., Filipek, P. A., Kemper, T. L., Normandin, J. J., et al. (2004). Localization of white matter volume increase in autism and developmental language disorder. *Ann. Neurol.* 55, 530–540. doi: 10.1002/ana.20032

Himberg, J., Hyvärinen, A., and Esposito, F. (2004). Validating the independent components of neuroimaging time series via clustering and visualization. *Neuroimage* 22, 1214–1222. doi: 10.1016/j.neuroimage.2004.03.027

Jiao, Y., Chen, R., Ke, X., Chu, K., Lu, Z., and Herskovits, E. H. (2010). Predictive models of autism spectrum disorder based on brain regional cortical thickness. *Neuroimage* 50, 589–599. doi: 10.1016/j.neuroimage.2009.12.047

Kana, R. K., Maximo, J. O., Williams, D. L., Keller, T. A., Schipul, S. E., Cherkassky, V. L., et al. (2015). Aberrant functioning of the theory-of-mind network in children and adolescents with autism. *Mol. Autism* 6, 59. doi: 10.1186/s13229-015-0052-x

Kaspárek, T., Marecek, R., Schwarz, D., Prikryl, R., Vanícek, J., Mikl, M., et al. (2010). Source-based morphometry of gray matter volume in men with first-episode schizophrenia. *Hum. Brain Mapp.* 31, 300–310. doi: 10.1002/hbm.20865

Kubera, K. M., Sambataro, F., Vasic, N., Wolf, N. D., Frasch, K., Hirjak, D., et al. (2014). Source-based morphometry of gray matter volume in patients with schizophrenia who have persistent auditory verbal hallucinations. *Prog. Neuropsychopharmacol. Biol. Psychiatry* 50, 102–109. doi: 10.1016/j.pnpbp.2013.11.015

Lee, T.-W. (1998). "Independent component analysis," in *Independent Component Analysis* (Boston, MA: Springer US), 27–66. doi: 10.1007/978-1-4757-2851-4_2

Levy, S. E., Mandell, D. S., and Schultz, R. T. (2009). Autism. *Lancet* 374, 1627–1638. doi: 10.1016/S0140-6736(09)61376-3

Libero, L. E., Maximo, J. O., Deshpande, H. D., Klinger, L. G., Klinger, M. R., and Kana, R. K. (2014). The role of mirroring and mentalizing networks in mediating action intentions in autism. *Mol. Autism* 5:50. doi: 10.1186/2040-2392-5-50

Lombardo, M. V., Chakrabarti, B., Bullmore, E. T., and Baron-Cohen, S. (2011). Specialization of right temporo-parietal junction for mentalizing and its relation to social impairments in autism. *Neuroimage* 56, 1832–1838. doi: 10.1016/j.neuroimage.2011.02.067

Lord, C., and Bishop, S. L. (2015). Recent advances in autism research as reflected in DSM-5 criteria for autism spectrum disorder. *Annu. Rev. Clin. Psychol.* 11, 53–70. doi: 10.1146/annurev-clinpsy-032814-112745

Lord, C., Cook, E. H., Leventhal, B. L., and Amaral, D. G. (2000). Autism spectrum disorders. *Neuron* 28, 355–363.

Minshew, N. J., and Williams, D. L. (2007). The new neurobiology of autism: cortex, connectivity, and neuronal organization. *Arch. Neurol.* 64, 945–950. doi: 10.1001/archneur.64.7.945

Misra, V. (2014). The social brain network and autism. *Ann. Neurosci.* 21, 69–73. doi: 10.5214/ans.0972.7531.210208

Müller, R.-A. (2007). The study of autism as a distributed disorder. *Ment. Retard. Dev. Disabil. Res. Rev.* 13, 85–95. doi: 10.1002/mrdd.20141

Nickl-Jockschat, T., Habel, U., Michel, T. M., Manning, J., Laird, A. R., Fox, P. T., et al. (2012). Brain structure anomalies in autism spectrum disorder–a meta-analysis of VBM studies using anatomic likelihood estimation. *Hum. Brain Mapp.* 33, 1470–1489. doi: 10.1002/hbm.21299

Oberman, L. M., Hubbard, E. M., McCleery, J. P., Altschuler, E. L., Ramachandran, V. S., and Pineda, J. A. (2005). EEG evidence for mirror neuron dysfunction in autism spectrum disorders. *Brain Res.* 24, 190–198. doi: 10.1016/j.cogbrainres.2005.01.014

Palmen, S. J. M. C., Durston, S., Nederveen, H., and Van Engeland, H. (2006). No evidence for preferential involvement of medial temporal lobe structures in high-functioning autism. *Psychol. Med.* 36, 827–834. doi: 10.1017/S0033291706007215

Pappaianni, E., Siugzdaite, R., and Grecucci, A. (2016). An abnormal cerebellar network in children with autistic spectrum disorder: a morphometric study. *Autism Open Access* 6:178. doi: 10.4172/2165-7890.1000178

Pelphrey, K. A., Morris, J. P., McCarthy, G., and Labar, K. S. (2007). Perception of dynamic changes in facial affect and identity in autism. *Soc. Cogn. Affect Neurosci.* 2, 140–149. doi: 10.1093/scan/nsm010

Pina-Camacho, L., Villero, S., Fraguas, D., Boada, L., Janssen, J., Navas-Sánchez, F. J., et al. (2012). Autism spectrum disorder: does neuroimaging support the DSM-5 proposal for a symptom dyad? A systematic review of functional magnetic resonance imaging and diffusion tensor imaging studies. J. Autism Dev. Disord. 42, 1326–1341. doi: 10.1007/s10803-011-1360-4

Rapin, I., and Tuchman, R. F. (2008). Autism: definition, neurobiology, screening, diagnosis. *Pediatr. Clin. North Am.* 55, 1129–1146, viii. doi: 10.1016/j.pcl.2008.07.005

Rogers, T. D., McKimm, E., Dickson, P. E., Goldowitz, D., Blaha, C. D., and Mittleman, G. (2013). Is autism a disease of the cerebellum? An integration of clinical and pre-clinical research. Front. Syst. Neurosci. 7:15. doi: 10.3389/fnsys.2013.00015

Rossion, B., Caldara, R., Seghier, M., Schuller, A.-M., Lazeyras, F., and Mayer, E. (2003). A network of occipito-temporal face-sensitive areas besides the right middle fusiform gyrus is necessary for normal face processing. *Brain* 126(Pt 11), 2381–2395. doi: 10.1093/brain/awg241

Saxe, R., and Wexler, A. (2005). Making sense of another mind: the role of the right temporo-parietal junction. *Neuropsychologia* 43, 1391–1399. doi: 10.1016/j.neuropsychologia.2005.02.013

Schaer, M., Ottet, M.-C., Scariati, E., Dukes, D., Franchini, M., Eliez, S., et al. (2013). Decreased frontal gyrification correlates with altered connectivity in children with autism. *Front. Hum. Neurosci.* 7:750. doi: 10.3389/fnhum.2013.00750

Schumann, C. M., Hamstra, J., Goodlin-Jones, B. L., Lotspeich, L. J., Kwon, H., Buonocore, M. H., et al. (2004). The amygdala is enlarged in children but not adolescents with autism; the hippocampus is enlarged at all ages. *J. Neurosci.* 24, 6392–6401. doi: 10.1523/JNEUROSCI.1297-04.2004

Smith, S. M. (2002). Fast robust automated brain extraction. *Hum. Brain Mapp.* 17, 143–155. doi: 10.1002/hbm.10062

Sparks, B. F., Friedman, S. D., Shaw, D. W., Aylward, E. H., Echelard, D., Artru, A. A., et al. (2002). Brain structural abnormalities in young children with autism spectrum disorder. *Neurology* 59, 184–192. doi: 10.1212/WNL.59.2.184

Tager-Flusberg, H., Rogers, S., Cooper, J., Landa, R., Lord, C., Paul, R., et al. (2009). Defining spoken language benchmarks and selecting measures of expressive language development for young children with autism spectrum disorders. *J. Speech Lang. Hear. Res.* 52, 643–652. doi: 10.1044/1092-4388(2009/08-0136)

Torres, E. B., Isenhower, R. W., Yanovich, P., Rehrig, G., Stigler, K., Nurnberger, J., et al. (2013). Strategies to develop putative biomarkers to characterize the female phenotype with autism spectrum disorders. *J. Neurophysiol.* 110, 1646–1662. doi: 10.1152/jn.00059.2013

Tzourio-Mazoyer, N., Landeau, B., Papathanassiou, D., Crivello, F., Etard, O., Delcroix, N., et al. (2002). Automated anatomical labeling of activations in SPM using a macroscopic anatomical parcellation of the MNI MRI single-subject brain. *NeuroImage* 15, 273–289. doi: 10.1006/nimg.2001.0978

Vander Wyk, B. C., Hudac, C. M., Carter, E. J., Sobel, D. M., and Pelphrey, K. A. (2009). Action understanding in the superior temporal sulcus region. *Psychol. Sci.* 20, 771–777. doi: 10.1111/j.1467-9280.2009.02359.x

Xu, L., Groth, K. M., Pearlson, G., Schretlen, D. J., and Calhoun, V. D. (2009). Source-based morphometry: the use of independent component analysis to identify gray matter differences with application to schizophrenia. *Hum. Brain Mapp.* 30, 711–724. doi: 10.1002/hbm.20540

Zilbovicius, M., Meresse, I., Chabane, N., Brunelle, F., Samson, Y., and Boddaert, N. (2006). Autism, the superior temporal sulcus and social perception. *Trends Neurosci.* 29, 359–366. doi: 10.1016/j.tins.2006.06.004

18

Variation in Gene Expression in Autism Spectrum Disorders: An Extensive Review of Transcriptomic Studies

Ashley Ansel, Joshua P. Rosenzweig, Philip D. Zisman, Michal Melamed and Benjamin Gesundheit *

Cell-El Ltd., Jerusalem, Israel

Edited by:
John Vijay Sagar Kommu, National Institute of Mental Health and Neurosciences, India

Reviewed by:
Munis Dundar, Erciyes University, Turkey
Anthony Luder, Bar-Ilan University, Israel

***Correspondence:**
Benjamin Gesundheit
b.gesund@gmail.com

Autism spectrum disorders (ASDs) are a group of complex neurodevelopmental conditions that present in early childhood and have a current estimated prevalence of about 1 in 68 US children, 1 in 42 boys. ASDs are heterogeneous, and arise from epigenetic, genetic and environmental origins, yet, the exact etiology of ASDs still remains unknown. Individuals with ASDs are characterized by having deficits in social interaction, impaired communication and a range of stereotyped and repetitive behaviors. Currently, a diagnosis of ASD is based solely on behavioral assessments and phenotype. Hundreds of diverse ASD susceptibility genes have been identified, yet none of the mutations found account for more than a small subset of autism cases. Therefore, a genetic diagnosis is not yet possible for the majority of the ASD population. The susceptibility genes that have been identified are involved in a wide and varied range of biological functions. Since the genetics of ASDs is so diverse, information on genome function as provided by transcriptomic data is essential to further our understanding. Gene expression studies have been extremely useful in comparing groups of individuals with ASD and control samples in order to measure which genes (or group of genes) are dysregulated in the ASD group. Transcriptomic studies are essential as a key link between measuring protein levels and analyzing genetic information. This review of recent autism gene expression studies highlights genes that are expressed in the brain, immune system, and processes such as cell metabolism and embryology. Various biological processes have been shown to be implicated with ASD individuals as well as differences in gene expression levels between different types of biological tissues. Some studies use gene expression to attempt to separate autism into different subtypes. An updated list of genes shown to be significantly dysregulated in individuals with autism from all recent ASD expression studies will help further research isolate any patterns useful for diagnosis or understanding the mechanisms involved. The functional relevance of transcriptomic studies as a method of classifying and diagnosing ASD cannot be underestimated despite the possible limitations of transcriptomic studies.

Keywords: autism spectrum disorders (ASD), gene expression, immune system, lymphoblastoid cell lines, monozygotic twins, Fragile X Syndrome, neurogenesis and inflammation

BACKGROUND

Autism spectrum disorders (ASDs) are a group of complex neurodevelopmental conditions that present in early childhood. Individuals with ASDs are characterized by having deficits in social interaction, impaired communication and a range of stereotyped and repetitive behaviors (Lord et al., 1994). In 2012, ASD has a current estimated prevalence of about 1 in 68 US children aged 8 years; estimated prevalence was significantly higher among boys (23.6 per 1000) than among girls (5.3 per 1000) (Christensen et al., 2016). ASDs are heterogeneous, and arise from epigenetic, genetic and environmental origins. The exact etiology of ASDs still remains unknown and ASD cases with a genetic etiology only collectively account for 10–20% at most (Abrahams and Geschwind, 2008). The precise role of genetics in the pathogenesis of ASD remains unclear. On the one hand, there are several hints that genetics play a role (Wang et al., 2009). For example, there are much higher concordance rates of ASDs in monozygotic twins (70–90%) than dizygotic twins (0–10%) (Abrahams and Geschwind, 2008). Similarly, the recurrence risk in families ranges from 12.9% (Sandin and Reichenberg, 2014) to 18.7% (Ozonoff et al., 2011; Yuen et al., 2015). Furthermore, more than 100 ASD-susceptibility genes have already been identified (Yuen et al., 2015). On the other hand, these specific genetic mutations account for less than 8% of cases (Alter et al., 2011). There are a number of explanations for this ambiguity ranging from gene-gene interactions, to the heterogeneity of the disease, to epigenetic factors (Alter et al., 2011). Broad gene expression screening of children diagnosed with ASD is one approach toward mitigating the challenge of the heterogeneity of ASD by separating those diagnosed with ASD into subclasses according to gene expression profiles.

In the most recent comprehensive review of gene expression studies in ASD in 2012, Voineagu et al. surveyed 10 major mRNA studies across two types of samples [lymphoblastic (LBL) and post-mortem brain tissue]. They found that transcriptome analysis was more efficient than DNA studies in identifying differences between ASD and controls. Focusing on human mRNA studies since 2011 in English that monitor up or down regulation of multiple genes in ASD, without comparing to other disorders, we find that 27 major new studies have been published. By considering both single gene studies and more complex studies looking at pathways, researchers will be able to compare their findings to individual lists of genes but also to attempt to place their findings in a broader context by looking at pathway networks implicated in ASD. For example, if a researcher identifies a single specific gene to be upregulated in a specific type of tissue in ASD, that can then be compared to other single gene studies across different tissue types to see if there is consistency in the directionality of regulation and across tissue types. Additionally, by looking at a variety of networks and pathways, researchers can see the interaction between various neurodevelopmental and immune processes. These studies follow similar methodology to the studies previously discussed; though some expand to a third tissue type namely, intestinal biopsy samples.

Abbreviations: ADI-R, autism diagnostic interview revised; ANOVA, analysis of variance; ASD, autism spectrum disorders; asdMO, mothers having children with ASD; CNV's-copy number variants; DAVID, Database for Annotation, Visualization and Integrated Discovery; DSM-5, Diagnostic and Statistical Manual of Mental Disorders, Fifth Edition; ELISA, Enzyme-Linked Immunosorbent Assay; IFNγ, interferon gamma; IL, interleukin; LCL, lymphoblastoid cell lines; mRNA, messenger ribonucleic acid; MGAM, maltase glucoamylase; NOS, nitric oxide synthetase; PCs, Purkinje cells; RT-qPCR, Real-time quantitative polymerase chain reaction; SAM, significance analysis of microarrays; SNP's, single nucleotide polymorphism; TD, typically developing/developed.

GENE EXPRESSION STUDIES IN ASD BY TISSUE TYPE

In reviewing the new gene expression studies since Voineagu's paper (**Table 1**), the classification according to sample source will prove helpful. Five sample sources were studied: post-mortem brain, peripheral blood, gastrointestinal tissue, adult olfactory stem cells, and scalp hair follicles. Before beginning with the post-mortem brain tissue studies, it is relevant to mention gross pathological and radiological brain findings that might provide context for the brain-related expression findings.

Neurological Background

Evidence for neurological involvement in ASD can be divided into neuroimaging and post-mortem pathology.

Neuroimaging

Neuroimaging studies of children with autism have revealed abnormal brain overgrowth in prefrontal, temporal and amygdala regions and abnormal functional asymmetry and activation in the cortex and cerebellum (Chow et al., 2012). Neuroimaging techniques such as functional MRI has shown altered patterns of functional specialization in autism in several domains of thinking, such as cognitive, linguistic, social, and visuospatial processing in children and adults with ASD (Maximo et al., 2014). Impaired functional connectivity may demonstrate inefficiency in maximizing network connections to execute tasks, yet the findings of over-connectivity have been interpreted to reflect hyper-specialized, rather than more efficient connectivity. Based on the abundance of information, inefficient connectivity may be the hallmark of ASD.

Pathology

Pathology on postmortem brains from subjects diagnosed with ASD have demonstrated abnormalities in neuronal organization of the cerebral cortex and decreased number of Purkinje cells in the cerebellum (Garbett et al., 2008). Children between 2 and 4 years old diagnosed with ASD have been found to have increased total cerebral gray and white matter, excess neurons in the pre-fontal cortex, and an increase in brain weight at autopsy (Courchesne et al., 2011; Hazlett et al., 2011). In some children diagnosed with ASD, the rate of head growth and brain growth is exceptionally rapid during the first few years of life. Additionally, although most children with autism are born normocephalic, during the first years of life, 15–20% will develop macrocephaly (Lainhart et al., 2006). However, by late adolescence and early

TABLE 1 | Gene Expression Studies of Autism: 2011 onwards (Year chosen since Voineagu et al. review paper is from 2012).

Study	Number of samples	Tissue source	Number of dysregulated genes listed
Alter et al., 2011	82 children with autism (mean: 5.5 years SD 2.1 $p < 0.0001$) and 64 controls (mean: 7.9 years SD 2.2 $p < 0.0001$)	PBL	Children w/autism/Children w/younger fathers: 2093 significantly downregulated & 641 significantly upregulated genes; Children w/older fathers: Children w/younger fathers: 1476 significantly downregulated & 764 significantly upregulated genes; 593 genes were downregulated and 145 genes were upregulated in both children with autism and children of with older fathers
Anitha et al., 2012	9 autism patients ant 8 controls	ACG, MC, THL	28 genes showed brain region-specific reduced expression in autism
Chien et al., 2013	PART I: Conducted comparative total gene expression profiling analysis between 16 male patients with ASD (age range 4–18 years) and 16 male control subjects (age range 18–67 years); PART II: compared transcript level of one particular gene (FOXP1) between 83 male patients with ASD and 83 male healthy controls	LCL derived from the EBV transformation of lymphocytes of peripheral blood	202 genes were differentially expressed in the ASD group, including 89 upregulated and 113 downregulated
Chow et al., 2012	16 from young postmortem males (2–14 years; autism = 9, control = 7) and 17 adult males (15–56 years, autism = 6, control = 11)	DLPFC	2017 genes across all autistic and control cases independent of age
Féron et al., 2016	9 adults with severe autism and low to very low developmental disabilities, plus two adults with mild or moderate autism and no or mild cognitive abilities (Asperger syndrome or high functioning autism) paired with 11 age and gender matched controls	Adult nasal olfactory stem cells	156 genes that were differentially expressed in at least one ASD patient, of which 31 were dysregulated in more than a third of the cohort
Ginsberg et al., 2012	9 autism and 9 control subjects	BA19 (occipital) brain tissues	876 unique, annotated genes differently expressed between autistic and control brains
Glatt et al., 2012	60 infants and toddlers at risk for ASDs (autistic disorder and pervasive developmental disorder), 34 at risk for LD, 17 at risk for DD, and 68 TD children	PBMCs	154 probes showed significant dysregulation in ASD
Chana et al., 2015	Utilized published microarray data from 30 control and 27 ASD individuals	DLPFC	3 downregulated genes and 1 upregulated gene in ASD samples
Ivanov et al., 2015	30 subjects with idiopathic autism (24 male, 6 female) aged 3 to 11 years (mean age of sample 6.86 years) and 30 healthy children age and sex matched	Peripheral blood	23 differentially expressed genes (10 upregulated, 13 downregulated)
James et al., 2014	13 autism and 13 unaffected control individuals	Cerebellar cortex	7 genes
Khan et al., 2014	11 control (4F,7M) and 10 ASD (3F,7M) cases were examined (Controls ranged between 5 and 16 years of age, while ASD ranged from 4 to 15 years of age)	CB, BST, CG, ORC, PT, Wer	15 genes showed brain-region specific dysregulated expression in ASD samples
Kong et al., 2013	20 proband-unaffected sibling pairs (5 probands-sib pairs were of the same gender, i.e., males, while 15 pairs were of the opposite gender including 12 male and 3 female probands) and 18 unrelated control (11 males, 7 females) individuals	Peripheral blood	163 unique genes were significantly changed between probands and siblings
Kuwano et al., 2011	GROUP 1: 21 Young adults with ASD (17 males and 4 females) aged 26.7 ± 5.5 years, age range: 18-38 years; GROUP 2: 21 age and gender matched healthy controls aged 27.0 ± 5.5 years, age range: 19–39; GROUP 3: 21 Healthy mothers having children with ASD (asdMO), aged 44.7 ± 6.7 years, age range: 33–58 years; GROUP 4: asdMO control, aged 44.7 ± 6.7 years, age range: 31–59 years	Peripheral blood	ASD/control: 19 genes were found to be significantly dysregulated (18 upregulated and 1 downregulated); asdMO/asdMO control: 57 genes were found to be significantly dysregulated (17 upregulated and 40 downregulated); 3 genes overlapped and were dysregulated both in individuals with ASD and in asdMO
Maekawa et al., 2015	24 male control subjects (Aged 32.60 ± 3.91) and 18 Autism subjects (16 male, 2 female; aged 25.61 ± 4.95)	Scalp hair follicles	1 gene

(Continued)

TABLE 1 | Continued

Study	Number of samples	Tissue source	Number of dysregulated genes listed
Prandini et al., 2014	Two separate series of sib-pairs totaling 36 children and adolescents between 4 and 18 years of age	LCLs	none found
Segura et al., 2015	21 adolescents and adults diagnosed as ASD (20 males, 1 female) as well as from 10 healthy controls (10 males)	Whole blood	3 genes
Stamova et al., 2011	33 boys with AU (mean age 45.3 months; age range of 31–60 months) and 51 age-matched TD control boys (mean age 43.3 months; age range 28–57 months)	Whole blood	11 genes
Talebizadeh et al., 2014	Autistic group included three females (6, 11, and 13 years old) and two males (5 and 12 years old) diagnosed with classical autism and 5 age and sex matched unrelated controls	LCL derived RNAs	57 genes
Taurines et al., 2011	51 children with ADHD, 26 children with ASD (19/26 comorbid with ADHD) and 39 TD	Whole blood cells	2 genes
Tian et al., 2011	37 children with autism (32 males, 5 females; average age 44.2 ± 10 months) compared to 15 typically developing controls (11 males, 4 females; average age 41.2 ± 6 months)	Whole blood	31 genes
Voineagu and Eapen, 2013	19 autism cases and 17 controls	STG, prefrontal cortex (BA9) and cerebellar vermis	444 genes showing significant expression changes in autism cortex samples, 2 genes differentially expressed in cerebellum
Walker et al., 2013	25 children with a diagnosis of ASD (mean age 5.0862.06 years; 23 male and 2 female, 16 had a diagnosis of autism; 9 had a diagnosis of autism spectrum disorder); 3 TD groups: (1) 15 children with no chronic GI symptoms (mean age 12.263.07 years; 6 male and 9 female); (2) children with a diagnosis of Crohn's disease (*n* = 8, mean age 12.9763.07 years; 3 male and 5 female); (3) children with a diagnosis of ulcerative colitis (*n* = 5, mean age 12.064.0 years; all female)	Tissue specimen from 7 anatomic locations (from terminal ileum to rectum)	Ileal mucosa: ASD-GI/TD -1409 differentially expressed transcripts • Colonic mucosa: ASD-GI/TD -1189 differentially expressed transcripts: Overlap between both sets ASD-GI (Ileum and Colon)/ TD -178 transcripts exclusively differentially-expressed
Williams et al., 2011	15 AUT-GI children (mean onset age 13.4+/25.4 months, median age at biopsy 4.5), 7 Control-GI patients (median age at biopsy 4.0)	Ileum and Cecum	6 genes
Yasuda et al., 2011	35 patients with ASD (mean age 12.9 years ± 12.4 SD) 35 healthy controls (mean age 34.8 years ± 9.7 SD)	LCLs	2 genes
Zhubi et al., 2014	10 ASD and 10 control samples	Cerebellar cortex	4 genes
Ziats and Rennert, 2013	Re-analyzed sex-specific gene-expression from a recent large transcriptomic study (Kang et al., 2011); *N* = 57, including 39 with both hemispheres; age, 5.7 post-conceptual weeks to 82 years; sex, 31 males and 26 females;	Transient prenatal structures and immature and mature forms of 16 brain regions (Kang et al., 2011; **Table 2**)	37 Female and 123 Male genes found to be differentially expressed by sex, and their brain region and developmental time point

PBL, Peripheral blood lymphocytes; LCL, lymphoblast cell line; PBMCs, peripheral blood mononuclear cells.
ACG, anterior cingulate gyrus; MC, motor cortex; THL, thalamus; DLPFC, Dorsolateral Prefrontal Cortex; CB, Cerebellar; BST, Brain stem.
CG, Cingulated gyrus; ORC, Orbitofrontal cortex; PT, Putamen; Wer, Wernicke's; STG, superior temporal gyrus.
LD, language delay; DD, global developmental delay; TD, typically developing.

adulthood, the autistic brain commonly displays neuron loss and cortical thinning and is no longer enlarged (Kates et al., 2004).

POST-MORTEM BRAIN TISSUE GENE EXPRESSION STUDIES

With the background provided by the neuroimaging and pathology findings in mind, gene expression studies in brain tissue can now be reviewed. There are nine gene expression studies that look at a variety of brain regions. The studies are all very small but produced large numbers of genes with variable expression between ASD and control. Chow et al. analyzed frozen samples of dorsolateral prefrontal cortex from 16 young postmortem males (9 autism, 7 control) and 17 adult males (6 autism, 11 control) in order to study age-dependent brain gene expression (Chow et al., 2012). They found 102 genes, which

TABLE 2 | Gene expression changes in ASD detected in multiple independent studies in various tissues.

Gene symbol	Blood/LCL study	Brain study	Intestinal biopsy study	Expression change in ASD
ABHD3	Kong et al., 2013	Garbett et al., 2008		Upregulated
ACTG2		Ziats and Rennert, 2013	Walker et al., 2013	Downregulated
ADM		Garbett et al., 2008; Voineagu and Eapen, 2013		Upregulated
AHI1		Garbett et al., 2008; Voineagu and Eapen, 2013		Downregulated
ALAD		Chow et al., 2012	Walker et al., 2013	Downregulated
ALPK1	Nishimura et al., 2007; Talebizadeh et al., 2014			Upregulated
ANKRD22	Glatt et al., 2012; Ivanov et al., 2015			Upregulated in Ivanov et al. Downregulated in Glatt et al.
ANXA1	Chien et al., 2013	Garbett et al., 2008; Voineagu and Eapen, 2013; Ziats and Rennert, 2013		Upregulated in Garbett et al. and Ziats et al. Downregulated in Chien et al.
AQP4		Garbett et al., 2008; Voineagu and Eapen, 2013		Upregulated
ATF3	Hu et al., 2006		Walker et al., 2013	Upregulated in Hu et al. Downregulated in Walker et al.
BAG3		Garbett et al., 2008; Voineagu and Eapen, 2013		Upregulated
C20orf7		Chow et al., 2012; Ginsberg et al., 2012		Downregulated
C5orf16		Garbett et al., 2008; Voineagu and Eapen, 2013		Downregulated
CCL17	Nishimura et al., 2007		Walker et al., 2013	Upregulated
CD160	Gregg et al., 2008; Enstrom et al., 2009			Upregulated
CHI3L1	Chien et al., 2013	Garbett et al., 2008		Upregulated in Garbett et al. Downregulated in Chien et al.
CLIC1		Garbett et al., 2008; Voineagu and Eapen, 2013		Upregulated
CMKOR1	Nishimura et al., 2007	Garbett et al., 2008; Voineagu and Eapen, 2013		Upregulated
CNN3		Garbett et al., 2008; Voineagu and Eapen, 2013		Upregulated
COL4A1		Garbett et al., 2008; Voineagu and Eapen, 2013		Upregulated
COX7B		Ginsberg et al., 2012; Anitha et al., 2012		Downregulated
CSDA		Garbett et al., 2008; Voineagu and Eapen, 2013		Upregulated
CTNNB1	Kong et al., 2013	Chow et al., 2012		Upregulated in Kong et al. Downregulated in Chow et al.
CX3CR1	Gregg et al., 2008; Enstrom et al., 2009	Ziats and Rennert, 2013		Upregulated
CXCL10	Chien et al., 2013	Chow et al., 2012		Upregulated
CXCR4	Chien et al., 2013	Chow et al., 2012		Upregulated
CYC1		Ginsberg et al., 2012; Anitha et al., 2012		Downregulated
CYFIP1	Nishimura et al., 2007; Talebizadeh et al., 2014			Upregulated
DLX1		Garbett et al., 2008; Voineagu and Eapen, 2013		Downregulated
DNASE1L3	Chien et al., 2013	Chow et al., 2012		Downregulated
DRD4	Emanuele et al., 2010; Taurines et al., 2011			Upregulated in Emanuele et al. Downregulated in Taurines et al.

(Continued)

TABLE 2 | Continued

Gene symbol	Blood/LCL study	Brain study	Intestinal biopsy study	Expression change in ASD
FAM46C	Nishimura et al., 2007; Chien et al., 2013			Upregulated in Chien et al. Downregulated in Nishimura et al.
FOSL1	Ivanov et al., 2015	Chow et al., 2012		Upregulated in Chow et al. Downregulated in Ivanov et al.
GAD1	Chien et al., 2013	Zhubi et al., 2014		Downregulated
GADD45B		Garbett et al., 2008; Voineagu and Eapen, 2013		Upregulated
GPR56	Gregg et al., 2008	Ginsberg et al., 2012		Upregulated
GRIA3	Chien et al., 2013	Chow et al., 2012		Downregulated
GZMB	Gregg et al., 2008; Enstrom et al., 2009; Chien et al., 2013			Upregulated
HCK	Hu et al., 2006; Chien et al., 2013; Talebizadeh et al., 2014			Upregulated in Talebizadeh et al., Downregulated in Hu et al. and Chien et al.
HIST1H1C		Garbett et al., 2008; Voineagu and Eapen, 2013		Upregulated
HIST1H2BD		Garbett et al., 2008; Voineagu and Eapen, 2013		Upregulated
HIST1H3H	Nishimura et al., 2007	Chow et al., 2012		Upregulated in Chow et al. Downregulated in Nishimura et al.
HLA-DQA1	Gregg et al., 2008; Stamova et al., 2011			Downregulated
HSPB1		Garbett et al., 2008; Ginsberg et al., 2012		Upregulated
IFITM2		Garbett et al., 2008; Voineagu and Eapen, 2013		Upregulated
IFITM3		Garbett et al., 2008; Voineagu and Eapen, 2013		Upregulated
IGF2BP1	Ivanov et al., 2015		Walker et al., 2013	Upregulated in Walker et al. Downregulated in Ivanov et al.
IGHA1	Gregg et al., 2008; Chien et al., 2013			Upregulated
IGHG1	Hu et al., 2006; Gregg et al., 2008; Chien et al., 2013			Upregulated in Chien et al. and Gregg et al. Downregulated in Hu et al.
IL2RA	Chien et al., 2013		Walker et al., 2013	Upregulated
IL2RB	Gregg et al., 2008; Enstrom et al., 2009			Upregulated
ITGB2	Gregg et al., 2008; Enstrom et al., 2009			Upregulated
KIF1B	Hu et al., 2006; Talebizadeh et al., 2014	Garbett et al., 2008		Upregulated in Garbett et al. and Talebizadeh et al. Downregulated in Hu et al.
KIR3DL2	Gregg et al., 2008; Enstrom et al., 2009			Upregulated
KSP37	Gregg et al., 2008; Enstrom et al., 2009			Upregulated
LAMP2		Chow et al., 2012	Walker et al., 2013	Downregulated
LRP6	Chien et al., 2013; Talebizadeh et al., 2014			Downregulated
MeCP2	Kuwano et al., 2011	James et al., 2014; Zhubi et al., 2014**		Upregulated in Kuwano et al. and Zhubi et al. Downregulated in James et al.
MIA	Nishimura et al., 2007		Walker et al., 2013	Upregulated in Nishimura et al. Downregulated in Walker et al. (Colon)
MKNK2		Garbett et al., 2008; Voineagu and Eapen, 2013		Upregulated
MSI2		Garbett et al., 2008; Voineagu and Eapen, 2013		Upregulated

(Continued)

TABLE 2 | Continued

Gene symbol	Blood/LCL study	Brain study	Intestinal biopsy study	Expression change in ASD
MSN		Garbett et al., 2008; Voineagu and Eapen, 2013		Upregulated
NDUFA2		Ginsberg et al., 2012; Anitha et al., 2012		Downregulated
NDUFB3		Ginsberg et al., 2012; Anitha et al., 2012		Downregulated
NDUFB5	Talebizadeh et al., 2014	Anitha et al., 2012		Upregulated in Talebizadeh et al., Downregulated in Anitha et al.
NEURL3	Kong et al., 2013; Chien et al., 2013			Upregulated in Chien et al. Downregulated in Kong et al.
NKG7	Gregg et al., 2008; Enstrom et al., 2009			Upregulated
NP		Garbett et al., 2008; Voineagu and Eapen, 2013		Upregulated
P2RX5	Hu et al., 2006; Chien et al., 2013			Upregulated
P4HA1		Garbett et al., 2008; Voineagu and Eapen, 2013		Upregulated
PALLD		Garbett et al., 2008; Voineagu and Eapen, 2013		Upregulated
PAM	Gregg et al., 2008; Enstrom et al., 2009			Upregulated
PARP9	Glatt et al., 2012	Garbett et al., 2008		Upregulated in Garbett et al. Downregulated in Glatt et al.
PIR		Garbett et al., 2008; Voineagu and Eapen, 2013		Upregulated
PITPNC1	Hu et al., 2006; Nishimura et al., 2007	Garbett et al., 2008; Voineagu and Eapen, 2013		Upregulated in Nishimura et al. Garbett et al. and Voineagu et al. Downregulated in Hu et al.
PLEKHC1		Garbett et al., 2008; Voineagu and Eapen, 2013		Upregulated
PRF1	Gregg et al., 2008; Enstrom et al., 2009			Upregulated
PTGDR	Gregg et al., 2008; Enstrom et al., 2009			Upregulated
PTTG1IP		Garbett et al., 2008; Voineagu and Eapen, 2013		Upregulated
PXDN	Stamova et al., 2011; Chien et al., 2013			Upregulated in Chien et al. Downregulated in Stamova et al.
RELN		Chow et al., 2012; Khan et al., 2014; Zhubi et al., 2014		Upregulated in Khan et al. Downregulated in Chow et al. and Zhubi et al.
RPS21		Garbett et al., 2008; Ginsberg et al., 2012		Upregulated in Garbett et al. Downregulated in Ginsberg et al.
S100A10		Garbett et al., 2008; Voineagu and Eapen, 2013		Upregulated
SCARA3		Garbett et al., 2008; Voineagu and Eapen, 2013		Upregulated
SDC2		Garbett et al., 2008; Ziats and Rennert, 2013		Upregulated
SERPINA1	Chien et al., 2013	Chow et al., 2012		Upregulated in Chow et al. Downregulated in Chien et al.
SERPINH1		Garbett et al., 2008; Chow et al., 2012; Ziats and Rennert, 2013		Upregulated
SERTAD1		Garbett et al., 2008; Voineagu and Eapen, 2013		Upregulated
SFTPA2		Chow et al., 2012	Walker et al., 2013	Upregulated in Chow et al. Downregulated in Walker et al.

(Continued)

TABLE 2 | Continued

Gene symbol	Blood/LCL study	Brain study	Intestinal biopsy study	Expression change in ASD
SH2DIB/EAT2	Gregg et al., 2008; Enstrom et al., 2009			Upregulated
SHANK3		Yasuda et al., 2011; Chana et al., 2015		Downregulated
SLC38A2	Hu et al., 2006; Kong et al., 2013			Upregulated
SLC9A9	Talebizadeh et al., 2014	Garbett et al., 2008; Voineagu and Eapen, 2013		Upregulated
SPON2	Gregg et al., 2008; Enstrom et al., 2009			Upregulated
STOM	Glatt et al., 2012	Garbett et al., 2008; Ziats and Rennert, 2013		Upregulated in Garbett et al. Downregulated in Glatt et al. and Ziats et al.
SYCE1	Kong et al., 2013	Chow et al., 2012		Downregulated
TAGLN2		Garbett et al., 2008; Voineagu and Eapen, 2013		Upregulated
TAP1	Glatt et al., 2012	Garbett et al., 2008; Voineagu and Eapen, 2013		Upregulated in Garbett et al. Downregulated in Glatt et al.
TBX21	Gregg et al., 2008; Enstrom et al., 2009			Upregulated
TET1		James et al., 2014; Zhubi et al., 2014		Upregulated
TIMP1		Garbett et al., 2008; Voineagu and Eapen, 2013		Upregulated
TMBIM1		Garbett et al., 2008; Voineagu and Eapen, 2013		Upregulated
TMEM40	Kong et al., 2013; Ivanov et al., 2015			Downregulated
TNFRSF19	Chien et al., 2013	Chow et al., 2012		Downregulated
TNPO1		Garbett et al., 2008; Voineagu and Eapen, 2013		Upregulated
UBD	Chien et al., 2013		Walker et al., 2013	Upregulated
WWTR1	Chien et al., 2013	Garbett et al., 2008		Upregulated in Garbett et al., Downregulated in Chien et al.
YAP1		Garbett et al., 2008; Voineagu and Eapen, 2013		Upregulated
ZFP36L1		Garbett et al., 2008; Voineagu and Eapen, 2013		Upregulated

***James et al. (2014). looked at MeCP2 binding to the EN-2 promoter, while Zhubi et al. (2014) looked at MeCP2 binding to the GAD1 & RELN promoters.*

contrasted between young children diagnosed with ASD and control groups, and 736 genes, which contrasted between adults diagnosed with ASD and control groups. Ginsberg et al. analyzed cerebellar and BA19 (Brodmann Area 19, occipital) brain tissues from 9 control and 9 autism patients (Ginsberg et al., 2012). After correcting for the region of the brain, they discovered 876 unique, annotated genes expressed differently between autistic and control brains. This was a false discovery rate of five percent. Anitha et al. compared the expression of 84 electron transport chain genes belonging to the 5 complexes in the post-mortem brains of 8 autism patients and 10 controls. They found that 11 genes of Complex I, 5 genes each of Complex III and Complex IV, and 7 genes of Complex V (28 genes in total) showed brain region-specific reduced expression in autism (Anitha et al., 2012). Voineagu et al. profiled post-mortem samples of the superior temporal gyrus, prefrontal cortex, and cerebellar vermis regions from 19 autism and 17 control cases (Voineagu and Eapen, 2013). They identified 444 genes, which showed significant expression changes in autism cortex samples as compared to the controls, while only 2 genes were differentially expressed in the cerebellum. Ziats et al. re-analyzed a large transcriptomic study in the developing brain that was done by (Kang et al., 2011; Ziats and Rennert, 2013). The study performed genome-wide microarray analysis on postmortem human brain tissues from 16 brain regions spanning preconception to adulthood, specifically looking to identify sex-biased gene expression in the developing brain. Thirty-seven female, and 123 male genes were found to be differentially expressed by sex, brain region, and developmental time point. Khan et al. analyzed altered thyroid hormone-dependent brain gene expression by studying various brain regions from 10 ASD and 11 control cases (Khan et al., 2014). They found 14 genes that were differentially expressed based on sex-specific brain area. For example, expression of the DIO2 gene, a gene involved in thyroid hormone activation, was increased in the putamen ($p < 0.05$) and there was a trend toward increase in cingulated gyrus ($p = 0.08$) of the female ASD cases, while expression of the Cirbp gene, a gene responsible for stabilizing transcripts of genes involved in cell survival, was decreased ($p < 0.05$) in the putamen of ASD male cases only. James et al. compared 1 sq cm blocks of cerebellar cortex from 13 individuals with ASD and 13 controls (James et al., 2014). They observed a significant increase in both 5-mC and 5-hmC in the cerebellum of individuals with ASD relative to control samples. DNMT3A, DNMT3B, TET1, TET3, which are all genes related to methylation and 8-oxo-deoxyguanosine (8-oxo-dG) (a major product of DNA oxidation) expression levels were significantly increased in the cerebellum of individuals with ASD relative to control samples. They also found that within the EN-2 promoter sequence there was a statistically significant positive association between 5-hmC (a gene important in epigenetics) and EN-2 gene expression. Additionally an association between 5-hmC and EN-2 gene expression in the 5′ promoter CpG Island was found in people diagnosed with ASD but not in controls. Studies of MeCP2 (a chromosomal protein that binds to methylated DNA) binding in the EN-2 promoter demonstrated a significant decrease in repressive MeCP2 binding to the identical 5′ promoter region that contained increased levels of 5-hmC in individuals with ASD relative to control samples. Zhubi et al. also compared blocks of cerebellar cortex from 10 individuals with ASD and 10 control samples. They found a one and a half to two time increase in binding of MeCP2 to GAD1 and RELN promoters in the cerebellum of individuals diagnosed with autism when contrasted to controls. RELN plays a role in layering of neurons in the cerebral cortex and cerebellum. They detected that levels of 5-hmC were significantly enriched at GAD1 and RELN promoters in individuals with ASD. The methylation changes they found lead to a remarkable increase in the amounts of 5-hmC relative to 5-mC. The 5-hmC/5-mC ratio at the GAD1 promoter is 5.5 in people diagnosed with ASD and only 1.2 in controls. Similar to James et al. (2014), they also found TET1 mRNA levels to be increased in the cerebella of individuals with ASD (Zhubi et al., 2014). Chana et al. (2015) compared data from brain tissue from 30 controls and 27 individuals diagnosed with ASD. They found that expression of mGluR5 was decreased in ASD when compared to controls. This gene has been found to be associated with the forming of synapses, activation of microglia, and other processes.

Immune System

One study demonstrated findings in post-mortem brain tissue that were specific to the immune system. Considering the extensive literature analyzing the relationship between the immune system and ASD (Gesundheit et al., 2013), this demands further attention. Garbett et al. analyzed frozen samples of superior temporal gyrus from 6 subjects with ASD and 6 controls (Garbett et al., 2008). Based on four parameters, they identified 152 differentially expressed gene products, and of these, 130 demonstrated increased expression while 22 showed decreased levels in the brains of individuals with ASD. Seventy-two annotated differentially expressed transcripts were either cytokine responsive transcripts or transcripts related to the immune system. Additionally, they noticed decreased transcript levels for a number of genes involved in outgrowth and neuronal differentiation. They used Gene Set Enrichment Analysis, which marks functional pathways in which gene expression changes are grouped together. This enabled the identification of 31 gene sets that were differentially expressed between individuals with autism and control samples. Of the 31, 19 genes were involved in immune system function.

PERIPHERAL BLOOD GENE EXPRESSION STUDIES

The second and most common source used in gene expression studies for autism was lymphoblastoid cell lines (LCLs). There is an apparent discrepancy between neuroanatomical and cellular abnormalities observed for autism at younger ages and molecular pathologies at more advanced ages. Hu et al. analyzed LCLs derived from lymphocytes of 3 pairs of monozygotic twins that were discordant with respect to clinical diagnosis of ASD (Hu et al., 2006). Twelve hundred genes were identified as significant with a false discovery rate of 26%, 25 genes were found to be up-regulated at least 1.5-fold in the more severely affected twin relative to the other twin (log2 (ratio) = 0.58) and 19 genes were down-regulated by at least 1.5-fold. Of these, eight of the 26 genes match genes connected to neurological function, development, or disease. In 2009, Hu et al. conducted microarray analysis on 116 LCLs from individuals with idiopathic autism who were separated into three phenotypic subcategories according to severity scores from the ADI-R questionnaire and age-matched, typically developing controls. They identified 530 significantly differentially expressed genes that distinguished controls from all samples with ASD. Hu et al. analyzed gene expression profiling and how it differentiates ASD from controls and phenotypic variants of ASD (Hu et al., 2009). Microarray analyses were conducted on 116 LCLs from individuals with idiopathic ASD who were separated into three phenotypic subgroups according to severity scores from the ADI-R questionnaire and age-matched, non-autistic controls. Five hundred and thirty significantly differentially expressed genes were found that distinguished the samples of ASD from controls. They also identified 123 significant genes from 4-class significance analysis of microarrays (SAM) analysis of data from gene expression from severe, mild, and savant subgroups and the non-autistic control groups. When the pathways of the overlapping genes were analyzed between the severe language and mild autism subgroups, a network of genes that affect common functional targets, such as synaptic transmission, neurogenesis, neurulation, long-term potentiation (learning), protein ubiquitination, and brain function was revealed. Additionally, 15 significant differentially expressed genes that regulate circadian rhythm were found, unique to the most severely affected ASD subgroup. Differential expression of these genes was observed only in the samples from severely language-impaired individuals (L subgroup), with each individual showing altered expression of multiple (but not all 15) genes. Emanuele et al. investigated increased dopamine DRD4 receptor mRNA expression in lymphocytes of individuals diagnosed with autism and musicians in order to explore the music-autism connection. The DRD4 receptor is known to be responsible for neuronal signaling in the mesolimbic system of the brain. They studied 20 ASD patients, 19 professional adult musicians, and 19 gender and age matched control individuals who were not interested in playing or listening to music. Analysis of variance (ANOVA) demonstrated significant differences in DRD4 mRNA expression between the groups ($P = 0.008$). *Post-hoc* analysis highlighted significant differences between the control group and both musicians ($P < 0.05$) and individuals diagnosed with ASD ($P < 0.05$) (Emanuele et al., 2010). Yasuda et al. measured mRNA expression levels in lymphoblastoid cells from 35 subjects with ASD and 35 controls. They found that in individuals diagnosed with autism, B-actin normalized NLGN3 expression levels or TATA-binding protein were decreased by 35 or 26% respectively. They also found that gene expression levels of the SHANK3 gene, a gene that codes for a major scaffold postsynaptic density protein, regulated by B-actin or TATA binding protein were also decreased in individuals with autism by 39 or 40% respectively (Yasuda et al., 2011).

Stamova et al. looked for correlations between gene expression and mercury level in blood of boys with and without ASD. They collected whole blood from 33 boys with ASD and 51 age-matched typically developed (TD) control boys. There was no significant difference in Hg levels between the ASD and TD groups. They found 11 genes whose expression correlated inversely with mercury levels in boys diagnosed with autism compared to typically developing children. One limitation of this study was that samples collected from children ages 2–5 do not consider the possible direct role of mercury as a causal factor for autism, which likely starts *in utero* or shortly after birth (Stamova et al., 2011).

Tian et al. looked for correlations of gene expression with blood lead levels in children diagnosed with autism contrasted to typically developed controls. They looked at 37 children with ASD, and 15 TD controls. There was no significant difference in blood lead levels. Forty-eight probe sets represent 31 genes, whose expression correlated with lead levels in each group, and the partial correlation coefficients were statistically different between the groups; most of the genes are negatively correlated with blood lead levels in typically developed children and positively correlated with blood lead levels in children diagnosed with autism. The conclusion of their study, however was that lead most likely does not explain the increasing incidence in ASD (Tian et al., 2011).

Alter et al. looked at ASD and changes related to paternal age in overall levels of gene expression regulation. They performed gene expression microarrays on RNA from peripheral blood lymphocytes of 82 children with ASD and 64 controls where parental age was similar between the 2 groups. They then performed a secondary analysis by analyzing paternal age difference as a risk factor for ASD and whether it was associated with variance. They found that the distribution of gene expression levels on microarrays from individuals with autism had a decreased variance when compared to microarrays from controls ($p = 0.006$). They also found that in controls, but not in children with ASD, overall variance in gene expression was found to be significantly and negatively associated with the age of the father ($p = 0.03$), so as predicted, the overall variance was the same in children of fathers who were older and children with ASD with fathers of any age. In the comparison of children with ASD to children with fathers of a younger age, there were 2093 genes that were significantly downregulated by at least 1.1-fold, and only 641 that were upregulated. In the blood of children with fathers who were older compared to the children with younger paternal age, there were 1476 downregulated and 764 upregulated genes. There were 593 genes that were downregulated in both children with ASD and children of with older fathers ($p< 0.000001$) and 145 genes that were upregulated in both comparisons (Alter et al., 2011).

Chien et al. looked at increased gene expression of FOXP1 by comparing LCL between 16 males diagnosed with ASD and 16 male controls. FOXP1 is a transcriptional repressor. A total of 252 differentially expressed probe sets corresponding to 202 genes were detected between the 2 groups, including 89 up- and 113 down-regulated genes in the group diagnosed with autism. Real-time quantitative polymerase chain reaction (RT-qPCR) verified significant elevation (1.89 ± 2.64, $P = 0.005$) of the FOXP1 gene transcript of LCL in a sample of 83 male patients, compared with 83 male controls. Using three platforms, they found several immune-related pathways showing significant differences between the ASD patients and controls (Chien et al., 2013).

Prandini et al. analyzed RBFOX1 gene expression in LCL of Italian discordant ASDs sib-pairs totaling 36 children and adolescents. Their data showed however, that RBFOX1 normalized mean values were not significantly different between controls and those diagnosed with ASD, they suggested a possible cause for this might have been due more subtle transcription level differences in RBFOX1 gene expression in LCL than in brain samples (Prandini et al., 2014).

Talebizadeh et al. performed a pilot study and looked at exon-level expression profiling and alternative splicing in ASD using LCL. They found 57 genes that were differentially expressed at the exon level between ASD and control samples. They also found differential splice variants of the gene CYFIP1 (which has 2 protein-coding transcripts in the literature), exon array analysis demonstrated a higher expression for the probe sets which binds to exon 16 in variant 1 (encoding a long form) in subjects with ASD vs. controls. DNA sequencing following RT-PCR for variant 1 also detected a product missing exon 16 inducing a premature stop codon, and qRT-PCR showed a higher expression of variant 1 in ASD compared with control samples. RT-PCR reactions were run for TRAP150 and ZMYM6 and DNA sequencing of the amplified products supported the fact that these exons undergo alternative splicing and enabled the indication of previously unreported alternative splicing isoforms for these two genes. These new variants included one isoform of TRAP150 (missing exon 4 resulting in an in-frame loss of 301 amino acid residues) and five alternatively spliced ZMYM6 variants that are labeled on the basis of the missing exons (isoforms missing exon 2, exon 4, exons 2&4, exons 2&5, and exons 2, 4, &5). ZMYM6 variants missing exon 2, the location of the start codon, most likely do not code for proteins and the exclusion of only exon 4 introduces a premature stop codon (Talebizadeh et al., 2014).

Immune System-Background

The role of the immune system in ASD is an active area of research. Evidence of an immune role in at least a subset of children diagnosed with ASD can be divided into brain antibodies, serum cytokines, family history and immunogenetics (Gesundheit et al., 2013).

Immune System-Gene Expression Studies

Gregg et al. subdivided the children into three groups based on various clinical criteria. Their sample size included 49 children on the autism spectrum and 12 controls. Unpaired *t*-tests detected a number of genes that were regulated more than 1.5-fold for autism vs. general population ($n = 55$ genes), for history of early onset vs. general population ($n = 140$ genes), and for developmental regression vs. general population ($n = 20$ genes). The three gene lists from the analysis were used to identify a small group of 11 genes that are shared between the three groups. These genes were all expressed in natural killer cells and many belonged to the KEGG natural killer cytotoxicity pathway. Database for Annotation, Visualization and Integrated Discovery (DAVID) and Ingenuity Pathway Analysis were used to analyze pathways, and notable pathway overlaps included natural killer cell signaling in all three comparisons, IL-2 signaling and serotonin receptor and dopamine receptor signaling in autism vs. general population and early onset vs. general population, and retinol and methionine metabolism in the early onset vs. general population analysis (Gregg et al., 2008).

Enstrom et al. analyzed peripheral blood from 35 children with ASD and 11 age and gender matched controls. They discovered that a total of 626 probes showed differential gene expression between the two groups (82 significantly higher and 544 significantly lower in the ASD group). The 82 upregulated probes in ASD correlated to 59 known genes, most of which have been connected to leucocyte function, more specifically the function of natural killer cells. Using microarray analysis, their studies demonstrated that 12 gene probes, corresponding to 11 different genes were differentially expressed in early onset and regressive types of ASD when compared with the control group. Flow cytometric analysis of natural killer cells demonstrated increased production of granzyme B, perforin, and interferon gamma (IFNγ) under resting conditions in children diagnosed with ASD (Enstrom et al., 2009).

Kuwano et al. looked at ASD-associated gene expression in peripheral leucocytes that were often noticed between subjects with ASD, and healthy mothers of children with ASD. They used DNA microarray to perform gene expression profiling in peripheral blood on 21 individuals from 4 groups: young adults with ASD, age and gender matched controls, mothers having children with ASD (asdMO), and age matched controls having healthy children. They found 19 genes that were significantly differentially expressed (18 up and 1 down-regulated) when comparing the ASD to the control group, and 57 genes that were differentially expressed between the asdMO group and the asdMO control group (17 up-regulated and 40 down-regulated genes fold change >2.0). Three genes overlapped and were dysregulated in both individuals diagnosed with ASD and in asdMO. An ASD-associated gene expression pattern was often observed in both asdMO and individuals with ASD even though they had no symptoms above clinical threshold of ASD (expression of the 19 and 57 genes was changed in a parallel direction; Kuwano et al., 2011).

Glatt et al. identified 60 infants and toddlers at risk for ASDs, 34 at risk for language delay, 17 at risk for global developmental delay, and 68 typically developing children. One hundred and fifty four probes showed significant dysregulation in ASD, and a log 2-fold change. The most accurate support vector machine utilized the magnitude of the expression of 48 probes to classify 71% of ASD and control subjects across 10 subsets of discovery sample into their appropriate diagnostic categories. Of 30 individuals diagnosed with ASD, 27 were correctly classified by this support vector machine as having ASD, 23/34 control subjects were correctly classified as controls. The list of 48 probes making up the best support vector machine classifier of ASDs was most significantly enhanced with genes related to immune responses, genes of the hemoglobin complex, and genes with guanine- or guanylate-binding affinity (Glatt et al., 2012).

Kong et al. performed a genome-wide expression profile of the blood from 20 proband-unaffected sibling pairs, and 18 unrelated controls. One hundred and eighty nine probe sets that represented 163 unique genes (including 2 previously reported ASD candidate genes) were significantly changed between probands and siblings—84 probands were up-regulated compared to unaffected siblings (Kong et al., 2013).

Segura et al. looked at neurotrophin blood-based gene expression and social cognition analysis by obtaining whole blood from 21 adults and adolescents diagnosed as ASD, as well as from 10 controls. Social cognition abilities of subjects with ASD and controls were determined according to three Theory of Mind tests (RME, Faux pas test, The Happé stories). They found that NT3 and NT4 mRNA expression in the whole blood was significantly lower in ASD patients compared to healthy controls ($P < 0.05$). They also found that P75NTR mRNA expression was significantly higher in ASD patients than in controls. The ASD group received lower scores in three Theory of Mind tasks compared to the control group, which indicates that social cognition impairments in association with the ASD phenotype, yet no correlations were observed between neurotrophins and their receptors expressions and measures of Theory of Mind (Segura et al., 2015).

GI AND ASD BACKGROUND

Gastrointestinal (GI) symptoms are common in children with ASD compared with typically developing children and those with other developmental delays. Some controversial studies suggest that as many as 70% of children with ASD exhibit chronic GI-related symptoms (Walker et al., 2013).

GASTROINTESTINAL TISSUE GENE EXPRESSION STUDIES

Williams et al. looked at impaired carbohydrate digestion and transport and mucosal dysbiosis in the intestines of children diagnosed with ASD and gastrointestinal disorders. They found that the levels of three brush border disaccharidases (sucrase isomaltase [SI], maltase glucoamylase [MGAM], and lactase [LCT]) were all significantly decreased in children with ASD and GI complaints (ASD-GI). Within the ASD-GI group, 86.7, 80, and 80% of children had lower transcript levels in SI, MGAM, and LCT respectively. Almost all (14/15, or 93.3%) ASD-GI children had deficiencies in at least one disaccharidase enzyme; 80% had deficiencies in 2 or more enzymes; and 73.3% had deficiencies in all three enzymes. Real-time polymerase chain reaction (RT-PCR) revealed a significant decrease in 2 hexose transporters: ileal SGLT1 mRNA and GLUT2 mRNA in ASD-GI children. For SGLT1, 73.3% of ASD-GI children had deficient transcript levels, and 73.3% of ASD-GI children had deficient GLUT2 transcript levels, relative to control-GI children. In total, 93.3% (14/15) of ASD-GI children had mRNA deficiencies in at least one of the five genes involved in carbohydrate digestion or transport; 66.7% (10/15) had mRNA deficiencies in all five genes (Williams et al., 2011).

Similarly, Walker et al. looked at subjects including children with ASD and three typically developing groups including (1) children who underwent diagnostic ileocolonoscopy for chronic GI symptoms in which no histopathology; (2) children with Crohn's disease (3) and children with ulcerative colitis. Pairwise analysis between the ileal mucosa from ASD-GI and non-inflamed control samples resulted in 1409 differentially expressed transcripts unique to the ASD-GI samples. Pairwise analysis between inflamed colonic mucosa from ASD-GI children and non-inflamed control samples resulted in 1189 differentially expressed transcripts unique to ASD-GI samples. The overlap between the 2 sets (ileum and colon) resulted in 178 transcripts that were exclusively differentially expressed in both ileal and colonic tissues form the ASDGI population. When these 178 transcripts were analyzed using Ingenuity Pathway Analysis software, three of the top associated biological functions were inflammatory disease, endocrine system development and function, and digestive system development and function (Walker et al., 2013).

ADULT OLFACTORY STEM CELL GENE EXPRESSION STUDIES

Féron et al. used adult nasal olfactory stem cells from nine adults with severe ASD and low developmental disabilities (DSM-5), plus two adults with mild ASD and no or mild cognitive abilities (Asperger syndrome or high functioning ASD) paired with 11 age and gender matched controls. Gene microarray analysis highlighted 156 genes that were differentially expressed in at least one ASD patient, of which 31 were dysregulated in more than 33% of the cohort (9 out of the 156 genes have been previously associated with ASD). They found that MOCOS, an enzyme involved in purine metabolism, is downregulated in most ASD individuals (8/11), compared to controls (Féron et al., 2016).

HAIR FOLLICLE GENE EXPRESSION STUDIES

Maekawa et al. utilized scalp hair follicles as a source of biomarker genes and found that the gene CNTNAP2 showed significantly decreased expression in samples from subjects with ASD compared with control follicles (Maekawa et al., 2015).

GENE EXPRESSION ANALYSIS: COMORBIDITIES

A few of the gene expression studies looked at people diagnosed with ASD and comorbidities.

ASD and Fragile X/Dup 15q

Nishimura et al. performed genome-wide expression profiling of LCL in order to distinguish different forms of ASD and to reveal shared pathways. Individuals with ASD both with and without FMR1-FM or dup (15q) were compared to TD male controls. The combination of ANOVA, SAM and RankProd, isolated 120 genes in ASD with FMR1-FM, and 80 genes in ASD dup (15q), 68 genes were found to be dysregulated in both ASD with FMR1-FM and dup (15q) (so 52 genes were selectively dysregulated only in ASD with FMR1-FM, and 12 genes were selectively dysregulated only in ASD with dup (15q). They also found a potential molecular connection between FMR1-FM and dup (15q), the cytoplasmic FMR1 interaction protein 1 (CYFIP1), which was up-regulated in dup (15q) patients. Expression of JAKMIP1 and GPR155 was significantly dysregulated in the 27 males with ASD when compared with their siblings without ASD. JAKMIP1 is a gene known to be related to microtubule transport. Genes related to chaperone and protein folding were enriched in the 52 genes selectively dysregulated in ASD with FMR1-FM; genes related to RNA binding and mRNA metabolism were also enriched in this set (this is consistent with FMRP protein's function as an RNA binding protein important in regulatory translation) (Nishimura et al., 2007).

ASD and ADHD

Taurines et al. looked at altered mRNA expression of monoaminergic specific genes in the blood of children with ADHD and ASD. They found a significant group difference with decreased DRD5- level in ASD patients when compared with controls and to patients diagnosed with ADHD. *Post-hoc* analyses demonstrated reduced DRD4-levels in the group of both ADHD patients and ASD patients when compared with healthy controls (Taurines et al., 2011).

GENE EXPRESSION IN ASD-SUMMARY (TABLE 2)

Sample Source Types

When the gene expression studies are viewed together independent of source type, over 100 genes are found in more than one study. Interestingly, whether the gene is up-regulated or down-regulated is independent of the source of the gene sampled and can even vary within the same source type in different studies. For example, the gene NDUFB5 was found to be upregulated in LCL derived cell line RNA's (Talebizadeh et al., 2014), but downregulated in three different regions of post-mortem brain tissue (Anitha et al., 2012). The gene NEURL3 was up-regulated in peripheral blood in a study conducted by Chien et al. (2013), but down-regulated in peripheral blood in a study conducted by Kong et al. (2013). However, most genes that were up or down-regulated followed the same pattern in different studies across sample source types.

Pathways (Table 3)

One of the aims of gene expression studies is to look for multiple genes in the same pathway. This should provide some clues to the underlying mechanism of the disease. From the studies surveyed, five pathways were found three times across different studies, and eight pathways were found twice. The pathways that were found three times included: cell cycle, cell death, GI disease, immune function, and neurogenesis. All of these areas are already areas of extensive research in ASD and therefore, they are not-surprising. The pathways that were found twice were: alternative splicing, arrhythmogenic right ventricular cardiomyopathy, cellular assembly and organization, cell-to-cell signaling and interaction, gap junction, inflammation, small molecule biochemistry, and ubiquitin mediated proteolysis. While inflammation and cell signaling are already areas of research for ASD, the potential relationship between the other pathways and ASD deserves further consideration. A more recent paper by Ivanov et al. (2015) highlights a number of other pathways and their importance in understanding the function of genes including the Wnt pathway and the calcium pathway, which is involved in the development of the nervous system and deserves further investigation regarding its potential role in ASD. Similarly, Wen et al. (2016) found the calcium signaling pathway to be a very active pathway in ASD. The precise role of calcium signaling in ASD and its potential relationship to other common metabolic disturbances in ASD demands further research.

Specific Genes/Pathways Already Implicated in ASD or in Processes Relevant to ASD

There are numerous examples of specific genes that have been shown to be altered between ASD and control samples. All have been shown to be directly related to important processes that when reduced or altered, can be connected to ASD. These genes can be roughly subdivided into genes related to the brain and genes related to the immune system.

Brain Related Genes

Hu et al. found the protein ASS to be upregulated in the autism samples. ASS controls the rate-limiting step involved in nitric oxide (NO) production via regeneration of arginine from citrulline, a by-product of the nitric oxide synthetase (NOS) reaction. Since NO is a important signaling molecule in the brain and has been implicated in several disorders, including ASD, thus the increased expression of ASS may be potentially relevant to the ASD phenotype (Hu et al., 2006).

Based on the findings of Nishimura et al., since CYFIP1, which was shown to be upregulated in dup (15q) patients is known to counteract FMRP, they reason that the induction of CYFIP1 in dup (15q) might elucidate some of the significant overlap between ASD with FMR1-FM and with dup (15q). They also found that JAKMIP1 was significantly induced in ASD with FMR1-FM and had a positive trend in ASD with dup (15q), suggesting that JAKMIP1 could represent a commonly dysregulated pathway. This gene is a particularly biologically important candidate, given its putative role in GABAB receptor expression and microtubule networks (Nishimura et al., 2007).

Since Taurines et al. found reduced expression in ASD probands of DRD5 which is expressed in the hippocampus associated areas and is thought to be important in the induction of long term potentiation related to novel events, it can be suggested that the reduced expression could give insight into the fact that probands have less expression of an important hippocampal gene (Taurines et al., 2011).

Kuwano et al. found that mRNA levels of ITGA2B encoding glycoprotein (GP) αIIβ were upregulated both in individuals with ASD and in asdMO; GPαIIβ forms αIIbβ3 integrin with ITGB3, an ASD-susceptible gene. Since αIIbβ3 integrin has an critical role in cell morphology, including synapse maturation, the increased expression of ITGA2B mRNA might change cellular morphology of peripheral cells in mothers having children with ASD as well as subjects with ASD (Kuwano et al., 2011).

Chow et al. showed that the A2A receptor-signaling pathway was the top dysregulated pathway in the young autistic brain. Adenosine receptors are crucial for both brain development and function including the regulation of neuronal stem cell proliferation, synaptic plasticity, motor function, cognition and emotion-related behaviors (Chow et al., 2012).

Voineagu et al. identified that A2BP1/FOX1, a neural and muscle specific alternative splicing regulator (and the only splicing factor previously implicated in ASD) was down-regulated in several individuals with ASD (Voineagu and Eapen, 2013).

The reports of James et al. showed that elevated 5-hmC in the EN-2 promoter is correlated with a significant decrease in repressive MeCP2 and histone H3K27me3 which appear to override 5-mC hypermethylation. These epigenetic changes are thought to loosen enhancer region chromatin which would facilitate enhancer binding and promote sustained upregulation of EN-2 expression. Since perinatal EN-2 downregulation is crucial for normal Purkinje cell differentiation and cerebellar patterning, the consistent postnatal overexpression of EN-2 suggests that the shutting of this programmed developmental

TABLE 3 | List of main pathways affected.

Paper	Software	List of main pathways affected
Alter et al., 2011	DAVID analysis	Alternative splicing, splice variant, zinc-finger, phosphoprotein, zinc, metal-binding, zinc-ion binding, dna-binding, ubiquitin mediated proteolysis, nucleus, transcription, transition metal ion binding, chromosomal rearrangement, ubl conjugation pathway, transcription regulation, coiled coil, regulation transcription, compositionally biased region: Ser-rich
Chien et al., 2013	DAVID analysis	Long-term depression, Cytokine-cytokine receptor interaction, Vascular smooth muscle contraction, Arrhythmogenic right ventricular cardiomyopathy (ARVC), glycerophospholipid metabolism, allograft rejection, Jak-STAT signaling pathway, Hematopoietic cell lineage, Gap junction, T cell receptor signaling pathway, RIG-I-like receptor signaling pathways, Ubiquitin mediated proteolysis, Intestinal immune network for IgA production, Type II diabetes mellitus, Leukocyte transendothelial migration, GnRH signaling pathway
	EMA (Easy Microarray data Analysis)	Long-term depression, Amoebiasis, Vascular smooth muscle contraction, Cytokine-cytokine receptor interaction, Arrhythmogenic right ventricular cardiomyopathy (ARVC), Intestinal immune network for IgA production, Endocytosis, Aldosterone-regulated sodium reabsorption, African trypanosomiasis, Graft-vs.-host disease
	GSEA Gene Set Enrichment Analysis	Arrhythmogenic right ventricular cardiomyopathy ARVC, terpenoid backbone biosynthesis, glycerophospholipid metabolism, vascular smooth muscle contraction, alpha linolenic acid metabolism, tight junction, inositol phosphate metabolism, cytosolic dna sensing pathway, renal cell carcinoma, cell receptor signaling pathway, chronic myeloid leukemia
Chow et al., 2012		
Young autistic/control	MetaCore software suite	DNA damage-response, cell cycle and apoptosis-related pathways
	DAVID analysis	DNA damage/cell cycle, apoptosis, and immune signaling and neurogenesis and neural development
Adult autistic/control	MetaCore software suite	Cell differentiation, mitogenic signaling and apoptosis genes
All autistic and control cases independent of age		DNA-damage response, apoptosis and immune system response functions
Enstrom et al., 2009	DAVID analysis	NK function, cellular proliferation, and leukocyte function
Féron et al., 2016	IPA analysis	Developmental disorders, gastrointestinal diseases, purine metabolism, inflammation
Garbett et al., 2008	GSEA Gene Set Enrichment Analysis	Antigen-specific immune response, inflammation, cell death, autoimmune diseases, migration, and targeting of the immune response to specific cells
Ginsberg et al., 2012	DAVID analysis	Mitochondrial oxidative phosphorylation, protein translation, synapse/neurotransmitters, vesicle transport, brain patterning,
	IPA analysis	Oxidative phosphorylation
Glatt et al., 2012	DAVID analysis	Genes related to immune response, genes of the hemoglobin complex, and genes with guanine- or guanylate-binding affinity
Gregg et al., 2008	DAVID analysis	Natural killer cell-mediated cytotoxicity
	IPA analysis	Natural killer cell signaling, IL-2 signaling, serotonin receptor and dopamine receptor signaling, retinol and methionine metabolism
Hu et al., 2006	IPA analysis	Neurological development and function, neuronal signaling, extension of neurites, myelination, VEGF-induced release of nitric oxide, neurogenesis, survival of Purkinje cells, apoptosis of neurons, development of septum, TNF and other cytokines
Hu et al., 2009	IPA analysis	Synaptic transmission, neurogenesis, neurulation, long-term potentiation (learning), protein ubiquitination, brain function, molecular and cellular functions, cell death, small molecule biochemistry, free radical scavenging, cellular function and maintenance, liver toxicity, circadian rhythm, and androgen sensitivity
Ivanov et al., 2015	KEGG pathway analysis	Calcium signaling pathway, Amphetamine addiction, Leishmaniasis, GABAergic synapse, Retrograde endocannabinoid signaling, MAPK signaling pathway, Arrhythmogenic right ventricular cardiomyopathy (ARVC), Cholinergic synapse, GnRH signaling pathway, Glutamatergic synapse, Serotonergic synapse, Dopaminergic synapse, Steroid biosynthesis, Steroid biosynthesis, Wnt signaling pathway, Leukocyte transendothelial migration, Hypertrophic cardiomyopathy (HCM), Dilated cardiomyopathy, Asthma, Influenza A, Carbohydrate digestion and absorption and Endocrine and other factor-regulated calcium reabsorption
Kong et al., 2013	GSEA Gene Set Enrichment Analysis	Ribosome and spliceosome pathways, neuroactive ligand receptor interaction pathway, calcium signaling pathway, and Gap junction
Kuwano et al., 2011		
ASD/control group	IPA analysis	Cell morphology, cellular assembly and organization, nerve system development and function
asdMO/asdMO	IPA analysis	Cancer, RNA post-transcriptional modification, reproductive system disease, protein synthesis, immune functions

(Continued)

TABLE 3 | Continued

Paper	Software	List of main pathways affected
Mahfouz et al., 2015	DAVID analysis	Synaptogenesis, regulation of apoptosis, regulation of cell death, GABAergic neurons, neuron projection, neuron differentiation, cell morphogenesis, learning/memory, behavior, mental retardation, epilepsy, mitochondrial function, protein translation, ubiquitination, synapse formation and elimination, protein turnover, ion channel, neurotransmitter receptor activity, and mitochondrial function
Nishimura et al., 2007	DAVID analysis	Cell communication and signal transduction, immune response, defense response
	IPA analysis	Cell cycle, cellular movement, and cell-to-cell signaling and interaction
Pramparo et al., 2015	Metacore GeneGo analysis	Apoptosis/Apoptotic nucleus, Immune response/Antigen presentation, Immune response/Phagocytosis, Immune Response/TCR signaling, Translation/Translation initiation, Inflammation/Interferon signaling, Apoptosis/Anti-Apoptosis via NF-kb, Cell Adhesion/Leukocyte chemotaxis, Inflammation/IFN-gamma signaling
Stamova et al., 2011	IPA analysis	Cellular Assembly and organization, cellular compromise, small molecule biochemistry, vitamin and mineral metabolism, cell death, neuronal development, neuronal survival
Talebizadeh et al., 2014	DAVID analysis	Protein-lipid modification
Tian et al., 2011	IPA analysis	Immunological and inflammatory disease processes, cell-cell signaling, antigen presentation, cell cycle, development and growth, proliferation, mitochondrial dysfunction pathways
Voineagu and Eapen, 2013	GO gene ontology enrichment analysis	Synaptic function, immune and inflammatory function
Walker et al., 2013		
Ileal Mucosa	PCA (Principal component analysis)	Gastrointestinal disease, inflammatory response, humoral immune response, tissue morphology, digestive system development and function, O-Glycan Biosynthesis, Propanoate Metabolism, Arginine and Proline Metabolism, and Alanine and Aspartate Metabolism
Colonic Mucosa	PCA (Principal component analysis)	Gastrointestinal disease, neurological disease, behavior, organ development, Atherosclerosis Signaling, Factors Promoting Cardiogenesis in Vertebrates and Mitotic Roles of Polo-Like Kinase
	IPA analysis	Inflammatory disease, endocrine system development and function and digestive system development and function, Granzyme A Signaling, Athersclerosis Signaling, Valine, Leucine and Isoleucine Degradation and Clathrin-mediated Endocytosis Signaling
Wen et al., 2016	KEGG Pathway Analysis	MAPK signaling pathway, Calcium signaling pathway, Cell signaling, cell structure/transport, metabolism, neural, immune, cancer, cardiac disease, metabolic disease, Cell Adhesion Molecules, Wnt signaling pathway, mTOR signaling pathway, Focal adhesion, Regulation of actin cytoskeleton, Ubiquitin mediated proteolysis, Long-term potentiation, Axon guidance, and neurodegenerative diseases
Ziats and Rennert, 2013	DAVID analysis	Extracellular matrix formation/glycoproteins, immune response, chromatin, and cell cytoskeleton

window may have been missed in some individuals with ASD because of epigenetic abnormalities (James et al., 2014).

NT3&NT4, which were down to have lower expression in ASD patients compared to controls by Segura et al. play a crucial role in the development of the climbing fiber system of the cerebellar Purkinje cells (PCs), and NT3 selectively increased their survival. PC's are the primary efferent neurons of the cerebellar cortex, and its potential involvement in ASD has long been proposed. Neuropathological studies have shown significant reductions in the number and size of PCs in ASD post-mortem brain. Therefore, they hypothesize that reduced NT3 levels in the periphery in ASD patients might reflect altered expression in the CNS which may be associated with a loss of PC that result in altered cerebellar cortical efferent signals (Segura et al., 2015).

CNTNAP2, which encodes the contactin associated protein-like 2, which was found have significantly decreased gene expression in Maekawa et al. is one of the most intense ASD susceptibility genes with supporting evidence from several independent studies (Peñagarikano and Geschwind, 2012). CNTNAP2, a neurexin family protein that acts as a neuronal adhesion molecule and receptor. It was found to be a direct neural target of the human FOXP2 protein, and mutations of FOXP2 and CNTNAP2 were linked to language and speech disorders in ASD (Maekawa et al., 2015). The FOXP1 gene, which was found to be elevated in ASD subjects according to Chien et al. functions as a transcription repressor, forms a heterodimer with FOXP2, and is co-expressed with FOXP2 in numerous brain regions, suggesting close functional cooperation between the two proteins. FOXP1 is extensively expressed in the developing and mature brain and has been suggested to be important for brain development and function. Based on their data, it indicates that associations among FOXP1, FOXP2, and CNTNAP2 genes may play an important role underlying the pathogenesis of syndromic and non-syndromic ASD. They inferred that increased FOXP1 gene expression may lead to increased FOXP2 gene expression through a feedback mechanism, which may in turn reduce the gene expression of CNTNAP2 in patients with ASD (Chien et al., 2013).

Feron et al. found MOCOS to be downregulated in most ASD individuals as compared to controls. *In vivo* and *in vitro* engineered models indicate that altered expression of MOCOS results in neurotransmission and synaptic defects. MOCOS expression also induces increased oxidative stress sensitivity. Metabolic disorders of purine metabolism have been shown to affect the nervous system and are able to induce autistic features (Féron et al., 2016).

Immune Related Genes

Gregg et al. found that SH2D1B/EAT2, one of the 11 differentially expressed genes they found to overlap in all 3 groups (AU vs. GP, A-E vs. GP, and A-R vs. GP), is mostly expressed in natural killer cells as well as macrophages, B cells, and dendritic cells, and has been theorized to suppress natural killer cell activity through the binding of protein tyrosine phosphatases, inhibitory kinases, or ubiquitin ligases. Abnormalities in RUNX3 (one of the 55 differentially expressed genes in AU vs. GP) function in leukocytes and is associated with sudden development of colitis and gastric mucosal hyperplasia and might be relevant to ASD since a small group of children with ASD appear to have gastrointestinal abnormalities (Gregg et al., 2008).

The findings of Enstrom et al. suggest possible dysfunction of natural killer cells in children with ASD, and the data suggests that circulating natural killer cells in ASD are persistently activated rather than quiescent (Enstrom et al., 2009).

Reduced expression of NLGN3 and SHANK3 genes in lymphoblasts of individuals with ASD is consistent with previous reports indicating that mutations of these genes cause reduced expression or loss of function of the protein. Yasuda et al. found that both these genes were found to be decreased in individuals in ASD (Yasuda et al., 2011).

One of the 48 biomarkers in the optimized support vector machine classifier by Glatt et al. IF116, was previously found to be dysregulated in the postmortem temporal cortex of subjects with ASD (Garbett et al., 2008; Glatt et al., 2012).

GENERAL LIMITATIONS IN RNA-GENE EXPRESSION STUDIES: A CRITICAL APPRAISAL OF THE DATA

Variance

One limitation of mRNA gene expression studies is variance. While gene specific approaches are helpful, they may ignore changes known as variance occurring at the global level of gene expression regulation. Global levels of gene expression regulation are crucial for understanding the underlying basis of diseases such as ASD where multiple systems are affected. For example, the associated increased risk of ASD in children of older fathers could be mediated by changes in global levels of gene expression regulation, or by paternally transmitted age related factors that are linked to changes in the global regulation of gene expression (Alter et al., 2011). Thus, it is possible that a common mediator, a change at the global level of gene expression regulation, could offer an all-encompassing explanation for multi-systemic effects of the disease.

Tissue Source

According to Chien et al. there are several disadvantages with the use of post-mortem brain tissue in gene expression studies (Chien et al., 2013). They point out that using fresh brain tissue from living patients is not always practical, and as a surrogate for brain tissue, several studies have instead utilized peripheral blood cells and LCL. They also state that there is a moderate correlation of gene expression has been reported between peripheral blood cells and brain tissue in humans which supports the usefulness of peripheral blood cells instead of brain-tissue for gene expression studies. Yet Mahfouz et al. (2015), argue that due to the nature of the pathology of ASD, which affects brain regions and the connection between various brain regions, there are advantages to post-mortem gene studies from brain tissue over peripheral blood studies. Kuwano et al. concluded that gene expression profiling of LCL are well documented because of their homogeneity (Kuwano et al., 2011).

Segura et al. explained that their rationale to use blood as opposed to post-mortem brain tissue was due to the limited access of tissue from the central nervous system (CNS) in humans (Segura et al., 2015). They also brought reports of a potential correlation between neurotrophin expression in CNS and the periphery, which would suggest that taking blood in order to study neurotrophins would be similarly effective to using brain tissue. Similarly, Pramparo et al. (2015) emphasized the advantages of peripheral blood, and were successful in identifying 2765 genes from a peripheral blood source from a variety of pathways including apoptosis, the immune response, and genes involved in translation.

According to Hu et al. while studies that used brain tissue to better understand the mechanistic basis for ASD could be informative; this method of study is not an appropriate target for diagnostic assays. They counter that diagnostic assays should ideally be taken from easily obtainable samples such as the patient's blood (Hu et al., 2006). However, Talebizadeh et al. acknowledge that LCL samples may not be ideal to use in order to investigate brain-related genes, but they may still be helpful for understanding at least a subset of brain-related changes (Talebizadeh et al., 2014).

LIMITATIONS SPECIFIC TO ASD GENE EXPRESSION STUDIES: A CRITICAL APPRAISAL OF THE DATA

The clinical heterogeneity of ASD presents a challenge any time studies attempt to find patterns across the spectrum. Complicating matters even more, the ASD gene expression studies relied on a variety of diagnostic methods to define ASD (**Tables 4A,B**). The lack of consistency between the diagnostic criteria and the subjectivity of the behavioral methods of diagnosis limit the ability to extrapolate the data to the broader ASD population.

Additionally, demographic variability between subjects and between subjects and controls complicates analysis. Considering that ASD is 4.5 times more common in males than females, the ratio of subjects in each study is of great importance if it is meant

TABLE 4A | Diagnostic tests part 1.

Paper/diagnostic test	DSM-4	DSM-5	ADOS	ADI-R	CARS	IQ scores	SCQ	CSBS DP	Mullen scales of early learning	Bayley scale of infant and toddler development	Vineland adaptive behavior scales	ToM social cognition test	Peabody Picture Vocabulary Test (PPVT)
Alter et al., 2011	✓		✓	✓									
Chien et al., 2013	✓			✓									
Chow et al., 2012			✓	✓									
Emanuele et al., 2010	✓				✓								
Enstrom et al., 2009	✓		✓	✓			✓						
Féron et al., 2016		✓									✓		
Ginsberg et al., 2012	✓		✓	✓		✓							
Glatt et al., 2012			✓					✓	✓				
Gregg et al., 2008	✓		✓	✓									
Hu et al., 2006			✓	✓									✓
Hu et al., 2009				✓									
Ivanov et al., 2015				✓	✓								
James et al., 2014	✓			✓									
Kong et al., 2013			✓	✓									
Kuwano et al., 2011	✓					✓							
Maekawa et al., 2015	✓			✓									
Nishimura et al., 2007			✓	✓		✓							
Pramparo et al., 2015	✓		✓						✓		✓		
Prandini et al., 2014	✓		✓	✓									
Segura et al., 2015	✓		✓	✓		✓						✓	
Stamova et al., 2011			✓	✓									
Talebizadeh et al., 2014 (taken from AGRE)			✓	✓							✓		
Taurines et al., 2011			✓	(ADI)									
Tian et al., 2011			✓	✓					✓		✓		
Walker et al., 2013	✓		✓	✓					✓	✓	✓		
Williams et al., 2011	✓			✓									
Yasuda et al., 2011	✓												

TABLE 4B | Diagnostic tests part 2.

Paper/diagnostic test	Social communication questionnaire	Shortened CPEA regression interview	ICD-10	PARS	Japanese version of the Asperger's questionnaire	Japanese version of the autism spectrum Quotient (AQ-J)	Japanese versions of WAIS-III	PPVT	Inclusion criteria	Exclusion criteria
Alter et al., 2011									For Probands: A negative Fragile X DNA test, impairment in language	For Probands: significant prenatal history (prematurity, 35 weeks, intraventricular hemorrhage, severe asphyxia, or cerebral palsy), serious CNS abnormality, known genetic or metabolic disorder, non-classic forms of autism were excluded, including autism with regression and Asperger's syndrome, a higher functioning form of autism where individuals have language skills within the normal range
Emanuele et al., 2010									For controls: no past or present history of any psychiatric disorder and none of them had ever taken medications for psychiatric conditions	For controls: subjects with axis-I diagnosis of first-degree relatives
Enstrom et al., 2009									ASD: children who scored above the cut-off for the ADOS modules 1 and 2 for ASD and met the criteria for autism	Children who were ill at the time of the study, or had a temperature above 98.9°F, or were prescribed anti-psychotics, or had a known medical disorder or primary diagnosis (e.g., Fragile X or Rett syndrome)
Féron et al., 2016			✓						For controls: neither presenting a neuropsychiatric disorder nor taking medication	
Ginsberg et al., 2012									Male gender; autism diagnosis by a validated psychiatric/psychologic instrument; and the availability of sufficient fresh frozen tissue available for genome-wide methylation analysis, bisulfite sequencing, and gene expression studies	Formalin-fixation of brains, brains from individuals with a medication history of medications known or suspected to have effects on methylation; gross structural abnormalities of the brain; brains from individuals with a complicated birth history and/or evidence of pre- or perinatal hypoxia; history of major head trauma; diagnosis of Rett syndrome, Fragile X syndrome, tuberous sclerosis, or other syndromic process; or any known or likely pathologic cytogenetic abnormality identified by either routine karyotyping or chromosomal microarray analysis
Hu et al., 2006								✓		

(Continued)

TABLE 4B | Continued

Paper/ diagnostic test	Social communication questionnaire	Shortened CPEA regression interview	ICD-10	PARS	Japanese version of the Asperger's questionnaire	Japanese version of the autism spectrum Quotient (AQ-J)	Japanese versions of WAIS-III	PPVT	Inclusion criteria	Exclusion criteria
Hu et al., 2009										All females, individuals with cognitive impairment, those with known genetic or chromosomal abnormalities (e.g., Fragile X, Retts, tuberous sclerosis, chromosome 15q11-q13 duplication), those born prematurely (<35 weeks gestation), those with diagnosed comorbid psychiatric disorders (e.g., bipolar disorder, obsessive compulsive disorder, severe anxiety)
James et al., 2014										For Case Donors: PDD-NOS, Asperger's, Rett or Fragile X For Control Donors: Previous medical history of neurologic disorders, seizures or mental retardation
Kong et al., 2013									ASD: No known genetic or syndromic disorders	For controls: chronic disease such as infectious disease, diabetes, cardiovascular disease, and developmental disorder or neurological disorder
Kuwano et al., 2011						✓	✓			For controls: serious physical or mental disorders including ASD in the past and at present
Prandini et al., 2014									ASD: meets Diagnostic and Statistical Manual of Mental Disorders, fourth edition criteria for Autistic Disorder, Asperger's Disorder, or Pervasive Developmental Disorder Not Otherwise Specified (PDD NOS); reaches the score cutoff in Autism Diagnosis Interview-Revised (ADI-R) and Autism Diagnostic Observation Schedule (ADOS); is at least 4 years old at the time of entering the research project; has at least one parent or legal guardian giving voluntary written consent for him/her to participate in the research project, and gives his/her assent when possible	For ASD: diagnosis of Rett syndrome or childhood disintegrative disorder, history of serious head injury, encephalitis or tumors, profound mental retardation (intelligence quotient <20), and age more than 18 years

(Continued)

TABLE 4B | Continued

Paper/ diagnostic test	Social communication questionnaire	Shortened CPEA regression interview	ICD-10	PARS	Japanese version of the Asperger's questionnaire	Japanese version of the autism spectrum Quotient (AQ-J)	Japanese versions of WAIS-III	PPVT	Inclusion criteria	Exclusion criteria
Segura et al., 2015									For ASD: Had a total IQ score above 70 For controls: no somatic or neurological disease and without medication	
Talebizadeh et al., 2014 (taken from AGRE)	✓									
Taurines et al., 2011										For controls: if had somatic or neurological disease or were taking medication
Tian et al., 2011	✓								For Autism: meeting criteria on the communication, social, and repetitive behavior domains of the ADI-R, and scoring at or above the total cutoff for autistic disorder on the ADOS module 1 or 2	
Walker et al., 2013										For controls: identifiable gastrointestinal pathology
Williams et al., 2011		✓								For controls: Developmental disturbances, including ASD
Yasuda et al., 2011				✓	✓					For healthy controls: neurological or medical conditions that could potentially affect the central nervous system, had any psychiatric diseases and/or received psychiatric medication, had first- or second-degree relatives with psychiatric disease or presented with an IQ < 70
Zhubi et al., 2014- brain samples taken from the Harvard Brain Tissue Resource Center									For Control donors: free of neurological disorders, seizures, mentalretardation, dementia	For Case Donors: Asperger's syndrome Fragile–X syndrome, RTT, pervasive developmental disorder not otherwise specified, and 15q11-q13 duplication

to represent the broader ASD population. While some studies took the disproportionate male incidence into consideration in choosing their subjects, others did not. The clinical presentation of ASD also varies by age. Therefore, significant age differences between ASD subjects and controls such as those in the study by Chien (Chien et al., 2013) deserve further attention.

CONCLUSION

One of the advantages of gene expression studies over whole genome sequencing studies or Enzyme-Linked Immunosorbent Assay (ELISA) based protein studies for ASD is that it allows for broad screening for unique aspects of the disorder while maintaining a level of specificity that the other modalities cannot provide. In whole genome sequencing studies, millions of base pairs are analyzed and often nothing significant is found, or the few sporadic single nucleotide polymorphisms (SNP's) or copy number variants (CNV's) lack any useful context. While admittedly, more than 100 ASD-susceptibility genes have been found, the utility of this information remains elusive. In gene expression studies, on the other hand, despite analyzing large amounts of genes, the thresholds for differences in expression enable a level of specificity and the ability to group specific genes together in order to identify specific pathways. Approximately 12,000 genes were differentially expressed between ASD compared to controls in gene expression studies since 2011. Most of studies can be subdivided by the source into three categories: brain (~3500 dysregulated genes), LCL (~5600 dysregulated genes), and GI (~2600 dysregulated genes). More specifically, in the gene expression studies of ASD surveyed, cell cycle, GI disease, immune function, and neurogenesis, were found to be the most common implicated pathways.

Most of the genes surveyed were shown to be consistently down or up-regulated across different source types in different studies. This strongly suggests that, in fact, these genes are not coincidentally higher or lower in ASD but might actually be active players in the underlying pathogenesis of the disorder.

Future Directions

Researchers might want to consider testing more than one sample source (peripheral blood, intestine, olfactory stem cell, and hair follicles) for each subject to help determine if up or downregulation is consistent amongst tissue types. In the absence of comparing across sample source types it remains unclear if differences between subjects in gene regulation are due to the different subjects or the different sample source.

Furthermore, researchers might consider including more healthy mothers of children with ASD in the gene expression studies and TD siblings in order to help isolate potential immunogenetic processes. This might help clarify why certain immune mechanisms affect only the child with ASD and not the mother or the siblings. Another idea could be to analyze the blood of daughters of women who have given birth to children with ASD in order to test whether they too have abnormal levels of certain proteins or immune markers that their healthy mothers have. If found, the abnormal levels could suggest that the healthy mother is passing something on to her daughter that would then make her more susceptible to having a child with ASD herself.

Additionally, now that certain pathways have been identified as being associated with ASD, researchers can work backwards and look for other genes involved in those pathways and test whether these specific genes play a role in ASD.

Finally, in order to help identify potential sub-groups of ASD, it might be fruitful to study correlations between subsection scores on ADOS and gene expression studies. This might unravel the heterogeneity of ASD into individual strands whose underlying pathology can be better understood at the genetic and epigenetic levels in order to develop targeted therapeutic approaches.

AUTHOR CONTRIBUTIONS

AA drafted the article, reviewed the relevant literature, made substantial contributions to conception and design, interpreted the data and approved final version. JR drafted drafted the article, reviewed the relevant literature, made substantial contributions to conception and design, interpreted the data, revised the article critically and approved final version. PZ and MM made substantial contributions to conception and design, participated in revising it critically, interpreted the data, and approved final version. BG participated in revising it critically, interpreted the data, and approved final version.

FUNDING

This study was supported by Cell-EL LTD.

REFERENCES

Abrahams, B. S., and Geschwind, D. H. (2008). Advances in autism genetics: on the threshold of a new neurobiology. *Nat. Rev. Genet.* 9, 341–355. doi: 10.1038/nrg2346

Alter, M. D., Kharkar, R., Ramsey, K. E., Craig, D. W., Melmed, R. D., Grebe, T. A., et al. (2011). Autism and increased paternal age related changes in global levels of gene expression regulation. *PLoS ONE* 6:e16715. doi: 10.1371/journal.pone.0016715

Anitha, A., Nakamura, K., Thanseem, I., Yamada, K., Iwayama, Y., Toyota, T., et al. (2012). Brain region-specific altered expression and association of mitochondria-related genes in autism. *Mol. Autism* 3:12. doi: 10.1186/2040-2392-3-12

Chana, G., Laskaris, L., Pantelis, C., Gillett, P., Testa, R., Zantomio, D., et al. (2015). Decreased expression of mGluR5 within the dorsolateral prefrontal cortex in autism and increased microglial number in mGluR5 knockout mice: Pathophysiological and neurobehavioral implications. *Brain Behav. Immun.* 49, 197–205. doi: 10.1016/j.bbi.2015.05.009

Chien, W. H., Gau, S. S., Chen, C. H., Tsai, W. C., Wu, Y. Y., Chen, P. H., et al. (2013). Increased gene expression of FOXP1 in patients with autism spectrum disorders. *Mol. Autism* 4:23. doi: 10.1186/2040-2392-4-23

Chow, M. L., Pramparo, T., Winn, M. E., Barnes, C. C., Li, H. R., Weiss, L., et al. (2012). Age-dependent brain gene expression and copy number anomalies in autism suggest distinct pathological processes at young versus mature ages. *PLoS Genet.* 8:e1002592. doi: 10.1371/journal.pgen.1002592

Christensen, D. L., Baio, J., Van Naarden Braun, K., Bilder, D., Charles, J., and Constantino, J. N. (2016). Prevalence and Characteristics of Autism Spectrum Disorder Among Children Aged 8 Years-Autism and Developmental Disabilities Monitoring Network, 11 Sites, United States, 2012. *MMWR. Surveill. Summ.* 65, 1–23. doi: 10.15585/mmwr.ss6503a1

Courchesne, E., Mouton, P. R., Calhoun, M. E., Semendeferi, K., Ahrens-Barbeau, C., Hallet, M. J., et al. (2011). Neuron number and size in prefrontal cortex of children with autism. *JAMA* 306, 2001–2010. doi: 10.1001/jama.2011.1638

Emanuele, E., Boso, M., Cassola, F., Broglia, D., Bonoldi, I., Mancini, L., et al. (2010). Increased dopamine DRD4 receptor mRNA expression in lymphocytes of musicians and autistic individuals: bridging the music-autism connection. *Neuro Endocrinol. Lett.* 31, 122–125.

Enstrom, A. M., Lit, L., Onore, C. E., Gregg, J. P., Hansen, R. L., Pessah, I. N., et al. (2009). Altered gene expression and function of peripheral blood natural killer cells in children with autism. *Brain Behav. Immun.* 23, 124–133. doi: 10.1016/j.bbi.2008.08.001

Féron, F., Gepner, B., Lacassagne, E., Stephan, D., Mesnage, B., Blanchard, M. P., et al. (2016). Olfactory stem cells reveal MOCOS as a new player in autism spectrum disorders. *Mol. Psychiatry* 21, 1215–1224. doi: 10.1038/mp.2015.106

Garbett, K., Ebert, P. J., Mitchell, A., Lintas, C., Manzi, B., Mirnics, K., et al. (2008). Immune transcriptome alterations in the temporal cortex of subjects with autism. *Neurobiol. Dis.* 30, 303–311. doi: 10.1016/j.nbd.2008.01.012

Gesundheit, B., Rosenzweig, J. P., Naor, D., Lerer, B., Zachor, D. A., Prochazka, V., et al. (2013). Immunological and autoimmune considerations of Autism Spectrum Disorders. *J. Autoimmun.* 44, 1–7. doi: 10.1016/j.jaut.2013.05.005

Ginsberg, M. R., Rubin, R. A., Falcone, T., Ting, A. H., and Natowicz, M. R. (2012). Brain transcriptional and epigenetic associations with autism. *PLoS ONE* 7:e44736. doi: 10.1371/journal.pone.0044736

Glatt, S. J., Tsuang, M. T., Winn, M., Chandler, S. D., Collins, M., Lopez, L., et al. (2012). Blood-based gene expression signatures of infants and toddlers with autism. *J. Am. Acad. Child Adolesc. Psychiatry* 51, 934-44 e2. doi: 10.1016/j.jaac.2012.07.007

Gregg, J. P., Lit, L., Baron, C. A., Hertz-Picciotto, I., Walker, W., Davis, R. A., et al. (2008). Gene expression changes in children with autism. *Genomics* 91, 22–29. doi: 10.1016/j.ygeno.2007.09.003

Hazlett, H. C., Poe, M. D., Gerig, G., Styner, M., Chappell, C., Smith, R. G., et al. (2011). Early brain overgrowth in autism associated with an increase in cortical surface area before age 2 years. *Arch. Gen. Psychiatry* 68, 467–476. doi: 10.1001/archgenpsychiatry.2011.39

Hu, V. W., Frank, B. C., Heine, S., Lee, N. H., and Quackenbush, J. (2006). Gene expression profiling of lymphoblastoid cell lines from monozygotic twins discordant in severity of autism reveals differential regulation of neurologically relevant genes. *BMC Genomics* 7:118. doi: 10.1186/1471-2164-7-118

Hu, V. W., Sarachana, T., Kim, K. S., Nguyen, A., Kulkarni, S., Steinberg, M. E., et al. (2009). Gene expression profiling differentiates autism case-controls and phenotypic variants of autism spectrum disorders: evidence for circadian rhythm dysfunction in severe autism. *Autism Res.* 2, 78–97. doi: 10.1002/aur.73

Ivanov, H. Y., Stoyanova, V. K., Popov, N. T., Bosheva, M., and Vachev, T. I. (2015). Blood-Based Gene Expression in children with Autism spectrum disorder. *BioDiscovery* 17:2. doi: 10.7750/BioDiscovery.2015.17.2

James, S. J., Shpyleva, S., Melnyk, S., Pavliv, O., and Pogribny, I. P. (2014). Elevated 5-hydroxymethylcytosine in the Engrailed-2 (EN-2) promoter is associated with increased gene expression and decreased MeCP2 binding in autism cerebellum. *Transl. Psychiatry* 4:e460. doi: 10.1038/tp.2014.87

Kang, H. J., Kawasawa, Y. I., Cheng, F., Zhu, Y., Xu, X., Li, M., et al. (2011). Spatio-temporal transcriptome of the human brain. *Nature* 478, 483–489. doi: 10.1038/nature10523

Kates, W. R., Burnette, C. P., Eliez, S., Strunge, L. A., Kaplan, D., Landa, R., et al. (2004). Neuroanatomic variation in monozygotic twin pairs discordant for the narrow phenotype for autism. *Am. J. Psychiatry* 161, 539–546. doi: 10.1176/appi.ajp.161.3.539

Khan, A., Harney, J. W., Zavacki, A. M., and Sajdel-Sulkowska, E. M. (2014). Disrupted brain thyroid hormone homeostasis and altered thyroid hormone-dependent brain gene expression in autism spectrum disorders. *J. Physiol. Pharmacol.* 65, 257–272.

Kong, S. W., Shimizu-Motohashi, Y., Campbell, M. G., Lee, I. H., Collins, C. D., Brewster, S. J., et al. (2013). Peripheral blood gene expression signature differentiates children with autism from unaffected siblings. *Neurogenetics* 14, 143–152. doi: 10.1007/s10048-013-0363-z

Kuwano, Y., Kamio, Y., Kawai, T., Katsuura, S., Inada, N., Takaki, A., et al. (2011). Autism-associated gene expression in peripheral leucocytes commonly observed between subjects with autism and healthy women having autistic children. *PLoS ONE* 6:e24723. doi: 10.1371/journal.pone.0024723

Lainhart, J. E., Bigler, E. D., Bocian, M., Coon, H., Dinh, E., Dawson, G., et al. (2006). Head circumference and height in autism: a study by the Collaborative Program of Excellence in Autism. *Am. J. Med. Genet. A* 140, 2257–2274. doi: 10.1002/ajmg.a.31465

Lord, C., Rutter, M., and Le Couteur, A. (1994). Autism Diagnostic Interview-Revised: a revised version of a diagnostic interview for caregivers of individuals with possible pervasive developmental disorders. *J. Autism Dev. Disord.* 24, 659–685. doi: 10.1007/BF02172145

Maekawa, M., Yamada, K., Toyoshima, M., Ohnishi, T., Iwayama, Y., Shimamoto, C., et al. (2015). Utility of Scalp Hair Follicles as a Novel Source of Biomarker Genes for Psychiatric Illnesses. *Biol. Psychiatry* 78, 116–125. doi: 10.1016/j.biopsych.2014.07.025

Mahfouz, A., Ziats, M. N., Rennert, O. M., Lelieveldt, B. P., and Reinders, M. J. (2015). Shared Pathways Among Autism Candidate Genes Determined by Co-expression Network Analysis of the Developing Human Brain Transcriptome. *J. Mol. Neurosci.* 57, 580–594. doi: 10.1007/s12031-015-0641-3

Maximo, J. O., Cadena, E. J., and Kana, R. K. (2014). The implications of brain connectivity in the neuropsychology of autism. *Neuropsychol. Rev.* 24, 16–31. doi: 10.1007/s11065-014-9250-0

Nishimura, Y., Martin, C. L., Vazquez-Lopez, A., Spence, S. J., Alvarez-Retuerto, A. I., Sigman, M., et al. (2007). Genome-wide expression profiling of lymphoblastoid cell lines distinguishes different forms of autism and reveals shared pathways. *Hum. Mol. Genet.* 16, 1682–1698. doi: 10.1093/hmg/ddm116

Ozonoff, S., Young, G. S., Carter, A., Messinger, D., Yirmiya, N., Zwaigenbaum, L., et al. (2011). Recurrence risk for autism spectrum disorders: a Baby Siblings Research Consortium study. *Pediatrics* 128, e488–e495. doi: 10.1542/peds.2010-2825

Peñagarikano, O., and Geschwind, D. H. (2012). What does CNTNAP2 reveal about autism spectrum disorder? *Trends Mol. Med.* 18, 156–163. doi: 10.1016/j.molmed.2012.01.003

Pramparo, T., Pierce, K., Lombardo, M. V., Carter Barnes, C., Marinero, S., Ahrens-Barbeau, C., et al. (2015). Prediction of autism by translation and immune/inflammation coexpressed genes in toddlers from pediatric community practices. *JAMA Psychiatry* 72, 386–394. doi: 10.1001/jamapsychiatry.2014.3008

Prandini, P., Zusi, C., Malerba, G., Itan Pignatti, P. F., and Trabetti, E. (2014). Analysis of RBFOX1 gene expression in lymphoblastoid cell lines of Italian discordant autism spectrum disorders sib-pairs. *Mol. Cell. Probes* 28, 242–245. doi: 10.1016/j.mcp.2014.05.001

Sandin, S., and Reichenberg, A. (2014). Recurrence rates in autism spectrum disorders–reply. *JAMA* 312, 1155. doi: 10.1001/jama.2014.9847

Segura, M., Pedreno, C., Obiols, J., Taurines, R., Pamias, M., Grunblatt, E., et al. (2015). Neurotrophin blood-based gene expression and social cognition analysis in patients with autism spectrum disorder. *Neurogenetics* 16, 123–131. doi: 10.1007/s10048-014-0434-9

Stamova, B., Green, P. G., Tian, Y., Hertz-Picciotto, I., Pessah, I. N., Hansen, R., et al. (2011). Correlations between gene expression and mercury levels in blood of boys with and without autism. *Neurotox. Res.* 19, 31–48. doi: 10.1007/s12640-009-9137-7

Talebizadeh, Z., Aldenderfer, R., and Wen Chen, X. (2014). A proof-of-concept study: exon-level expression profiling and alternative splicing in autism using lymphoblastoid cell lines. *Psychiatr. Genet.* 24, 1–9. doi: 10.1097/YPG.0b013e3283635526

Taurines, R., Grünblatt, E., Schecklmann, M., Schwenck, C., Albantakis, L., Reefschlager, L., et al. (2011). Altered mRNA expression of monoaminergic candidate genes in the blood of children with attention deficit hyperactivity disorder and autism spectrum disorder. *World J. Biol. Psychiatry* 12 (Suppl. 1), 104–108. doi: 10.3109/15622975.2011.600297

Tian, Y., Green, P. G., Stamova, B., Hertz-Picciotto, I., Pessah, I. N., Hansen, R., et al. (2011). Correlations of gene expression with blood lead levels in children with autism compared to typically developing controls. *Neurotox. Res.* 19, 1–13. doi: 10.1007/s12640-009-9126-x

Voineagu, I., and Eapen, V. (2013). Converging Pathways in Autism Spectrum Disorders: Interplay between Synaptic Dysfunction and Immune Responses. *Front. Hum. Neurosci.* 7:738. doi: 10.3389/fnhum.2013.00738

Walker, S. J., Fortunato, J., Gonzalez, L. G., and Krigsman, A. (2013). Identification of unique gene expression profile in children with regressive autism spectrum disorder (ASD) and ileocolitis. *PLoS ONE* 8:e58058. doi: 10.1371/journal.pone.0058058

Wang, K., Zhang, H., Ma, D., Bucan, M., Glessner, J. T., Abrahams, B. S., et al. (2009). Common genetic variants on 5p14.1 associate with autism spectrum disorders. *Nature* 459, 528–533. doi: 10.1038/nature07999

Wen, Y., Alshikho, M. J., and Herbert, M. R. (2016). Pathway network analyses for Autism Reveal Multisystem Involvement, major overlaps with other diseases and convergence upon MAPK and Calcium Signaling. *PLoS ONE* 11:e0153329. doi: 10.1371/journal.pone.0153329

Williams, B. L., Hornig, M., Buie, T., Bauman, M. L., Cho Paik, M., Wick, I., et al. (2011). Impaired carbohydrate digestion and transport and mucosal dysbiosis in the intestines of children with autism and gastrointestinal disturbances. *PLoS ONE* 6:e24585. doi: 10.1371/journal.pone.0024585

Yasuda, Y., Hashimoto, R., Yamamori, H., Ohi, K., Fukumoto, M., Umeda-Yano, S., et al. (2011). Gene expression analysis in lymphoblasts derived from patients with autism spectrum disorder. *Mol. Autism* 2:9. doi: 10.1186/2040-2392-2-9

Yuen, R. K., Thiruvahindrapuram, B., Merico, D., Walker, S., Tammimies, K., Hoang, N., et al. (2015). Whole-genome sequencing of quartet families with autism spectrum disorder. *Nat. Med.* 21, 185–191. doi: 10.1038/nm.3792

Zhubi, A., Chen, Y., Dong, E., Cook, E. H., Guidotti, A., and Grayson, D. R. (2014). Increased binding of MeCP2 to the GAD1 and RELN promoters may be mediated by an enrichment of 5-hmC in autism spectrum disorder (ASD) cerebellum. *Transl. Psychiatry* 4:e349. doi: 10.1038/tp.2013.123

Ziats, M. N., and Rennert, O. M. (2013). Sex-biased gene expression in the developing brain: implications for autism spectrum disorders. *Mol. Autism* 4:10. doi: 10.1186/2040-2392-4-10

19

Latent and Abnormal Functional Connectivity Circuits in Autism Spectrum Disorder

Shuo Chen[1*], *Yishi Xing*[1] *and Jian Kang*[2]

[1] Department of Epidemiology and Biostatistics, University of Maryland, College Park, MD USA, [2] Department of Biostatistics, University of Michigan, Ann Arbor, MI, USA

Edited by:
Alessandro Grecucci, University of Trento, Italy

Reviewed by:
Kathleen Susan Franco, Case Western Reserve University School of Medicine, USA
Don Hong, Middle Tennessee State University, USA
Keith Maurice Kendrick, University of Electronic Science and Technology of China, China

***Correspondence:**
Shuo Chen
shuochen@umd.edu

Autism spectrum disorder (ASD) is associated with disrupted brain networks. Neuroimaging techniques provide noninvasive methods of investigating abnormal connectivity patterns in ASD. In the present study, we compare functional connectivity networks in people with ASD with those in typical controls, using neuroimaging data from the Autism Brain Imaging Data Exchange (ABIDE) project. Specifically, we focus on the characteristics of intrinsic functional connectivity based on data collected by resting-state functional magnetic resonance imaging (rs-fMRI). Our aim was to identify disrupted brain connectivity patterns across all networks, instead of in individual edges, by using advanced statistical methods. Unlike many brain connectome studies, in which networks are prespecified before the edge connectivity in each network is compared between clinical groups, we detected the latent differentially expressed networks automatically. Our network-level analysis identified abnormal connectome networks that (i) included a high proportion of edges that were differentially expressed between people with ASD and typical controls; and (ii) showed highly-organized graph topology. These findings provide new insight into the study of the underlying neuropsychiatric mechanism of ASD.

Keywords: Autism spectrum disorder, biomarker, brain connectivity, fMRI, graph topology, network

1. INTRODUCTION

Autism spectrum disorder (ASD) is a neurodevelopmental disorder whose clinical symptoms include impaired social communication and language abilities, and repetitive behaviors (American Psychiatric Association, 2013). Its prevalence is increasing; one in 68 children were diagnosed with ASD in the United States in 2014 (CDC reports, 2014). However, the etiology of ASD remains unclear. Many recent studies have focused on the neural pathophysiology of brain structures and functions associated with ASD symptoms.

Neuroimaging techniques provide noninvasive methods of studying the neuropathology of ASD by learning about abnormal connectivity patterns. Mounting evidence suggests that ASD is associated with disturbances of neural connectivity rather than solely local neural activities (Di Martino et al., 2014; Hahamy et al., 2015). Resting-state functional magnetic resonance imaging (rs-fMRI) has become widely used to measure the functional connectivity between brain regions by calculating the correlations between time series of spontaneous low-frequency fluctuations in cerebral blood flow. The Autism Brain Imaging Data Exchange (ABIDE) consortium has contributed a publicly available set of existing rs-fMRI data from more than 1000 subjects, with the aim of improving the quality and reliability of functional connectivity research in ASD (Di Martino et al., 2014; Cheng et al., 2015). Many studies have yielded interesting, yet controversial, findings of altered connectivity patterns (Shih et al., 2010; Vissers et al., 2012; Chen et al., 2015a; Ecker et al., 2015; Ha et al., 2015; Hahamy et al., 2015). For example, hypoconnectivity is associated with ASD, particularly in long-range and cross-hemispheric connections, such as those between the left and right insula and left and right parieto-occipital regions, which are known as the default mode network (DMN) (Broyd et al., 2009; Anderson et al., 2010; Schipul et al., 2011; Just et al., 2012; Di Martino et al., 2014). However, these claims have been challenged by findings reporting hyperconnectivity within networks (including the DMN, and frontostriatal, frontotemporal, motor, visual, and salience networks), as well as between the striatum, insula, and superior temporal gyrus, in children with ASD compared with typical children (Di Martino et al., 2011; Müller et al., 2011; Keown et al., 2013; Lynch et al., 2013; Supekar et al., 2013; Uddin et al., 2013).

The conflicting evidence regarding differentially expressed connectome features may arise for many possible reasons, such as demographic variation between subjects recruited in the studies, preprocessing steps, network selection methods, and statistical analysis methods. Recently, Cheng et al. (2015) report reduced connectivity in ASD based on the ABIDE data (418 autism and 509 matched healthy controls) using a voxel-wise meta-analysis, and more importantly they also report that the reduced connectivity is significantly correlated with symptom severity. Building on these findings, we aim to further investigate whether the disrupted brain connections in ASD are systematically organized from a network perspective. However, the disrupted networks in ASD are not known prior to the experiment, making it even more challenging to examine them with statistical rigor.

Conventionally, seed voxel analysis, descriptive statistics and mass univariate analysis are used for group-level brain connectivity analyses (Yeo et al., 2011; Craddock et al., 2013; Sporns, 2014; Smith et al., 2015). Descriptive graph metrics denote brain regions as nodes, and connections between them as edges, and have yielded many interesting findings (Bullmore and Sporns, 2009; Rubinov and Sporns, 2010; Biswal et al., 2010; Achard et al., 2012; Crossley et al., 2013, 2014; Fornito et al., 2013, 2015; van den Heuvel and Sporns, 2013; Stam, 2014). However, such metrics (i.e., modularity, clustering coefficients, and rich-club coefficients) summarize all edges as individual measures and lose localized connectivity (edge-specific) information. Thus, they may lack specificity and sensitivity, making it difficult to interpret such data clinically (Simpson et al., 2015). Mass univariate analysis (e.g., network-based statistics—NBS and family-wise error control; Zalesky et al., 2010), based on the connectome of the whole brain or prespecified brain regions, retains localized information about differentially expressed features but is subject to the trade-off between false positives and a lack of statistical power, and does not account for organized or complex network properties.

Our goal is to detect the latent and abnormal networks that (i) exhibit well-organized topology; and (ii) have a high proportion of differentially expressed edges (hypo- and/or hyperconnections). This approach integrates topological, differentially expressed, and localized edge features, to identify altered connectivity patterns. Recently, network object-oriented algorithms have been developed to detect and test these hidden disease-related brain connectivity networks (Chen et al., 2015b, 2016).

Here, we apply these recently developed statistical techniques to the ABIDE rs-fMRI data sets. Using these new statistical graph methods, our aim was to ASD related abnormal connectivity networks by automatically detecting latent networks with well-organized topological structures. Our resulting edgewise findings converge with previous studies using ABIDE data sets (Cheng et al., 2015). Moreover, we detect networks showing idiosyncratic distortion (Hahamy et al., 2015), which may help uncover the underlying mechanisms responsible for the joint hypo- *and* hyperconnectivity observed in ASD in many topological organization studies. Our findings may improve the understanding of neuropathological machinery and identify biomarkers that assist with disease diagnosis and treatment selection.

2. MATERIALS AND METHODS

2.1. Data Sets and Preprocessing

The data set was collected at the University of Michigan, one of the ABIDE data collection sites (Monk et al., 2009; Weng et al., 2010; Di Martino et al., 2014). The publicly available data set comprises data from 48 people with ASD and 65 TCs, with no significant differences in demographics between the two groups. For example, the mean age of the people with ASD at scan was 13.85 years (standard deviation (sd) = 2.31; range, 9.2–18.6); the mean age of the TCs was 15.03 (sd = 3.66; range, 8.2–28.8). Thirty-nine of the 48 people in the ASD group were male, compared with 49 of the 65 TCs. The p values from the Wilcoxon rank sum test (age) and Pearson χ^2 test (sex) were both greater than the α level at 0.05. The study was approved by the local institutional review boards, and data were fully de-identified by removing all 18 Health Insurance Portability and Accountability (HIPAA)-protected health information identifiers as well as facial information from structural images, and data were carefully examined before release to the public (Di Martino et al., 2014). TCs had no behavioral or mental concerns; inclusion and exclusion criteria for TCs are described on the ABIDE project website (http://fcon_1000.projects.nitrc.org/indi/abide/), Typical controls (TCs) were included by the criteria that either verbal or non-verbal IQ was $\geq$ 85 and were aged at least 7 years, whereas TCs were excluded for those who received a score of 10 or higher on the Social Communication Questionnaire 14 or a score of 6 or higher on the Obsessive/Compulsive subscale of the Spence Children's Anxiety Scale (SCAS) 16.

Imaging was performed on a 3 Tesla GE Signa scanner. Data were obtained using a gradient echo T2*-weighted echo planar imaging sequence, echo time = 30 ms, repetition time = 2,000 ms, 64 × 64 matrix with 40 slices, each 4.0 mm thick, no skip, resulting in whole brain coverage with a voxel size of 3.4 × 3.4 × 3.0 mm. During the scan, all subjects were asked to lie as still as possible, keep their eyes open, look at a fixation cross, and to try not to think about anything in particular.

On these rs-fMRI data we performed preprocessing based on the Configurable Pipeline for the Analysis of Connectomes

(C-PAC, http://fcp-indi.github.io). The images were slice-time and motion corrected. The data were then registered to a standard Montreal Neurological Institute (MNI) space with voxel size 2 mm^3 and converted to percent signal change. Masks of white matter, gray matter and cerebrospinal fluid (CSF) were created in the standard MNI space. The mean time series of the white matter, CSF and the six movement parameters were regressed from the gray matter. The linear trend was removed from the signal, and the fMRI time series were bandpass filtered (0.009–0.08 Hz) and spatially smoothed with a 6 mm full width at half maximum Gaussian kernel. Using automated anatomical labeling (AAL), we then used the first 90 regions of interest (ROIs) as nodes (Tzourio-Mazoyer et al., 2002), and took the weighted average of the temporal profiles of all voxels within each ROI as the region level signal for all subjects. The Pearson correlation coefficients were calculated between the 90 nodes and then Fisher's Z transformation was performed on each correlation. In our analysis, we focused on detecting and testing alterations in connectivity networks by comparing connectivity matrices between TCs and people with ASD.

2.2. Group Level Analysis

The goal of group-level functional connectivity analysis is to examine whether different groups (or individuals) show differences in connectivity. Conventional brain connectivity and network methods are conducted from two distinct perspectives: testing which edges are differentially expressed, or whether the global graph descriptive metrics differ (Simpson and Laurienti, 2016). Hybrid analyses are more attractive because they enable the identification of well-organized (systematic) networks (subgraphs) where most contained edges are differentially expressed. Such findings may provide insight into systematic disruptions of the brain connectome in people with ASD. To achieve this goal, we used network object-oriented algorithms (Chen et al., 2015b, 2016).

We first compared the TC and ASD data by performing two-sample t tests on each of the 4005 edges. Whole-brain results were denoted as a graph, $G = (V, E)$, where the node set V represents a brain region, and an edge $e_{ij} \in E$ connects regions i and j. For each edge (e_{ij}) we assigned the weight as $W_{ij} = -\log(p_{ij})$. The greater the W_{ij} value, the greater the difference in this edge between the TC and ASD data. Thus, the weighted adjacency matrix **W** is our input data for the detection of altered networks.

Next, we applied parsimonious differential brain connectivity network detection (Pard, for community detection) and k-partite algorithms (Chen et al., 2015b, 2016). The joint use of these algorithms enabled the automatic detection of latent abnormal networks with organized clique and k-partite graph topology. For each altered network detected, we performed a permutation test to obtain the statistical significance (network-level p-value).

We specified null and alternative hypotheses for testing differentially expressed connectivity networks (Chen et al., 2016). H_0: There is no altered connectivity network when comparing the connectivity matrices across clinical subpopulations; this is equivalent to: (i) there are no differentially expressed edges (C1), or (ii) there *are* differentially expressed edges but they are randomly distributed in the graph G (C2). H_1: There are altered connectivity networks; this is equivalent to: (i) there are differentially expressed edges, or (ii) the differentially expressed edges are *not* distributed randomly in the graph G, but in an organized pattern.

Therefore, the statistical significance of an altered connectivity network is determined by two factors: (1) the significance levels of all individual edges within the network; (2) the distribution of the differentially expressed edges in G. If C2 in the null hypothesis is true and differentially expressed edges are distributed randomly in G, then the detected network/subgraph $G_k \subset G$ is expected to contain a similar proportion of differentially expressed edges in G. Thus, based on the combinatorics and graph theory, the probability that the detected subgraph includes a much larger proportion of differentially expressed edges is extremely low, so we reject the null hypothesis. In theory, there are numerous possible subgraphs with various topological structures in G and thus testing detected networks is subject to multiplicity. We accounted for this multiple testing issue by using permutation testing techniques (Nichols and Holmes, 2002). In each permutation, we recorded the detected network with the maximum test statistic, and then calculated the percentiles of observed networks among the maximum test statistics from all permutations. We collected the suprathreshold networks as our resulting object-oriented altered connectivity networks. We set the α level of the permutation test as 0.05.

3. RESULTS

We applied the above network analysis procedure to the ABIDE data sets. Below is a summary of the latent differentially expressed networks we identified.

We compared the connectivity metrics (i.e., Fisher's Z-transformed correlation coefficients) on each edge between TC and ASD data using two-sample t tests, and stored the p value as $W_{ij} = -\log(p_{ij})$ where i and j were the first 90 AAL brain region indices ($i \neq j \in \{1, \cdots, 90\}$). **Figure 1A** displays the input data: a 90×90 pairwise connectivity testing result matrix (**W**) with the entry $W_{ij} = -\log(p_{ij})$. The ROIs in the heatmap of **Figure 1B** are listed in ascending order of regions in the AAL atlas. Next, we applied the Pard algorithm to determine whether the informative edges were distributed in communities, to capture the most differentially expressed edges in parsimonious (clique) networks. We then implemented the k-partite graph detection algorithm to obtain multi-partite subgraphs. In the heatmap of **Figure 1B**, we list the ROIs in order of identified networks and highlight three diagonal blocks, each representing one network. We then performed the permutation test on these networks, which revealed that the first two were significantly different (both $p < 0.001$) whereas the third was not ($p = 0.068$). Therefore, the differentially expressed edges were not randomly distributed in the 90×90 graph, but instead they were clustered within well-organized subgraphs.

Next, we investigated the two significant networks in detail. **Figure 2** shows the altered connections in the first network in an enlarged heatmap and as 3D images. The region names and corresponding information are listed in **Tables 1, 2**. The heatmap

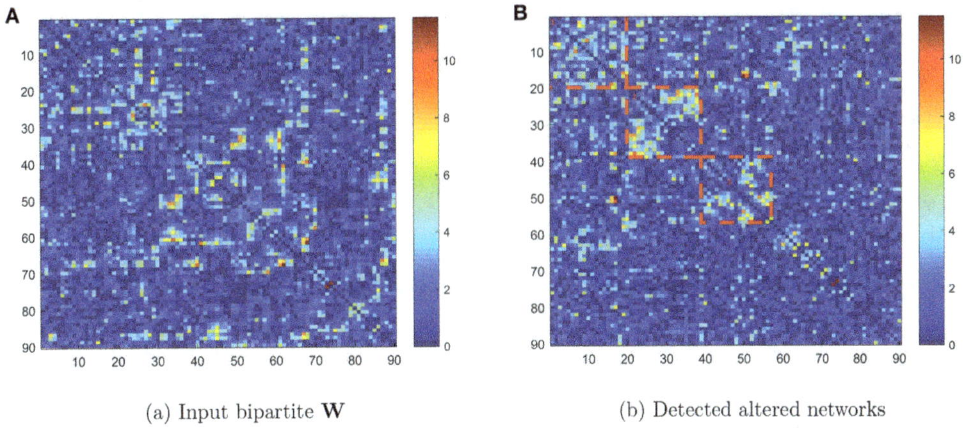

FIGURE 1 | (A) Heatmap of $-\log(p_{ij})$ values in the original order of the first 90 AAL regions; **(B)** heatmap of $-\log(p_{ij})$ values reordered to list the detected networks first.

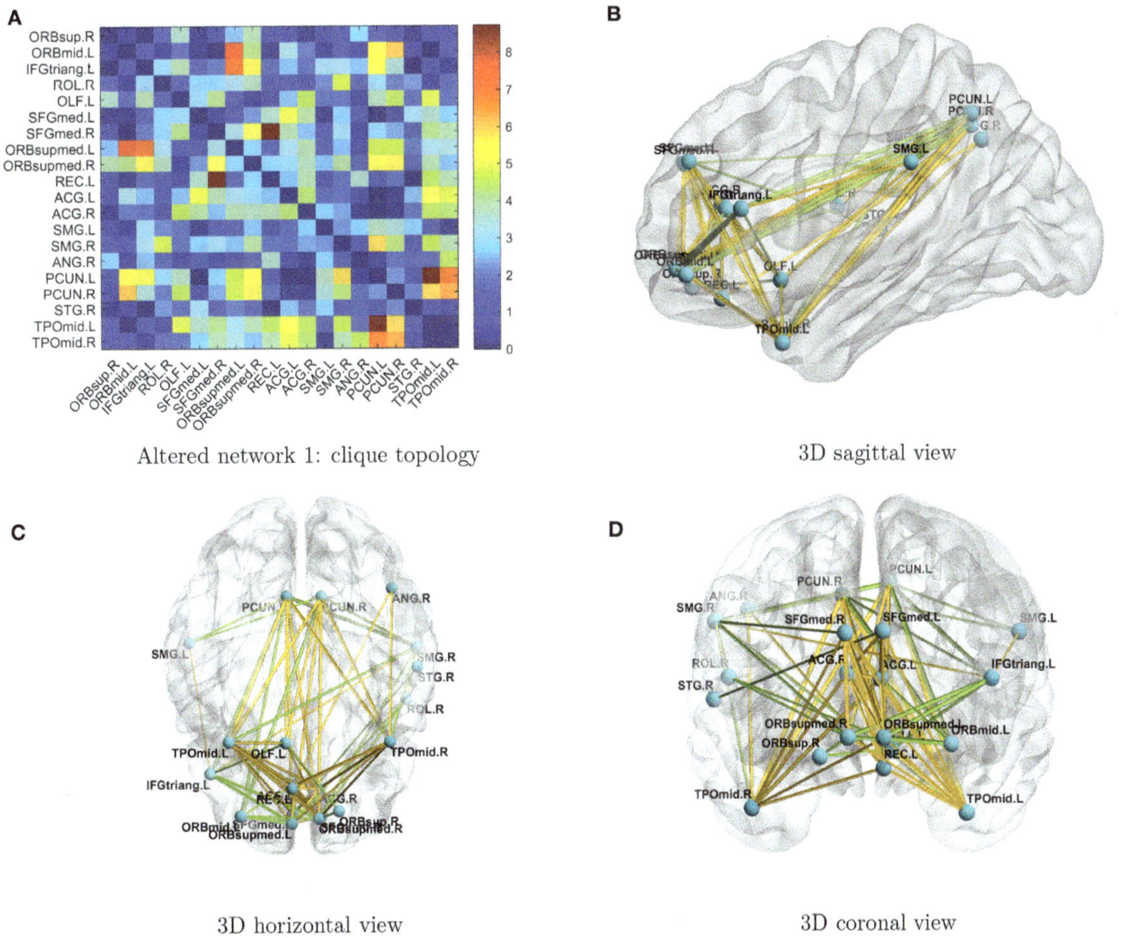

FIGURE 2 | (A) Enlarged heatmap showing altered connections between brain regions. **(B–D)** 3D images showing altered connections within the identified network. Yellow edge, TC > ASD; green edge, ASD > TC. The width of an edge reflects the statistical significance of the difference between TC and ASD data.

TABLE 1 | Altered network 1 with clique topology.

AAL region name	Abbreviation	Index	x	y	z
Superior frontal gyrus, orbital part Right	ORBsup.R	6	18	48	−14
Middle frontal gyrus, orbital part, Left	ORBmid.L	9	−31	50	−10
Inferior frontal gyrus, triangular part,Left	IFGtriang.L	13	−46	30	14
Rolandic operculum,Right	ROL.R	18	53	−6	15
Olfactory cortex, Left	OLF.L	21	−8	15	−11
Superior frontal gyrus, medial, Left	SFGmed.L	23	−5	49	31
Superior frontal gyrus, medial, Right	SFGmed.R	24	9	51	30
Superior frontal gyrus, medial orbital, Left	ORBsupmed.L	25	−5	54	−7
Superior frontal gyrus, medial orbital, Right	ORBsupmed.R	26	8	52	−7
Gyrus rectus, Left	REC.L	27	−5	37	−18
Anterior cingulate and paracingulate gyri, Left	ACG.L	31	−4	35	14
Anterior cingulate and paracingulate gyri, Right	ACG.R	32	8	37	16
Supramarginal gyrus, Left	SMG.L	63	−56	−34	30
Supramarginal gyrus, Right	SMG.R	64	58	−32	34
Angular gyrus, Right	ANG.R	66	46	−60	39
Precuneus, Left	PCUN.L	67	−7	−56	48
Precuneus, Right	PCUN.R	68	10	−56	44
Superior temporal gyrus, Right	STG.R	82	58	−22	7
Temporal pole: middle temporal gyrus, Left	TPOmid.L	87	−36	15	−34
Temporal pole: middle temporal gyrus, Right	TPOmid.R	88	44	15	−32

TABLE 2 | Altered network 2 with bipartite topology.

AAL region name	Abbreviation	Index	x	y	z	set
Precentral gyrus, Left	PreCG.L	1	−39	−6	51	2
Olfactory cortex, Right	OLF.R	22	10	16	−11	2
Median cingulate and paracingulate gyri, Left	DCG.L	33	−5	−15	42	1
Median cingulate and paracingulate gyri, Right	DCG.R	34	8	−9	40	1
Posterior cingulate gyrus, Left	PCG.L	35	−5	−43	25	1
Posterior cingulate gyrus, Right	PCG.R	36	7	−42	22	1
Superior occipital gyrus, Left	SOG.L	49	−17	−84	28	2
Superior occipital gyrus, Right	SOG.R	50	24	−81	31	2
Middle occipital gyrus, Left	MOG.L	51	−32	−81	16	2
Middle occipital gyrus, Right	MOG.R	52	37	−80	19	2
Inferior occipital gyrus, Left	IOG.L	53	−36	−78	−8	1
Inferior occipital gyrus, Left	IOG.R	54	38	−82	−8	1
Postcentral gyrus, Right	PoCG.R	58	41	−25	53	2
Superior parietal gyrus, Left	SPG.L	59	−23	−60	59	2
Superior parietal gyrus, Right	SPG.R	60	26	−59	62	2
Inferior parietal, but supramarginal and angular gyri, Left	IPL.L	61	−43	−46	47	2
Angular gyrus, Left	ANG.L	65	−44	−61	36	1
Paracentral lobule, Right	PCL.R	70	7	−32	68	2
Inferior temporal gyrus, Right	ITG.R	90	54	−31	−22	1

(**Figure 2A**) shows the symmetric brain regions related to the altered connections; these include the left and right precuneus (involved in self-consciousness; Margulies et al., 2009), middle temporal gyri (face recognition; Acheson and Hagoort, 2013), supramarginal gyri (empathy; Silani, 2013), superior frontal gyri (self-awareness; Goldberg et al., 2006), and anterior cingulate cortices (emotion Decety and Jackson, 2004). Therefore, the systematic differences may provide a more comprehensive image for us to compare connectomes between TCs and people with ASD. Generally, there are more over-connections across hemispheres in TCs than in people with ASD. Patients with ASD have hypoconnections for most edges linked with right and left middle temporal gyri and precuneus, consistent with that reported by Cherkassky et al. (2006), Anderson et al. (2010), and Lynch et al. (2013). Edgewise comparisons are shown in Supplementary Table 1.

We further validate the detected subnetwork features by performing classification analysis. We employ the support vector machine with radial basis function kernel and linear kernel as our classifier. The leave-one-out cross-validation results show that the accuracy rates are 89 and 84% correspondingly.

By implementing network detection and testing algorithms, we were able to conclude that the differentially expressed edges in the second abnormal connectivity network exhibited a k-partite topological structure (the algorithm selected $k = 2$ for this data set). The abnormal connectivity network is shown with a bipartite graph topological structure in **Figure 3**. In a bipartite graph there two disjoint sets of nodes; edges within each set are less differentially expressed than those between the two sets (**Figure 3A**). The first set of nodes includes lingual gyri, cingulate gyri, and the left angular gyrus, whereas the second set contains regions from the occipital, parietal, and frontal lobes. Interestingly, the brain regions in the second network are also fairly symmetric. The results suggest that people with ASD have hyperconnections for edges associated with the posterior cingulate gyrus (left and right), and hypoconnections for edges associated with the inferior occipital gyrus (left and right). In addition, all hyperconnections in our ASD group were associated with the angular and cingulate gyrus nodes. The hypo- and hyperconnected edges are in a well-organized topological structure and these results seem to be consistent with those of Monk et al. (2009), Just et al. (2012), Supekar et al. (2013), Uddin et al. (2013), Keown et al. (2013), and Di Martino et al. (2014). Overall, the findings may suggest that the coordination between the visual network (set two) and part of the DMN (set one) may be disrupted. A detailed edgewise comparison table and 3D video are presented as Supplementary Material.

4. DISCUSSION

Evidence of abnormal functional connectivity patterns in people with ASD has, to date, been inconsistent. The aim

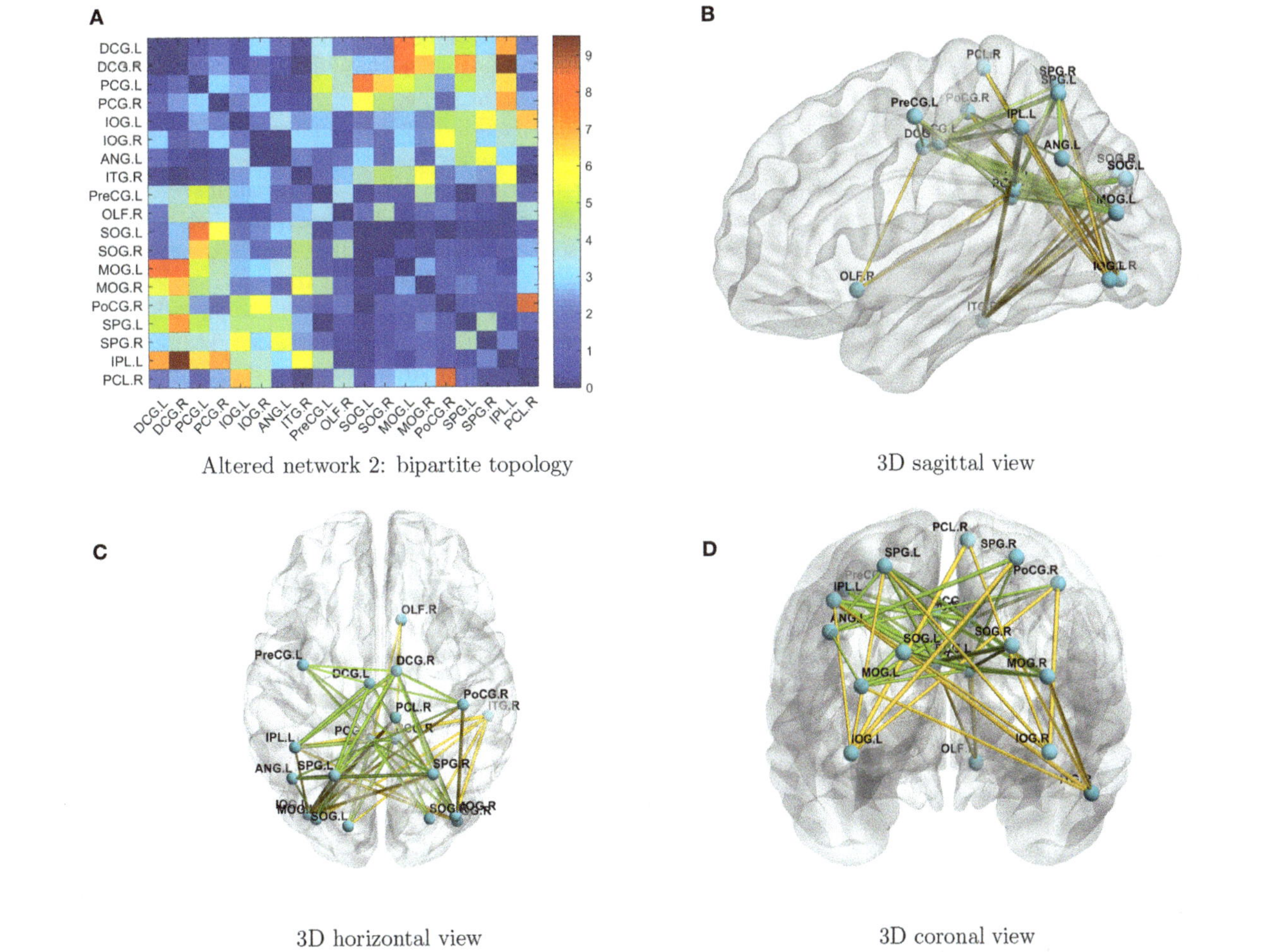

FIGURE 3 | (A) Enlarged heatmap showing altered connections between brain regions. **(B–D)** 3D images showing altered connections within the detected network. Yellow edge, TC > ASD; green edge: ASD > TC. The width of an edge reflects the statistical significance of the difference between the TC and ASD groups. Blue nodes, first disjoint set; red nodes, second disjoint set.

of the present study was to provide a novel strategy for brain connectivity analysis: to simultaneously uncover altered connectivity metrics and network structures. The findings of the present study suggest that unknown, systematic, and organized brain connectivity networks are disrupted in people with ASD. Within these aberrant networks, most edges are differentially expressed between TCs and people with ASD, and these differentially expressed edges show highly organized graph topology. Therefore, in the present study, we consider the altered connectivity as a network unit, rather than as individual edges or global graph summary metrics. This approach has several advantages: (i) the new statistical methods reveal specific nodes and edges within the abnormal networks; (ii) the statistical power is greatly increased while carefully controlling for multiple testing; and (iii) the topology of hypo- and hyperconnections in the abnormal networks could provide insight into the complex machinery underlying ASD. We used advanced graphical statistical methods to detect these hidden disease-related connectivity networks, and performed statistical tests to provide formal inferences.

From a statistical point of view, brain connectivity matrices are intercorrelated, high-throughput data. However, established statistical methods, including multiple-testing adjustment techniques (such as family error and false-positive discovery rate control) and shrinkage techniques (such as least absolute shrinkage and selection operator (Lasso) and elastic net) may not be directly applicable to connectivity analysis. The main reason is that connectivity edges are subject to spatial constraints and are thus dependent on each other in a highly complex, organized, yet unknown, topological structure. Without appropriately accounting for such a dependency structure, we risk a loss of statistical power and possible masking of significant findings. These new network-level connectivity analysis methods (Chen et al., 2015b, 2016) avoid the long-term trade-off between false positive findings and statistical power that arises from the universal cut-off in conventional statistical methods, because the edges borrow statistical strengths from each other through the topological structure. The latent topology provides additional information for statistical modeling and as a result we gain statistical power without increasing false positive error rates.

The topology of detected networks may reveal important underlying neuropathological mechanisms and provide valuable insight for future biological studies. In the networks we identified, most nodes were symmetric across hemispheres, and edges of hypo- and hyperconnections also seemed to be well organized. If we were to perform individual edge statistical analysis, only a small proportion of differentially expressed edges would pass the multiple testing adjustment threshold and no topological patterns would be detected. Interestingly, the two networks we identified include the functional hub nodes of the DMN, such as the posterior cingulate cortex, medial prefrontal cortex, and angular gyri, and the nodes from the dorsomedial subsystem, such as the temporoparietal junction (e.g., inferior parietal lobule and superior temporal gyrus; STG), lateral temporal cortex (e.g., inferior temporal gyrus), and anterior temporal pole (e.g., left and right middle temporal gyri). The first network also involved bilateral anterior, median, and posterior cingulate gyri and the occipital lobes. Our findings largely overlap with previously reported abnormalities in DMN, visual, and motor networks (Di Martino et al., 2011; Just et al., 2012; Uddin et al., 2013; Lynch et al., 2013; Ha et al., 2015; Cheng et al., 2015). The first network is mainly involved in the functional hubs of the DMN and is related to self-consciousness and emotion. The second network reflects the abnormal pattern of connections between parts of the DMN and the visual network. The first and second networks are jointly involved in many features of ASD including those related to receptive language, social cognition, joint attention, action observation, and empathy/emotion. The networks do not identify any consistent hypo- or hyperconnectivity in ASD; instead, the (significant) aberrant connectivities are organized systematically in topological structures. The organized topology of the altered connectivity networks identified here provides further evidence that these findings are promising clinical biomarker candidates.

Throughout this study, we limited our topological structure detection methods to clique and multipartite subgraphs. We are extending these methods to identify various other organized topological structures. We also focused on cross-sectional imaging data and did not address developmental changes of the brain connectome. Although we applied our methods only to fMRI data here, we may further extend these new network-based connectivity analysis tools to various other types of data including functional connectivity data (e.g., from EEG and fMRI) and structural connectivity data (e.g., from diffusion-weighted imaging) to investigate multimodal altered connectivity networks in ASD. The only requirements of the input data are an undirected graph, and that there is no restriction by the choice of connectivity metrics (such as in functional connectivity analysis correlation coefficients, maximum information coefficient, or spectral coherence). In addition, we only utilize a subset of ABIDE data base, and we plan to compare results from different study sites and perform meta-analysis in future work. We also plan to perform multivariate regression analysis to investigate association between brain connectivity and symptom severity at the network level.

We plan to develop more sophisticated algorithms for the automatic detection of complex latent topological structures that have explicit neurological significance, such as rich-club and hyper-graph topology. These new topological structure detection and statistical testing tools have the potential to become important research techniques for understanding the human connectome and its association with neuropsychiatric disorders.

5. AUTHOR CONTRIBUTIONS

SC and JK designed this work. SC, JK, and YX performed the data preprocessing and analysis. SC drafted the manuscript.

ACKNOWLEDGMENTS

We would thank the ABIDE initiative for aggregating and sharing the imaging and clinical data. Kang's work is supported by NIH 1R01MH105561-01.

REFERENCES

Achard, S., Delon-Martin, C., Vrtes, P. E., Renard, F., Schenck, M., Schneider, F., et al. (2012). Hubs of brain functional networks are radically reorganized in comatose patients. *Proc. Natl. Acad. Sci. U.S.A.* 109, 20608–20613. doi: 10.1073/pnas.1208933109

Acheson, D., and Hagoort, P. (2013). Stimulating the brain's language network: syntactic ambiguity resolution after TMS to the inferior frontal gyrus and middle temporal gyrus. *J. Cogn. Neurosci.* 25, 1664–1677. doi: 10.1162/jocn_a_00430

American Psychiatric Association. (2013). *Diagnostic and Statistical Manual of Mental Disorders, 5th Edn.* Washington, DC: American Psychiatric Association.

Anderson, J. S., Druzgal, T. J., Froehlich, A., DuBray, M. B., Lange, N., Alexander, A. L., et al. (2010). Decreased interhemispheric functional connectivity in autism. *Cereb. Cortex* 21, 1134–1146. doi: 10.1093/cercor/bhq190

Biswal, B. B., Mennes, M., Zuo, X. N., Gohel, S., Kelly, C., Smith, S. M., et al. (2010). Toward discovery science of human brain function. *Proc. Natl. Acad. Sci. U.S.A.* 107, 4734–4739. doi: 10.1073/pnas.0911855107

Bullmore, E., and Sporns, O. (2009). Complex brain networks: graph theoretical analysis of structural and functional systems. *Nat. Rev. Neurosci.* 10, 186–198. doi: 10.1038/nrn2575

Broyd, S. J., Demanuele, C., Debener, S., Helps, S. K., James, C. J., and Sonuga-Barke, E. J. (2009). Default-mode brain dysfunction in mental disorders: a systematic review. *Neurosci. Biobehav. Rev.* 33, 279–296. doi: 10.1016/j.neubiorev.2008.09.002

CDC reports, (2014). *Centers for Disease Control and Prevention (CDC) Report.* Available online at: http://www.cdc.gov/media/releases/2014/p0327-autism-spectrum-disorder.html

Chen, S., Kang, J., and Wang, G. (2015a). An empirical Bayes normalization method for connectivity metrics in resting state fMRI. *Front. Neurosci.* 9:316. doi: 10.3389/fnins.2015.00316

Chen, S., Kang, J., Xing, Y., and Wang, G. (2015b). A parsimonious statistical method to detect groupwise differentially expressed functional connectivity networks. *Hum. Brain Mapp.* 36, 5196–5206. doi: 10.1002/hbm.23007

Chen, S., Bowman, F. D., and Xing, Y., (2016). *Differentially Expressed Functional Connectivity Networks with K-partite Graph Topology.* arXiv:1603.07211.

Cheng, W., Rolls, E. T., Gu, H., Zhang, J., and Feng, J. (2015). Autism: reduced connectivity between cortical areas involved in face expression, theory of mind, and the sense of self. *Brain* 138, 1382–1393. doi: 10.1093/brain/awv051

Cherkassky, V. L., Kana, R. K., Keller, T. A., and Just, M. A. (2006). Functional connectivity in a baseline resting-state network in autism. *Neuroreport* 17, 1687–1690. doi: 10.1097/01.wnr.0000239956.45448.4c

Craddock, R. C., Jbabdi, S., Yan, C. G., Vogelstein, J. T., Castellanos, F. X., Di Martino, A., et al. (2013). Imaging human connectomes at the macroscale. *Nat. Methods* 10, 524–539. doi: 10.1038/nmeth.2482

Crossley, N. A., Mechelli, A., Vrtes, P. E., Winton-Brown, T. T., Patel, A. X., Ginestet, C. E., et al. (2013). Cognitive relevance of the community structure of the human brain functional coactivation network. *Proc. Natl. Acad. Sci. U.S.A.* 110, 11583–11588. doi: 10.1073/pnas.1220826110

Crossley, N. A., Mechelli, A., Scott, J., Carletti, F., Fox, P. T., McGuire, P., et al. (2014). The hubs of the human connectome are generally implicated in the anatomy of brain disorders. *Brain* 137, 2382–2395. doi: 10.1093/brain/awu132

Decety, J., and Jackson, P. L. (2004). The functional architecture of human empathy. *Behav. Cogn. Neurosci. Rev.* 3, 71–100. doi: 10.1177/1534582304267187

Di Martino, A., Kelly, C., Grzadzinski, R., Zuo, X. N., Mennes, M., Mairena, M. A., et al. (2011). Aberrant striatal functional connectivity in children with autism. *Biol. Psychiatry* 69, 847–856. doi: 10.1016/j.biopsych.2010.10.029

Di Martino, A., Yan, C. G., Li, Q., Denio, E., Castellanos, F. X., Alaerts, K., et al. (2014). The autism brain imaging data exchange: towards a large-scale evaluation of the intrinsic brain architecture in autism. *Mol. Psychiatry* 19, 659–667. doi: 10.1038/mp.2013.78

Ecker, C., Bookheimer, S. Y., and Murphy, D. G. (2015). Neuroimaging in autism spectrum disorder: brain structure and function across the lifespan. *Lancet Neurol.* 14, 1121–1134.. doi: 10.1016/S1474-4422(15)00050-2

Margulies, D. S., Vincent, J. L., Kelly, C., Lohmann, G., Uddin, L. Q., Biswal, B. B., et al. (2009). Precuneus shares intrinsic functional architecture in humans and monkeys. *Proc. Natl. Acad. Sci. U.S.A.* 106, 20069–20074. doi: 10.1073/pnas.0905314106

Monk, C. S., Peltier, S. J., Wiggins, J. L., Weng, S. J., Carrasco, M., Risi, S., et al. (2009). Abnormalities of intrinsic functional connectivity in autism spectrum disorders. *Neuroimage* 47, 764–772. doi: 10.1016/j.neuroimage.2009.04.069

Fornito, A., Zalesky, A., and Breakspear, M. (2013). Graph analysis of the human connectome: promise, progress, and pitfalls. *Neuroimage* 80, 426–444. doi: 10.1016/j.neuroimage.2013.04.087

Fornito, A., Zalesky, A., and Breakspear, M. (2015). The connectomics of brain disorders. *Nat. Rev. Neurosci.* 16, 159–172. doi: 10.1038/nrn3901

Goldberg, I., Harel, M., and Malach, R. (2006). When the brain loses its self: prefrontal inactivation during sensorimotor processing. *Neuron* 50, 329–339. doi: 10.1016/j.neuron.2006.03.015

Ha, S., Sohn, I. J., Kim, N., Sim, H. J., and Cheon, K. A. (2015). Characteristics of Brains in Autism Spectrum Disorder: structure, function and connectivity across the Lifespan. *Exp. Neurobiol.* 24, 273–284. doi: 10.5607/en.2015.24.4.273

Hahamy, A., Behrmann, M., and Malach, R. (2015). The idiosyncratic brain: distortion of spontaneous connectivity patterns in autism spectrum disorder. *Nat. Neurosci.* 18, 302–309. doi: 10.1038/nn.3919

Just, M. A., Keller, T. A., Malave, V. L., Kana, R. K., and Varma, S. (2012). Autism as a neural systems disorder: a theory of frontal-posterior underconnectivity. *Neurosci. Biobehav. Rev.* 36, 1292–1313. doi: 10.1016/j.neubiorev.2012.02.007

Keown, C. L., Shih, P., Nair, A., Peterson, N., Mulvey, M. E., and Mller, R. A. (2013). Local functional overconnectivity in posterior brain regions is associated with symptom severity in autism spectrum disorders. *Cell Reports* 5, 567–572. doi: 10.1016/j.celrep.2013.10.003

Lynch, C. J., Uddin, L. Q., Supekar, K., Khouzam, A., Phillips, J., and Menon, V. (2013). Default mode network in childhood autism: posteromedial cortex heterogeneity and relationship with social deficits. *Biol. Psychiatry* 74, 212–219. doi: 10.1016/j.biopsych.2012.12.013

Müller, R. A., Shih, P., Keehn, B., Deyoe, J. R., Leyden, K. M., and Shukla, D. K. (2011). Underconnected, but how? A survey of functional connectivity MRI studies in autism spectrum disorders. *Cereb. Cortex* 21, 2233–2243. doi: 10.1093/cercor/bhq296

Nichols, T. E., and Holmes, A. P. (2002). Nonparametric permutation tests for functional neuroimaging: a primer with examples. *Hum. Brain Mapp.* 15, 1–25. doi: 10.1002/hbm.1058

Rubinov, M., and Sporns, O. (2010). Complex network measures of brain connectivity: uses and interpretations. *Neuroimage* 52, 1059–1069. doi: 10.1016/j.neuroimage.2009.10.003

Schipul, S. E., Keller, T. A. and Just, M. A. (2011). Inter-regional brain communication and its disturbance in autism. *Front. Syst. Neurosci.* 5:10. doi: 10.3389/fnsys.2011.00010

Shih, P., Shen, M., Öttl, B., Keehn, B., Gaffrey, M. S., and Müller, R. A. (2010). Atypical network connectivity for imitation in autism spectrum disorder. *Neuropsychologia* 48, 2931–2939. doi: 10.1016/j.neuropsychologia.2010.05.035

Silani, G., Lamm, C., Ruff, C. C., and Singer, T. (2013). Right supramarginal gyrus is crucial to overcome emotional egocentricity bias in social judgments. *J. Neurosci.* 33, 15466–15476. doi: 10.1523/JNEUROSCI.1488-13.2013

Simpson, S. L., Burdette, J. H., and Laurienti, P. J. (2015). The brain science interface. *Significance* 12, 34–39. doi: 10.1111/j.1740-9713.2015.00843.x

Simpson, S. L., and Laurienti, P. J. (2016). Disentangling brain graphs: a note on the conflation of network and connectivity analyses. *Brain Connect.* 6, 95–98. doi: 10.1089/brain.2015.0361

Smith, S. M., Nichols, T. E., Vidaurre, D., Winkler, A. M., Behrens, T. E., Glasser, M. F., et al. (2015). A positive-negative mode of population covariation links brain connectivity, demographics and behavior. *Nat. Neurosci.* 18, 1565–1567. doi: 10.1038/nn.4125

Sporns, O. (2014). Contributions and challenges for network models in cognitive neuroscience. *Nat. Neurosci.* 17, 652–660. doi: 10.1038/nn.3690

Supekar, K., Uddin, L. Q., Khouzam, A., Phillips, J., Gaillard, W. D., Kenworthy, L. E., et al. (2013). Brain hyperconnectivity in children with autism and its links to social deficits. *Cell Reports* 5, 738–747. doi: 10.1016/j.celrep.2013.10.001

Stam, C. J. (2014). Modern network science of neurological disorders. *Nat. Rev. Neurosci.* 15, 683–695. doi: 10.1038/nrn3801

Tzourio-Mazoyer, N., Landeau, B., Papathanassiou, D., Crivello, F., Etard, O., Delcroix, N., et al. (2002). Automated anatomical labeling of activations in SPM using a macroscopic anatomical parcellation of the MNI MRI single-subject brain. *Neuroimage* 15, 273–289. doi: 10.1006/nimg.2001.0978

Uddin, L. Q., Supekar, K., Lynch, C. J., Khouzam, A., Phillips, J., Feinstein, C., et al. (2013). Salience networkbased classification and prediction of symptom severity in children with autism. *JAMA Psychiatry* 70, 869–879. doi: 10.1001/jamapsychiatry.2013.104

van den Heuvel, M. P., and Sporns, O. (2013). Network hubs in the human brain. *Trends Cogn. Sci.* 17, 683–696. doi: 10.1016/j.tics.2013.09.012

Vissers, M. E., Cohen, M. X., and Geurts, H. M. (2012). Brain connectivity and high functioning autism: a promising path of research that needs refined models, methodological convergence, and stronger behavioral links. *Neurosci. Biobehav. Rev.* 36, 604–625. doi: 10.1016/j.neubiorev.2011.09.003

Weng, S. J., Wiggins, J. L., Peltier, S. J., Carrasco, M., Risi, S., Lord, C., et al. (2010). Alterations of resting state functional connectivity in the default network in adolescents with autism spectrum disorders. *Brain Res.* 1313, 202–214. doi: 10.1016/j.brainres.2009.11.057

Yeo, B. T., Krienen, F. M., Sepulcre, J., Sabuncu, M. R., Lashkari, D., Hollinshead, M., et al. (2011). The organization of the human cerebral cortex estimated by intrinsic functional connectivity. *J. Neurophysiol.* 106, 1125–1165. doi: 10.1152/jn.00338.2011

Zalesky, A., Fornito, A., and Bullmore, E. T. (2010). Network-based statistic: identifying differences in brain networks. *Neuroimage* 53, 1197–1207. doi: 10.1016/j.neuroimage.2010.06.041

20

Genetic Syndromes, Maternal Diseases and Antenatal Factors Associated with Autism Spectrum Disorders (ASD)

Asher Ornoy[1*], *Liza Weinstein- Fudim*[1] *and Zivanit Ergaz*[1,2]

[1] *Laboratory of Teratology, Department of Medical Neurobiology, Hadassah Medical School, Hebrew University, Jerusalem, Israel,* [2] *Department of Neonatology, Hadassah-Hebrew University Medical Center, Jerusalem, Israel*

Edited by:
Benjamin Gesundheit, Cell El Ltd, Israel

Reviewed by:
Munis Dundar, Erciyes University, Turkey
Martine A. Jaworski, Carleton University, Canada

****Correspondence:***
Ornoy Asher
ornoy@cc.huji.ac.il

Autism spectrum disorder (ASD) affecting about 1% of all children is associated, in addition to complex genetic factors, with a variety of prenatal, perinatal, and postnatal etiologies. In addition, ASD is often an important clinical presentation of some well-known genetic syndromes in human. We discuss these syndromes as well as the role of the more important prenatal factors affecting the fetus throughout pregnancy which may also be associated with ASD. Among the genetic disorders we find Fragile X, Rett syndrome, tuberous sclerosis, Timothy syndrome, Phelan–McDermid syndrome, Hamartoma tumor syndrome, Prader-Willi and Angelman syndromes, and a few others. Among the maternal diseases in pregnancy associated with ASD are diabetes mellitus (PGDM and/or GDM), some maternal autoimmune diseases like antiphospholipid syndrome (APLS) with anti-β2GP1 IgG antibodies and thyroid disease with anti-thyroid peroxidase (TPO) antibodies, preeclampsia and some other autoimmune diseases with IgG antibodies that might affect fetal brain development. Other related factors are maternal infections (rubella and CMV with fetal brain injuries, and possibly Influenza with fever), prolonged fever and maternal inflammation, especially with changes in a variety of inflammatory cytokines and antibodies that cross the placenta and affect the fetal brain. Among the drugs are valproic acid, thalidomide, misoprostol, and possibly SSRIs. β2-adrenergic receptor agonists and paracetamol have also lately been associated with increased rate of ASD but the data is too preliminary and inconclusive. Associations were also described with ethanol, cocaine, and possibly heavy metals, heavy smoking, and folic acid deficiency. Recent studies show that heavy exposure to pesticides and air pollution, especially particulate matter <2.5 and 10 μm in diameter (PM2.5 and PM10) during pregnancy is also associated with ASD. Finally, we have to remember that many of the associations mentioned in this review are only partially proven, and not all are "clean" of different confounding factors. The associations described in this review emphasize again how little we know about the etiology and pathogenesis of ASD. It is obvious that we need more epidemiologic data to establish many of these associations, but if proven, they might be promising avenues for prevention.

Keywords: ASD, genetic syndromes, autoimmune diseases, prenatal factors, inflammation, drugs, chemicals, pollution

INTRODUCTION

ASD is defined by the DSM 5 as a neurobehavioral disorder manifested by persistent deficits in social and communication interaction, deficits in developing, understanding and maintaining relationships, as well as abnormal and fixed interests and repetitive behavior (Kogan et al., 2009; American Psychiatric Association, 2013). Symptoms must be present at early childhood and interfere with daily function. ASD is 4 times more prevalent in males than in females, but in experimental animal models where ASD is induced by neuro-teratogens, there are little gender differences. Mental impairment is common among children with ASD, and a variety of learning and behavioral changes are also prominent in autistic animals. The etiology is diverse, largely unknown, and seems to be the result of genetic and environmental interaction (Kogan et al., 2009; Tchaconas and Adesman, 2013).

Environmental exposures are increasingly being recognized as potential risk factors for ASD, and the possibility that the prenatal and perinatal environment affect fetal programming is an expanding direction for research. Prenatal environment include maternal use of medication, maternal infection and inflammations, and prenatal or perinatal exposure to various substances such as alcohol and heavy air pollution. Of special relevance are prematurity and maternal diabetes.

Epidemiology

The reported prevalence of autism has increased dramatically over time, from 4 to 5 cases per 10,000 in 1966 to ~1% today (Kogan et al., 2009; Tchaconas and Adesman, 2013). The increase is thought to result increased public awareness, changing diagnostic standards, earlier age of diagnosis, and development of treatment modes. It was also shown that many of the children and adults who were previously diagnosed as having mental retardation meet the DSM 4 and DSM 5 diagnostic criteria of ASD (Shattuck, 2006; Elsabbagh et al., 2012). Some increase, however, may result from "new" environmental causes such as pollution and changing life style.

In the US, for example, the autism and developmental disabilities monitoring network (ADDM network) found in children aged 8 years in 2008 an increase from 1/150 in year 2000 to 1/88 in 2008 and in the 2010 monitoring the rate increased to 1/68 children (Autism Developmental Disabilities Monitoring Network Surveillance Year Principal Centers for Disease Prevention, 2012).

In Israel, judging from the number of children who received childhood disability benefits by the Israeli Insurance Institute because of ASD, the cumulative incidence at 8 years of age at 2011 has increased 10-folds from 1991 and reached 0.49% with a ratio of males/females of about 5 (Raz et al., 2015b).

The more recent global prevalence of autism was estimated to be 0.62% (Autism Developmental Disabilities Monitoring Network Surveillance Year Principal Centers for Disease Prevention, 2012; Elsabbagh et al., 2012). In spite of a wide variation in prevalence between the studies, the authors conclude that there is no evidence of a significant impact of ethnic or socioeconomic factors on the rate of ASD.

It can be presumed that in developed countries the great progress in the diagnosis and treatment of ASD reached a relatively steady state at least in the last 10 years. However, both the incidence and prevalence of ASD continued to rise, implying that some of the increase results from a true increase in ASD rate. For example, in the UK in 1988–92 the incidence was 0.40/10,000 person years and it raised to 2.98/10,000 person years in 2000–2001 (Smeeth et al., 2004) and an in the US an increase was reported in the same states in the US between 2000 and 2008 and a further increase between 2008 and 2010 (Fombonne, 2009; Autism Developmental Disabilities Monitoring Network Surveillance Year Principal Centers for Disease Prevention, 2012). An increased incidence was also reported in Israel (Davidovitch et al., 2013). If this is correct, it may largely result from prenatal environmental causes because genetic, ethnic, socioeconomic, and geographic factors did not change significantly during that time. Recent meta-analysis of seven studies including 1,140,210 children evaluated the association between inter-pregnancy interval and increased risk of ASD, and found OR of 1.9 for interval <12 months and 1.37 interval >5 years. Proposed mechanisms included folate deficiency, maternal stress, and sustained post-partum inflammation from previous pregnancy for short interval and infertility, unintended pregnancy, and inflammation for long one (Conde-Agudelo et al., 2016). Genetic predisposition was offered by Darbro et al. who found decreased risk of cancer among ASD patients. Despite increased prevalence of rare coding single-nucleotide variations in oncogenes they tend to develop fewer neoplasms. They hypothesized that the protective effect may be due to defects in cellular proliferation and aging (Darbro et al., 2016).

The prenatal causes of ASD can be divided into environmental chemicals (i.e., drugs such as valproic acid, thalidomide, misoprostol; alcohol, cocaine, and toxic metals taken by the mother during pregnancy), exposure to particulate matter air pollution of up to 2.5 micron in diameter (PM2.5), maternal infections during pregnancy (i.e., rubella, CMV), maternal and fetal inflammation (Fox et al., 2012) and maternal diseases (i.e., diabetes mellitus), including autoimmune diseases (Brown et al., 2015) or allergic diseases such as asthma (Croen et al., 2005). In addition, perinatal factors such as perinatal asphyxia, IUGR, RDS, and others were also associated with an increase in the prevalence of ASD (Gardener et al., 2011).

Numerous mechanisms for ASD have been offered, based also on experimental animal models. In addition to complex genetic susceptibility, epigenetic changes have also been proposed (Kogan et al., 2009). Other mechanisms are: immune dysregulation that include abnormal levels of cytokines and growth factors and various fetal and maternal antibodies to brain tissue (Rossignol and Frye, 2012). Additional proposed mechanisms are increased oxidative stress, mitochondrial dysfunction, abnormalities in brain serotonin, abnormal white matter connectivity, decrease number of Purkinje cells in the cerebellum, and neuronal migration defects (Billeci et al., 2012; Grabrucker, 2012; Rossignol and Frye, 2012).

The purpose of the present review is to summarize the data describing genetic syndromes with ASD like behavior and the maternal diseases associated with increased prevalence of ASD.

In addition, we summarize the antenatal injurious factors that are known to be related to the etiology and pathogenesis of ASD.

GENETIC SYNDROMES ASSOCIATED WITH OR PREDISPOSING TO ASD

ASD phenomenology varies between syndromes, but in some it is more common than in the general population (Richards et al., 2015). Several human syndromes derived from a single gene mutation increase the risk for ASD. The more common aberrations are Fragile X syndrome, a mutation in FMR1 (Kaiser-McCaw et al., 1980), Rett syndrome, a mutation in MECP2 (Meloni et al., 2000), tuberous sclerosis, mutations in TSC1 or TSC2 (Green et al., 1994), Timothy syndrome, a mutation in CACNA1C (Gillis et al., 2012), and Hamartoma tumor syndrome, a mutation of the PTEN gene. Copy-number variants that lead to inherited maternal 15q11-13 duplication resulting in Prader-Willi and Angelman syndromes (Ogata et al., 2014) and other duplications like the NPHP1 gene (Yasuda et al., 2014) are also associated with autistic traits. Patients with other syndromes like 22q.11.2 deletion—DiGeorge syndrome (Swillen and McDonald-McGinn, 2015) and neurofibromatosis type 1 (Huijbregts et al., 2015) show behavioral changes that are also common among ASD patients. Multiple other syndromes were associated with ASD, however cases are sporadic (Moss and Howlin, 2009). The development in strategies for the identification of genetic variants led to the description of new syndromic forms of ASD and enabled the association between phenotype and genetic traits.

Fragile X (FMR1)

Children with Fragile X syndrome which is the most frequent inherited cause of mental retardation have increased rates of ASD. Current estimates suggest that ASD occurs in 21–50% of males with fragile X syndrome, with increased prevalence among individuals with a greater degree of intellectual disability (Moss and Howlin, 2009; Wadell et al., 2013). The Fragile Mental Retardation 1 locus (FMR1) resides in the X chromosome and expansion of triplet repeats in the untranslated region of the FMR1 gene prevents synthesis of the FMR1 gene product FMRP. FMRP is a RNA-binding protein that modulates mRNA trafficking, dendritic maturation and synaptic plasticity. FMRP deficiency leads to dysregulation of other pathways including metabotropic glutamate receptors (mGluR1 and 5), aminobutyric acid A and B pathways, phosphatidylinositol 3-kinase, and mammalian target of rapamycin pathways. FMRP regulates proteins known to be mutated in autism including neuroligins, neurorexins, SHANK, phosphatase, and tensin homolog (Darnell et al., 2011). Deficits in global network organization and decreased clustering with connectome that shift toward randomness were found by Bruno et al among fragile X patients by structural brain network topology evaluation with magnetic resonance imaging (MRI), a finding that was qualitatively similar to what has been described in ASD (Bruno et al., 2016). When 47 children and adolescents with fragile X were assessed for ASD symptoms, most were engaged in self injury behavior, aggression, and stereotypy (Newman et al., 2015). Compared to children with fragile X, those who also had ASD developed slower, had lower developmental level for age that improved over time and performed worse at language tasks (Ballantyne and Nunez, 2016). Boys with fragile X were found to have social smiling less impaired and complex mannerisms more impaired compared to boys with non-syndromic ASD (McDuffie et al., 2015). Besides behavioral Interventions that were proven beneficial, medical therapy based on the pathophysiology of fragile X is currently investigated (Newman et al., 2015). Waddell et al revised the medical treatment modalities based on the up-regulation of the metabotropic glutamate receptor 5 (mGluR5) pathway and down-regulation of the GABA A pathway. The mGluR5 antagonists evaluated in human studies, Fenobam and AFQ056, improved behavior. The GABA B agonist Arbaclofen which is the R-isomer of baclofen and a GABA B agonist that works at a presynaptic receptor improved social behavior of patients with fragile X and ASD. Minocycline, which lowers the levels of matrix metalloproteinase 9 (MMP9), one of a family of proteins important for synaptic plasticity, improved language and behavior among adolescents and young adults with fragile X, however minocycline may cause in young children graying of the permanent teeth when they emerge (Wadell et al., 2013). Human studies with antioxidants like melatonin (Karaaslan and Suzen, 2015; Kwon et al., 2015) and omega 3 fatty acid, vitamin C, vitamin E, and N acetyl cysteine have been tried in single cases. Acetylcarnitine (LAC) was proven beneficial among fragile x patients with ADHD (Wadell et al., 2013).

Rett Syndrome and MECP2 Mutations

Rett syndrome, an X linked disease that affects girls, is characterized by neurodevelopmental delay, ASD and seizures. Estimates of rates of ASD in Rett syndrome range from 25 to 40% and up to 97% in individuals with the preserved speech variant of Rett syndrome (Moss and Howlin, 2009). It is caused by mutations in the gene encoding for the methyl-CpG binding protein 2 (MeCP2) that binds to methylated-CpG dinucleotides and influences gene expression. MeCP2 is expressed widely, but is most abundant in neurons of the mature nervous system. MeCP2 duplication syndrome is characterized by autism, intellectual disability, motor dysfunction, anxiety, epilepsy, recurrent respiratory tract infections and early death. The MET receptor tyrosine kinase gene which is a part of the biological network that includes several ASD-associated transcriptional regulators, including FOXP2 and MeCP2 was found reduced in the temporal lobe of subjects with ASD. Regulation of MET transcription by MeCP2 was found *in vitro* in primary human neural progenitors from the olfactory epithelium. Analyses of postmortem temporal cortex samples from Rett syndrome and ASD cases demonstrated sex-based differences in reduced MET expression, with males' perturbation in ASD and females in Rett syndrome (Plummer et al., 2013). In a UK national sample of 91 women with Rett syndrome aged from 4 to 47 years behavioral disturbances included hand stereotypies (99%), low mood/changeable mood (77%), anxiety or inappropriate fear (73%), sleeping difficulties and night-time laughing (64%), teeth grinding (58%), and breath holding (63%) (Cianfaglione et al., 2015). Despite autistic traits Rett syndrome patients have some phenotypic features that differ from ASD patients like increased visual fixation at social stimuli (Schwartzman et al., 2015). Rett patients exhibited a decrease in visual evoked potential (VEP) amplitude that was most striking in the later stages of the disorder and a slower recovery from the peak of the VEP response that was impacted by MeCP2 mutation type (Leblanc et al., 2015). Based on animal studies in which IGF-1 and BDNF supplementation therapies improved neuronal developmental, synaptic maturation and plasticity exerted through the key cell-signaling pathways, PI3K/Akt and MAPK in MeCP2 mutant mice (Castro et al., 2013), a clinical trial in 10 Rett syndrome patients showed improvement in social and cognitive ability with recombinant human Insulin-Like Growth Factor 1 supplementation (Pini et al., 2016).

Tuberous Sclerosis TSC1 or TSC2

Tuberous sclerosis complex is an autosomal dominant disorder caused by mutations in either the TSC1 or TSC2 gene. The syndrome is associated with cerebral cortical tubers and may be complicated by astrocytomas. About 90% suffer from behavioral, intellectual, psychiatric and psychosocial difficulties and up to 60% have the diagnosis of ASD. There is disagreement regarding the association of ASD with the presence of temporal-lobe tubers (Moss and Howlin, 2009). The protein products of TSC1, hamartin and TSC2, tuberin, inhibit Ras homolog enriched in the brain (Rheb) that activates mammalian target of rapamycin (mTOR) complex 1 (mTORC1). Heterozygous defects in either TSC gene prevents the Rheb inhibition and allows for excessive mTOR activation, which induce cell growth and proliferation. Upregulation of the mTOR pathway leads to abnormal dendritic protein synthesis with reduced or dysmorphic dendritic spines and alterations in postsynaptic glutamate receptor-mediated long-term depression, similar to synaptic abnormalities described in ASD. Owing to the presence of cardiac rhabdomyomas being detected by pre/perinatal ultrasonography patients are diagnosed early, allowing prompt detection of ASD symptoms (Davis et al., 2015). In a recent study evaluating 42 patients aged 4–44 years that were diagnosed with Tuberous sclerosis 17 (40%) had ASD that worsened with intellectual disabilities. None of the patients with normal or borderline mental abilities had ASD. The Social Communication Questionnaire (SQL) score was positively associated with epilepsy, seizure onset before age 1 year, infantile spasms and mutations in TSC2, but not tubers localization and gender (Vignoli et al., 2015). The mTOR inhibitors used in treatment of TSC patients for various manifestations were also evaluated for ASD symptoms. Clinical trials with Rapamycin supplementation were inconclusive, some due to the severe intellectual deficits of the evaluated patients. TSC patients with infantile spasms had higher response rates compare to other patients when treated with Vigabatrin which increase GABA availability in the synaptic cleft. It is hypothesized that it may be associated with mTOR suppression found in a murine model (Davis et al., 2015)

Timothy Syndrome—CACNA1C Mutation

Timothy syndrome (TS) is a rare dysmorphic disease presenting with cardiac arrhythmias, syndactyly; immune deficiency, intermittent hypoglycemia and neurologic morbidities including seizures, mental retardation, and autism. It is a single nucleotide mutation in the gene encoding the pore-forming subunits of an L-type calcium channel (CaV1.2). The sporadic glycine-to-arginine mutation is located at position 406 in exon 8A (Splawski's terminology). Both variants of TS (the milder TS1 and the more severe TS2) arise from missense mutations in alternatively spliced exons that cause the same G406R replacement in the CaV1.2 L-type calcium channel. Association between non-syndromatic ASD and two SNPs in CACNA1C was found in families of Chinese Han ancestry (Li et al., 2015). Currently there is no specific treatment for ASD in patients with Timothy syndrome. Mexiletine, a voltage-gated sodium channel blocker improved cardiac symptoms in a 2 years old girl; however no data concerning her psychological situation is given (Gao et al., 2013).

Phelan–McDermid Syndrome—*SHANK3* Deletion

Deletion of the human *SHANK3* gene near the terminus of chromosome 22q13 is associated with Phelan–McDermid syndrome and autism. Clinical manifestations include dysmorphic face with wide nasal bridge, pointed chin, deep-set eyes, flat mid-face, large ears, long eyelashes, bulbous nose and high-arched palate, hypotonia, developmental delay, and delayed or absent speech. SHANK genes code for large synaptic scaffold proteins of the post-synaptic density. SHANK deletions or mutations were found in about 1% of cases of ASD. Among 760 ASD patients evaluated SHANK1 mutations were found in 0.04% and were present in males with normal IQ and autism, SHANK2 mutations were present in 0.17% of patients with ASD and mild intellectual disability and mutations in SHANK3 were present in 0.69% of the patients with ASD. Those with SHANK3 deletions presented manifestations of the Phelan–McDermid syndrome (Leblond et al., 2014). Using functional MRI to evaluate neural response to communicative vocal sounds, infants with Phelan–McDermid syndrome differed from infants with ASD by their better neural response to communicative vocal sounds in the right superior temporal gyrus (Wang et al., 2016). Children with Phelan–McDermid syndrome were found to have less sensory sensitivity as compared to children with ASD (Mieses et al., 2016).

Hamartoma Tumor Syndrome—PTEN Mutation

Phosphatase and tensin homolog on chromosome 10 (PTEN) is a tumor suppressor gene that has been reported in autistic individuals with macrocephaly, and also in some syndromes including the Hippocampus Cowdon, the Lhermitte-Duclos disease, and the Bannayan Riley Ruvalcaba Syndrome. More recently, the term PTEN Hamartoma Tumor Syndrome (PHTS) has been used to encompass the range of symptoms identified in PTEN mutation carriers (Leslie and Longy, 2016). McBride et al found in their ASD cohort that 7/99 (7.1%) of the ASD patients and 8/100 (8.0%) of those with mental retardation or developmental delay had PTEN mutations, all of them also had macrocephaly (McBride et al., 2010).

CNTNAP2 Mutations

The CNTNAP2 gene is located in chromosomal region 7q35. A recessive nonsense mutation in the contactin associated protein-like 2 (CNTNAP2) gene was shown to cause a syndromic form of ASD, cortical dysplasia and focal epilepsy syndrome (CDFE). This is a rare disorder resulting in epileptic seizures, language regression, intellectual disability, hyperactivity, and ASD. Neuronal migration defects were found in about half of the patients (Strauss et al., 2006). The CNTNAP2 variant that increases risk for the language impairments in autism was shown to lead to abnormal functional brain connectivity in human subjects (Scott-Van Zeeland et al., 2010). Besides ASD, mutations in the CNTNAP2 gene were also found among patients with Gilles de la Tourette syndrome, ADHD, language disturbances, epilepsy, and schizophrenia (Poot, 2015).

15q11-13 Deletion or Duplication Maternal/Paternal

Mutations in 15q11-13 are associated with either duplication or gene deletion. Prader-Willi syndrome results from the loss of imprinted genomic material within the paternal 15q11.2-13 locus and deletions, unbalanced translocations, or uniparental maternal disomy. The loss of maternal genomic material at the 15q11.2-13 locus results in Angelman syndrome since normally, only the maternal copy of the Ube3A gene is active in the brain (Lasalle et al., 2015). Region duplications are the most frequent genetic abnormality in autism and the penetrance rate in individuals with a maternally derived duplication is >85% (Cook and Scherer, 2008). Maternally inherited 15q11-13 duplications and triplications are among the most common genomic copy number variants identified in patients with autism. The dosage of an imprinted gene or genes within the duplicated region underlies the autism risk in these patients. E3 ubiquitin-protein ligase, Ube3a is the only gene within the 15q11-13 duplicated segment consistently expressed solely from the maternal allele in mature neurons, and inactivating mutations or deletions of Ube3a cause Angelman syndrome. Treatment attempts to hypermethylate the maternal locus by using pro-methylation oral supplements with folic acid and betaine (Peters et al., 2010) or L-5-methyltetrahydrofolate, vitamin B12, betaine, and creatine (Bird et al., 2011) failed to improve biochemical or behavioral parameters.

Oxytocin (OXT Gene)

Oxytocin is a hormone known for its role in childbirth and lactation. It is synthesized in neurons in the paraventricular and supraoptic nuclei of the hypothalamus and transported via axonal processing to the posterior pituitary, where it is stored in secretory vesicles for release into the portal vascular system to affect target organs, mainly the uterine and mammary glands. Additionally, oxytocin neurons directly project from the hypothalamus to the forebrain, the amygdala, the hippocampus, and the nucleus accumbens. Recent publications showed its role in interpersonal bonding behaviors and psychiatric disorders (Kirsch, 2015). The oxytocin receptor gene is a neuropeptide that contains many single-nucleotide polymorphisms (SNPs) with inconsistency in the effect of these variants on ASD. LoParo et al. revised data from eight studies evaluating 16 SNPs in oxytocin receptor using data from 3941 individuals with ASD from 11 independent samples and found significant associations between ASD and the SNPs rs7632287, rs237887, rs2268491, and rs2254298 (Loparo and Waldman, 2015). Another meta-analysis which also included data bases from Germany found an association with rs237889-A (Kranz et al., 2016). Studies on plasma oxytocin concentrations in children with ASD reported conflicting results, either lower levels (Modahl et al., 1998) or without significant difference to healthy controls (Taurines et al., 2014). Recently Francis et al showed association between OXT rs6084258 and ASD (Francis et al., 2016). Despite no difference between ASD children and controls, higher oxytocin blood levels were found in girls, and were associated with anxiety among the girls and less language impairment in the boys and girls of both groups (Miller et al., 2013). The validity of plasma oxytocin as a potential marker for brain levels was not evaluated among ASD patients, however, blood and CSF levels among non-psychiatric patients undergoing spinal anesthesia for minor procedures failed to show correlation between blood and CSF levels (Kagerbauer et al., 2013).

Oxytocin supplementation can be given either intravenously or intranasal with intranasal being superior due to its being well tolerated and easy to use. Reduction in repetitive behaviors (Hollander et al., 2003) and improved affective speech comprehension (Hollander et al., 2007) were found in ASD adults following oxytocin infusion. Studies evaluating ASD patients showed tasks improvement following a single dose (Aoki et al., 2015). However, some failed to show treatment effects (Althaus et al., 2015). Recent studies used continuous administration in order to evaluate treatment effects on daily life. Continuous intranasal administration over 6-weeks reduced autism core symptoms specific to social reciprocity among adults (Watanabe et al., 2015). Another study that failed to show improvement in social cognition and repetitive behaviors after 6 weeks of treatment found improvements in measures of social cognition and quality of life (Anagnostou et al., 2012). In a double-blind, randomized, placebo-controlled, crossover clinical trial, children with ASD at the age 3–8 years showed global improvement and significant improvement in caregiver-rated social responsiveness following a 5 week course of oxytocin (Yatawara et al., 2015).

The possible role of oxytocin in the etiology of ASD, and its potential use for the improvement of symptoms, is not yet understood and needs more studies.

MATERNAL DISEASES AND ASD IN THE OFFSPRING

Diabetes, several autoimmune diseases, infections and inflammatory diseases during pregnancy have been associated with an increased rate of ASD in the offspring. These diseases may apparently occur at any time during pregnancy.

ASD in Offspring of Diabetic Mothers

Diabetic pregnancies, both pregestational diabetes (PGD) and gestational diabetes (GD) are associated with a large number of pregnancy complications. While PGD may increase the rate of congenital anomalies in the offspring and affect fetal well-being and growth, GD is mainly associated with disturbed fetal growth and increased rate of a variety of pregnancy complications. Both PGD and GD are associated with slight disturbances in postnatal growth and development, also affecting fine and gross motor development and increasing the rate of learning difficulties and Attention Deficit Hyperactivity Disorder (Ornoy et al., 2001). Both also seem to be associated with a slight but significant increase in the rate of ASD in the offspring (Ornoy et al., 2015a).

Most, but not all studies on the possible association of maternal diabetes and ASD show an increased rate, and only recently is the type of diabetes in the mother (T1DM or T2DM or GDM) in relation to ASD in the offspring being considered. Lyall et al. (2012) assessed the possible association of maternal diabetes and ASD in 793 children with ASD from a cohort of 66,445 pregnancies. The highest association was found with maternal GD, as the OR of ASD among children born to mothers with GD was 1.76. This is in slight contrast to other studies which found that the risk for ASD is higher among offspring of mothers with PGD compared to mothers with GDM. Gardener et al. (2009) assessed the possible association of a variety of antenatal maternal factors with ASD in the offspring. Maternal diabetes was among the leading factors associated with ASD, with an odds ratio of 2.07 (95% CI 1.24–3.47). In a very recent study by Li et al. (2016) using the Boston Birth Cohort, both maternal diabetes and pregestational obesity were highly associated with ASD in the offspring. In mothers with PGD and obesity, the hazard ratio (HR) for ASD was 3.91 (95% CI 1.76–8.68) and in obesity and GD the HR was 3.04 (95% CI 1.21–7.63). As cohort and case-control studies are being published, there appears to be a more significant trend toward an association with ASD (Krakowiak et al., 2012). However, there are also studies that could not demonstrate such associations. For example, Hultman et al. (2002) in their case control study on 408 Swedish children with ASD compared to 2040 matched controls, found an association of ASD with a variety of pregnancy associated factors but not with maternal diabetes. Xiang et al. (2015) found in a recent study on pregnant women with preexisting type 2 diabetes. They found an adjusted odds ratio for ASD incidence in the offspring of only 1.21, that was insignificant, but in the offspring of women with GD diagnosed before the 26th week of pregnancy the HR was significant—1.42 (95% CI 1.15–1.74). Guinchat et al. (2012) in their review of 85 studies on the possible association between prenatal, perinatal and neonatal factors and ASD did not find a strong association of maternal diabetes and ASD. In contrast to this review, Xu et al. (2014) culled from 167 publications twelve; three cohort and nine case control studies. For the cohort studies, the pooled risk of maternal diabetes was 1.48 (1.25–1.75, $p < 0.001$), and for the case-control studies, the pooled odds ratio was 1.72 (1.24–2.41, $p = 0.001$). The OR for offspring of mothers with GD was generally lower than for that of mothers with PGD.

In a very recent study looking at the neuropsychiatric morbidity in offspring of 12,642 women with gestational diabetes compared to 218,629 non-diabetic women the investigators found an adjusted odds ratio of 4.4 (95% confidence interval: 1.55–12.69) for ASD. They examined children born during 1991–2014, and excluded prematurity, congenital anomalies, offspring of mothers with pregestational diabetes and other possible etiologic factors (Nahum Sacks et al., 2016).

The mechanism of the association between diabetes and ASD is largely unknown. We should remember that the increased risk found may be related to a variety of pregnancy complications that are common in diabetes, or to effects on fetal growth rather than to complications of hyperglycemia. Judging from the proposed mechanisms of the effects of maternal diabetes on the embryo and fetus, the increase in the rate of ASD in diabetic pregnancies may result from increased fetal oxidative stress, from epigenetic changes in the expression of several genes and it may also be related to the other neurodevelopmental changes induced by maternal diabetes (Ornoy et al., 2015b). It was shown repeatedly that good control of diabetes in pregnancy may reduce the different diabetic complications, but apparently will not completely prevent them. Hence, this is probably also the best way to reduce the diabetic—related ASD. There seem to be no studies relating the prevalence of ASD to the degree of diabetic control.

Maternal Autoimmune Diseases

In utero exposure to maternal antibodies and cytokines are known potential risk factors for ASD. Recent studies associated familial autoimmune diseases with the development of ASD. Most results come from cohort studies. However, due to the limited number of infants with ASD born to mothers with autoimmune diseases, many studies are small. Three Swedish registries including 1227 children with ASD [childhood autism, Asperger syndrome, or pervasive developmental disorder (PDD)] and 30,693 matched controls (25 controls for each case) evaluated linkage for 19 parental autoimmune disorders and found them weakly associated (maternal OR = 1.6, paternal OR = 1.4). A positive history of rheumatic fever was increased in both parents of ASD children, while type 1 diabetes, idiopathic thrombocytopenic purpura and myasthenia gravis were increased only among mothers (Keil et al., 2010). Out of 689,196 children born in Denmark from 1993 through 2004, a total of 3325 children were diagnosed with ASD. ASD diagnoses included infantile autism (1089 children), atypical autism, Asperger syndrome, and PDD. Children were evaluated for parental autoimmune diseases diagnosed before pregnancy. Increased ASD risk was found in offspring of families with type 1 diabetes, offspring of fathers with endocrine autoimmune diseases and mothers with rheumatoid arthritis and celiac disease. Thyrotoxicosis in the family and the mother, specifically, were related to lower risk of ASD (Atladottir et al., 2009).

Studies on the inter-relation of maternal autoimmune disorders with ASD also showed increased susceptibility to ASD among the offspring. A population-based cohort of 719 children born to 509 mothers with SLE, and a matched control group of 8493 children born to 5824 mothers without SLE found that children born to women with SLE had 1.4% recorded ASD diagnoses compared to 0.6% among the controls (OR 2.25). However, the numbers were small with 10 children of mothers with SLE and 53 children of controls. In addition to maternal SLE, other potential predictors of ASD in the adjusted multivariate analysis were gestational diabetes and male sex (Vinet et al., 2015). The association between maternal autoimmune thyroid disease and childhood autism was evaluated in 1.2 million singleton births with 1132 cases of childhood autism (not including Asperger disorder or PDD) in the Finnish cohort. The cases were matched 1:1 to comparison subjects drawn from the birth cohort who were without ASD. The odds of childhood autism were increased by nearly 80% among offspring of mothers who were positive for anti thyroperoxidase antibodies (TPO-Ab+) during pregnancy, compared to mothers negative for this autoantibody. The association was similar in males and females. There were no associations between maternal clinical or subclinical hypothyroidism or hyperthyroidism, maternal TSH or free T4 and autism (Brown et al., 2015). A follow-up study of 23 mothers with antiphospholipid syndrome (APLS) and their 36 children, and nine SLE mothers with 12 children revealed ASD in 3 children of the APLS mothers. Four children of the APLS mothers, of them the 3 ASD children had persistent anti-β2GP1 IgG antibodies. None of the offspring of the SLE mothers had either neurodevelopmental disorders or anti-β2GP1 IgG antibodies. The ASD cases born to mothers with APLS had normal birth weight, and normal genetic and metabolic work-up. Cerebral MRI performed at the ages of 2.5, 2.6, and 3.4 years were normal in two cases and revealed punctuate hyperintensities in the white matter of one case. None of the children had thrombosis or other antiphospholipid symptomatology (Abisror et al., 2013).

A prospective follow-up of a European multicenter cohort evaluated the long-term outcome and immunological status of children born to mothers with APLS at 3, 9, 24 months and 5 years. Of 134 children, four displayed behavioral abnormalities, which consisted with: autism (1), hyperactive behavior (1), feeding disorder with language delay (1), and axial hypotonicity with psychomotor delay (1). It is noteworthy that the mother of the ASD offspring also suffered from gestational diabetes (Mekinian et al., 2013).

Two large meta-analyses published lately found a significant increase in ASD prevalence among children born to parents with autoimmune diseases. Chen et al. evaluated nine case-control studies and one cohort study published from 1999 to 2015 and comprising of 9775 ASD cases born to mothers with autoimmune diseases and 952,211 controls. Of them, six studies reported a positive association while four did not reveal a substantially significant association. While evaluating the entire cohort they found that children of mothers with autoimmune diseases during pregnancy had a 30% greater risk of ASD. A positive association was identified between maternal autoimmune thyroid disease and ASD in the offspring. No significant difference was found for maternal SLE, inflammatory bowel disease, idiopathic thrombocytopenic purpura (ITP), psoriasis. and rheumatoid arthritis (Chen et al., 2016).

Wu et al evaluated the relationship between family history of autoimmune diseases and risk of ASD in children by a meta-analysis of 11 articles, including 3 cohort studies, 6 case-control studies. and 2 cross-sectional studies published up to Dec 2014. They found in the pooled analysis that family history of all autoimmune diseases combined was associated with a 28% higher risk of autism. Maternal autoimmune diseases were not associated with childhood autism and significant relative risks were only found in case-control studies. Type 1 diabetes in either of the parents, family history of rheumatoid arthritis, hypothyroidism, and psoriasis were significantly associated with higher risk of ASD in children (Wu et al., 2015).

In summary: there is insufficient data to associate maternal autoimmune diseases with increased rate of ASD. However, autoimmune diseases with specific IgG antibodies like TPO-Ab, or anti-β2GP1 that cross the placenta seem to increase significantly the rate of ASD in the offspring

Pre-Eclampsia

Preeclampsia may trigger aberrant neurodevelopment through placental, maternal, and fetal pathophysiologic mechanisms. Preeclampsia results from shallow placentation that may lead to fetal hypoperfusion. Association between pre-eclampsia and ASD was offered when brain MRI of 7–10 years old children (5 boys and 5 girls), offspring of pre-eclamptic pregnancies, revealed enlarged brain regional volumes in the cerebellum, temporal lobe, brain stem, and right and left amygdalae. These offspring also displayed reduced cerebral vessel radii in the occipital and parietal lobes. Enlarged left and right amygdalae were described in ASD and temporal lobe epilepsy (Ratsep et al., 2016).

Recent cohort studies suggested an association between pre-eclampsia and ASD. In the Swedish, population-based, case-control study that included 1216 subjects with autism who were born between 1987 and 2002 and 6080 controls, preeclampsia was associated with 50% increased risk of an autism spectrum disorder (Buchmayer et al., 2009). A recent study from the California Department of Developmental Services that compared 517 ASD cases to 350 controls found that pre-eclampsia complicated the pregnancy of children with ASD more than twice as often as those of controls and the association was more robust in those pregnancies complicated by severe disease (Walker et al., 2015). Two cohort data showed increased prevalence of ASD among pre-eclamptic pregnancies. Analysis of 87,677 births between 1996 and 2002, of the South Carolina Medicaid program, found greater odds of ASD with (OR = 1.69) or without (OR = 1.85) controlling for birth weight (Mann et al., 2010). Analysis of 218,890 singleton live births in Alberta, Canada, between 1998 and 2004 also found greater odds of ASD (OR = 1.49; Burstyn et al., 2010). Compared to these studies there was no association between pre-eclampsia and ASD among 28,967 children born between 1995 and 2008 in Aberdeen city and district (Love et al., 2012). A meta-analysis of 85 studies of pre-, peri,- and neonatal hazards related to PDD, including autism, concluded that there was not enough data in order to determine risk for PDD (Guinchat et al., 2012).

In conclusion: Preeclampsia seems to be an additional risk factor for ASD, but more studies are needed for the conclusive confirmation of such an association.

THE INFLAMMATORY AND INFECTIOUS ORIGIN OF ASD

Adverse intrauterine environment resulting from maternal bacterial and viral infections during pregnancy represent a significant risk factor for several neuropsychiatric disorders including ASD (Adams Waldorf and McAdams, 2013). The association between intrauterine inflammation, infection and ASD is based on both epidemiological studies and case reports.

Many studies associate maternal infection with ASD, and some studies even found that the season or month of birth was significantly related to the risk of ASD. For example, Gardener et al. (2011) found in a meta-analysis that March and August were both suggested as birth months associated with an elevated risk of ASD and hypothesized that a relationship may be caused by seasonal variation in viral or other infections.

Epidemiological Population Studies

An increased rate of ASD was found among children born to mothers that were hospitalized due to infection during pregnancy. Atladottir et al. (2010) matched the Danish Medical Birth Register of children born between 1980 and 2005, the Danish National Hospital Register and the cohort data in the Danish Psychiatric Central Register (1,612,342 children with 10,133 cases of ASD). They found that admission to hospital due to maternal viral infection in the first trimester of pregnancy increased the adjusted hazard ratio for ASD in the offspring by 2.98, and due to maternal bacterial infection in the second trimester by 1.42. No specific infectious category was associated with ASD in the offspring. Later, these authors (Atladottir et al., 2012) evaluated in the Danish cohort the association between self-reported maternal common infections and ASD among children born between years 1997–2003, and found that infection with influenza resulted in a hazard ratio of 2.3.

Lee et al. (2015) investigated the Swedish nationwide register-based birth cohort of children born in Sweden in 1984–2007 and followed until December 31, 2011. They found that 3.7% of ASD cases and 2.6% of non-ASD cases had mothers that were hospitalized with a diagnosis of infection during pregnancy. Maternal inpatient diagnosis of infection during pregnancy was associated with increased OR of ASD regardless of whether the infection was bacterial, viral, or other/unknown. The higher risk of ASD was observed during all trimesters: the 1st trimester (OR = 1.24), 2nd trimester (OR = 1.38), and 3rd trimester (OR = 1.36). In a subsample of the total Swedish population, the Stockholm Youth Cohort, the odds ratio for ASD with intellectual disability was 1.50, not related to the type of infection. Contradictory to these findings, Dodds et al. (2011) found that maternal infection during pregnancy did not increase the rate of ASD.

In a meta-analysis of 40 papers published until 2007 Gardener et al. (2009) evaluated the relationships between autism and pregnancy-related factors. Combined together there was no statistical increase in ASD except for maternal rubella with an OR of 1.66. However, when the analysis was limited to the four studies that controlled for multiple covariates or used sibling controls exposure to intra-uterine infections, a significant increase in risk for autism in OR was observed: 1.82 (1.01–3.30).

Case control studies comparing complications of pregnancy including maternal infection have also shown an association between viral maternal infections and ASD (Wilkerson et al., 2002). A similar association was found in women hospitalized during pregnancy due to bacterial infection (Zerbo et al., 2013). There were, however, case control studies that did not find any association of ASD with either maternal viral or bacterial infections (Langridge et al., 2013).

In summary: many but not all population or case control studies have shown a slight to moderate association of maternal infections with ASD. The controversy might be related to the fact that only several specific maternal infections (subgroups of women with infection during pregnancy) are associated with ASD. These are mainly Rubella, CMV and possibly influenza.

Congenital Rubella

The association between Rubella and ASD is based on few population studies and case reports. Berger et al. (2011) calculated that the rubella vaccination prevented an estimated number of congenital rubella cases that ranged from 8300 to 62,250 and that the corresponding ASD prevention estimates ranged from 614 to 4607 cases, depending on the infectious rate and prevalence of ASD among offspring of infected mothers. We should remember that at the time of the rubella epidemics, ASD definition was not the same as nowadays.

The largest study associating congenital rubella with ASD was reported in 1978 by Chess et al. (1978) who evaluated 243 children with congenital rubella, most of them followed until 9 years. Eighteen (7.4%) had autism compared to expected 0.07 (0.35/1000) in the general population at that time. All the children with autism also had other rubella associated anomalies including cardiac, neurologic, hearing and visual problems. Desmond et al. (1978) reported behavioral disturbances among 45% of *29* non-retarded children with congenital rubella at the age of 9–12 years. Carvill et al. (Carvill and Marston, 2002) described 12 young males with congenital Rubella who suffered from sensory imbalance and ASD. Associated morbidities included: visual and hearing impairment and seizures in three. Feldman et al. (1973) evaluated 12 children with autism or autistic traits and compared them with 25 children with a variety of psychiatric diagnoses, 21 children with language delay and 26 normal controls. None had a history of rubella. Sero-positivity for rubella was found to be significantly higher among the children with language delay, 8/21 and among children with autism, 3/12 compared to the other groups and the general population. All the mothers of the sero-positive children were sero-positive for rubella as well. Other reported cases of congenital rubella also described ASD children who suffered from hearing and visual impairment, iris hypoplasia, heart malformations, retinopathy, and seizures (Assumpcao and Kuczynski, 2002; Hwang and Chen, 2010).

CMV

The diagnosis of maternal CMV is based on medical history, serological studies for CMV or late diagnosis by preserved blood, mostly from Guthrie cards or dried umbilical cord. Koyano et al. (2004) and Sakamoto et al. (2015) used dried umbilical cords for retrospective diagnosis of congenital CMV infection in Japan where obstetric hospitals customarily provide dried umbilical cord to every parent as a symbol of the bond between mother and child.

Yamashita et al. studied seven children with congenital CMV, two of them had ASD. Neuroimaging studies did not vary between those who developed or did not develop autism when seven infants with congenital CMV were evaluated. Three had sub-ependymal cysts and two had calcifications. All had mental retardation (Yamashita et al., 2003).

When children with ASD were assessed, those seropositive for CMV tended to test worse in the major severity scales than the seronegative ones (Gentile et al., 2014). Additionally, Yamazaki et al. found that ASD cases with cochlear implants had lower language and social function than other children with corresponding developmental quotients (Yamazaki et al., 2012). Some studies showed that CMV DNA was detected among ASD cases in a higher prevalence than in the general population; however the numbers were small: 2/27 by Sakamoto et al. compared to incidence of ASD in Nagasaki which was 0.31%, $p = 0.004$ (Sakamoto et al., 2015); 3/76 by Stubbs et al. even though two had multifactorial prenatal causes for autism (Stubbs et al., 1984); 4/26 by Engman et al. with two of them also having cerebral cortical malformations (Engman et al., 2010). Townsend et al. (2013) evaluated 176 infants with congenital CMV born in Sweden and the United Kingdom between 1977 and 1986, and followed them until at least 5 years; none was diagnosed with ASD.

The role of individual placentas in the protection of the fetus against congenital CMV infection is exemplified by the different outcome in association with CMV stigmata, as described by Kitajima (Kitajima et al., 2012) in a triamniotic- trichorionic triplet born at 31 weeks after maternal febrile illness at 24 weeks. Two girls were asymptomatic; the third, a boy, had lower birth weight, increased IGM titer, thrombocytopenia, hepatosplenomegaly, retinitis, brain calcifications, and suffered from ASD. The triamniotic- trichorionic placentas had no fusion or structural abnormalities. Examination of the placenta of the third-born triplet showed that it was paler than the other two and had more severe villitis.

Other reported cases of ASD and congenital CMV also had associated anomalies including brain calcifications and chorioretinitis (Stubbs, 1978; Stubbs et al., 1984; Ivarsson et al., 1990; Sweeten et al., 2004; Lopez-Pison et al., 2005; Ikeda et al., 2006; Kawatani et al., 2010; Dogan et al., 2011).

In summary: There seem to be sufficient studies to associate maternal CMV infection in pregnancy to an increased rate of ASD in the offspring, especially in the children who suffer from other brain manifestations of congenital CMV.

Influenza

Studies associating maternal influenza and ASD are based on maternal reports. As stated above, Atladottir et al. (2012) found self-reported maternal infection with influenza to be associated with increased risk for infantile autism (adjusted HR: 2.3 [95% CI: 1.0–5.3]). The highest association was found with prolonged episodes of fever.

Zerbo et al. (2013) in a telephone interview, evaluated cases and controls in the Childhood Autism Risk from Genetics and Environment (CHARGE) Study. While comparing data from 538 children with ASD and 421 normal controls in association with maternal influenza during pregnancy, they found that the weighted odds ratio (wOR) between mothers of ASD children and those of children with normal development was 1.26. When they analyzed the association between fever and ASD, the odds ratio for mothers of children with ASD and fever during pregnancy doubled that of mothers of normal controls (wOR = 2.12). They also found that the wOR for ASD was 2.55, for children whose mothers reported fever but did not take anti-pyretic medication. For women who reported fever and took anti-pyretic medications, the wOR for ASD was only 1.30. Hence, if there is an association, it is weak, and apparently due to fever.

Inflammation

Maternal immune activation and cytokine dysregulation was also shown to be a mediator in the neuro-pathological behavior observed in autism. Maternal immune system and animal models were used to evaluate the role of cytokines in brain dysregulation together with *in-vitro* studies that evaluated the association between inflammatory mediators and neurological components.

Studies Evaluating Maternal Immune System

Increased levels of inflammatory mediators obtained from stored samples were found in large population studies. Abdallah et al. (2012, 2013) used a pool of samples from more than 100,000 pregnant women in Denmark and had their biologic samples stored from 1980 to 2004, and matched 421 singleton ASD cases born between 1982 and 2000 for gender and birth year with 820 controls. Levels of Monocyte Chemotactic Protein-1 (MCP-1) which play a role in the maturation of cerebellar Purkinje cells and may serve as a useful marker of abnormal neuronal development, were significantly elevated among ASD cases compared to controls. Using the same cohort amniotic fluid they found that samples from 331 ASD cases compared to 698 controls, had significantly elevated levels of IL-4, IL-10, TNF-α, and TNF- β. Goines et al. (2011) also found Increased levels of IL-4, IL-5, and IFN-gamma in banked serum collected from women at 15–19 weeks of gestation who gave birth to a child ultimately diagnosed with ASD ($n = 84$). Grether et al. (2010) found by examining screening filter paper blood specimens from the California Genetic Disease Screening Program of 213 ASD cases and 265 controls that children with ASD had lower total IgG and that the median value, for Herpes Simplex type 1 Virus IgG was significantly lower compared to controls.

Braunschweig et al. (2008) found reactivity to two protein bands against fetal brain at approximately 73kDa and 37kDa in plasma from 7 of 61 (11.5%) mothers of children with autism. These bands were not found in controls. These children also showed behavioral regression. It is assumed that the presence of specific anti-fetal brain antibodies in the circulation of mothers during pregnancy is a potential trigger to induce a downstream effect on neurodevelopment that may lead to autism. Mazina et al. (2015) investigated the gene-environment interaction by evaluating the interactive effects of maternal infection in pregnancy and the presence of copy number variants which are considered likely to play a contributing role in symptoms of ASD. Participants included 1971 children with ASD between the ages of 4 and 18 years with complete genetic, maternal pregnancy history, and phenotypic information. A statistically significant interactive effect of the presence of copy number variants and maternal infection on autistic symptomatology was observed.

C reactive protein (CRP) is an inflammatory marker that rises in response to infection or inflammation. Analysis of early gestational CRP levels in maternal sera and childhood autism in the Finish birth cohort (consisting of 1.2 million births from 1987–2007) revealed that increased maternal CRP levels were significantly associated with autism in the offspring (OR = 1.12). The increased risk was found in both sexes (Brown et al., 2014). Contradictory to these results, no association between maternal CRP blood levels during the first trimester of pregnancy and ASD in their offspring (children evaluated at 6 years) was found among 4165 pregnant women in Rotterdam that gave birth between 2002 and 2006 (Koks et al., 2016).

In Conclusion

In children affected by intrauterine infections with rubella or CMV, the association with ASD seems to result from the insult to the nervous system, as all also had other neurological problems as well as visual and hearing impairment, suggesting that ASD is secondary to the primary morbidity. Large population studies did not find a specific maternal infection to be associated with ASD, implying that the association between maternal infection during pregnancy and ASD is apparently related to maternal inflammatory process; hence, maternal immune activation may play a role in neuro-developmental perturbation.

EXPOSURE TO DRUGS AND CHEMICALS DURING PREGNANCY AND ASD IN THE OFFSPRING

Several drugs and chemicals have been associated with an increased rate of ASD following intrauterine exposure. However, the association was clearly demonstrated only in few drugs. In others, there are either few reports, or the existing literature is contradictory.

Exposure to SSRI's

Selective serotonin reuptake inhibitors (SSRIs) are among the most used drugs for the treatment of depression especially during pregnancy (Evans et al., 2001; Pereira et al., 2009). They increase extracellular serotonin and are recommended for first-line pharmacological management of depression because they are considered safer and better tolerated than other types of antidepressants. SSRIs and other antidepressant medications cross the placenta and are secreted in breast milk, thus raising concerns about possible adverse effects from fetal and infant exposure. Several studies show a possible association between SSRIs exposure during pregnancy and a higher risk of ASD in children (Croen et al., 2011b; Rai et al., 2013; Gidaya et al., 2014; Harrington et al., 2014). Three out of six recently published case–control studies reported a significantly positive association between SSRI exposure during pregnancy and ASD in children. Odds ratio in the different studies ranged from 2.2 (Croen et al., 2011b) with the strongest effect associated with treatment during the first trimester of pregnancy (OR, 3.8)—to 2.34 (Rai et al., 2013) and the highest was 2.91(Harrington et al., 2014). They found that the strongest association was following exposure in the first trimester of pregnancy. In addition, Gidaya et al. (2014) studied in Denmark a group of 5215 children diagnosed with ASD and 52,150 controls, all born between 1997 and 2006. The OR for ASD doubled among the children born to mothers who used SSRIs at any time during pregnancy.

Recently published large population based retrospective study by Boukhris et al. (2016) reported a significant association between maternal use of SSRI's during pregnancy and the risk of ASD in children. The study included 145,456 children born in Quebec, Canada from 1998 to 2009, of which1054 (0.72%) had at least one diagnosis of ASD. The authors reported that use of antidepressants during the second and/or third trimester was associated with the risk of ASD (31 exposed infants; adjusted hazard ratio, 1.87; 95% CI, 1.15–3.04). Stronger association was found if the mother used SSRI's antidepressants (22 exposed infants; adjusted hazard ratio, 2.17; 95% CI, 1.20–3.93) or used more than one class of antidepressants (5 exposed infants; adjusted HR, 4.39; 95% CI, 1.44–13.32). The risk was persistent even after taking into account maternal history of depression (29 exposed infants; adjusted hazard ratio, 1.75; 95% CI, 1.03–2.97). The use of other antidepressants during the first trimester or the year before pregnancy was not associated with the risk of ASD.

In contrast to these studies, Hviid et al. (2013) found no connection between the use of SSRIs during pregnancy and the increased risk for ASD (OR, 1.20; 95%CI, 0.90–1.61). Similarly, Sorensen et al. (2013) found that children who were exposed to SSRIs during pregnancy have indeed a 50% higher risk for ASD compared with unexposed children, but after controlling for important confounding factors such as maternal history of affective disorder and familial risk factors, they did not detect any significant association between maternal use of SSRI's during pregnancy and ASD in the offspring. Both researchers used data from the Danish civil registration system and Danish health registry systems about children who were born in Denmark between 1.1.96 and 31.12.2005 (Hviid) and until 31.12.2006 (Sorensen). The latest cohort study by Malm et al. from Finland (Malm et al., 2016) examined the rate of ASD among the offspring of 15,729 pregnant women exposed to SSRIs during pregnancy compared to 9651 women with psychiatric disease but no antidepressant treatment and 31,394 non-exposed women and without psychiatric disease. They did not find any increase in the rate of ASD among the SSRIs exposed children, as the rates of ASD were similar to the rate observed in the offspring of mothers with a psychiatric disorder but without treatment. The main finding in this study was an increase in the rate of depression in the SSRI exposed children at adolescence.

In summary: It is still unclear whether there is a direct association between the use of SSRIs during pregnancy and increased rate of ASD in the offspring. Alongside studies which show an association with ASD there are also negative studies. Of special importance is the recent negative study by Malm et al. (2016) as it examined the largest population of SSRI exposed children and adequately adjusted for confounders. It seems more reasonable that maternal depression itself, which is expressed by the use of antidepressants, or other causes, might be responsible for the association. Medical treatment during pregnancy of women with depression should apparently continue in spite of these, rather conflicting studies.

Exposure to Paracetamol

Several studies suggested a possible association between maternal use of paracetamol during pregnancy and a higher risk of ASD among the children. Bauer et al. (Bauer and Kriebel, 2013) examined the association between maternal paracetamol usage or early life paracetamol exposure in males and the prevalence of ASD. They reported positive correlations between ASD prevalence and indicators of both prenatal ($r = 0.80$) and very early life ($r = 0.98$) paracetamol exposures. Liew et al. (2015) followed 64,322 children and mothers enrolled in the Danish National Birth Cohort. They reported that maternal use of paracetamol in pregnancy was associated with ASD with hyperkinetic symptoms only (HR = 1.51 95% CI 1.19–1.92), but not with other types of ASD (HR = 1.06 95% CI 0.92–1.24). More than half of pregnant women in the USA and Europe report using paracetamol and it is the most common drug administered to children; as a result it is difficult to connect between these exposure and ASD). It is obvious that the data is insufficient to draw any conclusion from these studies.

Exposure to β2-Adrenergic Receptor Agonists

Connors et al. (2005) was the first to examine the effects of prenatal overstimulation of the beta2-adrenergic receptor (B2AR), in 37 dizygotic pair of ASD twins who were exposed to terbutaline, a B2AR agonists, commonly prescribed to treat asthma and other pulmonary disorders and to delay preterm labors. They found increased concordance for autism spectrum disorders in dizygotic twins (relative risk = 2.0), with a further increase in the risk for male twins with no other affected siblings (relative risk = 4.4) related to terbutaline exposure overall.

Croen et al. (2011a) examined maternal use of B2AR agonists during pregnancy among 291 children with and 284 without ASD. No evidence linking B2AR exposure during pregnancy with ASD risk was found. However, they reported that exposure to terbutaline only during the third trimester for more than 2 days may be associated with an increased risk of ASD.

A new case control study by Gidaya et al. (2016) investigated the associations between prenatal use of B2AR agonist drugs and the risk for ASD. They studied 5200 ASD diagnosed cases and 52,000 controls from the Denmark's health and population register. The frequency of B2AR agonist drug exposure in pregnancy was 3.7% (190) for cases and 2.9% (1489) in controls. B2AR agonist use during pregnancy was associated with increased risk of ASD, even after adjustment for maternal asthma and other covariates (OR: 1.3, 95% CI: 1.1–1.5). There was no difference regarding the trimesters of pregnancy during exposure.

Exposure to Valproic Acid

Antiepileptic drugs are among the most common teratogens prescribed to women of childbearing age, especially as some of them are also used for psychiatric indications and pain management. Prenatal exposure to antiepileptic drugs (AEDs) is associated with an increased risk of major congenital malformations and delayed cognitive development among the offspring, in a dose dependent manner (Meador et al., 2007; Tomson et al., 2011). Valporic acid (VPA), apparently the most teratogenic AED (Werler et al., 2011), was also found to be associated with impaired cognitive outcomes (Meador et al., 2009). Many reports demonstrate that prenatal exposure to VPA is also associated with a high risk for ASD in the prenatally exposed child in addition to other neurodevelopmental disorders, especially in language development (Moore et al., 2000; Williams et al., 2001; Rasalam et al., 2005; Bromley et al., 2008).

Christianson et al. (1994) were apparently the first to point to of a possible association between intrauterine exposure to VPA and ASD, as observed in four children exposed to VPA during pregnancy. All children had developmental delay and one of them had ASD.

Several years later, Williams et al. (2001) examined five children with ASD and found that VPA was used during pregnancy in all five, but in three in combination with another anticonvulsant. Moore et al. (2000) found among 57 children affected by antiepileptic drugs that four had autistic syndrome and two had Asperger syndrome. Five of them (10.8% of 46 exposed to VPA) were exposed to VPA alone or combined with another AED. Rasalam et al. (2005) evaluated the clinical features and frequency of autistic disorder or Asperger syndrome in 260 children exposed to anticonvulsant medication during pregnancy, by using the DSM IV criteria. They found that VPA was the drug most commonly associated with autistic disorder. The prevalence of ASD in children exposed to VPA alone was 8.9 and 11.7%, among children exposed to sodium valproate in combination with other AEDs. Bromley et al. (2008) examined 296 children of epileptic mothers and 336 children born to mothers without epilepsy. Out of the 632 children from both groups 10 have been diagnosed with ASD, 7 of them were exposed to AEDs. Of those seven children, four were exposed to VPA monotherapy (4/64 6.3%). In addition to these prospective studies, several large retrospective studies have also supported the findings that *in utero* VPA exposure may be linked to an increased risk of ASD (Ornoy, 2009).

Christensen et al. (2013) in a much larger Danish population-based study reviewed the National Population Register with prescription data, psychiatric register and birth records. Records were collated for 655,615 eligible children, with 508 exposed to VPA and 2136 to other anticonvulsants. An increased risk of ASD (Hazard Ratio-HR = 2.9, 95% CI, 1.7–4.9) was found in children exposed to VPA during pregnancy. The risk of ASD was elevated compared to non-exposure when VPA was taken in the first trimester of pregnancy or after the first trimester.

Animal models in rodents using different neurobehavioral measures fully support the human data. Exposure of mice and rats to VPA produced autism-like behaviors in the offspring (Schneider and Przewlocki, 2005; Wagner et al., 2006). Maternal exposure to VPA induced developmental delay, lifelong deficits in social behavior as well as motor deficits, anxiety-like behavior and alterations in postnatal growth and development in the offspring (Schneider and Przewlocki, 2005; Kolozsi et al., 2009; Bambini-Junior et al., 2011). As in humans, anatomical alterations such as reduced number of cerebellar Purkinje cells, damage to cranial nerve nuclei have been described (Rodier et al., 1997; Ingram et al., 2000) as well as enhanced synaptic plasticity of the prefrontal cortex (Sui and Chen, 2012).

In summary: VPA seems to be the drug with the highest association to ASD as proven in human and animal models and should therefore not be used as a first-line antiepileptic drug in pregnant women or in those who plan pregnancy. Similarly, it should not be used as a mood stabilizer for the treatment of psychiatric patients.

Exposure to Thalidomide

Thalidomide is a well-known human teratogen that caused multiple birth defects including limb reduction defects, ocular and cardiovascular anomalies. Thalidomide is still used in the treatment of leprosy and multiple myeloma (Ito et al., 2010). Stromland et al. (1994) have reported increased number of incidences of autism in children exposed prenatally to thalidomide. At least four of the 100 thalidomide embryopathy patients met full criteria for DSM III R autistic disorder- much higher prevalence then in the general population. The critical window of exposure to thalidomide was in the first trimester, mainly days 20–35 post fertilization. Because thalidomide is generally used in elder patients, no newer data was published regarding this possible effect, making it difficult to accept or deny this possible association, or to calculate the relative risk.

Exposure to Cocaine

Cocaine use during pregnancy has many deleterious effects on both the mother and the fetus, (Singer et al., 1993; Fox, 1994). Cocaine, which is used nowadays mainly as a recreational drug crosses the placenta and the fetal blood-brain barrier readily, and may affect the fetal central nervous system (Roe et al., 1990). Its use during pregnancy may have a variety of deleterious effects on the fetus including preterm delivery, intrauterine growth retardation, placental abruption, stillbirth, and neonatal death (Singer et al., 1993; Fox, 1994). Several studies reported a possible association between the use of cocaine during pregnancy and the development of ASD in the offspring.

Davis et al. (1992) examined 70 children with a history of prenatal cocaine exposure, in Harlem, New-York and found that nine of the children met the DMS III R criteria for autistic disorder—11.4%, much higher than the national average at that time. Harris et al. (1995) examined three, 25–36 month old children with prenatal exposure to cocaine, alcohol and other illicit drugs. They reported that all three children showed a notable pattern of autistic-like behaviors.

We could not find other studies associating prenatal cocaine exposure with ASD. Hence, judging from the paucity of studies, in spite of relatively high use, there seems to be insufficient data to support such association. Hence, the relative risk could not be calculated.

Exposure to Ethanol

Fetal alcohol syndrome (FAS) is a pattern of physical and neurodevelopmental abnormalities which develop in some of the children who were exposed to high levels of alcohol during pregnancy. It is characterized by prenatal and postnatal growth deficiency, CNS dysfunction including mental retardation and behavioral abnormalities, a distinctive pattern of facial features and major malformations of several organs. Some studies have shown a connection between FAS and an increased risk of ASD.

Nanson (1992) described six children aged 6–15 years, out of a data base of 326 FAS individuals who showed the physical phenotype of FAS and also presented a behavioral phenotype typical of autism spectrum disorder. The children also suffered from significant retardation of their cognitive and social skills. These data is representing an incidence of ASD in 1 of 54 cases of FAS.

Aronson et al. (1997) found that among 24 children born to mothers who used high doses of alcohol during pregnancy, two had Asperger syndrome and one had autistic-like behavior. There was a clear correlation between the occurrence and severity of ASD and the degree of alcohol exposure *in utero*. Landgren et al. (2010) assessed 71 children adopted from Eastern Europe between 4.8 and 10.5 years of age and found fetal alcohol syndrome in 37 of the children (52%) and autism in 6 of the children (9%), suggesting a positive association between prenatal alcohol consumption and ASD.

The association between maternal alcohol consumption in pregnancy and ASD does not seem to exist with low alcohol intake. In a large population-based cohort study Eliasen et al. (2010) evaluated a total of 80,522 mother-child pairs. Almost half of the women reported an average weekly intake of at least half a standard alcoholic drink (45%), and approximately one-quarter of the women reported at least one episode of binge drinking during pregnancy. They found no positive associations between ASD and average alcohol consumption or number of binge drinking episodes during pregnancy Adjusted hazard ratio for alcohol consumption of 0.5–1.5 glasses of wine per week (119 cases) = 0.84, 95% CI: 0.68–1.05; adjusted hazard ratio for single binge drinking episode (51 cases) = 0.72, 95% CI: 0.53–0.97.

In summary: Although the existing data of the association between high amounts of alcohol consumption in pregnancy and the risk for ASD in children (especially those with FAS) is well established, the relation to lower amounts ingested is not yet established.

Exposure to Misoprostol and Moebius Sequence

Misoprostol is a prostaglandin analog drug widely used to induce medical abortions (Gonzalez et al., 1998). It is also often prescribed for the prevention and treatment of gastric ulcers. Möbius sequence is a rare congenital disorder, characterized by uni-or bilateral eye-face palsy due to damage to cranial nerve nuclei, associated with muscle or skeletal malformations in the upper or lower limbs, with an estimated prevalence of 1:50,000 cases in the general population (Stromland et al., 2002; Verzijl et al., 2003). Among the etiological factors responsible for Möbius sequence, apart from genetic causes, is also intrauterine exposure to teratogens mainly misoprostol (Bandim et al., 2003; Vauzelle et al., 2013). Judging from the literature, it is expected that about 1% of children exposed *in utero* to misoprostol will have Möbius sequence (Gonzalez et al., 1993; Marques-Dias et al., 2003).

Johansson et al. (2001)analyzed 25 Swedish individuals with Möbius sequence. Six patients met all diagnostic DSM III R criteria for autism which is a much higher frequency than that of the general population. These findings suggest a strong association between Möbius sequence and ASD. All these patients also had mental retardation.

Bandim et al. (2003) examined 23 Brazilian patients with the age range of 1–11 years, which had been diagnosed as having Möbius sequence based on clinical findings. They identified seven children with ASD of whom four (57.1%) had a positive history of prenatal exposure to misoprostol during the first trimester of pregnancy. They concluded that the prevalence of ASD found in Möbius patients is around 26.1%, much higher than the general population, thus suggesting a strong association linking the two pathologies.

The correlation between misoprostol exposure during pregnancy and ASD is suggested on the basis of reports published in the literature. However, since most, if not all affected children also had Mobius syndrome, it is difficult to directly associate misoprostol exposure to ASD. We found no reports on an association of ASD to misoprostol exposure in exposed children that do not present the symptoms of Moebius syndrome. It should be remembered that the experimental models of VPA—induced ASD in rats and mice have also caused damage to the cranial nerve nuclei, similar to the damage observed in Mobius syndrome (Rodier et al., 1997; Ingram et al., 2000; Sui and Chen, 2012). Hence, it is possible that the relation of misoprostol—induced Mobius syndrome to ASD is not a result of the direct effects of misoprostol but rather from the damage to the cranial nerve nuclei.

Folic Acid Deficiency

Folic acid deficiency is associated with a variety of adverse outcomes in the offspring, especially Neural Tube Defects (NTD). Folic acid deficiency was therefore also proposed as a possible risk factor for ASD.

Schmidt et al. were the first to report that mothers of children with autism were less likely, than those of typically developing children, to report having taken prenatal vitamins, including folic acid, during the 3 months before pregnancy or the first month of pregnancy (OR, 0.62; 95% CI, 0.42–0.93). Later, Schmidt et al. (2012) examined the effect of maternal folic acid intake on the ASD risk in a group of 429 children with ASD and 278 normal children and found that mothers of normal children had a significantly greater mean folic acid intake during the first month of pregnancy compared to mothers of children with ASD. A mean daily folic acid intake of $\geq$600 μg during the first month of pregnancy was associated with reduced ASD risk (OR, 0.62), and risk estimates decreased with increased folic acid (P-trend = 0.001). The association between folic acid and reduced ASD risk was strongest for mothers and children with MTHFR 677 C > T variant genotypes.

In a prospective Norwegian cohort study, Surén et al. (2013) followed up 85,176 children of whom 270 had been diagnosed with ASD and found a significantly higher rate of Autism in children who were not exposed *in utero* to folic acid (0.21%) compared to children of mothers who took 400 μg or more folic acid (0.10%) during a month before and 2 month after the start of pregnancy (OR, 0.6).

Recently, DeVilbiss et al. (2015) summarized the existing literature regarding folic acid deficiency and ASD and discussed the limitations of the different studies. He concluded that the data associating Folate deficiency with a higher risk of autism is yet inconclusive. Hence, it is obvious that more studies are needed to elucidate the possible association of maternal folic acid deficiency with ASD.

EXPOSURE TO HIGH LEVELS OF ENVIRONMENTAL AGENTS

Exposure to Air Pollution

Increased air pollution is one of the more common signs of our modern life, and its possible effects on health are extensively investigated. In spite of great difficulties in measuring the extent of air pollution and the elucidation the large number of possible confounding factors, more and more studies are being published associating heavy air pollution to ASD.

The first study was apparently conducted in San Francisco Bay area in 2006 by Windham et al. (2006). They examined the effects of prenatal exposure to 19 hazardous air pollutants in 284 children with ASD compared to 657 controls. Elevated risk for ASD was found in adjusted analyses of the top quartile of exposure to chlorinated solvents and heavy metals [95% CI, 1.1–2.1]. In this study, however, the exposure was estimated 2 years after birth when ASD diagnosis was established. Hence the effects might be attributed to postnatal effects of these pollutants.

Kalkbrenner et al. (2010) examined prenatal exposure to 35 hazardous air pollutants in 383 children with ASD and 2829 control children with speech and language impairment. They found that prenatal exposure to hazardous air pollutants including methylene chloride (OR, 1.4; 95% CI, 0.7–2.5), quinoline (OR, 1.4; 95% CI, 1.0–2.2), and styrene (OR, 1.8; 95% CI, 1.0–3.1) were associated with a higher risk for ASD.

Volk et al. (2011) investigated the association between ASD and proximity of residence to freeways and major roadways during pregnancy and near the time of delivery, in a group of 304 children with ASD and 259 controls. They found that maternal residence during the third trimester (OR, 2.22; 95% CI, 1.16–4.42) and at the time of delivery (OR, 1.86; 95%CI, 1.04–3.45) were more likely to be near a freeway ($\leq$309 m) for the ASD children than for the controls. They also found (Volk et al., 2013) in an additional study that, during gestation, children with

ASD were more likely to live at residencies that had the highest quartile of exposure to traffic-related air pollution (OR, 1.98; 95% CI, 1.20–3.31) compared with control children. Regional exposure during pregnancy with nitrogen dioxide and particulate matter <2.5 and 10 μm in diameter (PM2.5 and PM10) were also associated with autism.

Similarly, Becerra et al. (2013) studied the influence of exposures to traffic-related air pollution during pregnancy on the occurrence of ASD with controls matched by sex, birth year, and gestational age. They found a small but significant 12–15% relative increase, per interquartile range, in odds of autism for ozone (OR, 1.12, 95% CI: 1.06–1.19; per 11.54-ppb increase) and particulate matter ≤2.5 μm when mutually adjusting for both pollutants.

Roberts et al. (2013) estimated the association between levels of hazardous air pollutants at the time and place of birth and ASD in 325 children with ASD and 22,101 controls. Prenatal exposures to the highest quintile of air pollutants, such as diesel, lead, manganese, mercury, and methylene chloride, were significantly associated with ASD, with odds ratios ranging from 1.5 (for overall metals measure) to 2.0 (for diesel and mercury). For most pollutants, associations were stronger for boys (279 cases) than for girls (46 cases) suggesting a significant gender difference.

Raz et al. (2015a) examined the association between maternal exposure to particulate matter (PM) air pollution during pregnancy and the risk of ASD compared to controls. They found that PM2.5 exposure during pregnancy was associated with increased risk of ASD, with an adjusted odds ratio for ASD per interquartile range of 1.57 (95% CI: 1.22, 2.03). The association between ASD and PM2.5 was stronger for exposure during the third trimester (OR, 1.42 per inter-quartile range increase in PM2.5, 95% CI, 1.09–1.86).

In a recent, population based case–control study in Pennsylvania, Talbott et al. (2015) found that living in areas with higher ambient levels of styrene and chromium during pregnancy and the first and second years of life is associated with increased risk of ASD with borderline effects for polycyclic aromatic hydrocarbons (PAHs) and methylene chloride.

In contrast to these studies mostly carried out in the United States, showing a consistently positive association between exposure to several air pollutants during pregnancy and diagnosis of ASD, a much larger, recently published analysis of four European population-based cohorts appears to contradict those findings, reporting no associations between ASD and prenatal air pollution exposure (Guxens et al., 2016).

This research compared between nitrogen oxides and various sizes of particulate matter concentrations at the participants' birth home addresses during pregnancy and the presence of autistic traits, but not formal diagnoses of ASD, in more than 8000 children. No associations were found between the presence of autistic traits and prenatal exposure to any of the air pollutants (odds ratio = 0.94; 95% CI: 0.81, 1.10 per each 10-μg/m3 increase in NO2 pregnancy levels). The researchers explained the contradictory findings by the fact that previous case–control studies selected children with a diagnosis of ASD, whereas this study examined children with autistic traits from population-based birth/child cohorts. An alternative explanation could be the possible differences in air pollution levels and sources.

It can therefore be concluded that air pollution might be a contributing factor in the risk for ASD, but the data is as yet inconclusive.

In summary: these case control studies suggest that there is a positive association between maternal exposure to air pollution during pregnancy and ASD in children, especially following exposure in the third trimester. Although small PM may cross the placenta, there might also be other factors in the air pollutants that are associated and were not measured.

Exposure to Pesticides

Few studies have examined the effects of *in utero* exposure to pesticides such as organophosphates and carbamates on the neurobehavioral development and the risk of ASD in children. Each study reported an association with ASD.

Roberts et al. (2007) examined the association between maternal residence near agricultural pesticide applications during key periods of gestation and ASD in children. They reported that ASD risk was higher in children whose mothers lived near agricultural applications of organochlorines during the first trimester of pregnancy (OR 6.1) and decreased with increasing distance from such fields.

Shelton et al. (2014) evaluated whether residential proximity to agricultural areas and therefore increased exposures to pesticides during pregnancy is associated with ASD. They found that residence near organophosphates at some point during gestation was associated with a 60% increased risk for ASD, higher for third-trimester exposures (OR, 2.0), and second-trimester chlorpyrifos applications (OR, 3.3). Also, children of mothers residing near pyrethroid insecticide applications just before conception or during the third trimester were at greater risk for ASD with ORs ranging from 1.7 to 2.0. We can summarize that due to the paucity of studies in spite of extensive use, an association between ASD and pesticides is plausible, but it was not yet established.

Exposure to Heavy Metals

Maternal exposure to heavy metals, such as mercury, lead, and cadmium, has been suggested to be associated with neurodevelopmental disorders including mental retardation, inattention, learning difficulties, and possibly ASD (Mendola et al., 2002). Although there is more data on mercury, most available data suggests that maternal exposure to mercury does not play an important role in the development of ASD. Moreover, several of the studies were carried out on the affected children and not on their mothers, hence making the association with pregnancy an unproven possibility (Kern et al., 2007). In that respect we should add that Kern et al. (2007) found that sulfhydryl reactive metals: arsenic, cadmium, and lead were reduced in the hair of 45 children with ASD compared to controls. They suggested that the children with ASD have a problem in secreting these sulfhydryl reactive metals and their accumulation may contribute to the symptoms of ASD.

Geier et al. (2009) examined the association between maternal dental amalgams (containing 50% mercury) and the severity of ASD diagnosis in a group of 100 autistic children. They found that a rise in autism severity correlated with an elevation in the number of dental amalgams in the mother during pregnancy.

However, Yau et al. (2014) investigated the association between ASD and levels of total mercury measured in maternal serum from mid-pregnancy and infant blood shortly after birth in 84 children with ASD and 159 control children. They found no significant associations between ASD and mercury levels in maternal serum samples (OR, 0.96; 95% CI, 0.49–1.90) or in newborn blood samples (OR, 1.18; 95% CI, 0.71–1.95).

Van Wijngaarden et al. (2013) examined prenatal exposure to methyl mercury in 1784 children and young adults, by measuring maternal hair samples collected at or near the time of birth. They found no significant association between ASD and prenatal methyl mercury exposure.

It can therefore be concluded that there in insufficient data to associate prenatal exposure to heavy metals, especially mercury, to a higher occurrence of ASD in the offspring.

Exposure to Cigarette Smoking

Heavy maternal cigarette smoking during pregnancy is associated with an increased rate of spontaneous abortions, preterm delivery, reduced birth weight, immune system difficulties such as asthma and allergies and a relatively high rate of learning disabilities and attention deficit disorders later in life (Castles et al., 1999; Stene-Larsen et al., 2009; Kiechl-Kohlendorfer et al., 2010). Several studies have examined whether prenatal exposure to heavy tobacco smoke is also associated with ASD, and the findings are inconsistent. Hultman et al. (2002) and Larsson et al. (2009) found a mild association between smoking during pregnancy and the risk of childhood autism (OR, 1.4 and 2.09, respectively).

Kalkbrenner et al. (2012) assessed the association between maternal smoking during pregnancy and ASD among 3315 children with ASD and 630,674 control children at 8 years of age. A slightly positive association (OR 1.26) was found only for "ASD not otherwise specified" (ASD-NOS), which disappeared after correcting for possible confounding factors. Similarly Tran et al. (2013) examined 4019 ASD cases and 16, 123 controls, in a nested case-control study based on the Finnish Prenatal Study of Autism (FIPS-A) and found no connection between maternal smoking and childhood autism or Asperger syndrome, but found a slight association with PDD (OR, 1.2, 95% CI, 1.0- 1.5).

Other large studies also did not find any association between tobacco exposure and ASD. In a large registry based Swedish case-control study, that included 3958 ASD cases and 38,983 controls, Lee et al. (2012) found that maternal smoking during pregnancy is not associated with increased risk of ASD after adjustments for parental education, occupation, and income.

Several additional studies (Maimburg and Vaeth, 2006; Burstyn et al., 2010) and two recently published meta-analyses by Rosen et al. (2015) and Tang et al. (2015), also reported no significant association between maternal smoking during pregnancy and ASD.

It can be summarized maternal smoking does not increase the rate of ASD in the offspring.

CONCLUSIONS

The observed increase in the incidence of ASD in the last decades is considered to result directly from changes in definitions and better ascertainment. However, it is also possible that it reflects a real increase in the occurrence of ASD. In addition to well-defined genetic causes for ASD, examples of which we discussed in this review, the current search for prenatal environmental etiologic factors demonstrated real associations with a number of causes that may affect the developing fetal brain raising the vulnerability for ASD. Based on the findings reviewed here, we may conclude—with caution—that: (1) A possible association exists with maternal influenza in pregnancy, exposure to pesticides and insecticides, exposure to misoprostol, thalidomide, cocaine, SSRIs, or folic acid deficiency. (2) A probable association was found for maternal fever, autoimmune diseases, diabetes, preeclampsia, and exposure to heavy air pollution. (3) A definite association of ASD with maternal Rubella and CMV infections in pregnancy, maternal inflammation and immune activation, or exposure in pregnancy to VPA, and high levels of ethanol. (4) Although sometimes suggested, there seems to be sufficient evidence that there is no association with ASD for many maternal infections in pregnancy (i.e., herpes viruses, Epstein Barr virus, varicella—zoster virus, parvovirus), smoking, exposure to heavy metals or vitamin D deficiency.

Despite the increasing efforts in recent years, and support from animal studies, we still seem to be in a stage where the etiology of ASD is largely unknown and the associations described in the literature are, for many agents, inadequately proven. Hence, more research is needed to unravel environmental contribution to the genetic etiology of ASD. This type of research may ultimately lead to the establishment of possibilities for prevention.

AUTHOR CONTRIBUTIONS

Following the request by Dr. Joshua Rosenzweig and Dr. Benjamin Gesundheit, we attach our manuscript entitled Genetic syndromes, maternal diseases and antenatal factors associated with Autism Spectrum Disorders (ASD) by EZ, WL, and OA for consideration for publication in the special topic of the Journal-Autism Spectrum Disorders (ASD)—searching for the biological basis for behavioral symptoms and new therapeutic targets.

REFERENCES

Abdallah, M. W., Larsen, N., Grove, J., Norgaard-Pedersen, B., Thorsen, P., Mortensen, E. L., et al. (2012). Amniotic fluid chemokines and autism spectrum disorders: an exploratory study utilizing a Danish Historic Birth Cohort. *Brain Behav. Immun.* 26, 170–176. doi: 10.1016/j.bbi.2011.09.003

Abdallah, M. W., Larsen, N., Grove, J., Norgaard-Pedersen, B., Thorsen, P., Mortensen, E. L., et al. (2013). Amniotic fluid inflammatory cytokines: potential markers of immunologic dysfunction in autism spectrum disorders. *World J. Biol. Psychiatry* 14, 528–538. doi: 10.3109/15622975.2011.639803

Abisror, N., Mekinian, A., Lachassinne, E., Nicaise-Roland, P., De Pontual, L., Chollet-Martin, S., et al. (2013). Autism spectrum disorders in babies born to mothers with antiphospholipid syndrome. *Semin. Arthritis Rheum.* 43, 348–351. doi: 10.1016/j.semarthrit.2013.07.001

Adams Waldorf, K. M., and McAdams, R. M. (2013). Influence of infection during pregnancy on fetal development. *Reproduction* 146, R151–R162. doi: 10.1530/rep-13-0232

Althaus, M., Groen, Y., Wijers, A. A., Noltes, H., Tucha, O., and Hoekstra, P. J. (2015). Oxytocin enhances orienting to social information in a selective group of high-functioning male adults with autism spectrum disorder. *Neuropsychologia* 79, 53–69. doi: 10.1016/j.neuropsychologia.2015.10.025

Anagnostou, E., Soorya, L., Chaplin, W., Bartz, J., Halpern, D., Wasserman, S., et al. (2012). Intranasal oxytocin versus placebo in the treatment of adults with autism spectrum disorders: a randomized controlled trial. *Mol. Autism* 3:16. doi: 10.1186/2040-2392-3-16

Aoki, Y., Watanabe, T., Abe, O., Kuwabara, H., Yahata, N., Takano, Y., et al. (2015). Oxytocin's neurochemical effects in the medial prefrontal cortex underlie recovery of task-specific brain activity in autism: a randomized controlled trial. *Mol. Psychiatry* 20, 447–453. doi: 10.1038/mp.2014.74

Aronson, M., Hagberg, B., and Gillberg, C. (1997). Attention deficits and autistic spectrum problems in children exposed to alcohol during gestation: a follow-up study. *Dev. Med. Child Neurol.* 39, 583–587. doi: 10.1111/j.1469-8749.1997.tb07493.x

American Psychiatric Association (2013). *Diagnostic and Statistical Manual of Mental Disorders (DSM-5).* Washington, DC: American Psychiatric Association.

Assumpcao, F. B. Jr., and Kuczynski, E. (2002). [Autism, bipolar disorder and mental retardation in a male adolescent with congenital rubella: case report]. *Arq. Neuropsiquiatr.* 60, 324–327.

Atladottir, H. O., Henriksen, T. B., Schendel, D. E., and Parner, E. T. (2012). Autism after infection, febrile episodes, and antibiotic use during pregnancy: an exploratory study. *Pediatrics* 130, e1447–e1454. doi: 10.1542/peds.2012-1107

Atladottir, H. O., Pedersen, M. G., Thorsen, P., Mortensen, P. B., Deleuran, B., Eaton, W. W., et al. (2009). Association of family history of autoimmune diseases and autism spectrum disorders. *Pediatrics* 124, 687–694. doi: 10.1542/peds.2008-2445

Atladottir, H. O., Thorsen, P., Ostergaard, L., Schendel, D. E., Lemcke, S., Abdallah, M., et al. (2010). Maternal infection requiring hospitalization during pregnancy and autism spectrum disorders. *J. Autism Dev. Disord.* 40, 1423–1430. doi: 10.1007/s10803-010-1006-y

Autism Developmental Disabilities Monitoring Network Surveillance Year Principal and Centers for Disease and Prevention (2012). *Prevalence of Autism Spectrum Disorders–Autism and Developmental Disabilities Monitoring Network, 14 Sites, United States, 2008.* MMWR. Surveillance Summaries. 61, 1–19.

Ballantyne, C. J., and Nunez, M. (2016). Developmental trajectories of hierarchical visuo-spatial processing in fragile X syndrome and ASD: within- and cross-syndrome variability. *Res. Dev. Disabil.* 51–52, 103–115. doi: 10.1016/j.ridd.2015.12.016

Bambini-Junior, V., Rodrigues, L., Behr, G. A., Moreira, J. C., Riesgo, R., and Gottfried, C. (2011). Animal model of autism induced by prenatal exposure to valproate: behavioral changes and liver parameters. *Brain Res.* 1408, 8–16. doi: 10.1016/j.brainres.2011.06.015

Bandim, J. M., Ventura, L. O., Miller, M. T., Almeida, H. C., and Costa, A. E. (2003). Autism and Mobius sequence: an exploratory study of children in northeastern Brazil. *Arq. Neuropsiquiatr.* 61, 181–185. doi: 10.1590/S0004-282X2003000200004

Bauer, A. Z., and Kriebel, D. (2013). Prenatal and perinatal analgesic exposure and autism: an ecological link. *Environ. Health* 12:41. doi: 10.1186/1476-0 69X-12-41

Becerra, T. A., Wilhelm, M., Olsen, J., Cockburn, M., and Ritz, B. (2013). Ambient air pollution and autism in Los Angeles county, California. *Environ. Health Perspect.* 121, 380–386. doi: 10.1289/ehp.1205827

Berger, B. E., Navar-Boggan, A. M., and Omer, S. B. (2011). Congenital rubella syndrome and autism spectrum disorder prevented by rubella vaccination–United States, 2001-2010. *BMC Public Health* 11:340. doi: 10.1186/1471-2458-11-340

Billeci, L., Calderoni, S., Tosetti, M., Catani, M., and Muratori, F. (2012). White matter connectivity in children with autism spectrum disorders: a tract-based spatial statistics study. *BMC Neurol.* 12:148. doi: 10.1186/1471-2377-12-148

Bird, L. M., Tan, W. H., Bacino, C. A., Peters, S. U., Skinner, S. A., Anselm, I., et al. (2011). A therapeutic trial of pro-methylation dietary supplements in Angelman syndrome. *Am. J. Med. Genet. A* 155A, 2956–2963. doi: 10.1002/ajmg.a.34297

Boukhris, T., Sheehy, O., Mottron, L., and Berard, A. (2016). Antidepressant use during pregnancy and the risk of autism spectrum disorder in children. *JAMA Pediatr.* 170, 117–124. doi: 10.1001/jamapediatrics.2015.3356

Braunschweig, D., Ashwood, P., Krakowiak, P., Hertz-Picciotto, I., Hansen, R., Croen, L. A., et al. (2008). Autism: maternally derived antibodies specific for fetal brain proteins. *Neurotoxicology* 29, 226–231. doi: 10.1016/j.neuro.2007.10.010

Bromley, R. L., Mawer, G., Clayton-Smith, J., Baker, G. A., Liverpool and Manchester Neurodevelopment Group (2008). Autism spectrum disorders following *in utero* exposure to antiepileptic drugs. *Neurology* 71, 1923–1924. doi: 10.1212/01.wnl.0000339399.64213.1a

Brown, A. S., Sourander, A., Hinkka-Yli-Salomaki, S., McKeague, I. W., Sundvall, J., and Surcel, H. M. (2014). Elevated maternal C-reactive protein and autism in a national birth cohort. *Mol. Psychiatry* 19, 259–264. doi: 10.1038/mp.2012.197

Brown, A. S., Surcel, H. M., Hinkka-Yli-Salomaki, S., Cheslack-Postava, K., Bao, Y., and Sourander, A. (2015). Maternal thyroid autoantibody and elevated risk of autism in a national birth cohort. *Prog. Neuropsychopharmacol. Biol. Psychiatry* 57, 86–92. doi: 10.1016/j.pnpbp.2014.10.010

Bruno, J. L., Hosseini, S. M., Saggar, M., Quintin, E. M., Raman, M. M., and Reiss, A. L. (2016). Altered brain network segregation in fragile x syndrome revealed by structural connectomics. *Cereb. Cortex.* doi: 10.1093/cercor/bhw055. [Epub ahead of print].

Buchmayer, S., Johansson, S., Johansson, A., Hultman, C. M., Sparen, P., and Cnattingius, S. (2009). Can association between preterm birth and autism be explained by maternal or neonatal morbidity? *Pediatrics* 124, e817–e825. doi: 10.1542/peds.2008-3582

Burstyn, I., Sithole, F., and Zwaigenbaum, L. (2010). Autism spectrum disorders, maternal characteristics and obstetric complications among singletons born in Alberta, Canada. *Chronic Dis. Can.* 30, 125–134.

Carvill, S., and Marston, G. (2002). People with intellectual disability, sensory impairments and behaviour disorder: a case series. *J. Intellect. Disabil. Res.* 46, 264–272. doi: 10.1046/j.1365-2788.2002.00400.x

Castles, A., Adams, E. K., Melvin, C. L., Kelsch, C., and Boulton, M. L. (1999). Effects of smoking during pregnancy. Five meta-analyses. *Am. J. Prev. Med.* 16, 208–215. doi: 10.1016/S0749-3797(98)00089-0

Castro, J., Mellios, N., and Sur, M. (2013). Mechanisms and therapeutic challenges in autism spectrum disorders: insights from Rett syndrome. *Curr. Opin. Neurol.* 26, 154–159. doi: 10.1097/WCO.0b013e32835f19a7

Chen, S. W., Zhong, X. S., Jiang, L. N., Zheng, X. Y., Xiong, Y. Q., Ma, S. J., et al. (2016). Maternal autoimmune diseases and the risk of autism spectrum disorders in offspring: a systematic review and meta-analysis. *Behav. Brain Res.* 296, 61–69. doi: 10.1016/j.bbr.2015.08.035

Chess, S., Fernandez, P., and Korn, S. (1978). Behavioral consequences of congenital rubella. *J. Pediatr.* 93, 699–703. doi: 10.1016/S0022-3476(78)80921-4

Christensen, J., Gronborg, T. K., Sorensen, M. J., Schendel, D., Parner, E. T., Pedersen, L. H., et al. (2013). Prenatal valproate exposure and risk of autism spectrum disorders and childhood autism. *JAMA* 309, 1696–1703. doi: 10.1001/jama.2013.2270

Christianson, A. L., Chesler, N., and Kromberg, J. G. (1994). Fetal valproate syndrome: clinical and neuro-developmental features in two sibling pairs. *Dev. Med. Child Neurol.* 36, 361–369. doi: 10.1111/j.1469-8749.1994.tb11858.x

Cianfaglione, R., Clarke, A., Kerr, M., Hastings, R. P., Oliver, C., Moss, J., et al. (2015). A national survey of Rett syndrome: behavioural characteristics. *J. Neurodev. Disord.* 7, 11. doi: 10.1186/s11689-015-9104-y

Conde-Agudelo, A., Rosas-Bermudez, A., and Norton, M. H. (2016). Birth spacing and risk of autism and other neurodevelopmental disabilities: a systematic review. *Pediatrics.* doi: 10.1542/peds.2015-3482. [Epub ahead of print].

Connors, S. L., Crowell, D. E., Eberhart, C. G., Copeland, J., Newschaffer, C. J., Spence, S. J., et al. (2005). beta2-adrenergic receptor activation and genetic polymorphisms in autism: data from dizygotic twins. *J. Child Neurol.* 20, 876–884. doi: 10.1177/08830738050200110401

Cook, E. H. Jr., and Scherer, S. W. (2008). Copy-number variations associated with neuropsychiatric conditions. *Nature* 455, 919–923. doi: 10.1038/nature07458

Croen, L. A., Connors, S. L., Matevia, M., Qian, Y., Newschaffer, C., and Zimmerman, A. W. (2011a). Prenatal exposure to beta2-adrenergic receptor agonists and risk of autism spectrum disorders. *J. Neurodev. Disord.* 3, 307–315. doi: 10.1007/s11689-011-9093-4

Croen, L. A., Grether, J. K., Yoshida, C. K., Odouli, R., and Hendrick, V. (2011b). Antidepressant use during pregnancy and childhood autism spectrum disorders. *Arch. Gen. Psychiatry* 68, 1104–1112. doi: 10.1001/archgenpsychiatry.2011.73

Croen, L. A., Grether, J. K., Yoshida, C. K., Odouli, R., and Van de Water, J. (2005). Maternal autoimmune diseases, asthma and allergies, and childhood autism spectrum disorders: a case-control study. *Arch. Pediatr. Adolesc. Med.* 159, 151–157. doi: 10.1001/archpedi.159.2.151

Darbro, B. W., Singh, R., Zimmerman, M. B., Mahajan, V. B., and Bassuk, A. G. (2016). Autism linked to increased oncogene mutations but decreased cancer rate. *PLoS ONE* 11:e0149041. doi: 10.1371/journal.pone.0149041

Darnell, J. C., Van Driesche, S. J., Zhang, C., Hung, K. Y., Mele, A., Fraser, C. E., et al. (2011). FMRP stalls ribosomal translocation on mRNAs linked to synaptic function and autism. *Cell* 146, 247–261. doi: 10.1016/j.cell.2011.06.013

Davidovitch, M., Hemo, B., Manning-Courtney, P., and Fombonne, E. (2013). Prevalence and incidence of autism spectrum disorder in an Israeli population. *J. Autism Dev. Disord.* 43, 785–793. doi: 10.1007/s10803-012-1611-z

Davis, E., Fennoy, I., Laraque, D., Kanem, N., Brown, G., and Mitchell, J. (1992). Autism and developmental abnormalities in children with perinatal cocaine exposure. *J. Natl. Med. Assoc.* 84, 315–319.

Davis, P. E., Peters, J. M., Krueger, D. A., and Sahin, M. (2015). Tuberous Sclerosis: a new frontier in targeted treatment of autism. *Neurotherapeutics* 12, 572–583. doi: 10.1007/s13311-015-0359-5

Desmond, M. M., Fisher, E. S., Vorderman, A. L., Schaffer, H. G., Andrew, L. P., Zion, T. E., et al. (1978). The longitudinal course of congenital rubella encephalitis in nonretarded children. *J. Pediatr.* 93, 584–591. doi: 10.1016/S0022-3476(78)80892-0

DeVilbiss, E. A., Gardner, R. M., Newschaffer, C. J., and Lee, B. K. (2015). Maternal folate status as a risk factor for autism spectrum disorders: a review of existing evidence. *Br. J. Nutr.* 114, 663–672. doi: 10.1017/S0007114515002470

Dodds, L., Fell, D. B., Shea, S., Armson, B. A., Allen, A. C., and Bryson, S. (2011). The role of prenatal, obstetric and neonatal factors in the development of autism. *J. Autism Dev. Disord.* 41, 891–902. doi: 10.1007/s10803-010-1114-8

Dogan, Y., Yuksel, A., Kalelioglu, I. H., Has, R., Tatli, B., and Yildirim, A. (2011). Intracranial ultrasound abnormalities and fetal cytomegalovirus infection: report of 8 cases and review of the literature. *Fetal Diagn. Ther.* 30, 141–149. doi: 10.1159/000330636

Eliasen, M., Tolstrup, J. S., Nybo Andersen, A. M., Gronbaek, M., Olsen, J., and Strandberg-Larsen, K. (2010). Prenatal alcohol exposure and autistic spectrum disorders–a population-based prospective study of 80,552 children and their mothers. *Int. J. Epidemiol.* 39, 1074–1081. doi: 10.1093/ije/dyq056

Elsabbagh, M., Divan, G., Koh, Y. J., Kim, Y. S., Kauchali, S., Marcin, C., et al. (2012). Global prevalence of autism and other pervasive developmental disorders. *Autism Res.* 5, 160–179. doi: 10.1002/aur.239

Engman, M. L., Lewensohn-Fuchs, I., Mosskin, M., and Malm, G. (2010). Congenital cytomegalovirus infection: the impact of cerebral cortical malformations. *Acta Paediatr.* 99, 1344–1349. doi: 10.1111/j.1651-2227.2010.01852.x

Evans, J., Heron, J., Francomb, H., Oke, S., and Golding, J. (2001). Cohort study of depressed mood during pregnancy and after childbirth. *BMJ* 323, 257–260. doi: 10.1136/bmj.323.7307.257

Feldman, R. B., Pinsky, L., Mendelson, J., and Lajoie, R. (1973). Can language disorder not due to peripheral deafness be an isolated expression of prenatal rubella? *Pediatrics* 52, 296–299.

Fombonne, E. (2009). Epidemiology of pervasive developmental disorders. *Pediatr. Res.* 65, 591–598. doi: 10.1203/PDR.0b013e31819e7203

Fox, C. H. (1994). Cocaine use in pregnancy. *J. Am. Board Fam. Pract.* 7, 225–228.

Fox, E., Amaral, D., and Van de Water, J. (2012). Maternal and fetal antibrain antibodies in development and disease. *Dev. Neurobiol.* 72, 1327–1334. doi: 10.1002/dneu.22052

Francis, S. M., Kistner-Griffin, E., Yan, Z., Guter, S., Cook, E. H., and Jacob, S. (2016). Variants in adjacent oxytocin/vasopressin gene region and associations with ASD diagnosis and other autism related endophenotypes. *Front. Neurosci.* 10:195. doi: 10.3389/fnins.2016.00195

Gao, Y., Xue, X., Hu, D., Liu, W., Yuan, Y., Sun, H., et al. (2013). Inhibition of late sodium current by mexiletine: a novel pharmotherapeutical approach in timothy syndrome. *Circ. Arrhythm. Electrophysiol.* 6, 614–622. doi: 10.1161/CIRCEP.113.000092

Gardener, H., Spiegelman, D., and Buka, S. L. (2009). Prenatal risk factors for autism: comprehensive meta-analysis. *Br. J. Psychiatry* 195, 7–14. doi: 10.1192/bjp.bp.108.051672

Gardener, H., Spiegelman, D., and Buka, S. L. (2011). Perinatal and neonatal risk factors for autism: a comprehensive meta-analysis. *Pediatrics* 128, 344–355. doi: 10.1542/peds.2010-1036

Geier, D. A., Kern, J. K., and Geier, M. R. (2009). A prospective study of prenatal mercury exposure from maternal dental amalgams and autism severity. *Acta Neurobiol. Exp. (Wars).* 69, 189–197.

Gentile, I., Zappulo, E., Bonavolta, R., Maresca, R., Messana, T., Buonomo, A. R., et al. (2014). Prevalence and titre of antibodies to cytomegalovirus and epstein-barr virus in patients with autism spectrum disorder. *In Vivo* 28, 621–626.

Gidaya, N. B., Lee, B. K., Burstyn, I., Michael, Y., Newschaffer, C. J., and Mortensen, E. L. (2016). *In utero* exposure to beta-2-adrenergic receptor agonist drugs and risk for autism spectrum disorders. *Pediatrics* 137, 1–8. doi: 10.1542/peds.2015-1316

Gidaya, N. B., Lee, B. K., Burstyn, I., Yudell, M., Mortensen, E. L., and Newschaffer, C. J. (2014). *In utero* exposure to selective serotonin reuptake inhibitors and risk for autism spectrum disorder. *J. Autism Dev. Disord.* 44, 2558–2567. doi: 10.1007/s10803-014-2128-4

Gillis, J., Burashnikov, E., Antzelevitch, C., Blaser, S., Gross, G., Turner, L., et al. (2012). Long QT, syndactyly, joint contractures, stroke and novel CACNA1C mutation: expanding the spectrum of Timothy syndrome. *Am. J. Med. Genet. A* 158A, 182–187. doi: 10.1002/ajmg.a.34355

Goines, P. E., Croen, L. A., Braunschweig, D., Yoshida, C. K., Grether, J., Hansen, R., et al. (2011). Increased midgestational IFN-gamma, IL-4 and IL-5 in women bearing a child with autism: a case-control study. *Mol. Autism* 2:13. doi: 10.1186/2040-2392-2-13

Gonzalez, C. H., Marques-Dias, M. J., Kim, C. A., Sugayama, S. M., Da Paz, J. A., Huson, S. M., et al. (1998). Congenital abnormalities in Brazilian children associated with misoprostol misuse in first trimester of pregnancy. *Lancet* 351, 1624–1627. doi: 10.1016/S0140-6736(97)12363-7

Gonzalez, C. H., Vargas, F. R., Perez, A. B., Kim, C. A., Brunoni, D., Marques-Dias, M. J., et al. (1993). Limb deficiency with or without Mobius sequence in seven Brazilian children associated with misoprostol use in the first trimester of pregnancy. *Am. J. Med. Genet.* 47, 59–64. doi: 10.1002/ajmg.1320470113

Grabrucker, A. M. (2012). Environmental factors in autism. *Front. Psychiatry* 3:118. doi: 10.3389/fpsyt.2012.00118

Green, A. J., Johnson, P. H., and Yates, J. R. (1994). The tuberous sclerosis gene on chromosome 9q34 acts as a growth suppressor. *Hum. Mol. Genet.* 3, 1833–1834. doi: 10.1093/hmg/3.10.1833

Grether, J. K., Croen, L. A., Anderson, M. C., Nelson, K. B., and Yolken, R. H. (2010). Neonatally measured immunoglobulins and risk of autism. *Autism Res.* 3, 323–332. doi: 10.1002/aur.160

Guinchat, V., Thorsen, P., Laurent, C., Cans, C., Bodeau, N., and Cohen, D. (2012). Pre-, peri- and neonatal risk factors for autism. *Acta Obstet. Gynecol. Scand.* 91, 287–300. doi: 10.1111/j.1600-0412.2011.01325.x

Guxens, M., Ghassabian, A., Gong, T., Garcia-Esteban, R., Porta, D., Giorgis-Allemand, L., et al. (2016). Air pollution exposure during pregnancy and childhood autistic traits in four european population-based cohort studies: the ESCAPE project. *Environ. Health Perspect.* 124, 133–140. doi: 10.1289/ehp.1408483

Harrington, R. A., Lee, L. C., Crum, R. M., Zimmerman, A. W., and Hertz-Picciotto, I. (2014). Prenatal SSRI use and offspring with autism spectrum disorder or developmental delay. *Pediatrics* 133, e1241–e1248. doi: 10.1542/peds.2013-3406

Harris, S. R., MacKay, L. L., and Osborn, J. A. (1995). Autistic behaviors in offspring of mothers abusing alcohol and other drugs: a series of case reports. *Alcohol. Clin. Exp. Res.* 19, 660–665. doi: 10.1111/j.1530-0277.1995.tb01564.x

Hollander, E., Bartz, J., Chaplin, W., Phillips, A., Sumner, J., Soorya, L., et al. (2007). Oxytocin increases retention of social cognition in autism. *Biol. Psychiatry* 61, 498–503. doi: 10.1016/j.biopsych.2006.05.030

Hollander, E., Novotny, S., Hanratty, M., Yaffe, R., Decaria, C. M., Aronowitz, B. R., et al. (2003). Oxytocin infusion reduces repetitive behaviors in adults with autistic and Asperger's disorders. *Neuropsychopharmacology* 28, 193–198. doi: 10.1038/sj.npp.1300021

Huijbregts, S. C., Loitfelder, M., Rombouts, S. A., Swaab, H., Verbist, B. M., Arkink, E. B., et al. (2015). Cerebral volumetric abnormalities in Neurofibromatosis type 1: associations with parent ratings of social and attention problems, executive dysfunction, and autistic mannerisms. *J. Neurodev. Disord.* 7, 32. doi: 10.1186/s11689-015-9128-3

Hultman, C. M., Sparen, P., and Cnattingius, S. (2002). Perinatal risk factors for infantile autism. *Epidemiology* 13, 417–423. doi: 10.1097/00001648-200207000-00009

Hviid, A., Melbye, M., and Pasternak, B. (2013). Use of selective serotonin reuptake inhibitors during pregnancy and risk of autism. *N. Engl. J. Med.* 369, 2406–2415. doi: 10.1056/NEJMoa1301449

Hwang, S. J., and Chen, Y. S. (2010). Congenital rubella syndrome with autistic disorder. *J. Chin. Med. Assoc.* 73, 104–107. doi: 10.1016/S1726-4901(10)70011-3

Ikeda, S., Tsuru, A., Moriuchi, M., and Moriuchi, H. (2006). Retrospective diagnosis of congenital cytomegalovirus infection using umbilical cord. *Pediatr. Neurol.* 34, 415–416. doi: 10.1016/j.pediatrneurol.2005.10.006

Ingram, J. L., Peckham, S. M., Tisdale, B., and Rodier, P. M. (2000). Prenatal exposure of rats to valproic acid reproduces the cerebellar anomalies associated with autism. *Neurotoxicol. Teratol.* 22, 319–324. doi: 10.1016/S0892-0362(99)00083-5

Ito, T., Ando, H., Suzuki, T., Ogura, T., Hotta, K., Imamura, Y., et al. (2010). Identification of a primary target of thalidomide teratogenicity. *Science* 327, 1345–1350. doi: 10.1126/science.1177319

Ivarsson, S. A., Bjerre, I., Vegfors, P., and Ahlfors, K. (1990). Autism as one of several disabilities in two children with congenital cytomegalovirus infection. *Neuropediatrics* 21, 102–103. doi: 10.1055/s-2008-1071471

Johansson, M., Wentz, E., Fernell, E., Stromland, K., Miller, M. T., and Gillberg, C. (2001). Autistic spectrum disorders in Mobius sequence: a comprehensive study of 25 individuals. *Dev. Med. Child Neurol.* 43, 338–345. doi: 10.1017/S0012162201000627

Kagerbauer, S. M., Martin, J., Schuster, T., Blobner, M., Kochs, E. F., and Landgraf, R. (2013). Plasma oxytocin and vasopressin do not predict neuropeptide concentrations in human cerebrospinal fluid. *J. Neuroendocrinol.* 25, 668–673. doi: 10.1111/jne.12038

Kaiser-McCaw, B., Hecht, F., Cadien, J. D., and Moore, B. C. (1980). Fragile X-linked mental retardation. *Am. J. Med. Genet.* 7, 503–505. doi: 10.1002/ajmg.1320070411

Kalkbrenner, A. E., Braun, J. M., Durkin, M. S., Maenner, M. J., Cunniff, C., Lee, L. C., et al. (2012). Maternal smoking during pregnancy and the prevalence of autism spectrum disorders, using data from the autism and developmental disabilities monitoring network. *Environ. Health Perspect.* 120, 1042–1048. doi: 10.1289/ehp.1104556

Kalkbrenner, A. E., Daniels, J. L., Chen, J. C., Poole, C., Emch, M., and Morrissey, J. (2010). Perinatal exposure to hazardous air pollutants and autism spectrum disorders at age 8. *Epidemiology* 21, 631–641. doi: 10.1097/EDE.0b013e3181e65d76

Karaaslan, C., and Suzen, S. (2015). Antioxidant properties of melatonin and its potential action in diseases. *Curr. Top. Med. Chem.* 15, 894–903. doi: 10.2174/1568026615666150220120946

Kawatani, M., Nakai, A., Okuno, T., Kobata, R., Moriuchi, M., Moriuchi, H., et al. (2010). Detection of cytomegalovirus in preserved umbilical cord from a boy with autistic disorder. *Pediatr. Int.* 52, 304–307. doi: 10.1111/j.1442-200X.2010.03027.x

Keil, A., Daniels, J. L., Forssen, U., Hultman, C., Cnattingius, S., Soderberg, K. C., et al. (2010). Parental autoimmune diseases associated with autism spectrum disorders in offspring. *Epidemiology* 21, 805–808. doi: 10.1097/EDE.0b013e3181f26e3f

Kern, J. K., Grannemann, B. D., Trivedi, M. H., and Adams, J. B. (2007). Sulfhydryl-reactive metals in autism. *J. Toxicol. Environ. Health Part A* 70, 715–721. doi: 10.1080/15287390601188060

Kiechl-Kohlendorfer, U., Ralser, E., Pupp Peglow, U., Reiter, G., Griesmaier, E., and Trawoger, R. (2010). Smoking in pregnancy: a risk factor for adverse neurodevelopmental outcome in preterm infants? *Acta Paediatr.* 99, 1016–1019. doi: 10.1111/j.1651-2227.2010.01749.x

Kirsch, P. (2015). Oxytocin in the socioemotional brain: implications for psychiatric disorders. *Dialogues Clin. Neurosci.* 17, 463–476.

Kitajima, J., Inoue, H., Ohga, S., Kinjo, T., Ochiai, M., Yoshida, T., et al. (2012). Differential transmission and postnatal outcomes in triplets with intrauterine cytomegalovirus infection. *Pediatr. Dev. Pathol.* 15, 151–155. doi: 10.2350/11-05-1034-CR.1

Kogan, M. D., Blumberg, S. J., Schieve, L. A., Boyle, C. A., Perrin, J. M., Ghandour, R. M., et al. (2009). Prevalence of parent-reported diagnosis of autism spectrum disorder among children in the US, 2007. *Pediatrics* 124, 1395–1403. doi: 10.1542/peds.2009-1522

Koks, N., Ghassabian, A., Greaves-Lord, K., Hofman, A., Jaddoe, V. W., Verhulst, F. C., et al. (2016). Maternal C-reactive protein concentration in early pregnancy and child autistic traits in the general population. *Paediatr. Perinat. Epidemiol.* 30, 181–189. doi: 10.1111/ppe.12261

Kolozsi, E., MacKenzie, R. N., Roullet, F. I., Decatanzaro, D., and Foster, J. A. (2009). Prenatal exposure to valproic acid leads to reduced expression of synaptic adhesion molecule neuroligin 3 in mice. *Neuroscience* 163, 1201–1210. doi: 10.1016/j.neuroscience.2009.07.021

Koyano, S., Araki, A., Hirano, Y., Fujieda, K., Suzutani, T., Yagyu, K., et al. (2004). Retrospective diagnosis of congenital cytomegalovirus infection using dried umbilical cords. *Pediatr. Infect. Dis. J.* 23, 481–482. doi: 10.1097/00006454-200405000-00028

Krakowiak, P., Walker, C. K., Bremer, A. A., Baker, A. S., Ozonoff, S., Hansen, R. L., et al. (2012). Maternal metabolic conditions and risk for autism and other neurodevelopmental disorders. *Pediatrics* 129, e1121–e1128. doi: 10.1542/peds.2011-2583

Kranz, T. M., Kopp, M., Waltes, R., Sachse, M., Duketis, E., Jarczok, T. A., et al. (2016). Meta-analysis and association of two common polymorphisms of the human oxytocin receptor gene in autism spectrum disorder. *Autism Res.* doi: 10.1002/aur.1597. [Epub ahead of print].

Kwon, K. J., Lee, E. J., Kim, M. K., Jeon, S. J., Choi, Y. Y., Shin, C. Y., et al. (2015). The potential role of melatonin on sleep deprivation-induced cognitive impairments: implication of FMRP on cognitive function. *Neuroscience* 301, 403–414. doi: 10.1016/j.neuroscience.2015.05.079

Landgren, M., Svensson, L., Stromland, K., and Andersson Gronlund, M. (2010). Prenatal alcohol exposure and neurodevelopmental disorders in children adopted from eastern Europe. *Pediatrics* 125, e1178–e1185. doi: 10.1542/peds.2009-0712

Langridge, A. T., Glasson, E. J., Nassar, N., Jacoby, P., Pennell, C., Hagan, R., et al. (2013). Maternal conditions and perinatal characteristics associated with autism spectrum disorder and intellectual disability. *PLoS ONE* 8:e50963. doi: 10.1371/journal.pone.0050963

Larsson, M., Weiss, B., Janson, S., Sundell, J., and Bornehag, C. G. (2009). Associations between indoor environmental factors and parental-reported autistic spectrum disorders in children 6-8 years of age. *Neurotoxicology* 30, 822–831. doi: 10.1016/j.neuro.2009.01.011

Lasalle, J. M., Reiter, L. T., and Chamberlain, S. J. (2015). Epigenetic regulation of UBE3A and roles in human neurodevelopmental disorders. *Epigenomics* 7, 1213–1228. doi: 10.2217/epi.15.70

Leblanc, J. J., Degregorio, G., Centofante, E., Vogel-Farley, V. K., Barnes, K., Kaufmann, W. E., et al. (2015). Visual evoked potentials detect cortical processing deficits in Rett syndrome. *Ann. Neurol.* 78, 775–786. doi: 10.1002/ana.24513

Leblond, C. S., Nava, C., Polge, A., Gauthier, J., Huguet, G., Lumbroso, S., et al. (2014). Meta-analysis of SHANK Mutations in Autism Spectrum Disorders: a gradient of severity in cognitive impairments. *PLoS Genet.* 10:e1004580. doi: 10.1371/journal.pgen.1004580

Lee, B. K., Gardner, R. M., Dal, H., Svensson, A., Galanti, M. R., Rai, D., et al. (2012). Brief report: maternal smoking during pregnancy and autism spectrum disorders. *J. Autism Dev. Disord.* 42, 2000–2005. doi: 10.1007/s10803-011-1425-4

Lee, B. K., Magnusson, C., Gardner, R. M., Blomstrom, A., Newschaffer, C. J., Burstyn, I., et al. (2015). Maternal hospitalization with infection during pregnancy and risk of autism spectrum disorders. *Brain Behav. Immun.* 44, 100–105. doi: 10.1016/j.bbi.2014.09.001

Leslie, N. R., and Longy, M. (2016). Inherited PTEN mutations and the prediction of phenotype. *Semin. Cell Dev. Biol.* 52, 30–38. doi: 10.1016/j.semcdb.2016.01.030

Li, M., Fallin, M. D., Riley, A., Landa, R., Walker, S. O., Silverstein, M., et al. (2016). The association of maternal obesity and diabetes with autism and other developmental disabilities. *Pediatrics* 137:e20152206. doi: 10.1542/peds.2015-2206

Li, J., Zhao, L., You, Y., Lu, T., Jia, M., Yu, H., et al. (2015). Schizophrenia related variants in CACNA1C also confer risk of autism. *PLoS ONE* 10:e0133247. doi: 10.1371/journal.pone.0133247

Liew, Z., Ritz, B., Virk, J., and Olsen, J. (2015). Maternal use of acetaminophen during pregnancy and risk of autism spectrum disorders in childhood: a Danish national birth cohort study. *Autism Res.* doi: 10.1002/aur.1591. [Epub ahead of print].

Loparo, D., and Waldman, I. D. (2015). The oxytocin receptor gene (OXTR) is associated with autism spectrum disorder: a meta-analysis. *Mol. Psychiatry* 20, 640–646. doi: 10.1038/mp.2014.77

Lopez-Pison, J., Rubio-Rubio, R., Urena-Hornos, T., Omenaca-Teres, M., Sans, A., Cabrerizo de Diago, R., et al. (2005). [Retrospective diagnosis of congenital infection by cytomegalovirus in the case of one infant]. *Rev. Neurol.* 40, 733–736.

Love, E. R., Crum, J., and Bhattacharya, S. (2012). Independent effects of pregnancy induced hypertension on childhood development: a retrospective cohort study. *Eur. J. Obstet. Gynecol. Reprod. Biol.* 165, 219–224. doi: 10.1016/j.ejogrb.2012.08.015

Lyall, K., Pauls, D. L., Spiegelman, D., Ascherio, A., and Santangelo, S. L. (2012). Pregnancy complications and obstetric suboptimality in association with autism spectrum disorders in children of the Nurses' Health Study II. *Autism Res.* 5, 21–30. doi: 10.1002/aur.228

Maimburg, R. D., and Vaeth, M. (2006). Perinatal risk factors and infantile autism. *Acta Psychiatr. Scand.* 114, 257–264. doi: 10.1111/j.1600-0447.2006.00805.x

Malm, H., Brown, A. S., Gissler, M., Gyllenberg, D., Hinkka-Yli-Salomäki, S., et al. (2016). Gestational exposure to selective serotonin reuptake inhibitors and offspring psychiatric disorders: a national register-based study. *J. Am. Acad. Child Adolesc. Psychiatry.* 55, 359–366. doi: 10.1016/j.jaac.2016.02.013

Mann, J. R., McDermott, S., Bao, H., Hardin, J., and Gregg, A. (2010). Pre-eclampsia, birth weight, and autism spectrum disorders. *J. Autism Dev. Disord.* 40, 548–554. doi: 10.1007/s10803-009-0903-4

Marques-Dias, M. J., Gonzalez, C. H., and Rosemberg, S. (2003). Mobius sequence in children exposed *in utero* to misoprostol: neuropathological study of three cases. *Birth Defects Res. Part A Clin. Mol. Teratol.* 67, 1002–1007. doi: 10.1002/bdra.10144

Mazina, V., Gerdts, J., Trinh, S., Ankenman, K., Ward, T., Dennis, M. Y., et al. (2015). Epigenetics of autism-related impairment: copy number variation and maternal infection. *J. Dev. Behav. Pediatr.* 36, 61–67. doi: 10.1097/DBP.0000000000000126

McBride, K. L., Varga, E. A., Pastore, M. T., Prior, T. W., Manickam, K., Atkin, J. F., et al. (2010). Confirmation study of PTEN mutations among individuals with autism or developmental delays/mental retardation and macrocephaly. *Autism Res.* 3, 137–141. doi: 10.1002/aur.132

McDuffie, A., Thurman, A. J., Hagerman, R. J., and Abbeduto, L. (2015). Symptoms of autism in males with fragile X Syndrome: a comparison to nonsyndromic ASD using current ADI-R scores. *J. Autism Dev. Disord.* 45, 1925–1937. doi: 10.1007/s10803-013-2013-6

Meador, K. J., Baker, G., Cohen, M. J., Gaily, E., and Westerveld, M. (2007). Cognitive/behavioral teratogenetic effects of antiepileptic drugs. *Epilepsy Behav.* 11, 292–302. doi: 10.1016/j.yebeh.2007.08.009

Meador, K. J., Baker, G. A., Browning, N., Clayton-Smith, J., Combs-Cantrell, D. T., Cohen, M., et al. (2009). Cognitive function at 3 years of age after fetal exposure to antiepileptic drugs. *N. Engl. J. Med.* 360, 1597–1605. doi: 10.1056/NEJMoa0803531

Mekinian, A., Lachassinne, E., Nicaise-Roland, P., Carbillon, L., Motta, M., Vicaut, E., et al. (2013). European registry of babies born to mothers with antiphospholipid syndrome. *Ann. Rheum. Dis.* 72, 217–222. doi: 10.1136/annrheumdis-2011-201167

Meloni, I., Bruttini, M., Longo, I., Mari, F., Rizzolio, F., D'adamo, P., et al. (2000). A mutation in the rett syndrome gene, MECP2, causes X-linked mental retardation and progressive spasticity in males. *Am. J. Hum. Genet.* 67, 982–985. doi: 10.1086/303078

Mendola, P., Selevan, S. G., Gutter, S., and Rice, D. (2002). Environmental factors associated with a spectrum of neurodevelopmental deficits. *Ment. Retard. Dev. Disabil. Res. Rev.* 8, 188–197. doi: 10.1002/mrdd.10033

Mieses, A. M., Tavassoli, T., Li, E., Soorya, L., Lurie, S., Wang, A. T., et al. (2016). Brief report: sensory reactivity in children with Phelan-McDermid syndrome. *J. Autism Dev. Disord.* 46, 2508–2513. doi: 10.1007/s10803-016-2754-0

Miller, M., Bales, K. L., Taylor, S. L., Yoon, J., Hostetler, C. M., Carter, C. S., et al. (2013). Oxytocin and vasopressin in children and adolescents with autism spectrum disorders: sex differences and associations with symptoms. *Autism Res.* 6, 91–102. doi: 10.1002/aur.1270

Modahl, C., Green, L., Fein, D., Morris, M., Waterhouse, L., Feinstein, C., et al. (1998). Plasma oxytocin levels in autistic children. *Biol. Psychiatry* 43, 270–277. doi: 10.1016/S0006-3223(97)00439-3

Moore, S. J., Turnpenny, P., Quinn, A., Glover, S., Lloyd, D. J., Montgomery, T., et al. (2000). A clinical study of 57 children with fetal anticonvulsant syndromes. *J. Med. Genet.* 37, 489–497. doi: 10.1136/jmg.37.7.489

Moss, J., and Howlin, P. (2009). Autism spectrum disorders in genetic syndromes: implications for diagnosis, intervention and understanding the wider autism spectrum disorder population. *J. Intellect. Disabil. Res.* 53, 852–873. doi: 10.1111/j.1365-2788.2009.01197.x

Nahum Sacks, K., Friger, M., Shoham-Vardi, I., Abokaf, H., Speigel, E., Sergienko, R., et al. (2016). Prenatal exposure to gestational diabetes mellitus as an independent risk factor for long- term neuropsychiatric morbidity of the offspring. *Am. J. Obstet. Gynecol.* doi: 10.1016/j.ajog.2016.03.030. [Epub ahead of print].

Nanson, J. L. (1992). Autism in fetal alcohol syndrome: a report of six cases. *Alcohol. Clin. Exp. Res.* 16, 558–565. doi: 10.1111/j.1530-0277.1992.tb01417.x

Newman, I., Leader, G., Chen, J. L., and Mannion, A. (2015). An analysis of challenging behavior, comorbid psychopathology, and attention-deficit/hyperactivity disorder in fragile X syndrome. *Res. Dev. Disabil.* 38, 7–17. doi: 10.1016/j.ridd.2014.11.003

Ogata, H., Ihara, H., Murakami, N., Gito, M., Kido, Y., and Nagai, T. (2014). Autism spectrum disorders and hyperactive/impulsive behaviors in Japanese patients with Prader-Willi syndrome: a comparison between maternal uniparental disomy and deletion cases. *Am. J. Med. Genet. A* 164A, 2180–2186. doi: 10.1002/ajmg.a.36615

Ornoy, A. (2009). Valproic acid in pregnancy: how much are we endangering the embryo and fetus? *Reprod. Toxicol.* 28, 1–10. doi: 10.1016/j.reprotox.2009.02.014

Ornoy, A., Ratzon, N., Greenbaum, C., Wolf, A., and Dulitzky, M. (2001). School-age children born to diabetic mothers and to mothers with gestational diabetes exhibit a high rate of inattention and fine and gross motor impairment. *J. Pediatr. Endocrinol. Metab.* 14(Suppl. 1), 681–689. doi: 10.1515/jpem.2001.14.s1.681

Ornoy, A., Reece, E. A., Pavlinkova, G., Kappen, C., and Miller, R. K. (2015a). Effect of maternal diabetes on the embryo, fetus, and children: congenital anomalies, genetic and epigenetic changes and developmental outcomes. *Birth Defects Res. C Embryo Today* 105, 53–72. doi: 10.1002/bdrc.21090

Ornoy, A., Weinstein-Fudim, L., and Ergaz, Z. (2015b). Prenatal factors associated with autism spectrum disorder (ASD). *Reprod. Toxicol.* 56, 155–169. doi: 10.1016/j.reprotox.2015.05.007

Pereira, P. K., Lovisi, G. M., Pilowsky, D. L., Lima, L. A., and Legay, L. F. (2009). Depression during pregnancy: prevalence and risk factors among women attending a public health clinic in Rio de Janeiro, Brazil. *Cad. Saude Publica* 25, 2725–2736. doi: 10.1590/S0102-311X2009001200019

Peters, S. U., Bird, L. M., Kimonis, V., Glaze, D. G., Shinawi, L. M., Bichell, T. J., et al. (2010). Double-blind therapeutic trial in Angelman syndrome using betaine and folic acid. *Am. J. Med. Genet. A* 152A, 1994–2001. doi: 10.1002/ajmg.a.33509

Pini, G., Congiu, L., Benincasa, A., Dimarco, P., Bigoni, S., Dyer, A. H., et al. (2016). Illness severity, social and cognitive ability, and eeg analysis of ten patients with rett syndrome treated with mecasermin (recombinant human IGF-1). *Autism Res. Treat.* 2016:5073078. doi: 10.1155/2016/5073078

Plummer, J. T., Evgrafov, O. V., Bergman, M. Y., Friez, M., Haiman, C. A., Levitt, P., et al. (2013). Transcriptional regulation of the MET receptor tyrosine kinase gene by MeCP2 and sex-specific expression in autism and Rett syndrome. *Transl. Psychiatry* 3, e316. doi: 10.1038/tp.2013.91

Poot, M. (2015). Connecting the CNTNAP2 networks with neurodevelopmental disorders. *Mol. Syndromol.* 6, 7–22. doi: 10.1159/000371594

Rai, D., Lee, B. K., Dalman, C., Golding, J., Lewis, G., and Magnusson, C. (2013). Parental depression, maternal antidepressant use during pregnancy, and risk of autism spectrum disorders: population based case-control study. *BMJ* 346:f2059. doi: 10.1136/bmj.f2059

Rasalam, A. D., Hailey, H., Williams, J. H., Moore, S. J., Turnpenny, P. D., Lloyd, D. J., et al. (2005). Characteristics of fetal anticonvulsant syndrome associated autistic disorder. *Dev. Med. Child Neurol.* 47, 551–555. doi: 10.1017/S0012162205001076

Ratsep, M. T., Paolozza, A., Hickman, A. F., Maser, B., Kay, V. R., Mohammad, S., et al. (2016). Brain structural and vascular anatomy is altered in offspring of pre-eclamptic pregnancies: a pilot study. *AJNR Am. J. Neuroradiol.* 37, 939–945. doi: 10.3174/ajnr.A4640

Raz, R., Roberts, A. L., Lyall, K., Hart, J. E., Just, A. C., Laden, F., et al. (2015a). Autism spectrum disorder and particulate matter air pollution before, during, and after pregnancy: a nested case-control analysis within the nurses' health study ii cohort. *Environ. Health Perspect.* 123, 264–270. doi: 10.1289/ehp.1408133

Raz, R., Weisskopf, M. G., Davidovitch, M., Pinto, O., and Levine, H. (2015b). Differences in autism spectrum disorders incidence by sub-populations in israel 1992-2009: a total population study. *J. Autism Dev. Disord.* doi: 10.1007/s10803-014-2262-z

Richards, C., Jones, C., Groves, L., Moss, J., and Oliver, C. (2015). Prevalence of autism spectrum disorder phenomenology in genetic disorders: a systematic review and meta-analysis. *Lancet Psychiatry* 2, 909–916. doi: 10.1016/S2215-0366(15)00376-4

Roberts, A. L., Lyall, K., Hart, J. E., Laden, F., Just, A. C., Bobb, J. F., et al. (2013). Perinatal air pollutant exposures and autism spectrum disorder in the children of Nurses' Health Study II participants. *Environ. Health Perspect.* 121, 978–984. doi: 10.1289/ehp.1206187

Roberts, E. M., English, P. B., Grether, J. K., Windham, G. C., Somberg, L., and Wolff, C. (2007). Maternal residence near agricultural pesticide applications and autism spectrum disorders among children in the California Central Valley. *Environ. Health Perspect.* 115, 1482–1489. doi: 10.1289/ehp.10168

Rodier, P. M., Ingram, J. L., Tisdale, B., and Croog, V. J. (1997). Linking etiologies in humans and animal models: studies of autism. *Reprod. Toxicol.* 11, 417–422. doi: 10.1016/S0890-6238(97)80001-U

Roe, D. A., Little, B. B., Bawdon, R. E., and Gilstrap, L. C. III. (1990). Metabolism of cocaine by human placentas: implications for fetal exposure. *Am. J. Obstet. Gynecol.* 163, 715–718. doi: 10.1016/0002-9378(90)91054-G

Rosen, B. N., Lee, B. K., Lee, N. L., Yang, Y., and Burstyn, I. (2015). Maternal smoking and autism spectrum disorder: a meta-analysis. *J. Autism Dev. Disord.* 45, 1689–1698. doi: 10.1007/s10803-014-2327-z

Rossignol, D. A., and Frye, R. E. (2012). A review of research trends in physiological abnormalities in autism spectrum disorders: immune dysregulation, inflammation, oxidative stress, mitochondrial dysfunction and environmental toxicant exposures. *Mol. Psychiatry* 17, 389–401. doi: 10.1038/mp.2011.165

Sakamoto, A., Moriuchi, H., Matsuzaki, J., Motoyama, K., and Moriuchi, M. (2015). Retrospective diagnosis of congenital cytomegalovirus infection in children with autism spectrum disorder but no other major neurologic deficit. *Brain Dev.* 37, 200–205. doi: 10.1016/j.braindev.2014.03.016

Schmidt, R. J., Tancredi, D. J., Ozonoff, S., Hansen, R. L., Hartiala, J., Allayee, H., et al. (2012). Maternal periconceptional folic acid intake and risk of autism spectrum disorders and developmental delay in the CHARGE (CHildhood autism risks from genetics and environment) case-control study. *Am. J. Clin. Nutr.* 96, 80–89. doi: 10.3945/ajcn.110.004416

Schneider, T., and Przewlocki, R. (2005). Behavioral alterations in rats prenatally exposed to valproic acid: animal model of autism. *Neuropsychopharmacology* 30, 80–89. doi: 10.1038/sj.npp.1300518

Schwartzman, J. S., Velloso Rde, L., D'antino, M. E., and Santos, S. (2015). The eye-tracking of social stimuli in patients with Rett syndrome and autism spectrum disorders: a pilot study. *Arq. Neuropsiquiatr.* 73, 402–407. doi: 10.1590/0004-282X20150033

Scott-Van Zeeland, A. A., Abrahams, B. S., Alvarez-Retuerto, A. I., Sonnenblick, L. I., Rudie, J. D., Ghahremani, D., et al. (2010). Altered functional connectivity in frontal lobe circuits is associated with variation in the autism risk gene CNTNAP2. *Sci. Transl. Med.* 2, 56ra80. doi: 10.1126/scitranslmed.3001344

Shattuck, P. T. (2006). Diagnostic substitution and changing autism prevalence. *Pediatrics* 117, 1438–1439. doi: 10.1542/peds.2005-2911

Shelton, J. F., Geraghty, E. M., Tancredi, D. J., Delwiche, L. D., Schmidt, R. J., Ritz, B., et al. (2014). Neurodevelopmental disorders and prenatal residential proximity to agricultural pesticides: the CHARGE study. *Environ. Health Perspect.* 122, 1103–1109. doi: 10.1289/ehp.1307044

Singer, L., Arendt, R., and Minnes, S. (1993). Neurodevelopmental effects of cocaine. *Clin. Perinatol.* 20, 245–262.

Smeeth, L., Cook, C., Fombonne, P. E., Heavey, L., Rodrigues, L. C., Smith, P. G., et al. (2004). Rate of first recorded diagnosis of autism and other pervasive developmental disorders in United Kingdom general practice, 1988 to 2001. *BMC Med.* 2:39. doi: 10.1186/1741-7015-2-39

Sorensen, M. J., Gronborg, T. K., Christensen, J., Parner, E. T., Vestergaard, M., Schendel, D., et al. (2013). Antidepressant exposure in pregnancy and risk of autism spectrum disorders. *Clin. Epidemiol.* 5, 449–459. doi: 10.2147/CLEP.S53009

Stene-Larsen, K., Borge, A. I., and Vollrath, M. E. (2009). Maternal smoking in pregnancy and externalizing behavior in 18-month-old children: results from a population-based prospective study. *J. Am. Acad. Child Adolesc. Psychiatry* 48, 283–289. doi: 10.1097/CHI.0b013e318195bcfb

Strauss, K. A., Puffenberger, E. G., Huentelman, M. J., Gottlieb, S., Dobrin, S. E., Parod, J. M., et al. (2006). Recessive symptomatic focal epilepsy and mutant contactin-associated protein-like 2. *N. Engl. J. Med.* 354, 1370–1377. doi: 10.1056/NEJMoa052773

Stromland, K., Nordin, V., Miller, M., Akerstrom, B., and Gillberg, C. (1994). Autism in thalidomide embryopathy: a population study. *Dev. Med. Child Neurol.* 36, 351–356. doi: 10.1111/j.1469-8749.1994.tb11856.x

Stromland, K., Sjogreen, L., Miller, M., Gillberg, C., Wentz, E., Johansson, M., et al. (2002). Mobius sequence–a Swedish multidiscipline study. *Eur. J. Paediatr. Neurol.* 6, 35–45. doi: 10.1053/ejpn.2001.0540

Stubbs, E. G. (1978). Autistic symptoms in a child with congenital cytomegalovirus infection. *J. Autism Child. Schizophr.* 8, 37–43. doi: 10.1007/BF01550276

Stubbs, E. G., Ash, E., and Williams, C. P. (1984). Autism and congenital cytomegalovirus. *J. Autism Dev. Disord.* 14, 183–189. doi: 10.1007/BF02409660

Sui, L., and Chen, M. (2012). Prenatal exposure to valproic acid enhances synaptic plasticity in the medial prefrontal cortex and fear memories. *Brain Res. Bull.* 87, 556–563. doi: 10.1016/j.brainresbull.2012.01.011

Suren, P., Roth, C., Bresnahan, M., Haugen, M., Hornig, M., Hirtz, D., et al. (2013). Association between maternal use of folic acid supplements and risk of autism spectrum disorders in children. *JAMA* 309, 570–577. doi: 10.1001/jama.2012.155925

Sweeten, T. L., Posey, D. J., and McDougle, C. J. (2004). Brief report: autistic disorder in three children with cytomegalovirus infection. *J. Autism Dev. Disord.* 34, 583–586. doi: 10.1007/s10803-004-2552-y

Swillen, A., and McDonald-McGinn, D. (2015). Developmental trajectories in 22q11.2 deletion. *Am. J. Med. Genet. C Semin. Med. Genet.* 169, 172–181. doi: 10.1002/ajmg.c.31435

Talbott, E. O., Marshall, L. P., Rager, J. R., Arena, V. C., Sharma, R. K., and Stacy, S. L. (2015). Air toxics and the risk of autism spectrum disorder: the results of a population based case-control study in southwestern Pennsylvania. *Environ. Health* 14, 80. doi: 10.1186/s12940-015-0064-1

Tang, S., Wang, Y., Gong, X., and Wang, G. (2015). A meta-analysis of maternal smoking during pregnancy and autism spectrum disorder risk in offspring. *Int. J. Environ. Res. Public Health* 12, 10418–10431. doi: 10.3390/ijerph120910418

Taurines, R., Schwenck, C., Lyttwin, B., Schecklmann, M., Jans, T., Reefschlager, L., et al. (2014). Oxytocin plasma concentrations in children and adolescents with autism spectrum disorder: correlation with autistic symptomatology. *Atten. Defic. Hyperact. Disord.* 6, 231–239. doi: 10.1007/s12402-014-0145-y

Tchaconas, A., and Adesman, A. (2013). Autism spectrum disorders: a pediatric overview and update. *Curr. Opin. Pediatr.* 25, 130–144. doi: 10.1097/MOP.0b013e32835c2b70

Tomson, T., Battino, D., Bonizzoni, E., Craig, J., Lindhout, D., Sabers, A., et al. (2011). Dose-dependent risk of malformations with antiepileptic drugs: an analysis of data from the EURAP epilepsy and pregnancy registry. *Lancet Neurol.* 10, 609–617. doi: 10.1016/S1474-4422(11)70107-7

Townsend, C. L., Forsgren, M., Ahlfors, K., Ivarsson, S. A., Tookey, P. A., and Peckham, C. S. (2013). Long-term outcomes of congenital cytomegalovirus infection in Sweden and the United Kingdom. *Clin. Infect. Dis.* 56, 1232–1239. doi: 10.1093/cid/cit018

Tran, P. L., Lehti, V., Lampi, K. M., Helenius, H., Suominen, A., Gissler, M., et al. (2013). Smoking during pregnancy and risk of autism spectrum disorder in a Finnish National Birth Cohort. *Paediatr. Perinat. Epidemiol.* 27, 266–274. doi: 10.1111/ppe.12043

Van Wijngaarden, E., Davidson, P. W., Smith, T. H., Evans, K., Yost, K., Love, T., et al. (2013). Autism spectrum disorder phenotypes and prenatal exposure to methylmercury. *Epidemiology* 24, 651–659. doi: 10.1097/EDE.0b013e31829d2651

Vauzelle, C., Beghin, D., Cournot, M. P., and Elefant, E. (2013). Birth defects after exposure to misoprostol in the first trimester of pregnancy: prospective follow-up study. *Reprod. Toxicol.* 36, 98–103. doi: 10.1016/j.reprotox.2012.11.009

Verzijl, H. T., van der Zwaag, B., Cruysberg, J. R., and Padberg, G. W. (2003). Mobius syndrome redefined: a syndrome of rhombencephalic maldevelopment. *Neurology* 61, 327–333. doi: 10.1212/01.WNL.0000076484.91275.CD

Vignoli, A., La Briola, F., Peron, A., Turner, K., Vannicola, C., Saccani, M., et al. (2015). Autism spectrum disorder in tuberous sclerosis complex: searching for risk markers. *Orphanet J. Rare Dis.* 10, 154. doi: 10.1186/s13023-015-0371-1

Vinet, E., Pineau, C. A., Clarke, A. E., Scott, S., Fombonne, E., Joseph, L., et al. (2015). Increased risk of autism spectrum disorders in children born to women with systemic lupus erythematosus: results from a large population-based cohort. *Arthritis Rheumatol.* 67, 3201–3208. doi: 10.1002/art.39320

Volk, H. E., Hertz-Picciotto, I., Delwiche, L., Lurmann, F., and McConnell, R. (2011). Residential proximity to freeways and autism in the CHARGE study. *Environ. Health Perspect.* 119, 873–877. doi: 10.1289/ehp.1002835

Volk, H. E., Lurmann, F., Penfold, B., Hertz-Picciotto, I., and McConnell, R. (2013). Traffic-related air pollution, particulate matter, and autism. *JAMA Psychiatry* 70, 71–77. doi: 10.1001/jamapsychiatry.2013.266

Wadell, P. M., Hagerman, R. J., and Hessl, D. R. (2013). Fragile X syndrome: psychiatric manifestations, assessment and emerging therapies. *Curr. Psychiatry Rev.* 9, 53–58. doi: 10.2174/157340013805289644

Wagner, G. C., Reuhl, K. R., Cheh, M., McRae, P., and Halladay, A. K. (2006). A new neurobehavioral model of autism in mice: pre- and postnatal exposure to sodium valproate. *J. Autism Dev. Disord.* 36, 779–793. doi: 10.1007/s10803-006-0117-y

Walker, C. K., Krakowiak, P., Baker, A., Hansen, R. L., Ozonoff, S., and Hertz-Picciotto, I. (2015). Preeclampsia, placental insufficiency, and autism spectrum disorder or developmental delay. *JAMA Pediatr.* 169, 154–162. doi: 10.1001/jamapediatrics.2014.2645

Wang, A. T., Lim, T., Jamison, J., Bush, L., Soorya, L. V., Tavassoli, T., et al. (2016). Neural selectivity for communicative auditory signals in Phelan-McDermid syndrome. *J. Neurodev. Disord.* 8, 5. doi: 10.1186/s11689-016-9138-9

Watanabe, T., Kuroda, M., Kuwabara, H., Aoki, Y., Iwashiro, N., Tatsunobu, N., et al. (2015). Clinical and neural effects of six-week administration of oxytocin on core symptoms of autism. *Brain* 138, 3400–3412. doi: 10.1093/brain/awv249

Werler, M. M., Ahrens, K. A., Bosco, J. L., Mitchell, A. A., Anderka, M. T., Gilboa, S. M., et al. (2011). Use of antiepileptic medications in pregnancy in relation to risks of birth defects. *Ann. Epidemiol.* 21, 842–850. doi: 10.1016/j.annepidem.2011.08.002

Wilkerson, D. S., Volpe, A. G., Dean, R. S., and Titus, J. B. (2002). Perinatal complications as predictors of infantile autism. *Int. J. Neurosci.* 112, 1085–1098. doi: 10.1080/00207450290026076

Williams, G., King, J., Cunningham, M., Stephan, M., Kerr, B., and Hersh, J. H. (2001). Fetal valproate syndrome and autism: additional evidence of an association. *Dev. Med. Child Neurol.* 43, 202–206. doi: 10.1017/S001216220100038X

Windham, G. C., Zhang, L., Gunier, R., Croen, L. A., and Grether, J. K. (2006). Autism spectrum disorders in relation to distribution of hazardous air pollutants in the san francisco bay area. *Environ. Health Perspect.* 114, 1438–1444. doi: 10.1289/ehp.9120

Wu, S., Ding, Y., Wu, F., Li, R., Xie, G., Hou, J., et al. (2015). Family history of autoimmune diseases is associated with an increased risk of autism in children: a systematic review and meta-analysis. *Neurosci. Biobehav. Rev.* 55, 322–332. doi: 10.1016/j.neubiorev.2015.05.004

Xiang, A. H., Wang, X., Martinez, M. P., Walthall, J. C., Curry, E. S., Page, K., et al. (2015). Association of maternal diabetes with autism in offspring. *JAMA* 313, 1425–1434. doi: 10.1001/jama.2015.2707

Xu, G., Jing, J., Bowers, K., Liu, B., and Bao, W. (2014). Maternal diabetes and the risk of autism spectrum disorders in the offspring: a systematic review and meta-analysis. *J. Autism Dev. Disord.* 44, 766–775. doi: 10.1007/s10803-013-1928-2

Yamashita, Y., Fujimoto, C., Nakajima, E., Isagai, T., and Matsuishi, T. (2003). Possible association between congenital cytomegalovirus infection and autistic disorder. *J. Autism Dev. Disord.* 33, 455–459. doi: 10.1023/A:1025023131029

Yamazaki, H., Yamamoto, R., Moroto, S., Yamazaki, T., Fujiwara, K., Nakai, M., et al. (2012). Cochlear implantation in children with congenital cytomegalovirus infection accompanied by psycho-neurological disorders. *Acta Otolaryngol.* 132, 420–427. doi: 10.3109/00016489.2011.653442

Yasuda, Y., Hashimoto, R., Fukai, R., Okamoto, N., Hiraki, Y., Yamamori, H., et al. (2014). Duplication of the NPHP1 gene in patients with autism spectrum disorder and normal intellectual ability: a case series. *Ann. Gen. Psychiatry* 13, 22. doi: 10.1186/s12991-014-0022-2

Yatawara, C. J., Einfeld, S. L., Hickie, I. B., Davenport, T. A., and Guastella, A. J. (2015). The effect of oxytocin nasal spray on social interaction deficits observed in young children with autism: a randomized clinical crossover trial. *Mol. Psychiatry.* doi: 10.1038/mp.2015.162. [Epub ahead of print].

Yau, V. M., Green, P. G., Alaimo, C. P., Yoshida, C. K., Lutsky, M., Windham, G. C., et al. (2014). Prenatal and neonatal peripheral blood mercury levels and autism spectrum disorders. *Environ. Res.* 133, 294–303. doi: 10.1016/j.envres.2014.04.034

Zerbo, O., Iosif, A. M., Walker, C., Ozonoff, S., Hansen, R. L., and Hertz-Picciotto, I. (2013). Is maternal influenza or fever during pregnancy associated with autism or developmental delays? Results from the CHARGE (CHildhood Autism Risks from Genetics and Environment) study. *J. Autism Dev. Disord.* 43, 25–33. doi: 10.1007/s10803-012-1540-x

21

Abnormalities of Inter- and Intra-Hemispheric Functional Connectivity in Autism Spectrum Disorders: A Study Using the Autism Brain Imaging Data Exchange Database

Jung Min Lee[1†], *Sunghyun Kyeong*[2†], *Eunjoo Kim*[3] *and Keun-Ah Cheon*[3*]

[1] *Division of Computational Mathematics, National Institute for Mathematical Sciences, Daejeon, South Korea,* [2] *Severance Biomedical Science Institute, Yonsei University College of Medicine, Seoul, South Korea,* [3] *Division of Child and Adolescent Psychiatry, Department of Psychiatry and Institute of Behavioral Science in Medicine, Yonsei University College of Medicine, Seoul, South Korea*

Edited by:
Roma Siugzdaite,
Ghent University, Belgium

Reviewed by:
David Cochran,
University of Massachusetts Medical Center, USA
Suhash Chakraborty,
Hindustan Aeronautics Limited Hospital, India

***Correspondence:**
Keun-Ah Cheon
kacheon@yuhs.ac

† These authors have contributed equally to this work.

Recently, the Autism Brain Imaging Data Exchange (ABIDE) project revealed decreased functional connectivity in individuals with Autism Spectrum Disorders (ASD) relative to the typically developing controls (TDCs). However, it is still questionable whether the source of functional under-connectivity in subjects with ASD is equally contributed by the ipsilateral and contralateral parts of the brain. In this study, we decomposed the inter- and intra-hemispheric regions and compared the functional connectivity density (FCD) between 458 subjects with ASD and 517 TDCs from the ABIDE database. We quantified the inter- and intra-hemispheric FCDs in the brain by counting the number of functional connectivity with all voxels in the opposite and same hemispheric brain regions, respectively. Relative to TDCs, both inter- and intra-hemispheric FCDs in the posterior cingulate cortex, lingual/parahippocampal gyrus, and postcentral gyrus were significantly decreased in subjects with ASD. Moreover, in the ASD group, the restricted and repetitive behavior subscore of the Autism Diagnostic Observation Schedule (ADOS-RRB) score showed significant negative correlations with the average inter-hemispheric FCD and contralateral FCD in the lingual/parahippocampal gyrus cluster. Also, the ADOS-RRB score showed significant negative correlations with the average contralateral FCD in the default mode network regions such as the posterior cingulate cortex and precuneus. Taken together, our findings imply that a deficit of non-social functioning processing in ASD such as restricted and repetitive behaviors and sensory hypersensitivity could be determined via both inter- and intra-hemispheric functional disconnections.

Keywords: Autism Spectrum Disorder (ASD), inter-hemisphere, intra-hemisphere, functional connectivity, resting state fMRI

INTRODUCTION

Autism Spectrum Disorder (ASD) is characterized by impairments in social interaction and communication, and restrictive and repetitive behaviors (American Psychiatric Association, 2013). ASD is caused by genetic and neurobiological factors (Frith and Happe, 1993; Bogdashina, 2006; Hughes, 2009; Amaral, 2011). Among the neurobiological mechanisms, the prevailing theory is that ASD is caused by abnormalities in the neuronal system and social brain network (Bogdashina, 2006; Minshew and Keller, 2010; Nebel et al., 2014). In functional neuroimaging studies, researchers have investigated the functional connectivity in subjects with ASD (Just et al., 2007), and the under-connectivity theory of ASD has been supported by many previous studies (Muller et al., 2011; Rudie et al., 2012; Vissers et al., 2012; Di Martino et al., 2014). A neuronal network study using electroencephalography showed long-range under-connectivity and short-range over-connectivity in patients with ASD (Barttfeld et al., 2011). The white matter integrity of the brain network has been examined with diffusion tensor imaging analysis. Furthermore, a decreased size of the corpus callosum was observed in the ASD group in a structural magnetic resonance imaging (MRI) study (Keary et al., 2009). Because the corpus callosum is the biggest part of the transcallosal connectivity in the human brain, a decreased corpus callosum size has been argued as an indication of long-range under-connectivity. Moreover, decreased volumes and abnormal integrity of the corpus callosum have been observed in diffusion tensor imaging studies (Alexander et al., 2007; Keller et al., 2007; Cheon et al., 2011).

Many researchers utilized the resting state functional MRI and found atypical brain activities in ASD (Cherkassky et al., 2006; Di Martino et al., 2014). Due to the restricted computational power, studies in the neuroimaging, and psychiatric research areas predominantly used a seed-based analysis by considering a default network alteration (Monk et al., 2009; Weng et al., 2010). Recently, voxel-wise data-driven functional connectivity density (FCD) mapping method was proposed (Tomasi and Volkow, 2010), in which all voxels in the whole brain region would be examined rather than using a specific seed region of interest for a connectivity analysis. The FCD method has been applied successfully to analyze the sex differences in functional connectivity in both healthy control subjects (Tomasi and Volkow, 2012b) and subjects with attention deficit hyperactivity disorder (ADHD) using large samples (Tomasi and Volkow, 2012a).

Due to the diverse symptoms and complexity of ASD, a large dataset is needed to investigate the characteristic features of ASD. Recently, the Autism Brain Imaging Data Exchange (ABIDE) collected 1112 resting state functional MRI datasets of subjects with ASD and typically developing control (TDC) subjects from 17 international sites. Previously, large datasets from multiple centers have been successfully analyzed to identify features of the functional human brain (Lord et al., 2000; Biswal et al., 2010; Tomasi and Volkow, 2012a). In particular, the FCD method was applied successfully to the ADHD-200 dataset to identify differences in the functional hubs among children with ADHD (Tomasi and Volkow, 2012a). A deeper understanding of the connectivity abnormalities in ASD has been achieved with the worldwide neuroimaging data sharing initiative. Di Martino et al. analyzed brain connectivity in 1000 subjects using global connectivity measures, and revealed over- and under-connectivity in the ASD group (Di Martino et al., 2014).

Several studies have examined the regional inter-hemispheric under-connectivity in ASD by evaluating the correlation between a voxel and its opposite hemispheric counterpart on a symmetric template (Anderson et al., 2011; Di Martino et al., 2014). However, the whole-brain inter- and intra-hemispheric functional under-connectivity studies have been rarely investigated to uncover the deficit of social and non-social functioning in ASD. Because the global FCD was originally proposed to identify the functional hub regions, the ipsilateral FCD and contralateral FCD measure the intra-hemispheric and inter-hemispheric functional hub regions, respectively. A recently published study using the ABIDE datasets examined both intra-hemispheric and inter-hemispheric connectivity in participants with ASD, and revealed both increased and decreased connectivity in the ASD groups in comparison to the control groups, depending on the different types of brain connectivity and distortions in connectivity patterns examined at the individual level (Hahamy et al., 2015). In the current study, we aimed to examine both inter- and inter-hemispheric connectivity in the brains of participants with ASD by decomposing the functional connectivity into ipsilateral and contralateral parts. These approaches would allow us to investigate how connectivity abnormalities in the ASD group would be determined by interactions between the intra- and inter-hemispheric functional connectivity. The results would also confirm that the abnormal regions of the resting state functional connectivity in ASD are related to the default mode network (Raichle and Snyder, 2007; Assaf et al., 2010; Weng et al., 2010; Lynch et al., 2013) and brain regions implicated in the non-social functioning processes such as restricted and repetitive behaviors (Di Martino et al., 2009; Supekar et al., 2013; von dem Hagen et al., 2013; Fishman et al., 2014).

MATERIALS AND METHODS

Dataset

We used resting state fMRI data of 458 subjects with ASD and 517 TDCs (see **Table 1** for additional demographic information) among 1112 datasets from the ABIDE datasets (http://fcon_1000.projects.nitrc.org/indi/abide). To minimize the institution dependent variability, our study included data from research centers that contributed to both the ASD and TDC groups. Therefore, the present study included neuroimaging datasets from California Institute of Technology (CALTECH), Kennedy Krieger Institute (KKI), Ludwig Maximilians University, Munich (MAX_MUM), New York University Langone Medical Center (NYU), Olin Institute of Living at Hartford Hospital (OLIN), Oregon Health & Science University (OHSU), University of Pittsburgh School of Medicine (PITT), San Diego State University (SDSU), Stanford University (STANFORD), Trinity Center for Health Sciences (TRINITY), University of California,

Los Angeles (UCLA), University of Leuven (LEUVEN), University of Michigan (UM), University of Utah School of Medicine (USM), and Yale Child Study Center (YALE). All experimental protocols were in compliance with the policies of site-specific institutional review boards. The demographic variables and scanning parameters are summarized in **Table 1**. The graphical illustration of the demographic variables can be found in elsewhere (Di Martino et al., 2014). We excluded datasets from the social brain Lab BCN NIC UMC Groningen and Netherlands Institute for Neurosciences due to the missing information of a full-scale intelligence quotient (IQ) for many subjects. After preprocessing, we found that a large part of the cerebellum was missing in the imaging dataset of Carnegie Mellon University, and all datasets from Carnegie Mellon University were excluded. To control for potential confounding effects of IQ in our analysis, we decided to exclude five datasets that included some subjects with IQ lower than 70. Finally, we performed voxel-wise group comparisons with 975 imaging datasets.

Image Preprocessing

Datasets were preprocessed with SPM8 (http://www.fil.ion.ucl.ac.uk/spm/software/spm8/). The first step was realignment for head motion correction. Images were realigned to the first image and a mean echo planar image (EPI) was created during this step. Subsequently, structural T1 images were coregistered to their mean EPI data. Registered EPI data of each subject were normalized to Montreal Neurological Institute (MNI) template and spatially smoothed with 8 mm of full-width at half-maximum. Then, in the temporal domain, the linearly increasing trend due to heat absorption was removed at each voxel, and the effects of the head motion, white matter, cerebrospinal fluid, and global signal were regressed out. Lastly, temporal band-pass filtering was applied (0.01–0.08 Hz).

Functional Connectivity Density Mapping

Preprocessed resting state fMRI data were normalized into the MNI template space with a voxel size of $2 \times 2 \times 2$ mm. At each voxel, we applied a voxel-wise data-driven FCD mapping method to calculate the global FCD, which was introduced by Tomasi and Volkow (2010). In this study, we divided the global functional connectivity density into two parts. One is the contralateral FCD and another is the ipsilateral FCD (**Figure 1**). The global FCD is the number of functional edges connected with all other voxels. For a given voxel *i*, a voxel *j* is said to be connected to the voxel *i* if the correlation coefficient between *i*-th and *j*-th time series is larger than 0.6 (Tomasi and Volkow, 2010, 2012a,b,c). Then the degree between the two voxels is defined to be 1 ($S_{ij} = 1$); and otherwise, the degree is zero ($S_{ij} = 0$). Likewise, we could obtain the degree from other voxels and the sum of all degrees at a given voxel *i* is defined as the global FCD at that voxel. At a voxel *i*, the global FCD is calculated as,

$$\text{global FCD}_i = \sum_{j=1}^{N} S_{ij},$$

where N is the number of voxels (or nodes) in the gray matter regions.

The contralateral (or inter-hemispheric) FCD is evaluated by counting the number of functional connectivity with all voxels in the opposite hemispheric brain regions as follows:

$$\text{contralateral FCD}_i = \sum_{j=1}^{N} h_{ij} S_{ij},$$

where h_{ij} is 1 if *j*-th voxels are in the opposite hemispheres and 0 otherwise.

Lastly, the ipsilateral (or intra-hemispheric) FCD was computed by subtracting the number of contra-lateral functional connectivity from the total number of functional connectivity as follows:

$$\text{ipsilateral FCD}_i = \text{global FCD}_i - \text{contralateral FCD}_i.$$

The graphical illustrations of global, contralateral, and ipsilateral functional connectivity densities are presented in **Figure 1**. Finally, the normalized contralateral FCD (cFCD), normalized ipsilateral FCD (iFCD), and normalized global FCD (gFCD) were obtained by normalizing the number of functional connections at each voxel with respect to the average value of the global functional connectivity of each subject.

$$\text{iFCD}_i = \frac{\text{ipsilateral FCD}_i}{mean\left(\text{global FCD}\right)},\ \text{cFCD}_i = \frac{\text{contralateral FCD}_i}{mean\left(\text{global FCD}\right)},$$
$$\text{and gFCD}_i = \frac{\text{global FCD}_i}{mean\left(\text{global FCD}\right)},$$

where *mean*(global FCD) is the average of the global FCD for all voxels.

The use of the normalized functional connectivity density minimizes the individual variability of the overall connectivity and makes it easier to detect the fractionally increased or decreased connectivity. Consequently, the average of the gFCD becomes one.

Statistical Analysis

The images of the gFCD, cFCD, and iFCD were used for a second-level analysis, comparing the subjects with ASD and TDCs using SPM8, in which a 2-tailed *t*-test design with two covariates of age and sex was used to compute the statistical significance of the FCD differences between the two groups. Statistical significance was based on the false discovery rate corrected $P < 0.05$ together with requiring 20 voxels for the minimum continuous voxel size within a cluster (corrected $P < 0.05$). For brain regions showing significantly decreased FCDs, we computed the partial correlations between the averages (or regional maximum) of the FCD values for each cluster and the scores from symptom severity scales while controlling for effects of age and sex. The Benjamini-Hochberg procedure was applied to control multiple comparison corrections (Benjamini and Hochberg, 1995). The significances of the correlation analysis were set at a threshold of (Benjamini–Hochberg) corrected $P < 0.05$.

TABLE 1 | Demographic variables and imaging parameters for the selected resting-state functional MRI datasets from Autism Brain Imaging Data Exchange database.

Center	No. of scans	TR(ms)	TDC			ASD		
			M/F	Age	FIQ	M/F	Age	FIQ
PITT	200	1500	23/4	18.9 ± 6.5	110.1 ± 9.2	26/4	18.9 ± 7.1	110.0 ± 14.1
OLIN	210	1500	14/2	16.9 ± 3.6	114.9 ± 16.0	16/2	16.3 ± 3.0	113.0 ± 17.4
OHSU	82	2500	15/0	10.1 ± 1.0	115.7 ± 10.7	10/0	10.9 ± 1.8	109.7 ± 18.4
SDSU	180	2000	16/6	14.2 ± 1.9	108.1 ± 10.3	13/1	14.7 ± 1.7	111.4 ± 17.4
TRINITY	150	2000	25/0	17.1 ± 3.7	110.9 ± 12.0	24/0	17.3 ± 3.5	109.3 ± 14.7
UM	300	2000	56/17	14.6 ± 3.6	108.0 ± 9.7	50/9	13.2 ± 2.5	107.3 ± 16.8
USM	240	2000	43/0	21.4 ± 7.6	115.1 ± 13.6	57/0	22.4 ± 7.5	100.9 ± 15.2
YALE	200	2000	20/8	12.7 ± 2.7	105.0 ± 17.1	18/8	12.7 ± 3.0	97.9 ± 17.8
LEUVEN	250	1667	15/0	23.3 ± 2.8	114.8 ± 12.4	14/0	21.9 ± 4.0	109.4 ± 12.6
KKI	156	2500	23/9	10.1 ± 1.2	113.8 ± 8.9	16/4	10.0 ± 1.5	97.8 ± 16.4
NYU	180	2000	79/26	15.8 ± 6.2	113.2 ± 13.1	68/10	14.5 ± 7.0	108.1 ± 16.5
STANDFORD	180	2000	16/4	10.0 ± 1.6	112.1 ± 15.0	16/3	9.9 ± 1.5	113.3 ± 17.5
UCLA	120	3000	38/6	13.0 ± 1.9	106.3 ± 10.8	46/6	13.1 ± 2.4	100.9 ± 13.2
MAX_MUN	120	3000	29/4	26.2 ± 9.7	111.5 ± 8.7	16/3	22.9 ± 14.1	107.6 ± 13.7
CALTECH	150	2000	15/4	28.9 ± 10.9	114.2 ± 9.4	14/4	27.8 ± 10.2	108.2 ± 12.2
Total			427/90	16.5 ± 7.3	111.2 ± 12.4	404/54	16.2 ± 7.4	106.0 ± 16.3

ASD, autism spectrum disorder; CALTECH, California Institute of Technology; F, female; FIQ, full scale IQ standard score; KKI, Kennedy Krieger Institute; M, Male; MAX_MUM, Ludwig Maximilians University Munich; NYU, New York University Langone Medical Center; OLIN, Olin Institute of Living at Hartford Hospital; OHSU, Oregon Health and Science University; PITT, University of Pittsburgh School of Medicine; SDSU, San Diego State University; STANFORD, Stanford University; TDC, Typically developed control group; TRINITY, Trinity Center for Health Sciences; UCLA, University of California, Los Angeles; LEUVEN, University of Leuven; UM, University of Michigan; USM, University of Utah School of Medicine; YALE, Yale Child Study Center.

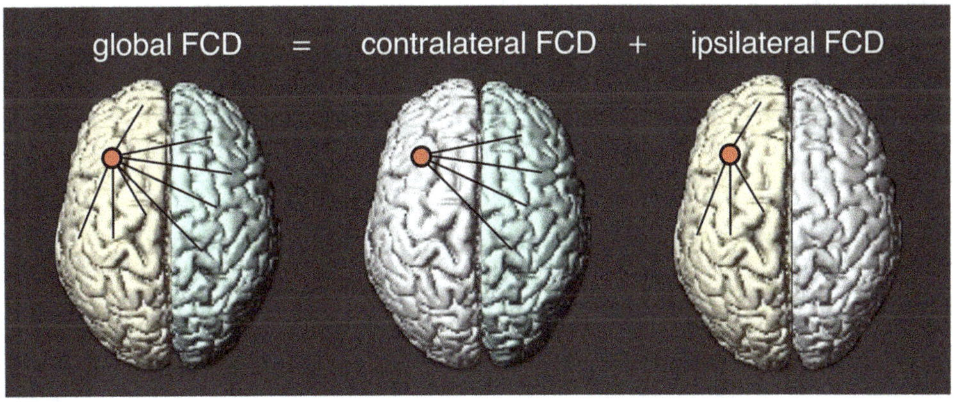

FIGURE 1 | Calculating three measures of functional connectivity density. cFCD (contralateral functional connectivity density) is the number of functional connectivity from the opposite hemisphere; iFCD (ipsilateral functional connectivity density) is from the same hemisphere; gFCD (global functional connectivity density) is computed as the sum of cFCD and iFCD.

RESULTS

Demographic Variables and Clinical Measures

We included data from 458 subjects (54 females) with ASD and 517 TDCs (90 females) in the data analysis. The two-sample t-test showed that the age distribution of subjects with ASD were not significantly different from that of TDCs, but the full-scale IQ score was significantly lower in the ASD group than that in the TDC group ($P < 0.05$).

Functional Connectivity Density

For both the ASD and TDC groups, the average values of gFCD, iFCD, and cFCD are presented (**Figure 2**), and the distribution of the functional connectivity density were bilateral. For each measure of the normalized gFCDs, iFCDs, and cFCDs, the two-sample t-test with covariates of age and sex found significantly decreased functional connectivity in multiple regions in the ASD group, but no significantly increased functional connectivity was detected (**Figure 3** and **Table 2**). For example, in the comparisons of gFCD, the ASD group showed a significantly decreased

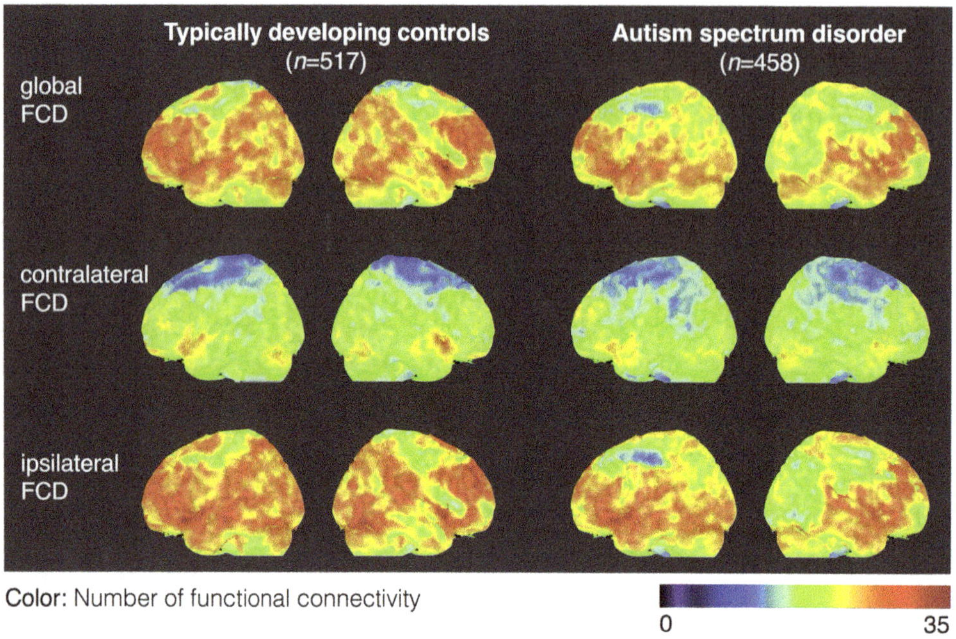

FIGURE 2 | Average maps of functional connectivity densities for the typically developing controls (TDCs) and autism spectrum disorders (ASDs). Distribution of gFCD, cFCD, and iFCD are averaged over 458 patients with ASDs and 517 TDCs. The color bar represents the number of functional connectivities.

functional connectivity in the default mode network regions including the medial prefrontal cortex, posterior cingulate cortex, and inferior parietal lobule, and the sensorimotor regions including the bilateral postcentral gyri, paracentral lobule, and parahippocampal gyrus (corrected $P < 0.05$; **Table 2** gFCD; **Figure 3**). The group differences in the iFCD showed similar patterns to that of the gFCD. Furthermore, iFCDs of the right inferior frontal gyrus, left superior frontal gyrus, and precuneus were significantly decreased in the ASD group (corrected $P < 0.05$; **Table 2** iFCD, **Figure 3**). Finally, the comparison of cFCD revealed regional under-connectivity of the ASD group in the posterior cingulate cortex, parahippocampal gyrus, precentral gyrus, and right angular gyrus (corrected $P < 0.05$; **Table 2** cFCD, **Figure 3**).

In particular, common brain regions showing under-connectivity in ASD across different institutions were the default mode network regions, such as the medial prefrontal cortex, posterior cingulate cortex, precuneus, and lingual/parahippocampal gyrus. The extent of regional overlaps in the normalized global, contralateral, and ipsilateral FCDs are presented in **Figure 4**.

Correlation between Clinical Data and FCD

In several sites, the datasets contained clinical information such as the Autism Diagnostic Interview-Revised (ADI-R), the restricted and repetitive behavior subscore of the Autism Diagnostic Observation Schedule (ADOS-RRB), and communication subscore of the ADOS (ADOS-COM). The average values of FCDs in each region of interest showed meaningful correlations with the ADI-R scores (Lord et al., 1994) and ADOS scores (Lord et al., 2000). **Figure 5** shows the significant correlations between the FCDs and the ADOS-RRB score. In the ASD group, the ADOS-RRB score showed significant negative correlations with the average gFCD ($\rho = -0.24$, corrected $P = 0.003$, $df = 217$), iFCD ($\rho = -0.23$, corrected $P = 0.006$, $df = 217$), and cFCD ($\rho = -0.24$, corrected $P = 0.003$, $df = 217$) in the lingual/parahippocampal gyrus cluster. Also, the ADOS-RRB score showed significant negative correlations with the average cFCD in the PCC ($\rho = -0.18$, corrected $P = 0.03$, and $df = 217$) and precuneus ($\rho = -0.15$, corrected $P = 0.05$, and $df = 217$). Moreover, significances of those correlations were preserved if we use a regional maximum value of FCDs instead of a regional mean within each region of interest (corrected $P < 0.05$).

DISCUSSION

Abnormalities in the neuronal systems of individuals with ASD have been reported in many studies over the last two decades, using small sample ASD groups. We used data from 517 TDCs and 458 patients with ASD from the ABIDE database to examine the abnormalities of functional connectivity in the ASD group relative to TDCs. We used a data-driven voxel-wise method, which examined all voxels in the entire brain. We computed the FCD maps by calculating the connectivity degree of each voxel with all other voxels. The FCD maps were used to compare the functional connectivity between the ASD and TDC groups. A group difference analysis showed regional under-connectivity in the ASD group relative to the TDC group. The abnormal

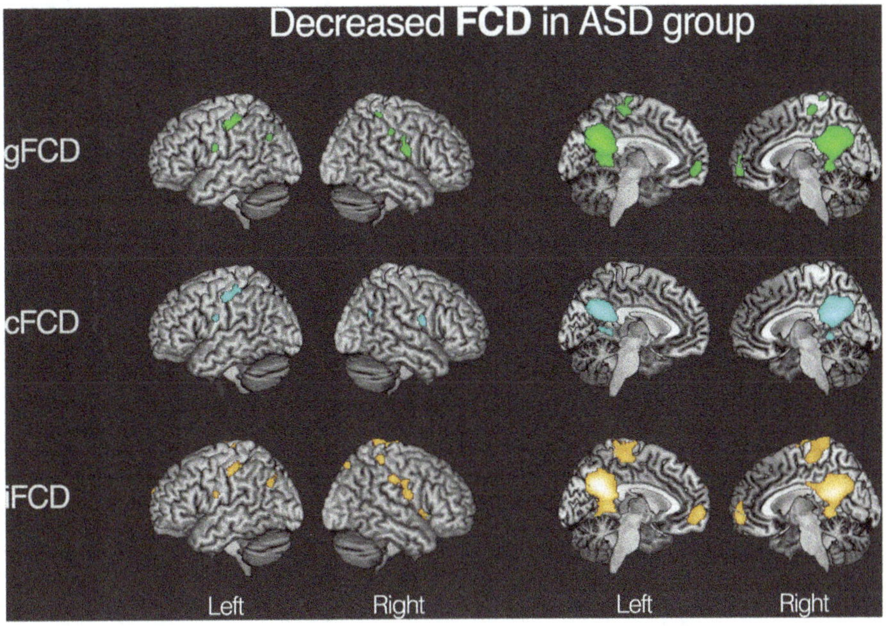

FIGURE 3 | Decreased functional connectivity density (FCD) in autism spectrum disorder (ASD) group. Group differences in the normalized global, contralateral, and ipsilateral FCDs were visualized with the statistical significance at corrected $P < 0.05$. Detailed information on each cluster is written in **Table 2**.

regions of intrinsic functional connectivity in the ASD group were the lingual/parahippocampal gyrus, posterior cingulate cortex, precuneus, postcentral gyrus, paracentral lobule, medial prefrontal cortex, precentral gyrus, angular gyrus, inferior frontal gyrus, superior frontal gyrus, and supplementary motor area, which are related to the default mode network and social functioning processes.

To the best of our knowledge, the present study is the first attempt to decompose the functional connectivity into ipsilateral and contralateral parts to explore abnormalities in the intrinsic neural networks of ASD. Inter-hemispheric connectivity in ASD was examined previously in several studies (Anderson et al., 2011), in which a correlation between each voxel and a corresponding voxel in the opposite hemisphere was calculated. The present study used all voxels in the opposite hemisphere to calculate the inter-hemispheric connectivity. Consequently, inter-hemispheric FCD is somewhat analogous to long distance connectivity. Intra-hemispheric FCD was used to identify the characteristics of the short distance connectivity. Global functional connectivity density was obtained by combining the inter- and intra-hemispheric FCDs.

Functional Under-Connectivity vs. Over-Connectivity

Neuroimaging studies have shown abnormal brain networks in ASD, but the issue of over-connectivity or under-connectivity in those findings remains controversial (Muller et al., 2011). Children with ASD showed both over-and under-connectivity (Lynch et al., 2013). The precuneus was underconnected with other brain regions, as we observed in this study, but the posterior cingulate cortex was overconnected, which was the opposite result from our study. For adolescents with ASD, functional connectivity between the medial prefrontal cortex and precuneus (theory of mind regions) and some regions in the mirror neuron system have been found to be overconnected (Northoff et al., 2006; Fishman et al., 2014). However, when the brains of adults with ASD were examined, the medial prefrontal cortex and precuneus were underconnected. This result may be explained by two reasons. First, including adult subjects may change the overall result from over-connectivity to under-connectivity. However, it is unlikely that the inclusion of adult subjects may change the connectivity pattern of subjects with ASD because the majority of subjects with ASD in our study were children and adolescents. Second, the medial prefrontal cortex and precuneus were overconnected with some regions in the mirror neuron system but underconnected with a majority of other brain regions. In summary, the medial prefrontal cortex and precuneus may appear underconnected in some specific brain regions.

In a prior study where the posterior cingulate cortex had been used as a single seed (Monk et al., 2009), the ASD group showed under-connectivity in the right superior frontal gyrus and over-connectivity in the right temporal pole and right parahippocampal gyrus, compared to the TDC group. In our results using the voxel-wise data-driven method, both the posterior cingulate cortex and parahippocampal gyrus in the ASD group showed reduced functional connectivity compared to TDCs. This result is consistent with the result from prior studies showing a weaker connectivity between the posterior cingulate cortex and precuneus in the ASD group compared to that of the TDC group (Cherkassky et al., 2006).

TABLE 2 | Group differences in the normalized global, contralateral, and ipsilateral FCDs (gFCD, cFCD, and iFCD) between the ASDs and TDCs.

Cluster Name	BA	gFCD	cFCD	iFCD
		Cluster Size (MNI)	Cluster Size (MNI)	Cluster Size (MNI)
Lt. Medial prefrontal cortex*	10	303 (0, 62, −6)		538 (0, 62, −6)
Lt. Superior frontal gyrus	10			58 (−14, 72, 28)
Rt. Inferior frontal gyrus	22			60 (54, 16, −4)
Lt. Supplementary motor area	6			49 (0, −6, 76)
Lt. Precentral gyrus	4	51 (−64, −4, 22)	29 (−62, −4, 22)	25 (−64, −4, 22)
Lt. Postcentral gyrus	2	648 (−64, −20, 50)	751 (−60, −18, 48)	387 (−64, −20, 48)
Rt. Postcentral gyrus	2	136 (40, −36, 58)	91 (66, −2, 16)	234 (44, −34, 60)
Rt. Lingual/parahippocampal gyrus	30		74 (12, −44, −2)	
Lt. Cerebellum (Culmen)	29	4014 (−6, −56, 28)	113 (−6, −44, 2)	4190 (−6, −56, 28)
Rt. Posterior cingulate cortex*	23		2682 (6, −50, 22)	
Rt. Precuneus	7			127 (24, −76, 56)
Lt. Angular gyrus*	39	43 (−54, −68, 32)		176 (−46, −78, 46)
Lt. Inferior parietal lobule*	39	46 (−48, −76, 46)		
Rt. Angular gyrus	39		29 (50, −62, 26)	
Rt. Supramarginal gyrus	40	24 (62, −22, 42)		224 (62, −22, 40)
Lt. Paracentral lobule	6	333 (0, −24, 60)		1338 (0, −24, 60)
Rt. Paracentral lobule	6	56 (8, −38, 76)		

The number of voxels and the corresponding center of mass in MNI for each cluster were described accordingly.
Cortical clusters that cover wide range of brain areas were highlighted in dark gray.
Asterisk(*) indicates the default mode network regions.
BA, Brodmann areas; Lt, left; Rt, right.

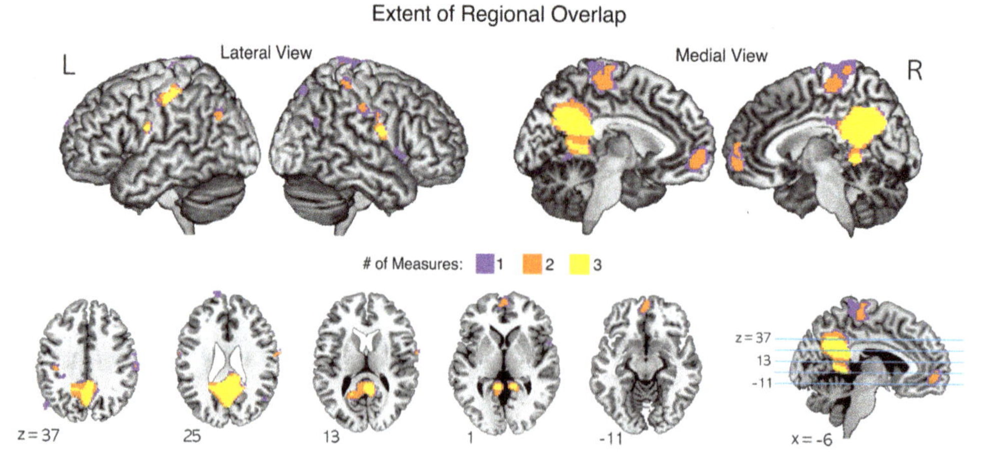

FIGURE 4 | The extent of regional overlaps for functional underconnectivities in the normalized global, contralateral, and ipsilateral FCDs (gFCD, cFCD, and iFCD). Yellow color represents the overlapping areas for functional underconnectivities observed in gFCD, cFCD, and iFCD. Orange color represents the overlapping areas of functional underconnectivities observed in any pairs of FCDs: gFCD and cFCD, gFCD and iFCD, or cFCD and iFCD. Purple color represents functional underconnectivities observed in gFCD, cFCD, or iFCD without overlapping areas.

Hypofunctional Connectivity Density

Functional connectivity differences between the ASD and TDC groups were found in the medial prefrontal cortex, posterior cingulate cortex, precuneus, and parahippocampal gyrus. The medial prefrontal cortex, posterior cingulate cortex, and precuneus have been reported to be an important parts of the default mode network, and abnormalities in the default mode network have been reported in subjects with ASD

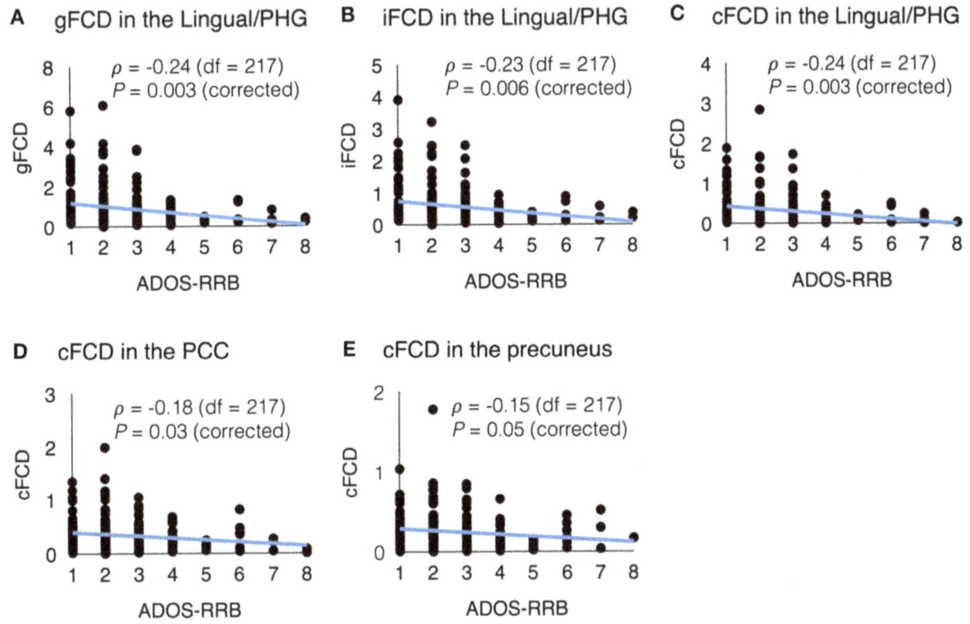

FIGURE 5 | Scatter plots of functional connectivity density (FCD) vs. clinical variable. (A) gFCD in the Lingual/PHG and ADOS-RRB score; **(B)** iFCD in the Lingual/PHG and ADOS-RRB score; **(C)** cFCD in the Lingual/PHG and ADOS-RRB score; **(D)** cFCD in the PCC and ADOS-RRB score; and **(E)** cFCD in the precuneus and ADOS-RRB score.

(Ochsner et al., 2005; Northoff et al., 2006). The above-mentioned brain regions are involved in many impaired mental functions seen in the ASD group, such as difficulty in decision making (Luke et al., 2012), lack of identification with self (Northoff et al., 2006), cognitive deficits (Baron-Cohen et al., 1985) and problems in self-referential thought (Ochsner et al., 2005) and mentalizing (Frith and Happe, 1993; Frith and Frith, 1999; Gallagher and Frith, 2003; Kana et al., 2009; Gotts et al., 2012; Schurz et al., 2014). Especially, the medial prefrontal cortex and posterior cingulate cortex are implicated in the theory of mind network, a key symptomatic feature of patients with ASD. Therefore, we assert that the under-connectivity in the medial prefrontal cortex and posterior cingulate cortex may cause the social functioning impairments in ASD.

Inter- and Intra-Hemispheric Connectivity

Using inter-hemispheric correlation, Anderson et al. showed a lower inter-hemispheric correlation in the sensorimotor cortex, superior parietal lobule, and frontal insula in subjects with ASD compared to that in controls (Anderson et al., 2011). Moreover, the mean corpus callosum volume in the ASD group was significantly smaller than that of TDCs. Although, both corpus callosum volume and gray matter inter-hemispheric functional connectivity were significantly reduced in autism, no direct relationship was observed between them, suggesting that the structural and functional imaging measure different aspects of inter-hemispheric connectivity (Anderson et al., 2011).

In our study, the inter-hemispheric differences between the two groups were computed by the difference in cFCDs between the two groups. Regions showing lower cFCD in the ASD group were the posterior cingulate/precuneus, somatosensory areas, parahippocampal gyrus, and angular gyrus. However, the mean cFCD in the ASD group was not significantly different from that of TDCs and the mean cFCD in the ASD group was even higher than that of TDCs after normalization. On the contrary, the examination of the mean iFCD showed that it is significantly reduced in the ASD group compared to that of TDCs. As intra-hemispheric under-connectivity contributed more to the overall results of our study, global under-connectivity in patients with autism may be a result of intra-hemispheric under-connectivity rather than inter-hemispheric under-connectivity. This result is consistent with that of a prior study showing altered intra-hemispheric connectivity in the autistic brains (Minshew and Williams, 2007). In reality, intra-hemispheric connectivity has been less studied than inter-hemispheric connectivity, due to the complex and time-consuming processes needed to calculate these values. However, our results suggest that the models of under-connectivity in autism should consider intra-hemispheric as well as inter-hemispheric connectivity for more sophisticated understanding of how connectivity abnormalities would be determined by interactions between the intra- and inter-hemispheric functional connectivity in the ASD group.

Correlation between Connectivity and Clinical Measures

We found that there were significant correlations between the average of gFCD, cFCD, and iFCD values in the lingual/parahippocampal gyrus and ADOS-RRB scores (**Figure 5**). The lingual/parahippocampal gyrus is connected with the amygdala and limbic structure in the brain, and is believed to play an important role in the processing of visual information about parts of the human faces (McCarthy et al., 1999) and processing high-emotion words or images, identifying visual scene and social context, and paralinguistic communication (Epstein and Kanwisher, 1998). These functions are the main areas in which individuals with ASD suffers from severe impairment, and the abnormality in the lingual/parahippocampal gyrus has been reported in individuals with autism (Weng et al., 2010). The significant correlation between gFCD and iFCD in the lingual/parahippocampal and ADOS-RRB scores can be explained by a theoretical framework provided by the salience landscape theory (Ramachandran and Oberman, 2006). Although autism is mainly considered a social disability, it also has non-social features, such as restricted and repetitive behavior/interests and sensory hypersensitivity. The salience landscape theory provides a compelling explanation for this symptom dimension of autism, suggesting that the altered connections between the limbic system and the sensory areas could cause extreme emotional responses and autonomic hyperactivity to the surrounding environment in patients with ASD, and repetitive behavior has a compensatory calming effect by reducing the child's autonomic arousal. The lingual/parahippocampal area is adjacent to, or a part of the limbic system. Therefore, our result suggests that the functional connectivity of this area might be altered in a different way in individuals with ASD, and these alterations may explain the restricted and repetitive behaviors in the ASD group.

Differences in a Recent Study Using ABIDE Dataset

Recently, a study using a large dataset from ABIDE was published with 360 male subjects with ASD and 403 male TDCs (Di Martino et al., 2014). They used four different imaging analysis methods. Among the four methods, the degree centrality was similar to gFCD used in this study. However, their results using the degree centrality were different from our results, in that the ASD group showed over-connectivity in the right middle frontal gyrus. In the right posterior cingulate cortex, no difference was observed between the two groups according to the degree centrality analysis, but in our analysis, the ASD group showed under-connectivity in the posterior cingulate cortex. Even though the degree centrality method and FCD methods are both data-driven voxel-wise methods, several factors may explain such different results. The degree centrality method used eight times lower resolutions in voxel dimensions (4 × 4 × 4 mm) (Zuo et al., 2012) than our method (2 × 2 × 2 mm). Their sample size was smaller than our sample size; they used only male subjects, whereas we used all subjects, including females and adults.

LIMITATIONS

There are several potential limitations in this study. First, the age of the subjects with ASD and TDCs are widely distributed from childhood through adolescence to adulthood. We considered only the average FCDs of all subjects from these broad age groups. Although we found average patterns of functional connectivity in the ASD group compared to those in the TDC group after setting age as a covariate, we may have missed age-related changes in the functional connectivity of the ASD group. Brain structure changes during human development (Sowell et al., 1999, 2003). In particular, adolescence is a time of human brain maturation as remarkable physical and behavioral changes occur (Paus et al., 2008; Koyama et al., 2011). Thus, future research should focus on the age effects on the neural system in ASD. The second limitation is that the FCD mapping analytical method found cortical hubs, but we did not examine which regions were strongly connected with those hubs after group comparison. This approach may require higher computational power. Third, the inconsistent findings regarding over- vs. under-connectivity in the brains of patients with ASD might be due to individualized alterations in the functional connectivity patterns, and the group comparison study like ours may not have taken functional idiosyncrasy into consideration as a possible source of these discrepant findings in functional connectivity (Hahamy et al., 2015).

CONCLUSIONS

In conclusion, we observed abnormalities of global functional connectivity in ASD by applying FCD mapping on data from 517 TDC subjects and 458 patients with ASD from the ABIDE datasets. We found regional under-connectivity in ASD by comparing of intra-hemispheric, inter-hemispheric, and global functional connectivity. Our findings suggest that a deficit of non-social functioning process in ASD, such as restricted and repetitive behaviors and sensory hypersensitivity, might be determined by both the inter- and intra-hemispheric functional disconnections in the posterior limbic and sensorimotor regions.

AUTHOR CONTRIBUTIONS

Equally contributed first authors: JL, SK. Conceived and designed the experiments: JL, SK, KC. Performed the experiments: JL, SK, KC. Analyzed the data: JL, SK. Contributed reagents/materials/analysis tools: JL, SK, EK, KC. Wrote the manuscript: JL, SK, EK, KC.

ACKNOWLEDGMENTS

This work was supported by the research grant from Korean Health Technology R&D Project of Ministry of health & welfare, Republic of Korea (Grant number: HI12C0021-A120029, HI12C0245).

REFERENCES

Alexander, A. L., Lee, J. E., Lazar, M., Boudos, R., DuBray, M. B., Oakes, T. R., et al. (2007). Diffusion tensor imaging of the corpus callosum in Autism. *Neuroimage* 34, 61–73. doi: 10.1016/j.neuroimage.2006.08.032

Amaral, D. G. (2011). The promise and the pitfalls of autism research: an introductory note for new autism researchers. *Brain Res.* 1380, 3–9. doi: 10.1016/j.brainres.2010.11.077

American Psychiatric Association (2013). *Diagnostic and Statistical Manual of Mental Disorders, 5th Edn.* Arlington, VA.

Anderson, J. S., Druzgal, T. J., Froehlich, A., DuBray, M. B., Lange, N., Alexander, A. L., et al. (2011). Decreased interhemispheric functional connectivity in autism. *Cereb. Cortex* 21, 1134–1146. doi: 10.1093/cercor/bhq190

Assaf, M., Jagannathan, K., Calhoun, V. D., Miller, L., Stevens, M. C., Sahl, R., et al. (2010). Abnormal functional connectivity of default mode sub-networks in autism spectrum disorder patients. *Neuroimage* 53, 247–256. doi: 10.1016/j.neuroimage.2010.05.067

Baron-Cohen, S., Leslie, A. M., and Frith, U. (1985). Does the autistic child have a “theory of mind”? *Cognition* 21, 37–46.

Barttfeld, P., Wicker, B., Cukier, S., Navarta, S., Lew, S., and Sigman, M. (2011). A big-world network in ASD: dynamical connectivity analysis reflects a deficit in long-range connections and an excess of short-range connections. *Neuropsychologia* 49, 254–263. doi: 10.1016/j.neuropsychologia.2010.11.024

Benjamini, Y., and Hochberg, Y. (1995). Controlling the false discovery rate: a practical and powerful approach to multiple testing. *J. R. Statist. Soc. Ser. B* 57, 289–300.

Biswal, B. B., Mennes, M., Zuo, X. N., Gohel, S., Kelly, C., Smith, S. M., et al. (2010). Toward discovery science of human brain function. *Proc. Natl. Acad. Sci. U.S.A.* 107, 4734–4739. doi: 10.1073/pnas.0911855107

Bogdashina, O. (2006). *Theory of Mind and the Triad of Perspectives on Autism and Asperger Syndrome.* Philadelphia, PA: Jessica Kingsley Publishers.

Cheon, K.-A., Kim, Y.-S., Oh, S.-H., Park, S.-Y., Yoon, H.-W., Herrington, J., et al. (2011). Involvement of the anterior thalamic radiation in boys with high functioning autism spectrum disorders: a diffusion tensor imaging study. *Brain Res.* 1417, 77–86. doi: 10.1016/j.brainres.2011.08.020

Cherkassky, V. L., Kana, R. K., Keller, T. A., and Just, M. A. (2006). Functional connectivity in a baseline resting-state network in autism. *Neuroreport* 17, 1687–1690. doi: 10.1097/01.wnr.0000239956.45448.4c

Di Martino, A., Ross, K., Uddin, L. Q., Sklar, A. B., Castellanos, F. X., and Milham, M. P. (2009). Functional brain correlates of social and nonsocial processes in autism spectrum disorders: an activation likelihood estimation meta-analysis. *Biol. Psychiatry* 65, 63–74. doi: 10.1016/j.biopsych.2008.09.022

Di Martino, A., Yan, C. G., Li, Q., Denio, E., Castellanos, F. X., Alaerts, K., et al. (2014). The autism brain imaging data exchange: towards a large-scale evaluation of the intrinsic brain architecture in autism. *Mol. Psychiatry* 19, 659–667. doi: 10.1038/mp.2013.78

Epstein, R., and Kanwisher, N. (1998). A cortical representation of the local visual environment. *Nature* 392, 598–601. doi: 10.1038/33402

Fishman, I., Keown, C. L., Lincoln, A. J., Pineda, J. A., and Müller, R. (2014). Atypical cross talk between mentalizing and mirror neuron networks in autism spectrum disorder. *JAMA Psychiatry* 71, 751–760. doi: 10.1001/jamapsychiatry.2014.83

Frith, C. D., and Frith, U. (1999). Interacting minds–a biological basis. *Science* 286, 1692–1695. doi: 10.1126/science.286.5445.1692

Frith, U., and Happe, F. (1993). Autism: beyond “theory of mind”. *Cognition* 50, 115–132. doi: 10.1016/0010-0277(94)90024-8

Gallagher, H. L., and Frith, C. D. (2003). Functional imaging of ‘theory of mind’. *Trends Cogn. Sci.* 7, 77–83. doi: 10.1016/S1364-6613(02)00025-6

Gotts, S. J., Simmons, W. K., Milbury, L. A., Wallace, G. L., Cox, R. W., and Martin, A. (2012). Fractionation of social brain circuits in autism spectrum disorders. *Brain* 135, 2711–2725. doi: 10.1093/brain/aws160

Hahamy, A., Behrmann, M., and Malach, R. (2015). The idiosyncratic brain: distortion of spontaneous connectivity patterns in autism spectrum disorder. *Nat. Neurosci.* 18, 302–309. doi: 10.1038/nn.3919

Hughes, J. R. (2009). Update on autism: a review of 1300 reports published in 2008. *Epilepsy Behav.* 16, 569–589. doi: 10.1016/j.yebeh.2009.09.023

Just, M. A., Cherkassky, V. L., Keller, T. A., Kana, R. K., and Minshew, N. J. (2007). Functional and anatomical cortical underconnectivity in autism: evidence from an FMRI study of an executive function task and corpus callosum morphometry. *Cereb. Cortex* 17, 951–961. doi: 10.1093/cercor/bhl006

Kana, R. K., Keller, T. A., Cherkassky, V. L., Minshew, N. J., and Just, M. A. (2009). Atypical frontal-posterior synchronization of theory of mind regions in autism during mental state attribution. *Soc. Neurosci.* 4, 135–152. doi: 10.1080/17470910802198510

Keary, C. J., Minshew, N. J., Bansal, R., Goradia, D., Fedorov, S., Keshavan, M. S., et al. (2009). Corpus callosum volume and neurocognition in autism. *J. Autism Dev. Disord.* 39, 834–841. doi: 10.1007/s10803-009-0689-4

Keller, T. A., Kana, R. K., and Just, M. A. (2007). A developmental study of the structural integrity of white matter in autism. *Neuroreport* 18, 23–27. doi: 10.1097/01.wnr.0000239965.21685.99

Koyama, M. S., Di Martino, A., Zuo, X. N., Kelly, C., Mennes, M., Jutagir, D. R., et al. (2011). Resting-state functional connectivity indexes reading competence in children and adults. *J. Neurosci.* 31, 8617–8624. doi: 10.1523/JNEUROSCI.4865-10.2011

Lord, C., Risi, S., Lambrecht, L., Cook, E. H. Jr., Leventhal, B. L., DiLavore, P. C., et al. (2000). The autism diagnostic observation schedule-generic: a standard measure of social and communication deficits associated with the spectrum of autism. *J. Autism Dev. Disord.* 30, 205–223. doi: 10.1023/A:1005592401947

Lord, C., Rutter, M., and Le Couteur, A. (1994). Autism Diagnostic Interview-Revised: a revised version of a diagnostic interview for caregivers of individuals with possible pervasive developmental disorders. *J. Autism Dev. Disord.* 24, 659–685. doi: 10.1007/BF02172145

Luke, L., Clare, I. C., Ring, H., Redley, M., and Watson, P. (2012). Decision-making difficulties experienced by adults with autism spectrum conditions. *Autism* 16, 612–621. doi: 10.1177/1362361311415876

Lynch, C. J., Uddin, L. Q., Supekar, K., Khouzam, A., Phillips, J., and Menon, V. (2013). Default mode network in childhood autism: posteromedial cortex heterogeneity and relationship with social deficits. *Biol. Psychiatry* 74, 212–219. doi: 10.1016/j.biopsych.2012.12.013

McCarthy, G., Puce, A., Belger, A., and Allison, T. (1999). Electrophysiological studies of human face perception. II: response properties of face-specific potentials generated in occipitotemporal cortex. *Cereb. Cortex* 9, 431–444. doi: 10.1093/cercor/9.5.431

Minshew, N. J., and Keller, T. A. (2010). The nature of brain dysfunction in autism: functional brain imaging studies. *Curr. Opin. Neurol.* 23, 124–130. doi: 10.1097/WCO.0b013e32833782d4

Minshew, N. J., and Williams, D. L. (2007). The new neurobiology of autism: cortex, connectivity, and neuronal organization. *Arch. Neurol.* 64, 945–950. doi: 10.1001/archneur.64.7.945

Monk, C. S., Peltier, S. J., Wiggins, J. L., Weng, S.-J., Carrasco, M., Risi, S., et al. (2009). Abnormalities of intrinsic functional connectivity in autism spectrum disorders. *Neuroimage* 47, 764–772. doi: 10.1016/j.neuroimage.2009.04.069

Muller, R. A., Shih, P., Keehn, B., Deyoe, J. R., Leyden, K. M., and Shukla, D. K. (2011). Underconnected, but how? A survey of functional connectivity MRI studies in autism spectrum disorders. *Cereb. Cortex* 21, 2233–2243. doi: 10.1093/cercor/bhq296

Nebel, M. B., Joel, S. E., Muschelli, J., Barber, A. D., Caffo, B. S., Pekar, J. J., et al. (2014). Disruption of functional organization within the primary motor cortex in children with autism. *Hum. Brain Mapp.* 35, 567–580. doi: 10.1002/hbm.22188

Northoff, G., Heinzel, A., de Greck, M., Bermpohl, F., Dobrowolny, H., and Panksepp, J. (2006). Self-referential processing in our brain—A meta-analysis of imaging studies on the self. *Neuroimage* 31, 440–457. doi: 10.1016/j.neuroimage.2005.12.002

Ochsner, K. N., Beer, J. S., Robertson, E. R., Cooper, J. C., Gabrieli, J. D., Kihsltrom, J. F., et al. (2005). The neural correlates of direct and reflected self-knowledge. *Neuroimage* 28, 797–814. doi: 10.1016/j.neuroimage.2005.06.069

Paus, T., Keshavan, M., and Giedd, J. N. (2008). Why do many psychiatric disorders emerge during adolescence? *Nat. Rev. Neurosci.* 9, 947–957. doi: 10.1038/nrn2513

Raichle, M. E., and Snyder, A. Z. (2007). A default mode of brain function: a brief history of an evolving idea. *Neuroimage* 37, 1083–1090. doi: 10.1016/j.neuroimage.2007.02.041

Ramachandran, V. S., and Oberman, L. M. (2006). Broken mirrors: a theory of autism. *Sci. Am.* 295, 62–69. doi: 10.1038/scientificamerican1106-62

Rudie, J. D., Brown, J. A., Beck-Pancer, D., Hernandez, L. M., Dennis, E. L., Thompson, P. M., et al. (2012). Altered functional and structural brain network organization in autism. *Neuroimage* 2, 79–94. doi: 10.1016/j.nicl.2012.11.006

Schurz, M., Radua, J., Aichhorn, M., Richlan, F., and Perner, J. (2014). Fractionating theory of mind: a meta-analysis of functional brain imaging studies. *Neurosci. Biobehav. Rev.* 42, 9–34. doi: 10.1016/j.neubiorev.2014.01.009

Sowell, E. R., Peterson, B. S., Thompson, P. M., Welcome, S. E., Henkenius, A. L., and Toga, A. W. (2003). Mapping cortical change across the human life span. *Nat. Neurosci.* 6, 309–315. doi: 10.1038/nn1008

Sowell, E. R., Thompson, P. M., Holmes, C. J., Batth, R., Jernigan, T. L., and Toga, A. W. (1999). Localizing age-related changes in brain structure between childhood and adolescence using statistical parametric mapping. *Neuroimage* 9, 587–597. doi: 10.1006/nimg.1999.0436

Supekar, K., Uddin, L. Q., Khouzam, A., Phillips, J., Gaillard, W. D., Kenworthy, L. E., et al. (2013). Brain hyperconnectivity in children with autism and its links to social deficits. *Cell Rep.* 5, 738–747. doi: 10.1016/j.celrep.2013.10.001

Tomasi, D., and Volkow, N. D. (2010). Functional connectivity density mapping. *Proc. Natl. Acad. Sci. U.S.A.* 107, 9885–9890. doi: 10.1073/pnas.1001414107

Tomasi, D., and Volkow, N. D. (2012a). Abnormal functional connectivity in children with attention-deficit/hyperactivity disorder. *Biol. Psychiatry* 71, 443–450. doi: 10.1016/j.biopsych.2011.11.003

Tomasi, D., and Volkow, N. D. (2012b). Gender differences in brain functional connectivity density. *Hum. Brain Mapp.* 33, 849–860. doi: 10.1002/hbm.21252

Tomasi, D., and Volkow, N. D. (2012c). Laterality patterns of brain functional connectivity: gender effects. *Cereb. Cortex* 22, 1455–1462. doi: 10.1093/cercor/bhr230

Vissers, M. E. X., Cohen, M., and Geurts, H. M. (2012). Brain connectivity and high functioning autism: a promising path of research that needs refined models, methodological convergence, and stronger behavioral links. *Neurosci. Biobehav. Rev.* 36, 604–625. doi: 10.1016/j.neubiorev.2011.09.003

von dem Hagen, E. A., Stoyanova, R. S., Baron-Cohen, S., and Calder, A. J. (2013). Reduced functional connectivity within and between 'social' resting state networks in autism spectrum conditions. *Soc. Cogn. Affect. Neurosci.* 8, 694–701. doi: 10.1093/scan/nss053

Weng, S. J., Wiggins, J. L., Peltier, S. J., Carrasco, M., Risi, S., Lord, C., et al. (2010). Alterations of resting state functional connectivity in the default network in adolescents with autism spectrum disorders. *Brain Res.* 1313, 202–214. doi: 10.1016/j.brainres.2009.11.057

Zuo, X. N., Ehmke, R., Mennes, M., Imperati, D., Castellanos, F. X., Sporns, O., et al. (2012). Network centrality in the human functional connectome. *Cereb. Cortex* 22, 1862–1875. doi: 10.1093/cercor/bhr269

Permissions

All chapters in this book were first published in ASDSBBBSNTT, by Frontiers; hereby published with permission under the Creative Commons Attribution License or equivalent. Every chapter published in this book has been scrutinized by our experts. Their significance has been extensively debated. The topics covered herein carry significant findings which will fuel the growth of the discipline. They may even be implemented as practical applications or may be referred to as a beginning point for another development.

The contributors of this book come from diverse backgrounds, making this book a truly international effort. This book will bring forth new frontiers with its revolutionizing research information and detailed analysis of the nascent developments around the world.

We would like to thank all the contributing authors for lending their expertise to make the book truly unique.

They have played a crucial role in the development of this book. Without their invaluable contributions this book wouldn't have been possible. They have made vital efforts to compile up to date information on the varied aspects of this subject to make this book a valuable addition to the collection of many professionals and students.

This book was conceptualized with the vision of imparting up-to-date information and advanced data in this field. To ensure the same, a matchless editorial board was set up. Every individual on the board went through rigorous rounds of assessment to prove their worth. After which they invested a large part of their time researching and compiling the most relevant data for our readers.

The editorial board has been involved in producing this book since its inception. They have spent rigorous hours researching and exploring the diverse topics which have resulted in the successful publishing of this book. They have passed on their knowledge of decades through this book. To expedite this challenging task, the publisher supported the team at every step. A small team of assistant editors was also appointed to further simplify the editing procedure and attain best results for the readers.

Apart from the editorial board, the designing team has also invested a significant amount of their time in understanding the subject and creating the most relevant covers. They scrutinized every image to scout for the most suitable representation of the subject and create an appropriate cover for the book.

The publishing team has been an ardent support to the editorial, designing and production team. Their endless efforts to recruit the best for this project, has resulted in the accomplishment of this book. They are a veteran in the field of academics and their pool of knowledge is as vast as their experience in printing. Their expertise and guidance has proved useful at every step. Their uncompromising quality standards have made this book an exceptional effort. Their encouragement from time to time has been an inspiration for everyone.

The publisher and the editorial board hope that this book will prove to be a valuable piece of knowledge for researchers, students, practitioners and scholars across the globe.

List of Contributors

Meredith C. Anderson
California Department of Public Health, Richmond, CA, USA

Lisa A. Croen
Division of Research, Kaiser Permanente of Northern California, Oakland, CA, USA

Judith K. Grether
California Department of Public Health, Richmond, CA, USA
Division of Research, Kaiser Permanente of Northern California, Oakland, CA, USA

Paul Ashwood
Department of Medical Microbiology and Immunology, University of California, Davis, CA, USA

Judy Van de Water
Department of Internal Medicine, University of California, Davis, CA, USA

Robert H. Yolken
Johns Hopkins School of Medicine, Johns Hopkins University, Baltimore, MD, USA

Anthony R. Torres and Jonna B. Westover
Center for Persons with Disabilities, Utah State University, Logan, UT, USA

Thayne Sweeten
Department of Biology, Utah State University, Brigham City, UT, USA

Robin L. Hansen
MIND Institute, University of California, Davis, CA, USA

Martin Kharrazi
Genetic Disease Screening Program, California Department of Public Health, Richmond, CA, USA

Robert Gougelet
Cognitive Science, University of California San Diego, La Jolla, CA, USA

Michael Datko and Jaime A. Pineda
Cognitive Science, University of California San Diego, La Jolla, CA, USA
Neurosciences, University of California San Diego, La Jolla, CA, USA

Alessandra Retico
Pisa Section of National Institute of Nuclear Physics, Pisa, Italy

Ming-Xiong Huang
Department of Radiology, University of California San Diego, La Jolla, CA, USA

Santosh Ganesan, Manuel Zetino and Manfred G. Keri-Lee A. Garel
Department of Neurology, Massachusetts General Hospital, Boston, MA, USA
Athinoula A. Martinos Center for Biomedical Imaging, MGH/MIT/Harvard, Boston, MA, USA

Javeria A. Hashmi, Fahimeh Mamashli, Hari M. Bharadwaj, Kitzbichler and Tal Kenet
Department of Neurology, Massachusetts General Hospital, Boston, MA, USA
Athinoula A. Martinos Center for Biomedical Imaging, MGH/MIT/Harvard, Boston, MA, USA
Harvard Medical School, Boston, MA, USA

Sheraz Khan
Department of Neurology, Massachusetts General Hospital, Boston, MA, USA
Athinoula A. Martinos Center for Biomedical Imaging, MGH/MIT/Harvard, Boston, MA, USA
Harvard Medical School, Boston, MA, USA
McGovern Institute for Brain Research, Massachusetts Institute of Technology, Cambridge, MA, USA

Konstantinos P. Michmizos
Department of Computer Science, Rutgers University, Piscataway, NJ, USA

Matti S. Hämäläinen
Athinoula A. Martinos Center for Biomedical Imaging, MGH/MIT/Harvard, Boston, MA, USA
Harvard Medical School, Boston, MA, USA
Department of Radiology, Massachusetts General Hospital, Boston, MA, USA,
Department of Neuroscience and Biomedical Engineering, Aalto University School of Science, Espoo, Finland

Tiago Simas
Department of Psychiatry, University of Cambridge, Cambridge, UK

John Suckling
Department of Psychiatry, University of Cambridge, Cambridge, UK
Cambridge and Peterborough NHS Foundation Trust, Cambridge

Ilaria Gori
Pisa Division National Institute for Nuclear Physics, Pisa, Italy
Department of Chemistry and Pharmacy, University of Sassari, Sassari, Italy

Alessia Giuliano
Pisa Division National Institute for Nuclear Physics, Pisa, Italy
Department of Physics, University of Pisa, Pisa, Italy

Sara Calderoni
Department of Developmental Neuroscience, IRCCS Stella Maris Foundation, Pisa, Italy

Filippo Muratori
Department of Developmental Neuroscience, IRCCS Stella Maris Foundation, Pisa, Italy
Department of Clinical and Experimental Medicine, University of Pisa, Pisa, Italy

Alix Thillay and Sylvie Roux
UMR Institut National de la Santé et de la Recherche Médicale U930, Université François-Rabelais de Tours, Tours, France

Mathieu Lemaire, Emmanuelle Houy-Durand, Catherine Barthélémy and Frédérique Bonnet -Brilhault
UMR Institut National de la Santé et de la Recherche Médicale U930, Université François-Rabelais de Tours, Tours, France
Centre Universitaire de Pédopsychiatrie, CHRU de Tours, Tours, France

Robert T. Knight
Helen Wills Neuroscience Institute and the Department of Psychology, University of California, Berkeley, CA, USA

Aurélie Bidet-Caulet
Institut National de la Santé et de la Recherche Médicale U1028, Centre National de la Recherche Scientifique UMR S5292, Centre de Recherche en Neurosciences de Lyon, Bron, France

Blythe A. Corbett
Department of Psychiatry and Behavioral Sciences, Vanderbilt University, Nashville, TN, USA
Vanderbilt Brain Institute, Neuroscience Graduate Program, Vanderbilt University, Nashville, TN, USA

Rachael A. Muscatello
Vanderbilt Brain Institute, Neuroscience Graduate Program, Vanderbilt University, Nashville, TN, USA

Scott D. Blain
Department of Psychology and Human Development, Vanderbilt University, Nashville, TN, USA

Maciel C. Vidal and André Fujita
Department of Computer Science, Institute of Mathematics and Statistics, University of São Paulo, São Paulo, Brazil

João R. Sato
Center of Mathematics, Computation, and Cognition, Universidade Federal do ABC, Santo André, Brazil

Joana B. Balardin
Hospital Israelita Albert Einstein, São Paulo, Brazil

Daniel Y. Takahashi
Deparment of Psychology and Princeton Neuroscience Institute, Princeton University, Princeton, NJ, USA

Ruth A. Carper, Jiwandeep S. Kohli and Ralph-Axel Müller
Brain Development Imaging Laboratory, Department of Psychology, San Diego State University, San Diego, CA, USA

Jeffrey M. Treiber
School of Medicine, University of California San Diego, La Jolla, CA, USA

Nathan S. White
Multimodal Imaging Laboratory, Department of Radiology, University of California San Diego, La Jolla, CA, USA

Richard E. Frye and John C. Slattery
Autism Research Program, Arkansas Children's Research Institute, Little Rock, AR, USA
Department of Pediatrics, University of Arkansas for Medical Sciences, Little Rock, AR, USA

Manuel F. Casanova
Department of Biomedical Sciences, University of South Carolina School of Medicine Greenville, Greenville, SC, USA

S. Hossein Fatemi, Timothy D. Folsom and Teri J. Reutiman
Department of Psychiatry, University of Minnesota Medical School, Minneapolis, MN, USA

Gregory L. Brown
Serenity Health Care Center, Waukesha, WI, USA

Stephen M. Edelson
Autism Research Institute, San Diego, CA, USA

James B. Adams
School for Engineering of Matter, Transport, and Energy, Arizona State University, Tempe, AZ, USA

Sara Calderoni and Antonio Narzisi
IRCCS Stella Maris Foundation, Pisa, Italy

Lucia Billeci
Department of Clinical and Experimental Medicine, University of Pisa, Pisa, Italy

Filippo Muratori
IRCCS Stella Maris Foundation, Pisa, Italy
Department of Clinical and Experimental Medicine, University of Pisa, Pisa, Italy

Paolo Brambilla
Department of Neurosciences and Mental Health, Fondazione IRCCS Ca' Granda Ospedale Maggiore Policlinico, University of Milan, Milan, Italy
Department of Psychiatry and Behavioral Sciences, University of Texas Health Science Center at Houston, Houston, TX, USA,

Alfredo Spagna and Laura J. Egan
Department of Psychiatry, Icahn School of Medicine at Mount Sinai, New York, NY, USA
Department of Psychology, Queens College, City University of New York, Flushing, NY, USA

Tingting Wu
Department of Psychology, Queens College, City University of New York, Flushing, NY, USA

Tehila Eilam-Stock
Department of Psychiatry, Icahn School of Medicine at Mount Sinai, New York, NY, USA
Department of Psychology, Queens College, City University of New York, Flushing, NY, USA
The Graduate Center, City University of New York, New York, NY, USA

Jin Fan
Department of Psychiatry, Icahn School of Medicine at Mount Sinai, New York, NY, USA
Department of Psychology, Queens College, City University of New York, Flushing, NY, USA
The Graduate Center, City University of New York, New York, NY, USA
Department of Neuroscience, Icahn School of Medicine at Mount Sinai, New York, NY, USA
Friedman Brain Institute, Icahn School of Medicine at Mount Sinai, New York, NY, USA

Bernard J. Crespi
Department of Biological Sciences and Human Evolutionary Studies Program, Simon Fraser University, Burnaby, BC, Canada

Kay Jann, Robert X. Smith, Edgar A. Rios Piedra and Danny J. J. Wang
Laboratory of FMRI Technology, Department of Neurology, University of California Los Angeles, Los Angeles, CA, USA

Mirella Dapretto
Department of Psychiatry and Biobehavioral Sciences, University of California Los Angeles, Los Angeles, CA, USA

Holger F. Sperdin
Office Médico-Pédagogique, Department of Psychiatry, University of Geneva School of Medicine, Geneva, Switzerland

Marie Schaer
Office Médico-Pédagogique, Department of Psychiatry, University of Geneva School of Medicine, Geneva, Switzerland
Stanford Cognitive & Systems Neuroscience Laboratory, Stanford University School of Medicine, Palo Alto, CA, USA

Moriya Gamliel
Department of Immunology and Cancer Research, Hadassah-Hebrew University Medical Center, Jerusalem, Israel

Karen L. Anderson and David Mankuta
Department of Obstetrics and Gynecology, Hadassah-Hebrew University Medical Center, Jerusalem, Israel

Richard P. Ebstein
Department of Psychology, National University of Singapore, Singapore

Nurit Yirmiya
Department of Psychology, The Hebrew University of Jerusalem, Jerusalem, Israel

Alessandro Grecucci, Luca Surian and Remo Job
Department of Psychology and Cognitive Sciences, University of Trento, Trento, Italy

Danilo Rubicondo
Department of Psychology and Cognitive Sciences, University of Trento, Trento, Italy
Center for Mind/Brain Sciences, University of Trento, Trento, Italy

Roma Siugzdaite
Department of Experimental Psychology, Faculty of Psychological and Pedagogical Sciences, Ghent University, Ghent, Belgium

Ashley Ansel, Joshua P. Rosenzweig, Philip D. Zisman, Michal Melamed and Benjamin Gesundheit
Cell-El Ltd., Jerusalem, Israel

Shuo Chen and Yishi Xing
Department of Epidemiology and Biostatistics, University of Maryland, College Park, MD USA

Jian Kang
Department of Biostatistics, University of Michigan, Ann Arbor, MI, USA

Asher Ornoy and Liza Weinstein- Fudim
Laboratory of Teratology, Department of Medical Neurobiology, Hadassah Medical School, Hebrew University, Jerusalem, Israel

Zivanit Ergaz
Laboratory of Teratology, Department of Medical Neurobiology, Hadassah Medical School, Hebrew University, Jerusalem, Israel
Department of Neonatology, Hadassah-Hebrew University Medical Center, Jerusalem, Israel

Jung Min Lee
Division of Computational Mathematics, National Institute for Mathematical Sciences, Daejeon, South Korea

Sunghyun Kyeong
Severance Biomedical Science Institute, Yonsei University College of Medicine, Seoul, South Korea

Eunjoo Kim and Keun-Ah Cheon
Division of Child and Adolescent Psychiatry, Department of Psychiatry and Institute of Behavioral Science in Medicine, Yonsei University College of Medicine, Seoul, South Korea

Index

www.ingramcontent.com/pod-product-compliance
Lightning Source LLC
LaVergne TN
LVHW080928210926
848485LV00004B/752